Social Research Methods

Social Research Methods

Third Canadian Edition

Alan Bryman

Edward Bell

James J. Teevan

OXFORD

UNIVERSITY PRESS

OXFORD
UNIVERSITY PRESS

Oxford University Press is a department of the University of Oxford.
It furthers the University's objective of excellence in research, scholarship,
and education by publishing worldwide. Oxford is a registered trade mark of
Oxford University Press in the UK and in certain other countries.

Published in Canada by
Oxford University Press
8 Sampson Mews, Suite 204,
Don Mills, Ontario M3C 0H5 Canada

www.oupcanada.com

First published 2012
First Canadian Edition published in 2005
Second Canadian Edition published in 2009

Social Research Methods, Second Edition was originally published in English in 2001.
This edition is published by arrangement with Oxford University Press.
Great Clarendon Street, Oxford, England 0X2 6DP

Library and Archives Canada Cataloguing in Publication

Bryman, Alan
Social research methods / Alan Bryman, Edward Bell, James J. Teevan.   3rd Canadian ed.

Includes bibliographical references and index.
ISBN 978–0–19–544296–0

1. Social sciences Research Textbooks. 2. Social sciences Methodology Textbooks.
I. Bell, Edward A. (Edward Allan), 1955– II. Teevan, James J., 1942– III. Title.

H62.B78 2012   300.72   C2012-900953-9

Cover image: © Eric Michaud/istockphoto.com

This book is printed on permanent (acid-free) paper ∞
which contains a minimum of 10% post-consumer waste.

Printed and bound in the United States of America

1 2 3 4 — 15 14 13 12

Brief Contents

Contents

PART V

PART VI

Chapter 18: Conducting a Research Project

Guide to the Book

An invitation to students

Why are you here?

That's a good question to ask yourself whenever you start something new.

So why are you here? Why are you reading this book? If you're like most students, you're here because you have to be. Methodology is a required course, and to do well on the exams and assignments you have to read this book.

If you're here out of necessity, that's all right. But what if there were more to social research methods than you thought? What if this book actually explored topics that were meaningful and useful to you? I'll be making the case that, with a little effort, you will find both intellectual stimulation and some valuable practical applications in this book.

What sort of intellectual payoff can you expect from learning about social research methods? In most courses in the social sciences, students spend their time absorbing, and sometimes challenging, claims made about the social world. For example, you may learn that men are more likely to commit violent crimes than women. You may come to understand what it feels like to be homeless. Or perhaps you'll encounter a theory explaining why some countries are rich and powerful while others are not. That sort of endeavour—learning about and reflecting on claims to knowledge—is clearly worthwhile, but it will not be what concerns us here. Instead, we will focus on how those types of claims are generated and how they gain acceptance as knowledge. In other words, instead of exploring the body of facts, concepts, theories, and interpretations that social scientists use to make sense of the world, we'll look at how all those things are created.

One of the most profound questions that can be asked of someone making a claim to knowledge is, 'How do you *know* that?' That simple question is at the heart of this book. And like so many simple questions, it has no simple answer. Since ancient times, philosophers, scientists, and others have been grappling with the questions of what knowledge is and how it is to be acquired. The branch of philosophy that addresses issues of that kind—the nature of truth, what sorts of things can be known, what should be accepted as knowledge, how knowledge is to be sought—is called *epistemology*.

It may come as a surprise to you, but epistemological debates are still alive and well in the social sciences. In fact, they rage on even among researchers in the same discipline, such as sociology. The epistemological issues we will examine in this book involve different and sometimes conflicting positions on what procedures should be used to know things about society. For example, should the methods used in the natural sciences (disciplines such as physics, chemistry, and biology) be used to study people and the social order? If not, what are the alternatives? To what extent should values affect the research process? Do human beings have some degree of free will? If so, does that make it impossible to predict their behaviour? These and many other issues impinge on social research in a variety of ways and will be confronted at different stages of the book. Although knowing how to do research—how to design a questionnaire, how to observe, how to analyze the mass media, and so on—is crucial to an education in research methods, so too is an appreciation of those wider issues.

A related division of philosophy, *ontology*, is concerned with the nature of reality and existence, what 'reality' means, and what should be considered real. Here again, age-old controversies have carried over into modern times. There is no shortage of opinions in the social sciences, especially in sociological circles, regarding what is real. We will explore some of the more salient disagreements on that topic and see how they are reflected in social research and the claims to knowledge made by social scientists.

Learning about various approaches to social knowledge and how such knowledge may be generated can be of immense benefit to you as a social thinker. Just as learning how clothes are made can help you tell the difference between a good pair of jeans and a shoddy one, understanding where social knowledge comes from will help you distinguish between sound ideas and fatuous ones.

The practical implications of improving your critical thinking skills in this way are many. First of all, having a solid background in social research methods will help you make sense of the material you will be expected to understand in your social science courses. Second, at various points in your university career you will probably be called on to do some small research projects. The knowledge you will gain here can put you at an advantage with that sort of assignment, and it could even be a starting point for more sophisticated research if you go on to graduate school or even become a professional social scientist.

Finally, in everyday life you will be inundated with claims about people, society, and the world at large: how men and women are different (or the same), why people divorce, how children should be educated, how the country should be governed, and so on. The knowledge and skills you can acquire through learning about various social research methods will be useful when you have to evaluate those types of claims in order to make decisions in your life. And you may not be the only beneficiary of what you will learn. The people who are affected by your decisions could benefit as well, and if you become active in your community or some larger social grouping, the ripple effects may be wide indeed.

Who would benefit from reading this book?

This book was written for undergraduate students taking a research methods course, most often in sociology departments but also in other social science disciplines, such as social work and education. It covers a wide range of methods, approaches to research, and ways of carrying out data analysis.

Research methods are not tied to any particular nation, and the principles underlying them transcend national boundaries. The same is true of this book. The original text by Alan Bryman was written with the needs of UK post-secondary students in mind, but it was widely adopted in Europe and Canada as well. Feedback from adopters and reviewers suggested that the book could be made even more useful for Canadian instructors and students through the addition of Canadian and, more broadly, North American examples, sources, and research studies. Edward Bell's and James Teevan's adaptations have preserved the qualities that contributed to the book's initial success—its clarity, comprehensiveness, and presentation of social research methods in an international context—while expanding on those strengths by incorporating elements that are integral to North American, and especially Canadian, courses in the social sciences.

Structure of the book

In social research, an important distinction is made between the quantitative and qualitative approaches to inquiry. This distinction lies behind the structure of the book and the way it approaches issues and methods. Since both perspectives are crucial in developing an understanding of social phenomena, both receive full-blown treatment and analysis.

The Introduction that begins this new edition has two purposes: to provide an entrée into the world of social research methods, and to make the case that research methods are something to get excited about. The rest of the text is divided into six parts, which are followed by two appendices.

Part One comprises two scene-setting chapters that deal with basic ideas about the nature of social research.

- Chapter 1 examines issues such as the nature of the relationship between theory and research and the degree to which a natural science approach is an appropriate framework for the study of society. It's here that the distinction between quantitative and qualitative research is first encountered: the two are presented as different *research orientations* with different ways of conceptualizing how people and society should be studied. This chapter also includes a discussion of *research questions*: what they are, why they are important, and how they are formulated.

- Chapter 2 introduces the idea of a *research design*, along with the basic frameworks within which social research is carried out (experimental, cross-sectional, longitudinal, and case study designs). These two chapters provide the basic building blocks for the rest of the book.

Part Two consists of five chapters concerned with quantitative research.

- Chapter 3 presents the fundamentals of quantitative research and provides the context for later chapters. The next two chapters are largely concerned with aspects of social survey research.
- Chapter 4 focuses on structured interviewing and the design of questionnaires. It also discusses how to compose a self-completion questionnaire.
- Chapter 5 examines how to ask questions in questionnaires and structured interviews.
- Chapter 6 covers structured observation, a method developed for the systematic observation of behaviour.
- Chapter 7 looks at how data collected by other researchers and by official bodies are analyzed.

Part Three presents three chapters on aspects of qualitative research.

- Chapter 8 plays the same role for Part Three that Chapter 3 does for Part Two. It provides an overview of the nature of qualitative research and hence the context for the other chapters in this part.
- Chapter 9 discusses ethnography and participant observation. The two terms are often used interchangeably to refer to the immersion of the researcher in a social setting, a technique that is the source of some of the best-known studies in social research.
- Chapter 10 examines the kinds of interview that qualitative researchers conduct (typically semi-structured or unstructured) and focus groups, in which groups of individuals are interviewed on a specific topic.

Part Four contains only Chapter 11, which deals with research ethics for all types of social research.

Part Five looks at sampling and data analysis in both quantitative and qualitative research.

- Chapter 12 deals with sampling: how to select a sample and the considerations involved in assessing what can be inferred from different kinds of samples. Although most texts place sampling near their discussions of quantitative research, this placement reflects the fact that sampling is crucial in qualitative work as well.
- Chapter 13 presents a range of basic non-technical tools for quantitative data analysis. The emphasis is on how to choose a method of analysis and how to interpret findings. In order to keep the focus on methodological concepts and interpretations, formulae are not discussed.
- Chapter 14 explores some approaches to the analysis of qualitative data, including grounded theory and coding.

Part Six moves beyond the quantitative/qualitative division to explore what the two approaches have in common, how they may complement each other, and how they may be combined in the same research project.

- Chapter 15 proposes that the distinction between quantitative and qualitative research may be less fixed than is sometimes supposed, and presents some ways in which they can be combined to produce multi-strategy research.
- Chapter 16 applies the multi-strategy approach to content analysis, a method that is generally considered quantitative and is used in the study of 'documents' ranging from books, letters, and newspapers to movies, chat lines, and television shows. It also examines two ways to analyze language: conversation analysis and discourse analysis.
- Chapter 17 provides guidance on writing up research, an often-neglected area in the teaching of the research process.
- Chapter 18 offers advice on conducting a research project, taking readers through the main steps involved.

Finally, the *appendices* present easy-to-access resources for successful research.

- Appendix A explains how to use SPSS and NVivo software to perform the quantitative data analyses described in Chapter 13 and the qualitative data analyses discussed in Chapter 14 respectively.
- Appendix B outlines the ideal stages of research.

Special features of the book

Several features make this third Canadian edition especially helpful to students:

- **NEW** *Chapter on Ethics.* A new chapter on Research Ethics, placed in its own section, emphasizes that ethics are relevant for all research methods and come to play at every stage of research.

CHAPTER 11

Research Ethics

CHAPTER OVERVIEW

Ethics are a primary concern in social research. They permeate every aspect of the research process, from the recruitment of subjects to the publishing of the results. This chapter discusses some general ethical principles and their applications to real research situations. The backdrop for the discussion is the *Tri-Council Policy Statement: Ethical Conduct for Research Involving Humans (TCPS2)* (2010), which governs most research practices in Canada. The *TCPS2* was prepared by the Canadian Institutes of Health Research (CIHR), the Natural Sciences and Engineering Council of Canada (NSERC), and the Social Sciences and Humanities Research Council of Canada (SSHRCC). It identifies three core principles, which are complementary and mutually reinforcing:

- *Respect for persons* stipulates that people's autonomy and their freedom to choose what will happen to them must be ensured. Research participants must therefore be made aware of everything the study will entail, so that their consent is not only freely given but fully informed. Consent must also be ongoing; thus participants should be allowed to withdraw from the study at any time.
- *Concern for welfare* covers all aspects of a person's life as well as the welfare of groups and communities. To protect

the welfare of individuals and groups, a favourable balance between the risks and benefits of research must be sought.

- *Justice* requires that people be treated fairly and equitably, so that no segment of the population bears an undue burden of the risk associated with research, and no part of society is excluded from the benefits that research may bestow.

Each of these principles provides valuable guidance and can be used to identify research activities and practices that should be avoided for moral reasons.

You may be surprised to learn that there are stringent formal policies in place to ensure that research in Canada is conducted in an ethical manner. Why, you ask? Surely researchers are decent people, not mad scientists who take pleasure in abusing the people who participate in their studies. Of course. Still, every research situation has an ethical dimension to it, and the history of the social sciences is riddled with studies in which well-meaning researchers harmed their subjects in some way. In many cases the studies seemed quite acceptable when they were done, and it was only with the passage of time that the consequences for participants were recognized. How could things possibly have gone so wrong? And why are ethical dilemmas still endemic to social research?

CHAPTER 1

General Research Orientations

CHAPTER OVERVIEW

The aim of this chapter is to examine the fundamental assumptions upon which social research is based. An important distinction commonly drawn by practitioners of social research—between the **quantitative** and **qualitative** approaches—is explored in relation to those considerations. We will consider:

- the relationship between theory and research—in particular, whether theories and the hypotheses derived from them are tested by gathering data (a **deductive** approach) or whether data gathering is used as a means to *create* theory (an **inductive** approach);
- **epistemological** issues, such as whether a natural science model like the one used in chemistry or biology is suitable for the study of the social world;
- **ontological** issues, such as whether the social world should be regarded as a reality external to individuals over which they have little or no control, or as something that social actors may fashion into their personal realities;
- how values and *practical* issues impinge on the research process; and
- how these issues relate to both quantitative and qualitative research; a preliminary discussion, followed up in Chapter 15, suggests that although the quantitative and qualitative orientations are different, they can complement each other.

Soon-Yi wants to find out why Aboriginal Canadians are more likely to live in poverty than other Canadians, but doesn't know where to begin. Should she start by gathering information on First Nations communities (residence patterns, economic activities, age structure)? Or should she examine the effects of land claims and treaties, or educational trajectories, or perceptions of Aboriginal people by non-Aboriginals? Once all those matters are explored, she thinks, it might be possible to come up with a theory that could shed some light on the question. But the list of topics she could gather information on seems endless.

Maybe it would be better to start out with some hunches and then gather information to see whether they are supported by evidence. She already has the beginnings of a theory in the form of the idea that the level of wealth individuals can acquire depends on the extent to which they accept mainstream cultural notions about what is important in life, in particular whether they believe that obtaining material things should take priority over other aspects of life. Perhaps she can see if First Nations people are more likely to buy into that cultural norm or to reject it. In that case, should she gather information from Aboriginal people only, or from non-Aboriginals as well in order to compare the two groups?

Then there is the question of how to gather the information. Should she design a questionnaire and send it out to a large number of Aboriginal people? Or would it be better just to interview a few people and encourage them to talk about their priorities in life without trying to steer the conversation in any particular direction? If she does the

- **NEW** *Chapter opening vignettes.* At the beginning of each chapter, the topics to be addressed are now introduced in an informal and provocative way designed to help students grasp their real-world relevance.

CHAPTER 13: Quantitative Data Analysis | 245

correlation is below 1, at least one other variable is affecting the relationship between them, possibly affecting variable 1 as well as variable 2.

The scatter diagram for variables 2 and 3 (Figure 13.7) shows a perfect negative relationship, which yields a Pearson's *r* correlation of –1. This means that as one variable increases, the other decreases, and that the values of one variable perfectly predict the values of the other. Here, as in the previous case, the line could be extended beyond the data to predict what would happen to either variable if the other moved beyond the range shown, although it is risky to go beyond what is known. Also, because social data usually include so many exceptions that few cases fall exactly on the line, predictions based on them tend to be general rather than specific.

If, as in Figure 13.8, there is no apparent pattern in the scatter diagram, there is no or virtually no correlation between the variables. In the case of variables 2 and 5, the correlation is close to zero, at –.041. This means that the variation in the dependent variable is probably associated with variables other than the one used in this analysis.

If a relationship is strong, a clear pattern will be evident in the variables. This is the case with variables 2 and 4, whose scatter diagram appears in Figure 13.9. There is clearly a positive

relationship; in fact, the Pearson's *r* is .88 (positive correlations are usually presented without the + sign). This means that the variation in the two variables is very closely connected, but that other variables also have some influence.

Going back to the gym survey, the correlation between *age* (var00002) and the time spent on

BOX 13.5 | Imaginary data from five variables to show different types of relationship

	Variables			
1	2	3	4	5
1	10	50	7	9
2	12	45	13	23
3	14	40	18	7
4	16	35	14	15
5	18	30	16	6
6	20	25	23	22
7	22	20	19	12
8	24	15	18	8
9	26	10	22	18
10	28	5	24	10

TABLE 13.5 | Correlations output for age, weimins, and cardmins (SPSS output)

CORRELATIONS

CORRELATIONS

Correlations of *p* < 0.05 are 'flagged' with asterisks

		AGE	WEIMINS	CARDMINS
AGE	Pearson Correlation	1.000	–.273 **	–.109
	Sig. (2-tailed)	.	.010	.311
	N	89	89	89
WEIMINS	Pearson Correlation	–.273 **	1.000	–.161
	Sig. (2-tailed)	.010	.	.130
	N	89	90	90
CARDMINS	Pearson Correlation	–.109	–.161	1.000
	Sig. (2-tailed)	.311	.130	.
	N	89	90	90

** Correlation is significant at the 0.01 level (2-tailed).

Shows strength of relationship as indicated by Pearson's *r*

Shows number of cases, less any cases for which there are missing data for either or both variables

Shows level of statistical significance of computed value of Pearson's *r*

- **NEW** *Vibrant full-colour design.* A visually appealing layout engages students and helps them to navigate the content.

- **NEW** *Methods in Motion: Applications to Canadian Society.* These boxes highlight recent Canadian research that illustrates how the methods discussed in the chapter have been used to study Canadian society.

Methods in Motion

Applications to Canadian Society

Why are some Canadians politically conservative and others liberal?

Bell and his colleagues (2009) did a behavioural genetic study of political attitudes and behaviours that addressed the issue of why some Canadians tend to have conservative or right-leaning attitudes, while others are more liberal or left-oriented in their political views. The methodology used in the study (the details of which go beyond the scope of this book) was a kind of natural experiment comparing monozygotic (identical) twins, who are essentially genetic clones of each other, with dizygotic (fraternal) twins, who share only about 50% of the genetic material that varies between human beings. The researchers examined how similar the identical twins were in their political attitudes, and compared that with how similar the fraternal twins were on that score. If identical twins are more similar on the characteristic under examination than the fraternal twins, that would indicate that genetic factors or other biological influences have some impact on the trait in question. The results of the study showed that the identical twins were in fact much more similar in their political attitudes than the fraternal twins, which suggests that genetic factors do play a role in the formation of these attitudes. The study also found that environmental factors (such as educational influences and media effects) influenced political orientations, although it did not test for specific environmental influences. Taken as a whole, the results indicate that 'nature' and 'nurture' *interact* in the formation of political attitudes.

These sorts of studies are uncommon in sociology, political science, or anthropology, although they are conducted more frequently in psychology and the health sciences. They have far-reaching implications for the social sciences, in particular for disciplines in which biological influences are seldom examined. The standard paradigm in the latter fields of study assumes that some combination of socialization, culture, and situational factors can explain the origins of most attitudes and behaviours. Researchers using behaviour genetic methods, on the other hand, acknowledge that those sorts of influences are crucial, but argue that a more complete understanding of the human condition can be achieved by considering both biological and environmental factors.

If behaviour genetics and other approaches that consider both biological and environmental influences were to be more widely adopted in the social sciences, that could have a major impact on the theoretical perspectives that are developed and rise to prominence in academe. For example, a blend of Darwinian evolutionary theory and sociological conflict theories is a possibility (e.g., Sanderson 2001). Such approaches have the potential to promote *consilience* or the unity of knowledge, which in this case would take the form of a closer relationship between the social and biological sciences.

CHAPTER 3

The Nature of Quantitative Research

CHAPTER OVERVIEW

This chapter is concerned with **quantitative research**, an approach used by a large number of people in the social sciences. The emphasis here is on what quantitative research typically entails, though departures from this ideal type will be outlined later on. This chapter explores:

- the main steps of quantitative research, presented as a linear succession of stages;
- the importance of measurement in quantitative research, and the ways in which measures are devised for **concepts**;
- procedures for checking the **reliability** and **validity** of those measures;
- the main goals of quantitative research: measurement, establishing **causality**, **generalization**, and **replication**; and
- some criticisms of quantitative research.

For his class project, Mario wants to ask some fellow students questions about a topic that's always fascinated him: drug and alcohol use, and how it might affect a person's self-image. But how will he get the information he needs? He quickly jots down a few notes, but soon realizes that coming up with effective questions is more difficult than he imagined. His first question reads: 'Do you take drugs?'; but he quickly realizes that 'drugs' is too vague, since for some people that would include things like aspirin and cough medicine. And what about alcohol? Isn't alcohol a kind of drug too? Now he begins to think about other potential problems. What if some people refuse to say what their level of drug and alcohol consumption is? Would some people be offended by the question? And when they do answer, how will he know if they're telling the truth? Is there a second method he could use, such as observing people in a local pub, to see if their behaviour is consistent with the survey data? And once he's asked the basic questions about consumption, how will he approach the self-image part of his research question? What exactly should he be asking about? Should the information be recorded in numeric form? If so, how do you do that? When he has finished analyzing the data, will he be able to say that his findings have wider applications? In this chapter we will explore how researchers deal with the kinds of issues that Mario is facing.

- *Chapter overviews.* Each chapter opener includes an overview that serves as a route map, alerting readers to what they can expect to learn.

BOX 3.3 | A multiple-indicator measure of another concept

In Kelley and De Graaf's (1997) research on religious beliefs, national religiosity and family religious orientation were each measured by a single indicator (see Box 1.3). However, religious orthodoxy was measured by four survey questions; answers to each of the four were given a value and then added together to form a religious belief score for each respondent. The questions were as follows:

Please indicate which statement below comes closest to expressing what you believe about God:

- I don't believe in God. (1)
- I don't know whether there is a God and don't believe there is a way to find out. (2)
- I don't believe in a personal God, but I do believe in a higher power of some kind. (3)
- I find myself believing in God some of the time, but not at others. (4)
- While I have doubts, I feel that I do believe in God. (5)
- I know God really exists and I have no doubts about it. (6)

Which best describes your beliefs about God?

- I...

- I don't believe in God, but I used to. (2)
- I believe in God now, but I didn't used to. (3)
- I believe in God now and I always have. (4)

How close do you feel to God most of the time?

- Don't believe in God. (1)
- Not close at all. (2)
- Not very close. (3)
- Somewhat close. (4)
- Extremely close. (5)

There is a God, one personally concerned with every human being.

- Strongly agree. (5)
- Agree. (4)
- Neither agree nor disagree. (3)
- Disagree. (2)
- Strongly disagree. (1)

Notice the values attached to each answer. A person whose answers add up to 20 (6 + 4 + 5 + 5) has the highest level of religious belief possible on this measure, and a person with a sum of 4 (getting a 1 on each question) has the lowest.

- *Examples.* In general, undergraduates lack both the time and the resources required to carry out a full-scale research project. This makes it all the more important to include examples of how professional researchers have done their work and the lessons they have learned in the process. Most of the major topics discussed in the text are illustrated with several examples from published research.

BOX 1.2 | The need for theory

Teevan and Dryburgh (2000) collected data from 57 male adolescents concerning their participation in deviant activities such as truancy, theft, vandalism, and fighting, and asked them why they acted the way they did. Then the boys were read specially adapted sociological explanations of such behaviour and asked what they thought of them. In effect, they were asked to evaluate the sociologists' theories as if they were sociologists themselves. The idea was to give marginalized people a voice and to see the issue in question from the point of view of those studied—two common approaches in qualitative research. Some journal reviewers liked the idea but thought that the findings' relevance for sociological theory needed to be explored. Eventually the authors brought a variety of social theories to bear on the data they had gathered, and in doing so provided a critical assessment of existing explanations for delinquency and conformity.

A young man painting graffiti on a wall. Some call this behaviour vandalism, while others consider it art. What social theories might you invoke to explain what he is doing? How might the young man himself explain it? Do you think his explanation would have anything in common with your social theories?

- *Boxes.* These provide in-depth examples of how the various research methods discussed in the book have been employed in real research situations. The boxes also list the advantages and disadvantages of a particular method, summarize important points, discuss methodological controversies, and offer practical advice.

BOX 7.3 | The Mackenzie King Diaries

William Lyon Mackenzie King was prime minister of Canada for 21 of the 27 years between 1921 and 1948. He was an avid diarist for most of his life, recording his thoughts and feelings about both personal issues and national and international events. The contents of the diaries suggest that he did not expect them to be made public. They reveal his political views in considerable detail, but also a side of the man that shocked many people when the transcripts were

that he could commune with his deceased dog Pat. (The practice of spiritualism was quite common when King was a young man in the late nineteenth and early twentieth centuries.) Sensationalism aside, the King diaries are a valuable primary source of information for a significant portion of Canadian and world history.

Nevertheless, the publication of the King diaries does raise ethical questions. Is it a violation of privacy rights to publish or quote from someone's diary,
d cannot raise
e now available
of Canada at
g/index-e.html

BOX 12.1 | Basic terms and concepts in sampling

- *Element* or *unit*: a single case in the population. In the social sciences that element or unit is usually a person, but many other things can be sampled as well: nations, cities, regions, schools, firms, etc. Finch and Hayes (1994), for example, based part of their research on a random sample of wills of deceased people.

- *Population*: all the cases about which you are seeking knowledge, or all the cases to which your conclusions are meant to apply. For example, if you are studying voting behaviour, the population might be all the people in a particular jurisdiction who are eligible to vote. If the topic is hyperactivity among young children, the population might be all children aged 2 to 11. (Note that 'population' in this context means something different from 'population' in the everyday sense.)

- *Sampling frame*: the list of elements from which the sample will be selected.

- *Sample*: the elements selected for investigation, a subset of the population. The method of selection may involve probability or non-probability sampling (see below).

- *Representative sample*: a sample that is a microcosm of the population, one that 'represents' its essential characteristics. A sample like this is most likely to be selected when a probability sampling process is used (see next).

- *Probability sample*: a sample selected using a random process such that each unit in the population has a known chance of being selected. The aim of probability sampling is to keep sampling error (see below) to a minimum.

- *Non-probability sample*: a sample selected using a non-random method. Essentially, this implies that some units in the population are more likely to be selected than others.

- *Sampling error*: an error of estimation that occurs if there is a difference between the characteristics of a sample and those of the population from which it was selected. Sampling error can occur even when a random method is used. For example, if valid measures indicate that 45 per cent of a national probability sample is in favour of more public funding for the arts, but the actual figure in the population is 49 per cent, the difference is caused by sampling error.

- *Non-response*: occurs whenever some unit selected for the sample refuses to participate in the study, cannot be contacted, or for some other reason does not supply the required data.

- *Census*: if an attempt is made to collect data from all elements in the population rather than from a sample, the data are a census. The phrase 'the census' typically refers to the enumeration of all (or nearly all) members of the population of a nation state—that is, a national census.

Practical **TIP** ▶▶▶▶

Sample size and probability sampling for students

For most quantitative researchers sample size does matter: the bigger the sample, the more representative it is likely to be (provided the sample is randomly selected), regardless of the size of the population from which it is drawn. However, students have to do their research with very limited resources and a truly random sample may not be feasible for them. The crucial point is to be clear about your sampling decisions and to justify what you have done. Explain the difficulties that you would have encountered in generating a random sample. Explain why you could not increase your sample size. Above all, though, don't make claims about your sample that are not warranted. Never claim that your sample is representative, or randomly selected, unless that is true. Also, even if your sample is small, it may have some good features: the range of people included, a good response rate, high levels of honesty. Make sure to play up these positive features while being honest about the sample's limitations. This is what professional researchers do.

- *Practical tips.* Most chapters include at least one box of practical tips on how to approach certain tasks or avoid common mistakes.

- *Checklists.* Most chapters also include checklists of points to keep in mind when engaging in a particular activity, whether devising a structured interview schedule, conducting a focus group, or doing a literature review. Checklists reinforce key points and remind students of things they need to consider when doing their own research.

☑ **Checklist** *of ethical issues to consider before going into the field to collect data*

✔ Have you submitted your project to your institution's research ethics board? If only certain types of research need to be submitted for formal approval, is your research exempt, or does it require clearance?

✔ Have you ensured that there is no prospect of serious harm to participants?

✔ Does your research conform to the principle of informed consent, so that research participants understand:
  – what the research is about?
  – the purposes of the research?
  – the nature of the participant's involvement in the research?
  – how long their participation is going to take?
  – that participation is voluntary?

  – that they can withdraw from the study at any time, even after the research starts?
  – what is going to happen to the data (for example, how it will be kept, when it will be destroyed)?

✔ Are you sure that the privacy of the people involved in your research will not be violated and that the confidentiality of the data will be maintained?

✔ If deception is involved, have you ensured that research participants will be debriefed in a timely matter—that is, that they will get an explanation of the true purposes of the study as soon as possible?

✔ After the data have been collected, have you ensured that the names of research participants and/or organizations involved will be made unidentifiable? Do you have a strategy for archiving data in electronic form that complies with data protection legislation?

Key Points

- Quantitative research can be characterized as a linear series of steps moving from theory to conclusions, but the process described in Figure 3.1 is an ideal from which there are many departures.
- Examining the reliability and validity of measures is important for assessing their quality.

- Quantitative research has the following key goals: measurement, the establishment of causality, generalization, and replication.
- Quantitative research has been criticized by qualitative researchers. These criticisms tend to revolve around rejecting the view that a natural science model is appropriate for studying the social world.

Relevant Websites

The *Statistics Canada* site provides access to a wide variety of quantitative information about Canada. It also offers up-to-date figures on things like the inflation rate, the level of unemployment, and Canada's population.
http://www.statcan.gc.ca/start-debut-eng.html

The *Alberta Survey* (discussed in Box 3.2) conducted annually by The Population Research Lab at the University of Alberta in Edmonton since 1987. This site provides copies of the questionnaires

used, a description of the sampling procedures, and even raw data that can be downloaded for analysis.
http://www.uofaweb.ualberta.ca/prl/AlbertaSurvey.cfm

Examples and discussion of *Likert Scaling*:
http://www.socialresearchmethods.net/kb/scallik.php

[Websites accessed 20 July 2011]

Questions for Review

THE MAIN STEPS IN QUANTITATIVE RESEARCH
- What are the main steps in quantitative research?
- To what extent do the main steps follow a strict sequence?
- Do the steps suggest a deductive or an inductive approach to the relationship between theory and research?

CONCEPTS AND THEIR MEASUREMENT
- Why is measurement important to a quantitative researcher?
- Why may multiple indicators of a concept be preferable to using a single indicator?

RELIABILITY AND VALIDITY
- Are some forms of reliability more important than others?
- 'Whereas validity presupposes reliability, reliability does not presuppose validity.' Discuss.

- Name and define four different kinds of measurement validity, providing an illustration of each one.
- What are the main criteria for evaluating measurement validity?

THE MAIN GOALS OF QUANTITATIVE RESEARCHERS
- Outline the main goals of quantitative researchers. What is to be gained by achieving them?
- Why is replication especially important to quantitative researchers, in spite of the tendency for replication to be very rare in social research?

THE CRITIQUE OF QUANTITATIVE RESEARCH
- 'The crucial problem with quantitative research is its failure to adequately address the issue of meaning.' Discuss.
- 'The natural science model of research should not be used to study society.' Discuss.

- *Key points.* Each chapter concludes with a summary of its most significant points.
- *Relevant websites.* A list of websites offering further information or elaboration is provided at the end of each chapter.
- *Questions for review.* Questions designed to test understanding of key concepts are grouped under headings that reflect the structure of the chapter.

- *Glossary.* Learning a new subject usually involves learning some new terminology, or at least new meanings for familiar words and phrases. To help you keep track of new terms and concepts, key terms are **bolded** the first time they appear in each chapter and are defined in the Glossary at the end of the book.

Glossary

Terms in *italic* type are defined elsewhere in the Glossary.

action research   An approach in which the researcher and client collaborate to diagnose a problem and develop a solution based on the diagnosis.

adjacency pair   Two kinds of talk activity that are linked together, such as an invitation and a response.

analytic induction   An approach to the analysis of qualitative data in which the collection of data continues and the hypothesis is modified until no cases inconsistent with it are found.

arithmetic mean   What everyday language refers to as the 'average': the sum of all the scores divided by the number of scores. Also known simply as the **mean.**

biographical method   See *life history method.*

bivariate analysis   Examination of the relationship between two variables, as in *contingency tables; correlation.*

CAQDAS   An abbreviation of computer-assisted (or -aided) qualitative data analysis software.

case study   A *research design* that entails detailed and intensive analysis of either a single case or (for comparative purposes) a small number of cases.

causality   A causal connection between variables, as opposed to a mere *correlation* between them.

cells   The areas in a table where the rows and columns intersect and data are inserted.

census   A count of an entire *population;* by contrast, a *sample* counts only some units of a population.

chi-square test   Chi-square (χ^2) is a test of *statistical significance* used to establish confidence that a finding displayed in a *contingency table* can be generalized from a *probability sample* to the *population* from which it is drawn.

closed, closed-ended question   A question in an *interview schedule* or *questionnaire* that presents the respondent with a fixed set of possible answers to choose from; also called a **fixed-choice question.**

cluster sampling   A procedure in which the researcher first samples sets of cases ('clusters') and then samples units within them, usually using a *probability sampling* method.

code, coding   In *quantitative research,* codes are the tags used to assign the data on each *variable* to a category of the variable in question. Numbers are usually assigned to each category to allow easier computer processing. In *qualitative research,* coding is the process in which data are broken down into component parts, which are then assigned names.

coding frame or **coding manual**   A list of the codes to be used in the analysis of a particular set of data. For answers to a structured interview schedule or questionnaire, the coding frame delineates the categories used for each *open question.* With *closed questions,* the coding frame is essentially incorporated into the fixed answers from which respondents must choose; hence the term 'pre-coded question.'

concept   A general or abstract idea; a category that serves to organize observations and ideas about some aspect of the social world.

concurrent validity   A type of validity that is tested by relating a measure to an existing criterion or a different indicator of the concept to see if one predicts the other: one of the main forms of *measurement validity.*

connotation   A term used in *semiotics* to refer to the meanings of a *sign* associated with the social context within which it operates: a sign's connotations are supplementary to its *denotation* and less immediately apparent.

constant   An attribute on which cases do not differ; compare with *variable.*

constructionism, constructionist   An *ontological* position (the antithesis of *objectivism*) according to which social phenomena and their meanings are continually being created by social actors; also known as **constructivism.**

construct validity   1) Same as measurement validity; 2) a type of measurement validity that is established by determining whether the concepts being measured relate empirically in a manner that would be predicted by relevant theories.

content analysis   An approach to the analysis of documents and texts that seeks to quantify content in terms of predetermined categories in a systematic and replicable manner. The term is sometimes used in connection with qualitative research as well; see *qualitative content analysis.*

contingency table   A table made up of rows and columns that shows the *relationship* between two *variables.* Usually, at least one of the variables is a *nominal variable* or *ordinal variable.* Each *cell* in the table shows the number or (more often) the percentage of cases for that specific combination of the two variables.

control group   See **experiment.**

convenience sample   A sample that is selected because of its availability to the researcher; a form of *non-probability sample.*

conversation analysis   The fine-grained analysis of talk (recorded in naturally occurring situations and then transcribed) to uncover the underlying structures in

Companion website

Textbooks today do not stand on their own: they are only the central elements in a complete learning and teaching package. *Social Research Methods* is no exception. This third Canadian edition is supported by an outstanding array of ancillary materials for both students and instructors.

www.oupcanada.com/SocialResearch3e

COMPANION WEBSITE

Alan Bryman, Edward Bell and The late James J. Teevan

Social Research Methods, Third Canadian Edition
ISBN 13: 9780195442960

Social Research Methods

Inspection copy request

Ordering information

Contact & Comments

About the Book

Now in its third Canadian edition, the market-leading Social Research Methods is an engaging and straightforward introduction to conducting quantitative and qualitative research in the social sciences. Building on the success of previous editions, the authors deftly guide students through all aspects of the research process, while providing useful tips on how to effectively collect, analyze, and interpret data, and disseminate those findings to others.

Sample Material

Get Adobe PDF reader [US | UK]

Instructor Resources

You need a password to access these resources. Please contact your local Sales and Editorial Representative for more information.

Student Resources

For Students

- *Companion Website*
  A comprehensive online study guide site provides detailed chapter summaries, self-assessment quizzes, and links to useful media resources.

For Instructors

- *Online Instructor's Manual*
  This fully revised online resource includes comprehensive outlines of the text's chapters, additional assignments, classroom activities designed to encourage student engagement, and teaching aids that will enhance the learning experience.

- *PowerPoint Slides*
  Hundreds of slides for classroom presentation—newly updated and enhanced for this edition—summarize key points from each chapter and can be edited to suit individual instructors' needs.

- *Online Test Generator*
  A comprehensive electronic test item file—employing cutting-edge test generator technology that gives instructors a wide array of options for sorting, editing, importing, and distributing questions—provides approximately 1,500 questions in multiple-choice, short-answer, and true/false formats.

How to use this book

Social Research Methods can be used in many ways. Some instructors, for reasons of time or preference, may not want to include all chapters or all sections of a specific chapter. Following is an overview of the major topic areas and the parts of the book where they are addressed:

- *Wider philosophical and methodological issues* are discussed at some length in Chapter 1. Instructors who do not wish to use this contextual material can largely ignore the chapter, except for the section on formulating a research question. Those who do want to emphasize issues of context should also see Chapter 15.

- *Practical issues involved in doing quantitative research* are the subject of Part Two. Chapter 2 is a useful introduction because it maps out the main research designs used in both quantitative and qualitative research.

- *Practical issues involved in doing qualitative research* are the subject of Part Three. Again, Chapter 2 maps out the most common designs.

- *Data analysis* is covered in Chapters 13 (quantitative) and 14 (qualitative), and a guide to the use of computer software for these purposes can be found in Appendix A. Even if the module is taught without actual computer applications, exposure to them will reinforce the textual material and may be useful for later work.

- *The quantitative/qualitative distinction* is used in two ways: to organize the discussion of research methods and data analysis, and to introduce some wider philosophical issues that have a bearing on social research. Chapter 1 outlines the main areas of difference between quantitative and qualitative research, while Chapter 15 explores ways of integrating the two. If time is a concern, the latter chapter can be skimmed.

- *Writing up research* is as much a part of the research process as data collection and analysis. Chapter 17 discusses a variety of issues related to writing and should be drawn to students' attention even if it is not discussed in class.

- *Specific advice on doing a research project.* As we have already noted, the whole book is relevant to student projects, but Chapter 18 addresses this subject directly.

Acknowledgements

Many people have helped me with this book, many of them unwittingly. Generations of research methods students at the University of Western Ontario have tested its contents. I wish to thank several people at or connected with OUP: David Stover, who had to persevere to initiate the project, Phyllis Wilson, who guided its early phases and never complained of my missing deadlines, and a dedicated copy editor, Pamela Erlichman, for her suggestions. I am grateful to Sarah Pink for her permission to use an image from her research on women and bullfighting.

Two people deserve the greatest appreciation: Alan Bryman and my wife, Bonnie. He wrote the British text on which this book is based. He put into clear prose the many things I tried to impart to my students in lectures, from philosophy of science issues to showing the common aspects of qualitative and quantitative methods, making my adaptation so much easier. My wife put up yet again with the late nights and daily tensions that a book like this entails. Thank you both.

James J. Teevan

Many thanks must go to Alan Bryman, who wrote the original version of this book, and to James J. Teevan, who produced the First Canadian Edition. It's an honour to be associated with them. Their diligent work made the Second and now the Third Canadian Edition possible.

At Oxford University Press, Allison McDonald and Caroline Starr did a very good job of getting this latest edition off the ground, and Patricia Simoes did a wonderful service in guiding it through to completion. I'm especially grateful for Patricia's calm patience and understanding as complications arose. A big thank you also goes out to Sally Livingston, who did fine work as the copy editor.

Many of the changes to this edition were made in response to the very constructive comments provided by the reviewers, which are deeply appreciated.

I would also like to thank my family—Jennifer Wakefield and Ted and Angelica Bell—for their support and inspiration.

Edward Bell

This book is dedicated to James J. Teevan, who died on 7 September 2010. The fact that Jim spent a great deal of his time writing textbooks is a testament to his devotion both to scholarship and to the sharing of that scholarship with students. His fingerprints are all over this book. He was especially resourceful in providing examples of Canadian research that illustrate key methodological concepts, and in outlining the countless challenges that researchers face as they go about their work. In 2007 he very kindly invited me on board as a co-author of this work; it proved to be the beginning of a memorable experience, for which I am very grateful. He will be greatly missed.

Edward Bell

Introduction

As I write this Introduction, much of the Middle East is in revolution. After decades of 'domestic peace' in which citizens showed very little opposition to their rulers, the 'Arab Spring' has blossomed. Ordinary people are taking to the streets in anger and frustration, clamouring for more open and democratic societies. Why this reaction, and why now? Did Facebook and Twitter help to mobilize the dissidents? Can liberal democracy become the norm in the Middle East, or is that way of organizing society able to take root only in countries where Western cultural and economic influences predominate? If the movement is successful, what are the implications for Islamist movements like al-Qaeda? And how will gender relations in Muslim countries be affected? The Arab Spring presents a seemingly endless list of questions that could be investigated by social researchers.

At the same time, there is no shortage of questions to be asked about Western societies. In Canada and several other countries, for instance, women now form a clear majority of university students, and that pattern holds true in highly prestigious faculties like medicine and law. Yet only a few decades ago, women were a minority on most university campuses. How did this change come about, and what are the implications for gender relations and society as a whole? Does this mean that gender discrimination in Canada is a thing of the past? Tellingly, women do *not* form a majority of students in disciplines such as mathematics and engineering. Is that evidence that gender discrimination is still present on our campuses and in the way we raise young girls and boys? Or does it suggest that men and women have innate differences that lead them to make different choices when deciding on a program of study? Do both explanations have some merit?

Any number of social phenomena shape the contours of the society in which we live—crime, single motherhood, ethnic tensions, labour disputes, racism, inequality, the living conditions of First Nations people, changing notions of the family, homelessness, sexual mores, and many more. It is crucial both for the individuals directly affected by such things and for society at large that these realities be examined and understood.

Social scientists have gone a long way towards improving our understanding of such issues, but we still have a lot to learn. In order to come up with informed, thoughtful analyses of these topics, and to be capable of evaluating the assessments offered by others, it is crucial to be familiar with the different *research methodologies* used to come up with that knowledge. As you will see as you make your way through this book, the range of research methods used in the social sciences is broad, but much of the work that is done involves acquiring information and organizing it in useful ways. In research as in art, the final product depends partly on the choice of materials, and partly on the methods and skills employed. In both endeavours, however, the end result is most beautiful when creativity and the imagination are allowed to flourish.

Personal experience with both research and art tells me that what is created can vary from the exquisite to the downright awful, depending on what raw materials are used and how the work is done. Experience also tells me that knowledge, practice, and constructive feedback are invaluable if one wants to create things that are truly beautiful; those who do the best work use all three to their advantage. This book will focus on the first two: acquiring knowledge (about research methods) and gaining practical experience. It will be up to your instructor or some other mentor to provide feedback on your work. The more you discuss your projects with others, the better they will be, so share your creations with the world.

The creation of knowledge through research involves more than just coming up with new ideas or novel ways of looking at life: it is also tied in with the exercise of power. To produce or acquire knowledge is a *political* act. We often hear that 'knowledge is power,' and in many ways that is true. Dictators know this best; they all try to limit access to knowledge in order to preserve their control over others. But the 'knowledge is power' maxim leaves several questions unanswered. What is knowledge? How can it be acquired? How are we to tell the difference between a sound idea and one that should be ignored? How can we gather information that will help us understand our subject matter, and what sort of information should we seek? How should that information be analyzed and evaluated? Are there some things that we will never fully understand, regardless of how hard we try?

This book explores a variety of answers to those questions. It takes the view that knowledge is *created*, just as statues, paintings, bridges, music, and loaves of bread are created. To produce knowledge, we need a methodology—a way of creating it. This book will explore how knowledge of society is created and evaluated. And if you accept the premise that knowledge is power, then learning about research methods means learning about how to become powerful, or at least more powerful. You could even say that 'methodology is power,' and you wouldn't be far off the mark.

How could methodology be power? For one thing, if you know how knowledge is created, you won't be as easily fooled as someone who doesn't know. Just as people who design computers usually make excellent judges of a particular computer's strengths and weaknesses, those who spend a lot of time thinking about research methodologies are often astute judges of whether claims made about society or human behaviour deserve serious consideration or should be dismissed. In other words, learning about research methodologies is

an excellent way to enhance your critical thinking skills—skills that are essential in any situation where power is exercised (i.e., everywhere).

Methodology can also be power insofar as it makes you a producer of ideas. Start thinking of yourself not only as someone who absorbs ideas and evaluates them, but also as someone who projects ideas onto the world. Start thinking of yourself as a *researcher*: someone who has the potential to look at societies and contribute to our understanding of them. That's far more interesting than just reading other people's work, although reading is an essential part of the process.

So if you do a study of the 'Arab Spring' and find that Facebook and Twitter did in fact help to mobilize the resistance movements in the Middle East, you will have made a contribution to the existing knowledge on political revolts and may even, in some small way, have made it more likely that those kinds of movements will succeed. If you do a study of the medical and mental health status of people living in poverty, you are in effect joining the chorus that is calling for change. If you conduct an inquiry into how boys and girls adopt their gender identities, you may help women and men understand each other better—something that could have far-reaching implications for human happiness.

Social research always has political ramifications, because it always implies (subtly or not so subtly) that some ways of organizing society are better than others. Some researchers are happy to leave their political involvement at that level: an *implication* in their work that existing social structures or practices should either change or be preserved. Others go so far as to engage in *advocacy*, taking part in public campaigns to persuade governments and the public at large that some sort of action should be taken. Whichever position the researcher takes, the politics of research cannot be avoided. What varies is how loudly the trumpet is sounded, which is a matter for the individual researcher to decide. Debates about the wisdom of social researchers' becoming advocates are part of the storied history of the social sciences, some of which will be told in this book.

If you want to learn how knowledge is created in the social sciences, or if you aspire to make an impact on the world by doing social research yourself, reading this book is a good way to start. If your goal is limited to passing a research methods course, you can take consolation in the fact that most of the people in your class are probably like you in that respect. Just remember that you can change your mind; the opportunity to delve deeper is always there. I hope that reading this book will at least pique your interest in how social researchers do what they do, and what the implications of social research are. To paraphrase Gore Vidal: the more one learns, the more interesting consciousness becomes.

Edward Bell
May, 2011

Social Research Methods

PART I

Part I of this book is concerned with two ideas that recur again and again throughout the text: the idea of general research orientation and the idea of research design. In Chapter 1, two general orientations are identified—the quantitative and qualitative approaches—along with a variety of considerations that affect the practice of social research. Chapter 2 presents different kinds of research design and identifies the criteria used to evaluate social research. Together these chapters provide the basic conceptual building blocks that we will return to later in the book. Some of the issues may seem remote from actual research practices, but they are in fact crucial for understanding them.

CHAPTER 1

General Research Orientations

CHAPTER OVERVIEW

The aim of this chapter is to examine the fundamental assumptions upon which social research is based. An important distinction commonly drawn by practitioners of social research—between the **quantitative** and **qualitative** approaches—is explored in relation to those considerations. We will consider:

- the relationship between theory and research—in particular, whether theories and the hypotheses derived from them are tested by gathering data (a **deductive** approach) or whether data gathering is used as a means to *create* theory (an **inductive** approach);

- **epistemological** issues, such as whether a natural science model like the one used in chemistry or biology is suitable for the study of the social world;

- **ontological** issues, such as whether the social world should be regarded as a reality external to individuals over which they have little or no control, or as something that social actors may fashion into their personal realities;

- how *values* and *practical issues* impinge on the research process; and

- how these issues relate to both quantitative and qualitative research; a preliminary discussion, followed up in Chapter 15, suggests that although the quantitative and qualitative orientations are different, they can complement each other.

Soon-Yi wants to find out why Aboriginal Canadians are more likely to live in poverty than other Canadians, but doesn't know where to begin. Should she start by gathering information on First Nations communities (residence patterns, economic activities, age structure)? Or should she examine the effects of land claims and treaties, or educational trajectories, or perceptions of Aboriginal people by non-Aboriginals? Once all those matters are explored, she thinks, it might be possible to come up with a theory that could shed some light on the question. But the list of topics she could gather information on seems endless.

Maybe it would it be better to start out with some hunches and then gather information to see whether they are supported by evidence. She already has the beginnings of a theory in the form of the idea that the level of wealth individuals can acquire depends on the extent to which they accept mainstream cultural notions about what is important in life, in particular whether they believe that obtaining material things should take priority over other aspects of life. Perhaps she can see if First Nations people are more likely to buy into that cultural norm or to reject it. In that case, should she gather information from Aboriginal people only, or from non-Aboriginals as well in order to compare the two groups?

Then there is the question of how to gather the information. Should she design a questionnaire and send it out to a large number of Aboriginal people? Or would it be better just to interview a few people and encourage them to talk about their priorities in life without trying to steer the conversation in any particular direction? If she does the latter, should she conduct a series of conversations at specified places and times? Or would it be better to live in a First Nations community for the summer and gather information through observation?

Soon-Yi also wonders what she would do if it turned out that Aboriginal people have ideas about the acquisition of material wealth that are different from her own. Should she try to determine whose perspective offers a more accurate view of reality? Can those sorts of issues ever be resolved? Are there 'right' and 'wrong' positions on such matters? She wonders whether, in general, social reality is whatever you make it to be, or whether there is a social reality 'out there' that is independent of the person who perceives it, and that can be known through careful observation and analysis. Could it be that the latter position is one that is appropriate for 'facts' but not for 'values'?

Then there are the broader questions: What, if anything, can be done about the issue of poverty among Aboriginal Canadians? Can society be changed so that Aboriginal poverty is eliminated, or at least reduced? Or are the social forces that affect our lives so strong that we have no choice but to conform to them, like leaves in a windstorm?

It turns out that a great many social thinkers and researchers have confronted the same issues that Soon-Yi is pondering. In fact there are a number of rich, if sometimes conflicting, intellectual traditions that can be drawn on to make sense of these matters and to assist people like Soon-Yi in making the kinds of practical decisions that all researchers have to make. In this chapter you will be introduced to that body of ideas and the debates surrounding them.

Introduction

This book is about social research. It would be easy to 'cut to the chase' and get on with explaining what the various research procedures are, when each is appropriate, and how to implement them. But the practice of social research does not exist in a vacuum, sealed off from philosophical and political debates, and contested assumptions. Several questions may arise; for example: Are people passive reactors to the social world or active creators of social reality? Can the methods of the natural sciences be applied to the social world, or does social science need unique methods to deal with its subject matter? Must past research be the source for current research? The explanations of social phenomena that scholars offer and their choices of research methods often depend on how they answer those sorts of questions.

Social research can be driven by a variety of motives. Quite often the goal is to assess the adequacy of a particular social theory, such as a theory of prejudice or crime. In other cases the aim is to gather information to create theories; for example, a sociologist may pose as a street person to find out how the homeless are treated by the public. Sometimes simple 'fact-finding' or exploratory work is carried out. For instance, Milgram's (1963) famous study of obedience was done partly to see how far subjects would go in obeying an authority figure's commands, and the results were astounding—many people appeared to be willing to inflict pain on innocent others. Similarly, Bell's (2007) study of the western-Canadian separatist movement was motivated in part by a desire to know how much public support the movement had, and it produced evidence that the movement was more popular than previously thought.

In other instances, research is driven by what is seen as a pressing social problem. In fact the discipline of sociology came into being in the eighteenth and nineteenth centuries partly as a way of understanding the social crises associated with modern life, and that tradition continues to this day. Hier (2002), for example, investigated raves when they became a subject of official concern following the ecstasy-related deaths of three young adults in Toronto in 1999. Yet another stimulus for research is personal experience (Lofland and Lofland 1995). Sugiman (2004), who is a 'sansei' or third-generation Japanese, investigated Japanese-Canadian women's experiences of internment during the Second World War after hearing about the personal histories of her family and friends.

Regardless of the motivation for doing research, the data gathered are usually viewed in relation to theories of some kind. That's because theories are an attempt to 'make sense of it all,' to find order and meaning in a seemingly infinite mass of information. How is that done?

Theory and research

The connection between theory and research is not straightforward. There are several issues at stake here, but two stand out: first, the form of the theory; and second, the relationship between data and theory.

DEGREE OF ABSTRACTION

The term 'theory' is used in a variety of ways, but its most common meaning is *an explanation of observed regularities or patterns*: for example, the finding that schizophrenia is more common in the working class than in the middle class, or that more men than women are alcoholics. Theories are composed of interrelated and usually verifiable statements or propositions. The statements and propositions come in varying forms, and different types may be combined in the same theory. Here are three common components of a theory:

1. *Definitions* specify what the key terms in the theory mean; for example, 'Crime is any violation of the *Canadian Criminal Code* and includes arson, embezzling, etc.'

2. *Descriptions* outline the characteristics of the phenomena of interest; for example, 'Arson involves the illegal setting of fires and is often done at night, either to abandoned buildings or houses when no one is home. There were 438 cases of arson last year, with estimated damage over $2 billion.'

3. *Relational statements* connect two or more **variables**, so that knowing the value of one variable conveys information about the other; for example, 'As the economy experiences a downturn, the arson rate increases.' Relational statements come in two forms:

   a. *deterministic*, which means the two variables always go together in a particular way; for example, 'as the economy shrinks by 1 per cent, the arson rate increases by 5 per cent.' If research uncovers an instance in which the variables are not related in this way, the relational statement must be modified.

   b. *probabilistic*, which means the two variables go together with some degree of regularity, but the relationship is not inevitable; for example, 'regions of the country with growing economies are more likely to experience a decrease in the arson rate than regions in which the economy is shrinking.' Here, finding a case that does not fit the pattern does not mean that the theory must be modified; this could simply be one of the times when the variables are not related in the usual way.

There are different types of theories. One distinction that is sometimes made is between *theories of the middle range* (Merton 1967) and *grand theories*. The former are more limited in scope, and can be tested directly by gathering empirical evidence. For instance, Durkheim's (1952 [1897]) theory of suicide, which maintains that suicide is a function of the level of social integration, is a theory of the middle range. One way to test it would be to compare suicide rates for married people with those for single, divorced, or widowed individuals. Merton's (1938) anomie theory, which suggests that crime is more common when a society instils a desire for wealth in everyone but provides insufficient means for all to achieve it, is another theory of the middle range. Such theories represent attempts to understand and explain a limited aspect of social life.

Grand theories, by contrast, are general and abstract. They include theories such as structural-functionalism, symbolic interactionism, critical

---

BOX 1.1   Grand theory and social research

Giddens' (1984) structuration theory attempts to bridge the gulf between notions of structure and agency in social life. This theoretical issue is explored in empirical research by Dinovitzer *et al.* (2003) on the educational attainment of immigrant youth. The specific focus of their research was suburban Toronto immigrants in the years 1976 to 1995. The data were quantitative, generated through structured interviews. The goal of the researchers was to tease out the relative influence on educational attainment of structural variables (such as class, gender, and the youths' family background) and individual variables over which the young people had more control (such as studying and cutting classes).

The authors found that educational achievement is affected by two structural variables (gender and father's occupation) and one individual factor (intellectual investment), and that bilingual ESL students do better than young immigrants for whom English is a first language. They are not brighter, nor do they work harder, but they have greater parental supervision, and—perhaps partly as a consequence—they plan better.

theory, post-structuralism, feminism, and so on. Grand theories generally offer few direct indications of how to collect evidence to test them, but they provide ways of looking at the world that can be the inspiration for a wide variety of research programs. For example, *standpoint theory* was developed by Dorothy Smith (2004; 2005) and others from a general feminist perspective. This theory maintains that the way we view the world and make our way in it is largely determined by our placement in various hierarchies of status and power. One offshoot of standpoint theory has been an increased willingness to examine the views and perceptions of poor or marginalized groups in society. Similarly, Box 1.1 shows how an abstract theory like Giddens' structuration theory (1984) can be applied to a specific situation and yield some important insights.

Although theory plays a crucial role in the social sciences, not all studies make reference to it. For example, some qualitative writers focus on providing a rich description of the experiences of a group of people without trying to come up with a comprehensive theory that would explain those experiences. Nonetheless, as Box 1.2 shows, social scientists are often under pressure from their peers to relate their work to theories of some kind.

As Box 1.2 indicates, some social scientists will reject research that has no direct connection to theory in either the grand or the middle-range sense of the term. However, non-theoretical work can provide insights that are useful or revealing in their own right. McKeganey and Barnard's (1996) research on British prostitutes and their clients is a case in point. The authors related their research findings to investigations of prostitutes in several other countries, and what they describe offers good illustrations of ideas that form an important part of the sociologist's conceptual toolkit. Although it is not possible to tell whether the authors had the **concept** in mind when they collected their data, their work offers real-life examples of Goffman's (1963) notion of 'stigma' and the way stigmatized individuals, in this case prostitutes and their clients,

---

BOX 1.2 : The need for theory

Teevan and Dryburgh (2000) collected data from 57 male adolescents concerning their participation in deviant activities such as truancy, theft, vandalism, and fighting, and asked them why they acted the way they did. Then the boys were read specially adapted sociological explanations of such behaviour and asked what they thought of them. In effect, they were asked to evaluate the sociologists' theories as if they were sociologists themselves. The idea was to give marginalized people a voice and to see the issue in question from the point of view of those studied— two common approaches in qualitative research. Some journal reviewers liked the idea but thought that the findings' relevance for sociological theory needed to be explored. Eventually the authors brought a variety of social theories to bear on the data they had gathered, and in doing so provided a critical assessment of existing explanations for delinquency and conformity.

A young man painting graffiti on a wall. Some call this behaviour vandalism, while others consider it art. What social theories might you invoke to explain what he is doing? How might the young man himself explain it? Do you think his explanation would have anything in common with your social theories?

manage a spoiled identity. Their work also sheds light on Hochschild's (1983) concept of 'emotional labour,' a term she coined to refer to the work that flight attendants do when they feign friendliness in order to deal with difficult passengers. Similarly, several other non-theoretical studies provide data that could eventually be used to evaluate or devise a theory. Our discussion of what theory is and its importance invites consideration of another question: What is the relationship between theory and research? Up to this point we have focused primarily on how theory can guide research, in particular on how the collection and analysis of data can be used to test theories. But this notion of research as essentially 'theory testing' does not provide a complete picture of what social scientists do. Theory may also *follow upon* or *arise from* the collection and analysis of data. Here we begin to see two different ways to go about acquiring knowledge: the **deductive** and **inductive** approaches.

Deductive and inductive approaches

The deductive method is the most common approach to social research. The sequence of steps taken in deductive research is depicted in Figure 1.1. Note that the researcher starts by coming up with a theory that seeks to explain a particular phenomenon, and then deduces specific hypotheses from it that are tested with empirical data (see Box 1.3 for a concrete example) and then are either confirmed or rejected. In the case of the research described in Box 1.3, the hypotheses were supported. If the data gathered do not support the researchers' hypotheses, however, the theory has to be revised or rejected.

It is also important to bear in mind that when the deductive approach is put into operation, the researcher does not necessarily follow the exact linear sequence shown in Figure 1.1. For example, a new hypothesis may come to mind during the data-gathering stage; or the relevance of the data for a *second* theory may become apparent *after* the data have been collected. Although the sequence outlined in Figure 1.1 is a common one, it is only a general model, one that is not strictly followed in all cases.

In fact, some research makes no attempt to follow the sequence outlined in Figure 1.1. Some investigators prefer an *inductive* approach in which theory is the *outcome* of research. In inductive social science, the researcher begins not by coming

FIGURE 1.1   The process of deduction

up with a theory to be tested, but by *gathering or examining data* relevant to the phenomenon being investigated; see Figure 1.2, which illustrates the difference between induction and deduction. Box 1.4 provides an example: Wilson (2002) offered theories to explain raves only *after* he had gathered qualitative information on the topic.

When the inductive method is used, data are gathered not to test a theory, but to come up with the information required to *construct* a theory. That's why with induction, data gathering comes first, and the effort to create concepts and theories out of it comes later. After some theoretical reflection a researcher may decide to collect more data to establish the conditions under which the newly developed theory does or does not hold. This strategy of moving back and forth between data and theory is often described as *iterative*. The practice of deriving theories from qualitative data is sometimes referred to as **grounded theory**.

In actual research situations it is impossible to conduct a study that is purely deductive or purely inductive. Just as deduction always entails an element of induction (theories do not emerge from a pristine mind unaware of previous findings) so the inductive process always entails a modicum of

BOX 1.3　A deductive study

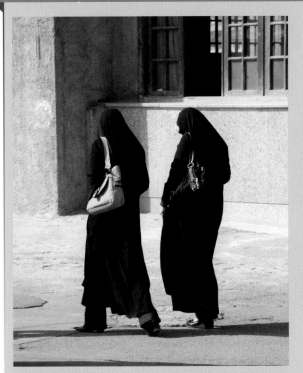

Veiled women in Iran. Do you think that Iran's strict religious environment, which makes wearing the hijab compulsory for women, has an effect on the personal religious beliefs of Iranian women, as Kelley and De Graff's (1997) theory would predict? Specific predictions can be derived from a general theory when the deductive approach is used.

Based on their readings of previous studies of what affects religious beliefs—factors such as parents, schools, and friends—Kelley and De Graaf (1997) argued that there are good grounds to think that the nation into which someone is born is also an important influence. These reflections constitute what they referred to as the 'theory' that guided their research and from which the following hypothesis was derived: 'People born into religious nations will, in proportion to the orthodoxy of their fellow-citizens, acquire more orthodox beliefs than otherwise similar people born into secular nations' (1997: 641). The authors hypothesized further that the religious orientation of the individual's family (whether devout or secular) would have a stronger effect in secular countries.

To test their hypotheses, Kelley and De Graaf examined large-sample survey research from 15 nations. Religious orthodoxy was measured by four survey questions about religious belief: (1) whether the person believed in God; (2) past beliefs about God; (3) how close the individual felt to God; and (4) whether the person believed that God cares about everyone. To measure national religiosity, each of the 15 nations was classified in one of five categories, from secular to religious. The classification was derived by averaging parental religious attendance measured on a scale of five levels and religious belief in the nation as a whole (1997: 647). The hypotheses were broadly confirmed, with the authors concluding that the 'religious environment of a nation has a major impact on the beliefs of its citizens' and that 'in relatively secular nations, the effect of family religiosity on children's religiosity is strong' (1997: 654, 655).

Note that this study demonstrates how hypotheses are deduced from existing theory and then are used to guide the process of data collection so that the theory can be tested.

deduction (no researcher will be totally unaware of theories that might be applicable to the phenomenon he or she is observing). Often some combination of both can be found in the same research.

Although some researchers using induction undoubtedly try to develop theories, sometimes the results of their research are little more than empirical **generalizations**, however useful they may be. An example is a recent Statistics Canada finding that from 1997 to 2007, salaries stagnated for blue-collar employees in manufacturing and for clerical employees and retail salespeople, while the earnings of private-sector managers grew by 20 per cent in that period (http://www.statcan.gc.ca/daily-quotidien/080222/dq080222b-eng.htm, accessed 28 Oct. 2010).

The next section examines some epistemological issues that affect the conduct of social research.

Epistemological considerations

Those who do social research base their work on a number of epistemological assumptions—notions of what can be known and how knowledge can be acquired. One important epistemological issue in sciences should follow the same principles and procedures as the natural sciences.

Positivism

One epistemological position that affirms the importance of following the natural sciences is **positivism**. Although definitions of the term vary, positivism is generally taken to entail the following:

1. Only phenomena confirmed by the senses (sight, hearing, etc.) can be accepted as knowledge: this is the principle of **empiricism**. Ideas must be subjected to the rigours of empirical testing before they can be considered knowledge.

2. A key purpose of theory is to generate hypotheses that can be tested and thereby allow explanations of observed laws and principles to be assessed (*deduction*).

3. Knowledge can also be arrived at through the gathering of facts that provide the basis for generalizations or laws (*induction*).

4. Science must (and presumably can) be 'value-free.' That is, it must be conducted in such a way that different researchers, given the same data, will always reach the same conclusions, no matter how different their values might be. In the past this 'value-free' quality was called 'objectivity'; today it is more likely to be called 'intersubjectivity.'

5. There is a clear distinction between scientific statements, which describe how and why certain social phenomena operate the way they do, and normative statements, which outline whether certain acts or social conditions are morally acceptable. Only scientific statements have a place in the domain of science; normative statements belong in the realm of philosophy or religion. This idea is implied by point 1 above, because the truth of moral claims cannot be confirmed by the senses.

It is possible to see in these five points a link with some of the issues already raised about the relationship between theory and research. Positivism assumes a fairly sharp distinction between theory and research and includes elements of both deduction and induction. One role of research is to test theories and gather the information necessary for the development of scientific laws. Positivism also implies that it is possible to collect observations without any reference to pre-existing theories, and

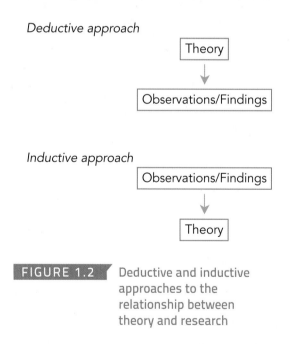

Deductive approach

Theory

↓

Observations/Findings

Inductive approach

Observations/Findings

↓

Theory

FIGURE 1.2 Deductive and inductive approaches to the relationship between theory and research

the social sciences is the question of what should be regarded as acceptable knowledge. A fundamental debate in this context is whether the social to develop new theories purely on the basis of those observations. Finally, theories and propositions not directly testable through empirical observation are often not considered to be genuinely scientific.

A common mistake is to treat positivism as synonymous with science and the scientific. In fact, philosophers of science and social science differ quite sharply over how best to characterize scientific practice, and since the early 1960s positivism has acquired some negative connotations. One reason for dissatisfaction was the fact that certain researchers in the positivist tradition ignored some fundamental differences between human beings and the often inanimate or not fully conscious entities studied by natural scientists. Unlike subatomic particles or plants, for example, we humans have thoughts, feelings, and values — perhaps even some capacity for volition. Those aspects of human behaviour were often not addressed in the leading positivistic theories of the day. The positivist idea that science can or should be value-free was also a source of dissatisfaction. Critics pointed out that 'neutral' social scientists often took moral positions on social issues, at least implicitly. For example, theories implying that social equilibrium or harmony is normal seemed to suggest that social change is not needed or not desirable. Some critics went so far as to claim that it is the duty of the social scientist to help bring about social change in order to create a better world.

Interpretivism

Interpretivism to some extent grew out of the epistemological critique of positivism, and provides an alternative to the sort of social science typically done by positivists. Interpretive researchers maintain that it is the role of social scientists to grasp the subjective *meanings* of people's actions. They make the point that people act on the basis of the meanings that they attribute to their acts and to the acts of others. Individuals use their own common-sense constructs to interpret the reality of their daily lives, and it is these thoughts that motivate their behaviour.

Interpretivists claim that it is the job of the social scientist to gain access to the 'common-sense thinking' of the people they study and hence to interpret people's actions and their social world *from the point of view of the actors*. Thus any thoughts constructed by the social scientist to grasp this social reality must be founded on the common-sense interpretations of those they study: people living their daily lives within their own social world (Schutz 1962:

59). Many interpretive social scientists argue that the subject matter of the social sciences — people, groups, and institutions — is fundamentally different from that of the natural sciences. For them it follows that the study of the social world requires a different logic and research procedure, one that reflects what they see as the distinctiveness of humans as against other living things or inanimate objects. This clash reflects a division between the positivist emphasis on the *explanation* of human behaviour and the interpretivist preference for an *empathetic understanding* and *interpretation* of human behaviour. This division, which precedes the emergence of modern social science, finds expression in Max Weber's (1864–1920) notion of *Verstehen* (which means 'empathetic understanding'). Weber described sociology as a 'science which attempts the interpretive understanding of social action in order to arrive at a causal explanation of its course and effects' (1947: 88). Weber's definition seems to embrace both explanation *and* understanding, but the crucial point is that the task of 'causal explanation' is undertaken with reference to the 'interpretive understanding of social action.' This is a different emphasis from a more Durkheimian view in which the external forces that affect behaviour may not be perceived by those involved, or at least may have no meaning for them. For a Marxist view, see Box 1.5.

Symbolic interactionism is an example of a sociological perspective that falls under the heading of interpretivism. The ideas of the founders of symbolic interactionism — in particular George Herbert Mead (1863–1931), who maintained that the individual's *self-concept* emerges through an appreciation of the perceptions of others — have been hotly debated. Symbolic interactionists argue that interaction takes place in such a way that individuals are continually interpreting the symbolic meaning of their environment (including the actions of others) and acting on the basis of that imputed meaning (cf. Collins 1994). In research terms, according to Blumer (1962: 188), 'the position of symbolic interaction requires the student to catch the process of interpretation through which [actors] construct their actions.'

Taking an interpretative stance can result in surprising findings, or at least findings that appear surprising if the researcher's position is outside the particular social context being studied. Box 1.6 provides an interesting example.

BOX 1.5 | Research methods used by Marxists

Almost all social scientists who adopt a Marxist approach are critical of the positivist notion that researchers should take a value-neutral stance regarding their subject matter. But they are also critical of narrowly interpretive perspectives on social life, arguing that social research has to go beyond acquiring knowledge of how people in society interpret their world. Marxists argue that those who own the means of production deceive, constrain, and exploit the weak. The masses could be free if social scientists, by asking embarrassing questions and making pointed arguments, would uncover exploitation, expose hypocrisy, and reveal to the general populace the nature and extent of their oppression. This would transform the masses from what Marx called a *class an sich* (a class in itself, an objective reality) into a *class für sich* (a class for itself, one with an awareness of its exploitation).

Marxists reject the idea that it is the role of the scientist to be detached. Instead, they see it as the role of social scientist to unmask the unjust conditions in the world, thus allowing the downtrodden to see the sources of their ills. They maintain that research should be action-oriented, that it should involve *praxis*: putting one's theoretical and academic positions into practice. The idea of praxis is contained in Marx's famous dictum that 'philosophers have only *interpreted* the world in various ways; the point, however, is to *change* it' (Marx 1998 [1845]: 574 [emphasis in original]). Smashing myths and uncovering contradictions are just the first part of that process (cf. Neuman 2003).

Of course, as the example in Box 1.6 suggests, when social scientists adopt an interpretive stance, they are not simply revealing how members of a social group interpret the world around them. The social scientist almost certainly aims to place those interpretations into a social scientific framework. Thus there is a double interpretation going on: the researcher is interpreting others' interpretations. Indeed, there is even a third level of interpretation, because the researcher's interpretations have to be further interpreted in terms of the concepts, theories, and literature of the social sciences. Thus, in Box 1.6 the idea that Riverside was not perceived as a high-crime area by residents was Foster's interpretation of her subjects' interpretations. She then had the additional job of placing her findings into a social scientific framework, which she accomplished by relating them to existing concepts and discussions in criminology: concepts such as informal social control, neighbourhood watch schemes, and the role of housing style as a possible cause of criminal activity.

The aim of this section has been to outline how epistemological considerations—especially those relating to whether a natural science or positivist approach can supply legitimate knowledge of the social world—are related to research practice. Among its key points is the idea that positivists often use the deductive approach, although they concede that it is possible to generate theories using induction. By contrast, we've seen that interpretive researchers typically adopt an inductive strategy. However, it is important not to overstate the connections between epistemological issues and research practice: they represent tendencies only. Particular epistemological principles and

BOX 1.6 | Interpretivism in practice

Foster (1995) conducted **ethnographic** research using **participant observation** and semi-structured interviews in a housing estate in East London referred to as Riverside, a residential complex experiencing a high level of crime according to official statistics. However, she found that residents did not perceive the estate to be a high-crime area; nor were they overly anxious about becoming victims of crime. Those perceptions could be attributed to a number of factors, but a particularly important one was 'informal social control,' which was used in conjunction with more formal methods such as policing. People expected a certain level of crime, but felt fairly secure because informal social control worked to keep the level of crime contained.

Informal social control has several aspects. One is that neighbours often look out for each other. In the words of one of Foster's interviewees: 'If I hear a bang or shouting I go out. If there's aggravation I come in and ring the police. I don't stand for it.' Another aspect of informal social control is that people often feel secure because they know each other. A second respondent said: 'I don't feel nervous . . . because people do generally know each other. We keep an eye on each other's properties. . . . I feel quite safe because you know your neighbours and you know they're there . . . they look out for you' (Foster 1995: 575).

research practices do not necessarily go hand in hand in a neat, unambiguous manner. Often hybrid approaches are taken, which combine different positions and approaches. This point will be made again on several occasions.

Ontological considerations

There are two ontological debates that are of particular interest to social scientists. The first is concerned with the following questions: Do social phenomena have an objective reality, independent of our perceptions? Or is what passes for reality merely a set of mental constructions? If you answer 'yes' to the first question, you are in the **objectivist** camp. People on this side of the debate maintain that there is such a thing as social reality, and that it is the job of social scientists to discover what that reality is. An affirmative answer to the second question means that you agree with the **constructionist** position. People holding this view are in sympathy with Nietzsche's famous aphorism that there are no facts, only interpretations (1910: 12). Such people maintain that there is no objective social reality against which our conceptions and views of the world may be tested. (The discussion of postmodernism in Chapter 17 further

examines this viewpoint.) A middle ground or 'soft constructionist' position is also possible, and is held by many. It maintains that there may be an objective social reality, but that many of our ideas do not reflect it: instead those ideas are constructed to justify or rationalize various forms of domination. Box 1.7 provides two illustrations of the less stringent form of constructionism.

A second debate revolves around these questions: Is social reality akin to the physical world as most people see it—largely fixed and 'out there,' something that individuals and groups have to confront but over which they have little or no control, like a snowstorm? Or is social reality not necessarily pre-existing and fixed, but rather created through our actions? A 'yes' to the first question indicates support for a variant of objectivism, while a 'yes' to the second affirms a kind of constructionism. In this chapter we'll focus mainly on this second debate: whether social reality can be created.

Some social scientists suggest that social phenomena confront individuals as external facts beyond their reach or influence. For example, an organization has rules and regulations and adopts standardized procedures for getting things done. A division of labour assigns people to different jobs. There is a hierarchy of authority, a mission

---

BOX 1.7 | Constructionism in action

Lantz and Booth (1998) examined media treatment of the apparent rise in the incidence of breast cancer that began in the early 1980s and found that its depiction as epidemic can be treated as a social construction. They analyzed a variety of popular magazines and noted that many of the articles drew attention to the lifestyles of modern women, such as delaying first births and having careers. The authors also argued that the articles ascribe blame: 'Women are portrayed as victims of an insidious disease, but also as victims of their own behaviours, many of which are related to the control of their own fertility' (1998: 915).

This article concludes that, as a social category, the breast cancer epidemic was represented in popular magazines in a particular way—one that blamed the victims and their lifestyles, particularly in the case of young women. Yet in fact fewer than 20 per cent of cases of breast cancer were in women under the age of 50. Lantz and Booth's study is fairly representative of a constructionist ontology in suggesting that the idea

that young women's lifestyles cause breast cancer was constructed as a social fact by popular magazine writers.

Similarly, Hallgrimsdottir et al. (2006: 266) argue that the media 'contributes to constructing, reproducing and deepening the social stigmas associated with working in the sex industry.' The authors compared media depictions of sex-trade workers in Victoria, BC, from 1980 to 2004 with the interpretations the street prostitutes, escorts, and others provided themselves. Whereas the media portrayed these people as wicked and blameworthy in the earlier years, and as exploited, trapped, and innocent girls more recently, the sex workers interpreted their experiences very differently. Although there was considerable heterogeneity in their experiences and attitudes towards their trade, many saw sex work as a largely mundane matter of earning a living. Because they are marginalized and stigmatized, however, their voices are seldom heard; most people have their ideas about prostitution constructed for them by the media.

statement, and so on. Objectivists see any organization as possessing a reality external to any of the specific individuals who inhabit it; they may leave, but it will stay. Moreover, the organization represents a social order in that it exerts pressure on individuals to conform to organizational requirements. People learn and apply the rules and regulations and follow the standardized procedures. They do the jobs to which they are appointed. If they do not do these things, they may be reprimanded or even fired. The organization is therefore a constraining force that acts on and inhibits its members. To a large extent, this is the 'classic' way of conceptualizing an organization.

An alternative ontological position challenges the suggestion that things such as organizations are external realities confronting social actors who have limited power to influence or change them. Strauss and colleagues (1973), for example, carried out research in a psychiatric hospital and proposed that its organization was best conceptualized as one of 'negotiated order.' Instead of viewing order as a pre-existing characteristic, they argued that it is worked at and created to some extent, and that the rules are far less extensive and less rigorously imposed than might be supposed from an objectivist account of organizations.

Indeed, Strauss and colleagues saw rules more as general understandings than as commands (1973: 308). Precisely because relatively little of the activity of doctors, nurses, and other personnel is specifically set down or prescribed, the social order of a hospital is an outcome of agreed-upon patterns of action that are themselves the products of negotiations among the different parties involved. For instance, the official rules may say that only a doctor can increase medication; however, some nurses are routinely given this power, even though this is never actually stated in the regulations. The social order is in a constant state of change because the hospital is 'a place where numerous agreements are continually being terminated or forgotten, but also are continually being established, renewed, reviewed, revoked, [and] revised. . . . In any pragmatic sense, this is the hospital *at the moment* [our emphasis]: this is its social order' (1973: 316–17). The authors argued that a preoccupation with the formal properties of organizations (rules, organizational charts, regulations, and roles) makes it hard to recognize the degree to which order in organizations has to be *established* in everyday interaction. This *informal* organization arises because there cannot be rules for every possible contingency, and because the existing rules are sometimes problematic. However, this is not to say that the formal properties of organizations have *no* effect on individual action.

Although Strauss and colleagues stressed the active role of individuals in the social construction of social reality, they did not push the argument to an extreme. For example, they did not claim that nurses can negotiate their roles to the point where they are allowed to operate on patients. But not all writers adopting a constructionist position are similarly prepared to acknowledge the existence or importance of an objective reality. It is precisely this split between seeing the social world as an objective reality and seeing it as a subjective reality in a continuous state of flux that Giddens sought to straddle in formulating his idea of structuration (recall Box 1.1).

The constructionist perspective that maintains that social reality can be negotiated also suggests that the concepts people employ to help them understand the natural and social world are social products whose meaning is constructed in and through social interaction. For example, a concept such as 'masculinity' is treated as a social construction. This implies that masculinity is not a distinct, timeless, and universal entity, but something whose meaning is built up through interaction. That meaning is likely to be ephemeral, in that it will vary over time and place. This tendency can be seen particularly well in **discourse analysis**, examined in Chapter 16. As Potter (1996: 98) observed: 'The world . . . is *constituted* in one way or another as people talk it, write it, and argue it [emphasis in original].' This sense of constructionism frequently sparks an interest in how social phenomena are represented.

RELATIONSHIP TO SOCIAL RESEARCH

Questions of social ontology cannot be divorced from issues concerning the conduct of social research. Ontological assumptions and commitments affect both the way research questions are formulated and the way the research is carried out. For example, a researcher who sees organizations as objective social entities that act on individuals is likely to emphasize their formal properties. Alternatively, a researcher who is interested in the negotiated, changing nature of organizations is likely to focus on the active involvement of people in reality construction. In each case, a different research design is required.

General orientations: quantitative and qualitative research

Many writers on methodological issues distinguish between quantitative and qualitative research. The most basic distinction is that quantitative research uses numbers and statistics in the collection and analysis of data, while qualitative research relies mainly on words and other non-numerical symbols. Some writers see the distinction between the two types of research as fundamental; others believe it to be no longer useful or even 'false' (Layder 1993: 110). Although this issue has been vigorously debated, we're convinced that there is a meaningful difference between quantitative and qualitative research. That difference will be a recurring theme in this book, both because it is a useful way of classifying different research methods and because it is a helpful reference point for a range of issues in the practice of social research.

On the surface, it seems that the main difference between quantitative and qualitative research is that quantitative researchers rely more on formal and mathematical measurement and analysis techniques than qualitative researchers do. But many sociologists and others suggest that the differences are deeper than merely the amount of quantification. For many writers, quantitative and qualitative research differ in their epistemological foundations and in other respects too. Indeed, when we look at the areas that were the focus of the last three sections—the relationship between theory and research, epistemological considerations, and ontological issues—we can see quantitative and qualitative research as forming two distinctive *general orientations* to the conduct of social research. Table 1.1 outlines the differences between quantitative and qualitative research in terms of the three areas.

Thus quantitative research:

- usually entails a deductive approach to the relationship between theory and research in which theory testing is a prime objective;
- incorporates the practices and norms of the natural science model and of positivism in particular; and
- generally embodies a view of society as an external, objective reality.

By contrast, qualitative research:

- takes a predominantly *inductive* approach to the relationship between theory and research, in which the *generation of theories and interpretations* is the main goal;
- rejects the use of the natural science and positivist models in social research and replaces them with methodologies that seek to determine how individuals interpret their social world; and
- embodies a view of social reality as a constantly shifting and emergent property of individuals' creations.

There is even more to the quantitative/qualitative distinction than this contrast suggests. The nature of quantitative and qualitative research respectively will be outlined in greater detail in Chapters 3 and 8. Then in Chapter 15 their contrasting features will be further explored as we examine the effects of the commitment to a positivist epistemology in quantitative research and the rejection of that epistemology by qualitative researchers.

Finally, although it is useful to contrast the two general orientations, it is important not to hammer a wedge between them. For example, although quantitative research tends to be deductive and qualitative work inductive, there are notable exceptions to that general rule. It may seem perverse to introduce a basic set of distinctions and then suggest that they are problematic, but a recurring theme of this book is that discussing the nature of social research is just as complex as conducting research itself. We can outline the typical philosophical assumptions and research practices of the two general orientations, but the full reality is messier than those neat categories would suggest. Issues become more complicated the deeper we delve into them.

For example, we've seen that qualitative research is typically described as being more concerned with generating theories than testing them. However, there are many studies in which qualitative research is used to test rather than generate theories. An example is Hier's (2002) investigation of Ontario rave scenes, with their all-night dancing and amphetamine use. Hier wanted to show that the regulation of raves was a contest between a city that feared increased drug use and rave supporters, who eventually won the day by arguing that banning raves would drive the drugs underground with even worse consequences. Similarly, although Wilson's (2002) study of the same topic (outlined in Box 1.4) is broadly interpretivist, with its examination of how ravers view their social situation, it includes some objectivist overtones. For example, in exploring the effects of technology, including the Internet, on the scene, he was describing a world that is 'out there' and as having a formal, objective quality. It is thus another example of qualitative research that does not have *all* the features outlined in Table 1.1.

The point here is that quantitative and qualitative research represent different research orientations, and that the two approaches may be quite different in terms of the role of theory, epistemological issues, and ontological concerns. Once again, however, the distinction is not hard-and-fast: studies that have the broad characteristics of one research strategy may also have some of the characteristics of the other. Also, many writers argue that the two can be combined within a single research project, as we will see in Chapter 15.

Influences on the conduct of social research

You can now see how social research is influenced by a variety of factors. Figure 1.3 summarizes the influences examined so far, but adds three more: the impact of *values*, *politics*, and *practical considerations*.

VALUES

How might the values, personal beliefs, and feelings of researchers affect their work? Perhaps one would expect social scientists to be completely value-free and objective in their studies. Research that simply reflects the personal views of its practitioners would be biased and invalid, and thus unscientific. Durkheim (1858–1917) wrote that *social facts* are objects whose study requires that all 'preconceptions must be eradicated' (1938: 31). Since values are a form of preconception, his point implies that they should be suppressed when conducting research. But is that humanly possible? Social researchers never work in a moral or evaluative vacuum: they are always influenced by value presuppositions that have implications

for the conduct of social research. This view is increasingly accepted among social researchers. Indeed, it is now recognized that values can intrude at any or all points in the process of social research, including the following:

- choice of research area;
- formulation of the research question;
- choice of method;
- formulation of the research design and data collection techniques;
- data collection;
- analysis of data;
- interpretation of data; and
- conclusions.

There are, therefore, numerous points at which bias and the intrusion of values can occur during the course of research. For example, researchers may develop affection or sympathy for the people they are studying. It is quite common for researchers working within a qualitative research strategy, in particular when they use very intensive interviewing, to become so close to their subjects that they find it difficult to disentangle their role as social scientists from their concern for the subjects' well-being. As noted in Box 1.8, this risk may be heightened by the tendency for sociologists to be sympathetic to underdogs.

Equally, social scientists may be repelled by the people they are studying. In his research into an African society known as the Ik, a social anthropologist was appalled by what he saw: a loveless (and for him unlovable) group that left its young and very old to die (Turnbull 1973). Although he was able to identify the conditions that led to these practices, he was very honest in his disgust for what he witnessed, particularly during his early time with them.

One way of dealing with the problem of values and bias is to recognize that research cannot be value-free, and to try to ensure that values in

TABLE 1.1	Fundamental differences between quantitative and qualitative research strategies	
	QUANTITATIVE	**QUALITATIVE**
Role of theory in research	Mainly deductive; testing of theory	Mainly inductive; generation of theory
Epistemological orientation	Natural science model; positivism	Interpretivism
Ontological orientation	Objectivism	Constructionism

Methods in Motion

Applications to Canadian Society

Women in male-dominated occupations: How do they fare?

Demaiter and Adams (2009) did a qualitative study of how Canadian women cope in the male-dominated world of information technology (IT) workplaces. As is typical of qualitative research, the study involved only a relatively small number of people: interviews were conducted with eleven successful women in eight IT organizations located in four different provinces. The authors acknowledge that the 'small sample size and the uniqueness of study participants prevent generalization' (39), which is commonly the case with this sort of research. However, as we will see in later chapters, it is not necessarily the goal of qualitative research to come up with findings that can be generalized to some larger population. Instead, qualitative researchers seek to find out how the subjects of the study perceive their world by allowing them to speak for themselves. The sorts of insights that can be derived from research of this kind are difficult to attain in quantitative research, which normally requires research participants to choose from a fixed set of responses.

For the interviews, Demaiter and Adams used a semi-structured format that included open-ended questions. The interviews were conducted in three different ways: eight by telephone, two in person, and one by email. Here again the authors were open about the limitations of their methods: 'We acknowledge the fact that the mixed format [for interviews] . . . is not ideal' (40). The authors are not alone in having to settle for a methodology that wasn't exactly what they would have preferred. In fact, virtually all studies in the social sciences involve methodological compromises of one sort or another, partly because the resources available to do the research are always limited. Nevertheless, the results can still be highly informative if wise methodological decisions are made.

The authors found that, by and large, the women they interviewed did not perceive their gender to be a barrier to their career advancement. One database analyst, for example, stated: 'Yes, I've never felt that I was at a disadvantage (or an advantage) because I am a woman' (41). Yet when asked to elaborate on their experiences, many of the women suggested that gender was in fact an issue in their workplace. For example, one interviewee said, 'I mean you have to be super smart, super intelligent, like way above average to go beyond a certain level because the glass ceiling is definitely there' (43). Demaiter and Adams concluded that the women in their study may have been successful in their careers partly because they were, to a certain extent, oblivious to the gendered nature of their workplace—they forged ahead undaunted by the gender barriers they faced.

In addition to providing a window from which to view women's experiences in male-dominated occupations, this study illustrates a point raised in the Introduction to this book, namely that issues of power and politics inevitably enter the picture whenever social research is done. What differs from study to study is the extent to which the political implications are explicit. In the case of this project, the political elements of the study are never far from the surface. For instance, the authors write that the women's 'tendency to downplay the significance of gender' in their career histories may serve to 'prevent meaningful change' (31), which suggests that the researchers see their work as informing a larger discussion on gender relations in Canadian society, an issue that has important political dimensions. Again, virtually all research in the social sciences is to some degree relevant to politics in the larger sense of the word.

---

the research process are acknowledged and made explicit. This is part of a larger process of **reflexivity** or self-reflection that researchers are encouraged to carry out. As Turnbull (1973) put it at the beginning of his book on the Ik:

> The reader is entitled to know something of the aims, expectations, hopes, and attitudes that the writer brought to the field [in his case, Western values about the

FIGURE 1.3   Influences on social research

BOX 1.8 | Taking sides in social research

Over forty years ago, an interesting debate took place between Becker and Gouldner, two prominent figures in American sociology. It raised many issues concerning the role of values in research, including the issue of taking sides. Becker (1967) argued that it is almost impossible to do research without being affected by personal sympathies. For example, much research is undertaken in the context of hierarchical relationships (police/criminals, managers/workers, doctors/patients, or teachers/students). Becker felt it would be difficult in such instances not to take sides, but argued that the bigger dilemma involved deciding which side to take.

Becker recognized that within his field, the sociology of deviance, the sympathies of many practitioners lay with the underdogs in hierarchical relationships, leading them (at a minimum) to seek to express or represent the underdogs' point of view. However, Becker argued that sociologists siding with the underdog were more likely to be accused of bias than their colleagues who identified with the more powerful. (There was greater respect for the powerful when Becker wrote than there is today.)

Gouldner (1968) countered that Becker had exaggerated the problem and that it was possible to take the point of view of a section of society seriously without sympathizing with that group. More recently, Liebling (2001) added that it is possible to see the merits of more than one side. Taking the case of prison research, she showed not only that it is possible to recognize the virtues of different perspectives (in her case, those of prison officials and prisoners) but that a researcher can do so without incurring the wrath of either side.

family], for these will surely influence not only how he sees things but even what he sees (13).

Researchers are increasingly prepared to forewarn readers of their biases and assumptions and to explain how these may have influenced their findings. Since the mid-1970s many researchers have published 'insider' accounts of what doing research is really like, as opposed to the generalities presented in social research methods textbooks (like this one). These accounts frequently function as 'confessions' of personal biases and reveal the pride that researchers take in telling readers how open they are in revealing them.

Still another approach is to argue for consciously value-laden research. Some writers on social research celebrate what Mies (1993: 68) called a 'conscious partiality.' For example, Tastsoglou and Miedema (2003) clearly adopted a feminist, anti-racist approach in studying immigrant women in the Maritimes. A similar perspective allowed Pratt and Valverde (2002) to describe a large Canadian newspaper as a 'notorious tabloid,' 'obsessed' with what it called bogus refugees. It is also exemplified in Hallgrimsdottir et al.'s (2006) condemnation of the media's role in stigmatizing sex workers in BC. In fact, some feminist researchers would consider it inappropriate (as well as difficult) to do research on women in an objective, value-neutral way because that would be incompatible with their values. Instead, many feminist researchers argue for research that exposes the conditions of women's disadvantage in a male-dominated society, as Demaiter and Adams (2009) did in their study of women in the IT sector, featured in the Methods in Motion box on page 15. Some feminist writers argue that only research on women intended *for* women is consistent with women's wider political needs.

The significance of feminism in relation to values goes further than this, however. Several feminist social researchers in the early 1980s proposed that quantitative research is incompatible with feminist ideals. For writers such as Oakley (1981), quantitative research is bound up with the male value of *control*, as seen in the researcher's control both of the research subject/respondent and of the research context and situation. Moreover, the research process is seen as a one-way affair in which researchers extract information from their subjects and give little if anything in return. For many feminists, such a strategy borders on exploitation and is incompatible with the value that feminism attributes to sisterhood and non-hierarchical relationships.

The antipathy towards quantitative research resulted in a preference for qualitative research among certain feminists. Qualitative research was seen not only as more consistent with the values of feminism, but as more adaptable to those values. Feminist qualitative research came to be associated with refusing to take a value-neutral approach and relating to the people under study as human beings rather than research instruments. This stance demonstrates how strongly values can affect the process of social investigation. In more recent years, however, feminist attitudes towards quantitative research have been softening, especially when it is employed in conjunction with qualitative research (Oakley 1998). This issue will be revisited in Chapters 9, 15, and 16.

There are, then, different positions that can be taken in relation to values and value-free research. Few writers today believe it is possible to be truly objective. There is a greater awareness of the limits of objectivity, and some of the more categorical pronouncements on the subject, such as Durkheim's, have fallen into disfavour. At the same time, giving free rein to one's political beliefs and value positions can be problematic. Researchers today still have to fight the all-too-human propensity to demonize those whose values are different from their own, and they still struggle with the temptation to summarily reject research findings when the researcher's ideological or moral positions are not compatible with their own.

POLITICS IN SOCIAL RESEARCH

If values and moral positions can influence social research, so can politics. Here are some of the ways in which social research may be political:

- Social researchers sometimes *take sides*, as we have seen. This is precisely what many feminist researchers do when they focus on the disadvantages that women face and the possibilities for improving the position of women. But taking sides occurs among other researchers as well. For example, some social scientists may favour government intervention in economic affairs, while others may defend the free market.

- A related issue involves research *funding*. Much social research is funded by organizations such as private firms or government departments that may have a vested interest in the outcomes of the research. The very fact that these organizations fund some research projects but not others opens the door to political influence. Such organizations may seek to invest in studies that will be useful to them or supportive of their operations and world views. They will often call for researchers to tender bids for an investigation in a certain area. When social researchers take part in such exercises, they enter a political arena, since their research may be designed to please the funding body. As a result, as Hughes (2000) observed in relation to

research in the field of crime, an investigation of gun crimes among the 'underclass' is more likely to receive funding than one concerned with misdemeanours committed by agents of the state. Morgan (2000) pointed out that research funded by government is typically empirical and quantitative; it tends to be concerned with the short-term costs and benefits of a particular policy or innovation; and it is generally uncritical in the sense that the underlying government policies are not questioned: all the government wants to know about is the effectiveness of their implementation. Political issues often arise when the funding agency itself is trying to secure a continuous stream of government funding.

- Gaining *access* to research subjects can also be a political process, especially in the case of organizations. Access to organizations is usually mediated by **gatekeepers** concerned not only about the researcher's motives but also about what the organization stands to gain from the investigation, what it will lose by participating in terms of staff time and other costs, and the potential risks to its image. Often, gatekeepers seek to influence how the investigation will take place: what kinds of questions can be asked; who can and cannot be a focus of study; the amount of time to be spent with each research participant; the interpretation of the findings; and the form the reports will take, even to the point of asking to approve drafts.

- Public institutions such as police departments, schools, and hospitals, as well as most commercial firms, are concerned with how they are going to be represented in publications. Consequently, gaining access is almost always a matter of *negotiation* and as such inevitably turns into a political process. The product of such negotiations is often referred to as 'the research bargain,' and in many cases there is more than one bargain that has to be struck. Once in the organization, researchers often discover layers of gatekeepers. For example, let's say the provincial government grants a research team permission to talk to the boys in a group home. Before the research can begin, the head of the home has to be brought onside, then the staff, and then the actual adolescents. Frequently, one of the staff is then given the responsibility of dealing with the fieldworkers. A suspicion that the researchers are really working for management then has to be overcome. And it is unwise to assume that simply because gatekeepers have granted access, a smooth passage will ensue in subsequent dealings with the people to be studied. Perhaps the most powerful of the boys will turn out to be the key gatekeeper. Researchers may find themselves used as pawns if subgroups attempt to enlist them in advancing a particular goal. Research participants who doubt the utility of social research may even try to obstruct the research process. For example, some of Beagan's (2001) medical students refused to participate when they heard she was asking about gays and lesbians, and one student who did cooperate nevertheless reported annoyance with being asked about sexual preference.

- There may be pressure to restrict the *publication* of findings. Hughes (2000) cited a study of plea-bargaining in the British criminal justice system as a case in point. The researchers had uncovered what were deemed at the time to be disconcerting levels of informal plea-bargaining, and they concluded that the formal judicial process was being weakened. The English legal establishment sought to thwart the dissemination of the findings and was persuaded to allow publication only when a panel of academics confirmed the **validity** of the findings. Similarly, the editors of academic journals may refuse to publish pieces that do not conform to their own ideological or political preferences.

These are just a small handful of the ways in which politics intrudes in the research process.

PRACTICAL CONSIDERATIONS

There are also a number of *practical issues* to be confronted in carrying out social research, many of which will be addressed in detail in later chapters. One important practical consideration is that the choice of research orientation, design, or method has to match the specific research question being investigated. For instance, if a researcher is interested in measuring the impact of various possible causes of a social phenomenon, a quantitative strategy is probably appropriate. Alternatively, if the focus is on the world views of members of a certain social group, a qualitative research strategy—one sensitive to the way participants interpret their social world—may be the way to go. If a researcher is interested in a topic on which little or no research

has been done, a quantitative strategy may be difficult to employ because there is little prior literature from which to draw leads about possible causes. A more qualitative, exploratory approach may be preferable because that type of investigation is typically associated with the generation of theory rather than theory testing (see Table 1.1) and with a relatively unstructured approach to the research process.

Another dimension involves the nature of the topic and of the people being investigated. A researcher who wants to study individuals involved in illicit activities—for example, price fixing, shoplifting, or drug dealing—may find it difficult to develop the rapport with them that is needed to conduct a social survey. It is not surprising, therefore, that researchers in these areas tend to use a qualitative strategy. On the other hand, it's unlikely that the hypothesis in Box 1.3 on the effects of societal religiosity on individual religious orthodoxy could have used a qualitative approach.

Although practical considerations may seem mundane and uninteresting compared with the lofty philosophical debates surrounding epistemology and ontology, they are important. All social research is a coming together of the ideal and the feasible. The nature of the topic, the type of people one may be investigating, and the related constraints on a researcher loom large in decisions about how to proceed.

Research questions   The last practical considerations involve choosing a research question. In many ways, this is like picking a destination for a hike: the route you take and what you will experience along the way are largely determined by where you want to go. Similarly, what you stand to accomplish with a particular research study and how you will accomplish it are profoundly affected by your formulation of the research question.

A research question states the purpose of the study in the form of a question. This is useful because a question can often be more evocative and stimulating than a simple declarative statement. A question arouses curiosity and challenges the researcher to find ways to answer it. Here are some examples of research questions taken from a study of voluntary associations in Canada: 'Does individual income level affect whether an individual is a voluntary association member? Does this effect differ between neighbourhoods?' (Duncan 2010: 578)

The process of formulating and assessing research questions is something of an art, but here are some general thoughts. Research often starts with the choice of a general area of interest: for example, male homosexuality. At this stage, a very general research question might be 'How do people in general feel about gays?' This broad research area has to be narrowed down: for example, to 'How does the Canadian adult population react to the portrayal of gays on television dramas?' But even that is too broad, so the next level of specification might be something like: 'Do young straight men react differently than young straight women to the portrayal of gay male romance on television program X? If so, do those differences reflect a more fluid sexual identity on the part of young women as compared to young men?' Such questions could be linked to larger theories of sex roles, sexual orientation acquisition, socialization, or the tolerance of difference in society.

No single study can answer all the research questions that will occur to the researcher. Only a small number of them can be selected. The need to narrow the topic is not only a matter of the time available and the cost of doing research. It is also a reflection of the need for a clear focus.

As suggested above, the research question may change as the study progresses, for a number of reasons. The discovery of a new data source may change the focus a bit, as might some of the initial findings. For instance, if in the study of male homosexuality the researchers find that having a gay relative in the immediate family makes a large difference in people's attitudes, the research question and the attendant methodology and theoretical orientation may be changed. The research question may also change because of limitations in time and other resources available to the researcher. Box 1.9 offers some tips on developing research questions.

Research questions in quantitative research are sometimes more specific than those in qualitative research. Indeed, some qualitative researchers advocate a very open approach with *no* research questions or only very broad ones. This is a risky approach and can be a recipe for collecting masses of data without a clear sense of what to observe or what to ask interviewees. There is a growing tendency among qualitative researchers to take a more focused approach to their craft, as, for example, in Parnaby's (2003) study of Toronto's squeegee kids.

Research questions set realistic boundaries for research. A poorly formulated research question can result in unfocused and substandard research. No matter how well designed a questionnaire is or how skilled the interviewers are, clear research questions are required to avoid going off in unnecessary directions and tangents. Research questions are crucial because they guide:

- the literature search;
- decisions about the kind of research design to employ;
- decisions about what data to collect and from whom;
- the analysis of the data; and
- the writing up of the findings.

BOX 1.9 : Considerations when developing research questions

A good research question will

- be as clear as possible so that it will be understandable to others;

- be researchable: it must allow for the development of a research design and the collection of data; this means that extremely abstract terms are not suitable;

- relate in some way to established theory and research that suggests how your question may be approached. Even with a topic that has not been widely studied, there will probably be some relevant literature (for example, on related or parallel topics); making connections with existing theory and research will help to show how your research can contribute to knowledge and understanding;

- be linked to the other research questions in the study, so that you can develop a single argument or at least a set of related arguments; this is hard to do with unrelated research questions;

- have the potential to make a contribution, however small, to the existing knowledge on the topic;

- be neither too broad (no research project can do justice to all aspects of a topic) nor too narrow (unable to make a significant contribution to an area of study).

If you are unsure about how to formulate research questions (or about other aspects of research), look at journal articles or research monographs to see how other researchers have handled them.

Key Points

Quantitative and qualitative research constitute different approaches to social investigation and carry with them important epistemological and ontological assumptions.

Epistemological considerations loom large in the choice of a research strategy. To a great extent, the issues revolve around the advantages and disadvantages of a natural science approach (in particular positivism) versus an interpretivist approach.

Ontological considerations, such as objectivism versus constructionism, also constitute important dimensions of the quantitative/qualitative contrast.

Theory can either precede research and data gathering (the deductive method) or emerge out of it (induction).

Feminist researchers in the past have tended to prefer a qualitative approach, although this situation is changing now.

Values can impinge on the research process in various ways; as a consequence, research often has political dimensions.

The political dimensions of research relate to the exercise of power at different stages of an investigation.

Practical considerations can also affect decisions about research methods. Clear research questions improve the chances of success.

Relevant Websites

A good way to become familiar with how research is done is to read articles published in academic journals. You may not be able to fully understand the methodologies and data analyses at this stage in your academic career, but reading articles will help you become familiar with formal research presentations. Below are the web addresses for some leading Canadian and international social science journals. You may not be able to access articles in a particular journal directly; it may be necessary to sign on to your institution's library server first.

Canadian Journal of Sociology
   http://ejournals.library.ualberta.ca/index. php/CJS/index

Canadian Review of Sociology
   http://www.wiley.com/bw/journal. asp?ref=1755-6171&site=1

Canadian Political Science Review
   http://ojs.unbc.ca/index.php/cpsr

Canadian Journal of the Humanities and Social Sciences
   http://www.cjhss.org/

Canadian Journal of Political Science
   http://journals.cambridge.org/action/ displayJournal?jid=CJP

Canadian Social Work Review
   http://www.caswe-acfts.ca/en/Canadian_ Social_Work_Review_32.html

Native Social Work Journal
   https://zone.biblio.laurentian.ca/dspace/ handle/10219/378

Canadian Journal of Education
   http://ojs.vre.upei.ca/index.php/cje-rce/

American Journal of Sociology
   http://www.journals.uchicago.edu/toc/ajs/ current

American Sociological Review
   http://www.asanet.org/journals/asr/index. cfm

Social Forces
   http://socialforces.unc.edu/

Qualitative Sociology
   http://www.springer.com/social+sciences/ journal/11133

British Journal of Sociology
   http://www2.lse.ac.uk/BJS/Home.aspx

International Journal of Sociology
   http://www.mesharpe.com/mall/results1. asp?ACR=ijs

[Websites accessed 20 July 2011]

Questions for Review

THEORY AND RESEARCH

- If you were to conduct some social research, what would the topic be and what factors would influence your choice?

- Can you find, in your other courses, additional examples of middle-range theories?

- List the names of three social researchers not discussed in this chapter who have been influenced by grand theory, and explain how their work is an extension of grand theory.

- What are the differences between inductive and deductive logic? Why is the distinction important?

EPISTEMOLOGICAL CONSIDERATIONS

- What is meant by the terms 'positivism' and 'interpretivism'? Why is it important to understand each of them?

- How might a positivist and an interpretivist differ in conducting research on illegal drug use?

ONTOLOGICAL CONSIDERATIONS

- What are the main differences between epistemological and ontological considerations?

- What do the terms 'objectivism' and 'constructionism' mean?

GENERAL RESEARCH ORIENTATIONS: QUANTITATIVE AND QUALITATIVE RESEARCH

- Outline the main differences between quantitative and qualitative research in terms of the relationship between theory and data, epistemological considerations, and ontological considerations.

- Under what circumstances might qualitative research be more concerned with testing theories and quantitative research with generating theories?

INFLUENCES ON THE CONDUCT OF SOCIAL RESEARCH

- What are some of the main influences on social research?

POLITICS IN SOCIAL RESEARCH

- What is meant by the suggestion that politics play a role in social research?

- In what ways are politics manifested in social research?

RESEARCH QUESTIONS

- Why are research questions so important in the overall research process?

- What are the main characteristics of a good research question?

- Pick a topic of interest to you and devise a question that could be used as a starting point to research it.

CHAPTER 2

Research Designs

CHAPTER OVERVIEW

A research design is a framework for the collection and analysis of the data that will be used to answer the research question. It must satisfy certain criteria, and the form it takes depends on the research questions being asked. This chapter will discuss:

- **reliability**, **replicability**, and **validity**: these are criteria for assessing the quality of social research, and are crucial to consider when choosing a research design; the various kinds of validity—**measurement validity**, **internal validity**, and **external validity**—are illustrated;

- the idea that such criteria are relevant mainly to **quantitative** research, and that alternative criteria should be employed for **qualitative** research; and

- four prominent research designs:

  - experimental and related designs (such as the quasi-experiment);

  - **cross-sectional designs**, including survey research, its most common form;

  - **longitudinal** designs, such as panel and cohort studies; and

  - **case study** designs.

'Would you tell me, please, which way I ought to go from here?'

'That depends a good deal on where you want to get to,' said the Cat.

'I don't much care where—' said Alice.

'Then it doesn't matter which way you go,' said the Cat.

'—so long as I get *somewhere*,' Alice added as an explanation.

'Oh, you're sure to do that,' said the Cat, 'if you only walk long enough.'

*Alice's Adventures in Wonderland
(Carroll 2009 [1865]: 56)*

It's not hard to feel a little like Alice when you start out on the journey that is a research project, especially if the voyage is one you are somewhat reluctant to undertake (this is not at all uncommon). Where should I be going with this study? How can I get there? How can I tell if I'm on the right track? Such questions flood the mind at the beginning of the trip. As Alice learned, finding the right way starts with knowing where you want to end up. In research, a lot depends on what you want to accomplish with the project, which in turn depends on the sort of research question you have posed. In this chapter we'll explore what kinds of destination are possible, some ways of getting to them, and some techniques for determining whether you are on the right path.

Introduction

A research design is a broad structure that guides the collection and analysis of data. Choosing a research design involves decisions about what you want to accomplish with the study. Is one of your goals to describe the causal connections between **variables**? Will you explore how a social phenomenon changes over time, and how it may be linked to other events and situations? Will it be important to search out the meanings that the research subjects attach to certain things? Do you want to be able to generalize your findings to people and groups that were not part of the study? How these questions are answered will affect your choice of research design.

Another important consideration in choosing a research design is the kind of explanation you would like to develop. Quantitative researchers often explain a phenomenon in terms of causes and effects that are expressed in *laws* and *principles*. Such laws and principles are usually fairly general, and are meant to apply to people who were not part of the study. For example, a study that finds that men are more likely than women to approve of pornography may explain that result with a Darwinian theory of erotic attraction. This sort of explanation is supposed to apply to humanity in general, not just to the people who participated in the study. This approach to explanation is called *nomothetic*.

Nomothetic explanations have to satisfy *three criteria of causation*. In other words, three conditions have to be satisfied before the explanation is considered acceptable. Suppose you are trying to explain why some people are more violent than others, and your explanation involves the idea that the propensity to be violent is influenced by watching violent movies. For this to be accepted as a causal explanation, it would have to meet the following criteria:

1. *Correlation*: the proposed cause and the proposed effect have to vary together. In our example, as the number of violent movies watched changes, the level of violence would have to change as well. You would have to observe that, in general, the greater the number of violent movies watched, the higher the level of violence.

2. *Time order*: the proposed cause must precede the effect in time. Assume that you do find a correlation between watching violent movies and real violence. You would also have to show that the increase in the watching of violent movies came *before* the increase in violence. If you found that the increase in the watching of violent movies occurred after the level of violence went up, your explanation would have to be rejected.

3. *Non-spuriousness*: alternative explanations for the correlation observed have to be ruled out. 'Spurious' literally means false or illegitimate. A common source of spuriousness is a variable that influences both the proposed cause and the effect. Suppose our data reveal that people who are violent tend to watch a lot of violent movies, and that people who reject violence watch very few violent films, i.e., that the two variables are correlated. Can we conclude from this that watching violent movies *causes* people to be more violent? In order to answer that question, we would try to determine whether some third factor is the cause of the correlation between the number of violent movies watched and the level of violence. For instance, could it be that people who are violent to begin with seek out violent movies? If so, then pre-existing violent tendencies affect both the watching of violent movies (your proposed cause) and the level of violence (the effect). If that is the case, the correlation between watching violent movies and the level of real violence is spurious, and your explanation does not hold up. As a further illustration of spuriousness, imagine that you live in a summer resort community where there is ample opportunity for swimming. Throughout the calendar year, there is probably a correlation between the number of ice-cream cones sold on a particular day and the number of people swimming: as one increases the other also increases. But does purchasing ice-cream cones *cause* people to go swimming? Of course not. Those two things are influenced by a third factor: warm weather.

Quantitative researchers choose research designs that help to satisfy these three criteria. Qualitative researchers, on the other hand, aim for different kinds of explanations. They usually seek to produce a rich description of a person or group based on the perceptions and feelings of the people studied, rather than to discover general laws and principles. The description usually involves or implies proximate, specific causes that are not meant to explain other situations or the behaviour of people who were not part of the research. For instance, a qualitative analysis of a group of homeless teenagers may find that they avoid sleeping in the local homeless shelter because they value their privacy. That finding is not meant to apply to other homeless people or other shelters; it simply helps to explain why these particular teenagers behave the way they do. These sorts of accounts are called *idiographic* explanations, and they usually involve a detailed 'story' or description of the people studied that is based on *empathetic understanding*. Qualitative researchers will choose research designs that will produce idiographic explanations.

Once a design has been selected, a specific method for collecting data has to be chosen. There are many different ways of gathering data. One way is to use a preset instrument, such as a self-completion **questionnaire** or a structured **interview schedule**. Another is to utilize a less formalized method like **participant observation** in which the researcher takes part in the activities of a group of people, sometimes even living among them for a time.

Consider one of the research designs to be covered in this chapter: the case study. It entails a detailed exploration of a specific case, which could be a community, organization, person, or event. Once you've selected a case to investigate, how will you get data on it? Do you use participant observation? Do you observe from the sidelines? Do you conduct interviews? Do you examine documents? Do you administer questionnaires? Any or all of these methods can be used.

Before we consider various research designs, some basic issues surrounding data gathering and assessing the quality of social research will be outlined.

Criteria for evaluating social research

Much of the discourse in the social sciences, in particular discussions of theories and **causality**, revolve around *variables*. A variable is simply a characteristic or attribute that varies, such as gender, income, fondness for mathematics, or athletic ability. Several of the criteria for evaluating research involve the measurement of variables. Three of the most prominent criteria are *reliability*, *replicability*, and *validity*. Each will be examined in greater detail in later chapters, but a brief treatment here will be helpful.

RELIABILITY

Quantitative researchers are concerned with whether measures of social science **concepts** (for example, poverty, racial prejudice, or religious orthodoxy) are reliable. Would the same results be achieved if the same measurement technique were administered several times to the same research subject? If the answer is yes, the measure is reliable. For example, if scores on a new intelligence test are unstable, fluctuating when administered to the same people on two or more occasions, or if different findings are produced when different psychologists use the test on the same people, that would mean that the test is unreliable.

REPLICABILITY

The idea of reliability is related to another research criterion: *replicability*. A study is replicable if others are able to repeat it and get the same results. Sometimes replications are conducted to make sure that the original research was carried out properly; this is especially important if a study's results do not match prior findings on the topic. For replication to be possible, the initial researcher must spell out all the research procedures in great detail.

VALIDITY

A crucial criterion in the evaluation of social research is *validity*, which is concerned with the integrity of the conclusions generated by a piece of research. There are three main types of validity:

- *Measurement or construct validity* applies primarily to quantitative research and its measures of social concepts. Essentially, it refers to whether a particular **indicator** actually does measure what it is supposed to measure. The question, 'Do IQ tests really measure intelligence?' is asking whether IQ tests are a *valid* measure of intelligence. To take another example, in the study reported in Box 1.3, three concepts needed to be measured: national religiosity, religious orthodoxy, and family religious orientation. The question is, do the measures used by the researchers really gauge those concepts? If they do not, the study's findings are questionable. Measurement validity is related to reliability: if a measure of a concept is unstable and hence unreliable, it cannot be a valid measure of the concept in question.

- *Internal validity* relates to causality (discussed in more detail in Chapter 3). For example, in the study examined in Box 1.3, the authors concluded that a nation's religious environment affects the religious beliefs of its citizens. Internal validity asks whether the religious environment really does influence people's religious beliefs. Could the cause be something else? Might there be a network of causes? If so, does that network really include the religious environment? In discussing issues of causality, it is common to refer to proposed causes as **independent variables** and the corresponding effect as the **dependent variable**. In this case, the 'religious environment of a nation' is an independent variable, and religious belief the dependent. Internal validity raises the issue of how confident you can be that the independent variable really does have an impact on the dependent variable.

- *External validity* involves two things. One is whether a study's findings are applicable in settings outside the research environment—in particular, everyday or natural social settings. Sometimes the research setting is so artificial or so different from real life that we may question whether the results actually tell us anything about the sorts of things that people normally experience. The more the social scientist intervenes in natural settings or creates unnatural ones, such as a laboratory (or even just a special room for interviews), the greater the chance that the findings will be externally *in*valid. Measurement validity and a reasonable level of internal validity cannot guarantee this form of external validity.

  Qualitative research tends to fulfill this requirement of external validity because it usually takes a **naturalistic** stance. **Naturalism** in this context refers to a style of research that seeks to minimize the use of artificial methods of data collection. It implies that the social world should be disturbed as little as possible when it is studied (Hammersley and Atkinson 1995: 6). A naturalistic researcher collects data in naturally occurring situations and environments as opposed to artificial ones: for example, by living with people for months to observe their behaviour or by conducting intensive interviews.

A second concern with external validity is whether the results of a study can be generalized beyond the people or cases analyzed by the researcher. The study in Box 1.2 asked 57 adolescent male volunteers about their delinquency and if any of the currently popular sociological theories of delinquency could explain their behaviour. How far can the findings of this study be generalized? To other male adolescents who attended the same school? To all Canadian male adolescents? If the findings are fully externally valid, they can be applied to any population of interest. If they possess no external validity, the findings apply only to the 57 boys studied and to no one else. Usually, external validity falls somewhere between these extremes, and it is in this context that *how* people are selected to participate in research becomes crucial. If a **representative sample** of people is selected (see Chapter 12), the researcher can be confident that the results of the study may be applied to the population from which the sample was drawn.

RELATIONSHIP WITH THE GENERAL RESEARCH ORIENTATION

One striking feature of the discussion so far is that it seems to downplay qualitative research. Both reliability and measurement validity are essentially concerned with how adequately concepts have been measured, which is more of an issue in quantitative research. Internal validity is also more pertinent to quantitative research. External validity has considerable relevance to both qualitative and quantitative work, but the representativeness of samples has a more obvious application to the latter, given the desire of quantitative researchers to generalize beyond the people or cases they are studying.

Some qualitative researchers even argue that it is inappropriate to apply the concepts of reliability and validity to their research. They propose that their studies be judged or evaluated according to different criteria. For example, Lincoln and Guba (1985) recommend *trustworthiness* as a criterion of how good a qualitative study is. Each aspect of trustworthiness has a parallel with the criteria mentioned earlier:

- *credibility*, which parallels measurement and internal validity: how believable are the findings? Did the investigator allow personal values to ruin any chance of **intersubjectivity**?

- *transferability*, which parallels external validity: do the findings apply to other people and other contexts?

- *dependability*, which parallels reliability: are the findings likely to be consistent over time?

- *confirmability*, which parallels replicability: would another investigator reach the same conclusions?

The distinctive features of qualitative research will be explored in depth in later chapters.

Research designs

EXPERIMENTAL DESIGN

True experiments are fairly rare in sociology, but they can be found in areas such as social psychology and studies of organizations. Researchers in social policy may also use them to assess the impact of reforms or new policies. The main reason for discussing experiments here is that a true experiment is often used as a yardstick against which non-experimental research is measured. This does not mean that an experiment is necessarily the *best* or the *only* yardstick to use. As we shall see below, experimental designs, like other methodological approaches, have their strengths and weaknesses and are better suited to some research topics than others. Their greatest strength is that they tend to be very high in internal validity, especially when they are used to isolate the effects of a small number of factors.

Manipulation   If experiments are so strong in this respect, why do social researchers not make more use of them? The reason is simple: to conduct a true experiment, it is necessary to do something to people and observe the effects. To put the matter more formally, an experiment *manipulates* an independent variable to determine its influence on a dependent variable. Typically, some subjects are allocated to a 'treatment' group in which the independent variable is changed or manipulated, while others are placed in a 'control' group where no manipulation takes place. The dependent variable is then observed and measured. The problem is that many of the independent variables of concern

to social researchers cannot be manipulated. For example, some sociologists maintain that a country's national character is affected by whether the country came into existence through revolution (for example, Lipset 1990). In order to test this idea experimentally, revolution would have to be induced in some randomly selected areas to produce a new country, while in others no revolution would be fomented. The researcher would then compare the national characters of the revolutionary countries with the non-revolutionary ones. Needless to say, such experimental manipulations would usually be impossible to carry out.

This example also illustrates a second reason why experiments are so rare in sociology: ethical concerns often preclude them. Suppose you are interested in the effect of nutrition on children's academic performance. In order to examine this issue experimentally, you could select a number of six-year-olds at **random** and place them in two groups. Those in the first group would be fed unhealthy foods for a month, while those in the second would be given nutritious diets. Then you would test the two groups to see if they differed in academic ability. Although sound from a methodological standpoint, such a study would raise serious ethical problems. In fact, as we will see in Chapter 11, ethical issues may arise even when the experimental manipulation is of very short duration.

Another reason why experiments are uncommon in sociology is that many of the things of interest to sociologists—gender roles, political preferences, the formation of social movements, and so on—have complex, long-term causes that cannot be easily simulated in experiments. Could the experimental method be used to explain the rise of second-wave feminism in the 1960s? Unfortunately not: experiments are generally limited to relatively simple, short-term manipulations of independent variables (see Brannigan 2004). A further reason is that even where social scientists are successful in using experiments to identify causal variables, the perceptions and feelings of the participants—which provide information vital to a full understanding of the phenomenon in question—are usually not examined in depth (Dobash and Dobash 2000).

Before moving to a more complete discussion of experimental designs, it is important to introduce a basic distinction between *laboratory* and ***field experiments***. The former take place in artificial settings, whereas the latter occur in real-life surroundings such as classrooms and factories. The Rosenthal and Jacobson (1968) study described below is a well-known example of a field experiment.

Classic experimental design   Rosenthal and Jacobson (1968) tried to determine what effect teachers' expectations had on their students' academic performance. In addition to illustrating the classical experimental design, their study is a good example of research that gets a lot of attention, is then subject to intense methodological scrutiny (see Brannigan 2004: 80–9 for critiques), and ultimately provides the impetus for further research designed to improve on the original.

The research was conducted in a US school where many poor and minority-group children were enrolled. In the spring all the students were given a test and told it was designed to identify 'spurters'—that is, students who were likely to experience a sudden improvement in their academic performance. At the beginning of the following academic year, the teachers were given the names of the spurters in their classes. In fact, a random 20 per cent of the students had been identified as spurters. The test was re-administered eight months after the original one, allowing the authors to compare the so-called spurters with the other students on things such as IQ scores, reading ability, and intellectual curiosity. Since they believed that there was no initial difference in ability between the spurters and the others, any improvements were attributed to the fact that the teachers had been led to expect the spurters to perform better. The authors report that the teachers' expectations that the spurters would show superior academic performance actually caused those students to do better than the others, presumably because they received differential treatment from the teachers.

The Rosenthal and Jacobson study includes most of the essential features of what is known as the classical experimental design. Subjects (in this case, students) are randomly assigned to two groups. The experimental manipulation (different levels of the independent variable, here heightened teacher expectations) is carried out on the **experimental group** or *treatment group* (the spurters). The other group is not given the treatment and thus forms a **control group**. The dependent variable—academic performance—is measured

before the experimental manipulation to make sure that the two groups really are, on average, equal at the start (see Figure 2.1). If they are equal, and because of **random assignment** they should be, the researchers can feel confident that any differences in student performance found between the two groups *after* the manipulation is due to the treatment. Everything else about the two groups is presumed to be the same, leaving differences in teacher expectations as the only possible explanation for any differences that are found between the spurters and non-spurters.

FIGURE 2.1   Classical experimental design

To capture the essence of the classical experimental design, the following simple notation is used:

- **Obs**: an **obs**ervation made of the dependent variable. There may be more than two observations but, to simplify, the design shows the most common configuration: *pre-test* and *post-test* (here, IQ test scores before the experimental manipulation and after).

- **Exp**: the **exp**erimental treatment (independent variable), here the creation of teacher expectancies. **No Exp** refers to the absence of an experimental treatment and represents the experience of the control group.

- **T**: the **t**iming of the observations made in relation to the dependent variable, here, the time when an IQ test is administered.

Classic experimental design and validity   What is the purpose of the control group? Surely it is what happens to the spurters (the experimental group) that really matters. For this study to be a true experiment, however, it must control for (in other words, eliminate) rival explanations of its causal findings, leaving teacher expectations as the only factor that could have created any differences in performance between the two groups. Of course, student performance is a complex phenomenon, with many causes, but the present study wanted to examine only one of those causes (teacher expectations). The presence of a control group *and* the random assignment of subjects to the experimental and control groups help to eliminate rival explanations for differences in academic performance, which in this case are any explanations other than different teacher expectations. By doing so, these procedures contribute to the study's internal validity. To see this, consider some threats to internal validity that would pose serious challenges to the study's conclusions if there were *no* control group or random assignment. The following list of threats is based on a book written by Cook and Campbell (1979). In each situation, the possibility of a rival interpretation of Rosenthal and Jacobson's findings is proposed, but the presence of both a control group and random assignment greatly reduces the threat. As a result, confidence in the finding that teacher expectations influence student performance is enhanced.

- *History*. This refers to events other than the manipulation of teacher expectations that might have caused the spurters' scores to rise. For example, suppose that the school's principal had taken steps to raise standards in the school. Without a control group, we could not be sure whether it was the teachers' expectations or the principal's action that produced the increase in spurters' grades. With a control group, we can say that the principal's action should have had an effect on the control subjects too, and therefore that the differences between the experimental and control groups can be attributed to the effect of teacher expectations alone.

- *Testing*. This threat refers to the possibility that subjects may become more experienced at taking a test or sensitized to the aims of the experiment as a result of the pre-test. The presence of a control group, which presumably would also experience the same things, diminishes this possibility.

- *Instrumentation*. This threat refers to the possibility that changes in the way a test is administered can account for an increase (or decrease) in scores between a pre-test and post-test; for example, perhaps the teachers know their students better or are more friendly the second time they give the test. Again, if there is a control group, the people in that group should be affected as well.

- *Mortality*. A particular problem for studies that span a long period of time is the risk that some subjects will leave the experiment before it is over: for example, some students might move to a different school, or experience a long-term illness. Since this problem is likely to affect the control group too, it may not make a difference to the results. However, experimenters should try to determine whether mortality has affected the experimental and control groups differently.

- *Maturation*. Quite simply, people change over time and the ways in which they change may have implications for the dependent variable. The spurters might have improved anyway as they got older, regardless of the effect of teacher expectancies. But the control group would also mature, so maturation effects cannot explain the differences between it and the control group.

- *Selection*. When subjects are not assigned randomly to the experimental and control groups, variations between them in the post-test may be due to pre-existing differences between the two groups. For example, if all the best students were given the spurter label, it might have been their pre-existing academic ability rather than teacher expectations that caused them to do better. However, since a random selection process was employed here, the 'selection' risk is greatly reduced. With random assignment, the top students would make up roughly the same proportion of the spurter group as the non-spurter group, cancelling out the effect of pre-existing academic ability. However, even with the use of random assignment, if the number of people in each group is relatively small, there is still a risk of pre-existing differences between the experimental and control groups.

Even if research is deemed to be internally valid, that does not mean that questions cannot be raised about it. First there is the question of measurement validity. In the case of the Rosenthal and Jacobson (1968) study, there are potentially two aspects to this question. First, has academic performance been adequately measured? Reading scores seem to possess **face validity**, in the sense that they appear to correspond to what they are supposed to be measuring. However, given the controversy surrounding IQ tests and what they measure, we may feel unsure that gains in IQ test scores can be regarded as strongly indicative of academic performance. Similarly, to take another of the authors' measures, is intellectual curiosity a valid measure of academic performance? Does it really measure what it is supposed to measure?

Another question relating to measurement validity is whether the experimental manipulation really worked. In other words, was the identification of some schoolchildren as spurters enough to create the conditions needed for the hypothesis about teacher expectations to be tested? The study depended on the teachers' remembering the 'information' they were given about the spurters for the duration of the experiment, but it is possible that as time went on some of them came to doubt or forget it; in that case, the manipulation would have been contaminated.

Second, is the research externally valid? The fact that Rosenthal and Jacobson carried out their research as a field experiment in a real school rather than a laboratory enhances this aspect of their work. Also, the fact that the students and the teachers seem to have been unaware that they were participating in an experiment may also have enhanced external validity, although such deception raises *ethical* concerns (a topic to be discussed in Chapter 11).

Cook and Campbell (1979) identified five major threats to the external validity and hence the generalizability of findings derived from an experiment:

- *Interaction of selection and treatment*. To what social and psychological groups can a finding be generalized? Can it be generalized to a wide variety of individuals who differ in ethnicity, social class, religion, gender, and type of personality? In the Rosenthal and Jacobson study, the students were largely from poorer groups and a large proportion from ethnic minorities. This may limit the generalizability of the findings.

- *Interaction of setting and treatment*. Can the results of a study be applied to other settings (in Rosenthal and Jacobson's case, to other schools)? There is also the wider issue of whether expectation effects can also be discerned in non-educational settings.

- *Interaction of history and treatment*. This threat raises the question of whether the findings can be generalized to the past and into the future. The Rosenthal and Jacobson research was conducted more than 40 years ago. Would the findings still apply today? Also, their investigation was conducted at a particular juncture in the school year. Would the same results have been obtained if the research had been conducted at different points in the year?

- *Interaction effects of pre-testing*. As a result of being pre-tested, subjects in an experiment may become sensitized to the experimental treatment, with the result that their responses are affected as they become more test-wise. Consequently, the findings may not be generalizable to groups that have not been pre-tested, and, of course, in the real world people are rarely pre-tested. This may have occurred in the Rosenthal and Jacobson research, since all students were pre-tested at the end of the previous academic year, so the students new to the school in the fall (when the teachers were told about spurters) presumably were not pre-tested.

- *Reactive effects of experimental arrangements*. People are frequently, if not invariably, aware of the fact that they are participating in an experiment. Their awareness may influence how they respond to the experimental treatment; for example, they may try to behave in a socially acceptable manner rather than sincerely and spontaneously, which could affect the generalizability of the findings. Since Rosenthal and Jacobson's subjects do not appear to have been aware that they were participating in an experiment, this problem is unlikely to have been significant. The issue of reactivity and its potentially damaging effects is a recurring theme in many types of social research.

A third issue relates to the question of replicability. Rosenthal and Jacobson laid out their procedures and measures, and anyone carrying out a replication could obtain further information from them. Consequently, their research is replicable, although there has never been an exact replication. Clairborn (1969) conducted one of the earliest replications and followed a procedure very similar to Rosenthal and Jacobson's, although the study was carried out in three middle-class suburban schools, and the timing of the creation of teacher expectancies was different from the original study. Clairborn failed to replicate Rosenthal and Jacobson's findings, casting doubt on the external validity of the original research and suggesting that the first two threats to external validity referred to earlier in this chapter may have limited the applicability of the findings.

Virtually all experiments in the social sciences involve deception of some kind. In the Rosenthal and Jacobson study, for example, the experimenters told the teachers that certain students were spurters, which simply was not true. But could the experiment have been carried out without any deception? For example, could the experimenters have told the teachers that they were testing the effects of teacher expectations on student achievement? Could they have given the teachers a list of students and said, 'Pretend that these students are gifted, although they are not any more gifted, on average, than the students not on the list. We want to see whether you would treat such children differently, and whether differential treatment affects their academic performance.' Surely, that sort of approach would not have produced authentic behaviour on the part of the teachers, and the teachers might well have refused to participate under those conditions for ethical and practical reasons. Clearly, some form of deception was necessary for the experiment to work.

But deception raises ethical concerns—it is basically a form of lying. Chapter 11 will discuss the ethical implications of using deception in social research, as well as other sorts of ethical dilemmas facing researchers in the social sciences.

The laboratory experiment   One of the main advantages of laboratory over field experiments is the researcher's greater control over the research environment. In particular, it is easier to randomly assign subjects to different experimental conditions in the laboratory than in a real-life situation, which enhances the internal validity of the study. For example, Walsh and colleagues (1999) were able to tell some randomly assigned university students in Eastern Canada that previous results on the mathematics test they were about to take showed that women perform less well than men on such tests. Other students, also randomly assigned, were not told this. The data showed that women scored lower than men when informed of this 'fact.' When told that the test

was to compare Canadians and Americans, there was no gender difference. Without the chance to randomly assign subjects, there would always be some doubt that the treatment (being told that women score lower than men on the test) rather than a pre-existing difference between the two sets of subjects actually caused the women to do less well than the men. Also, laboratory experiments are more easily replicated because they are less bound to a natural milieu that could be difficult to reproduce.

However, laboratory experiments like the one described in Box 2.1 also suffer from a number of limitations. First, the external validity is probably low, since the laboratory setting may not mirror real-world experiences and contexts, despite the fact that the subjects are very involved in most experiments and take them very seriously. In addition, the treatment effects may be unique to the people in the study; others may not react the same way. In technical terms, there may be an interaction of selection and treatment. In the case of Howell and Frost's (1989) study described in Box 2.1, for example, there are a number of difficulties. As students, the subjects were not representative of the general population, if only because of their youth, so their responses to the experimental treatment may have been distinctive. They were also volunteers, who generally differ from non-volunteers (Rosnow and Rosenthal 1997: ch. 5); in addition, the fact that they were given an incentive to participate might have further distinguished them from others since not everyone would be equally motivated to earn the reward given to those who participate. There was no effect of pre-testing because, as in many experiments, there was none. However, it is quite possible that reactive effects occurred: the subjects knew they were in an experiment, and that may have affected their behaviour.

Quasi-experiments   *Quasi-experiments* have some characteristics of the experimental model but do not fulfill all the internal validity requirements. Several different types of quasi-experiments have been identified (Cook and Campbell 1979). Not all of them can be covered here, but a particularly interesting type are 'natural experiments,' in which experiment-like conditions are produced by naturally occurring phenomena or changes brought about by people not doing research. When that occurs, researchers can gather data in

BOX 2.1 | A laboratory experiment

Howell and Frost (1989) were interested in whether 'charismatic' leadership is more effective than two other leadership approaches: 'considerate' and 'structuring.' They conducted a laboratory experiment to test a number of hypotheses, among them the idea that individuals working under a charismatic leader will have higher task performance than those under a considerate leader (Howell and Frost 1989: 245). Course grades were enhanced by 3 per cent for the 144 students who volunteered for the experiment (what ethical issue does that raise?). They were randomly assigned to work on a simulated business task under one of the three types of leadership, all three of which were performed by two female actresses. In broad conformity with the hypotheses, subjects working under charismatic leaders generally scored higher on measures of task performance than those working under other leadership types, particularly the considerate leader.

much the same way they do in experiments. For example, if an earthquake hit a particular city, but a city of comparable size and composition a short distance away was spared, the conditions for a natural experiment would be present. The effects of the natural disaster on civic pride or attitudes toward local political leaders could be measured by comparing the two cities on those variables. However, in natural experiments, it is usually impossible to randomly assign subjects to experimental and control groups. The absence of random assignment casts doubt on the study's internal validity, since the groups may not have been equivalent on all relevant characteristics before the independent variable was introduced. For instance, in the earthquake example, there may have been some pre-existing differences between the two cities before the earthquake struck that contributed to post-earthquake differences: for instance, if the stricken city showed an increase in civic pride, perhaps that was not because of the earthquake, but because it had a more charismatic mayor than the neighbouring city. However, the results of such studies are still compelling because they are real rather than artificial interventions in social life, making them high in external validity.

St Helena in the South Atlantic provided a fascinating natural laboratory for the examination of various claims regarding the effect of television violence on children when TV was introduced to the island for the first time in the mid-1990s. The findings—from video footage showing young children at play during school breaks, from **diaries** kept by about three hundred of the children, and from ratings by teachers—suggested that the introduction of television was not followed by an increase in the number of aggressive acts observed (Charlton *et al.* 1998, 1999). The researchers suggest that in environments such as St Helena, where children are closely watched by the community and are expected to avoid violence or aggression, television may have little effect on their behaviour.

Another type of natural experiment can be found in *twin studies*, which are commonly used in *behavioural genetic* research. Monozygotic (popularly known as 'identical') twins share 100 per cent of their genetic structure, whereas dizygotic ('fraternal') twins have in common only about 50 per cent of the genes that vary between human beings. This natural difference allows researchers to estimate the strength of environmental and genetic influences on a variety of attitudes and behaviours (Plomin *et al.* 2008). The presence of greater behavioural or attitudinal similarities among monozygotic than dizygotic twins suggests a genetic influence. For example, recent behavioural genetic studies indicate that social and political attitudes are affected not only by societal and situational factors, but also by genes (Alford *et al.* 2005; Bell *et al.* 2009). Additional examples of quasi-experiments are presented in Box 2.2.

Quasi-experimental designs have been particularly prominent in **evaluation research** studies, which examine the effects of organizational innovations such as a longer school day or greater worker autonomy in a plant (see Box 2.3). Sometimes the results are surprising. A quasi-experimental investigation on the effect of support for people who take care of the elderly (Demers 1996) showed that the extra support made caregivers feel less depressed, but *more* burdened. She was not sure why, although she speculated that perhaps the help was seen as something else to be coordinated and managed. The situation that Demers found herself in—not being sure how to interpret her findings—is actually quite common. It's one thing to come up with findings like hers, but another to explain them. The solution usually involves doing more research.

BOX 2.2 : Quasi-experiments

A common type of quasi-experiment compares data collected before and after a policy shift by government or industry. For example, the numbers of car accidents before and after the lowering of a speed limit can be compared. If the number goes down after the speed limit has been lowered, the policy would appear to be a success, but one cannot be sure because there is no control group not experiencing the change. Perhaps the change was caused by something other than the reduction in the speed limit, such as increased media coverage of car accidents.

Another example might involve the installation of cameras to detect speeding. If the cameras are placed only in randomly selected places and not in others, the research changes from a quasi- to a real experiment, since the locations without cameras would constitute a control group. Governments find it difficult, however, to subject some people to one condition and others to another. The prison system, schools, and other institutions controlled by governments are part of

the real social world, and as such have to meet goals that are very different from those of experimental research. That makes it next to impossible for governments to randomly assign people to different conditions. Therefore, they usually have to make do with quasi-experimental evaluations of policy changes. A criminologist may want to randomly assign criminals to jail or home custody and then compare the two forms of detention, but the potential for some of the at-homes to reoffend would be seen as too great a risk. Because minor criminals are more likely to get home custody than are more serious criminals, a fair test is not possible without random assignment. Similarly, when Canada abolished the death penalty, it was not for the purpose of conducting an experiment: abolition was a policy decision. Data could be examined as if the change were part of a quasi-experiment, for example, by comparing the murder rate before and after capital punishment was abolished; but the legislation was definitely not intended for that purpose.

Quasi-experiments are also used to evaluate the effectiveness of institutional policies. For example, Hanson *et al.* (2004) wanted to know whether treating sex offenders after they are released from prison has any effect on their chances of reoffending. A total of 724 convicted male sex offenders were divided into two groups: those who underwent mandatory treatment after release to community supervision, and those who were released prior to the implementation of the mandatory treatment program. (Some of the latter group had received treatment during or prior to incarceration, although the extent of that treatment was not known.) This division was not perfect, since the men in the first group may have differed in some relevant way from those in the second; the fact that some in the latter category received treatment is also an issue. In any case, the results showed that, after an average twelve-year follow-up period, there were equal rates of reoffending in both groups: about 20 per cent for sex crimes, which was not very encouraging for the professionals who treat offenders.

Significance of experimental design   As we noted at the outset of this section, true experiments are rare in sociology, but they are worth discussing

because, where they are practicable, they allow researchers to isolate the causal influence of a particular variable—a goal to which researchers using other designs also aspire. Cross-sectional designs of the kind associated with survey research (see p. 33) offer another way of evaluating causal hypotheses.

Logic of comparison   It is important to draw attention to a significant general lesson that an examination of experiments reveals. A central feature of any experiment is a *comparison*: at the very least, an experiment allows the researcher to compare the results obtained from an experimental group with those obtained from a control group. In the case of the Howell and Frost (1989) experiment in Box 2.1, the research compared the effects of three different types of leadership. The advantage of such comparisons is that they permit a better understanding of the phenomenon in question than would be possible if it were examined under one condition alone. The argument that charismatic leadership is an efficient, performance-enhancing form of leadership is much more persuasive when its effects can be compared with those produced by other forms of leadership. While the experimental design is typically associated with a quantitative research strategy, the

BOX 2.3 | Evaluation research

An example of evaluation research comes from the Pivot Legal Society in BC, which urged the repeal of Canadian prostitution laws. Based on interviews with 91 prostitutes, the society found, for example, that the law against communicating for the purpose of prostitution (prostitution itself is not illegal) is problematic. It forces prostitutes to make their arrangements in back alleys, where they are vulnerable to assault by their clients and others. It may also lead them to jump into cars before they have fully ascertained how safe they will be. Other groups objected to any change in the law, saying it would increase the number of prostitutes, make them more of a public nuisance, or even expose underage boys to their lure. Which side should win is a political and moral issue, but the validity of the claims regarding the social consequences of prospective changes in public policy is for evaluation research to determine.

The essential question asked by such studies is whether the new policy initiative or organizational change achieved its goals. Ideally, the design would have one group that is exposed to the treatment—the new initiative—and a control group that is not. Since it is often not feasible or ethical to randomly assign research participants to the two groups (certainly not in the situation just described), such studies are usually quasi-experimental. For instance, data gathered from people before a change may be compared with data acquired after; the 'before' people become the control group, the 'after' people the experimental group. This approach has the added advantage that the two groups are basically the same, making random assignment unnecessary. Such a design could be used for the prostitution study if prostitution were ever legalized.

Experimental designs are fairly entrenched in evaluation research, but in recent years evaluations based on qualitative research have emerged. Although there are differences of opinion about how qualitative evaluation should be carried out, there is consensus on the importance of, first, understanding the context in which an intervention occurs and, second, hearing the diverse viewpoints of the stakeholders (Greene 2000). For example, Pawson and Tilley (1997) advocate a pluralistic methodology that examines not only the context but also the mechanisms that allow programs to work. Tilley (2000) later outlined an example of the approach in an evaluation of the use of closed-circuit television (CCTV) in parking lots. He observed that there are several ways in which CCTV deters car crime. For instance, it serves as a direct deterrent to offenders (fewer people are willing to commit crimes if they think they will be filmed and caught), which encourages greater usage of car parks, which in turn increases personal surveillance, which itself deters crime. Examples of contexts relevant to the intervention include time (such as when the car park fills up and empties during rush-hour periods, or slow times during the day); blind spots in car parks; and the availability of other nearby venues for offenders to commit car crimes. The kind of evaluation research advocated by Pawson and Tilley maps the different combinations of cause and context in relation to different outcomes.

---

specific logic of comparison provides lessons of broad applicability and relevance.

CROSS-SECTIONAL DESIGN

Many people associate cross-sectional designs with questionnaires and **structured interviewing**. However, other data-gathering techniques may also be used in cross-sectional research, including **structured observation** and analysis of official statistics or diaries. These will be covered in later chapters, but we will outline the basic structure of the cross-sectional design here. In cross-sectional studies, observations are taken *at one point in time*—there are no before and after comparisons. Also, cross-sectional designs *do not involve any manipulation of the independent variable*: they are like snapshots taken of a group or phenomenon at one point in time.

A cross-sectional design entails the collection of data (usually quantitative) on more than one case. Researchers are interested in variation between different people, families, nation states, and so on, and variation can be established only when more than one case is examined. Researchers employing this design usually select many cases, for at least two reasons. For one thing, a larger number makes it more likely that variation will be encountered in *all* the variables of interest. A second reason is that certain statistical techniques are likely to require large sample sizes (see Chapter 12).

Data are collected on two or more variables, which are then examined to detect patterns of association. This approach sometimes makes it difficult to show cause and effect because the independent and dependent variables are measured

Methods in Motion

Applications to Canadian Society

Why are some Canadians politically conservative and others liberal?

Bell and his colleagues (2009) did a behavioural genetic study of political attitudes and behaviours that addressed the issue of why some Canadians tend to have conservative or right-leaning attitudes, while others are more liberal or left-oriented in their political views. The methodology used in the study (the details of which go beyond the scope of this book) was a kind of natural experiment comparing monozygotic (identical) twins, who are essentially genetic clones of each other, with dizygotic (fraternal) twins, who share only about 50% of the genetic material that varies between human beings. The researchers examined how similar the identical twins were in their political attitudes, and compared that with how similar the fraternal twins were on that score. If identical twins are more similar on the characteristic under examination than the fraternal twins, that would indicate that genetic factors or other biological influences have some impact on the trait in question. The results of the study showed that the identical twins were in fact much more similar in their political attitudes than the fraternal twins, which suggests that genetic factors do play a role in the formation of these attitudes. The study also found that environmental factors (such as educational influences and media effects) influenced political orientations, although it did not test for specific environmental influences. Taken as a whole, the results indicate that 'nature' and 'nurture' *interact* in the formation of political attitudes.

These sorts of studies are uncommon in sociology, political science, or anthropology, although they are conducted more frequently in psychology and the health sciences. They have far-reaching implications for the social sciences, in particular for disciplines in which biological influences are seldom examined. The standard paradigm in the latter fields of study assumes that some combination of socialization, culture, and situational factors can explain the origins of most attitudes and behaviours. Researchers using behaviour genetic methods, on the other hand, acknowledge that those sorts of influences are crucial, but argue that a more complete understanding of the human condition can be achieved by considering both biological and environmental factors.

If behaviour genetics and other approaches that consider both biological and environmental influences were to be more widely adopted in the social sciences, that could have a major impact on the theoretical perspectives that are developed and rise to prominence in academe. For example, a blend of Darwinian evolutionary theory and sociological conflict theories is a possibility (e.g., Sanderson 2001). Such approaches have the potential to promote *consilience* or the unity of knowledge, which in this case would take the form of a closer relationship between the social and biological sciences.

---

simultaneously, making any demonstration of time order (showing that the cause actually precedes the effect in time) hard to prove. For example, there is a well-supported negative relationship between social class and serious forms of mental illness: more poor people are mentally ill than rich people. But there is also a debate about the nature of that relationship: Does being poor lead to stress and therefore to mental illness? Or does being mentally ill lead to difficulties in holding down a job and thus poverty? Or is it a bit of both? To take another example, a study of 1000 men found that those who had two or more orgasms a week exhibited a 50 per cent lower mortality risk compared with men who had on average less than one orgasm per week. It may be tempting to conclude that male orgasm leads to

longer life expectancy, but it is also possible that the causal arrow points in the other direction: men who are ill (and thus at greater mortality risk) are less likely to be sexually active in the first place (Houghton 1998: 14). This finding and the preceding one are similar, showing what Blaxter (1990) called 'an ambiguity about the direction of causal influence.' There is only an *association* between the two variables—no clear causal link. However, as will be shown below and in Chapter 13, there are a number of ways for researchers to draw cautious inferences about causality using cross-sectional designs.

Reliability, replicability, and validity   How does cross-sectional research measure up in terms of the previously outlined criteria for evaluating quantitative research: reliability, replicability, and validity?

- The issues of reliability and measurement validity primarily relate to the quality of the measures employed to tap the concepts in which the researcher is interested, rather than to a research design. This will be covered in the next chapter.

- Replicability characterizes most cross-sectional research, so long as the researcher spells out the procedures for selecting respondents, administering research instruments (structured interview or self-completion questionnaire, etc.), and the analysis of data.

- Internal validity can be problematic. As was just suggested, it may be difficult to establish causal direction from the resulting data. Cross-sectional research designs can identify associations that are indicative of causation, but other designs may have to be employed to substantiate causal inferences.

- External validity is strong when the sample is a random one. When non-random methods of sampling are employed, external validity becomes questionable, an issue addressed in Chapter 12.

Variables that cannot be manipulated   As noted in the section on experimental design, in much (if not most) social research it is not possible to manipulate the variables of interest. This is a key reason why most quantitative social research employs a cross-sectional design rather than an experimental one. To more or less all intents and purposes, ethnicity, age, gender, and social backgrounds are 'givens' and not really amenable to the kind of manipulation necessary for a true experimental design (but see Box 2.4). For example, an experimenter with makeup and a fake accent can create a fictional man or a woman—say, a Scot or a Swede—perhaps to see the effects on job offers, but the manipulation is limited to the external signs of gender and ethnicity, missing the more subjective and experiential aspects.

However, the very fact that certain variables are givens provides a clue as to how to make causal inferences in cross-sectional research. Many of the variables of interest can be assumed to be temporally prior to other variables. For example, in a relationship between ethnic status and alcohol consumption, the latter cannot be the independent variable because it occurs after ethnicity. Ethnicity still cannot be said with certainty to be the cause, however: it is just a possible cause. In other words, even though researchers are unable to manipulate things like ethnic status or gender, causal inferences can still be cautiously drawn from cross-sectional data.

BOX 2.4 | Manipulating 'non-manipulable' variables: body weight, ethnicity, and race

A researcher was interested in how people respond to 'overweight' as against 'normal weight' people. She could have compared accounts given by people of different body weights or even directly observed how others responded to them. Instead, because she had filled her short frame to almost 100 kilograms, she conducted a personal experiment. She gradually slimmed down and at the same time looked for changes in the reactions of others as she did. Apparently, the effects of being fat were not as negative as anticipated, because she claimed that early on she 'had the most unbelievably good-looking man chat her up' (reported in Wilkinson and Whitworth 1998: 3). Such studies could be made less personally invasive by showing respondents pictures of individuals, first fat and then slim, and asking for their opinions of each.

Ethnicity too can be studied experimentally. Identical résumés could be sent out to prospective employers, but the names and birthplaces would vary. The researcher could then monitor the calls for personal interviews. This is a watered-down version of what Griffin (1961) did in the 1950s when he blackened his face and visible parts of his body and travelled around the American South as a person of colour, always keeping his eyes averted to show due deference to whites. Griffin's aim was to experience what it was like to be a black person in a period and region of racial segregation. While Griffin's study is interesting, and he was treated as a black man in various ways (having to use segregated water fountains, etc.), it is doubtful that such a brief sojourn adequately captured the experience of being black in the American South at that time, a condition of subordination formed by many years of personal encounters and the knowledge that they would be ongoing.

The current discussion of the cross-sectional design places it firmly in the context of quantitative research. But qualitative research can also use a form of cross-sectional design. For example, Beardsworth and Keil (1992) carried out a study of the dietary beliefs and practices of vegetarians. They administered 'relatively **unstructured interviews**,' which were 'guided by an inventory of issues,' with 76 vegetarians and vegans (1992: 261). The interviews were taped and **transcribed**, yielding a large body of qualitative data.

The research was not preoccupied with quantitative criteria such as internal and external validity, replicability, measurement validity, and so on. In fact, the conversational interview style made the study more externally valid than research using more formal instruments of data collection. The study was concerned with the factors that influence food selection, like vegetarianism. The very notion of an 'influence' carries a strong connotation of causality, suggesting that qualitative researchers are also interested in the investigation of causes and effects, although they do not use the language of quantitative research with its talk of independent and dependent variables. As well, the emphasis was much more on understanding the experience of something like vegetarianism than is often the case with quantitative research.

This qualitative research bears many similarities to the cross-sectional design in quantitative research. It entailed interviewing quite a large number of people at a single point in time. And, as with many quantitative studies using a cross-sectional design, the examination of people's past and current eating habits was based on the subjects' retrospective accounts of factors that affected their past and present behaviour.

Structure of cross-sectional designs   A cross-sectional design collects data on a series of variables (Obs_1 Obs_2 Obs_3 Obs_4 Obs_5 ... Obs_n) for different cases (people, households, cities, nations, etc.) at a single point in time. The effect is to create a data set that comprises variables Obs_1 to Obs_n and cases $case_1$ to $case_n$, as in Figure 2.2. Each cell in the matrix has data in it.

LONGITUDINAL DESIGN(S)

With a longitudinal design, cases are examined at a particular time (T1) and again at a later time or times (T2, T3, and so on), but without the

	Obs_1	Obs_2	Obs_3	. . .	Obs_n
$Case_1$					
$Case_2$					
$Case_3$					
$Case_4$					
$Case_5$					
. . .					
$Case_n$					

FIGURE 2.2   The data rectangle in cross-sectional research

manipulation of an independent variable that characterizes experiments (see Box 2.5). It thus allows insight into the time order of variables and is better able to deal with the problem of 'ambiguity about the direction of causal influence' that plagues cross-sectional designs. Because potential independent variables can be identified at T1, the researcher is in a better, if not perfect, position to infer that the effects identified at T2 or later occurred *after* changes occurred in the independent variables. In all other respects, the points made above about cross-sectional designs are the same as those for longitudinal designs. In spite of its heightened ability to show cause and effect, the longitudinal design is not frequently used in social research because of the additional time and cost involved.

Longitudinal studies can take different forms. For example, Goyder *et al.* (2003) examined how gender-influenced evaluations of occupational prestige had changed over 25 years. Some of the earlier male advantage had disappeared; indeed, some occupations showing a female incumbent were rated more highly than the same occupation with a male incumbent. Baer *et al.* (2001) did a 15-nation study examining whether membership in clubs and associations had changed over time. Kerr (2004) and Kerr and Michalski (2007) investigated hyperactivity in Canadian children as they grew older and its sources in poverty and family structure.

There are two basic types of longitudinal design: the *panel study* and the *cohort study*. With the former, the same people, households, or other groups are studied on at least two different

BOX 2.5 | Longitudinal research and the case study

Case study research frequently includes a longitudinal element. The researcher is often a participant observer in an organization or a member of a community for many months or years, or may conduct interviews with individuals over a lengthy period. Moreover, the researcher may be able to inject an additional longitudinal element by analyzing archival information and asking respondents to recall events that occurred before the study began, thus discovering some history.

A longitudinal element also occurs when a case that has been studied is returned to at a later time. A particularly interesting example of this occurred in 'Middletown,' a pseudonym for an American Midwest town first studied by Lynd and Lynd (1929) in 1924–5 and restudied in 1935 during the Depression to see what changes had occurred (Lynd and Lynd 1937). In 1977, the community was again restudied, this time in a post–Vietnam War setting (Bahr *et al.* 1983), using the same research instruments but with minor changes.

occasions. An example is the National Longitudinal Survey of Children and Youth (NLSCY), described in Box 2.6, in which the same children were studied in successive years. A panel study, especially one at the household level, needs rules for handling new entrants (e.g., as a result of marriage or elderly relatives moving in) and exits (e.g., as a result of marital break-up or children leaving home).

In a cohort study people sharing the same experience, such as being born in the same year or graduating from a particular school at the same time, are studied over time, but the same people may not be studied each time. For example, Walters (2004) used the 1982, 1986, 1992, and 1995 National Graduates Surveys to examine trends in the economic fortunes of Canadians graduating from post-secondary institutions. The same people were not selected for the sample each year, but the information was still useful in understanding each graduating cohort, as well as the similarities and differences between cohorts.

Panel and cohort studies share similar features. In social sciences such as sociology, social policy, and human geography, both are usually in the form of repeated survey research using a self-completion questionnaire or structured interview. They have a similar design structure and are concerned both with illuminating social change and improving the understanding of causal influences.

Panel and cohort studies also share similar problems. First, there is the problem of sample attrition: some subjects may die, some may move away, and some may simply choose to withdraw at later stages of the research. For instance, in the study by Dinovitzer *et al.* (2003) on the educational attainment of immigrant youth, researchers were able to talk to only 65 per cent of those originally surveyed 19 years earlier. Comparing those who participated in the second round with those who were lost from the study, the authors found no significant differences. That sort of comparison is a common practice; when no difference is found, the losses are treated as random and thus acceptable to ignore. The main problem with attrition is that those who leave the study may differ in some important respects from those who remain, so that the latter do not form a representative group. However, there is some evidence from panel studies that attrition declines with time (Berthoud 2000*a*); in other words, those who do not drop out after the first wave or two of data collection tend to stay on the panel.

Second, there are few guidelines for determining the best timing for further waves of data collection. Finally, there is evidence of a *panel conditioning* effect, whereby continued participation in a longitudinal study affects respondents' behaviour. Menard (1991) cited a study of family caregiving in which 52 per cent of respondents

BOX 2.6 | The National Longitudinal Survey of Children and Youth

This panel study is a long-term effort to monitor Canadian children's development and well-being as they mature from infancy to adulthood. It began with a representative sample of children 11 years of age or younger in 1994–5 being interviewed, with follow-ups every two years. Statistics Canada collects the data, with direction provided by Human Resources Development Canada. The study hopes to follow the subjects until they are 25 years old, and to make a contribution to the development of policies that help children live healthy, active, and rewarding lives (see Michaud 2001). The data for Cycle 8, which began in September 2008, were released in November 2010.

attributed a change in the way they cared for relatives to their participation in the research.

It is easy to associate longitudinal designs more or less exclusively with quantitative research. However, qualitative research sometimes incorporates elements of a longitudinal design. This is especially noticeable in ethnographic research when the ethnographer is in a location for a lengthy period of time or when interviews are carried out on more than one occasion in order to examine change. In an example of the latter, Smith *et al.* (2004) described a study of the experiences of citizenship for 110 young people. They were interviewed in depth in 1999 and then re-interviewed at two-year intervals to examine changes in their lifestyles, feelings, opinions, and ambitions in relation to citizenship issues. Only 64 people participated in all three waves of data collection, illustrating the high rate of sample attrition in this style of research.

CASE STUDY DESIGN

The basic case study design entails a detailed and intensive analysis of a single case. A case may be:

- a single community, as in Hughes's classic study of Drummondville, a textile town in Quebec (1943), or in Pratt and Valverde's (2002) research on Somalis in Toronto;

- a single family, as in Lewis's (1961) study of the Sánchez family in Mexico;

- a single organization, such as the automobile factory studied by Rinehart (1996), or a group within an organization, like the nurses in a Hamilton hospital researched by White (1990);

- a person, as in Nemni and Nemni's (2006) study of Pierre Trudeau or Foran's book on Mordecai Richler (2010); such research is characterized by use of the **life history** or biographical approach (see Chapter 10);

- a single event, like the fight against locating a home for recovering addicts in a Richmond, BC, neighbourhood (Huey 2003), or the Alberta election analyzed by Bell *et al.* (2007); or

- a state or province, as in Laplante's (2006) study of the rise of cohabitation in Quebec.

There is a tendency to associate case studies with qualitative research, such as Pratt and Valverde's (2002) study of the Toronto Somali community. Exponents of the case study design often favour methods like participant observation and unstructured interviewing, which are viewed as particularly helpful in generating an intensive, detailed examination of a case. However, case studies can also use quantitative methods, or some combination of quantitative and qualitative.

With a case study, the case is an object of interest *in its own right* and the researcher aims to provide an in-depth elucidation of it. Sometimes it is difficult to distinguish case studies from other research designs because almost any kind of research can be construed as a case study. Even research based on a national, **random sample** of Canadians could be considered a case study of Canada.

What distinguishes a true case study is the goal of finding and revealing the features of the case. Collecting in-depth, often qualitative data that may be unique to time and place is characteristic of this sort of research. Case studies are often idiographic in nature, seeking to provide a rich description of the subject matter, like Shalla's (2002) study of how Air Canada's customer sales and service agents became victims of airline restructuring.

When the predominant research orientation is qualitative, a case study tends to take an **inductive** approach to the relationship between theory and research. If a mainly quantitative strategy is adopted, the research is often **deductive**, guided by specific research questions derived from social theories.

Reliability, replicability, and validity of case studies   The question of how the case study fares on the research design criteria of measurement validity, internal validity, external validity, reliability, and replicability depends in large part on whether the researcher feels these criteria are appropriate for their work. Writers of qualitative case study research tend to play down or ignore the salience of these factors (cf. Stake 1995). Those influenced by the quantitative research tradition see them as more significant, and usually try to develop case studies that meet the criteria.

One question that has generated a great deal of discussion concerns the *external validity* or *generalizability* of case study research. How can a single case possibly be representative of other cases? For example, would the findings from a study of the Toronto police department be generalizable to all large urban police departments in Canada? The answer, of course, is that the findings probably cannot be applied to other police departments. Case study researchers do not usually delude themselves into thinking that it is possible to identify typical cases that can represent a class of objects, whether factories, mass media reporting, police services, or communities. In other words, they typically do not think that a case study is a sample of one.

Types of case   Yin (1984) distinguished three types of case, each of which relates to the issue of external validity:

- The *critical case*. Here the researcher has a clearly specified hypothesis, and a case is chosen on the grounds that it will allow a better understanding of the circumstances under which the hypothesis does or does not hold. The classic study by Festinger *et al.* (1956) of a doomsday/UFO cult is an example. The fact that the world did not end allowed the researchers to test propositions about how people respond to thwarted expectations. What did cult members do when, after quitting their jobs, leaving their homes, and waiting on a mountaintop, nothing happened? Did they sneak down and move to another town? No: they decided that their faith had saved humankind and that their new role was to tell others of that miracle so more people could be converted to their religion.

- The *extreme*, even *unique*, *case* is a common focus in clinical studies. Margaret Mead's (1928) well-known (albeit controversial) study of growing up in Samoa seems to have been motivated by her belief that it represented a unique case and thus could challenge the then popular nature-over-nurture hypothesis. She reported that, unlike adolescents in most other societies, Samoan youth did not suffer a period of anxiety and stress in their teenage years. She explained this by their culture's strong, consistently enforced standards of conduct and morality. These factors were of interest because many readers thought they might contain lessons for the West.

- The *revelatory case*. The basis for the revelatory case exists 'when an investigator has an opportunity to observe and analyse a phenomenon previously inaccessible to scientific investigation' (Yin 1984: 44). This can happen when previously unavailable evidence becomes accessible, as was the case with certain KGB files after the fall of the Soviet Union.

Cases may also be chosen for mundane reasons, such as convenience, and still provide an adequate context for answering certain research questions or examining key social processes. To take a concrete example, Russell and Tyler (2002) studied a Girl Heaven store in the UK (which caters to 3- to 13-year-old girls) not because it was a critical or unique case, or because it offered a context never before studied, but because of its capacity to illuminate the links between gender and consumption and the commodification of childhood in modern society. Indeed, often it is only at a very late stage in the research that the singularity and significance of the case becomes apparent (Radley and Chamberlain 2001).

As we have mentioned, one of the standard criticisms of the case study is that its findings cannot be generalized. Case study researchers argue strenuously that this is not the purpose of their craft. A valid picture of one case is more valuable than a potentially less valid picture of many. Their aim is to generate an intensive examination of a single case, which may or may not be used for theoretical analysis. Pratt and Valverde (2002) studied only Somalis and expressed a hope that others would study other immigrant groups in other places. Their central concern was the richness of the data and the quality of the theoretical reasoning that the case allowed. As we have noted, sometimes case studies are primarily inductive, used as information to generate theories. Other times they may be deductive in nature, providing the data required to assess theories.

Problems can arise when the research involves comparison of two or more cases. Dyer and Wilkins (1991), for example, argued that a multiple-case study approach means that less attention is paid to the specific details of a particular case, and more to the ways in which multiple cases can be contrasted. Furthermore, the need for comparison often leads the researcher to choose an explicit focus at the outset, when it might be advantageous to adopt a more open-ended approach. A preference for contextual insight and a less structured research approach is associated with a qualitative research strategy. As illustrated in Boxes 2.7 and 2.8, comparative case study work is often quantitative in orientation.

The strength of comparative designs is that they highlight the similarities and differences between cases, which can be used to assess or generate theories. They exhibit certain features similar to experiments and quasi-experiments, which also rely on the capacity to establish comparisons.

BOX 2.7 Comparative research: cross-cultural studies

Phenomena such as voting behaviour or crime victimization in two or more countries can be compared using the same research instruments, seeking similarities and differences and a deeper understanding of social reality in different national contexts. At the very least such research supplies a replication. The research by Kelley and De Graaf (1997) referred to in Box 1.3 is an illustration of cross-cultural survey evidence collected in 15 nations.

Cross-cultural research is more expensive than other approaches. It also presents other problems. When using existing data such as official statistics or survey evidence, the researcher must ensure that the variable categories and data-collection methods are comparable. When new data are being collected, the researcher must ensure that data-collection instruments (for example, questionnaires and interview schedules) are translated properly. Even when translation is carried out competently, there may

still be a problem with insensitivity to specific national and cultural milieus. For example, the London 'tube,' the Toronto 'subway,' and the Montreal 'métro' differ in more than name: public transit experiences in the three cities may be very different in terms of ridership, safety, cleanliness, and so on.

A strength of cross-cultural research is that it helps to illustrate how social scientific findings may be culturally specific. For example, Wilson's (2002) examination of Ontario raves made frequent comparisons to the earlier rave scene in Britain. However, the UK scene was primarily an outgrowth of working-class struggles, whereas Canadian raves appealed more to middle-class, culturally alienated youths. Similarly, Baer *et al.* (2001) found that joining clubs and voluntary organizations increased towards the end of the last century in the US, West Germany, and the Netherlands, was stable in Canada and 10 other countries, but decreased in Spain.

BOX 2.8 Managing cross-cultural research

As its name implies, cross-cultural research entails the collection and/or analysis of data from two or more cultures. For example:

1. A researcher, perhaps in conjunction with a research team, collects data in a number of countries. A related option is for a coordinator to recruit researchers in participating nations and to direct their investigations. The work is coordinated to ensure comparability of research questions, survey questions, and procedures for administering the research instruments. Sometimes the foreign team leaders have

considerable autonomy in deciding which cases they will study, provided that they meet pre-determined criteria (for example, organizational level or size).

2. A lone researcher or small team replicates work done in a foreign country in his or her own country. For instance, a 2004 Ipsos-Reid survey for Canadian Blood Services found that only 3.7 per cent of Canadians are blood donors—less than half the rate in Taiwan, and below the US rate of about 5 per cent.

Bringing research orientation and design together

Finally, we can bring together the two general research orientations covered in Chapter 1 with the research designs outlined in this chapter. Table 2.1 shows the typical form associated with each combination of research orientation and research design, along with a number of examples that either have been encountered so far or will be covered in later chapters. Table 2.1 also refers to research methods to be introduced in later

chapters, but not referred to so far. The glossary provides a quick reference for unfamiliar terms.

The distinctions are not always perfect. In particular, in some qualitative research it is not obvious whether a study is an example of a longitudinal design or a case study design. Life history studies, research that concentrates on a specific issue over time, and **ethnography**, in which the researcher charts change in a single case, contain elements of both designs. Such studies are perhaps better conceptualized as longitudinal case studies rather than as belonging to one category or another. A further point is that there is no typical form in the qualitative research orientation/experimental research design cell. Qualitative research in the context of true experiments is very unusual; a quasi-experimental design is a more realistic alternative.

TABLE 2.1	Research strategy and research design	
RESEARCH DESIGN	**GENERAL RESEARCH ORIENTATION**	
	Quantitative	*Qualitative*
Experimental	Typical form: Most experiments involve quantitative comparisons between experimental and control groups on the dependent variable. Example: the Rosenthal and Jacobson (1968) study discussed in this chapter.	Experiments are not used in qualitative research, although they may inspire or be inspired by qualitative findings. For example, a qualitative study of the teachers who participated in the Rosenthal and Jacobson (1968) study discussed in this chapter would be enlightening.
Cross-sectional	Typical form: Survey research and structured observation on a sample at a single point in time are two forms; content analysis of a sample of documents is another. Sometimes there is a comparison, as in cross-cultural research. Example: Box 1.3.	Typical form: Qualitative interviews or focus groups at a single point in time are two forms; qualitative content analysis of a set of documents relating to a single period is another. Example: the Beardsworth and Keil (1992) study of vegetarianism discussed in this chapter.
Longitudinal	Typical form: Survey research on a sample on more than one occasion, as in panel and cohort studies is one form; content analysis of documents relating to different time periods is another. Example: Box 2.8.	Typical form: These include ethnographic research over a long period, qualitative interviewing on more than one occasion, or qualitative content analysis of documents relating to different time periods. Such research is longitudinal when the main purpose is to map change. Examples: the Lynd and Lynd (1929) study of 'Middletown' discussed in this chapter.
Case study	Typical form: Survey research is conducted on a single case with a view to revealing important features about its nature. Example: Bell *et al.* (2007) study of the 2004 Alberta provincial election.	Typical form: The intensive study is done by qualitative interviewing of a single case, which may be an organization, person, family, or community. Example: Box 1.6.

Key Points

- There is an important distinction between a general research orientation (quantitative vs qualitative) and a research design.
- The nomothetic approach to explanation involves discovering general laws and principles.
- Nomothetic explanations must satisfy three criteria of causation: correlation, time order, and non-spuriousness.
- Qualitative researchers usually take the idiographic approach to explanation, which entails creating a rich description of a person or group based on the perceptions and feelings of the

people studied.

- Reliability, replicability, and validity (measurement, internal, and external) are important criteria for evaluating the quality of social research.

- Four key research designs are experimental, cross-sectional, longitudinal, and case study.

- Threats to internal validity are of particular

importance in non-experimental research.

- External validity is a concern with case studies (generalizability) and laboratory experiments (findings may not be applicable outside the research environment).

Relevant Websites

The *National Longitudinal Study of Children and Youth* site provides information on an ongoing, longitudinal study in Canada.

http://www.statcan.gc.ca/cgi-bin/imdb/ p2SV.pl?Function=getSurvey&SDDS=4450&la ng=en&db=imdb&adm=8&dis=2

The *Online Dictionary of the Social Sciences* site, maintained by Athabasca University, 'has 1000 entries covering the disciplines of sociology, criminology, political science and women's study with a commitment to Canadian examples and events and names.'

http://bitbucket.icaap.org/dict.pl

The *Research Methods Knowledge Base* provides a detailed discussion of various types of experimental design:

http://www.socialresearchmethods.net/kb/ desexper.php

The *Human Genome Project* site offers some basic information on behavioural genetics:

http://www.ornl.gov/sci/techresources/ Human_Genome/elsi/behavior.shtml

[Websites accessed 20 July 2011]

Questions for Review

CRITERIA FOR THE EVALUATION OF SOCIAL RESEARCH

- Provide an original example of a spurious relationship between two variables.

- How do qualitative researchers produce idiographic explanations? Pick a topic of interest to you and explain how you could research it using the idiographic approach.

- What are the differences between reliability and validity, and why are both criteria important in social research?

- Give an example of each of the following: measurement validity, internal validity, and external validity.

- Why have some qualitative researchers sought to devise alternative criteria for reliability and validity to assess their investigations?

RESEARCH DESIGNS

- Which research design would be most appropriate for examining the use of illegal drugs in a local high school? Explain.

- A researcher reasons that people who read broadsheet newspapers (wider than they are tall) are likely to be more knowledgeable about personal finance than readers of tabloid newspapers (taller than they are wide). One hundred people are interviewed about which type they read and their level of financial knowledge: 65 readers of tabloids and 35 of broadsheets. The latter are on average considerably more knowledgeable about personal finance than tabloid readers, so the researcher concludes that reading broadsheets enhances knowledge of personal finance. Assess that conclusion.

EXPERIMENTAL DESIGN

- How are true experiments able to establish causal connections between variables? Explain.

- Following from the last question, if experiments are so useful and important, why are they not used more in disciplines such as sociology or political science?

- What are the drawbacks to using true experiments in the social sciences?

- What is a quasi-experiment?

- Give a new example of a situation in which a natural experiment could be conducted. What could be learned by doing research in this situation?

CROSS-SECTIONAL DESIGN

- What is meant by a cross-sectional research design?

- In what ways does the survey exemplify the cross-sectional research design?

- Assess the degree to which survey research can achieve internal validity.

- To what extent is the survey design exclusive to quantitative research?

LONGITUDINAL DESIGN(S)

- Why might a longitudinal research design be superior to a cross-sectional one?

- What are the main differences between panel and cohort designs?

CASE STUDY DESIGN

- What is a case study?

- Is case study research exclusive to qualitative research?

- What are some of the principles by which cases might be selected?

PART II

Part II of this book is concerned with quantitative research. Chapter 3 sets the scene by exploring its main features. Chapter 4 focuses on structured interviews and questionnaires—two of the most widely used data-gathering techniques in quantitative research. Chapter 5 provides guidelines on how to ask questions using those instruments, while Chapter 6 discusses structured observation, a method that takes a systematic approach to the study of people in their natural surroundings. Chapter 7 examines other data sources, such as the information collected by other researchers and government agencies. These chapters describe the essential tools for doing quantitative research, from basic methodological principles to practical applications.

CHAPTER 3

The Nature of Quantitative Research

CHAPTER OVERVIEW

This chapter is concerned with **quantitative research**, an approach used by a large number of people in the social sciences. The emphasis here is on what quantitative research typically entails, though departures from this ideal type will be outlined later on. This chapter explores:

- the main steps of quantitative research, presented as a linear succession of stages;
- the importance of measurement in quantitative research, and the ways in which measures are devised for **concepts**;
- procedures for checking the **reliability** and **validity** of those measures;
- the main goals of quantitative researchers: measurement, establishing **causality**, **generalization**, and **replication**; and
- some criticisms of quantitative research.

For his class project, Mario wants to ask some fellow students questions about a topic that's always fascinated him: drug and alcohol use, and how it might affect a person's self-image. But how will he get the information he needs? He quickly jots down a few notes, but soon realizes that coming up with effective questions is more difficult than he imagined. His first question reads: 'Do you take drugs?'; but he quickly realizes that 'drugs' is too vague, since for some people that would include things like aspirin and cough medicine. And what about alcohol? Isn't alcohol a kind of drug too? Now he begins to think about other potential problems. What if some people refuse to say what their level of drug and alcohol consumption is? Would some people be offended by the question? And when they do answer, how will he know if they're telling the truth? Is there a second method he could use, such as observing people in a local pub, to see if their behaviour is consistent with the survey data? And once he's asked the basic questions about consumption, how will he approach the self-image part of his research question? What exactly should he be asking about? Should the information be recorded in numeric form? If so, how do you do that? When he has finished analyzing the data, will he be able to say that his findings have wider applications? In this chapter we will explore how researchers deal with the kinds of issues that Mario is facing.

Introduction

In Chapter 1, quantitative research was outlined as a distinctive research strategy involving particular **epistemological** and **ontological** assumptions. It should be clear by now that much more than the presence of numbers distinguishes a quantitative from a qualitative research strategy. In very broad terms, quantitative research entails the collection of numerical data, a **deductive** relationship between theory and research, a preference for the natural science approach to research (**positivism** in particular), and an **objectivist** conception of social reality. This chapter spells out the main steps in quantitative research, and outlines how some of its principal concerns, such as **measurement validity**, are addressed.

The main steps in quantitative research

Figure 3.1 outlines the main steps in quantitative research. This is very much an ideal account of the process: research is rarely as linear or straightforward as the figure implies. However, it represents a useful starting point for coming to grips with the main facets of the quantitative approach.

Some of the steps were covered in the previous chapters. The fact that the model starts off with theory signifies a broadly deductive approach to the relationship between theory and research. Similarly, it is common for outlines of quantitative research to suggest that a hypothesis is deduced from a theory and is tested, another notion incorporated into Figure 3.1. However, a great deal of quantitative research does not specify a hypothesis beforehand; instead there may simply be a loosely defined set of concerns in relation to which the social researcher collects data. This was the case for Gazso-Windlej and McMullin's (2003) study of how time, resources, and patriarchy contribute to the unequal spousal sharing of domestic labour in Canada. The specification of testable hypotheses is more common in experimental research.

In step 3 a research design is selected, a topic explored in Chapter 2. This choice has implications for a variety of issues, such as the **external validity** of the findings and the ability to impute causality. Step 4 entails devising measures of

1. Theory
2. Hypothesis
3. Research design
4. Devise measures of concepts
5. Select research site(s)
6. Select research subjects/respondents
7. Administer research instruments/collect data
8. Process data
9. Analyze data
10. Findings/conclusions
11. Write up findings/conclusions

FIGURE 3.1   The process of quantitative research

concepts, a process often referred to as **operationalization**, a term derived from physics to refer to the operations performed to measure a concept such as temperature or velocity (Bridgman 1927). Further aspects of this issue are explored later in this chapter.

The next two steps are the selection of a research site or sites and the selection of subjects/respondents. (Experimenters tend to call the people on whom they conduct research 'subjects,' whereas social survey researchers typically call them 'respondents.') In the study of delinquency among male adolescents described in Box 1.2, Teevan and Dryburgh's (2000) first choice as a research site was a school where they had connections. When they had to arrange for permission slips to be signed, however, they decided to restrict their study to boys old enough to give their own permission. Finally, because of a less-than-eager response, all boys who were willing to participate became part of the study. In bigger studies, especially those in which the findings are expected to be applicable to some larger population, an elaborate sampling process (discussed in Chapter 12) may be used to select people for the project, although this approach is rare in experimental research.

Step 7 is the administration of the research instruments. In experimental research, this usually means pre-testing subjects, manipulating the **independent variable** for the experimental group only, and post-testing. In cross-sectional research using survey research instruments, it involves interviewing the members of the **sample** with a structured **interview schedule** (a list of questions or statements to which the person being interviewed responds) or distributing a self-completion **questionnaire**. In research using **structured observation**, this step involves watching the setting of interest and the people in it, and then recording the types of behaviours observed.

Step 8 simply refers to the fact that the information collected must be systematically recorded so that it can be analyzed. With some information this can be done in a relatively straightforward way. For example, for information relating to matters such as people's ages, incomes, and the number of years they spent at school, the information does not have to be transformed: the scores can simply be recorded in a computer file. For other variables, processing the data entails **coding** the information—that is, transforming it into numbers to facilitate quantitative data analysis. This consideration leads into step 9: analysis of the data. In this step, the researcher chooses among various statistical techniques to test for relationships between variables, tries to determine whether the measures are reliable, and so on.

Next, in step 10, the researcher must interpret the results of the analysis; it is at this stage that the 'findings' emerge. Here the researcher must consider the reasons why the research was done in the first place, in particular how the results may be used to answer the research question(s). If there is a hypothesis, is it supported? What are the implications of the findings for the theoretical ideas that were the background to the research? Do the findings support the theory? If not, should the theory be revised? Should it be abandoned entirely?

Then the research must be written up in step 11. Until it enters the public domain in some way, as a paper to be read at a conference, a report to the agency that funded the research, or as a book or journal article to be read by other researchers or students, it cannot have an impact beyond satisfying the researcher's personal curiosity. In writing up the findings and conclusions, researchers must do more than simply relay their results to others: they must convince readers that the research conclusions are important and the findings robust. A significant part of doing research is convincing others of the relevance and validity of one's findings.

Once the findings have been published they become part of the stock of knowledge in their domain. Thus there is a feedback loop from step 11 back to step 1. The presence of both an element of **deduction** (steps 1 and 2) and **induction** (the feedback loop) is indicative of the **positivist** foundations of quantitative research. The emphasis on the translation of concepts into measures (step 4) is also a feature of positivism, and it is to that important phase of the research that we now turn. As we will see, certain considerations follow from the need for measurement in quantitative research—in particular, finding valid and reliable ways to measure concepts.

Concepts and their measurement

WHAT IS A CONCEPT?

Concepts are ideas or mental representations of things. They are the building blocks of theory and represent the points around which social research is conducted. Just think of the numerous concepts that have already been mentioned so far in this book:

> emotional satisfaction, religious orthodoxy, religious orientation, hyperactivity, academic achievement, teacher expectations, charismatic leadership, crime, research ethics, healthy lifestyle, drug and alcohol use, and self-image.

Each represents a label given to elements of the social world that seem to be significant and to have common features. As Bulmer succinctly put it, concepts 'are categories for the organization of ideas and observations' (1984: 43). One item mentioned in Chapter 2 but missing from the list above is IQ. It has been omitted because it is not, strictly speaking, a concept. It is a *measure* of the concept of intelligence. This is a rare case for social science, a measure so well known that the measure and the concept are almost synonymous.

A concept can be either an independent or a **dependent variable**. In other words, a concept can be presented as a possible cause of a certain aspect of the social world (independent), or it can represent something needing an explanation (dependent). Often the same concept will be an independent variable in one context and a dependent variable in another. The concept 'social mobility,' for example, can be used in either capacity: as a possible explanation of certain attitudes (are there differences between the downwardly mobile and others in their political attitudes?) or as something to be explained (why are some people upwardly mobile and others not?). Equally, concepts may be used for descriptive or comparative purposes. For instance, a researcher might be interested in changes in the amount of social mobility in Canada over time, or in variations among comparable nations in their levels of social mobility.

WHY MEASURE?

There are three main reasons for the attention given to measurement in quantitative research:

- Measurement allows for delineation of *fine differences* between people in terms of the characteristic in question. This is very useful since, although it is often easy to distinguish between people in terms of extreme categories, finer distinctions are much more difficult to recognize. Clear variations in levels of job satisfaction—people who love their jobs and people who hate their jobs—are easy to see, but small differences are much more difficult to detect.

- Measurement provides a *consistent device* or yardstick for gauging such distinctions. This consistency relates both to time and to the people using the measure. A measure's results should not be affected by either the time when it is administered or the person who administers it. With regard to time, this rule means that the measure should generate consistent results *unless* the phenomenon or characteristic being measured has changed. For example, measures of worker morale administered at different times should indicate the same level of morale unless the morale itself has changed. Similarly, those measures and the data they produce should be the same regardless of who is using

them. Whether a measure actually possesses this consistency pertains to the issue of *reliability*, introduced in Chapter 2 and examined again later in this chapter.

- Measurement provides the basis for *estimates of the nature and strength of the relationship between concepts* (for example, through **correlation** analysis, which will be examined in Chapter 13).

INDICATORS

Concepts used in quantitative research are given two types of definition. One is a *nominal* definition, which describes in words what the concept means, much as a dictionary definition does. For example, a nominal definition of 'crime' might be: 'any violation of the *Criminal Code of Canada*.' By contrast, a concept's **operational definition** (from the idea of operationalization, discussed above) spells out the operations the researcher will perform to measure the concept. For example, one way to measure the incidence of crime is to use statistics provided by police forces; another is to ask a sample of people whether they have been victims of certain crimes.

To measure a concept it is necessary to have an indicator or indicators that stand for or represent the concept. Sometimes the term 'indicator' simply refers to a measure in the ordinary sense: for example, the total income reported on a tax return is an indicator of a person's wealth. However, sometimes it refers to an indirect measure of a concept that cannot be tapped easily or directly. For example, absenteeism may be used as an indirect measure of employee morale. Income declared for tax purposes may be a direct measure of personal income, but if used as an indicator of social class, it becomes an indirect measure.

There are a number of ways to devise indicators. For example:

- through questions that are part of a structured interview schedule or self-completion questionnaire. The questions can be concerned with the respondents' attitudes (e.g., job satisfaction), their personal experiences (e.g., stress), their behaviours (e.g., leisure pursuits), and so on;

- by developing criteria for classifying observed behaviour (e.g., pupil behaviour in a classroom);

- through the use of official statistics (e.g., Statistics Canada);

- by developing classification schemes to analyze the content of written material (e.g., Hallgrimsdottir *et al.*'s (2006) examination of how newspapers in Victoria, BC, characterized sex-trade workers at different times).

Indicators can be derived from a wide variety of sources and methods. Very often a researcher has to consider whether one indicator of a concept suffices. Instead of relying on a single indicator, the researcher may use several to tap a concept (see Boxes 3.1 and 3.3 for examples).

USING MULTIPLE-ITEM MEASURES IN SURVEY RESEARCH

The main advantage in using a multiple-indicator measure of a concept is that there are potential problems in relying on just a single indicator:

- A single indicator may misclassify some individuals if the wording of the question leads to misunderstanding of its meaning. If there are several indicators, however, it is possible that the other items will allow proper classification of the person.

- A single broad, general indicator may not capture all the meaning in the underlying concept.

If you were to ask people how satisfied they are with their work, for instance, you might miss the complexity of the situation. People who answer 'not satisfied' may like some parts of their work, just as those who claim to be 'satisfied' may dislike specific aspects of their work.

- Alternatively, a more specific question may cover only one dimension of a particular concept. For example, to measure job satisfaction, is it sufficient to ask people how satisfied they are with their pay? Almost certainly the answer is 'no,' because for most people there is more to job satisfaction than just satisfaction with pay. In this case, a single indicator will miss things like satisfaction with benefits, with the work itself, and with other aspects of the work environment. By asking a number of questions, the researcher can get access to a wider range of issues covered by the concept.

- Multiple indicators allow for fine distinctions. Take the Christakis *et al.* (2008) measure of attitudes toward affirmative action as an example (see Box 3.1). If we were to use just one of the items as our measure, the scores for this variable could vary from 1 to 5 (since

---

BOX 3.1 | A multiple-indicator measure of a concept

Christakis *et al.* (2008) did a study of University of Toronto medical students who were applying for a residency position in ophthalmology. One goal of the study was to determine how the medical students felt about the issue of affirmative action. Another was to get an ethnic, racial, and gender breakdown of applicants to see whether a program of affirmative action was necessary. To measure attitudes towards affirmative action, respondents were given a series of statements on the role of gender and ethnicity in university admissions. They were asked to indicate whether they 'strongly agree, agree, neither agree nor disagree, disagree, or strongly disagree' with the statements. These sorts of attitude measures are called **Likert items** or **Likert scales** (in some cases researchers use a seven-point rather than a five-point scale for responses). See Box 3.2 for an outline of what a Likert scale entails. Here are some examples of the statements used by Christakis *et al.*:

- Admissions committees should be permitted to take race and ethnicity into account in their admissions process to achieve the educational benefits of a diverse student body.

- There should be quotas (fixed numbers or percentages of available places) for minority applicants.

- In Ontario some ethnic groups are being given an advantage in the admissions process.

- In Ontario some ethnic groups are being discriminated against in the admissions process.

- Sex plays a role in the admissions process.

- Sex should play a role in the admissions process.

The authors found that only 24 per cent of the medical students supported affirmative action and only 12 per cent were in favour of quotas for minority applicants, in spite of the fact that 62 per cent considered themselves to be members of an ethnic minority and 57 per cent were members of a visible minority. Given the attitudes of the students and their ethnic and racial breakdown, the researchers concluded that the ophthalmology program was not in need of an affirmative action program.

answers indicating strong disagreement are assigned a value of 1 and answers indicating strong agreement a value of 5). With six indicators, however, the range becomes 6 (6 x 1) to 30 (6 x 5).

- Multiple indicators of a concept allow for sophisticated data analyses such as *factor analysis*. Although such techniques are beyond the scope of this book, they provide an indication of the extent to which (a) multiple measures really are measuring a single concept as opposed to more than one concept, and (b) individual items are measuring the concept in question. Bell *et al.* (2009), for example, used factor analysis to develop measures of political attitudes.

DIMENSIONS OF CONCEPTS

As we suggested earlier, the concept of interest may have multiple facets or dimensions, which are often revealed in the theories and research associated with it. In developing a measure for a concept, its different aspects or components should be considered. Bryman and Cramer (2001) demonstrated this approach with reference to the concept of 'professionalism.' The idea is that people scoring high on one dimension of the concept (e.g., respecting confidentiality) may not necessarily score high on other dimensions (e.g., fiscal honesty or continuing education), so that for each respondent one can have a multidimensional 'profile.' Box 3.4 demonstrates the use of dimensions in connection with the concept of 'de-skilling' in the sociology of work.

However, in much quantitative research, there is a tendency to rely on a single indicator for each concept. This is quite adequate for some purposes, in particular when one is measuring an uncomplicated variable such as age. Some studies, like Kelley and De Graaf's (1997; see Box 3.3), employ both single- and multiple-indicator measures of concepts. What is crucial is that the measures be reliable and valid representations of the concepts they are supposed to be gauging.

Reliability and measurement validity

RELIABILITY

Reliability is concerned with the *consistency* of measures. The term has at least three different meanings.

BOX 3.2   Likert scales

The investigation of attitudes is a prominent area in survey research. One of the most common techniques for investigating attitudes is the Likert scale. Named after Rensis Likert, who developed the method, it is essentially a multiple-indicator measure of the intensity of feelings about a particular topic. In its most common format, it comprises a series of statements (known as 'items') on an issue or theme. Usually, each respondent is asked to indicate his or her level of agreement with the statement. The format for indicating level of agreement is normally a five-point scale from 'strongly agree' to 'strongly disagree,' but seven-point and other formats are used as well. There is usually a middle position of 'neither agree nor disagree' or 'undecided' indicating neutrality on the issue. A respondent's reply on each item is scored and then the scores are aggregated to form an overall score. Variations on the typical format of agreement are scales referring to frequency (for example, 'never' through 'always') and evaluation (for example, 'very poor' to 'very good').

There are several points to remember in constructing a Likert scale. The following are particularly important:

- The items must be statements, not questions.
- The items must all relate to the same object (for example, a particular organization, the issue of unemployment).
- The items that make up the scale should be inter-related.
- It is useful to vary the phrasing so that some items imply a positive view of the phenomenon of interest and others a negative one. For example, in the 2007 Alberta Survey conducted by the Population Research Laboratory at the University of Alberta, attitudes towards body checking in minor hockey were measured using five-point Lickert items. One item read: 'Body checking is the main cause of injuries for children in organized minor hockey.' A second was: 'Body checking is an essential part of the game of organized minor hockey.' The first implies a negative view of body checking, the second a more positive one.

BOX 3.3 : A multiple-indicator measure of another concept

In Kelley and De Graaf's (1997) research on religious beliefs, national religiosity and family religious orientation were each measured by a single indicator (see Box 1.3). However, religious orthodoxy was measured by four survey questions; answers to each of the four were given a value and then added together to form a religious belief score for each respondent. The questions were as follows:

Please indicate which statement below comes closest to expressing what you believe about God:

- I don't believe in God. (1)
- I don't know whether there is a God and don't believe there is a way to find out. (2)
- I don't believe in a personal God, but I do believe in a higher power of some kind. (3)
- I find myself believing in God some of the time, but not at others. (4)
- While I have doubts, I feel that I do believe in God. (5)
- I know God really exists and I have no doubts about it. (6)

Which best describes your beliefs about God?

- I don't believe in God and I never have. (1)

- I don't believe in God, but I used to. (2)
- I believe in God now, but I didn't used to. (3)
- I believe in God now and I always have. (4)

How close do you feel to God most of the time?

- Don't believe in God. (1)
- Not close at all. (2)
- Not very close. (3)
- Somewhat close. (4)
- Extremely close. (5)

There is a God, one personally concerned with every human being.

- Strongly agree. (5)
- Agree. (4)
- Neither agree nor disagree. (3)
- Disagree. (2)
- Strongly disagree. (1)

Notice the values attached to each answer. A person whose answers add up to 20 (6 + 4 + 5 + 5) has the highest level of religious belief possible on this measure, and a person with a sum of 4 (getting a 1 on each question) has the lowest.

Stability over time 'Stability' refers to whether the results of a measure fluctuate as time progresses, assuming that what is being measured is not changing. This means that if one administers a measure to a group and then re-administers it perhaps an hour later, there should be little variation in the results. Most thermometers have this kind of reliability.

The most obvious way of testing for the stability of a measure is the *test–retest* method. This involves administering a test or measure on one occasion and then re-administering it to the same sample on another occasion, that is:

$$T_1 \qquad T_2$$
$$Obs_1 \qquad Obs_2$$

One would expect to find a high correlation between Obs_1 and Obs_2. For example, those who score high on the first observation should also score high on

the second, and those who score low on the first should score low on the second. Imagine a multiple-indicator measure that is supposed to tap a concept called 'designerism' (a preference for buying goods and especially clothing with 'designer' labels). The measure would be administered to a sample of respondents and then later re-administered. If the correlation between Obs_1 and Obs_2 is low, the measure is unstable, implying that it cannot be relied upon.

However, there are a number of problems with this approach to evaluating reliability. Respondents' answers at T_1 may influence how they reply at T_2: for instance, perhaps answering a question on designer goods increases some respondents' interest in them. Yet giving an answer at T_1 is not supposed to affect later measurements. Second, events may intervene between T_1 and T_2 that influence the degree of consistency. For example, if a long span of time is involved, changes in the

BOX 3.4	Specifying dimensions of a concept: the case of de-skilling

Based on a reading of the literature on the topic of de-skilling, Marshall *et al.* (1988) argued that the concept has two important components or dimensions—'skill as complexity and skill as freedom'—which 'are central to the thesis that work is being proletarianized through the de-skilling of tasks' (1988: 116). 'Skill as complexity' was measured by a single interview question asking respondents whether their current jobs require more, less, or about the same amount of skill as when they first started. 'Skill as freedom' was measured by seven indicators treated separately and not added together. The questions asked about issues such as whether respondents can reduce the pace of the work done or initiate new tasks in their work. Neither dimension offered significant support for the de-skilling thesis.

economy or in respondents' personal financial circumstances can influence their views about designer goods and their predilection for them.

There are no clear solutions to these problems, other than introducing a complex research design and so turning the investigation of reliability into a major project in its own right. Perhaps for these reasons, many, if not most, research projects do not include tests of stability over time.

When such tests are done, they may indicate that there is no problem, even when a substantial amount of time has elapsed. Berthoud (2000*b*), for example, was pleased that an index of illness achieved high test–retest reliability even though the tests were conducted a year apart.

Internal reliability (or internal consistency)   The key issue here is whether multiple measures that are *administered in one sitting* are consistent—in other words, whether respondents' scores on any one indicator tend to be related to their scores on the other indicators. For example, on a scale created to measure attitudes toward liberal democracy, people who agree with the statement that voting is an important right should also agree that freedom of speech is an important right.

Cronbach's alpha coefficient is a commonly used test of **internal reliability**. Its value varies from 1 (denoting perfect internal reliability)

to 0 (denoting none). The figure .80 is typically employed to mark the minimum acceptable level of internal reliability, though many writers work with a lower figure. Berthoud (2000*b*: 169), for instance, wrote that a minimum level of .60 is 'good.' In the case of Kelley and De Graaf's (1997) measure of religious orthodoxy (see Box 3.3), which used four indicators, alpha ranged from .79 to .95 for each of the 15 national samples that made up the data. In a study of environmental values among Chinese- and Anglo-Canadians by Deng *et al.* (2006), the alphas ranged from .50 to .89 for various variables. The study of domestic labour by Gazso-Windlej and McMullin (2003) could only achieve alphas averaging .50 for its Likert-style items measuring gender ideology, although the study was only exploratory. The use of Cronbach's alpha has grown as a result of its incorporation into computer software for quantitative data analysis.

Another way of testing for internal reliability is the *split-half* method. Take the attitude toward affirmative action measure developed by Christakis *et al.* (2008) as an example (see Box 3.1). The six indicators would be divided into two halves of three, allocated on a random or an odd-numbered item/even-numbered item basis. The degree of correlation between the scores on the two halves for all respondents would then be calculated. If the six items are consistent, a respondent's score on the two groups of indicators should be similar, perhaps high on both, or low on both. A perfect positive correlation and therefore complete internal consistency would yield a correlation coefficient of 1; no correlation and therefore no internal consistency would produce a coefficient of 0. The meaning of correlation and correlation coefficients will be explored in much greater detail later on. The chief point at this stage is that the correlation coefficient establishes how closely respondents' scores on the two groups of indicators are related.

Inter-observer consistency   When more than one researcher is taking part in an activity involving subjective judgment, such as the recording of observations or the translation of data into categories, their judgments may differ. This problem can arise in a number of contexts: for example, if answers to **open-ended** questions have to be categorized, or in structured observation when observers have to decide how to classify subjects' behaviour. Is the person under observation 'afraid,' 'concerned,' or 'just thinking' when reading about the spread of yet another deadly new virus? Problems arise if all observers do not classify a particular behaviour in the same way. Cramer (1998: ch. 14) provides a very detailed treatment of inter-observer consistency and the techniques that can be used to maximize it.

MEASUREMENT VALIDITY

As we noted in Chapter 2, measurement validity refers to whether an indicator (or set of indicators) devised to gauge a concept really does so. When people argue about whether an IQ score really measures or reflects someone's level of intelligence, they are raising questions about the measurement validity of the IQ test in relation to the concept of intelligence. Whenever students and their teachers debate whether multiple-choice examinations provide an accurate measure of academic ability, they too are raising questions about measurement validity. Establishing **face validity**, **concurrent validity**, predictive validity, **construct validity**, and convergent validity shows that you have in fact measured what you wanted to measure.

Face validity   At the very minimum, a researcher who develops a new measure should establish that it has *face validity*—that is, that it appears to reflect the content of the concept in question. Face validity can be established by asking those with expertise in a field to act as judges to determine whether, *on the face of it*, the measure seems to reflect the concept concerned. Face validity is essentially an intuitive process.

Concurrent validity   The researcher can also seek to gauge the concurrent validity of the measure by employing a *criterion* relevant to the concept in question but on which cases (for example, people) are known to differ. Assuming that as job satisfaction goes down, absenteeism goes up, a researcher seeking to establish the concurrent validity of a new measure of job satisfaction might look to see if people who are satisfied with their jobs are less likely to be absent from work than those who are not satisfied. If there is no difference in absenteeism between those who are satisfied and those who are not, doubt is cast on whether the new measure is really gauging job satisfaction.

Construct validity   Some writers advocate that researchers estimate the *construct validity* of a measure, which involves seeing whether the concepts used in the research relate to each other in a way that is consistent with what their theories would predict. For example, suppose that a researcher wants to establish the construct validity of the new measure of job satisfaction. Drawing on a theory maintaining that job satisfaction is influenced by the stimulation that comes from performing several *different* activities, he or she may anticipate that people who do routine jobs are less satisfied with their jobs than those who have greater opportunities for variety, complexity, and creativity. If these variables correlate in the expected way, then the measure in question has construct validity. On the other hand, some caution is required if the relationship is weak or non-existent; for example, if those who do routine jobs are just as satisfied as those with jobs involving a lot of variety. If so, the measures used may be invalid, or the deduction that is made from the theory may be misguided, or the theory itself may be in need of revision. Whatever the problem may be, it's probably best to seek another measure and try again.

Convergent validity   In the view of some methodologists, the validity of a measure ought to be gauged by comparing it to measures of the same concept developed through other methods. For example, if a questionnaire asks managers how much time they spend on various activities (attending meetings, touring their organization, informal discussions, and so on), its validity may be determined by directly observing the managers to see how much time they actually spend on those activities.

An interesting instance of convergent *in*validity is described in Box 3.5. Crime surveys were consciously devised to serve as a check on official police statistics. The two sets of data are collected in quite different ways: official crime statistics are collected as part of the bureaucratic processing of offenders in the criminal justice system, whereas crime victimization surveys provide data from interviews with members of the general public. In the case reported in Box 3.5, a lack of convergent validity was found. This illustrates a problem with the convergent approach to testing validity: it's

BOX 3.5 | A case of convergent invalidity: crime statistics

Police gathering evidence at a murder scene. This crime will definitely be entered into the official crime statistics. Why will it become part of the official record while other crimes might not?

Official police reports and national crime victimization studies often provide very different indications of the amount of crime in society. As part of the General Social Survey (GSS), Canadians are asked about their victimization experiences. It is widely known that the victimization data show more crime than the official police reports because many Canadians do not report their experiences with crime to the police, for a variety of reasons (inconvenience, embarrassment, etc.). To take one example, for robbery the victimization rate reported in the surveys is almost three times the official rate. But for auto theft, the police data show 50 per cent more thefts, because the GSS does not gather data on the theft of company cars or cars taken from car dealerships (Silverman *et al.* 2000: 58). So there will probably always be a discrepancy between police statistics and victimization surveys on the amount of crime that exists. Another illustration of a lack of concurrence between two methods of data gathering pertains to murder rates. The police report 15 per cent more homicides in Canada than does the Mortality Database drawn from death certificates (Gabor *et al.* 2002); some officials in charge of the latter may be reluctant to classify certain deaths as homicides because doing so might upset the relatives of the victims.

not easy to establish which of the two measures provides the more accurate picture. In the case of crime statistics, the two methods are really measuring somewhat different things. Victimization surveys measure the crimes that people experience, as well as some things that may not be crimes; they also omit certain crimes (for example, when a stolen item is presumed to be 'lost'). Police statistics, on the other hand, measure the crimes that people are willing to call the police about, plus the crimes the police themselves discover; and not all crimes end up in official police statistics. In any case, the 'true' volume of crime at any one time is almost always a contested notion (Reiner 2000*a*). Box 3.6 presents some more examples of the ways in which reliability and validity are assessed.

Reflections on reliability and validity

There are, then, a number of ways to investigate the merit of measures devised to represent social scientific concepts. However, the discussion of reliability and validity is potentially misleading because not all new measures of concepts are submitted to the rigours just described. In fact, the reliability and validity of many measures are never tested. When a new multiple-indicator measure is devised, there may be an examination of face validity and a test for internal reliability, but in many cases no further testing takes place.

It should also be remembered that, although reliability and validity are analytically distinguishable, they are related: if a measure is not reliable, it cannot be valid. For example, a multiple-indicator measure lacking internal reliability is probably measuring two or more different things and therefore is not a valid indicator of the single concept it is supposed to be measuring.

The main goals of quantitative researchers

MEASUREMENT

To understand the social order one must be able to go into the world and measure things like prejudice, the incidence of homelessness, attitudes towards the federal government, or the distribution of wealth in society. It would be awfully hard to make sense of such phenomena or to evaluate theories and interpretations of them without acquiring data on them: that is, without measuring them. It's not

BOX 3.6 Developing a Likert scale: the case of attitudes to vegetarians

Noting that some non-vegetarians treat vegetarians with suspicion if not hostility, Chin *et al.* (2002) developed a scale to measure pro- or anti-vegetarian attitudes. It comprised 33 statements to which respondents were asked to indicate their strength of agreement or disagreement on a seven-point scale. The items were developed from interviews with both vegetarians and non-vegetarians, a review of the literature on vegetarianism, field observations, brainstorming sessions within the team, and attitude scales measuring other forms of prejudice (for possible wording and presentation). The items were meant to tap four areas:

- forms of behaviour on the part of vegetarians that others find irritating; for example, 'Vegetarians preach too much about their beliefs and eating habits';

- disagreement with vegetarians' beliefs; for example, 'Vegetarians are overly concerned with animal rights';

- disagreement with vegetarians' beliefs regarding health; for example, 'Vegetarians are overly concerned about gaining weight'; and

- appropriate treatment of vegetarians; for example, 'It's okay to tease someone for being a vegetarian.'

The scale was tested on a sample of US undergraduates. Some items were dropped because of poor internal consistency with other items. Cronbach's alpha for the remaining 21 items was .87.

The construct validity of the scale was also tested. Respondents completed other scales on variables thought to be associated with pro- or anti-vegetarian attitudes. For example, the authors hypothesized that people scoring high on an authoritarian attitude scale would be more likely to be anti-vegetarians. This was confirmed, although the relationship was weak. Worse, they had hypothesized that liberals would be more tolerant of vegetarians, but attitude-towards-vegetarianism scores were not related to political conservatism measures. Thus their scale emerged as internally reliable but of slightly questionable construct validity.

surprising, then, that the reliability and validity of such measurement are matters of concern.

ESTABLISHING CAUSALITY

Most quantitative research involves a search for causal explanations. Quantitative researchers are rarely satisfied with merely describing *how* things are: they are keen to find out *why* things are the way they are—an emphasis also found in the natural sciences. Researchers examining prejudice, for instance, may want not only to describe it but also to *explain* it, which means finding its causes. They may seek to explain prejudice in terms of personal characteristics (such as a low level of education) or social characteristics (such as low social mobility). In the resulting reports, prejudice is the dependent variable, the one to be explained, and levels of education and social mobility are independent variables, the ones tested as possible causal influences on prejudice.

When an experimental design is employed, the independent variable is the one that is manipulated, and there is little ambiguity about the direction of causal influence. However, with cross-sectional designs of the kind used in most

social survey research, there is ambiguity about the direction of causal influence because the data on all variables are collected simultaneously: this means that we cannot say with full confidence that a particular independent variable preceded the dependent one in time. To refer to independent and dependent variables in the context of cross-sectional designs, we must *infer* the temporal sequence of variables based on common sense or prior theory, as in the example concerning level of education and prejudice in the previous paragraph. However, there is always the risk that the inference is wrong, that the variable purported to be the cause did not precede the dependent variable in time (see Box 3.7).

Good quantitative research inspires confidence in the researcher's causal inferences. Research of the more experimental type is often better able to establish causality than cross-sectional research because with the former it is easier to demonstrate the direction of causal influence and to control for other independent variables. However, quantitative researchers who employ cross-sectional designs often use techniques that allow them to make causal inferences, such as statistical controls (see Chapter

| BOX 3.7 | The case of displayed emotions in convenience stores |

Following a review of the literature, Sutton and Rafaeli (1992) hypothesized a positive relationship between the display of positive emotions by staff to retail shoppers (smiling, friendly greeting, eye contact) and the level of retail sales. In other words, when retail staff are friendly and give time to shoppers, higher sales follow. Sutton and Rafaeli had data from 576 convenience stores in a US national retail chain. Structured observation of the retail workers provided data on the display of positive emotions, and quantitative sales data provided information for the other variable.

The hypothesis was not supported; indeed, stores in which retail workers were less inclined to smile, be friendly, and so on, had better sales. Sutton and Rafaeli (1992: 124) considered restating their hypothesis to make it seem that they had found what they had expected (which would have raised ethical concerns) but fortunately resisted the temptation. Instead, they conducted a qualitative investigation of four stores in order to understand what was happening. They used several methods: unstructured observation of interactions between staff and customers;

semi-structured interviews with store managers; and casual conversations with store managers, supervisors, executives, and others, as well as data gathered through posing as a customer. The qualitative investigation suggested that the relationship between the display of positive emotions and sales was indeed negative, but that sales were likely to be a cause rather than a consequence of the display of emotions. In stores with high levels of sales, staff were under greater pressure and encountered longer lineups at checkouts. Therefore they had less time and inclination for the pleasantries associated with the display of positive emotions.

Thus the causal sequence was not

More positive emotions → More retail sales

but

More retail sales → Less positive emotions.

This study highlights the main difficulty associated with inferring causal direction from a cross-sectional research design.

13). The rise of longitudinal research almost certainly reflects a desire on the part of quantitative researchers to improve their ability to generate findings that permit a causal interpretation.

GENERALIZATION OF FINDINGS TO THOSE NOT STUDIED

In quantitative research, researchers usually want to generalize their findings beyond the particular context in which the research is conducted. Thus, if a study of prejudice required respondents to fill out a questionnaire, can the results apply to individuals other than those who actually participated in the study? Since it is rarely feasible to send questionnaires to (let alone interview) a whole population (whether all residents of a town, all citizens of a country, or even everyone in an organization), the individuals surveyed are only a *sample* of the larger population. A sample must be as representative as possible of the population from which it is drawn in order for the researcher to have confidence that the results are not unique to the particular group on whom the research is conducted (that is, the sample). The goal of arriving at generalizable findings can be seen as a

parallel to the goal of developing scientific 'laws' in the natural sciences.

Probability sampling, explored in Chapter 12, is normally the first choice among researchers seeking a representative sample. This procedure largely eliminates bias by using a random selection process. Random selection does not guarantee a representative sample, but it does improve the chances of getting one. Here it is important to emphasize that even a perfectly representative sample would be representative *only* of the population from which it was selected: strictly speaking, therefore, results obtained from that sample cannot be generalized beyond that population. This means that, if the population from which a sample is taken is all inhabitants of a particular town, city, or province, generalizations should be made only to the inhabitants of that town, city, or province. It may be very tempting to see the findings as having a wider applicability, so that results from a sample representing a city such as Vancouver or Toronto could be considered relevant to similar cities. Even so, no inferences should be made beyond the population from which the sample is selected.

The concern with the **generalizability** of research findings is particularly strong among quantitative researchers using cross-sectional and longitudinal designs. Experimental researchers are concerned about generalizability too, as the discussion of external validity in Chapter 2 suggested, but people doing experiments usually give greater attention to **internal** than external **validity**.

REPLICATION

The natural sciences are often depicted as seeking to reduce to a bare minimum the contaminating influence of the scientist's biases, values, characteristics, and expectations. Were those influences allowed to affect research, the claims of the natural sciences to provide a definitive picture of the world would be seriously undermined. Scientists also try to minimize if not eliminate routine errors in the conduct of their research. To guard against such problems, scientists believe that they should be able to replicate one another's research. If a certain finding cannot be reproduced after repeated tries, serious questions are raised about its validity. Likewise, researchers in the social sciences often regard the ability to replicate as an important criterion for judging research. It's easy to see why: the risk that the researcher's values will affect his or her findings would appear to be all the greater in the case of the social world. Consequently, researchers

Methods in Motion

Applications to Canadian Society

Ricciardelli and Clow (2009) examined two rarely studied topics: men's attitudes toward their physical appearance and their views on whether it is appropriate for men to have cosmetic surgery. The purpose of the study was to determine whether men's self-confidence, self-deprecation (feelings of low self-esteem), and levels of comfort regarding their bodies affected their assessment of their physical appearance and their acceptance of cosmetic surgery. The people participating in the research were 103 Canadian men who lived in the greater Toronto area. Although the sample was small in size and not selected at random (which meant that the results could not be generalized to any larger population; see Chapter 12), the findings were informative nonetheless.

One of the strengths of the study was that it combined quantitative and qualitative methods. For the former, the authors used 18 Likert items (see Box 3.2 for examples of these sorts of measures) administered online. The items were used to gauge the men's perceptions of their physical appearance, their satisfaction with their bodies, how others judged their bodies, and their views on cosmetic surgery. The items were analyzed using multiple regression (a topic discussed in Chapter 13). The qualitative element of the study was a single, open-ended question that asked the men to 'please describe your feelings towards cosmetic surgery.' The answers were analyzed with the intention of identifying common themes.

The quantitative findings indicated that the men expressing high self-confidence were less likely to believe that their physical appearance made other people think they were lazy, and that men with higher levels of self-deprecation were more likely to believe that their appearance decreased their self-confidence. The results also showed that the men with high scores on the self-deprecation measure were more likely to dislike and be embarrassed by their bodies, while lower self-confidence was associated with a higher willingness to have cosmetic surgery. In the open-ended responses, those who were in favour of cosmetic surgery often used the third person to describe their feelings: for example, 'if surgery could boost their esteem they should do it' (123). The authors speculated that such men were distancing themselves from the notion of cosmetic surgery because the culture around them deemed such body modifications to be appropriate for women but not for men. By using the third person, the authors suggest, the men were seeking to protect their male gender identity.

Following Bourdieu (1987), the authors saw their results as illustrating the impact of the 'field'—the totality of the individual's social networks as well as the society at large—on self-evaluation, in this case on judgments about the acceptability of one's body and physical appearance. They also suggest that their study shows social and self-acceptability to be closely associated with the body, and the field as influencing the value and meaning given to certain physical attributes. They also conclude that it is a mistake to think that only women are highly conscious of their bodies and feel judged on the basis of their physical characteristics; men too face negative consequences if they have the 'wrong' kind of physical features.

usually take care to spell out all research procedures so that others can replicate them.

Unfortunately, replication tends to be considered pedestrian and uninspiring. It is not a high-status activity in either the natural or social sciences, and standard replications are rarely accepted for publication in many academic journals. A further reason for the low incidence of published replications in the social sciences is the difficulty of ensuring that the conditions are precisely the same as those in the original study. If there is room for doubt on that score, any differences in findings may be attributed to the design of the replication rather than to a deficiency in the original study. Nonetheless, it is crucial that the methods used to generate findings are made explicit, so that replication is *possible*. Providing all the information needed to conduct a replication is often regarded as an important quality of quantitative research.

An example of the benefits of replication can be found in Goyder *et al.*'s (2003) study of occupational prestige conducted in the Kitchener–Waterloo area of Ontario. The authors replicated research done 25 years earlier (Guppy and Siltanen, 1977), taking great pains to ensure that the methodologies of the two studies were as similar as possible. The replication not only provided a check for biases and routine errors; given that a quarter-century had passed since the original study, it also provided a measure of how much attitudes had changed with regard to occupational prestige and gender. As reported in Chapter 2, the authors concluded that the earlier male advantage in occupational prestige had disappeared by the time the replication was done; in fact, women in people-oriented jobs enjoyed higher prestige than men did in the more recent study. If the authors had not taken care to ensure accurate replication of the original study, it would be impossible to know whether the differences in the findings represented actual social change or were simply a by-product of using different methodologies.

Critiques of quantitative research

Every approach to research has its strengths and weaknesses. Over the years quantitative research, along with its epistemological and ontological foundations, has been the focus of criticism, particularly from exponents of qualitative research. The criticisms pertain to quantitative research as a general research strategy, and to specific methods and research designs with which quantitative research is associated.

CRITICISMS OF QUANTITATIVE RESEARCH

To give a flavour of the critique of quantitative research, six criticisms are covered briefly here:

- *Quantitative researchers fail to distinguish people and social institutions from 'the world of nature.'* Some critics object to the idea of treating the social world as if it were no different from the natural order. They argue that because people interpret the world around them, their actions and experiences cannot be studied using the methods employed in the natural sciences. They claim that science is applicable only to entities and processes lacking this sort of self-reflection, such as chemical elements, photosynthesis, and the circulation of blood. But many quantitative researchers maintain that humans (and other animals) really are part of the world of nature, and that it is simply wrong to think that our existence cannot be usefully analyzed using science. For instance, they would claim that consciousness itself is amenable to the scientific method, as are emotions, decision-making processes, and so on. The debate continues.

- *The measurement process produces an artificial and false sense of precision and accuracy.* For example, quantitative research presumes that different individuals responding to the same question on a survey are interpreting its key terms in the same way. Yet a question such as 'What is your social class?' can be interpreted in at least two ways: as a reference to current wealth, or as a reference to ancestry going back generations. Many methodologists find significant variations in respondents' interpretations of such terms. Researchers often attempt to solve this problem by using questions with fixed-choice answers—'Are you upper class, middle class, working class, etc.?'—but this approach provides 'a solution to the problem of meaning by simply ignoring it' (Cicourel 1964: 108). Quantitative social researchers counter that there are ways to test for shared meanings, although they would concede that this issue deserves more attention than it usually gets.

- *The reliance on instruments and procedures produces a disjuncture between research and everyday life.* This issue relates to the question of external validity. For example, many methods of quantitative research rely heavily on research instruments such as structured interviews and self-completion questionnaires. As Cicourel (1982) pointed out, researchers tend to assume that survey respondents have both the knowledge they need to answer the questions and a sense that the topic matters in their everyday lives. But is this the case? How can researchers who pose a set of questions designed to measure attitudes toward federal–provincial relations, for example, be sure that respondents have sufficient interest in the topic to produce meaningful responses? Similarly, there may be an important difference between what people say to researchers and what they actually do in real life (see Box 3.8). Another criticism, introduced in Chapter 2, is directed at experimental research that relies on controlling situations to determine causal connections. According to Brannigan (2004), such research can produce only small, short-term manipulations of independent variables; yet much of everyday life is affected by long-term, ongoing social processes.

- *The analysis of relationships between variables promotes a view of social life that is remote from everyday experience.* Blumer argued that studies designed to bring out the relationships between variables omit 'the process of interpretation or definition that goes on in human groups' (1956: 685). This **symbolic interactionist** assessment incorporates the first and third criticisms above, that the meaning of events to individuals is ignored and that the connection to everyday contexts is missing. Quantitative researchers recognize those risks, but claim that their research does not preclude a search for how people interpret their everyday existence. For example, quantitative sociologists sometimes ask respondents what they think about social inequality, and try to link the responses with variables such as age, gender, class, and ethnicity. Nonetheless, more thorough and subject-centred research into questions of meaning is usually undertaken by qualitative sociologists.
- *Explanations for findings in quantitative studies may be provided without examining the perceptions of the people to whom the findings purportedly pertain.* A related issue arises when

---

BOX 3.8 : Gap between stated and actual behaviour

A study of racial prejudice conducted many years ago by LaPiere (1934) illustrates that there may be a difference between what people say and what they actually do. LaPiere spent two years travelling with a young Chinese student and his wife, observing from a distance to see if they were refused entry at hotels and restaurants. Of 66 hotels approached, only one turned the couple away; of 184 restaurants and diners, none refused entry.

LaPiere then allowed six months to elapse before sending questionnaires to the hotels and restaurants visited. One question asked: 'Will you accept members of the Chinese race as guests in your establishment?' Of the establishments that replied, 92 per cent of restaurants and 91 per cent of hotels said no. LaPiere's simple though striking study clearly illustrated a gap between reports of behaviour and actual behaviour. The fact that the question asked was somewhat unclear is not usually noted in connection with this widely cited study. 'Will you . . .?' can be interpreted in two ways: as a question about the future or as a question about current policy. Why the more obvious formulation 'Do you . . .?' was not used is not clear,

though it is unlikely that this point had a significant bearing on the findings and their implications for survey research. On the other hand, the results might have been just another example of the widespread difference between holding a prejudiced attitude and engaging in a discriminatory act. An experimental study of prejudice among college students (Frazer and Wiersma 2001) showed that in hypothetical situations the students hire black and white applicants of varying abilities equally, but a week later recall the black applicants as less intelligent than the whites even though the two groups were equal. In the real world, peer pressure can make an unprejudiced person discriminate, to 'go along,' while a prejudiced person may not discriminate for fear of a lawsuit.

The gap is usually worst when predictions of future behaviour are involved. In 2004 the Canadian Blood Services reported that 28 per cent of Canadians said they intended to give blood in the next year, but only 3.7 per cent actually did. And in any election many people say that they intend to vote—and even reveal their preferences to pollsters—but then do not follow through.

valid quantitative findings are achieved, but the explanation for them is not informed by an empathetic understanding of the people involved. For example, it's empirically true that in many developed countries today much larger proportions of children are born to unwed parents than was the case in previous decades. Many researchers conclude from this that marriage is losing its popularity in certain sectors of society, such as among the poor in inner-city areas. However, in-depth field research conducted by Edin and Kefalas (2005) suggests that among the poor single mothers they studied in Philadelphia, marriage is in fact highly valued, but is expected to happen later in life, after the children have been born. 'What is striking about the body of social science evidence,' they write, 'is how little of it is based on the perspectives and life experiences of the women who are its subjects. . . . [S]urveys, though they have meticulously tabulated the trend, have led us to a dead end when it comes to fully understanding the forces behind it' (5).

- *Quantitative researchers tend to assume an objectivist* **ontology**. As we saw in Chapter 1, quantitative researchers often assume that a reality exists that may be independent of the observer or of individual consciousness. They may also see the social order as fixed or given—at least at a particular point in history—rather than created by individuals through negotiation, although the latter view is not universal among quantitative researchers. People on the quantitative side reply that it is not a mistake to assume that some things may exist and have certain characteristics regardless of how we perceive them. Again, the debate is ongoing.

Is it always like this? Reality and practice

One of the problems with characterizing any research orientation, design, or method is that to a certain extent each has to be presented in its pure form—a form that is rarely seen in actual research practice. The model of the process of quantitative research presented here is really a general *tendency* rather than a definitive description of all quantitative research. The gap between the ideal and actual can arise as a result of several factors. The failure to follow the procedures associated with good practice is not necessarily due to incompetence on the part of social researchers, though in some cases it is. More likely it is associated with matters of time, cost, and feasibility—in other words, the unavoidable pragmatic concerns of conducting research.

An illustration of how ideal and actual research practice may differ concerns reliability and validity. Analyses of published quantitative research in organization studies (Podsakoff and Dalton 1987) revealed that writers rarely reported tests of the stability of their measures and even more rarely included evidence of measurement validity (only 3 per cent). Although a large proportion of articles did refer to Cronbach's alpha, a measure of internal consistency for multiple-item measures, for non-scale items the stability and validity of many measures used in the field of organizations are unknown. This is not to say that the measures used are necessarily *un*stable and *in*valid: those features are simply unknown or not demonstrated. The reasons for these omissions are almost certainly the time and expense that would be required to pursue them. Researchers tend to be more concerned with theoretical and conceptual issues and less with the work required to accurately determine measurement quality. As Cicourel (1964) said, much measurement in sociology is 'measurement by fiat.'

These remarks on the rarity of assessments to determine measurement quality should not be taken as a justification for students and researchers to neglect this aspect of their work. The aim here is merely to draw attention to the fact that the practices described in this book are not always followed, and to suggest some reasons why that is the case.

A similar point can be made in relation to sampling. As we have noted, good research practice often requires **random** or *probability sampling*. However, a lot of research is based on inferior alternatives. Sometimes the use of non-probability samples is due to the difficulty of obtaining probability samples. Another reason is that the time and money required to secure a probability sample are too great relative to the resources available. An additional reason is that sometimes the opportunity to study a certain group arises and represents too good an opportunity to miss. Such reasons do not justify ignoring the principles of sampling, but they do help to explain why actual research practice often falls short of the recommendations in books such as this one.

Key Points

- Quantitative research can be characterized as a linear series of steps moving from theory to conclusions, but the process described in Figure 3.1 is an ideal from which there are many departures.

- Examining the reliability and validity of measures is important for assessing their quality.

- Quantitative research has the following key goals: measurement, the establishment of causality, generalization, and replication.

- Quantitative research has been criticized by qualitative researchers. These criticisms tend to revolve around rejecting the view that a natural science model is appropriate for studying the social world.

Relevant Websites

The *Statistics Canada* site provides access to a wide variety of quantitative information about Canada. It also offers up-to-date figures on things such as the inflation rate, the level of unemployment, and Canada's population.

> **http://www.statcan.gc.ca/start-debut-eng. html**

The *Alberta Survey* (discussed in Box 3.2) has been conducted annually by The Population Research Laboratory at the University of Alberta in Edmonton since 1987. This site provides copies

of the questionnaires used, a description of the sampling procedures, and even raw data that can be downloaded for analysis.

> **http://www.uofaweb.ualberta.ca/prl/ AlbertaSurvey.cfm**

Examples and discussion of *Likert Scaling*:

> **http://www.socialresearchmethods.net/kb/ scallik.php**

[Websites accessed 20 July 2011]

Questions for Review

THE MAIN STEPS IN QUANTITATIVE RESEARCH

- What are the main steps in quantitative research?

- To what extent do the main steps follow a strict sequence?

- Do the steps suggest a deductive or an inductive approach to the relationship between theory and research?

CONCEPTS AND THEIR MEASUREMENT

- Why is measurement important to a quantitative researcher?

- Why may multiple indicators of a concept be preferable to using a single indicator?

RELIABILITY AND VALIDITY

- Are some forms of reliability more important than others?

- 'Whereas validity presupposes reliability, reliability does not presuppose validity.' Discuss.

- Name and define four different kinds of measurement validity, providing an illustration of each one.

- What are the main criteria for evaluating measurement validity?

THE MAIN GOALS OF QUANTITATIVE RESEARCHERS

- Outline the main goals of quantitative researchers. What is to be gained by achieving them?

- Why is replication especially important to quantitative researchers, in spite of the tendency for replication to be very rare in social research?

THE CRITIQUE OF QUANTITATIVE RESEARCH

- 'The crucial problem with quantitative research is its failure to adequately address the issue of meaning.' Discuss.

- 'The natural science model of research should not be used to study society.' Discuss.

CHAPTER 4

Survey Research: Structured Interviewing and Questionnaires

CHAPTER OVERVIEW

Survey research is one of the most commonly used data-gathering techniques in the social sciences. Surveys normally involve either structured interviews or written questionnaires that respondents fill out themselves. One of the strengths of survey research is that it allows for standardization in the asking of questions and the categorization of the answers given.

This chapter explores:

- the reasons for the widespread use of surveys, including a consideration of the importance of standardization to the process of measurement;
- the different ways to do survey research, such as using more than one interviewer, conducting interviews by telephone, or using the Internet or email to administer questionnaires;
- various prerequisites of structured interviewing, including establishing rapport with the interviewee; asking questions exactly as they appear on the interview schedule; keeping to the question order as it appears on the schedule; and recording exactly what is said by interviewees;
- problems with survey research, including: the influence of the interviewer on respondents, and the possibility of systematic bias in answers (known as **response sets**);

- the advantages and disadvantages of the questionnaire compared to the structured interview;
- researcher-driven **diaries** as a form of survey research; and
- a feminist critique of structured interviews and questionnaires.

'I never do surveys,' said Anna-Lise as she hung up the phone.

'Why?' I asked.

'For one thing, they always call at dinner time, when I'm tired and hungry.'

'Maybe that's because most people are home at dinner time,' I said.

'That doesn't make it any more comfortable. And they always ask questions in the weirdest ways, like: "On a scale from 1 to 5, with 1 being strongly dislike and 5 being strongly like, how do you feel about blah, blah, blah." Why can't they just ask you your opinion on something and let you say what you want? That would be way more interesting.'

'Well, sometimes they give you a statement to respond to rather than a question. And I guess they do the "On a scale from 1 to 5' thing because they want to compare responses between individuals in a way that is meaningful, or they may want to put a number on what people in general think of the issue, by calculating a mean or something.'

'They turn phone conversations into numbers? Very weird.'

'Ever step on a scale to weigh yourself? Hey, there's another kind of 'scale'! Or how about the numbers that appear on the gas pump when you're filling up, or numbers showing the time in the bottom right-hand corner of your computer? Same idea—turning things into numbers.'

'I still say the whole thing is very weird.'

Introduction

Doing interviews and completing questionnaires are common occurrences in social life. There are job interviews, media interviews, and police interviews, and one is often asked to complete a questionnaire before getting medical treatment or after using a service of some kind. Research interviews and questionnaires share some common features with the everyday variety, although greater care is usually taken to elicit information that is valid and reliable. The information gathered often pertains to matters such as behaviour, attitudes, norms, beliefs, and values.

The structured interview

In a structured interview (sometimes called a standardized interview), the interviewer asks questions listed on an interview schedule: basically a formalized script that must be followed closely. Interviewers are supposed to read out the questions exactly as they are phrased and in the same order as they appear in the schedule. This is to ensure that all interviewees experience the same form of questioning and receive exactly the same interview stimulus. The goal is to allow interviewees' replies to be aggregated (added together to form group rates), and this can be achieved reliably only if those replies are in response to identical cues. Questions are usually very specific and offer the interviewee a fixed range of answers from which to choose.

The main reason why survey researchers use structured interviews is that they promote standardization in both the asking of questions and the recording of answers. This feature has two closely related virtues: it reduces error due to variations in the way questions are posed, and it ensures greater accuracy and ease in processing respondents' answers.

Reducing error due to interviewer variability

Properly executed, standardization in both asking questions and recording answers means that variations in replies are due to 'true' or 'real' variations in the characteristic being measured rather than extraneous factors. Still, there is always a chance that some responses will be inaccurately measured, and there are a number of reasons for this. Some prominent sources of error in survey research are:

1. poorly worded questions;
2. interviewer error in asking a question;
3. misunderstanding on the part of the interviewee;
4. interviewee lapses in memory;
5. interviewer error in recording information;
6. mistakes in entering the data into a computer file; and
7. biases caused by the innate characteristics (such as gender or race) of the interviewers and/or the interviewees.

To take a simple illustration, a question on alcohol consumption among students will show that students vary in the amount of alcohol they consume. Most measurement will contain an element of error, so it is helpful to think of the measured variation in alcohol consumption as made up of two components: true variation and error. In other words: measured variation = true variation + variation due to error. The aim is to keep the error portion to a minimum (see Figure 4.1), since error reduces the validity of a measure. Standardization in the structured interview means that two sources of variation due to error—items 2 and 5 in the preceding list—are likely to be less pronounced.

Variation due to error can come from several other sources. One is *intra-interviewer variability*,

FIGURE 4.1   A variable with little error and one with considerable error

whereby an interviewer is not consistent in asking questions or recording answers, either with different respondents or with the same respondent. For example, an interviewer may treat respondents differently depending on the respondents' personal characteristics or the interviewer's level of fatigue. Another source of error is *inter-interviewer variability*, which may occur when there is more than one interviewer (the usual case). If interviewers are not consistent with each other in the ways they ask questions and/or record answers, measurement error can occur. Needless to say, these two sources of error are not mutually exclusive; they can coexist, compounding the problem even further.

Accuracy and ease of data processing

Like questionnaires, most structured interviews contain questions that are variously referred to as **closed**, closed-ended, **pre-coded**, or fixed-choice. With a closed question, the respondent is given a limited choice of possible answers from which to choose. Once an answer has been selected, the interviewer simply puts a tick on a form or does the equivalent using a keypad. The advantage is that the potential for interviewer variability is reduced: there is no problem with the interviewer not being able to write down everything that the respondent says, or with the interviewer misinterpreting the reply given. By contrast, with what are called open or **open-ended questions**, the interviewer generally cannot write down everything that is said, may embellish what is said, or may misinterpret the response given.

An additional advantage of closed questions is that they greatly facilitate the processing of data. When an open question is asked, answers can run to several sentences. These answers have to be examined and then categorized, so that each person's answer can be aggregated with other respondents' answers to the same question. A number is then allocated to each category of answer for quantitative analysis. This process is known as coding and will be examined in greater detail in Chapter 5. Not only is coding laborious, particularly if there are many open questions and/or respondents, but it also introduces the potential for another source of error: variability in the coding of answers.

If the rules for assigning answers to categories, collectively known as the **coding frame**, are flawed, observed variations may not reflect the true variation in interviewees' replies but instead may result from the shortcomings of the coding frame. Variation may also occur in the ways in which answers are categorized, because of the way the interview schedule was administered and/or the way responses were recorded. As with other forms of interviewing, this kind of variation can come from two sources: *intra-coder variability*, whereby a coder varies over time in applying the rules for assigning answers to categories, and *inter-coder variability*, in which different coders categorize the same answer in different ways. If either or both of these sources of variability are present, at least part of the measured variation in interviewees' replies is caused by error rather than true variation.

Closed questions sidestep this problem neatly, because respondents allocate *themselves* to categories. The coding process is a simple matter of attaching a different number to each category of answer and entering the numbers into a computer database (as in Strongly agree = 1, Agree = 2, etc.). It is not surprising, therefore, that this type of question is often referred to as pre-coded because coding decisions are typically made before any respondent has actually been asked a question. There is very little opportunity for interviewers or coders to differ in how they record answers. Of course, if any of the terms in the answers presented are misunderstood by respondents, or if the answers do not adequately cover the appropriate range of possibilities, the question cannot provide a valid measure. Nonetheless, when compared to open questions, closed questions reduce potential sources of error and are easier to process for quantitative analysis.

Dealing with interviewer effects

Some interviewer characteristics will affect the responses given. Sex and race are the key **reactive** issues that may have an impact, although their effects are generally confined to sexual and racial issues.

To illustrate, take the topic of whether certain jobs should be set aside for female applicants only. Here are some hypothetical results (percentage who approve): male talking to male interviewer, 37; male talking to female interviewer, 48; female talking to female interviewer, 58; female talking to male interviewer, 50. Something is wrong, but where? One might assume that some men are not being truthful with the female interviewer and are offering responses that they think will please her. But maybe some men are not being candid with the male interviewer—a man may believe in employment equity but hide his real views because the subject is controversial. Similarly, some of the women who say they agree may actually disagree. They may feel that the time for employment equity is past and that women should be hired strictly on their merits, but keep that idea to themselves when talking to another woman so that they don't appear to be deserting the feminist cause; sharing a common status does not always lead to candour.

What can be done? A first step is to train interviewers carefully to be professional and to stress that any answer is acceptable. A second is to conduct a pilot study (see Chapter 5) to see if any interviewers are getting responses that are very different from the others. The data collected by any one interviewer should be fairly similar to the data collected by the others. It's important to check for this problem early in the process. Any interviewers who stand out in terms of the responses they collect should be retrained or, as a last resort, replaced. However, if the problem arises primarily from deeply felt biases on the part of respondents, there may be limits to what the researcher can do.

Interview contexts

In a traditional interview, an interviewer stands or sits in front of the respondent, asks a series of questions, and writes down or keys in the answers. However, there are several possible departures from this pattern.

MORE THAN ONE INTERVIEWER OR INTERVIEWEE

Multiple interviewers are rare in social research because of the considerable cost involved in dispatching more than one person to interview someone. In the case of **focus groups** it is more common, but in that instance there is more than one interviewee as well. However, to conduct a structured interview with a focus group would be very unusual: in most cases a specific individual is the object of questioning by one interviewer. Indeed, it is usually advisable to *discourage* as far as possible the presence or intrusion of others during the interview. Studies in which more than one person is being interviewed tend to be conducted by qualitative researchers, though that is not always the case. For example, Pahl's (1990) study of patterns in the control of money among couples employed

structured interviewing first of the couples and then of husbands and wives separately.

IN PERSON OR BY TELEPHONE?

It is customary in academic social research not involving national samples to conduct research with face-to-face interviews. However, telephone interviewing is the norm in fields such as market or government research. Telephone interviews have several advantages of over the face-to-face variety:

- They are far cheaper and quicker to administer than in-person interviews, which may require the interviewers to spend a great deal of time travelling to meet with respondents; this is a particular problem when a sample is geographically dispersed. Telephone interviews take time and hired interviewers have to be paid, but the cost of conducting a telephone interview is still lower than a comparable face-to-face one. Moreover, the general efficiency of telephone interviewing has been enhanced with the advent of computer-assisted telephone interviewing (CATI).

- Telephone interviews are easier to supervise than the personal kind. This is a particular advantage when several interviewers are calling from the same location at the same time, since supervisors may be able to detect interviewer errors, such as rephrasing questions or probing inappropriately. Face-to-face interviews can be tape-recorded for the purpose of assessing data quality, but the taping of interviews raises issues of confidentiality and so must be treated with caution.

- Telephone interviewing can also reduce bias arising from the characteristics of the interviewers or interviewees (for example, gender, class, and ethnicity). The remoteness of the interviewer in telephone interviewing removes this potential source of bias to a significant extent, since the interviewers' race and general appearance cannot be seen, although their gender is usually apparent.

On the other hand, telephone interviewing suffers from certain limitations when compared to the personal interview:

- People who do not have a telephone or otherwise cannot be contacted by phone cannot be part of the study. Since lack of a phone is most likely to be a feature of poorer households, the potential for sampling bias exists. Also, many people choose to be ex-directory (they pay to have their telephone numbers *not* listed in a telephone book) or they use cell phones only and for that reason are not listed. This presents a problem if the researcher is using a directory to select respondents. A solution to the latter problem is *random digit dialling*. With this technique (used in the annual Alberta Survey conducted at the University of Alberta, as well as in the General Social Survey administered by Statistics Canada), a computer randomly selects telephone numbers within a predefined geographical area. This method can give you access to ex-directory households, though it's important to note that in some areas it is prohibited by law to contact cell phones in this way.

- Respondents with hearing impairments are likely to find telephone interviews more difficult than personal interviews.

- A telephone interview is unlikely to be sustainable beyond 20 to 25 minutes, whereas personal interviews can be conducted for longer periods of time (Frey 2004).

- There is some evidence that telephone interviews fare less well than personal interviews in obtaining data on sensitive issues such as drug and alcohol use, income, tax payments, and health. The evidence is not entirely consistent on this point, but when many questions of this kind are to be asked, a personal interview may be superior (Shuy 2002).

- Telephone interviewers cannot see the respondents and therefore cannot respond to signs of puzzlement or unease on their faces. In a personal interview, the interviewer may respond to such signs by restating the question or attempting to clarify its meaning, though this has to be handled in a standardized way as far as possible. A further issue is that interviewers may be able to collect subsidiary information, such as whether the home in which the interview was conducted is in need of repair. That sort of information cannot be acquired over the telephone.

- Frequently, the target of the research is a specific individual in a household or firm: for example, the person in a certain role or position, or someone with particular characteristics. It is probably more difficult to ascertain by telephone interview whether the correct person is replying.

- The telephone interviewer cannot employ visual aids such as show cards from which respondents select their replies (see Box 4.1). Similarly, diagrams or photographs cannot be used.

There is some evidence that the quality of the data gathered through telephone interviews is inferior to that produced by face-to-face interviews. According to Holbrook *et al.* (2003), a series of experiments in the US using long questionnaires found that respondents interviewed by telephone were more likely to express no opinion or give 'don't know' as an answer; give the same answer to a series of linked questions; express socially desirable opinions; be apprehensive about the interview; and be dissatisfied with the time taken by the interviews (even though they were shorter than the face-to-face kind). Also, telephone interviewees tend to be less engaged in the interview process.

COMPUTER-ASSISTED INTERVIEWING

Today it is common to use computers in the interview process. There are two main formats for such interviews: computer-assisted personal interviewing (CAPI) and computer-assisted telephone interviewing (CATI). The use of CAPI has been growing lately, mainly because of the increased portability and affordability of laptop computers and other electronic devices, and the availability of quality software packages.

With computer-assisted interviewing, the questions in the interview schedule appear on the screen, the interviewer keys in the reply, and the computer shows the next question. This approach is especially useful when *filter questions* are asked. Filter questions are used to determine whether it is appropriate to ask certain questions of a particular respondent. For example, a question asking respondents to name the party they voted for in the last election would be inappropriate for people who did not in fact vote in that election. Asking a filter question beforehand would eliminate those respondents. In the 2008 Canadian Election Study (funded by Elections Canada), respondents were asked the filter question, 'Did you vote in the [2008] election?' Only those who said yes were then asked, 'Which party did you vote for?' Similarly, in a study of eating habits, there is no point in asking vegetarians a lot of questions about eating meat: it's probably best to filter them out—that is, to skip the questions about meat and go on to the next series of questions. Once the response to the filter question has been keyed in, the computer will automatically go to the next relevant question, eliminating inappropriate items where necessary. This removes the possibility of interviewers inadvertently asking meaningless questions or failing to ask some that should be asked. In this way, computer-assisted interviewing enhances the researcher's control over the interview process and improves standardization in the asking and recording of questions.

Computer-assisted interviewing may make it easier to perform other tasks as well. For example, sometimes it is beneficial to randomize the order in which certain items are presented to the respondent because the responses given may depend on the order in which the items are listed. Automatic randomization was used in the Goyder *et al.* (2003) study of occupational prestige done in southwestern Ontario. As the authors put it: 'The deck was electronically shuffled for each new respondent.' Another advantage of computer-assisted interviews is that if interviewers are out in the field all day, the data can be sent to the research office electronically.

CAPI and CATI have not been incorporated into academic survey research to the same degree that they have been in commercial survey research, although that picture is changing because of their many advantages. Many of the large datasets available for analysis now come from computer-assisted interviews conducted by large social research organizations.

USING ONLINE PERSONAL INTERVIEWS

Online interviews run a higher risk of respondent dropout than other forms do. However, Mann and Stewart (2000: 138–9) have suggested that it is possible to develop a relationship of mutual trust when using them. This can be accomplished by regularly sending messages to respondents assuring them that their responses are helpful and significant, especially since online interviewing is still an unfamiliar experience for most people and takes longer than other forms. It is worth the trouble because online interviews make it relatively easy for the researcher to go back to interviewees for further information or reflections—something difficult to do with face-to-face interviews.

A further issue for the online personal interviewer is whether to send all the questions at once or to conduct the interview on a question-followed-by-reply basis. The problem with sending all at once is that respondents may read through them and reply only to the most interesting ones. Asking one question at a time is likely to be more reliable. Nonetheless, Bampton and Cowton (2002) reported that conducting email interviews by sending questions in small batches takes the pressure off interviewees to make a quick reply, gives them the opportunity to provide considered replies (although there can be a loss of spontaneity), and gives the interviewers greater opportunity to respond to interviewee answers.

There is evidence that prospective online interviewees are more likely to agree to participate if agreement is solicited prior to sending the actual questions. Another way to encourage respondents to participate is for the researcher to use some form of self-disclosure, such as directions to a website that contains detailed contact information. It also helps to provide personal material about the researcher (such as a photo), as well as information relevant to the research topic (Curasi 2001; O'Connor and Madge 2001, 2003). Such steps are necessary because unsolicited emails ('spam') are often seen as a nuisance and can result in an immediate refusal to take the message seriously.

Curasi (2001) conducted a comparison in which 24 interviews carried out through email correspondence were contrasted with 24 parallel face-to-face interviews. The interviews were concerned with shopping on the Internet. She found that:

- face-to-face is better than online for maintaining rapport with respondents;

- because greater commitment and motivation are required to complete an online interview, replies are often more detailed than in face-to-face interviews; and

- online interviewees' answers tend to be more considered and grammatically correct because they have more time to ponder and tidy up answers. Whether this is a positive feature is debatable. There is the obvious advantage of a 'clean' transcript, but there may be some loss of spontaneity.

On the other hand, Curasi found that some online responses were short on detail, perhaps because replies had to be typed, not just spoken. The full significance of the difference between online and face-to-face interviewing is still being explored by researchers.

The webcam may offer further possibilities for online personal interviews, making the online interview similar to the telephone version and quite comparable to an in-person interview because those involved in the exchange can see each other. However, one of the main advantages of the online interview is lost: respondents' answers need to be transcribed.

Conducting interviews

KNOW THE INTERVIEW SCHEDULE

Before interviewing anybody, an interviewer should have a thorough knowledge of the interview schedule. Interviewing can be stressful, and it is possible that under strain standard interview procedures can cause interviewers to get flustered and leave questions out or ask the wrong questions. All interviewers need to be fully trained to reduce interviewer variability in asking questions, a potential source of error.

INTRODUCING THE RESEARCH

Prospective respondents have to be offered a credible rationale for participating in the research, in particular for giving up their valuable time. This aspect of conducting interviews is of special significance at a time when survey response rates appear to be declining. The introductory rationale may be either spoken by the interviewer or printed for the respondent to read. It is usually spoken if interviewers 'cold call' potential respondents at their homes, either in person or by telephone. A written rationale is common to alert respondents that someone will be contacting them to request an interview. In many cases, respondents may be presented with both modes—for example, researchers will send respondents a letter inviting them to participate in a study and then call or speak to them in person.

RAPPORT

It is frequently suggested that interviewers need to establish a *rapport* with respondents. A relationship must be forged fairly quickly to encourage respondents to participate in and persist with the interview. If an element of rapport is not established, some

Methods in Motion

Applications to Canadian Society

Beres *et al.* (2009) wanted to determine the extent to which the process of institutionalization has affected sexual assault and rape crisis centres (SAC/RCCs) in Canada. 'Institutionalization' refers to the adoption of formal organizational and operational procedures, and is something that many social movements experience over time. The process has advantages and disadvantages; the former include more efficient use of resources and the generation of more predictable organizational outcomes. But very often institutionalization is accompanied by a dilution of the movement's ideology, which makes its ideas less oppositional and more in keeping with conventional thinking. Institutionalization also tends to make charismatic leadership less likely, and can reduce the willingness of the organization to achieve large-scale social change.

Beres and colleagues noted that the SAC/RCCs that sprang up in Canada in the 1970s were dedicated to feminist principles and sought fundamental social change in order to eradicate sexual violence against women. As organizations they eschewed hierarchy and tended to

favour collective decision-making. To find out whether those principles, political goals, and operating policies had been abandoned in recent years, the authors mailed a questionnaire to 115 Canadian SAC/RCCs, of which 53 (46%) responded. Centres in all provinces except Prince Edward Island participated in the study, as did organizations in both urban and rural areas. Unusually, for research involving questionnaires, the unit of analysis in this study was the organization rather than the individual.

The authors found that even though there was some evidence of institutionalization—in particular, a drift toward a non-gendered social service model rather than a social change orientation—SAC/RCCs in Canada for the most part retained their feminist identity and called for political and social change. For example, a majority of centres presented themselves as 'feminist' to the communities in which they operated, and 68% were involved in organizing for political and social causes. However, recent funding shortages have led many of them to rely increasingly on the unpaid efforts of women volunteers to achieve their political goals.

respondents who have agreed to be interviewed may decide to back out because of the time the interview is taking, or perhaps because of the nature of the questions being asked. While this injunction essentially invites the interviewer to be friendly with respondents and put them at ease, it is important not to take it too far. Too much rapport can result in the interview going on too long and the respondent suddenly deciding that too much time is being spent on the activity. Too much friendliness can also lead respondents to tailor their answers to please the interviewer. Thus, achieving the appropriate rapport between interviewer and respondent is a delicate balancing act. It is probably somewhat easier to achieve in a face-to-face interview than over the telephone. In the latter situation the interviewer is unable to offer the visual cues of friendliness—such as smiling or maintaining good eye contact—that help to create and sustain rapport.

TOPICS AND ISSUES TO INCLUDE IN AN INTRODUCTORY STATEMENT

In an introductory statement to a prospective interviewee:

- Clearly identify yourself.
- Identify the auspices under which the research is being conducted (for example, a university, a government agency).
- If you are a student doing research for a thesis, make that fact clear.
- Indicate what the research is about in broad terms and why it is important, and give an indication of the kind of information to be collected.
- Indicate how the respondent has been selected (for example, by a random process, by convenience, because of special characteristics).
- Provide reassurance about the confidentiality of any information given by the respondent.
- Explain that participation is voluntary.
- Reassure respondents that they will not be identified or identifiable. This can usually be achieved by pointing out that when the data are aggregated or analyzed at the group level, individual participants cannot be identified.
- Give the respondent the opportunity to ask questions; be sure to provide a contact telephone number or email address. If in person, simply ask if the respondent has any questions.

These suggestions are also relevant to the covering letter that should accompany mailed questionnaires. The latter should also include a stamped, pre-addressed return envelope.

ASKING QUESTIONS

We suggested earlier that one aim of the structured interview is to ensure that each respondent is asked exactly the same questions, so as to eliminate a potential source of variation in replies that does not reflect 'true' variation. The structured interview is meant to reduce the risk of such 'error' variation, but there is no guarantee that it will not occur because there is always the possibility that some interviewers will embellish or otherwise change a question when it is asked. There are many reasons why interviewers may vary the question wording, including reluctance to ask certain questions, perhaps because of embarrassment (Collins 1997). Therefore, training interviewers, paying them well, and monitoring them is very important.

Does it really matter? Do small variations in wording on the part of the interviewer make a significant difference to people's replies? While the impact of variation in wording obviously differs from context to context, and in any case is difficult to quantify exactly, three experiments suggested that even small variations in wording can affect replies (Collins 1997).

RECORDING ANSWERS

Interviewers should write down respondents' replies as exactly as possible. Not to do so can distort respondents' answers and introduce errors. Such errors are less likely to occur if interviewers merely have to allocate respondents' replies to a category, as in a closed question, than if they are required to write down the answers to open questions (Fowler and Mangione 1990).

QUESTION ORDER

Interviewers should also be alerted to the importance of asking questions in their proper order. For one thing, varying the question order can result in certain questions being accidentally omitted, because the interviewer may forget to ask the ones that have been leapfrogged during the interview. Variation in question order can also have an impact on replies. If some respondents have been asked a question on unemployment and others have not, the latter's responses to other questions may reflect this omission. For example, if a later question asks about the causes of increasing crime, those who were previously asked about unemployment may mention that as a cause of crime more often than those who were not asked about it.

PROBING

A highly problematic area for researchers employing a structured interview method is probing respondents who need help with their answers. This may occur if respondents do not understand the question and then struggle to provide an adequate answer, or if they do not provide a complete answer and have to be probed for more information. For example, in the 2007 Alberta Survey, respondents were asked questions about AADAC (the Alberta Alcohol and Drug Abuse Commission). One open-ended question read: 'To the best of your knowledge, what does AADAC do?' The probe available for all interviewers is: 'What services does AADAC provide?' A potential problem with any probe is that some interviewers may be more inclined to use it than other interviewers, and the probe itself may affect the response given, which could lead to reliability problems. A bigger problem arises if different interviewers use different probes, although proper organization and training should preclude that.

Some general tactics with regard to probes are as follows:

- If further information is required, usually in the context of an open-ended question, standardized probes should be employed, such as 'Can you say a little more about that?' or 'Are there any other reasons why you think that?'

- If, with a closed question, the respondent replies in a way that does not match one of the pre-designed answers, the interviewer should repeat the fixed-choice alternatives and make it clear that the answer must be chosen from those provided.

- When the interviewer needs to know about something that requires quantification, such as the number of visits made to a doctor in the last four weeks or the number of banks in which the respondent has accounts, but the respondent answers in general terms ('quite often' or 'I have several'), the interviewer needs to persist for a more precise answer. With fixed-response surveys, this will usually entail repeating the response options. The

interviewer should not suggest an answer on the basis of the respondent's reply since the respondent may not be comfortable with the idea of disagreeing with the interviewer.

In a face-to-face interview, the interviewer may use 'show cards' (see Box 4.1) instead of reading out a series of fixed-choice alternatives. Sometimes called 'flash cards,' they display all the answers from which the respondent is to choose and are handed to the respondent at different points in the interview. There are several situations in which it may be beneficial to use show cards:

- Sometimes there is a very long list of possible answers; for example, respondents may be asked about which magazines they read most frequently. To read out a list of magazines would be tedious and it is probably better to hand the respondent a list from which to choose.

- Some people are not keen to divulge personal details such as their age or income. One way of reducing the impact of such questioning is to present respondents with age or income ranges with a letter or number attached to each (see Box 4.1). A similar approach may be used with other sensitive topics such as sexual practices. However, this procedure will obviously not be appropriate if the research requires *exact* figures pertaining to sensitive topics.

- Sometimes, during the course of an interview, respondents will be presented with a series of statements or questions to which the same possible responses apply—for example: 'strongly agree, agree, neutral, disagree, and strongly disagree.' It would be time-consuming and

---

BOX 4.1 | Two show cards

Card 4 (Age)	Card 6 (for various items)
(a) Less than 20	(1) Strongly agree
(b) 20–29	(2) Agree
(c) 30–39	(3) Undecided
(d) 40–49	(4) Disagree
(e) 50–59	(5) Strongly disagree
(f) 60–69	
(g) 70 and over	

off-putting to read out all five possible answers over and over again, but it might also be expecting too much of respondents to ask them to keep all the possible answers in their heads for the entire batch of questions to which they apply. Providing a show card listing the possible responses is an obvious solution.

PROMPTING

Prompting occurs when the interviewer suggests a specific answer to a particular interviewee. It is very rare and should be used only as a last resort. An example of unacceptable prompting would be to ask an open-ended question and then suggest a possible answer to a respondent who appears to be struggling to think of an appropriate reply. In all situations, interviewers should do what they can to allow respondents to come up with their own replies. Otherwise the data gathered will not be authentic—they may also reveal more about the interviewer than the interviewee.

LEAVING THE INTERVIEW

It's important to remember common courtesies, such as thanking respondents for giving up their time. However, the period immediately after the interview also calls for some care if respondents try to engage the interviewer in a discussion about the purpose of the interview. Interviewers should have a standard response prepared and resist further elaboration, since the respondents may communicate what they are told to others, which could bias the results if the latter later become interviewees themselves.

TRAINING AND SUPERVISION

As we have noted, interviewers must be properly trained to ensure that the research is carried out correctly. Fowler (1993) cited evidence to suggest that a training period shorter than one full day is rarely sufficient. Researchers use various ways to determine whether an interviewer has been trained properly, including:

- checking individual interviewers' response rates;
- tape-recording a sample of interviews;
- examining completed schedules to determine whether any questions are being left out and ensure that they are being completed properly; and

- making call-backs on a sample of respondents (usually about 10 per cent) to make sure they were interviewed and to ask about the interviewer's conduct.

Questionnaires

A questionnaire is essentially a structured interview without an interviewer. Questionnaires can be delivered and retrieved in several different ways. Probably the most common way is by mail. That is how Anderson *et al.* (2006) studied family physicians in southwestern Ontario, and how Bell *et al.* (2009) distributed questionnaires to twins in their research on the heritability of political attitudes. Sometimes respondents will be asked to deposit their completed questionnaires at a specified location: for a study conducted in a business organization, for instance, the location might be their supervisor's office. Researchers may hand out questionnaires to students in a class and collect them there as well, as Smith and McVie (2003) did in their longitudinal cohort study on crime.

In many ways the questionnaire and structured interview are very similar. The obvious difference is that with questionnaires, respondents must read the questions themselves and record their own answers. Because there is no interviewer to administer it, the research instrument has to be especially easy to follow and the questions particularly easy to answer. As a result, questionnaires tend to differ from structured interviews in the following ways:

- they have fewer 'open' questions because 'closed' questions are easier to answer;
- they have easy-to-follow designs to minimize the risk that a respondent will inadvertently miss a question or part of one; and
- they are shorter to reduce the risk of 'respondent fatigue' (it's much easier for a tired respondent facing a long questionnaire to throw it out than it is for a tired interviewee to ask an interviewer to leave).

ADVANTAGES OF THE QUESTIONNAIRE OVER THE STRUCTURED INTERVIEW

Cheaper, quicker, more convenient to administer Interviewing is expensive, and the low cost of the questionnaire is especially advantageous if a sample is geographically dispersed. This advantage is obviously less pronounced when compared to telephone interviews, but even there the mailed questionnaire enjoys cost advantages.

A thousand questionnaires can be sent through the post in one batch; a class of four hundred students can fill out questionnaires in one class period. Even with a team of telephone interviewers, it takes a long time to conduct personal interviews with samples of that size. However, it is important to remember that the questionnaires may not come back immediately (respondents usually fill them in at *their* convenience) and may take several weeks to be returned. Also, in many situations it is necessary to send out follow-up letters and/or duplicate questionnaires to those who fail to respond.

Absence of interviewer effects   We have already noted that interviewer characteristics may affect respondent answers. Obviously those sorts of effects are not an issue with questionnaires, since there is no interviewer present. Similarly, with a questionnaire, no one is there to read the questions to the subject in the wrong order, to present them in different ways to different respondents, or to state the items with varying emphases from person to person; the problems those practices can cause are precluded.

Probably of greater importance is the tendency for people to exhibit a social desirability bias when an interviewer is present, giving 'politically correct' rather than genuine responses. There is also a tendency for interview respondents to underreport activities that induce anxiety, or about which they are sensitive. By contrast, research summarized by Tourangeau and Smith (1996) strongly suggests that respondents tend to report more drug use and alcohol consumption and higher numbers of sexual partners and abortions when responding to questionnaires than in structured interviews.

DISADVANTAGES OF QUESTIONNAIRES VERSUS STRUCTURED INTERVIEWS

Cannot explain the question   It's always important to ensure that the questions asked are clear and unambiguous, but this is especially true with questionnaires, since there is no interviewer to help respondents with questions they cannot understand. Also, as we saw earlier in this chapter, great attention must be paid to ensure that the questionnaire is easy to complete; if the instructions are not clear, questions may be inadvertently omitted.

Greater risk of missing data   Incomplete questionnaires are more common (because of a lack of probing or supervision) than incomplete interviews. It is also easier for respondents to decide not to answer a question when they are on their own than when they are with an interviewer; questions that respondents find boring or irrelevant are especially likely to be skipped. Questionnaire respondents are more likely than interview participants to become tired of answering questions that are not fully salient to them, and to abandon the project entirely. Put positively, when a research issue is important to the respondent, a high response rate is possible. This means that when the questions are highly relevant, a questionnaire may be a good choice, especially because of its much lower cost.

Cannot probe   There is no opportunity to probe respondents to elaborate on an answer. However, this problem mainly applies to open questions, which are not widely used in questionnaire research.

Difficult to ask a lot of questions   Long questionnaires are rarely feasible because of the risk of 'respondent fatigue.' They may also discourage prospective respondents from participating at all.

Difficult to ask other kinds of questions   It's also important to avoid asking more than a very small number of open questions, because respondents frequently do not want to write very much. Questions with complex structures, such as filters, should be avoided as far as possible, since some respondents find them difficult to follow.

Questionnaire can be read as a whole   When respondents are able to read the whole questionnaire even before answering the first question, none of the questions asked is truly independent of the others. It also means that the researcher cannot be sure that questions have been answered in the correct order, raising the possibility of question-order effects.

Not appropriate for some kinds of respondents   Respondents whose literacy is limited or whose facility with the language used is restricted may not be able to answer a questionnaire. The second of these difficulties cannot be entirely overcome with an interview, but the difficulties are likely to be greater with a questionnaire.

One last problem: who filled out the questionnaire? With mailed questionnaires, the researcher can never be sure whether the questions were answered by the designated respondent or someone else. It is also impossible to prevent other members of a household (for example) from helping the respondent answer the questions. Similarly, if a questionnaire is sent to the manager of a firm, the task may simply be delegated to someone else. The same problem arises with structured interviews when they are administered by telephone.

ONLINE SOCIAL SURVEYS

The number of surveys being administered online has grown considerably. It is uncertain whether online research instruments should be regarded as structured interviews or as questionnaires—in a sense they are both. So far as online social surveys are concerned, there is a crucial distinction between surveys administered by email (email surveys) and surveys administered via the web (web surveys). In the case of the former, the questionnaire is sent via email to a respondent, whereas with a web survey, the respondent is directed to a website in order to answer it. Sheehan and Hoy (1999) suggested that there has been a tendency to use email surveys to study 'smaller, more homogeneous groups of on-line user groups' and web surveys to study 'large groups of online users.'

Email surveys With email surveys it is important to distinguish between embedded and attached questionnaires. In the case of the former, the questions are embedded in the body of the email. There may be an introduction to the questionnaire followed by a graphic that partitions the introduction from the questionnaire itself. Respondents may be asked either to indicate their replies using simple notation, such as an 'X,' or to delete alternatives that do not apply to them. If a question is open, they are asked to type in an answer. When finished, they simply hit the reply button to return the completed questionnaire.

An attached questionnaire arrives as an attachment to an email that introduces it. As with the embedded questionnaire, respondents must select and/or type their answers. To return the questionnaire, it must be attached to a reply email, although respondents may also be given the opportunity to fax it back or to return it through the regular mail (Sheehan and Hoy 1999).

The chief advantage of the embedded questionnaire is that it requires less computer expertise. Knowing how to read and then return an attachment requires a certain facility with online communication that is still not universally possessed. Also, the recipients' operating systems or software may not be able to handle attachments, or respondents may refuse to open them because of concerns about viruses. On the other hand, since most email software allows only limited formatting, the appearance of embedded questionnaires tends to be rather dull and featureless, although this situation is rapidly changing. Furthermore, it is slightly easier for respondents to type answers into an attachment that uses well-known software such as Microsoft Word because if the questionnaire is embedded in an email the alignment of questions and answers may be lost.

Dommeyer and Moriarty (2000) compared the two forms of email survey in connection with an attitude study. The attached questionnaire was given a much wider range of embellishments in terms of appearance than was possible with the embedded one. Before conducting the survey, undergraduate students were asked to compare the two formats in terms of appearance. The attached questionnaire was deemed to be better-looking, easier to complete, clearer in appearance, and better organized. The two formats were then administered to two random samples of students, all active email users. The researchers found a much higher response rate with the embedded than with the attached questionnaire (37 per cent versus 8 per cent), but little difference in terms of speed or omitted responses. Although Dommeyer and Moriarty (2000: 48) concluded 'the attached e-mail survey presents too many obstacles to the potential respondent,' the study was conducted during what were still early days in the world of online surveys. It may be that as prospective respondents become more adept at using online communication methods, and as virus-checking software improves in terms of accessibility and cost, the concerns that led to the lower response rate for the attached questionnaire will be less pronounced.

Web surveys Web surveys invite prospective respondents to visit a website where the questionnaire can be found and completed online. The web survey has an important advantage over the email survey in that it can use a much wider variety of embellishments, including colour (see Box 4.2). Plate 4.1 presents a section of a questionnaire in a web-survey format (the full questionnaire will appear in Chapter 13). Common features include 'radio buttons' (used to choose among two or more closed-question answers, as in Question 8 in Plate 4.1) and pull-down menus of possible answers (see Plate 4.2). With open questions, the respondent is invited to type directly into a boxed area (for example, Question 2 in Plate 4.1).

However, the advantages of the web survey go beyond appearance and format. The questionnaire can be designed so that when there is a filter question (for example, 'if yes, go to question 12; if no, go to question 14'), it skips automatically to the next appropriate question.

The questionnaire can also be programmed either to show only one question at a time or to allow the respondent to scroll down and look at all the questions in advance. Finally, respondents' answers can be automatically programmed to download into a database, eliminating the daunting task of coding a large number of questionnaires. Software packages designed to produce questionnaires with all the features just described are now widely available.

Web surveys are also advantageous in that they may give researchers access to unique populations, such as people who share a particular interest (e.g., in virtual dating, cyber-stalking, or political conservatism). It would be hard from a purely logistical standpoint to conduct face-to-face interviews with the large numbers of people

---

BOX 4.2 | Advantages and disadvantages of online surveys compared to mailed questionnaires

This box summarizes the main advantages and disadvantages of online surveys, both email and web varieties, compared to mailed questionnaires. Note that all three share one disadvantage relative to personal and telephone interviews: namely, that the researcher can never be certain of who is actually answering the questions.

Advantages

- *Low cost*. Even though mailed questionnaires are inexpensive to administer, online surveys cost even less. They require no postage, paper, or envelopes, and they save time because there is no need to stuff covering letters and questionnaires into envelopes.

- *Faster response and processing*. Online surveys can be returned considerably faster than mailed questionnaires. Researchers also appreciate the automatic skipping of irrelevant questions that is possible when they use filter questions, as well as the opportunity for immediate downloading of replies into a database.

- *Fewer unanswered questions*. There is evidence that online questionnaires are completed with fewer unanswered questions than mailed questionnaires.

- *Better response to open questions*. Open questions are more likely to be answered online, and online replies are usually more detailed.

Disadvantages

- *Low response rate*. Typically, response rates for online surveys are lower than those for comparable mailed questionnaires.

- *Restricted to online populations*. Only people who are available online can reasonably be expected to participate in an online survey. This restriction should ease over time, but since the online population still differs in significant ways from the non-online population, it remains a difficulty.

- *Requires motivation*. Because online survey respondents must pay for the connection and could be tying up their telephone lines, they may need a higher level of motivation than mailed questionnaire respondents. This suggests that the invitation to participate must be especially persuasive.

- *Confidentiality and anonymity issues*. It is standard practice for survey researchers to indicate that replies will be kept anonymous. However, with email surveys the addresses of the respondents are known, which may make it difficult for people to believe that their identity really will be protected.

- *Multiple replies*. With web surveys, there is a risk that some people may mischievously complete the questionnaire more than once. There is much less risk of this with email surveys.

Source: Adapted from Cobanoglu *et al.* (2001); Kent and Lee (1999); Schaeffer and Dillman (1998); Sheehan and Hoy (1999); Tse (1998).

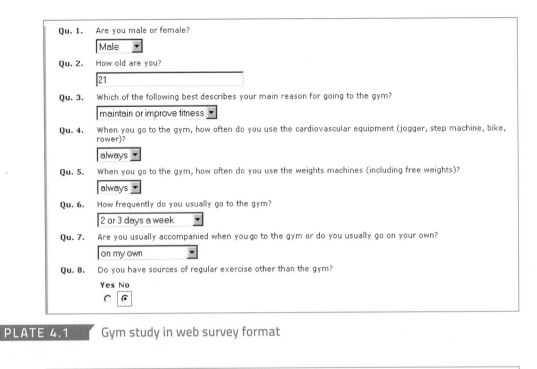

Gym study in web survey format

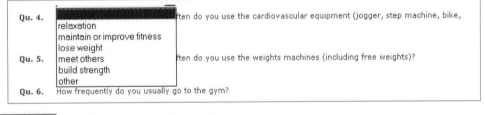

A pull-down menu for Qu. 3

who share such interests. Web surveys are particularly useful for reaching stigmatized populations who are difficult to reach offline, such as people with eating disorders or extreme political views (Wright 2005).

Potential respondents need to be directed to the website containing the questionnaire. One way to do this is to email them, as Andrews *et al.* (2007) did in their study of academic integrity (i.e., cheating and plagiarism) in Canadian and American dental schools. It may be most efficient to send the email invitation to someone who can forward it to large numbers of potential participants. In the Andrews *et al.* study the invitation was sent to academic deans who then forwarded it to faculty members and students. For surveys in which participation must be restricted, it may be necessary to set up a password system to filter out people for whom the questionnaire is not appropriate.

RESEARCHER-DRIVEN DIARIES AS A FORM OF QUESTIONNAIRE

When the researcher is interested in precise accounts of behaviour, what Elliott (1997) called the *researcher-driven diary* can be used as a kind of questionnaire. The researcher asks participants to record their perceptions, feelings, or actions with regard to certain experiences shortly after they occur. Laurenceau and Bolger (2005) used the diary method to study marital and family processes. Hessler *et al.* (2003) used researcher-driven diaries in an email study of adolescent risk behaviour that produced rich narratives of everyday life as perceived by adolescents. Sometimes this method is supplemented by a personal interview in which the researcher will follow up on points raised in the diary: for example, by asking the diarist what he or she meant by certain remarks.

Corti (1993) distinguished between 'structured

diaries' and 'free text diaries.' Either can be employed by quantitative as well as qualitative researchers. The research on the domestic division of labour by Sullivan (1996) is an illustration of a structured diary. This type of diary has the general appearance of a questionnaire with largely closed questions. The kind of diary Sullivan used is often described as a 'time-use' diary because it is designed for recording, more or less at the time of the actual behaviour, how long people engage in activities such as food preparation, childcare, or eating. Sullivan also asked couples to record on a five-point scale the amount of enjoyment they derived from those kinds of activities.

Recording events as they happen is often considered a more accurate approach than recording them at the end of the day, largely because there is less risk of forgetting. However, it is more intrusive than answering a questionnaire because it is a constant interruption and it may even change people's behaviour. For example, one can become preoccupied with the behaviours under study and thus engage in them in a more thoughtful or premeditated way.

Sometimes diaries can be constructed as part of a larger structured interview. This was the approach taken in the 2010 Time Use study, which was part of the General Social Survey conducted for Statistics Canada. A 24-hour diary was produced by asking people what they were doing on a certain day. The first question is: 'On [diary day], at 4:00 am, what were you doing?' (Most people say 'sleeping' and are then asked what time they got up.) 'And then, what did you do?' is asked repeatedly until the entire day is covered. Sometimes questions such as 'Where were you?' or 'Who was with you?' are asked as well.

An example of a free-text diary is provided in Coxon's (1994) study of how the risk of HIV/AIDS affects the sexual activities of gay men. One of several advantages of the diary method for this research is that it provided information on the time sequencing of events (for example, which practice followed which) and context—information that is more difficult to glean from questionnaires. The method involved recording, for one week, the following information:

- location of the activity;
- nature and sequence of each separate sexual act (who did what to whom);

- whether drugs accompanied the activity;
- what activities—sexual or otherwise—preceded each item of sexual activity;
- whether any sexual aids were employed; and
- whether the diarist or his partner achieved orgasm.

Crook and Light (2002) employed time-use diaries within a free-text format. University students were asked to keep a diary for a week, divided into 15-minute intervals, of the different kinds of study and learning activity in which they engaged, where the activity took place, and the study resources used (for example, the library). The various activities were grouped into three types: classes, private study, and social study (that is, study with a peer). They were able to show the very different amounts and patterns of study typically undertaken during a day.

Using free-text recording of behaviour carries the same kinds of coding problems as those associated with open-ended interview questions—namely, the time-consuming nature of the exercise and the risk of introducing error while coding answers. However, the free-text approach is less likely to be problematic when, as in the case of Coxon's (1994) research, diarists are given instructions about what is required and the behaviours of interest are specific and concrete. It would be much more difficult to code free-text entries relating to more general behaviours such as the domestic activities studied by Sullivan (1996).

Corti (1993) recommended that people doing research involving diaries should:

- provide explicit instructions for diarists;
- be clear about the time periods in which the behaviour of interest is to be assessed (for example, daytime, certain 24-hour periods, particular weeks), and indicate that in the diary template;
- supply a model of a completed section of a diary;
- provide brief checklists of 'items, events or behaviour' to jog the memory.

Advantages and disadvantages of the diary as a method of data collection   The studies illustrating the use of diaries discussed above suggest potential advantages:

- When fairly precise estimates regarding frequency of and/or amount of time spent in different forms of behaviour are required, the diary may provide more valid and reliable data than questionnaires.
- When information about the sequencing of different types of behaviour is required, it is likely to perform better than questionnaires or interviews.
- A diary is useful for collecting data on behaviour that is personally sensitive, such as sexual activity.

On the other hand, the diary method may present the following problems:

- Diaries tend to be more expensive than personal interviews because of costs related to recruiting diarists and ensuring that they are using their diaries properly.
- There is a risk of attrition as diarists tire of the task, which raises reliability issues.
- Failure to record details quickly enough can result in errors or omissions.

However, diary researchers such as Coxon and Sullivan argue that the information collected through diaries is more accurate than that collected through interviews or questionnaires on the same topic.

Respondent problems

A number of problems with structured interviews, questionnaires, and diaries have been identified.

RESPONSE SETS

This problem is especially relevant to multiple-indicator measures, where respondents reply to a battery of related questions or items. A response set occurs when someone responds to a series of items in the same way, suggesting that the responses are motivated by something other than the person's actual feeling about the items. Three of the most prominent types of response set involve the 'acquiescence,' 'social desirability,' and 'laziness or boredom' effects.

Acquiescence   Acquiescence refers to the tendency among some people to either agree or disagree with a set of questions or items, regardless of content, just to be 'cooperative' or to please the researcher. Imagine a respondent agreeing

to both items from the 2007 Alberta Survey discussed in Chapter 3: 'Body checking is the main cause of injuries for children in organized minor hockey,' and 'Body checking is an essential part of the game of organized minor hockey.' Agreement with the first implies a negative view of body checking, while agreement with the second suggests the opposite. If someone agrees with both, at least one of those responses is probably not authentic. To weed out respondents with an 'acquiescence' response set, researchers using multiple-item measures may include some items that logically call for opposite positions, so that if respondents are consistent in their attitudes, they can neither agree with all the items nor disagree with all of them. Those who persist in choosing the same answer regardless of the question may have to be removed from the study.

Social desirability   The social desirability effect occurs when respondents provide replies that are not sincere or genuine, but that make them appear to be respectable or likeable people. An answer perceived as socially undesirable is less likely to be given than one perceived as desirable. This phenomenon has been demonstrated in studies on mental health using psychiatric inventories of minor neuroses and anxieties: many respondents will not admit that they have those afflictions. The problem is compounded by the fact that some categories of people may be more truthful than others about certain issues. Women, for example, are less likely than men to conceal their illnesses, while men are more likely than women to be frank about certain sexual issues.

Laziness or boredom   Sometimes respondents will provide a series of answers just to get the interview or questionnaire over with. For example, when visiting a doctor's office for the first time, patients usually have to fill out a form with a long list of diseases, indicating whether they have ever suffered from them. Someone may begin carefully, reading the list and checking off 'No, No, No, . . . ,' but eventually tire of the task and just tick 'No' for the remaining items without reading them closely. To avoid this sort of problem, researchers may have to devise a set of questions that cannot be answered truthfully or consistently with a single response, whether 'yes' or 'no'—a tack similar to the one used to test for the acquiescence response set.

When these forms of response error go undetected, they represent sources of error in concept measurement. Some have suggested that the structured interview is particularly prone to them. Awareness of these potential problems has led researchers to limit their impact by removing cases obviously affected by them, or by instructing interviewers to avoid both becoming overly friendly with respondents and appearing judgmental about their replies.

THE PROBLEM OF MEANING

Another issue that survey researchers have to deal with is the 'problem of meaning': the fact that when humans communicate they not only draw on commonly held meanings but also create new ones. 'Meaning' in this sense is not a given but something that must be worked at and achieved. In structured interviewing this requires drawing attention to the presumption that interviewers and respondents attach the same meanings to the terms employed in the interview question and answer options, when in fact this may not be the case. For example, respondents who say they 'hate' body piercing may use forceful language for everything, and so their 'hate' may be the same as a milder person's 'dislike.' Conversely, when a mild person says 'hate' in an interview or on a questionnaire, the meaning may be much stronger than someone prone to colourful speech might assume.

The feminist critique

Some feminist social researchers maintain that standard survey research methods create an asymmetrical relationship in which the researcher extracts information from the subject and gives nothing in return. For example, textbook advice of the kind offered in this chapter says that it is important to establish a rapport with respondents, but that interviewers should guard against becoming too familiar with respondents. Thus, participants who ask questions (for example, about the topic of the study or the research process) should be politely but firmly rebuffed lest the answers bias their subsequent answers. Feminist scholars in the past have criticized such practices as hierarchical and even exploitative.

On the other hand, as we noted in Chapter 1, there has been some softening of attitudes towards quantitative research among feminist researchers. Paying more attention to issues such as privacy in the interview and providing special training in the handling of sensitive topics has contributed to this change. Moreover, survey research in some countries has proven to be highly instructive about issues of concern to feminists, such as the frequency and causes of phenomena such as violence against women (cf. Walby and Myhill 2001), and the challenges faced by sexual assault and rape crisis centres (Beres *et al.* 2009; see the 'Methods in Motion' box in this chapter). Such research, based on structured interviews, would seem to be consistent with the goals of most feminist researchers, and is potentially of great value for both women and men.

Key Points

The structured interview is a research instrument used to standardize the wording and order of questions and the recording of answers, which minimizes interviewer-related error.

- Structured interviews can be administered in person, over the phone, or online.
- It is important for interviewers to keep to the wording and order of questions. Training in the asking of questions, the recording of answers,

and how to establish rapport with respondents is essential.

- Questionnaires reduce some of the problems encountered in structured interviews, but they also have weaknesses.
- Online surveys take two major forms: web surveys and email surveys.
- The researcher-driven diary is an alternative to using questionnaires and interviews, especially

when the research questions are concerned with specific behaviours rather than attitudes or opinions.

- Response sets are a potential problem in both structured interviews and questionnaires, but steps can be taken to lessen their impact.

Relevant Websites

The *Canadian Election Study* site gives you access to structured interviews and questionnaires and the numerical data derived from them for Canadian elections going back as far as 1965.

http://ces-eec.org/

The *Online Survey Design Guide* provides guidelines on using colours, sound effects, video clips and screen layouts in online surveys. It also provides examples of more commonly used survey features such as Likert scales, filter questions, and open-ended questions.

http://lap.umd.edu/survey_design/index.html

In the *Statistics Canada 2010 General Social Survey Time Use Questionnaire* one can find an example of a research diary that forms part of a larger structured interview.

http://www.statcan.gc.ca/imdb-bmdi/instrument/4503_Q2_V1-eng.htm#a3

[Websites accessed 20 July 2011]

Questions for Review

THE STRUCTURED INTERVIEW

- Why is it important to keep interviewer variability to a minimum?
- How successful is the structured interview in reducing interviewer variability?
- Why might a survey researcher prefer a structured interview to an unstructured one?
- Why do structured interview schedules typically include mainly closed questions?

INTERVIEW CONTEXTS

- In what circumstances is it preferable to conduct structured interviews with more than one interviewer?
- 'Given that telephone interviews generally cost less to conduct than face-to-face interviews, they are generally preferable.' Discuss.

CONDUCTING INTERVIEWS

- Prepare an opening statement for a school study of student shoplifting.
- To what extent is rapport an important ingredient of structured interviewing?

- What is the difference between probing and prompting? What danger does each pose?

QUESTIONNAIRES

- What advantages do questionnaires have over structured interviews?
- What disadvantages do they have compared to structured interviews?
- What ethical issues are involved when professors ask their students to fill out a questionnaire in class?

ONLINE SOCIAL SURVEYS

- How are email and web surveys different? Are those differences important? Explain.
- Are there circumstances in which embedded email questionnaires are more likely to be effective than attached questionnaires?
- What advantages do online surveys have over traditional research methods for collecting data?
- What disadvantages do they have compared to traditional research methods for collecting data?

THE DIARY AS A FORM OF QUESTIONNAIRE

- Are there circumstances in which a diary approach is preferable to a questionnaire?

PROBLEMS WITH SURVEY RESEARCH

- What are response sets and why is it important to know about them?

- Name and define three kinds of response set, providing an example of each one.

- What are the main issues behind the feminist critique of survey research?

CHAPTER 5

Asking Questions

This chapter is concerned with the questions used in **structured interviews** and **questionnaires**, two data-gathering techniques discussed in Chapter 4. We will explore:

- the issues involved in deciding whether to use **open** or **closed questions**;
- different kinds of questions that can be asked in structured interviews and questionnaires;
- rules to bear in mind when designing questions;
- optimal question order;
- how questionnaires can be designed to minimize error and make answering easier for respondents;
- projection or **vignette** questions in which respondents are asked to reflect on a hypothetical scenario presented to them;
- the importance of pre-testing questions; and
- the use of questions taken from previous research.

For his class project, Tom decided to get an indication of Canadians' attitudes toward the monarchy. Since his instructor had told the class not to be concerned about sample selection procedures, he turned on his cell phone and dialled the local area code, followed by a common three-digit prefix. Then he closed his eyes and hit the number pad four times. He repeated this procedure 50 times in all, and asked everyone he reached the same question: 'Do you think the monarchy should be abolished in Canada, or should it be allowed to say?' However, for half the calls he prefaced the question with this statement: 'Many Canadians watched coverage of the recent wedding of Prince William and Kate Middleton, which led people to talk about the relevance of the monarchy in the modern age.' And for the other half of the calls he introduced the question this way: 'Prince Charles and Camilla Parker Bowles recently announced their plans to embark on a world tour, which led people to talk about the relevance of the monarchy in the modern age.' Tom found that 65 per cent of the first group were in favour of keeping the monarchy, while only 45 per cent of the second group were. What gives?

Introduction

As we suggested in Chapter 4, there is much more involved in survey research than an optimal phrasing of questions. However, question wording is a crucial concern and will be the focus of our attention here.

Open or closed questions?

One of the most significant considerations in survey research is whether to ask a question in an 'open' or 'closed' format, a distinction introduced in the last chapter.

With an open question, respondents can reply however they wish. With a closed question, they are presented with a set of fixed alternatives from which they have to choose an appropriate answer. All the questions in Box 5.5 (p. 92) are of the closed kind. So too are the **Likert scale** items in Box 5.7 (p. 95). What, then, are some of the advantages and limitations of the two formats?

OPEN QUESTIONS

Open questions present both advantages and disadvantages to a survey researcher. By and large, however, problems associated with the processing of answers tend to limit their use, especially in **quantitative research**.

Advantages   Open questions have certain advantages over closed ones:

- Respondents can answer in their own terms, not just those chosen by the researchers.
- They allow unusual responses, replies that the survey researcher might not have contemplated and therefore might not have offered as fixed-choice options.
- Because the questions do not suggest answers, they make it possible to tap the participants' knowledge and understanding of issues. The salience of particular issues for respondents can also be examined.
- They are useful for exploring new or changing areas.
- They can generate fixed-choice format answers (a point we will return to later in this chapter).

Disadvantages   Open questions also present problems for a survey researcher:

- It's time-consuming to record the answers, since interviewees are likely to give longer answers to an open question than to a comparable closed question.
- The answers have to be **coded**, which can also take a lot of time and effort. (The next section discusses coding and outlines how it is done.)
- Many prospective respondents are likely to be put off by the need to compose an answer, because of the greater time and effort required. This may exacerbate the problem of low response rates with questionnaires.
- Because of the difficulty of writing down exactly what respondents say, there may be inaccuracies in the recording of answers. One obvious solution is to use a tape recorder, but this can make some respondents nervous, and transcribing tape-recorded answers takes a long time. Transcription is a constant challenge for **qualitative researchers** using **semi-structured** and **unstructured** interviews (to be discussed in Chapter 10), but they work with only a small number of respondents, in contrast to the large numbers typical of survey research.

Coding   Coding is a key stage in quantitative research. Many forms of social science data are essentially unstructured and unorganized, including answers to open questions in interviews and questionnaires, and the content of newspaper articles. To make sense of the information, researchers must go through it all, deriving themes or categories of behaviour to form the basis for **codes** (the labels or titles given to the themes or categories): for example, 'hostile to outsiders,' or 'not hostile to outsiders.' Next, the researcher usually assigns numbers to the codes. This may be a largely arbitrary process in the sense that the numbers are simply tags to allow the material to be stored quantitatively. Then it is necessary to go through the information again to look for incidences of the theme or category, and to record the appropriate numbers on a computer spreadsheet. This approach is sometimes called *post-coding*. Post-coding can be an unreliable procedure because there may be inconsistencies in the judgments of different coders, which leads to both measurement error and lack of validity.

When Schuman and Presser (1981, see Box 5.3) asked an open question about the features of a job that people like, the answers were to be grouped into 11 codes: pay; feeling of accomplishment; control of work; pleasant work; security; opportunity for promotion; short hours; working conditions; benefits; satisfaction; other responses. Each of these 11 categories was assigned a number: 1 for pay; 2 for feeling of accomplishment; 3 for control of work; 4 for pleasant work, and so on.

Charles and Kerr (1988) conducted interviews with 200 women concerning the consumption of food in the home. Their interviews were of the semi-structured kind, and the questions were open-ended. Charles and Kerr were working with a qualitative research strategy, but for several of their questions they found it helpful to quantify respondents' answers. For example, one of their concepts was responsibility for meal preparation, which they divided into five categories: self prepares all meals; self mainly, partner sometimes; either self or self and partner together equally; self mainly with help from partner and/or children sometimes; and other. See Box 5.1 for another example.

Pre-coding, on the other hand, is a process in which the researcher designs a **coding frame** in advance of administering the survey instrument (as in Box 5.2). Closed questions in survey research are, by definition, pre-coded (as in the left-hand column in Box 5.3). This means that respondents are asked to assign their answers to a category, with a number already set up by the researcher. In post-coding, the response or behaviour is elicited without reference to any classification scheme.

When coding, three basic principles need to be observed (Bryman and Cramer 2004):

- The categories must not overlap. If they do, the numbers assigned to them will not denote distinct behaviours or types of responses.

- The list of categories must be exhaustive, covering all possibilities. If it does not, some material cannot be coded. That is why many classification schemes, such as those used to code open questions, include the category 'other.'

- There should be clear rules about how codes are to be applied, with examples of the kinds of answers that may be subsumed under a particular category. Such rules are meant to ensure that coders are consistent over time in how they assign the material to categories

and, if more than one person is coding, that the various coders are consistent with each other. The term 'coding frame' also describes the lists of categories that should be applied to unstructured data and the rules for their

---

BOX 5.1 | Coding an open question

Foddy (1993) asked a small sample of his students to state their fathers' occupations; then he requested three details: nature of business, size of business, and whether owner or employee. The replies to the 'size of business' question were particularly varied, including 'big,' 'small,' 'very large,' '3000 acres,' 'family,' 'multinational,' '200 people,' and 'Philips.' The problem here is obvious: these categories do not provide a useful measure of size. The problem has only partly to do with the difficulty of coding an open question; it is also due to a lack of specificity in the question. If Foddy had asked, 'How many employees are (were) there in your father's place of employment?' a more meaningful set of answers would have been forthcoming. Whether his students would have known this information is, of course, yet another issue. However, his experience illustrates some potential problems with asking an open question, particularly one that lacks a clear reference point.

BOX 5.2 | Processing a closed question

Which party did you like the most [in the 2008 Canadian federal election campaign]?
 [Interviewer: do not read list!]

1 Liberals (Grits)
2 Conservative (Conservative Party, new Conservative Party)
3 NDP
4 Bloc Québécois
5 Green Party
0 Another party, specify
97 None of them
d Don't know
r Refused

Source: *2008 Canadian Election Study—Post Election Survey-Joint French and English Version* available at http://130.15.161.127:82/ webview/?v=2&study=http%3A//130.15.161.127%3A82/obj/ fStudy/CES08&mode=documentation&submode=ddi&node= 0&top=yes [accessed November 16, 2011]

application. In **content analysis** and **structured observation**, the term '**coding manual**' is often preferred.

Coding is also used in qualitative research, but its role and significance are somewhat different.

CLOSED QUESTIONS

The advantages and disadvantages of closed questions are in many respects implied in the considerations relating to open questions.

Advantages   Closed questions offer the following advantages:

- The answers they elicit are easy to process: questionnaire respondents or interviewers using a structured interview schedule can simply place a tick on the form or circle an answer to indicate the appropriate response. The mark can then be scanned by an optical reader (see Box 5.7, p. 95, for an example). Similarly, responses may be typed directly into a computer file with the appropriate software.

- Closed questions enhance the comparability of answers. As we have mentioned, post-coding can be unreliable, even with inter- and intra-coder checks designed to ensure that coders do not vary their coding conventions. Closed questions circumvent this problem.

- Some respondents may not be clear about what a question is getting at; the available answers may provide some clarification.

- Because interviewers and respondents are not expected to write extensively and instead are to place ticks, circle answers, or enter the response using a keyboard, closed questions can be answered quickly and easily.

- As we noted in Chapter 4, if interviewers cannot write down exactly what respondents say, a source of bias and hence of invalidity is introduced. Closed questions reduce the risk of this problem, though if a respondent refuses to select one of the answers provided, the interviewer may have to *interpret* what is said in order to assign it to a category; alternatively, the response may have to be coded 'refused' or 'no answer.'

Disadvantages   Closed questions also present certain disadvantages, however:

- Respondents' answers may lack spontaneity and authenticity. It is also possible that the answers provided do not cover all the potential replies. One solution is to use an open question to generate the categories (see Box 5.3). Another is to include 'other' as a response option and category and then invite respondents who choose it to elaborate on their choice.

- Care must be taken to ensure that the response categories don't overlap: for example, when the age categories offered are '20–30,' '30–40,' and '40–50.' Because the forced-choice answers are not mutually exclusive, 30- and 40-year-old respondents will not know which category to select because they fit into two. Pre-tests and careful selection of categories usually eliminate this problem.

- It may be difficult to make forced-choice answers exhaustive. In theory, all possible answers should be provided, but a common compromise is to list the ones most likely to be chosen and then an 'other' category to avoid excessively long lists of possible answers. Should a particular 'other' response appear frequently in the pre-test, it can be added to the actual list.

- Respondents may differ in their interpretation of forced-choice answers; for example, the understanding of the word 'soon' in a question can vary widely from person to person. This problem can reduce the validity of the research.

- Closed questions may irritate respondents who are unable to find an answer category that they feel applies to them.

- In interviews, a large number of closed questions reduces conversation and gives the interview an impersonal feeling, reducing rapport. On the other hand, closed questions may represent a welcome break from open ones.

Types of questions

Structured interviews and questionnaires generally contain several different types of question. There are various ways of classifying them, but here are the main forms:

- *Personal, factual questions.* These are questions that ask respondents to provide personal information, such as their age, occupation, marital status, and income. This kind of

BOX 5.3 | A comparison of results for closed and open questions

Schuman and Presser (1981) conducted an experiment to determine whether responses to closed questions could be improved by asking the questions first in open-ended format and then developing categories of reply from respondents' answers. They asked a question about what people look for in work in both open and closed formats, using different samples for each. They found considerable disparities between the two sets of answers. They then revised the closed categories to reflect the answers they had received to the open-ended question, and re-administered the questions to two large samples. The question (with revised response categories) and the answers they received were as follows:

'This next question is on the subject of work. People look for different things in a job. Which one of the following five things do you most prefer in a job? [closed question]. What would you most prefer in a job? [open question].'

CLOSED FORMAT		OPEN FORMAT	
Answer	**%**	*Answer*	**%**
Work that pays well	13.2	Pay	16.7
Work that gives a feeling of accomplishment	31.0	Feeling of accomplishment	14.5
Work where there is not too much supervision and you make most decisions yourself	11.7	Control of work	4.6
Work that is pleasant and people who are nice to work with	19.8	Pleasant work	14.5
Work that is steady with little chance of being laid off	20.3	Security	7.6
	96% of sample		57.9% of sample
		Opportunity for promotion	1.0
		Short hours/lots of free time	1.6
		Working conditions	3.1
		Benefits	2.3
		Satisfaction/liking a job	15.6
Other/dk/na	4.0	Other responses	18.3
	100%		100%

With the revised form of the closed question, Schuman and Presser found that a much higher proportion of the answers to the open question corresponded to the closed categories. They argued that the new closed question was superior to its predecessor and also superior to the open question. However, it was still disconcerting to find that only 58 per cent of the answers given to the open question matched the categories offered in the closed one. Also, the distributions were somewhat different: for example, twice as many respondents cited a feeling of accomplishment with the closed format as with the open one. Nonetheless, the experiment demonstrated the desirability of generating forced-choice answers from open questions.

question also includes questions about behaviour. Respondents often have to rely on their memories to answer these sorts of questions, as when they are asked about the frequency of their attendance at religious services or how often they go out to a movie.

- *Factual questions about others.* These questions should be used only as a last resort, not only because there may be problems of recall, as above, but because respondents' knowledge of others' behaviour may be distorted or inaccurate (Beardsworth and Keil 1997). It's better to interview the person directly than to rely on the second-hand accounts of others. However, if the researcher is interested in the respondent's own perceptions of how someone else acts or feels, questions on that topic are appropriate.

- *Factual questions about an entity or event.* Sometimes respondents will act as informants about some phenomenon or event with which they are familiar. Asking people about what they witnessed at a riot—how many people were there, whether the police took appropriate action, the approximate ages of people engaged in looting—is an example. Although more defensible than factual questions about others, since the information may not be readily available from other sources, this sort of question can lead to problems because in everyday life most people are not careful and systematic observers, and they may have biases that affect their perceptions and recollections.

- *Questions about attitudes.* Questions about attitudes are very common in both structured interviews and questionnaire research. A five-point Likert scale (see Box 5.7, p. 95 for an example) is one of the most common formats for measuring attitudes.

- *Questions about beliefs.* Respondents are often asked about their social, political, moral, or religious beliefs. For example: 'Should Canada maintain its military presence in Afghanistan? Choose one: definitely yes, yes, unsure, no, definitely no.'

- *Questions about knowledge.* Sometimes questions are designed to 'test' respondents' knowledge in a certain area. For example, the Dominion Institute often tests Canadians' knowledge of Canada and its history. A poll done in 2007 showed that 91 per cent of respondents knew who Canada's largest trading partner was, and 82 per cent were able to name the prime minister. But only 70 per cent could name the three oceans that border on Canada, and just 5 per cent could name four different rights or freedoms protected by the *Canadian Charter of Rights and Freedoms* (see www.dominion.ca/Dominion_Institute_Press_Release_Mock_Exam.pdf) [accessed January 18, 2012].

Most structured interview schedules and questionnaires include more than one type of question. When doing research, it's important to keep the distinctions in mind, for the following reasons:

- It will help you to clarify what it is that you're asking, albeit in rather general terms.

- It will prevent you from asking questions in an inappropriate format. For example, a Likert scale is generally not suitable for asking certain factual questions about behaviour.

- It will help you avoid mixing different types of questions in a single scale. For example, attitudes and beliefs may seem similar, but they are different things and should be measured on different scales; otherwise measurement validity will be threatened.

Rules for designing questions

Over the years, numerous rules have been devised in connection with the dos and don'ts of asking questions. Yet mistakes persist. So here are three simple rules of thumb, followed by some more specific guidelines.

GENERAL RULES OF THUMB

Keep the research questions in mind   The questions you ask in a questionnaire or structured interview should be designed specifically to answer your research questions. Focusing on the research questions will help protect you against the pain of realizing too late that a particular research question was not addressed in your study. It will also reduce the risk of pursuing issues that are irrelevant, which would be a waste of your time as well as your respondents.'

What exactly do you want to know?   Rule of thumb number two relates to the first one. It's important to focus on exactly what you want to know. Consider this seemingly harmless question:

Methods in Motion

Applications to Canadian Society

In a study conducted in Alberta, Van Brunschot *et al.* (2009) examined the hypothesis that the global social changes that have occurred in recent years have produced a generalized sense of anxiety and insecurity in many people. A related issue that the study considered was whether such anxiety influences how people live their daily lives, in particular whether general anxiety affects people's behaviours with regard to crime prevention, health promotion, and home protection, which they set up as dependent variables. The participants were 1200 adult Albertans, selected using random digit dialling, who took part in a 45-minute telephone survey.

To measure general anxiety, 14 different survey items were combined to form a single composite measure. They were recorded on a scale from 1 to 10, with the items measuring the extent to which respondents believed it was likely that: 'Someone will break into your home while you are away? You will be physically attacked? . . . You will be exposed to HIV or contract AIDS?' and so forth. Eight items, scored as yes (1) or no (0), were combined to measure crime prevention; for example, 'Do you routinely: Carry something (weapon, pepper spray) to defend yourself? . . . Keep lights on when home alone? Hold your keys defensively when walking alone at night?' Health promotion was gauged with questions such as 'Do you avoid fat in your diet? . . . Do you avoid loud noise? . . . Do you regularly smoke?' Home protection items included: 'Do you have a first aid kit at home? Do you have a working fire extinguisher at home? Do you have a plan to follow in case of a house fire?'

The researchers found that there was no simple relationship between generalized anxiety and the behaviours examined. For example, substantial differences in these relationships were observed for men and women. Also, anxiety was a significant predictor of crime prevention behaviours, but not health promotion activities. They also found that factors other than general anxiety, such as local, personal experience with crime, illness, and natural disasters had an impact on the precautionary actions that people took, as did individual biographical characteristics such as age, education, income, and marital status. The authors suggest that their findings illustrate the complexity of the relationship between generalized anxiety and personal behaviours in modern societies, and point to the need for further research.

Do you have a car?

What is that question seeking to tap? Car ownership? Access to a household car? Use of a company car? The ambiguity of the word 'have' means that a 'yes' answer could signify any of the three. If you want to find out whether a respondent owns a car, you need to ask specifically about ownership. Similarly, consider the question:

How many children do you have?

That may seem straightforward, but does 'children' include stepchildren? Adopted children? Grown children? Be as specific as possible. And if what you are trying to address is the standard of living of a person or household, the crucial question may well be how many children are living at home.

How would you answer it? Rule of thumb number three is to put yourself in the position of the respondent. Ask yourself the question and try to work out a reply. If you do this, there is at least a chance that the ambiguities inherent in a question like 'Do you have a car?' or 'How many children do you have?' will become evident. For example, you may remember that you have access to a car that you don't actually own, or wonder whether your partner's children from a previous relationship should be factored into your answer. Putting yourself in the position of the respondent can reveal the difficulty of answering poorly constructed questions.

SPECIFIC RULES WHEN DESIGNING QUESTIONS

Avoid ambiguous terms in questions If possible, avoid terms such as 'often' and 'regularly' as measures of frequency. They are ambiguous, and different respondents will take them to mean different things. It may not always be possible to get a specific number from respondents, but that should be your goal. Consider a question asked of people who have said that they own a cell phone:

How often do you use your cell phone?

Very often	_____
Quite often	_____
Not very often	_____
Not at all	_____

The problem with this question is that, with the exception of 'not at all,' all the terms in the response categories are ambiguous. Instead, ask about actual frequency, such as:

How often do you use your cell phone?

(Please tick whichever category comes closest to the number of times you use your cell phone.)

More than 10 times per day	_____
5–9 times per day	_____
1–4 times per day	_____
A few times a week	_____
A few times a month	_____
Almost never	_____

Alternatively, you could simply ask respondents to estimate the number of times per day they use their cell phone.

It's also important to bear in mind that certain common words, such as 'dinner' and 'book,' mean different things to different people. For some, dinner is a light midday meal, whereas for others it is a substantial evening meal. Similarly, some people refer to magazines, catalogues, or brochures as 'books,' while others work with a more restricted definition. In such cases it is necessary to clearly define the terms that are being used.

Avoid long questions   Most methodologists agree that long questions are undesirable. Interviewees can lose track of long questions, and respondents completing a questionnaire may be tempted to skim or even skip over them. However, Sudman and Bradburn (1982) suggested that this advice is more applicable to attitude questions than to those asking about behaviour. They argued that when the focus is on behaviour, longer questions can have certain positive features in interviews: for example, they are more likely to provide memory cues and facilitate recall because of the time it takes to ask them. By and large, however, it's best to keep questions short.

Avoid double-barrelled questions

How satisfied are you with your pay and working conditions?

The problem here is obvious: people may be satisfied with one but not the other. Not only will the respondent be unclear about how to reply, but the answer provided may pertain to pay, to conditions, or to both. The following question poses the same problem:

How frequently does your husband help with cooking and cleaning?

A husband may provide extensive help with the cooking but be totally uninvolved in the cleaning, so that any stipulation of frequency of help is ambiguous.

The same rule applies to fixed-choice answers. In Box 5.3, one of Schuman and Presser's (1981) answers is:

Work that is pleasant and people who are nice to work with.

While there may well be symmetry between the two ideas in this answer—pleasant work and nice people—there is no *necessary* correspondence between them. Pleasant work may be important for people who are indifferent to their co-workers. For an example of a triple-barrelled question, see Box 5.4.

Avoid very general questions   It may be tempting to ask a very general question when what is needed is a response to a specific issue. A question such as

How satisfied are you with your job?

seems harmless, but it lacks specificity. Does it refer to pay, working conditions, the nature of the work, or all of these? Respondents are likely to vary in their interpretation of the question, and this will be a source of error. A favourite general question comes from Karl Marx's *Enquête ouvrière*, a questionnaire sent to 25 000 French socialists and others (whether any were returned is unknown). The final question (the one-hundredth!) reads:

What is the general, physical, intellectual, and moral condition of men and women employed in your trade? (Bottomore and Rubel 1963: 218).

BOX 5.4   Matching questions and answers in closed questions

A publisher inserted a feedback questionnaire into copies of a novel, including a series of Likert-style items regarding the book's quality. In each case, readers were asked to indicate whether a particular attribute was 'poor,' 'acceptable,' 'average,' 'good,' or 'excellent.' However, the items were presented as questions that, strictly speaking, demanded 'yes' or 'no' answers. For example:

Was the writing elegant, seamless, imaginative?

Given a range of gradations such as 'definitely,' 'to a large extent,' 'to some extent,' 'not at all,' some readers might have been able to respond. However, none of the response options provided by the publisher could be considered logical answers to the questions that were posed. The questions would have been better presented as statements; for example:

Please indicate the quality of the writing in each of the following categories:

Elegance:

Poor   Acceptable   Average   Good   Excellent

Seamlessness:

Poor   Acceptable   Average   Good   Excellent

Imaginativeness:

Poor   Acceptable   Average   Good   Excellent

This approach would also solve the additional problem of the 'triple-barrelled' question that asks about three distinct aspects of the writing, leaving the reader unable to express differing opinions of each.

It could be argued that readers would understand that they were being asked to rate the book in terms of each attribute. The problem is that the impact of a disjunction between question and answer is simply not known—which means that any conclusions drawn by the publisher might well be wrong.

If you find it difficult to come up with precise questions to replace very broad, general ones, you might take inspiration from Blauner (1964), who provides a very detailed and nuanced description of job satisfaction among American factory workers based on some eighty specific questions.

Avoid leading questions   Leading or loaded questions push respondents in a particular direction; for example:

Would you agree to cutting taxes, even though welfare payments for the neediest sections of the population might be reduced?

Phrasing the question in this way is likely to make it difficult for some people to disagree, even if they do feel that taxes are too high. Once again, Marx is the source of a favourite leading question:

If you are paid piece rates, is the quality of the article made a pretext for fraudulent deductions from wages? (Bottomore and Rubel 1963: 215).

Avoid questions that actually ask two (or more) questions   The triple-barrelled question in Box 5.4 clearly transgresses this rule, but there are also more subtle versions of the problem. A question such as

Which party did you vote for in the 2011 federal election?

provides an illustration. What if the respondent did not vote in that election? The question is really two questions, which should be asked separately:

Did you vote in the 2011 federal election?

Yes   _____
No   _____

If YES, for which political party did you vote? Following is another type of double-barrelled question:

How effective have your different job search strategies been?

Very effective   _____
Fairly effective   _____
Not very effective   _____
Not at all effective _____

One problem here is that a respondent may or may not have used different job search strategies. Another is that judgments regarding effectiveness may well vary for each strategy. A mechanism is needed to assess the success of each strategy so that respondents aren't forced to average out their assessments of how successful the various strategies were.

Avoid questions that include negatives The problem with questions that include negative terms such as 'not' is that some respondents may miss the negative and give answers opposite to what they intended. There may be situations when it's impossible to avoid using a negative, but questions like the following should be avoided as far as possible:

> Do you agree with the view that university students should not have to take out loans to finance their education?

Instead, the question should be asked in a positive form; for example: 'Some university students have to take out loans to finance their education. Is that fair?' Questions with double negatives are never appropriate, because it's impossible to be sure that respondents have interpreted them correctly. Take the following example:

> Would you rather not drink non-alcoholic beer?

Minimize technical terms Use simple, plain language and avoid jargon. Don't ask a question like this:

> Do you sometimes feel alienated from your work?

The problem here is that many respondents may not be familiar with the term 'alienated,' and even if they are, they may not understand it in the same way. The same goes for acronyms and abbreviations: avoid them whenever possible. Consider the following question:

> The influence of the CAUT on national politics has declined in recent years.
>
> | | |
> |---|---|
> | Strongly agree | _____ |
> | Agree | _____ |
> | Undecided | _____ |
> | Disagree | _____ |
> | Strongly disagree | _____ |

The use of abbreviations such as CAUT (the Canadian Association of University Teachers) is a problem because many people will not know what the initials stand for.

Ensure that respondents have the requisite knowledge There is little point in asking about matters unfamiliar to respondents. For example, it would not be useful to ask the general public questions about CAUT, because very few people have heard of the organization. Similarly, it's doubtful that meaningful data regarding opinions on foreign affairs can be gained from people who do not follow international political issues.

Ensure symmetry between a closed question and its answers A common mistake is to pose a question with answers that are out of phase with it, as in: 'Do you believe in God? Select one: strongly agree, agree, neither agree nor disagree, disagree, strongly disagree.' When the response format doesn't match the question, one or the other has to change. See Box 5.4 for another example of this problem.

Ensure that the answers provided for a closed question are balanced It's important that the range of answers provided for a closed question be properly balanced between positive and negative options. A set of responses like this

Excellent	_____
Good	_____
Borderline	_____
Poor	_____

is weighted towards a favourable response. 'Excellent' and 'Good' are both positive; 'Borderline' is a neutral or middle position; and 'Poor' is a negative response. A second negative response choice, such as 'Very poor' is needed.

Memory problems Don't overstretch people's memories. It might be useful to know exactly how many times respondents have used their cell phones in the previous month, but few people will be able to give you an accurate answer for such an extended period of time. For this reason it's important to choose a suitable time frame, such as per day in the case of cell phone use.

Don't know One area of controversy regarding closed questions is whether the answer set should include a 'don't know' or 'no opinion' option. This issue chiefly relates to survey questions concerning attitudes. The main argument for including a 'don't know' option is to ensure that respondents will not be forced to express views that they don't actually hold. Many recommend offering the 'don't know' option in the form of a filter question to remove those respondents who have no opinion on the topic. This means that the interviewer needs to ask the filter question 'Do you have an opinion on this issue?' of everyone and then ask the second question only of those who say that they do have an opinion.

The alternative argument in connection with the 'don't know' option is that it offers an easy way out for respondents who can't be bothered to do the required thinking on the issue. A series of experiments conducted in the US found that many respondents who claim to have no opinion on a topic do in fact hold one (Krosnick *et al.* 2002). Respondents with lower levels of education are especially likely to select the 'don't know' option; and later questions in a questionnaire are the most likely to elicit a 'don't know' response. The latter finding implies a kind of question order effect (to be addressed in the next section): respondents may become increasingly tired or bored as the questioning proceeds and therefore more lazy in their answers. The researchers concluded that data quality is not enhanced by the inclusion of a 'don't know' option and that it may prevent some respondents from expressing an opinion that

they do actually hold. Consequently, these researchers would *not* offer a 'don't know' option unless it was absolutely necessary.

Question order   Quite a lot of research has been directed at finding out how responses are affected by asking questions at different points in an interview schedule. Results have varied and few if any consistent effects have been found. Mayhew (2000) tells an interesting anecdote on question order in a crime survey. By mistake, half of the respondents were asked the question 'Taking everything into account, would you say the police in this area do a good job or a poor job?' twice: once early on, and once again later, in the context of questions on contact with the police. Almost a quarter (22 per cent) of those respondents gave a more positive rating the second time. Mayhew suggests that as the interview wore on, respondents became more sensitized to crime-related issues and more sympathetic to the pressures on the police. As appealing as this explanation sounds, it cannot account for the 13 per cent who gave a lower rating the second time around. That is quite a reliability issue. (See also Box 5.5.)

BOX 5.5 | About question order

Imagine that there are two pollsters: one who favours the federal New Democratic Party and another who favours the Conservatives. The key question in both their surveys is: 'In the upcoming federal election, which party do you intend to vote for?' That question would be followed by an alphabetical list of the main political parties. Look at the two sets of Likert items that follow (assume there are five response options ranging from 'strongly agree' to 'strongly disagree'), and imagine that the items immediately *preceded* the voting question. Try to determine whether these items would influence responses to the voting question and, if so, how:

Set One:

1. Canada must do more to reduce global warming.
2. Tax cuts should wait until we clean up the environment.
3. Too many Canadian soldiers have died in Afghanistan.
4. A national daycare program would help most working families.

Set Two:

1. The Harmonized Sales Tax (HST) will have a positive effect on the Canadian economy.
2. Canada's mounting debt is mortgaging the future of its children.
3. Canada's military presence in Afghanistan has helped the Afghan people, especially women and children.
4. The government should register criminals, not guns.

For those who do not follow politics closely: the first set would probably increase the number of respondents saying they would vote NDP, while the second would likely do the same for the number declaring their intention to vote Conservative. Although most pollsters avoid such blatant biases, sometimes more subtle influences on respondents go unnoticed. Also, did you notice the 'response set' problem? In any event, this is an interesting exercise because it illustrates the importance of question order in survey research: if it was necessary to use these Likert items, they ought to be presented *after* the voting question.

It's hard to draw any general lessons from question order research, at least in part because experiments do not always reveal clear-cut effects, even in cases where effects might legitimately have been expected. Nonetheless, two general lessons have emerged:

- All respondents in a survey should receive questions in the same order.
- Researchers should be sensitive to the possible effects that a question could have on subsequent questions.

In addition, the following rules about question order are sometimes proposed:

- Early questions should be directly related to the announced research topic. This removes the risk that respondents will be put off by apparently irrelevant questions asked at an early stage in the interview. It also means that personal questions about age, social background, and so on should *not* be asked at the beginning of an interview.

- As far as possible, questions likely to be important or meaningful to respondents should be asked early in the interview, to stimulate their interest and attention. This suggestion may conflict with the previous one if questions about the research topic are not of interest to respondents. In any case, questions relating to the research topic that may grab participants' attention should be asked at or close to the start of the interview.

- If possible, questions that may cause embarrassment or anxiety should be left for later in the schedule—though not to the very end. Respondents should not leave the interview (or complete the questionnaire) with misgivings or negative feelings about the research.

- With a long schedule or questionnaire, questions should be grouped logically in related sections, and should not jump back and forth from one topic to another.

- Within each group of questions, general questions should precede specific ones. If a specific question comes first, the aspect of the general question that it highlights may be discounted by respondents who feel they have already covered it. For example, if a question asking how people feel about their salary precedes a general question about job satisfaction, some respondents may discount the issue of pay when responding to the job satisfaction question, since they have already addressed it. Similarly, an item about whether abortion is morally acceptable in cases where the mother's life is threatened may affect answers to a later, more general item such as 'Abortion is a matter of individual personal choice.' Some respondents who would otherwise disagree with that statement might have second thoughts about it because of the earlier item.

- It is sometimes recommended that questions dealing with opinions and attitudes precede questions about behaviour and knowledge. This is because questions that tap opinions and attitudes may be affected by the latter sorts of questions. For instance, if a husband reports that he does only 20 per cent of the housework, making that statement can affect how he responds when asked if housework should be shared equally between spouses.

- If a respondent provides an answer to a question that is to be asked later in the interview, the question should still be asked later on, when the interviewer arrives at the scheduled point. A different answer may be offered at the latter juncture because of question order effects.

Designing the questionnaire

CLEAR PRESENTATION

Make sure that the layout is easy on the eye and that it facilitates answering all the questions applicable to the respondent. Using a variety of print styles (different fonts and print sizes, boldface, italics, capitals, etc.) can enhance the questionnaire's appearance *so long as they are used consistently.* Thus all general instructions should appear in one style, all headings in a second, all specific instructions (e.g., 'Go to question 7') in a third, and so on. Mixing print styles or uses (e.g., using a particular style for both general instructions and specific questions) may confuse respondents.

VERTICAL OR HORIZONTAL CLOSED ANSWERS?

Bearing in mind that most questions in a questionnaire are likely to be closed, you will need to decide whether to arrange the fixed answers vertically or horizontally. Usually a vertical arrangement is used unless respondents are asked to choose their answer from a row of numbers or abbreviations, as is often done with Likert scales (see Box 5.7 for examples). Many writers prefer a vertical format because it reduces the risk of confusion. With a horizontal format there is a significant risk, especially if the respondent is in a hurry, that the required tick will be placed in the wrong space (for an example, see Box 5.6). Also, a vertical format more clearly distinguishes questions from answers. Although potential problems can be reduced through judicious use of spacing and print variation, a further advantage of the vertical format is that it may facilitate coding, especially when pre-codes appear on the questionnaire.

IDENTIFYING RESPONSE SETS IN A LIKERT SCALE

One of the advantages of using closed questions is that they are pre-coded, which simplifies the data entry for computer analysis. However, the scoring of the items still requires some thought. For example, items 3, 4, and 6 in Box 5.7 could be scored as follows:

Strongly agree = 5
Agree = 4
Undecided = 3
Disagree = 2
Strongly disagree = 1

Using that setup, a high score for the items (a score of 5 or 4) indicates satisfaction with the job, and a low score (1 or 2) indicates an absence of job satisfaction. However, the pattern is different for question 5. Here, agreement indicates a *lack* of job satisfaction, and disagreement indicates satisfaction. Therefore the scoring for this item would have to be reversed:

Strongly agree = 1
Agree = 2
Undecided = 3
Disagree = 4
Strongly disagree = 5

Now, with this reverse coding, the scoring for all four items follows the same pattern: the higher the score, the greater the job satisfaction. If you wanted to combine the four items to form a job satisfaction index, you would simply add their scores together.

A researcher may intentionally create a scale in which agreement with some items indicates high job satisfaction, but agreement with the others indicates low satisfaction. The purpose here is to identify *response sets*, mentioned in the last chapter. Under these conditions, it would be logically inconsistent to answer every question the same way: thus

---

BOX 5.6 : Closed question with a vertical or a horizontal format?

The following question is adapted from the 2008 Canadian Election Study—Post Election Survey:

Which party did you like most in the 2011 Canadian federal election campaign?

1. Liberal   ____
2. Conservative   ____
3. NDP   ____
4. Bloc Québécois   ____
5. Green Party   ____
6. Another party, please specify: _____
7. None of them   ____
8. Don't know   ____

Which party did you like most in the 2011 Canadian federal election campaign?

1. Liberal ____ 2. Conservative ____ 3. NDP ____ 4. Bloc Québécois ____
5. Green Party ____ 6. Another party, please specify: _____
7. None of them ____ 8. Don't know ____

BOX 5.7 | Formatting a Likert scale

In the next section you are presented with a set of statements. Please indicate your level of agreement or disagreement with each by indicating whether you: Strongly Agree (sa), Agree (a), are Undecided (u), Disagree (d), or Strongly Disagree (sd).

(Please indicate your level of agreement by circling the appropriate response.)

3. My job is like a hobby to me.

   sa   a   u   d   sd

4. My job is usually interesting enough to keep me from getting bored.

   sa   a   u   d   sd

5. It seems that my friends are more interested in their jobs than I am in mine.

   sa   a   u   d   sd

6. I enjoy my work more than my leisure time.

   sa   a   u   d   sd

a respondent who either agreed or disagreed with all the items could not be answering truthfully, and might have to be excluded from the study.

CLEAR INSTRUCTIONS ABOUT HOW TO RESPOND

Always be clear about how respondents should indicate their replies to closed questions. Are they supposed to place a tick by the appropriate answer, or are they to underline it? Should they circle it? Is it acceptable to choose more than one answer? If not, this should be indicated in the instructions; for example:

> *(Please choose the ONE answer that best represents your views by placing a tick in the appropriate box.)*

If this is not made clear and some respondents choose more than one answer, their replies cannot be counted and will have to be treated as if they were missing. If choosing more than one category is acceptable, this too must be made clear, for example:

> *(Please choose ALL answers that represent your views by placing a tick in the*

appropriate boxes. You may tick more than one box for each question—choose as many as apply to you.)

It is a common error for such instructions to be omitted and for respondents to be unsure about how to reply.

KEEP QUESTION AND ANSWERS TOGETHER

This simple rule may seem obvious, but it is often transgressed: a question, or the question and the answers that accompany it, should not be split between two separate pages. A common error is for a question to appear at the bottom of a page and the responses on the next page. The danger here is that the respondent will either (a) fail to answer the question or (b) pay insufficient attention to the question and give a superficial answer (this problem is especially likely when a series of questions with a common answer format is being used, as with a Likert scale).

Vignette questions

A form of closed question that is often used to examine ethical standards and beliefs is the **vignette technique**. It involves presenting respondents with one or more scenarios and asking them how they would respond if confronted with the circumstances depicted in the scenario. For example, Achille and Ogloff (1997) used vignettes of dying patients in a study of assisted suicide (they found lethal injection to be less acceptable than withdrawal of life support).

Box 5.8 outlines a vignette designed to tease out respondents' norms concerning several aspects of family obligations, including the nature of the assistance required (direct involvement or simple provision of resources); geographical considerations; the choice between paid work and unpaid care; and the gender question (should it be the man or the woman who gives up paid work for unpaid care?). The specificity of the situation facing Jim and Margaret increases as the vignette develops. The first question (a) does not say whether they are prepared to move; the second (b) says that they are; and in the last question (d) they have in fact moved and are facing a new dilemma.

Many aspects of the issues tapped by the questions in Box 5.8 can be accessed through attitude items. For example:

Practical Tip ▶ ▶ ▶ ▶

Common mistakes when asking questions

Over the years, the authors of this book have read many projects and dissertations based on structured interviews and questionnaires. A number of mistakes recur regularly, among them the following:

- Excessive use of open questions. While resistance to closed questions is understandable, open questions are likely to reduce the response rate and cause analysis problems. Keep them to a minimum.

- Excessive use of yes/no questions. Sometimes students include lots of questions that call for a yes/no response (usually a sign of inadequate thinking and preparation). The world rarely fits into this kind of response. Take a question like:

Are you satisfied with the opportunities for promotion in your firm?

Yes _____   No _____

Attitudes are complex, and most respondents will not be simply 'satisfied' or 'not satisfied.' For one thing, people's feelings about such things vary in intensity. An improvement would be to rephrase the item as:

How satisfied are you with opportunities for promotion in your firm?

Very satisfied	_____
Satisfied	_____
Neither satisfied nor dissatisfied	_____
Dissatisfied	_____
Very dissatisfied	_____

This sort of format also makes it possible to calculate some widely used statistics that are discussed in Chapter 13.

- Too many questions that allow respondents to choose more than one answer. Although there are times when such questions are unavoidable, the replies they produce are often difficult to analyze.

- Overlapping or missing categories. In spite of constant warnings, students (and some professional researchers who should know better) still formulate response choices that are not mutually exclusive or that omit some categories. For example:

How many times per week do you use public transport?

0 times	_____
1–3 times	_____
3–6 times	_____
6–9 times	_____
More than 10 times	_____

Here respondents whose answer is 3 or 6 will not know which category to choose, and there is no category at all for those whose answer is 10.

Answers that do not correspond to the questions asked. For example:

Do you go to your gym or fitness centre regularly?

Every day	_____
5–6 times per week	_____
2–4 times per week	_____
Once per week	_____
Once per month	_____
Less than once per month	_____

The only logical answer to the question is either 'yes' or 'no.' However (as noted above), 'yes or no' questions are rarely satisfactory, and the answers provided suggest that the point of the question is to gain some idea of frequency. The problem is that the question and the response categories are out of kilter. A better question would be:

How frequently do you go to your gym or fitness centre?

Every day	_____
5–6 times per week	_____
2–4 times per week	_____
Once per week	_____
Once per month	_____
Less than once per month	_____

When two working spouses decide that one of them should quit work to care for ailing parents, the wife should be the one to give up her job.

Strongly agree	_____
Agree	_____
Undecided	_____
Disagree	_____
Strongly disagree	_____

BOX 5.8   A vignette to establish family obligations

Jim and Margaret Robinson are a married couple in their early forties. Jim's parents, who live several hundred kilometres away, have had a serious car accident and they need long-term daily help. Jim is their only son. He and his wife both could get transfers to work nearer his parents.

(a) What should Jim and Margaret do?
 - Move to live near Jim's parents
 - Have Jim's parents move to live with them
 - Give Jim's parents money to help them pay for daily care
 - Let Jim's parents make their own arrangements
 - Do something else (specify)
 - Don't know

(b) In fact, Jim and Margaret are prepared to move and live near Jim's parents, but teachers at their children's school say that moving right now could have a bad effect on their children's education.

What should Jim and Margaret do? Should they move or should they stay?
 - Move
 - Stay

(c) Why do you think they should move/stay?

(d) Jim and Margaret do go to live near Jim's parents. A year later Jim's mother dies and his father's condition gets worse so that he needs full-time care.

Should one of either Jim or Margaret take an extended leave from work to take care of Jim's father?
IF YES: Who should, Jim or Margaret?
 - Yes, Jim should give up his job
 - Yes, Margaret should give up her job
 - No, neither should give up their jobs
 - Don't know/Depends

Source: Adapted from Finch (1987: 108).

The advantage of the vignette over this kind of attitude question is that it anchors the choice in a more realistic situation and thus reduces the risk of an unreflective reply. Finch (1987) also argued that on a sensitive topic like this, some respondents may feel uncomfortable or fear that they will be judged on their replies. The fact that the vignette is about other people (and imaginary ones at that) creates a certain distance between the questioning and the respondent, and hence the chance for a more candid answer. One obvious requirement of the vignette technique is that scenarios must be believable.

Finch also pointed to some limitations with this style of questioning, however. It may be impossible to establish what assumptions are being made by the respondents about the characters in the scenario (such as their age, ethnicity, and number of children at home) and the significance of those assumptions for the validity and comparability of people's replies. It is also difficult to establish how far respondents' answers reflect their own normative views or indeed how they themselves would act when confronted with the kinds of choices outlined in the scenarios.

Practical **Tip**   ▶ ▶ ▶ ▶

Getting help in designing questions

When designing questions, be empathetic: put yourself in the position of the people who will be answering them. This can be difficult, because the questions may not always apply to the person producing them—for example, to a young student doing a survey of retired people. Even so, you need to think about how you would reply. This means concentrating not just on the questions themselves but also on the links between the questions. For example, do filter questions work in the expected way?

Then try the questions out on some friends or classmates, as in a pilot study (see the next section). Ask them to be critical and to consider how well the questions connect to each other. Also, look at some questionnaires and structured interview schedules designed by experienced researchers. Those researchers may not have asked questions on your particular topic, but the way they have asked their questions should give you an idea of what to do and what to avoid.

Often what people say they would do in a particular situation turns out to be very different from what they actually do. People are not necessarily being dishonest—predicting behaviour, whether our own or someone else's, is often more difficult than we would imagine. That's why experiments, structured observation, historical analysis, and other research techniques are so important. In spite of these reservations, the vignette technique can provide useful information, or at least a starting point for further research.

Pilot studies and pre-testing questions

It is always desirable to conduct a pilot study before collecting data from respondents: not just to ensure that individual questions operate well but also to ensure that the research instrument as a whole is appropriate. Pilot studies may be particularly crucial in research using questionnaires, since there will be no interviewer present to clear up any confusion.

Here are some specific uses of pilot studies in survey research:

- If the study is going to employ mainly closed questions, a researcher can pose open questions in pilot qualitative interviews and then use them to generate the fixed-choice answers.

- Piloting an interview schedule can give interviewers some experience in using it and help them develop confidence.

- If everyone (or virtually everyone) who answers a question gives the same answer, the resulting data are not likely to be useful. A pilot study gives you an opportunity to identify such questions and modify them as necessary to elicit more varied answers.

- In survey interviews, it may be possible to identify questions that make respondents feel uncomfortable and to detect any junctures where interest tends to flag.

- Questions that respondents tend to skip or have difficulty understanding (more easily recognizable in an interview than in a questionnaire context) should become apparent. If

---

BOX 5.9   A bad questionnaire

How would you fix this questionnaire?

'Hello. I am taking a sociology course on research methods and would like to ask you some questions. Would that be ok?'

1. Were you ever scared that you were HIV-positive?
    Yes ____   No ____

For questions 2 to 6, please answer Agree or Disagree.

2. As a religious person, I feel sorry for AIDS victims.

3. I think victims of any disease deserve compassion.

4. I think the new legislation will be a boon to AIDS victims.

5. The government should not allocate more money to AIDS research.

6. People with AIDS and other sexual diseases should be quarantined.
    If you agree, has your viewpoint changed since the 1980s when AIDS first widely emerged?
    Yes ____ . No ____

Now there are just a few more questions.

7. If one were planned, would you fight having an AIDS hospice on your street?
    Yes ____   No ____

8. How does your spouse feel about AIDS victims?
    Compassionate ____   Sympathetic ____
    Concerned ____   Angry ____   Don't know ____

9. Elizabeth Taylor has raised much money for AIDS research. Should people be doing more fund-raising in this area?
    Yes ____   No ____

10. Do you know any AIDS victims?
    Yes ____ No ____

Finally I need a few facts for comparison purposes.

11. How old are you? ____

12. Did you graduate from high school?
    Yes ____   No ____

13. Did you ever have yourself tested for AIDS?
    Yes ____   No ____

Thank you for your cooperation.

certain questions are frequently skipped, it may be because of unclear or threatening phrasing, poorly worded instructions, or confusing positioning in the interview schedule or questionnaire (see Box 5.9). Whatever the cause, missing data are undesirable and a pilot study may be very helpful in identifying problems.

- Pilot studies allow the researcher to determine the adequacy of the instructions given to the interviewers, or to respondents completing a questionnaire.

- A pilot study may also offer an opportunity to consider the overall structure of the study. If the questions do not flow well, it may be necessary to move some of them around.

The pilot should not be carried out on people who may become members of the sample in the full study, since participation in the pilot could affect their responses in the study proper. If the population you are investigating is small, you don't want to be forced to exclude certain people, since that could affect the representativeness of sample. If this is an issue, do the pilot study on respondents from a different but similar population. Beagan (2001) did this in her study of medical students.

Using existing questions

Finally, it is sometimes possible to use questions that have been employed by other researchers for at least part of the questionnaire or interview schedule. This may seem like stealing, but it is a legitimate research practice so long as the original

---

☑ Checklist *of issues to consider for a structured interview schedule or questionnaire*

- ✔ Is a clear and comprehensive introduction to the research provided for respondents?
- ✔ Are there any questions used by other researchers that would be useful?
- ✔ Will the questions provide answers to all the research questions?
- ✔ Are there any questions not strictly relevant to the research questions that could be dropped?
- ✔ Has the questionnaire been pre-tested with some appropriate respondents?
- ✔ If a structured interview schedule is used, are the instructions clear? For example, with filter questions, is it clear which question(s) should be omitted?
- ✔ Are instructions about how to record responses clear (for example, whether to tick or circle; whether more than one response is allowable)?
- ✔ Has the number of open questions been limited?
- ✔ Can respondents indicate levels of intensity in their replies, or are they forced into 'yes or no' answers?
- ✔ Have questions and their answers been kept on the same page?
- ✔ Have socio-demographic questions been left until near the end of the interview or questionnaire?
- ✔ Are questions relating to the research topic asked near the beginning of the interview or questionnaire?

- ✔ Have the following been avoided?
  Ambiguous terms in questions or response choices
  Long questions
  Double-barrelled questions
  Very general questions
  Leading questions
  Questions that include negatives
  Questions using technical terms
- ✔ Do respondents have the knowledge required to answer the questions?
- ✔ Is there an appropriate match between questions and response choices?
- ✔ Are the response choices properly balanced?
- ✔ Do any of the questions depend too much on respondents' memory?
  If using a Likert scale approach:
- ✔ Are some items that have to be reverse-scored included, in order to identify response sets?
- ✔ Is there evidence that the items really do relate to the same underlying cluster of attitudes, so that the items can be aggregated?
- ✔ Are the response choices exhaustive and not overlapping?

source is cited. One advantage of using existing questions is that they may have already been piloted and tested for their reliability and validity. Robinson *et al.* (1999), for example, provide an extensive set of survey questions that have been used to measure political attitudes, along with measures of their reliability and validity. A further advantage is that existing questions allow for comparisons with other research. For instance, in psychology it is quite common to use standardized personality and intelligence tests; these permit comparisons between different samples and allow different researchers to make consistent measurements. Existing questions can also be used to investigate whether change has occurred over time by comparing current results with those arrived at in earlier time periods. At the very least, examining

questions used by others may provide ideas about how best to approach your own research questions, even if you eventually decide to modify them.

The use of existing questions is actually a common practice among social researchers. For example, the researchers who designed the scale measuring attitudes towards vegetarians (Box 3.6) used several existing questions devised for measuring other concepts in which they were interested, such as authoritarianism and political conservatism. These other measures had known levels of reliability and validity. Similarly, Walklate (2000: 194) described how in developing a survey instrument for victims of crime, she and her colleagues used 'tried and tested questions taken from pre-existing criminal victimization surveys amended to take account of our own more localized concerns.'

Key Points

- While open questions undoubtedly have advantages in survey research, closed ones are typically preferable. They facilitate the asking of the questions, the recording of answers, and coding. This point applies especially to questionnaires.

- Open questions of the kind used in qualitative interviewing can play a useful role in formulating fixed-choice answers.

- Learning the rules of question-asking will help you avoid some serious problems.

- Question order is very important and some general rules should be followed.

- The visual presentation of closed questions and their general layout are important considerations in designing questionnaires.

- Always put yourself in the position of the respondent when devising questions.

- Ensure that the survey questions generate data appropriate to the research questions.

- A pilot study can identify problems in question formulation.

Relevant Websites

Statistics Canada: General Social Survey 2009 (Victimization Study)

> http://www.statcan.gc.ca/cgi-bin/imdb/
> p2SV.pl?Function=getSurvey&SDDS=4504&la
> ng=en&db=imdb&adm=8&dis=2

Here you can look at the questions used by Statistics Canada to assess criminal victimization in Canada.

Inter-University Consortium for Political and Social Research

> http://www.icpsr.umich.edu/icpsrweb/
> ICPSR/

This international consortium of about 700 academic institutions and research organizations 'provides leadership and training in data access, curation, and methods of analysis for the social science research community.' Click on 'Find & Analyze Data' to access over 500,000 digital files for examples of questions used in a wide variety of social research projects.

Survey Resources Network: Survey Question Bank

http://surveynet.ac.uk/sqb/

This site provides a searchable databank of questions used on social surveys in the UK.

[Websites accessed 17 November 2011]

Questions for Review

OPEN OR CLOSED QUESTIONS?

- Why are closed questions preferred to open ones in survey research?
- What are the limitations of closed questions and how can each limitation be reduced?

TYPES OF QUESTIONS

- What are the main types of question likely to be used in a structured interview or questionnaire?

QUESTION ORDER

- How strong is the evidence that question order can significantly affect answers?

QUESTION LAYOUT

- Why is a vertical format usually preferable to a horizontal format for presenting the answers to closed questions?

VIGNETTE QUESTIONS

- In what circumstances are vignette questions especially appropriate? Make one up to examine an addiction of your choice.

PRE-TESTING QUESTIONS

- Why is it important to pre-test questions?

USING EXISTING QUESTIONS

- Why should researchers consider using questions devised by others?

CHAPTER 6

Structured Observation

CHAPTER OVERVIEW

Structured observation is a relatively under-used method in social research. It entails the direct observation of behaviour, which is analyzed using categories that are devised before the observation begins. This chapter explores:

- the limitations of **survey research** for the study of behaviour;
- different forms of observation in social research;
- the potential of structured observation to contribute to our understanding of social behaviour;
- how to devise an **observation schedule**;
- different strategies for conducting structured observation;
- issues of **reliability** and **validity** in structured observation;
- field studies, in which a researcher intervenes in actual social life and records what happens as a consequence of the intervention;
- ethical issues in the above; and
- some criticisms of structured observation.

Kate has just arrived at a 'meet and greet' reception held by her university's Social Sciences Division as part of Orientation Week. The invitation said that professors and even the Dean would be in attendance. Laid out on a long table in the centre of the room are fruit and vegetable snacks, cheese and crackers, wine, beer, and fruit juices, as well as tea and coffee. Being naturally curious, Kate decides that instead of schmoozing she will take a glass of wine and make her way to a deserted part of the room.

She notices that the people who look middle-aged tend to be talking to other people who look middle-aged. Are they profs? A group has gathered around a middle-aged woman in a business suit who is holding forth about student grades in the social sciences compared to the humanities. Is she the Dean? Kate also notices that in the past ten minutes, the woman who might be the Dean has talked to seven people who appear to be profs, but only two who look like students. The people who look like students seem far more likely to be talking to other students than to profs. Shifting her attention to the table in the centre of the room, Kate notices that the middle-agers who are drinking alcohol have almost all chosen wine rather than beer, and that the women prefer white to red by a factor of two to one. As a test of the latter observation she sets the timer on her watch so she can do a formal count for ten minutes. To her horror, the woman who appears to be the Dean walks all the way across the room and asks her brusquely, 'Are you doing some kind of study?'

Introduction

Structured observation is a technique in which the researcher follows explicitly formulated rules for the observation, categorization, and recording of behaviour. One of its main advantages is its emphasis on the direct observation of behaviour. In survey research, by contrast, behaviour must be inferred from what the respondent reports. As we have noted in previous chapters, such inferences can be problematic, since what people say and what they do are not always the same thing. Structured observation offers a possible solution to that problem.

Although structured observation may appear to be a logical alternative to survey research, it has not attracted a large following and tends to be used only in research settings such as classrooms, courts, and hospitals. One reason for this is that certain types of behaviour—such as criminal activity—are inherently difficult to observe. Another reason is that many social researchers want to generalize their findings, which means selecting large, random samples to provide information that can be extrapolated to some population of interest. Normally it is not feasible to adopt that sort of methodology in a structured observation study.

Problems with survey research

Chapter 4 dealt with several aspects of survey research, including the problems typically associated with it. Box 6.1 summarizes some of the main problems. Also recall that practitioners have developed, with varying degrees of success, ways of dealing with these shortcomings or at least of reducing their impact.

So why not just observe behaviour directly?

An obvious solution to the problems identified in Box 6.1 is not to rely on research instruments such as surveys, but to observe people's behaviour directly. Structured observation (sometimes called 'systematic observation') is one way to do that. (See Box 6.2 for other types of observation research.) Using this method, the researcher formulates explicit rules outlining what behaviours are to be observed and how the observations are to be recorded. Each person in the study is observed for a predetermined period of time following rules set out in a document (similar to a structured **interview schedule**) that is usually called an *observation schedule*. The data collected in this way, like survey data, can then be treated as variables for analysis.

One of the classic schedules for the observation of small-group behaviour was developed by Bales (1951) (see Figure 6.1). Suppose you wanted

---

BOX 6.1   Problems with using survey research to investigate behaviour

- *Problems of meaning.* People may vary in their interpretations of key terms in a question. Does 'watching television' include having it on in the background while you are making dinner?

- *Problems of memory.* Respondents may not remember certain aspects of their behaviour, or they may have false memories of it. For example, people may underestimate the number of alcoholic drinks they consume in a typical week.

- *Social desirability bias.* Perhaps the most important shortcoming of survey research is that respondents will often give answers that they think will reflect well on them; for example, overestimating donations to charity or underreporting traffic tickets.

- *Threatening or embarrassing questions.* These may lead to replies that are not fully truthful. For example, men who recently underwent surgery for prostate cancer may not want to admit to any incontinence.

- *Gap between stated and actual behaviour.* How people say they would behave and how they actually behave is often inconsistent (see Box 3.8). Husbands, for example, traditionally overestimate how much time they devote to housework. Perrucci *et al.* (2000) found two quite different kinds of racial relations on a predominantly white university campus, behaviours they described as 'front stage' and 'back stage.' The 'back stage' behaviour, which showed less than full acceptance of racial minorities, did not become apparent until questionnaires were supplemented by direct observation.

BOX 6.2 | Other types of observation research

- **Participant observation**. This is one of the best-known methods of social science research, especially in sociology and anthropology. It is primarily qualitative and entails the relatively prolonged immersion of the observer in a particular social setting (for example, a group, organization, or community). The main goal is usually to elicit the meanings that the people being observed attribute to their environment and behaviour. Participant observers vary considerably in how much they participate in the social settings in which they locate themselves. (For a more detailed discussion, see Chapter 8.)

- *Non-participant observation*. This term applies to situations in which the observer does not take part in what is going on in the social setting.

Bell's (2007) study of western Canadian separatists is an example of this sort of observation. If the subjects are not aware that they are being observed and analyzed, such research can be called '**unobtrusive observation**.' However, Bell's subjects knew that he was studying them. Non-participant observation may be either structured or unstructured (see below); Bell's approach was unstructured.

- *Unstructured observation*. As its name implies, unstructured observation does not follow formal rules for either making or recording observations. Instead, the observer records the subjects' behaviour in as much detail as possible, and then develops a narrative account (story) of that behaviour. Most participant observation is unstructured.

---

① Helps, rewards, affirms others

② Tension release, jokes, shows satisfaction

③ Agrees, concurs, complies

④ Gives direction

⑤ Gives opinion, evaluation

⑥ Gives orientation, repeats, clarifies

⑦ Asks orientation, for repetition/clarification

⑧ Asks opinions

⑨ Asks for direction, possible ways of action

⑩ Disagrees, withholds help

⑪ Shows tension, withdraws

⑫ Shows antagonism, deflates, defends self

Sum of 13: Balancing task areas (neutral affect)
    6 + 7 Communication
    5 + 8 Evaluation
    4 + 9 Decision

Sum of 13: Balancing socio-emotional reactions
    (−) (+)
    10 + 3 (Dis)agreement
    11 + 2 Tension (reduction)
    12 + 1 (Dis)integration

Adapted from Bales (1951)

FIGURE 6.1 Small group interaction process
Observation schedule for an imaginary study of small-group interaction

to compare leaders and followers in terms of their behaviour: using Bales' observation schedule, it would be possible to examine the frequency with which each group asks questions and answers them, talks or keeps silent, and so forth. Similarly, age and gender differences could be explored in relation to Bales' categories 11 ('Shows tension') and 2 ('Tension release'). Or the same categories could be used to compare 'authoritarian' and 'shared' leadership styles. For example, is there less tension and thus less need for tension relief with an 'authoritarian' leadership style, or with a 'shared' one? A scheme like this could also be used to help leadership trainees improve their leadership skills.

If an observer coded what was happening in the group as a whole every 15 seconds, the coding for a 12-minute period might look something like Figure 6.2. Notice how often a question tends to be followed by an answer and a negative affect by a smoothing positive affect (the way Bales organized his categories, the codes assigned to linked behaviours such as these add up to 13). In many cases, two types of leaders emerge: a task specialist and a socio-emotional leader who is more responsible for group members' feelings.

The observation schedule

Devising a schedule for recording observations is clearly a crucial step in a structured observation project. The considerations are very similar to

7	7	6	6	6	7	6	6	8	5	10	2
5	8	5	12	1	9	9	4	4	5	4	4
10	11	12	12	2	1	1	11	2	8	8	5
5	10	10	2	1	3	2	1	3	6	2	1

FIGURE 6.2   Coding sheet for imaginary study of small group

Note: Each cell represents a 15-second interval and each row is 3 minutes.

those involved in creating a structured interview schedule. For example:

- A clear focus is necessary, meaning that the research problem needs to be clearly stated. The observer must know exactly who is to be observed and which specific behaviours are to be recorded.

- As with the production of a closed question for a structured interview schedule, the categories of behaviour must be both mutually exclusive (not overlapping) and exhaustive (everything must have a category). What if someone knocks on the door to ask about emptying the trash can while the study is underway? Perhaps the best approach is to have a category of behaviour coded 'other' or 'interruption.' Pilot studies help to reveal possible problems associated with a lack of exhaustiveness.

- The classification scheme must be easy to use. Complex systems listing many types of behaviour may be unworkable. Much like interviewers using a structured interview schedule, observers need to be trained, but even a well-trained observer can become flustered or confused if faced with too many options.

- Problems can arise if the observation schedule requires too much interpretation on the part of the observer. For example, in Bales' scheme it can be difficult to distinguish between a category 10, *withholds help*, and a category 11, *withdraws*. If interpretation is needed, clear guidelines and considerable training and experience are required.

Strategies for observing behaviour

There are different ways to observe and record behaviours:

- Recording *incidents* means waiting for something to happen and then recording what follows from it. Essentially, this is what LaPiere (1934, Box 3.8) did when he waited for a Chinese couple to negotiate entry to a hotel or restaurant and then noted whether they were allowed in or not.

- A wide variety of behaviours can be observed and recorded in either short or long periods of time. In research reported in Chapter 2, children in St Helena were videotaped over a two-week period during their morning, lunch, and afternoon breaks. The tapes were then coded using 'the Playground Behaviour Observation Schedule, an instrument for recording the occurrence of 23 behaviours (e.g., games; fantasy play; character imitation; anti-social and pro-social behaviour) and their behaviour groupings (i.e., whether the behaviour was undertaken by an individual, a pair, by 3 to 5 children, or 6 or more). . . . A separate schedule was completed for each 30-second segment' (Charlton *et al.* 1998: 7).

- *Time sampling* is another approach to the observation of behaviour. Since it is usually not possible to observe a situation continuously for extended periods of time, researchers generally sample the times at which they make their observations. The times at which the observations are made are chosen in advance, either systematically or randomly. An example is a study of schools known as the ORACLE (Observational Research and Classroom Learning Evaluation) project (Galton *et al.* 1980). In this research, eight children (four of each gender) and their teacher were observed at regular intervals. A mechanical device made a noise every 25 seconds, signalling the observer to record what the teachers

BOX 6.3 | A study of shoplifting

The young man is looking at CDs, while the older man is inspecting shirts. Which do you think is more likely to shoplift? Why?

Buckle and Farrington (1994) reported a replication of a study of department store shoplifting. Customers were selected at random as they entered the store and were followed by two observers until they left. The observers recorded details such as the cost of items bought; gender, race, and estimated age of the people observed; and shopping behaviour. In the original study of 486 people, 9 people shoplifted; in the replication it was 6 out of 502. Most of the items taken were small and of relatively low monetary value, and most shoplifters purchased some other things before walking out with the stolen goods. In each instance the shoplifters were likely to be male, but they were under 25 years of age in the first study and over 55 in the replication. Does this discrepancy mean that the study should be redone? Are larger sample sizes needed?

or pupils were doing (in accordance with the observation schedule).

Issues of reliability and validity

Compared with interviews and questionnaires, structured observation 'provides (a) more reliable information about events; (b) greater precision regarding their timing, duration, and frequency; (c) greater accuracy in the time ordering of variables; and (d) more accurate and economical reconstruction of large-scale social episodes' (McCall 1984: 277). This is a very strong endorsement, but there are issues of reliability and validity to consider. Some of them are similar to those faced by any researcher seeking to develop measures in social research (especially survey research), while others are specific to structured observation.

RELIABILITY

One thing practitioners of structured observation have been concerned with is *inter-observer consistency*. Essentially, this entails considering how closely two or more observers of the same behaviour agree on how to code it (see Boxes 6.3 and 6.4).

A second consideration is *intra-observer consistency*: the degree of consistency in the application of the observation schedule by a single observer over time. Consistency is difficult to achieve because people tend to behave differently depending on the context. Reliability may also be threatened by factors such as observer fatigue and lapses in attention. However, observers can be trained to get highly reliable results using complex coding schedules. The procedures for assessing intra-observer reliability across all possibilities are broadly similar to those used to assess inter-observer consistency.

VALIDITY

Faulty administration of any measure can obviously affect its validity. However, ensuring **measurement validity**—that is, ensuring that an

BOX 6.4 | Cohen's kappa

Cohen's kappa is a measure of the level of agreement between two people's coding decisions that takes into consideration the possibility that agreement will occur by chance. It can be applied to any coding. Much like Cronbach's alpha (see Chapter 3), the coefficient varies from 0 to 1. The closer it is to 1, the higher the agreement and the better the inter-observer consistency. As a rough rule of thumb, a coefficient over .75 is considered 'very good'; from .6 to .75, 'good'; 'fair' ranges from .4 up to .59.

BOX 6.5 | Reactive effects in social research

Webb *et al.* wrote about 'reactive measurement effect' (1966: 13). It occurs when subjects' awareness that they are participating in research leads to changes in their behaviour that confound the investigator's data. **Response sets**, social desirability bias, and political correctness can all cause **reactive effects**. If a respondent reacts to some characteristic of the interviewer (e.g., gender or ethnicity), that is another example of a reactive effect. Here are a few more:

- *The Hawthorn effect*. The classic studies illustrating this effect were done at the Hawthorne Works (located near Chicago) in the 1920s (see Roethlisberger and Dickson, 1939). A series of **quasi-experiments** showed that each time working conditions improved (e.g., through improved lighting), productivity went up, at least temporarily. But it also went up after working conditions deteriorated! It appeared that performance improved simply because the workers were aware of being observed and analyzed, not because of the experimental manipulation itself: this is known as the 'Hawthorne effect.' A well-known general problem in experimental studies is that some individuals will seek out cues about the aims of the research, and then adjust what they say and do to conform with what they believe to be the purpose of the study. That is a problem, even if such subjects are mistaken about the aims of the research.

- *Role selection*. Webb *et al.* argued that participants may be tempted to adopt a particular kind of role in research. Some people with no strong opinion on a particular item may develop one when asked, in order to appear knowledgeable. Even telling them how important they are to the research can encourage some display of 'expertise.' Other, fairly opinionated individuals may back off a bit, scared by the tape recorder, perhaps, or not wanting to come on too strongly to a stranger.

- *Researcher presence as a change agent*. The simple fact that the researcher is present may change the situation that is being observed. For example, if an observer is sitting in a classroom, that means a chair is being occupied that otherwise might have been empty, which in turn may cause changes in space and privacy for those sitting nearby. When Whyte (1955), in his study of 'Cornerville,' joined one of the neighbourhood's bowling teams, he in effect removed one of his subjects from the team and turned that person into a rival on an opposing team.

- *Trying to help or to be nice to the researcher*. Although it is often assumed that research participants are always passive, this is not true, even in experiments. Some research subjects may try to please the researcher. An old saying holds that if you ask friends to do push-ups, they will ask 'what?' or 'why?' But subjects in an experiment (especially students, the usual pool from which subjects are drawn) will ask 'where?'! In fact, subjects generally try to do what they think they are supposed to do, although a few may deliberately do the opposite. Some will even ask 'Was I good?' at the end of the experiment. Such behaviour can be problematic if it affects the phenomenon being studied.

- Different researchers may elicit different reactions. Some may get the data they want by communicating, often unconsciously, their expectations. This is why experiments are supposed to be *double blind*, so that no one (not even the person administering the experiment) knows certain crucial details, such as which subjects have received the treatment and which have not (*single blind* means that only the subjects are kept in the dark). Here, hiring others to collect the data can help.

Reactive effects are likely to occur in any research in which participants know they are the focus of investigation. Webb *et al.* called for greater use of what they called **unobtrusive measures**: non-reactive methods that leave participants unaware that they are being studied. Records can be checked at hospitals and courts, for instance, removing the reactivity, but for ethical reasons permission must first be obtained, and getting such permission may be difficult or impossible.

Alternatively, the usual tools of social research can be used. A confidentiality guarantee backed up by reminders may help, as may anonymous questionnaires and telephone (rather than in-person) interviews, although these have their own downsides. It also helps to phrase questions so that they are as non-threatening and non-judgmental as possible; for example: 'Many people did not have time to vote in the referendum or could not make up their minds. Did you vote?' If you want to allow more men to admit they fear being out late at night, don't ask how afraid they are. Use a vignette: 'John does not like to walk alone at night in his neighbourhood. There is a lot of crime there, and police officers are rarely if ever seen. Is John almost a copy of you, a lot like you, a bit like you, not at all like you?'

Finally, although it is good to be aware of the shortcomings resulting from reactive effects, remember that no study is perfect, and that an imperfect study can still be an important source of knowledge. Also, maintain the same level of skepticism when the results you encounter please you as when they displease you. For example, research showing that university men are more violent than university women on dates should be held to the same methodological standards as research showing that women are more violent (for example, Katz *et al.* 2002).

indicator is measuring what it is supposed to measure—can be difficult even when the measure is administered properly.

The second point simply means that structured observation demands attention to the same kinds of issues (assessing **face validity**, **concurrent validity**, and so on) that interviews and questionnaires do. The first —error in implementation—relates to two matters in particular:

- Is the observation schedule being administered as directed? This is the equivalent of ensuring that structured interviewers follow instructions exactly. Variability between observers or over time makes the measure unreliable and therefore invalid. Observers should have a thorough understanding of how the observation schedule is to be implemented.

- Do people change their behaviour when they know they are being observed? If they do, that would constitute one of several kinds of 'reactive effect' that can occur in various forms of research (see Box 6.5). If people adjust the way they behave because they know they are being observed (perhaps because they want to be seen in a favourable light by the observer), their behaviour would have to be considered atypical or not authentic. However, as McCall (1984) noted, there is evidence that participants become accustomed to being observed and that researchers tend to become less intrusive the longer they are in the field. However, these effects are likely to persist when the behaviour under observation involves sensitive issues such as sexuality or deviance.

Field experiments as a form of structured observation

A **field experiment** is a study in which a researcher directly intervenes in a natural setting to observe the consequence of that intervention. That's what LaPiere (1934) did when he arranged for a Chinese couple to seek entry to hotels and restaurants in order to observe the effects (although his study was an imperfect experiment because there was no control group of non-Chinese people). In a field experiment—unlike most types of structured observation—participants do not know that they are being studied.

Another famous field experiment was conducted by Rosenhan (1973). He was one of eight researchers who posed as patients and were admitted to mental hospitals in the US. Each pseudo-patient was instructed to claim that he or she was 'hearing voices,' and each was accordingly diagnosed with schizophrenia. As soon as they were admitted, the pseudo-patients were instructed to cease exhibiting any symptoms. Even though they were all 'sane,' it took many of them quite a long time to be released. The length of hospitalization varied between 7 and 52 days, with an average of 19 days. In four of the hospitals, pseudo-patients approached psychiatrists and nurses with a request for release and recorded the nature of the response: 71 per cent of psychiatrists moved on with their heads averted and 88 per cent of nurses did likewise. To Rosenhan this indicated that a mental patient becomes powerless and depersonalized. This study is highly controversial, in part because of its use of *deception*, the ethical implications of which are discussed in Chapter 11. Also, in this sort of research, opportunities to employ an observation schedule are limited because excessive use will blow the observer's cover. The most that can usually be done is limited coding.

Criticisms of structured observation

Some problems with structured observation have already been mentioned in our discussion of its reliability, validity, and generalizability. Other criticisms include the following:

☑ Checklist *for structured observation research*

- ✔ Are the research questions stated clearly?
- ✔ Does the observation schedule indicate precisely the kinds of behaviour to be observed?
- ✔ Have observation categories been designed to minimize the need for observers to interpret what is going on?
- ✔ Has any overlap in the categories of behaviour been eliminated?

- ✔ Are the categories of behaviour exhaustive?
- ✔ Do the different categories of behaviour allow an answer to the research questions?
- ✔ Has a pilot study using the observation schedule been conducted?
- ✔ Are the coding instructions clear?
- ✔ Is it easy to log the behaviour while it is happening?

Methods in Motion

Applications to Canadian Society

Nippard and Murphy (2007) used both structured and unstructured observation techniques to study the establishment of 'social presence'—a social bond resulting from informal interactions that have some emotional content—in an online high school class for students in Newfoundland and Labrador. Earlier research indicated that the creation of social presence, by both teachers and students, is an essential ingredient in creating an effective learning environment.

Two methods of communication were available to both students and teachers: direct messaging (DM), which is text-based, and a voice-based communication tool that operated like a two-way radio. Students largely favoured the DM feature, while the teachers almost exclusively used the audio technology. The researchers found many instances in which the students used DM to create social presence, much as they would through text messaging on their cell phones or communicating in Internet chat communities. Examples included DM comments such as 'Ha Ha ha great job [student name] lol' and 'noooooooo test!!!!!!!!!!' Students used capitalization, acronyms, stretched text, and shortened words to establish mood and tone in their communications: 'LOL' (laugh out loud); 'ROFL' (roll on floor laughing); 'j/k' (just kidding);

'nvm' (never mind); 'Reeally pretty.' In addition to using emoticons such as :-) and :), the students used asterisks and characters in order to convey body language (e.g., **grins**). The teachers used the audio feature to promote social presence, saying things like 'Sorry my love' or 'I love it when people question things alright?' They also varied the tone and volume of their spoken words to foster social presence.

The researchers noted that another way of establishing social presence was through digressions from the course content, instigated by both teachers and students. For example, people would name their favourite hockey team or express their desire to take art classes. One teacher mentioned that he had played in a reggae band in Jamaica.

The authors concluded that if DM is used as a teaching medium, teachers may have to tolerate more informal and relaxed forms of written communications in order to allow for the development of social presence on the part of their students and themselves, and thus to enhance learning. They also suggested that teachers may have to tolerate or even actively encourage digressions from the academic subject of the day in order to promote social presence.

- There is a risk of imposing an inappropriate observation schedule on the setting in question; this risk is especially great in settings about which little is known. This problem is similar to the problem of closed-question answer categories that do not fit the question format. One solution is to precede the structured observation with a period of unstructured observation, so that appropriate variables and categories can be identified in advance.

- Because it concentrates on directly observable behaviour, structured observation in itself cannot get at the *intentions* behind behaviour. When intentions are of interest, observers must impute them. Essentially, the problem is that structured observation cannot tell the observer very much about the *meanings* that people attach to their behaviours—information that according to Weber (1947) is crucial in understanding human thought and action. In a similar vein, contextual factors such as events in the larger world may be given

insufficient attention as possible influences on the observed behaviour.

- There is a tendency for structured observation to generate many small bits of data. As a result it can be difficult to find general themes that illustrate the bigger picture behind the scattered bits of data. This problem is compounded by the fact that observers may not know the meanings the actors attach to their behaviours.

ON THE OTHER HAND . . .

The previous section made it clear that there are limitations to structured observation. However, it's also important to remember that when overt behaviour is the focus of analysis and issues of meaning are less salient, structured observation is almost certainly more accurate and effective than asking people to report their behaviour in a survey. Structured observation may work best when accompanied by another method, especially one that can probe for the reasons behind people's behaviours.

Key Points

- Structured observation is an alternative to survey-based measures of behaviour.
- It involves explicit rules for recording behaviour.
- Structured observation has generally been applied to a narrow range of behaviours, such as that occurring in schools, courts, and hospitals.
- It shares with survey research many common problems concerning reliability, validity, and generalizability.

- Reactive effects must be taken into account, but should not be exaggerated.
- The field experiment is a form of structured observation, but can involve ethical difficulties.
- Problems with structured observation include determining the meaning that people give to their behaviour, and ensuring that the framework for recording the observations is valid.

Relevant Websites

At *Bonkers Institute*, Rosenhan describes the famous field experiment he conducted in mental hospitals.

http://www.bonkersinstitute.org/rosenhan. html

A short video clip of *structured observation* being done on children.

http://www.youtube.com/ watch?v=VgTpAoJEXaE

[Websites accessed 20 July 2011]

Questions for Review

OBSERVING BEHAVIOUR

- What are the chief characteristics of structured observation?
- To what extent is it a better way to gather data than questionnaires or structured interviews?

THE OBSERVATION SCHEDULE

- 'An observation schedule is much like a questionnaire or structured interview except that it was not designed for asking questions.' Discuss.
- With a partner, devise an observation schedule for a setting you are familiar with, such as a popular student hangout. Ask other people you know how well they think the schedule matches what goes on, and if it missed anything.

STRATEGIES FOR OBSERVING BEHAVIOUR

- What are the main ways to record behaviour in structured observation?

ISSUES OF RELIABILITY AND VALIDITY

- How do the considerations of reliability and validity in structured observation mirror those encountered in question-based survey research?
- What are reactive effects and how can they be problematic in structured observation research?

FIELD EXPERIMENTS AS A FORM OF STRUCTURED OBSERVATION

- What are field experiments and what ethical concerns do they pose?

CRITICISMS OF STRUCTURED OBSERVATION

- 'The chief problem with structured observation is that it does not reveal the intentions that lie behind behaviour.' Discuss.

CHAPTER 7

Other Sources of Data

CHAPTER OVERVIEW

This chapter examines sources of data not considered in previous chapters, including personal documents, state records, and data collected by other researchers. We will discuss:

- personal documents in both written and visual form (**diaries**, letters, photographs);
- official government documents;
- official documents from private sources;
- mass media outputs, such as radio or television scripts;
- virtual outputs, such as Internet resources;
- criteria for evaluating each of the above sources;
- **secondary analysis**: the use of data collected by other researchers or government agencies;
- the advantages and disadvantages of secondary analysis;
- the growing recognition of the value of official statistics, following a period in which such statistics were considered seriously flawed; and
- the notion that official statistics are **unobtrusive measures** insofar as research participants are unaware of being studied and therefore behave naturally.

Few of us will ever be the subject of a full-length biography or autobiography, but suppose for a moment that you've decided to write a book about your life. What episodes would you include? Are there some things you've done that you would rather not share with posterity? Are there things you would like to describe in detail—your feelings at various stages of your life, the goals you set for yourself, the people you've met, the places you've visited, your triumphs, your disappointments? Would you seek out any documents for information—old report cards, emails you've saved, videos of yourself, essays you wrote? Would you interview relatives, friends, workmates, former teachers or employers to get their impressions of you or to fill in the gaps in your memory?

Now think of a different scenario. Suppose someone else took on the task of writing your biography, making every effort to be objective and to get as much information as possible. Would that version of your life story differ substantially from the one you would write yourself? Why might the two biographies be different? Would it be possible for a third party to determine which of the two accounts was more accurate or informative? Why? What criteria could be used to make the judgment?

Introduction

This chapter explores a fairly heterogeneous set of data sources: letters, diaries, autobiographies, newspapers, television shows, websites, photographs, and so on. For convenience, we will refer to all these sources as 'documents.' With sources such as these, the search for relevant data can often be highly protracted. Moreover, once these materials have been collected, considerable interpretative skill is required to ascertain their meaning.

In this chapter, a 'document' is any data source that:

- can be 'read' (including visual materials such as photographs); and
- was *not* produced specifically for the purpose of social research.

Documents are important because they are unobtrusive and non-**reactive**. The fact that the subjects don't know they are being studied removes a common threat to the **validity** of the data.

In discussing the different kinds of documents used in social science, Scott (1990) distinguished between personal and official documents and, within the latter group, between private and state documents. These distinctions are used in much of the discussion that follows. Scott also enumerated four criteria for assessing the quality of documents (1990: 6):

- *Authenticity*. Is the evidence genuine and of unquestionable origin?
- *Credibility*. Is the evidence free from error and distortion?
- *Representativeness*. Is the evidence typical of what it is supposed to represent (for example, social life at a particular time and place)? If not, is the extent of its uniqueness known?
- *Meaning*. Is the evidence clear and comprehensible?

These are extremely rigorous criteria, and we will refer to them frequently in the discussion that follows.

Personal documents

DIARIES, LETTERS, AND AUTOBIOGRAPHIES

Diaries and letters are often used by historians, but they have been given less attention by other social researchers (see Box 7.1). Whereas letters are written to communicate with other people, diarists presumably write for themselves. When written for wider consumption, diaries are difficult to distinguish from another kind of personal document: the autobiography. Used with a **life history** or **biographical method**, diaries, letters, and

autobiographies (whether solicited or unsolicited) can be either primary sources of data or adjuncts to other sources such as life story interviews. However, this chapter is primarily concerned with unsolicited documents.

The distinction between biographies and autobiographies can sometimes break down. Walt Disney provides a case in point. The first biography of Disney, written by his daughter, Diane Disney Miller (1956), almost certainly included information from Mr Disney himself. Subsequent biographies were very similar, because of the tight control exercised by the Walt Disney Corporation over the primary materials in the Disney archive (letters, notes of meetings, and so on) out of which the biographies were fashioned. As a consequence, even though Walt Disney never wrote an autobiography in the conventional meaning of the term, he (and, later, his company) clearly controlled what was written about him.

In evaluating personal documents, the *authenticity* criterion is obviously important. Is the purported author of the letter or diary the real author? In the case of autobiographies, the increasing use of 'ghost' writers has made this a standard question. But the same kind of problem can arise with other documents. For example, in the case of Augustus Lamb (Box 7.1), Dickinson (1993: 126–7) noted that there are 'only three letters existing from Augustus himself (which one cannot be certain were written in Augustus's own hand, since the use of amanuenses was not uncommon).' This raises the question of whether Augustus was in fact the author of the letters, especially in the light of his apparent learning difficulties.

Turning to the issue of *credibility*, Scott (1990) observed that there are at least two major concerns with respect to personal documents: their factual accuracy and whether they express the true thoughts and feelings of the writer (see Box 7.2). The case of Augustus Lamb suggests that a definitive, factually accurate account is at the very least problematic. Scott recommended a healthy skepticism regarding the sincerity with which the writer reports his or her feelings. Famous people who are aware that their letters or diaries will be of interest to others may be very careful about how much of themselves they reveal in their writings. Similarly, adolescent diary-keepers are often aware that their parents could 'accidentally' read what they write. In short, what is *not* said can

---

BOX 7.1 | Using historical personal documents: the case of Augustus Lamb

Dickinson (1993) provided an interesting account of the use of historical personal documents in the case of Augustus Lamb (1807–36), the only child of the novelist Lady Caroline Lamb and her husband, the second Viscount Melbourne, who was prime minister of the UK from 1834 to 1841. It is possible that the boy suffered from epilepsy, though he seems to have had other medical problems as well throughout his short life. Dickinson was drawn to him because of her interest in nineteenth-century reactions to non-institutionalized people with mental handicaps. In fact, Dickinson doubted that Augustus was mentally handicapped, and suggested the somewhat milder diagnosis of 'learning difficulties.' At the same time, she found that the people around him had difficulty coming to terms with his conditions, in large part because of the challenge of finding words to describe him that were consistent with his high social status.

The chief sources of data were 'letters from family and friends; letters to, about and (rarely) from Augustus' (1993: 122). Other sources included the record of the post-mortem examination conducted on his remains and extracts from the diary of his resident tutor and physician for the years 1817–21. Despite the many sources she consulted, Dickinson still could not conclude with certainty that she understood definitively what the boy was like.

BOX 7.2 | Letters: a dying art in hard copy

The potential of letters as sources for historical and social research is limited to a certain time period. As Scott (1990) observed, letter writing became common only after the introduction of an official postal service in the mid-nineteenth century. The emergence of the telephone in the twentieth century reduced letter writing, and the growing popularity of email communication is likely to mean that the role of letters in research will continue to decline, since relatively few emails are saved in either electronic or printed form.

On the other hand, there is growing interest in email in its own right. For example, Sharf (1999) reported how, while conducting research into rhetoric about breast cancer, she joined a listserv (a managed list of email addresses around a specific theme) devoted to breast cancer and gradually realized that electronic communications had considerable potential for her research.

wealthy, literate people. Moreover, because boys were more likely to receive an education than girls, the voices of women tended to be underrepresented in documents of that kind. Some researchers also argue that women in the past were less likely than men to have had the self-confidence to write diaries and autobiographies. Therefore such historical documents are likely to be biased in terms of their applicability to the society as a whole.

A further problem is the selective survival of documents like letters. What proportion are damaged, lost, or thrown away? How representative are suicide notes of the thoughts and feelings of all suicide victims? It seems that only a relatively small percentage of suicide victims leave notes, and some of the notes that are written may be destroyed by the victims' relatives, especially if they contain accusations against family members.

Finally, understanding the meaning of the documents we do have is often problematic. Some pages in a letter or diary may be missing or damaged, or the writer may have used abbreviations or codes that are difficult to decipher. Also, as Scott (1990) observed, letter writers tend to leave much unsaid when they take it for granted that the people they are writing to have the same values, assumptions, and information as they do.

Researchers often have to search long and hard for new or surprising materials in diaries. However, this was not the case with the diaries of William Lyon Mackenzie King. When the King diaries were first released to the public in the 1970s, they caused a sensation (see Box 7.3).

be of great importance. A particularly poignant illustration is Sugiman's (2004) suggestion that the reason many Japanese-Canadian women interned during the Second World War did not write down their experiences was to shield their children from that painful episode in their family histories.

Representativeness is clearly a major concern in assessing these materials. Since literacy rates were very low in the past, letters, diaries, and autobiographies were largely the preserve of a small class of

BOX 7.3 The Mackenzie King Diaries

William Lyon Mackenzie King was prime minister of Canada for 21 of the 27 years between 1921 and 1948. He was an avid diarist for most of his life, recording his thoughts and feelings about both personal issues and national and international events. The contents of the diaries suggest that he did not expect them to be made public. They reveal his political views in considerable detail, but also a side of the man that shocked many people when the transcripts were released. King believed strongly in psychic phenomena and spiritualism—he attended séances, consulted mediums, and believed that he was in communication with various deceased persons, including Franklin Delano Roosevelt and his own mother. He also believed that he could commune with his deceased dog Pat. (The practice of spiritualism was quite common when King was a young man in the late nineteenth and early twentieth centuries.) Sensationalism aside, the King diaries are a valuable primary source of information for a significant portion of Canadian and world history.

Nevertheless, the publication of the King diaries does raise ethical questions. Is it a violation of privacy rights to publish or quote from someone's diary, especially if the person is deceased and cannot raise objections? Mackenzie King's diaries are now available online through the National Archives of Canada at http://www.collectionscanada.gc.ca/king/index-e.html [accessed July 4, 2011].

VISUAL OBJECTS

There is a growing interest in the use of visual materials, especially photographs, in social research (see Box 7.4). One of the main reasons why photographs are of interest to social researchers is their potential to reveal important information about families.

As Scott (1990) observed, many family photos are taken as records of ceremonial occasions such as weddings and graduations, or of recurring events such as reunions and holidays. Scott distinguished three types of home photograph: *idealization* (a formal portrait of a wedding party or the family in its finery); *natural portrayal* (an informal snapshot capturing action as it happens, though there may be a contrived component); and *demystification* (depicting the subject in an atypical—often embarrassing—situation). Scott suggested that researchers need to be aware of these different types in order to avoid being deceived by the superficial appearance of images. One must probe beneath the surface:

> There is a great deal that photographs do not tell us about their world. Hirsch [1981: 42] argued, for example, that 'The prim poses and solemn faces which we associate with Victorian photography conceal the reality of child labour, women factory workers, whose long hours often brought about the neglect of their infants, nannies sedating their charges with rum, and mistresses diverting middle class fathers' (Scott 1990: 195).

As Scott argued, this means not only that the photograph must not be taken at face value when used as a research source, but that the viewer must have considerable knowledge of the social context in order to get its full meaning. Sutton (1992) makes a similar point in Box 7.5. In fact, we may wonder whether photographs in such situations can be of any use to a researcher. At the same time, a researcher's interpretations should not be accepted uncritically. For example, the 'prim poses and solemn faces' of Victorian portraits might well 'conceal' a bleak and miserable reality; but is that all? Could they not also conceal moments of human warmth or compassion? Or fun?

A particular problem for the analyst of photographs, according to Scott, is judging *representativeness*. Photos that survive the passage of time—in archives, for example—are very unlikely to be representative for the simple reason that somebody at some time decided they should be preserved. The discussion in Box 7.5 suggests that decisions about which photos to keep may reflect the needs and biases of the people who make those decisions. Another problem relates to the issue of what is *not* photographed, as suggested by Sutton's idea that unhappy events at Disney theme parks may not be photographed at all. Awareness of what is not photographed can reveal the 'mentality' of the person(s) behind the camera. It's clear that the question of representativeness is much more fundamental than the issue of what survives, because it points to how the selective survival of photographs

BOX 7.4 | Photographs in social research

This photo was taken in 1905 as part of a project to catalogue the facial tattoos of different Aboriginal peoples in Canada. How might it be used as data?

Photographs can play a variety of roles in social research. They can be used in qualitative research, as well as in questionnaires and as prompts in connection with an experiment. Three prominent roles photographs can play are the following:

- *As illustrations.* Photographs may be used to illustrate points and thus to enliven what might otherwise be rather dry discussions of findings. This was certainly the case with some classic reports by anthropologists.

- *As data.* Photographs may be data in their own right. When produced for research purposes, they essentially become part of the researcher's field notes. When based on extant photographs, they may become the main source of data about the field in which the researcher is interested, as in the work of Blaikie (2001) and Sutton (1992, see Box 7.5).

- *As prompts.* Photographs may be used as prompts to entice people to talk about what they see in them. Both researcher-created photographs and previously existing ones may be used in this way. Sometimes research participants may volunteer their own photographs. For example, Riches and Dawson (1998) found in their interviews with bereaved parents that many parents showed them pictures of their deceased children, likely the same pictures they had shown to neighbours and friends when they were first grieving their loss.

BOX 7.5 | Photographs of the Magic Kingdom

Sutton (1992) noted a paradox about visitors to Disney theme parks. The Magic Kingdom is supposed to be 'the happiest place on Earth,' and employees ('cast members') are trained to enhance visitors' experiences. Yet it is clear that some people do not enjoy themselves while visiting. Time spent waiting in lines is a particularly common gripe for 'guests' (Bryman 1995). Nonetheless, because people expect their visit to be momentous, they take photographs that support their assumption that Disney theme parks are happy places. When they return home, they 'discard photographs that remind them of unpleasant experiences and keep those that remind them of pleasant experiences' (Sutton 1992: 283). In other words, positive feelings about the experience are a post-visit reconstruction, substantially aided by the photos that are not thrown away. Thus the photographs provide an incomplete, somewhat distorted record.

Similar observations can be made with regard to pictures posted on social media. How common is it to see Facebook photographs of people having unpleasant experiences on their holidays? With social media, the purpose of photo-assisted reconstruction seems to be expanding: now photos may be used not only to create happy memories, but also to present a public image of oneself as a fun-loving, interesting person. Clearly, holiday photos represent more than an objective account of a vacation.

may be part of a reality that family members (or others) deliberately seek to fashion. As in Sutton's example, that manufactured reality itself may then become a focus of interest for the social researcher.

An important challenge for the researcher is recognizing the different ways in which an image may be comprehended. Blaikie (2001) found some fascinating photographs in the local museums of the Northern Isles of Orkney and Shetland taken by local photographers and found in donated family albums. As Blaikie observed, both the images themselves and the ways in which they were presented by the museums suggested that the 'apparently raw "reality" of island culture has already been appropriated and ordered' (2001: 347). For example, the image of a crofter standing by his home can suggest either respectability or poverty. Was the photographer offering a social commentary, depicting a disappearing way of life, or merely recording an image with no subtext? Any or all of these interpretations might be applicable. While acknowledging the diversity of the interpretations that

could be attached to the images he examined, Blaikie argued that they offer a perspective on the emergence of modernity and a sense of the loss of a way of life. Coming to this kind of understanding requires sensitivity to the contextual nature of images and the variety of ways in which they can be interpreted.

Government documents

The state is a source of much information of potential significance for social researchers. It produces a great deal of quantitative statistical information. For example, Bell *et al.* (2007) used government voting records as well as census information to analyze the issue of one-party dominance in Alberta. The state is also the source of a great deal of textual material of potential interest, such as official reports. For instance, in his study of the issues surrounding synthetic bovine growth hormone, Jones (2000) used transcripts of a Canadian senate inquiry on the topic. Briefly, Monsanto, the manufacturer, lost the battle to have the hormone accepted for use; health groups

Methods in Motion

Applications to Canadian Society

The question of 'who marries whom?' has long fascinated social researchers as well as people in general. A popular idea among both groups is that *homogamy* (similarity) may play an important role in our choice of marriage partners. Do we tend to marry people from the same social class as ourselves? Does physical propinquity play a role in our choice of partners? Do we seek out mates who have personalities similar to our own? Hamplová and Le Bourdais (2008) wanted to find out how common it is for married couples to have similar levels of education. Given that cohabitation is becoming increasingly common in Canada, especially in Quebec, they also wanted to know whether cohabiting couples differed from married couples in their levels of educational homogamy, and whether regional differences, in particular differences between Quebec and the rest of Canada, affected those patterns.

The researchers used data from the 2001 Canadian census. The study focused on heterosexual couples in which the woman was from 25 to 34 years of age, and the age difference between the partners did not exceed ten years. The results indicated that couples who marry do tend to have similar levels of education. Cohabiting

couples had lower levels of educational homogamy than married couples, and this finding held for Quebec and for the rest of Canada. These findings supported the 'double-selection hypothesis' that cohabitation serves as a trial stage for prospective marriage partners. The hypothesis assumes that homogamous couples are more likely to find themselves compatible and end up marrying, while heterogamous pairings either split up or remain in a cohabiting relationship. This interpretation also assumes that some people may consider their mates 'good enough to live with, but not good enough to marry' (849).

Hamplová and Le Bourdais suggest that as cohabitation becomes more common in Canada and hence more socially acceptable, two different trends may develop. Cohabitation may come to include more and more people who want a committed relationship, but who choose not to formalize the relationship through marriage. On the other hand, with growing prevalence, cohabitation may become an extension of the dating scene, and increasing numbers of couples may live together with no expectation of developing a long-term relationship or having children.

claimed that it was unnecessary and worse, that it posed a health risk both to cows and to the humans who drink their milk. Abraham (1994) used similar materials in his research on the role of self-interest and values in scientists' evaluations of the safety of medicines, specifically the drug Opren. The author described his sources as 'publicly available transcripts of the testimonies of scientists, including many employed in the manufacture of *Opren*, Parliamentary debates, questions and answers in *Hansard*, and leaflets, letters, consultation papers and other documentation disposed by the [drug regulatory authority]' (Abraham 1994: 720). His research showed inconsistencies in the scientists' testimonies, suggesting that self-interest can play an important role in such situations. He also used his findings to argue that the scientific ethos of 'objectivity' has limited applicability in areas where self-interest may be a factor.

In terms of Scott's (1990) four criteria, such materials can certainly be seen as authentic and as having meaning (in that they are clear and comprehensible to the researcher). However, the credibility criterion requires us to consider whether the documentary source is biased. This is exactly the point of Abraham's (1994) research: such documents can be interesting precisely because of the bias they reveal. Equally, this point suggests that caution is necessary in attempting to treat them as depictions of reality.

Official documents from private sources

Official documents available from 'private sources' vary widely, but a common category is company documents. Companies (and organizations generally) produce many documents, some of which are in the public domain; the latter include annual reports, press releases, advertisements, and public relations material both in printed form and on the Web. Other documents, such as company newsletters, organizational charts, minutes of meetings, memos, correspondence (internal and external), and manuals for new recruits, may not be accessible to the public. This kind of material is often used by organizational ethnographers in their investigations, but the difficulty of gaining access to it means that many other researchers have to rely on public domain documents. Even if the researcher is an insider with the organization, certain private documents may remain inaccessible.

Private documents also need to be evaluated using Scott's four criteria. As with the materials considered in the previous section, documents deriving from private sources such as companies are likely to be authentic and meaningful (in the sense of being clear and comprehensible to the researcher). However, issues of credibility and representativeness are still likely to require scrutiny.

People who write documents generally want to convey a particular point of view. An interesting illustration is provided by a study of career development issues in a major retail company (Forster 1994). Forster analyzed company documentation as well as interviews and a questionnaire. Because he was able to interview many of the authors of the documents, 'both the accuracy of the documents and their authorship could be validated by the individuals who had produced them' (1994: 155). In other words, the authenticity of the documents was confirmed and apparently the credibility as well. However, Forster also said that the documents revealed divergent interpretations of key events and processes:

> One of the clearest themes to emerge was the apparently incompatible interpretations of the same events and processes among the three sub-groups within the company—senior executives, HQ personnel staff, and regional personnel managers. . . . These documents were not produced deliberately to distort or obscure events or processes being described, but their effect was to do precisely this (1994: 160).

The perspectives that members of the different groupings expressed in the documents reflected their positions in the organization. Consequently, although the authors of the documents were able to confirm their authenticity, their contents could not be regarded as 'free from error and distortion,' as Scott put it. In other words, the accounts that documents provide may not be completely objective. They have to be analyzed critically and compared with other sources of data. As Forster's study suggests, the different stances taken by the authors of documents can be used to develop insights into the processes and factors that lie behind their creation.

Issues of representativeness are also important. Did Forster have access to a complete set of documents? It could be that some had been destroyed, or that he was not allowed access to certain sensitive ones. This is not to say that such documents necessarily exist, but a healthy skepticism is often warranted.

Mass media outputs

Newspapers, magazines, television programs, films, and other mass media are potential sources for social scientific analysis. For example, Parnaby's (2003) study of how Toronto tried to deal with its squeegee kids examined 200 newspaper articles that appeared between 1995 and 2000, mostly in the *Toronto Sun*, *The Toronto Star*, and *The Globe and Mail*—three papers that he categorized as 'mass,' 'popular,' and 'quality,' respectively. Similarly, Hier's (2002) study of the ecstasy panic surrounding raves in Toronto looked at hard-copy news stories in all four major Toronto papers (2002). And Hallgrimsdottir *et al.* (2006) looked at how newspapers in Victoria, BC, characterized sex-trade workers in the province.

Films, television shows, and magazines have similar potential for research. For example, when Coté and Allahar (1994) examined magazines aimed at adolescents, they concluded that these 'teenzines' turned adolescents into uncritical consumers and diverted them from protesting against their lack of adult privileges.

Authenticity is sometimes difficult to ascertain in the case of mass media outputs. The authors are not always identified, as in the case of a TV news report, so it is sometimes difficult to know whether a given account was prepared by someone in a position to know all the facts. Credibility is frequently an issue, and as the examples used in this section show, it is often the uncovering of error or distortion that is the objective of the analysis. Representativeness may not be an issue with newspaper or magazine articles, since many publications make a point of maintaining a consistent tone or ideological bent. Finally, some evidence may require considerable awareness of contextual factors; for an example, see Box 7.6.

Virtual outputs and the Internet as objects of analysis

There is a word that this chapter has avoided so far. **Text** has traditionally been used to mean a written document, but in recent years it has been

---

BOX 7.6 | Aberdeen football 'fanzines'

Giulianotti (1997) examined the 'fanzines' devoted to the Aberdeen Football Club, one of several teams he studied in the course of his ethnographic research. He found that the fanzines helped to create a sense of identity among supporters, especially during a period when the sport was in decline. He also found that they 'combine[d] the more traditional sense of [Aberdeen's] cultural differences from the rest of Scotland with the North-East's self-deprecating, often self-defeating humour' (1997: 231). The evidence for this finding consisted of the fanzines' frequent references to sheep in stories and cartoons. Recognizing the significance of the sheep motif required the contextual knowledge that Aberdeen supporters are accused by their rivals' fans of having an interest in sheep that extends beyond their potential as sources of food and wool. Hence the traditional insult directed at the Aberdeen team by fans of their rivals: 'Sheep-shagging bastards . . .' (1997: 220). Supporters of Aberdeen turned this allegation of bestiality on themselves and made it a central part of their identity in their fanzines.

---

applied to an increasingly wide range of phenomena including theme parks, technologies, paintings, and buildings. Contemporary writers and researchers regard such 'texts' as materials that can be interpreted to produce 'readings.'

Websites and web pages are further examples of 'texts' that can be 'read.' The vastness of the Internet and its growing accessibility make it a valuable source of documents for both quantitative and qualitative data analysis. Hier (2000), for example, examined a Toronto-based racial supremacy website and found that it allowed people access to racist ideas in a relatively anonymous way (e.g., without having to subscribe to a hard-copy newsletter). For that reason he feared that it might be more successful in reaching ordinary citizens than non-Internet sources would be.

The use of images on websites can also be quite revealing. Crook and Light (2002) analyzed the photographs in 10 university prospectuses and found that although there were many photos of students apparently studying, the setting was rarely a library carrel or a dorm room. Instead, students were usually shown in 'social' learning situations that allowed them to appear active and engaged, frequently out of doors. The authors argued that those less typical learning contexts were chosen because they are more seductive.

Other forms of Internet-based communication (such as listservs, discussion groups, and chat rooms) have also been used as objects of analysis. For their study of online social support groups, Nettleton *et al.* (2002) examined the interactions between people who use those sorts of virtual communications. In a study of the use of email in two organizations, Brown and Lightfoot (2002) found that online communication is strongly influenced by pre-existing, non-online forms of communication (such as written memos), meaning that earlier ways of working are not fully displaced. In addition, they noted that email is often used to establish who is responsible for certain actions (and who is not).

Websites clearly have huge potential, but it's important to keep Scott's criteria in mind. First, authenticity: anyone can set up a website, so you have no guarantee that a person offering information (such as financial advice) is an authority. Second, credibility: is the information on the site credible, or might it be distorted for some reason? For example, a site that encourages you to buy stock held by its author might exaggerate its value. Third, given the constant flux of the Internet, it's doubtful that one can ever know how representative websites on a certain topic are. As Ho *et al.* (2002) pointed out, new websites are continually appearing, others disappearing, still others being modified. Online searching is like trying to hit a target that is not only moving but also in a constant state of metamorphosis. In a related vein, any one search engine can provide access to only a portion of the web; there is evidence that even the combined use of several search engines gives access

> ### *Practical* Tip ▶ ▶ ▶ ▶
>
> **Referring to websites**
>
> It is becoming the common practice in academic work, when referring to websites, to include the date they were consulted. This convention is closely associated with the fact that websites often disappear and frequently change, so that if subsequent researchers want to check or follow up a web reference, they may find that the site has changed or even disappeared. Citing the date(s) the site was visited can help to relieve anxieties about citing web sources.

to just under half of the sites that exist, and there is no way of knowing if they are a biased sample. Finally, websites are notorious for a kind of 'web-speak' that makes it difficult to comprehend what is being said without some insider knowledge.

Researchers basing their investigations on websites need to recognize these limitations as well as the opportunities available. Scott's suggestions invite consideration of why a website was constructed in the first place. For commercial reasons? Political reasons? In other words, you should be no less skeptical about websites than about any other kind of document. Employing both traditional printed documents and website materials will allow you to cross-validate sources.

Introduction to secondary analysis

Survey research and **structured observation** can be extremely time-consuming and expensive to conduct, and are usually well beyond the

☑ Checklist *for evaluating documents*

Have the following questions been answered?

✔ Who produced the document?

4 Why was the document produced?

✔ Was the person or group who produced the document in a position to write authoritatively about the subject?

✔ Is the material genuine?

4 Did the author have an axe to grind or a particular slant to promote?

4 Is the document typical of its kind? If not, is it possible to establish how atypical it is and in what ways?

4 Is the meaning of the document clear?

4 Can the events or accounts presented in the document be corroborated?

4 Are there different interpretations of the document from the one you offer? If so, what are they? Have you discounted them? If so, why?

means of most students. This is where *secondary analysis* comes in. Large amounts of quantitative data already exist, collected by individual social scientists and by organizations such as government departments and university-affiliated research centres (see Box 7.7). The latter include the Institute for Social Research at York University, the Population Research Laboratory at the University of Alberta, and the Institute of Urban Studies at the University of Winnipeg. Sources such as these make raw statistical data available on topics such as income, fertility, crime, and unemployment, as well as a host of other social and political issues. Using secondary data rather than collecting your own has the additional advantage of sparing an already over-surveyed public yet another round of questions. For this reason, secondary analysis should be considered not just by students but by all social researchers. Indeed, some granting agencies require applicants proposing to collect new data to demonstrate that relevant data are not already available in an archive. On the other hand, the use of official statistics for social research has been controversial; aspects of that debate are addressed later in this chapter.

ADVANTAGES OF SECONDARY ANALYSIS

There are several reasons for considering secondary analysis a serious alternative to collecting new data. Its advantages have been enumerated by Dale *et al.* (1988):

- *Cost and time.* As we noted above, secondary analysis offers good-quality data for a tiny fraction of the cost involved in collecting new data.

- *High-quality data.* Most of the data sets employed for secondary analysis are of extremely high quality. First, the sampling procedures have often been rigorous, in many cases producing samples that are as close to representative as is reasonably possible. Although those responsible for these studies face the same problems of non-response as anyone else, well-established procedures are usually in place for following up non-respondents and thus keeping this problem to a minimum. Second, the samples are often national in scope, or at least cover a wide variety of regions, which is a highly desirable—and costly—feature. Third, many data sets have been generated by highly experienced researchers and, in the case of some of the large data sets, gathered by social research organizations with strong control procedures to check on data quality.

- *Opportunity for longitudinal analysis.* Another valuable feature of secondary analysis is that it can provide an opportunity for longitudinal research. Sometimes, as with the General Social Survey (GSS; see Box 7.8), a panel format (in which the same subjects are examined at different times) is used to chart trends over time. Similarly, because certain interview questions are recycled and asked of different samples each year, shifting opinions or changes in behaviour can be identified. See Box 7.9 for an example of the creative use of longitudinal secondary data.

- *Subgroup analysis.* When samples are large (as in the GSS) there is an opportunity to study subgroups. A sample of 100 people, for

---

BOX 7.7 | Existing data sets

Many important studies have been conducted through secondary analysis of existing data. Among the high-quality data sets used by researchers in Canada are the following:

1. The National Longitudinal Survey of Children and Youth, which contains data on young people up to age 25; used by Brannigan *et al.* (2002) and Kerr (2004).

2. The National Population Health Survey, begun in 1994–5 and planned to continue for 20 years; it examines health and health care in Canada.

3. National Graduates Surveys, which ask graduates about their employment two years after finishing their post-secondary education; used by Walters (2004).

4. The Longitudinal Immigration Data Base (IMDB) developed by Citizenship and Immigration Canada and Statistics Canada to provide data for the study of immigrants' long-term earnings; used by Li (2003).

5. The Canadian National Election surveys, which provide data for all federal elections from 1965 to the present; they are available through the Inter-University Consortium for Political and Social Research; scores of publications have been produced using these surveys; for example, Gidengil *et al.* (2006).

These are only a few of the available data sets.

BOX 7.8 | General Social Survey features

INTRODUCTION

In 1985, Statistics Canada introduced the General Social Survey (GSS), which covers major topics such as the health of Canadians and their levels of social support. The GSS has two principal objectives: first, to gather data regularly on Canadian social trends; and second, to provide information on specific policy issues of current interest. The GSS is a continuing research project that operates on an annual cycle. Each annual survey classifies subjects by age, sex, education, and income. Core content areas, however, cannot be treated adequately every year. Therefore they are usually covered every five years. The content by cycle is as follows:

CYCLE	YEAR	TOPICS
1	1985	Health, Social Support
2	1986	Time Use, Social Mobility, Language
3	1988	Personal Risk, Victim Services
4	1989	Education and Work
5	1990	Family and Friends
6	1991	Health (Various Topics)
7	1992	Time Use, Culture, Sport and Unpaid Activities
8	1993	Personal Risk, Alcohol and Drug Use
9	1994	Education, Work, Transition into Retirement
10	1995	Family Effects of Tobacco Smoke
11	1996	Social Support, Tobacco Use
12	1998	Time Use
13	1999	Victimization, Spousal Violence, Senior Abuse, and Public Perceptions of Alternatives to Imprisonment
14	2000	Access to and Use of Information Communication Technology
15	2001	Family History
16	2002	Social Support and Aging
17	2003	Social Contact with Family, Friends, and Neighbours; Involvement in Formal Organizations; Political Activities and Volunteer Work; Values and Attitudes; Trust in Public Institutions
18	2004	Criminal Victimization
19	2005	Replication of Time-use Study
20	2006	Family Life in Canada
21	2007	Life transitions experienced by Canadians over the age of 45, such as those relating to employment, family composition, social networks and housing
22	2008	Social networks; social and civic participation

COLLECTION METHODS

Telephone interviewing is the major form of data collection for three reasons: low cost, ease of monitoring interviewers, and data quality. The sample size for each cycle of the GSS is approximately 10 000 households, generally one person per household.

AVAILABILITY

GSS findings form the basis of a series of publications that present national and regional summary data, primarily in the form of tables and charts, along with initial analyses and findings. Public-use microdata files, together with supporting documentation, are available for secondary analyses. These files contain individual records, screened to ensure confidentiality.

Source: Statistics Canada (http://www.statcan.gc.ca/dli-ild/data-donnees/ftp/gss-esg-eng.htm), accessed on 18 October 2010.

Walters (2004) was interested in Canadian post-secondary education and whether incomes for graduates with highly specialized technical skills were greater than those for people with liberal arts backgrounds. Pooling national graduate surveys from 1982, 1986, 1990, and 1995, he found that fine arts graduates made the least money after graduation, followed by those in the humanities and the social sciences respectively; engineering, math, and business graduates all made more than people in the first three groups. However, he found that the gap was generally consistent in that the liberal arts were not losing ground to more technical areas. Although his work was not applied research, it probably has some policy implications—for instance, in areas such as repayment of student loans and variable tuition. A study like this one sheds light on an important topic using a relatively large, representative sample that would be beyond the reach of most individual researchers.

example, might include only three people over age 85. No quantitative researcher wants to talk about those three seniors, as in 'only 33 per cent of the aged are in good health': that amounts to one person. With a national sample of 2000, the numbers are increased twentyfold to 60. Even though his number is still small, it will allow a more meaningful estimate of seniors' health. It is impossible to reach such a number in a small study unless the group in question is the specific focus of the research.

Myles and Hou (2004) used a 20 per cent sample of 1996 census data to study 18 000 blacks and similar numbers of South Asian and Chinese respondents in their investigation of the spatial assimilation of new racial minority immigrants in Toronto. They found a clear pattern for blacks and South Asians: when they come to Canada they move into ethnic enclaves, and then as they become more affluent they disperse into the wider society. Chinese immigrants were different, however, buying houses sooner than the other two groups and choosing either to stay in existing Chinese communities or to form new ones. Box 7.10 provides a further example of subgroup analysis.

• *Opportunity for cross-cultural (international) analysis.* It's easy to forget that many findings may not apply to countries other than the ones in which the research was conducted. Cross-cultural research can address that issue. The research on religiosity by Kelley and De Graaf (1997) described in Box 3.3 (p. 52) is an example. The authors described the process as follows:

Ginn and Arber (1995) were interested in the declining labour force participation of married women in the 15 or so years before they reached pensionable age. To explore some of the factors behind this tendency, national surveys for 1988, 1989, and 1990 were pooled to create a sample of more than 11 000 women aged 40 to 64 and living in private households. The authors were especially interested in the relative importance of women's personal characteristics (such as age, health, and social class) and the characteristics of their households (number of children, whether the husband was employed and, if so, his income). One of the most significant variables for women of all mid-life ages was whether their partner was employed; if their partner was not in paid employment, they tended not to be working either. The authors also noted the significance of not having information on certain issues: 'The correlation between partners' non-employment may be due to several factors, which cannot be distinguished with these data; husbands and wives may synchronize their retirement in order to avoid the wife being employed when the husband is at home, or their joint non-employment may reflect the [similar] local labour market conditions faced by couples' (1995: 90).

Data are from the 1991 'Religion' module of the International Social Survey Programme (ISSP) . . . a module containing exactly the same questions, answer categories, and sequencing for all countries surveyed. . . . The samples are all large, representative national samples of adults. The most common procedure is to hold face-to-face interviews . . . followed by a leave-behind self-completion questionnaire containing the ISSP module . . . (1997: 642).

Kelley and De Graaf's results were based on a secondary analysis of data from 15 nations. Opportunities for such cross-cultural analysis appear to be increasing. For example, common core questions may be used in national surveys conducted in several countries. Both the US and Britain have the equivalent of our GSS. This allowed Grabb and Curtis (2004) to create a body of literature comparing the US and Canada, revealing cross-national regional differences where national differences were widely expected.

- *More time for data analysis.* Precisely because data collection is time-consuming, the analysis of the data is often rushed. It might seem that data collection would be the difficult phase and the analysis relatively straightforward, but this is not always the case. Working out what to make of the data requires considerable thought and, often, willingness to learn unfamiliar statistical techniques. While secondary analysis invariably entails a lot of data management—partly to get to know the data and partly to put it into an appropriate form (see later in this chapter)—the analysis phase should not be underestimated. Freedom from the task of collecting fresh data means that data analysis can be better planned and executed.

- *Reanalysis can offer new interpretations.* It's easy to think that once a set of data has been analyzed, the data have in some sense been used up. In fact, data can be analyzed in so many different ways that there is almost always additional insight to be gained from them. For example, a secondary analyst may look at relationships between variables that have not been previously considered, prompting a reconsideration of the data's relevance

(see Box 7.11). Also, new methods of quantitative data analysis, with the potential of allowing different interpretations of the data, are continuously emerging. As awareness of such techniques spreads, and their potential relevance is recognized, researchers can apply them to existing data sets.

- *The wider obligations of the social researcher.* For all types of social research, research participants give up some of their time, usually for no reward. It's not unreasonable that the public should expect the data they provide to be mined to the fullest. Indeed, much social research is chronically under-analyzed because primary researchers tend to focus on only their own research questions, or to lose interest in the existing data when they think of a new set of research questions that requires new data. Making data available for secondary analysis enhances the chances that they will be put to additional use.

LIMITATIONS OF SECONDARY ANALYSIS

The foregoing list of benefits sounds almost too good to be true. But there are some drawbacks to analyzing data gathered by others:

- *Lack of familiarity with the data.* With data collected by others, a period of familiarization is necessary to come to grips with a wide array of variables, the ways in which they were coded, and various aspects of their organization. With large data sets this period can be quite prolonged.

- *Complexity of the data.* Some of the best-known data sets employed for secondary analysis, such as the GSS, are very large both in the numbers of cases and in the numbers of variables they contain. Sometimes the sheer volume of data can present problems, and here too a period of acclimatization may be required. Also, some of the most prominent data sets employed for secondary analysis are *hierarchical*, meaning that the data are collected and presented at the level both of the household and of the individual (and sometimes at other levels as well). Different data may apply to each level. Thus at the household level, data on variables such as the number of cars may be included, while at the individual level, data on income and occupation are found. The secondary analyst must decide which level of analysis to use; if the decision is to analyze individual-level data, the individual-level data must then be extracted from the data set.

- The **ecological fallacy**. This can be a problem if data gathered by region or neighbourhood (such as census data) are used to make statements about *individuals*. The term 'ecological fallacy' comes from the common practice of acquiring data for a geographical area, such as the crime rate in a particular neighbourhood. Coleman and Moynihan (1996) provided an example of this fallacy as it relates to the relationship between ethnicity and crime. They observed that findings showing a higher incidence of crime in neighbourhoods with high concentrations of ethnic minorities had been used to imply that members of such minority groups were more likely than others to commit crimes. However, *individual* data are needed to examine this hypothesis, which may or may not be true. For example, it may not be the members of the minority groups who are responsible for the high levels of offending, but their non-minority neighbours. Similarly, people could be coming from adjoining neighbourhoods to commit crimes in a community they perceive as more vulnerable than their own. Group data cannot evaluate these possibilities. To avoid the ecological fallacy, the unit of analysis (individual, group, neighbourhood, etc.) of the data must be the same as the unit of analysis of the statement or hypothesis. For example, to test the hypothesis that people in group X are more likely to commit crimes than people not in group X, you would need data on *individuals*, not neighbourhoods or regions.

- *No control over data quality.* The point has been made on several occasions that secondary analysis offers researchers the opportunity to examine data of far higher quality than they could collect themselves. However, this point applies mainly to reputable data sets such as the GSS and others. With lesser-known data sets, more caution may be necessary with regard to data quality, although certain fundamental checks on quality are usually undertaken by the archives in which the data are deposited.

- *Absence of key variables.* Because secondary analysis entails the analysis of data collected

---

BOX 7.11 | Secondary analysis and new research questions

Secondary analysis can involve topics that in all likelihood were not envisaged by those responsible for the data collection. In a secondary analysis of data on dietary choices, attitudes, and practices, Beardsworth *et al.* (2002) added gender as a focus that had not been examined in previous analyses. The analysis showed that women were more likely than men to adopt a 'virtuous' pattern of eating, one in keeping with Western ethical and nutritional principles. The article also showed that adherence to these principles had a negative side in that it may be related to feelings of guilt, irregular eating patterns, and concerns about body shape. This work is an example of a profitable extension of prior research using existing data.

---

by others for their own purposes, one or more of the secondary analysts' key variables may not be present, or may be measured differently in different years. Walters (2004) had this problem in the study described in Box 7.9; therefore he had to modify the original data. Similarly, an analyst might want to see if a known relationship between two variables holds even when other variables are taken into account, but find that those other variables are not part of the data set. Considering more than one independent variable at a time is a form of *multivariate analysis*, a topic we will touch on in Chapter 13.

Official statistics

Agencies of the state are often required to keep running records of their activities. For example, in Canada the police compile data that are used to calculate the crime rate, and Statistics Canada collects data that are used to estimate unemployment levels. These are just two sets of statistics that can be subsumed under the general category of 'official statistics.'

The use of official statistics for social research has been controversial for many years. Still, official statistics offer the social researcher certain advantages over some other forms of quantitative data, such as data based on surveys:

- The data are often based on whole populations rather than samples, making it possible to obtain a complete picture of the population in question.

- Since the people who are the source of the data are not being asked questions as part of a research project, the problem of **reactivity** is less pronounced than when data are collected by interview or questionnaire.

- There is a greater prospect of analyzing the data both longitudinally and cross-culturally. Because the data are compiled over many years, it's possible to chart trends over time and perhaps to relate them to broader social changes. As well, official statistics from different nations can be compared for a specific area of activity. Durkheim's ([1897] 1952) famous study of suicide, for example, was the result of a comparative analysis of official statistics from several countries.

However, as we mentioned earlier in this book, official statistics can be very misleading because they record only those individuals who are processed by the agencies responsible for compiling the statistics. Crime and other forms of deviance have been a particular focus of attention and concern among critics of the use of official statistics. Figure 7.1 illustrates some of the factors of concern in connection with crime and the crime rate.

Taking a criminal offence as the starting point (step 1), consider the factors that determine whether it will be included in calculations of the crime rate. For a crime to be included in the crime rate, a victim or a witness has to be aware of it (step 2). Would you notice that $5 was missing from your wallet? A crime has to be recognized as such before it can be reported to the police (step 3). Did you lose that money, or was it stolen? Next, if the event is recognized as a criminal offence, the victim or the witness still must choose to bring it to the notice of the police (step 4). But sometimes that does not happen. Male victims of sexual assault, for instance, rarely report their experiences. So far this means that if a criminal act goes unnoticed, or is noticed but not recognized as criminal, or is noticed and recognized as criminal but is not reported to the police, it does not enter the official statistics.

Even if the crime is reported it may not be counted in the crime statistics, because the police have considerable discretion about whether to proceed officially and may choose to let a suspect off

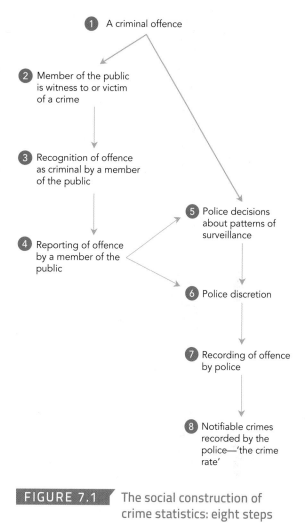

FIGURE 7.1   The social construction of crime statistics: eight steps

with a warning (step 6). The police may be influenced by factors such as the severity of the crime, the perpetrator's previous record, the perpetrator's demeanour or suggestions of contrition, even the victim's demeanour (do argumentative drunks get as much attention as sober victims?), the officer's volume of work at the time, or how close it is to quitting time.

Alternatively, a crime may be committed in a place that is under police surveillance, which itself is a product of decisions about how best to deploy police officers (step 5). However, the crime will not become part of the crime rate if it was not actually witnessed by a police officer. And even with a witness, the police must decide to proceed with prosecution (step 6) in order for the offence to be recorded (step 7) and become a part of the crime rate (step 8).

For these reasons a substantial amount of crime—often referred to as 'the dark figure'—is not included in crime statistics (Silverman *et al.* 2000). Other official statistics suffer from the same problem. As we have noted, suicide statistics almost certainly fail to include many cases. Determining whether a death was intentional can be difficult in the absence of a suicide note. Moreover, those responsible for concluding whether or not a death is a suicide may come under considerable pressure not to record it as such, perhaps because of religious taboos or potential social stigma.

The deficiencies of official statistics extend beyond areas such as crime and suicide. For example, official unemployment statistics may misrepresent the 'real' level of unemployment. People who have given up trying to find work are often missed in the statistics, while those who work in the 'underground or informal economy' (and thus are not actually unemployed) may be included in the unemployment statistics. In addition, the definition of 'unemployment' used by those who compile official statistics may not be exactly the same as the one used by social researchers.

RELIABILITY AND VALIDITY

Issues of **reliability** and validity loom large in official statistics. Reliability is jeopardized when the definitions and policies regarding the phenomenon to be counted vary over time. For example, if a local government decides to devote more police resources to monitoring an activity such as drug use, prostitution, or driving while intoxicated, those rates will almost certainly 'increase.' Moreover, during such crackdowns police officers may be less likely than usual to let perpetrators off with a warning. Zero tolerance programs have the same result. This illustrates how variations over time in official levels of particular activities may not be the result of variations in the incidence of those activities, but may simply reflect variations in the willingness to expend resources on surveillance or to proceed with prosecutions. A final factor that can impair the reliability of crime statistics is 'fiddling' by police officers (see Box 7.12). To the extent that such factors are in play, the reliability of crime statistics is adversely affected and, as a result, validity is impaired.

Problems with official statistics extend to the examination of variables associated with crime. Variations in criminal activity among particular

---

> ### BOX 7.12 | Fiddling the crime figures
>
> In 1998 an article in *The Times* [of London] reported growing evidence that senior police officers frequently massage crime statistics. The author (Leake 1998) argued that many officers deliberately 'lose' crimes in order to make their detection rates look better. As a result, official crime rates are often lower than they should be. The article cited the following methods of reducing the numbers of crimes recorded:
>
> - classifying multiple offences as a single incident;
> - excluding common assaults from the figures for violent crime when the victims are not seriously injured; and
> - excluding drug offences in which suspects were only cautioned.
>
> These methods of reducing the official crime rate adversely affect its reliability and thus its validity as a crime statistic, but they also hurt longitudinal analyses. Variations over time in the propensity to massage the data make meaningful comparisons of different time periods problematic.

ethnic groups or social classes may be a product of many factors, including:

- variations in the likelihood that members of the public will report a crime when the perpetrator is a member of a particular ethnic group or class (are First Nations people more likely than others to be noticed and reported?);
- variations in the degree of police surveillance devoted to different areas, so that areas with high concentrations of certain ethnic or social groups are more likely than others to be the focus of activity (do police spend more time patrolling some neighbourhoods than others?);
- variations in the propensity of police officers to exercise discretion when dealing with particular ethnic groups or social classes; and
- the fact that police may have particular difficulty identifying and investigating certain types of crime for reasons related to ethnicity or class (for example, white-collar crime).

With regard to suicide rates, variations among ethnic groups may in part reflect differences in the ability to pressure officials such as coroners not to treat a death as a suicide. In addition, the fact that different religious groups have different views of suicide affects the probability that a suicide note will be written, and this too affects official statistics.

OFFICIAL STATISTICS: CHANGING ATTITUDES

The 1960s saw a torrent of criticism directed at official statistics, especially those connected with crime. In fact, the belief that official statistics were of dubious value became so entrenched in some quarters that social researchers were often advised to analyze the organizational processes responsible for the deficient data rather than the data themselves. As a consequence, official statistics were consigned to the sidelines of social research; although some work continued, those involved were sensitive to the fact that official statistics were not tailored to their needs.

Not until Bulmer (1980) questioned the relative neglect of official statistics did many researchers begin to reconsider this source of data (Levitas and Guy 1996). For one thing, Bulmer argued that most of the problems identified by the critics had involved statistics relating to crime and deviance. Since these areas are known to be subject to special problems, there was no justification for generalizing those problems to the full range of official statistics. Moreover, the flaws in many of the official statistics on matters other than crime and deviance were probably no worse than the flaws that occur in measurements based on

surveys, if only because of the latter's high non-response rates. Indeed, some official statistics, such as those relating to births, marriages, and deaths, are probably very accurate by almost any set of criteria. All social measurement is prone to error; what is crucial is taking steps to keep the error to a minimum.

Today, the wholesale rejection of official statistics by social researchers has been tempered. Although there is widespread recognition that problems remain with certain forms of official statistics, each type should be evaluated on its own merits.

Official statistics as an unobtrusive measure

One of the most compelling, and most frequently cited, bases for the continued use of official statistics is that they are an *unobtrusive measure* (sometimes called an '**unobtrusive method**') (Lee 2000). An unobtrusive measure removes the observer from the behaviour under study. There are three main types (Webb *et al.* 1966):

1. *Physical traces.* These are the physical 'signs left behind by a group' and include things such as graffiti and trash, or paper trails of financial transactions.

2. *Archive materials.* This category includes documents and other information collected by governmental and non-governmental organizations.

3. *Simple observation.* This refers to 'situations in which the observer has no control over the behaviour . . . in question, and plays an

---

BOX 7.13   Using unobtrusive measures: the case of New York taxi drivers

Following his informal observation of the behaviour of New York taxi drivers ('cabbies'), Camerer (1997) tested two theories about the relationship between the number of hours that drivers work and their average hourly earnings. One theory—the law of supply—predicted that cabbies would want to work more when their average hourly earnings were high (for example, during bad weather or on weekdays when more businesspeople are looking for cabs). The second theory—daily income targeting—suggested that cabbies set an income target for the day and stop work once they reach it; this means that on a good day (when hourly income is higher) they will go home earlier.

Camerer obtained taximeter readings from the New York Taxi and Limousine Commission. The data covered 3000 observations of cabbies' behaviour for 1988, 1990, and 1994. Tips were not recorded, so they had to be estimated. The data provided unequivocal support for the daily income targeting theory. However, further analysis revealed a difference between newer and more experienced drivers: the former behaved very much as the income targeting theory predicted, but the experienced drivers were more variable and in general their behaviour was closer to the pattern predicted by the law of supply theory. Overall, if cabbies were to obey the law of supply, their mean incomes would rise by around 15 per cent.

unobserved, passive, and non-intrusive role in the research situation' (1966: 112).

Official statistics belong in Category 2, as does the example in Box 7.13. Structured observation of the kind covered in Chapter 6 typically does not fall into Category 3, because the observer is usually known to those being observed.

It's important to note that Webb *et al.* were not recommending that unobtrusive methods supplant conventional methods in social research. They were simply advising greater use of 'triangulation,' employing conventional (reactive) and unobtrusive (non-reactive) methods in conjunction with one another. As they put it, unobtrusive methods are 'ways in which the investigator may shore up reactive infirmities of the interview and questionnaire' (1966: 174).

Key Points

- Documents (as the term is used here) provide many different kinds of information and can take the form of personal documents, official documents from state or private sources, and output from the mass media.
- Such materials can be used for both quantitative and qualitative research.
- Documents may be in printed, visual, digital, or any other retrievable format.
- Many researchers believe that almost anything can be 'read' as a text.
- Criteria for evaluating the quality of documents include authenticity, credibility, representativeness, and meaning; some may be more relevant than others, depending on the nature of the document.
- Secondary analyses allow researchers to conduct their inquiries without having to collect new data.

- Very often, secondary analysis focuses on high-quality data sets taken from large, representative samples.
- Secondary analysis presents a few disadvantages, such as the absence of theoretically important variables.
- Official statistics, especially those relating to crime and deviance, can be problematic for secondary analysis because of reliability and validity concerns.
- The problems associated with official data relating to crime and deviance should not be generalized to all official statistics. Many types of official statistics are not prone to the kinds of errors associated with crime and deviance data.
- Official statistics are a form of unobtrusive measure and as such enjoy certain advantages (especially lack of reactivity).

Relevant Websites

The *Diary of William Lyon Mackenzie King* is online at Library and Archives Canada:

http://www.collectionscanada.gc.ca/king/index-e.html

Statistics Canada is a good source of data contained in official government documents:

http://www.statcan.gc.ca/start-debut-eng.html

The *Inter-University Consortium for Political and Social Research* offers a huge number of data sets that can be used in secondary analyses:

http://www.icpsr.umich.edu/icpsrweb/ICPSR/

[Websites accessed 20 July 2011]

Questions for Review

- What types of material may serve as 'documents' in social research?
- Should there be a fifth criterion for assessing documents? If so, what should it be?

PERSONAL DOCUMENTS

- List the different kinds of personal documents and rank them in terms of Scott's four criteria.
- What is the role of personal documents in the life history method?
- What uses can family photographs have in social research?
- Go online and take a look at the King diaries. What themes would you want to analyze if you were to do a study of King's life?

OFFICIAL GOVERNMENT DOCUMENTS

- How might official government documents be biased?
- How do these documents fare in terms of Scott's criteria?

OFFICIAL DOCUMENTS DERIVING FROM PRIVATE SOURCES

- What kinds of documents may be considered private official documents?
- How do these documents fare in terms of Scott's criteria?

MASS MEDIA OUTPUTS

- How might mass media outputs be biased?
- How do they fare in terms of Scott's criteria?

VIRTUAL OUTPUTS

- Can anything be treated as a text? Explain.
- Do Internet documents and other virtual outputs raise special problems in satisfying Scott's criteria? Explain.

OTHER RESEARCHERS' DATA

- What is secondary analysis?
- Outline the main advantages and limitations of secondary analysis.
- Examine recent issues of a periodical such as the *Canadian Journal of Sociology* and locate an article that uses secondary analysis. How closely are the advantages and limitations outlined here reflected in the article?

OFFICIAL STATISTICS

- What reliability and validity issues do official statistics pose?
- What other unobtrusive measures can be used in secondary analysis?

PART III

Part III of this book is concerned with qualitative research. Chapter 8 explores its main features, while Chapter 9 deals with ethnography and participant observation, two important ways of collecting qualitative data. Chapter 10 is concerned with qualitative interviewing and focus groups. The discussion provides the background knowledge needed to understand this sort of research, as well as some practical instructions on how to conduct it.

The Nature of Qualitative Research

CHAPTER OVERVIEW

Qualitative analysis focuses mainly on words and images rather than numbers. Qualitative researchers tend to produce **inductive**, **constructionist**, and **interpretivist** studies, although they do not necessarily subscribe to all three of those perspectives. This chapter will consider:

- the main steps in qualitative research (although they are not followed as closely as the stages of **quantitative** research);

- the relationship between theory and research in qualitative studies;

- the role of **concepts** in qualitative research;

- whether **reliability** and **validity** are appropriate criteria for qualitative researchers, and whether alternative criteria tailored to qualitative research are necessary;

- the main goals of qualitative researchers: seeing through the eyes of research participants; rich description; presentation of context; and concepts and theories as outcomes of the research process;

- some common criticisms of qualitative research; and

- the main contrasts between qualitative and quantitative research.

Imagine that you are a detective trying to solve the murder of a rich heiress who was killed after a long night of partying. You know the date and time of the murder and even have the murder weapon. The problem is that there are several people who were angry with the victim at the time of her death, including two ex-husbands and her current boyfriend's ex-girlfriend—so singling out the perpetrator is going to be a challenge. To complicate matters further, the victim had an extended network of friends, family members, and business partners who could also be considered potential suspects. Imagine as well that you're free to 'gather the facts' of the crime—time of death, physical cause of death, the victim's whereabouts before the murder, etc.—but that none of the people she knew will speak to you for fear of incriminating themselves. Do you think it would be possible to figure out what happened and why without speaking at length with the people who knew the murdered woman? What if they spoke to you, but only on the condition that you made up the questions in advance, and that the answers were limited to 'yes,' 'no,' 'agree,' 'disagree,' and so forth?

Social research has a lot in common with detective work. Qualitative researchers argue that doing social research without having in-depth discussions with the people involved is akin to investigating a murder without talking to anyone who knew the victim—not a complete waste of time, but very limiting.

Introduction

A focus on words and images rather than numbers is not the only distinguishing feature of qualitative research. The following are also significant:

- It usually involves an **inductive** view of the relationship between theory and research: qualitative researchers usually start with field research and then develop theories and concepts from it.

- It is normally *interpretivist* in that it seeks to understand the social world through other people's interpretations of it.

- Qualitative writers are often *constructionist* in that they understand social life to be an outcome of the interactions and negotiations between individuals, rather than a fixed structure to which individuals must conform and adapt.

- Its approach is **naturalistic** in that qualitative researchers try to minimize the disturbance they cause to the social worlds they study.

Although all qualitative research tends to share these features, qualitative researchers can also differ significantly in both approach and subject matter. The following are all varieties of qualitative research:

- **Ethnography/participant observation**. These are two very similar approaches to qualitative data collection. In both cases, the researcher is immersed in a social setting for some time, observing and listening to people in order to gain an appreciation of their culture. It has been employed in such social research classics as Whyte's (1955) study of street corner life in a slum community and Gans's (1962) research on residents in the throes of urban redevelopment.

- *Qualitative interviewing.* This is a very broad term used to refer to in-depth, semi-structured or **unstructured interviewing**. Qualitative researchers conducting ethnographic or participant observation research typically also engage in a substantial amount of qualitative interviewing.

- **Focus groups**. Several people are interviewed together, often using a semi-structured format.

- Language-based approaches such as **discourse** and **conversation analysis**.

- Qualitative analysis of **texts** and documents.

Each of these approaches will be examined in detail in later chapters. Quite often, qualitative studies will use a multi-method approach. For example, in addition to conducting qualitative interviews, an ethnographer may analyze texts and documents as well.

The main steps in qualitative research

The sequence of steps in the qualitative research process is outlined in Figure 8.1. To illustrate those steps, we will use Foster's (1995) study of crime on a housing estate in east London (previously encountered in Box 1.6):

- *Step 1. General research question(s).* It is frequently assumed that communities with public housing and high levels of crime tend to have low levels of social control. But Foster (1995) argued that little is known about how informal social control operates in such communities and what its significance is for crime. Foster formulated a set of general concerns about public housing and criminality, and the possible role of social control among residents.

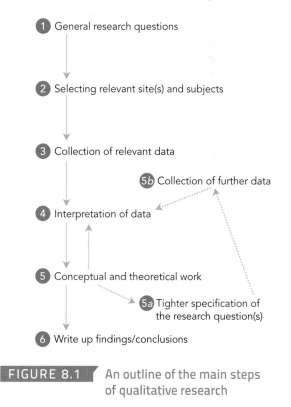

FIGURE 8.1   An outline of the main steps of qualitative research

Methods in Motion

Applications to Canadian Society

What happens to the institution of marriage when the law changes to allow same-sex couples to marry? Since Ontario and British Columbia introduced gay marriage in 2003, a move that was followed by other provinces and was made into national law in 2005, this is no longer a hypothetical question. Green (2010) used qualitative methods to examine three different predictions regarding same-sex marriage. Social conservatives maintain that gay marriage will contribute to further decline in the nuclear family, increase marital infidelity, and lead to less stable marriage bonds. Critical feminists and queer theorists argue that it will produce same-sex marriage institutions with the same problematic characteristics as those found in heterosexual marriage: obligatory monogamy, gender-specific social roles, and conventional expectations for childrearing. Lesbian and gay assimilationists offer a similar prediction, but one that sees conventional marriage norms as largely positive: same-sex marriage will strengthen ties between gay couples, encourage monogamy, and help to stabilize queer families.

Green explored the various positions on gay marriage by conducting 30 semi-structured interviews with people from two Ontario cities who were in same-sex marriages; half the interviewees were lesbians and the other half gay men. Contrary to the social conservative position, many interviewees reported that their relationships with their spouses were strengthened after they exchanged marriage vows, and that they came to value stability and permanence in their relationship more after they were married. One gay man said: 'I think it's just the sense of commitment that you feel. You've made a vow and, it's hard to describe, it definitely feels different than prior to [marriage]' (411). The people studied also mentioned that being married bestowed a sense of legitimacy on their relationship and on themselves as individuals. Extended family members, people at work, and society in general seemed more accepting of them after they were married. One lesbian remarked, 'It was absolutely incredible, overwhelming, just, even my mother. . . . [P]eople we hadn't talked to in years would phone and ask if it was okay to come to the wedding. . . . ' (413).

But contrary to both the critical feminist/queer theory position and the lesbian and gay assimilationist views, married same-sex couples did not completely buy into the conventional heterosexual idea of marriage. For one thing, there was more support for non-monogamous sexual relationships among those interviewed than in the public at large, although the support was more pronounced among the male interviewees. In fact, some couples were monogamous before marriage but not after. Said one gay man, 'So, it sounds kind of backwards to the traditional model, but the fact that we're legally married to each other and permanently committed makes us both feel very secure about [having sexual relations outside of marriage]' (419). Green also found that the people in same-sex marriages claimed to have an egalitarian division of labour regarding household chores and yard work, and relatively equal power relationships within the marriage, although he emphasized that further research was needed to substantiate those claims. Green speculated about the future of same-sex marriage, in particular whether it can retain its unique characteristics if queer institutions continue to gain acceptance by the larger society and in the process lose their oppositional tenor. Like other predictions for social change, those regarding gay marriage can be tested only with the passage of time.

She also noted that some writers suggest high levels of crime are attributable not just to the tenants and the people in the neighbourhood, but to flaws in the design of public housing.

- *Step 2. Selecting relevant site(s) and subjects.* Foster's research was conducted in a community (with the fictitious name 'Riverside') that had both a high level of crime and many of the housing features frequently associated with crime. Relevant research participants, mainly residents of the estate, were identified.

- *Step 3. Collection of data.* Foster described her research as 'ethnographic.' She spent 18 months 'getting involved in as many aspects of life there as possible from attending tenant meetings, the mothers and toddlers' group, and activities for young people, to socializing with some of the residents in the local pub' (1995: 566). She also reported 'extended interviews' with 45 residents of Riverside (and a few more from a contiguous area) and 25 'officials' such as police and housing officers. Foster's account of her research methods suggests that she used two types of data: fieldwork notes based on her ethnographic observation of life in the community, and detailed notes of her interviews.

- *Step 4. Interpretation of data.* One of the key findings to emerge from Foster's data was that, in spite of Riverside's high crime rate, its residents did not perceive crime to be a major problem. For example, she quoted from an interview with an elderly tenant: 'They used to say that they couldn't let [rent] the [apartments] here ... but I mean as far as muggings or anything like that you don't hear of nothing like that even now' (Foster 1995: 568). Residents were more concerned about housing problems than about crime. She also found that 'hidden economy' crimes (such as hiding income from welfare inspectors) was quite common, and that much of the crime in the complex was tolerated by residents. Finally, she observed that, contrary to expectations about places like Riverside, there was clear evidence of informal social control mechanisms (such as shaming) that helped to reduce or prevent crime.

- *Step 5. Conceptual and theoretical work.* No new concepts emerged from Foster's research, but her findings enabled her to tie together some of the elements outlined under step 1. For example, she wrote:

> Crime ... need not be damaging *per se* providing other factors cushion its impact. On Riverside these included support networks in which tenants felt that someone was watching out for their properties and provided links with people to whom they could turn if they were in trouble. Consequently while generalized fears about crime remained prevalent, familiarity and support went some way to reducing the potential for hostile encounters (1995: 580).

- *Step 5 a. Tighter specification of the research question(s)*, and

- *Step 5b. Collection of further data.* Usually the initial collection and interpretation of data lead to a sharpening of the research question(s), which is followed by additional data gathering to address the more specific concerns contained in the revised research

questions. Foster's account does not say whether she collected any additional data after starting to interpret the information she had gathered. When this does occur, however, there can be an interplay between interpretation and theorizing on the one hand, and data collection on the other. For instance, once a particular interpretation has been made, further data may be collected to determine whether the interpretation is valid. This strategy is frequently described as *iterative*. At one point Foster did state that some residents and officials were interviewed two or even three times in the course of her research. This suggests that she may have re-interviewed certain individuals in the light of her developing ideas.

- *Step 6. Writing up findings/conclusions.* In any form of research, an audience has to be convinced of both the credibility and the significance of the interpretations offered. Researchers are more than just conduits for what they see and hear. Foster made clear to her readers that her findings had implications for policies regarding public housing and crime, and for understanding the links between housing, communities, and crime. A key point to emerge from her work, which she emphasized throughout the article and hammered home in her concluding section, was that studying Riverside from the perspective of an insider allowed her to see that residents of communities perceived by outsiders as having a high propensity for crime do not necessarily share that perception.

An important part of qualitative research concerns how the theory and concepts of the study relate to the research data. It is to that issue that our discussion now turns.

Theory and concepts in qualitative research

Most qualitative researchers treat theory as something that emerges out of the collection and analysis of data. As we will see in Chapter 14, practitioners of **grounded theory**—a common approach to the analysis of qualitative data—stress the importance of using data to *develop* theoretical ideas. But some qualitative researchers argue that qualitative data can and should play a role in *testing* theories as well. Silverman (1993) maintains that there is no reason why qualitative research cannot be employed to test theories specified in advance of data collection.

Besides, much qualitative research entails the testing of theories in the iterative process described above. In Figure 8.1, the loop back from step 5a 'tighter specification of the research question(s)' to step 5b 'collection of further data' implies that a theoretical position may emerge in the course of research that spurs the collection of further data to test it. This oscillation between testing emerging theories and collecting data is a defining feature of grounded theory. However, it is presented as a dashed line in Figure 8.1 because it is not always carried out: generation of theory still tends to be preferred over theory testing.

Unlike quantitative researchers, most qualitative researchers do not consider the measurement of concepts to be a central part of their work, although concepts are still very much a part of the landscape. Other differences can be seen in the way concepts are developed and employed. Blumer's (1954) distinction between 'definitive' and 'sensitizing' concepts captures one of those differences. Blumer argued that fine nuances in the form a concept can assume and alternative ways of viewing its manifestations may be lost in the process of operationalization. For that reason, Blumer recommended that social researchers regard their concepts not as 'definitive' but as 'sensitizing'—providing 'a general sense of reference and guidance in approaching empirical instances' (1954: 7). For Blumer, concepts should provide a very general idea of what to look for, allowing the researcher to discover the variety of forms that the phenomenon identified by the concept can take.

But Blumer's distinction is not without problems. It is not clear how useful a very general formulation of a concept can be as a guide to empirical inquiry. If it is too general, it will fail to provide a useful starting point because its guidelines are too broad. If it is too narrow, it is likely to repeat some of the difficulties he identified with 'definitive' concepts. However, his view is important in that it illustrates the value of beginning with a broad definition of a concept and then narrowing it down during the course of data collection (for an example, see Box 8.1).

Reliability and validity in qualitative research

In Chapters 2 and 3 we noted that reliability and validity are important criteria for establishing and assessing the quality of quantitative research. But many qualitative writers argue that these criteria are not directly applicable to their work. For example, since measurement is not a major concern among qualitative researchers, measurement validity seems to have little bearing on their investigations. As was foreshadowed briefly in Chapter 2, qualitative researchers have taken a variety of stances on these issues.

ADAPTING RELIABILITY AND VALIDITY FOR QUALITATIVE RESEARCH

One approach to reliability and validity in qualitative research is to adopt most of the core ideas used in quantitative research without making any special adjustments. This is what Mason (2002a) does using terms such as validity, reliability, and generalizability (external validity) in much the same way that quantitative researchers do; for example: 'If your research is valid, it means you are observing, identifying, or "measuring" what you say you are' (2002a: 39).

Others have used terms similar to those employed in quantitative research but invested them with somewhat different meanings. LeCompte and Goetz (1982), for instance, discussed qualitative uses of the following terms:

- *External reliability*: the degree to which a study can be replicated. This is a difficult criterion to meet in qualitative research since, as LeCompte and Goetz recognized, it is impossible to 'freeze' the social setting and circumstances of an initial study to make it replicable in the usual sense of the term (see Chapter 3). However, they pointed to several strategies that can be used to satisfy the requirements of external reliability. For example, they suggested that a qualitative researcher replicating ethnographic research should adopt a social role similar to the one adopted by the original researcher, in order to increase the chances of seeing and hearing the same things that were observed in the original research.

- *Internal reliability*: whether, when there is more than one observer, members of the research team agree about what they see and hear. This is similar to the notion of *inter-observer consistency* (see Chapter 3).

- *Internal validity*: whether there is a good match between the researchers' observations and the

BOX 8.1 | The emergence of a concept in qualitative research: the case of emotional labour

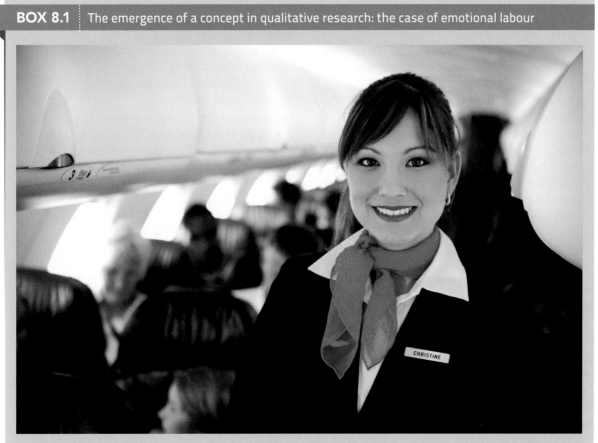

Is this woman's smile spontaneous and sincere, or is she just doing her job?

Hochschild's (1983) concept of emotional labour—labour that 'requires one to induce or suppress feelings in order to sustain the outward countenance that produces the proper state of mind in others' (1983: 7)—has become very influential in the sociology of work and in the developing area of the sociology of emotions. Hochschild gathered data on emotional labour by exploring how airline workers manage to keep smiling at truly obnoxious customers. Somewhat ironically for a mainly qualitative study, Hochschild's initial conceptualization emerged from a **questionnaire** she had created on a related topic. To develop the idea of emotional labour Hochschild gained access to Delta Airlines. In the course of her investigations she:

- watched training sessions for flight attendants and had many conversations with both trainees and experienced attendants;

- interviewed airline personnel such as managers and advertising agents;

- examined Delta advertisements spanning 30 years;

- observed the flight attendant recruitment process at Pan American Airways (because she had not been allowed to do this at Delta); and

- conducted 'open-ended interviews lasting three to five hours each with thirty flight attendants in the San Francisco Bay Area' (1983: 15).

For a contrasting occupational group also involved in emotional labour, she interviewed five debt collectors. Her book explored topics such as the human costs of emotional labour and the issue of gender in relation to it. It's clear that Hochschild's concept of emotional labour began with a somewhat imprecise idea that was gradually developed to address its wider significance. The concept has been picked up by other qualitative researchers in the sociology of work. For example, Leidner (1993) did an ethnographic study of a McDonald's restaurant and an insurance company to investigate how organizations seek to 'routinize' emotional labour.

theoretical ideas they develop. LeCompte and Goetz argued that internal validity tends to be a strength of qualitative research, particularly ethnographic research, because prolonged participation in the social life of a group allows the researcher to ensure a high level of congruence among theories, concepts, and observations.

- *External validity*: the degree to which findings can be generalized across social settings. LeCompte and Goetz argued that, unlike internal validity, external validity is a problem for qualitative researchers because of their tendency to rely on case studies and small samples, which makes it difficult to know whether the findings can be applied to other people or other locations.

ALTERNATIVE CRITERIA FOR EVALUATING QUALITATIVE RESEARCH

Some writers take a different approach, suggesting that qualitative studies should be judged or evaluated according to criteria quite different from those used in quantitative research. Lincoln and Guba (1985) and Guba and Lincoln (1994), for instance, argued that it is necessary to assess the quality of qualitative research in new ways, using new terms. They proposed two primary criteria for assessing a qualitative study: **trustworthiness** and *authenticity*.

Trustworthiness is made up of four criteria, each of which has a parallel in quantitative research:

- *credibility* parallels **internal validity**;
- *transferability* parallels **external validity**;
- *dependability* parallels reliability; and
- *confirmability* parallels objectivity.

Let's consider these terms in more depth.

Credibility   The idea of credibility is tied in with the notion that different people may interpret the social world in different ways. Since there can be several possible accounts of an aspect of social reality, the researcher has to ensure that the interpretations presented in the study ring true to the people observed. The establishment of credibility entails both following proper research procedures *and* submitting the findings to the people studied for confirmation that the account is consistent with the way they see their world. The researcher

is, after all, describing their reality. This technique is referred to as **respondent validation** or **member validation**.

The aim of respondent or member validation is to seek corroboration or criticism of the researcher's observations and interpretations. It can take several different forms:

- Each research participant may be provided with an account of what he or she said to the researcher or others, and a description of the behaviours observed. For example, Bloor (1997) reported that after he carried out observations of ear, nose, and throat (ENT) consultants concerning their assessment of patients, he submitted a report to each consultant on his or her practices and asked for feedback. Bloor said that for his research on therapeutic communities, he conducted taped group discussions with community members to gauge reactions to draft research reports.

- Researchers may show pre-publication versions of their articles, books, etc., to their subjects. Skeggs (1994), for example, asked the young working-class women who were the focus of her ethnographic study to comment on draft chapters (see Box 9.10 for further details).

In each case, the goal is to confirm that the researcher's findings and impressions are congruent with those of the people on whom the research was conducted and, if there are discrepancies, to find out why. However, the idea is not without practical difficulties:

- Respondent validation may lead some research participants to respond defensively and even demand censorship.

- Bloor (1997: 45) observed that research participants who develop relationships of 'fondness and mutual regard' with the researcher may be reluctant to criticize the study.

- It's doubtful that research participants can validate all of a researcher's analysis, since it will be written for social scientists and will therefore include many specialized references concepts, theories, and contextual issues unfamiliar to them. Hobbs (1993), for example, gave some of his scholarly publications to his informants, but they could make little sense of what he had written. Similarly, Skeggs (1994: 86) reported that the 'most common response' among her subjects was 'Can't understand a bloody word it says.'

Transferability   Because qualitative research typically entails in-depth, intensive study of a small number of people, qualitative findings tend to flow out of the context in which the observations are made. As Lincoln and Guba (1985: 316) put it, whether the findings 'hold in some other context, or even in the same context at some other time, is an empirical issue.' Instead of trying to come up with findings that can definitely be applied to other times, places, and people, qualitative researchers are encouraged to produce what Geertz (1973) called **thick description**: rich, detailed accounts of a group's culture or people's experiences. Lincoln and Guba argued that thick description provides others with the database they need in order to assess the possible transferability of findings to other milieus.

Dependability   As a parallel to reliability in quantitative research, Lincoln and Guba proposed that to establish dependability, researchers should adopt an 'auditing' approach. That is, they should keep complete records of all phases of the research process—problem formulation, selection of research participants, fieldwork notes, interview transcripts, data analysis decisions, and so on—and ensure that the records are accessible. Peers would then act as auditors, possibly during the course of the research and certainly at the end, to make sure that proper procedures have been followed and to assess the degree to which the study's interpretations and theoretical inferences can be justified.

Auditing has not, however, become a popular approach to enhancing the dependability of qualitative research. A rare example is a study of behaviour at an American 'swap meet,' where second-hand goods are bought and sold (Belk *et al.* 1988). A team of three researchers collected data over four days through observation, interviews, photography, and video records. The researchers conducted several trustworthiness tests, including respondent validation. In addition, they submitted their draft manuscript and data set to three peers whose task it 'was to criticize the project for lack of sufficient data for drawing its conclusions, if they saw such a void' (1988: 456). The same study highlighted some problems with this approach, among them the fact that, because qualitative research generates extremely large data sets, validation is very demanding for the auditors. That may be the major reason why auditing has not been widely used.

Confirmability   Objectivity is a difficult if not impossible standard to live up to in social research. For that reason, the confirmability criterion is designed to ensure that the researcher has acted in good faith. In other words, it should be apparent that personal values or theoretical inclinations did not blatantly and unduly sway either the conduct of the research or the findings derived from it. Lincoln and Guba suggest that establishing confirmability should be one of the objectives of auditors.

OVERVIEW OF THE CRITERIA ISSUE

There is a general recognition that quantitative researchers' notions of reliability and validity cannot be applied to qualitative research without some modification, although critics vary in their views on how much modification is necessary. To bolster their accounts, most qualitative researchers use some of the strategies advocated by Lincoln and Guba, such as thick description and respondent validation exercises.

Meanwhile, traditional quantitative research criteria have made something of a comeback. One reason is that a researcher who rejects the notion of reliability or validity risks being seen as lacking scientific rigour—not a desirable impression to create, especially when research funds are at stake. Consequently, there has been some increased concern with these issues. Armstrong *et al.* (1997), for example, reported the results of an 'inter-rater reliability' exercise in which six experienced researchers analyzed a transcript of a focus group session conducted with sufferers of cystic fibrosis (CF). These 'raters' were asked to find prominent themes in the transcript—one of the main ways of analyzing qualitative data. The six tended to identify similar themes, but they differed in the way they 'packaged' them. For example, all six identified 'visibility' as a theme: CF sufferers feel disadvantaged relative to other disabled groups because the public are more inclined to be sympathetic towards those whose disabilities are more visible. However, two analysts linked this theme with stigma and one with managing invisibility. In any case, this study illustrates the concern that issues such as reliability raise among qualitative researchers. A similar exercise is described in Box 8.2.

The main goals of qualitative researchers

SEEING THROUGH THE EYES OF THE PEOPLE BEING STUDIED

Many qualitative researchers try to view the social world through the eyes of the people they study. Hiller and DiLuzio (2004) went so far as to analyze the interview experience itself from the perspective of the interviewees. Studying internal migrants in Canada, they examined what interviewees got out of the process and found, for example, that they liked the fact that it allowed them to meet people who valued them and validated their life experiences.

Qualitative researchers maintain that '(1) . . . face-to-face interaction is the fullest condition of participating in the mind of another human being, and (2) . . . you must participate in the mind of another human being (in sociological terms, "take the role of the other") to acquire social knowledge' (Lofland and Lofland 1995: 16). This tendency reveals itself in frequent references to *empathy*. Here are some examples:

- Armstrong carried out research on British soccer hooliganism through participant observation. He described his work as rooted in

Verstehende sociology—trying to think oneself into the situations of the people one is interested in . . . in this case the 'hooligan.' This approach involves recognizing social phenomena as due not to any single or simply identifiable cause and attempting to make sense from the [multi-causal] social actors' viewpoint (Armstrong 1993: 5–6).

- For their research on teenaged girls and violence, Burman *et al.* (2001: 447) 'sought to ground the study in young women's experiences of violence, hearing their accounts, and privileging their subjective views.'

The goal of seeing through the eyes of the people under study is often accompanied by the closely related goal of probing beneath surface appearances. After all, by taking the position of those under study, researchers may be able to see things in a way that an outsider with little direct contact would not. This insight is revealed in:

- Foster's (1995) research on crime in a housing complex in east London (discussed earlier in this chapter), which found that the residents do not see crime as a serious problem where they live;
- Taylor's (1993: 8) study of female intravenous drug users, which showed that they are not 'pathetic, inadequate individuals' but 'rational, active people making decisions based on the contingencies of both their drug-using careers and their roles and status in society';
- Armstrong's (1993: 11) finding that, contrary to the popular view, hooligans are not a highly organized group led by clearly identifiable ringleaders;
- Atkinson's (2004) ethnography of tattooing, which rejected the view that it is a form of pathological self-injury and instead interpreted it as a pro-social and regulated act of communication; and
- Hallgrimsdottir *et al.*'s (2006) study of sex-trade workers, which revealed that, contrary to media depictions, prostitutes often see their occupation in a mundane light (for example, as simply a way to make a living).

On the other hand, sometimes qualitative research confirms popular notions of a particular group. For example, Bell (2007) found that

---

BOX 8.2 | Reliability in qualitative research

Gladney *et al.* (2003) reported an exercise in which two multidisciplinary teams of researchers were asked to analyze qualitative interviews conducted with 80 Texas school students on three topics: violence on television, the reasons for violence among some young people, and the reasons why some young people are not violent. One group of raters read transcripts of the interviews; the other group listened to the audiotaped recordings. Despite the different media, the two groups were remarkably consistent in the themes they identified. For example, in response to the question 'Why are some young people violent?', Group One listed: family/parental influence; peer influence; social influence; media influence; and coping. Group Two came up with: the way the young people were raised; media influence; appearance; anger, revenge, protection; and peer influence. This exercise shows how a concern for reliability can be found in qualitative research.

media depictions of the western Canadian separatist movement as decidedly right-wing were essentially correct.

The empathetic effort to see the world through the eyes of their subjects can present researchers with practical problems. For example: how far should one go to develop empathy? What if the research subject's experience includes participation in illegal or dangerous activities? There is also the risk that the researcher will be able to see through the eyes of some of the people in a particular social scene but not those of others, such as people of another gender or culture. These and other practical difficulties will be addressed in later chapters.

Description and the emphasis on context   Qualitative researchers are much more inclined than their quantitative colleagues to include descriptive detail when reporting their research. However, they are not exclusively concerned with description. They also try to explain. For example, Skeggs (1997) tried to answer this question: 'Why do women who are clearly not just victims of some ideological conspiracy, consent to a system of class and gender oppression which appears to offer few rewards and little benefit?' (1997: 22).

Nonetheless, many qualitative studies do provide a detailed account of what goes on in the setting under investigation. On the surface, some of this detail may appear irrelevant; indeed, there is a risk of becoming too embroiled in descriptive detail. Lofland and Lofland (1995: 164–5), for example, warned against what they called 'descriptive excess' in qualitative research, whereby the amount of detail overwhelms or inhibits the analysis of the data.

One of the main reasons for providing descriptive detail is that it permits a contextual understanding of social behaviour. This implies that we cannot understand the behaviour of members of a social group without some knowledge of the specific environment in which they operate. Behaviour that appears odd or irrational may make perfect sense when understood in the context within which it takes place. The emphasis on context in qualitative research goes back to the classic studies in social anthropology, many of which demonstrated how seemingly illogical practices (e.g., a magical ritual that accompanies the sowing of seeds) make sense when they are understood as part of the society's belief system. The provision of descriptive detail is also a manifestation of qualitative researchers' desire for naturalism: that is, their belief that researchers should study the social world as it actually is, rather than relying on contrived settings such as formal interviews or experiments.

EMPHASIS ON PROCESS

Qualitative research tends to view social life in terms of processes. This tendency reveals itself in a number of ways, but the main one is the qualitative researcher's concern with showing how events and patterns unfold over time. Qualitative evidence often conveys a strong sense of change and flux. As Pettigrew (1997: 338) put it, process is 'a sequence of individual and collective events, actions, and activities unfolding over time in context.' Qualitative research using participant observation is particularly well suited to the study of process. Ethnographers are typically immersed in a social setting for a long time—in many cases, for years. Consequently, they are able to observe how events develop over time and how the different elements of a social system (such as values, beliefs, and behaviour) interconnect. Tracing interdependent streams of actions and events allows the researcher to present social life as a process (see Box 8.3).

A sense of process can also be developed through semi-structured and unstructured

---

BOX 8.3 | Process in youth shelters

Karabanow (2002) described his experiences in two Canadian shelters for homeless and runaway youth. As a participant observer, he was able to monitor routine activities there and describe the shelter culture. In addition he carried out in-depth interviews with three levels of shelter workers and used agency archival materials. The dramatic transformations in the shelters' external environment and internal operations that took place over a period of years provided the basis for an analysis of the evolution of their organizational processes. This example shows the development of a sense of process in at least two ways. First, observation of the shelters over time made it possible to bring out developments and interconnections between events. Second, connecting these events with historical and other data made it possible to show how the shelters were affected by the larger society.

interviewing in which participants are asked to reflect on the activities leading up to or following an event. McKee and Bell (1985: 388), for example, used a 'largely unstructured, conversational interview style' with 45 couples in which all the husbands were unemployed, to show how both husbands and wives adapted to the situation. The various accommodations they made were not an immediate effect of unemployment but were gradual and incremental responses over time. The **life history** approach is another form of qualitative research that can be used to show process. One of the best-known studies of this kind is Lewis's (1961) classic study of a poor Mexican family, in which he conducted extended taped interviews with family members to reconstruct their life histories.

FLEXIBILITY AND LIMITED STRUCTURE

Many qualitative researchers are disdainful of approaches that impose a predetermined set of assumptions on the social world. This position is closely related to the preference for seeing the world through the eyes of the people under study. After all, a structured method of data collection must be planned ahead of time on the basis of the *researcher's* prior ruminations and expectations regarding the nature of a social reality that he or she may never have encountered before. This structure limits the degree to which the researcher can genuinely adopt the world view of those being studied, and can lead to serious misunderstandings. Keeping structure to a minimum is supposed to enhance the likelihood that the research will reveal the perspectives of the people being observed. This approach allows aspects of people's social world that are particularly important to them to come to light—aspects that might never even cross the mind of a researcher using a more structured method. For that reason, qualitative research tries to avoid limiting areas of inquiry, and the research questions it asks tend be fairly general (see step 1 in Figure 8.1).

Ethnography, with its emphasis on participant observation, is particularly well suited to an unstructured approach. It allows researchers to immerse themselves in a social setting with a general research idea in mind and then gradually, through observation, narrow it down to a more specific topic.

Another advantage of the unstructured nature of most qualitative inquiry is that it offers the prospect of flexibility. The researcher can change the direction of the investigation much more easily than in quantitative research, which tends to have a built-in momentum once the data collection is underway. (If you send out hundreds of postal questionnaires and realize only after getting some back that you left out an important issue, it's not easy to rectify the situation.) **Structured interviewing** and **structured observation** can offer some flexibility, but it will be limited by the requirement that interviews be as comparable as possible. O'Reilly (2000) wrote that the focus of her research on British people on the Costa del Sol (in Spain) shifted in two ways over the duration of her participant observation: from the elderly to expatriates of all ages; and from permanent residents to less-permanent populations such as tourists. She made these changes because the elderly and permanent migrants turned out to be less distinctive than she had supposed. See Box 8.4 for a further illustration of how the unstructured data collection style of qualitative research can suggest alternative avenues of inquiry or ways of thinking.

Critiques of qualitative research

Just as quantitative research has been criticized by people in the qualitative tradition, the latter has been taken to task by quantitative social scientists. Some of the more common criticisms of qualitative research are discussed below.

TOO SUBJECTIVE

Quantitative researchers sometimes criticize qualitative research for being too impressionistic and subjective. By this they usually mean that qualitative findings depend too much on the researchers' values and opinions about what is significant. A related problem stems from the close personal relationships that many researchers strike up with the people they study, which can lead to bias. Also, because qualitative researchers often begin in a relatively open-ended way and then gradually narrow down their research questions or problems, they may not explain clearly why they came to focus on one area rather than another. By contrast, quantitative researchers typically discuss problem formulation explicitly, usually justifying the topic of their research in terms of gaps in the existing literature or potential contributions to key theoretical ideas.

BOX 8.4 | Emerging concepts

Along with some colleagues, Bryman undertook an evaluation of new staff appraisal schemes in four universities. The research entailed collecting both quantitative and qualitative data, the former derived from large numbers of interviews with appraisers, appraisees, senior managers, and many others. In the course of conducting the interviews and analyzing the data, the team became increasingly aware that many of those interviewed expressed a certain cynicism about the appraisal project. For some it was a belief that nothing of any significance happens as a result of an appraisal meeting; for others it was a feeling that the appraisal process itself is not very meaningful. As one of the interviewees said: 'It's like going through the motions of it [appraisal]. It's just get it over with and signed and dated and filed and that's the end of it' (Bryman *et al.* 1994: 180).

On the basis of these findings the researchers suggested that the attitudes towards appraisal and the behaviour of those involved in it were characterized by 'procedural compliance'—a term that the researcher coined and defined as 'a response to an organizational innovation in which the technical requirements of the innovation . . . are broadly adhered to, but where there are substantial reservations about its efficacy and only partial commitment to it' (1994: 178).

DIFFICULT TO REPLICATE

Some quantitative researchers argue that the problem of subjectivity is made worse by the difficulty of replicating a qualitative study, even though replication is uncommon in the social sciences, regardless of the research methods used. Because it is unstructured and relies on the researcher's ingenuity, qualitative work is almost impossible to replicate. What is observed and heard often depends on the researcher, as does the choice of what to concentrate on; different researchers may choose to observe different things and as a result they may come up with different findings. Also, the behaviour of the people being observed or interviewed is likely to be affected by the characteristics of the researcher (personality, age, gender, and so on). The difficulties that qualitative social scientists experience when they revisit ground previously covered by another researcher (often referred to as a 'restudy') do not inspire confidence in the replicability of qualitative research (Bryman 1994).

PROBLEMS OF GENERALIZATION

It is often suggested that the scope of qualitative findings is restricted. Because research based on participant observation or unstructured interviews typically involves only a small number of individuals in a single organization or locality, many argue that it is impossible to know if the findings can be applied to other people or other settings. Can just one or two cases be representative of some larger population? Can Karabanow's (2002) study of two Canadian shelters for homeless youth (Box 8.3) be considered generalizable to all youth shelters in the country? In the case of research based on interviews rather than participation, are those who were interviewed representative of some larger population? Do the interview findings from sex-trade workers in Victoria (Hallgrimsdottir *et al.* 2006), for example, apply to prostitutes in Toronto? Are the prostitutes from three western provinces in the Nixon *et al.* (2002) study representative of their counterparts in other regions of the country?

The answer to these questions in most qualitative research studies is 'probably not.' But a case study is not a sample of one drawn from a known population. The people interviewed in qualitative research are not necessarily meant to be representative of some larger group. In fact, with some social groups, such as prostitutes, it may be impossible to enumerate the population in any precise manner, which makes the selection of a representative sample impracticable.

In most cases it is not the purpose of qualitative research to produce generalizable knowledge. Such research normally stands on its own, providing in-depth analysis of a person or a small group of people—something that quantitative research rarely does. Also, qualitative research can contribute to the creation of generalizable knowledge insofar as it produces theories or concepts that can be assessed using other research methods. For instance, Williams (2000) argued that qualitative researchers are often in a position to produce generalizations regarding the people or events studied (a group of drug users or soccer hooligans, a strike) that 'can be seen to be instances of a broader set of recognisable features' (2000: 215). In addition, Williams argued that a researcher studying the hooligans who follow a certain soccer club will often draw comparisons with the findings of other researchers who have studied comparable groups. He or she might also draw comparisons with followers of other professional sports teams, or with violent groups in contexts other than sport. However, such generalizations will always be limited and somewhat more tentative than the statistical generalizations produced by quantitative research.

LACK OF TRANSPARENCY

Another frequent criticism of qualitative research is that it is less than transparent about what the researchers actually did and how they arrived at their conclusions. For example, qualitative research reports are sometimes unclear about how the subjects were chosen for observation or interview. This deficiency contrasts sharply with the tendency of quantitative researchers to include detailed accounts of sampling procedures in their reports.

Is it always like this?

There can be departures from the qualitative research practices described above. One of the main differences is that qualitative research is sometimes much more focused than is implied by the idea that the researcher begins with general questions and then narrows them down as theories and concepts begin to emerge in the course of data collection. There is no reason why qualitative research cannot be used to investigate a specific research problem. For example, Hammersley *et al.* wanted to evaluate the claim that 'external examinations lead to lecturing and note-taking on the part of secondary-school teachers and instrumental attitudes among their pupils' (1985:

58). They did so by comparing two schools that varied considerably in the emphasis they placed on examinations.

Similarly, not all qualitative research is as unstructured and informal as the standard model suggests. As we will see in Chapter 16, techniques such as conversation analysis follow a highly codified method. Moreover, the growing use of computer-assisted qualitative data analysis software is leading to greater transparency in the procedures used for data analysis, which may in turn lead to greater standardization.

Some contrasts between quantitative and qualitative research

Several writers have used tables to contrast quantitative and qualitative research (for example, Hammersley 1992b). Table 8.1 highlights the main differences. As with any summary of a large body of material, the table outlines general tendencies. The full picture is more nuanced: there are exceptions to these general points, as we will see in Chapter 15.

- *Numbers vs. Words*. Quantitative researchers set great store by precise, numerical measurements of social phenomena. They use those measurements to calculate statistics to understand social life, whereas qualitative researchers use mainly words in their analyses of society.

- *Point of view of researcher vs. Points of view of participants*. In quantitative research, investigators are in the driver's seat; their concerns structure the investigation. In qualitative research, the

---

TABLE 8.1 Common contrasts between quantitative and qualitative research

QUANTITATIVE	QUALITATIVE
Numbers	Words
Point of view of researcher	Points of view of research participants
Researcher distant	Researcher close
Theory testing	Theory development
Structured	Unstructured
Generalizable knowledge	Contextual understanding
Hard, reliable data	Rich, deep data
Macro	Micro
Behaviour	Meaning
Artificial settings	Natural settings

investigation is structured by the people being investigated: their perspective—what they see as important—provides the point of orientation.

- *Researcher is distant vs. Researcher is close.* In quantitative research, researchers tend to be less involved with their subjects and in some cases, as in research based on mailed questionnaires, they may have no direct contact at all. Quantitative researchers often consider this distance desirable, because they want to be as objective as possible and feel their objectivity would be compromised if they were to become too involved with the people they study. By contrast, qualitative researchers seek involvement with the people they study, so that they can see the world through their eyes.

- *Theory and concepts tested in research vs. Theory and concepts developed from data.* Before data collection begins, quantitative researchers typically have a theory in mind that they want to test. In qualitative research, concepts and theories develop as the data are collected.

- *Structured vs. Unstructured.* Quantitative research is typically highly structured to maximize validity and reliability; in qualitative research, the approach is less structured in order to allow the researcher to get a sense of the meanings people derive from their everyday lives, and to permit the development and elaboration of concepts and theories as the data are collected.

- *Generalizable knowledge vs. Contextual understanding.* Whereas quantitative researchers want their findings to be applicable to some larger population, qualitative researchers focus on understanding the behaviour, values, and beliefs of the people in their study. Qualitative findings usually develop out of the context these people find themselves in; hence the insights gained may or may not apply to other people.

- *Hard, reliable data vs. Rich, deep data.* Quantitative researchers often describe their data as 'hard'—robust and unambiguous—because their measurement techniques are so precise. Qualitative researchers, by contrast, claim that their contextual approach and often-prolonged involvement in a setting mean that the information they collect is rich, nuanced, and very detailed.

- *Macro vs. Micro.* Quantitative researchers often seek to uncover large-scale social trends and connections between variables; as we noted above, their research is generally designed to be applicable to large populations. Qualitative researchers are usually concerned with in-depth analysis of small-scale aspects of social reality, such as personal interaction.

- *Behaviour vs. Meaning.* It is sometimes suggested that quantitative researchers focus more on people's behaviour, and qualitative researchers more on the meaning of that behaviour for the actor.

- *Artificial settings vs. Natural settings.* Whereas quantitative research is conducted in a contrived context, such as an experiment or a formal interview setting, qualitative researchers investigate people in their natural environments, such as social gatherings or workplaces.

Key Points

- Qualitative research does not lend itself to a clear set of linear steps. As a research strategy it tends to be more open-ended than is typically the case with quantitative research.

- In qualitative research, theories and concepts are outcomes of the research process.

- There is considerable unease about the direct application of reliability and validity criteria to qualitative research. Some writers prefer alternative criteria.

- Lincoln and Guba (1985; 1994) propose two key criteria to evaluate a qualitative study: trustworthiness and authenticity. Trustworthiness requires four conditions: credibility, transferability, dependability, and confirmability.

- Most qualitative researchers try to see the social world through the eyes of their research participants.
- Like all approaches to social research, qualitative methods have both strengths and weaknesses. Their major strengths include the development of empathetic understanding, rich description of context, and emphasis on process. Weaknesses include excessive reliance on the researcher's values and opinions when making research decisions, difficulties in replication, problems of generalization, and lack of transparency.

Relevant Websites

The *International Institute for Qualitative Methodology*, based at the University of Alberta in Edmonton, sponsors conferences and research training programs involving qualitative research methods. It also publishes the *International Journal of Qualitative Methods*, which is available free online:

http://www.uofaweb.ualberta.ca/iiqm/

Examples of qualitative studies can be found in the journal *Qualitative Research* and in the *Qualitative Sociology Review* (You may have to access these journals through your institution's library server):

http://qrj.sagepub.com/

http://www.qualitativesociologyreview.org/ENG/index_eng.php

[Websites accessed 20 July 2011]

Questions for Review

THE MAIN STEPS IN QUALITATIVE RESEARCH

- Do research questions have the same characteristics and significance in qualitative research as in quantitative research? Explain.

THEORY AND CONCEPTS IN QUALITATIVE RESEARCH

- Is the approach to theory in qualitative research primarily inductive or deductive? What do the terms 'inductive' and 'deductive' mean?
- What is the difference between 'definitive' and 'sensitizing' concepts?

RELIABILITY AND VALIDITY IN QUALITATIVE RESEARCH

- How have some writers adapted the notions of reliability and validity to qualitative research?
- Why have some writers sought alternative criteria for evaluating qualitative research?
- How far do Lincoln and Guba's criteria stray from quantitative criteria?
- What is respondent validation?

THE MAIN GOALS OF QUALITATIVE RESEARCHERS

- How do the main goals of qualitative researchers differ from those of quantitative researchers?

THE CRITIQUE OF QUALITATIVE RESEARCH

- What are some of the main criticisms of qualitative research? Are those criticisms valid? Explain.
- To what extent do the criticisms of qualitative research reflect the concerns of quantitative researchers?
- Can qualitative research be used to test hypotheses?

SOME CONTRASTS BETWEEN QUANTITATIVE AND QUALITATIVE RESEARCH

- 'The difference between quantitative and qualitative research revolves entirely around the concern with numbers in the former and with words in the latter.' To what extent do you agree with this statement? Why?

CHAPTER 9

Ethnography and Participant Observation

CHAPTER OVERVIEW

Ethnography and **participant observation** require extended involvement in the activities of the people under study. This chapter explores:

- the problems of gaining access to different settings and ways of overcoming them;

- whether **covert research** is practicable and acceptable;

- the role of **key informants**;

- the different roles that ethnographers can assume in the course of their fieldwork;

- the function of **field notes** and the forms they can take;

- the role of visual materials in ethnography;

- bringing an ethnographic study to an end; and

- the controversy over feminist ethnography.

Ever thought of becoming a spy? Some kinds of qualitative research are not unlike espionage, although they may not have the glamour of a James Bond adventure or the drama of Mata Hari's life. Also, ethical constraints typically mean that the research can't be entirely covert, and the purposes behind the information-gathering are usually academic and intellectual rather than political.

Nevertheless, if the idea of inserting yourself into a social setting and getting to know the people there over an extended period of time appeals to you, you might well consider trying ethnography and participant observation. What kinds of groups or social settings intrigue you? Sports teams? Criminal gangs? Strippers? Hospital emergency rooms? Women's shelters? All of these can be subjects of ethnographic and participant observation research.

Introduction

Discussions about *participant observation* have been fairly standard in textbooks on social research. For some time, however, writers on research methods have preferred the term '*ethnography*.' In both cases, a researcher is immersed in a group of people for an extended period of time (sometimes for years), observing behaviour, listening to what their subjects say in conversation, and asking questions. Typically, participant observers and ethnographers gather further data through documents and interviews, especially on matters that are not directly observable, or about which they are unclear. Desroches (1990), for example, included interviews with 15 investigating officers with his video recordings of sexual activities in public washrooms.

The terms 'participant observation' and 'ethnography' are essentially synonymous, although here ethnography will be used in a broader sense, including participant observation; the latter will refer specifically to the observational component of ethnographic research.

This chapter outlines some of the main decisions that ethnographers must make, along with some of the many contingencies they face. However, given the diversity of the experiences that confront ethnographers and the variety of ways in which they deal with those experiences, it's difficult to generalize about this kind of research or to provide specific recommendations about it. The following comment makes this point well:

> Every field situation *is* different and initial luck in meeting good informants, being in the right place at the right time, and striking the right note in relationships may be just as important as skill in technique. Indeed . . . many unsuccessful episodes are due as much to bad luck as to bad judgement (Sarsby 1984: 96).

However, this statement should not be taken to mean that forethought and an awareness of alternative approaches are irrelevant. It is with those issues that the rest of this chapter is concerned. Issues involving the conduct of interviews by ethnographers are reserved for Chapter 10.

Access

One of the most important and yet most difficult steps in ethnography is gaining access to the social

---

> ### Practical **Tip** ▶▶▶▶
>
> **Micro-ethnography**
>
> In doing research for an undergraduate project or master's thesis, it's generally not feasible to conduct a full-scale ethnographic study, if only because of time limitations. Nevertheless, it may be possible to carry out a form of micro-ethnography (Wolcott 1990), focusing on one specific aspect of a group. For example, if you were interested in call centres, you might focus on how staff members manage to interact and discuss work problems with one another despite continuous incoming calls and monitoring by supervisors. A shorter period of time (from a couple of weeks to a few months) can be spent in the organization—on either a full- or a part-time basis—to achieve this more limited goal.

setting one wants to research. How to gain access depends on several things, one of which is whether the setting is relatively open (public) or closed (private or restricted) (see Lofland and Lofland 1995). Closed settings generally include organizations of various kinds, such as firms, schools, cults, and social movements. Open settings are areas where anyone can gain access, such as libraries, parks, and sidewalks, but even there it can be quite difficult to make observations and talk to people. 'Open' does not necessarily mean easy access to people.

OVERT VERSUS COVERT ETHNOGRAPHY

One way to ease the access problem is to assume a *covert* role: in other words, not to disclose that you are a researcher. Getting access can be very problematic, and the adoption of a covert role removes some of the difficulties. These two distinctions—open versus closed setting, and overt versus covert role—suggest a fourfold distinction in forms of ethnography (see Figure 9.1); an example of Canadian research is given for each of the four types.

Three points should be noted about Figure 9.1. First, the 'open versus closed setting' distinction is not hard and fast. Sometimes the process of gaining access in 'open' settings can take on an almost formal quality: for instance, if you are talking to a gang leader in the street, you may have to answer some pointed questions about your goals. Also, 'closed' organizations and social movements sometimes create contexts that have a public character, such as meetings arranged for members or prospective recruits. Bell (2007) attended many western

	Open/public setting	Closed setting
Overt role	*Type 1* • Wilson's (2002) study of Toronto raves • Totten's (2001) study of youth gang members (Box 9.6)	*Type 2* • Karabanow's (2002) study of two Canadian youth shelters (Box 8.3) • Clancey's (2001) study of scientists in the Arctic (Box 9.10)
Covert role	*Type 3* • Desroches's (1990) updates on homosexual activities in public washrooms	*Type 4* • Lauder's (2003) discussion of covert research on the Heritage Front

FIGURE 9.1   Four types of ethnography

Canadian separatist meetings and rallies that were open to the public, and was able to get a lot of information on the movement and its leaders that way.

Second, the 'overt versus covert' distinction can vary from context to context even within the same research project. Although ethnographers may seek access through an overt route, many of the people with whom they come into contact may be unaware of their status as researchers. Atkinson (1981: 135) noted in connection with his research on the training of doctors in a medical school that although he was 'an "open" observer with regard to doctors and students,' he was 'a "disguised" observer with regard to the patients.' Also, some ethnographers move between the two roles (see Box 9.1).

Another interesting case is provided by Glucksmann (1994), who in the 1970s left her academic post for a job on a factory assembly line in an effort to find out why feminism appeared not to be relevant to working-class women. In a sense, she was a covert observer, but her motives for the research

---

BOX 9.1   Perils of covert observation: field notes in the lavatory

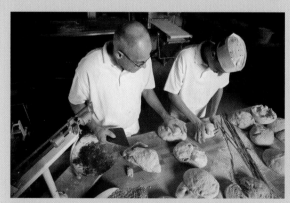

One of these bakers is a covert observer. What kinds of difficulties might researchers face when attempting to collect information without revealing their true identity and purpose?

Ditton's (1977) research in a bakery provides an interesting case study of the practical difficulties involved in taking notes during covert observation, as well as an illustration of an ethnographer who shifted positions from covert to overt observer at least in part because of those difficulties:

> Right from the start, I found it impossible to keep everything that I wanted to remember in my head until the end of the working day . . . and so had to take rough notes as I was going along. But I was stuck 'on the line,' and had nowhere to retire to privately to jot things down [except the washroom]. [Eventually] . . . my frequent requests for 'time out' after interesting happenings or conversations in the bakehouse and the amount of time I was spending in the lavatory began to get noticed. I had to pacify some genuinely concerned work-mates . . . and 'come out' as an observer—albeit in a limited way. I eventually began to scribble notes more openly, but still not in front of people when they were talking. When questioned about this, as I was occasionally, I coyly said that I was writing things down that occurred to me about 'my studies' (Ditton 1977: 5).

were primarily political, not academic. At the time she was undertaking the research she had no intention of writing the book, which was eventually published under a pseudonym. Was she an overt or a covert observer (or neither or both)? Whichever description applies, this is an interesting case of what might be termed 'retrospective ethnography': using observations that were gathered before the decision was made to conduct a study.

A third point with regard to Figure 9.1 is that the preferred choice is an overt role. There are several reasons for this. As Box 9.2 reveals, these reasons have to do with practical and especially ethical considerations. The ethics of covert research, which are addressed in depth in Chapter 11, involve issues of deception, lack of informed consent, and invasion of privacy, since the researcher has essentially fooled the participants into believing that they are not being observed for research purposes. Because of the ethical problems (and some of the practical difficulties) that beset covert research, the bulk of the following discussion of access issues focuses on overt research.

ACCESS TO CLOSED SETTINGS

Gaining access to most organizations requires strategic planning, hard work, and sometimes luck. In selecting a case study for an ethnographic investigation, the researcher may employ several criteria, depending on the research area of interest. One may choose a certain case or setting because of its 'fit' with the research questions, but there is no guarantee of access. Sometimes sheer perseverance pays off. Leidner (1993) was determined that McDonald's would be one of the organizations in which she conducted ethnographic research on the routinization of service work:

> The company was a pioneer and exemplar of routinized interaction, and since it was locally based, it seemed like the perfect place to start. McDonald's had other ideas, however, and only after tenacious pestering and persuasion did I overcome corporate employees' polite demurrals, couched in terms of protecting proprietary information and the company's image (1993: 234–5).

This kind of determination is necessary whenever the target is a specific organization or group

(e.g., a particular religious sect or social movement). Rejection can mean having to find a completely different research topic.

On the other hand, for many research questions you are likely to find that several potential cases will be suitable. Organizational researchers have developed a range of tactics, some of which may seem rather unsystematic but are still worth considering:

- Use friends, contacts, and colleagues to help gain access; as long as the organization is relevant to the research question, the route should not matter.

- If possible, get someone in the organization to vouch for you and the value of your research. Such people are considered 'sponsors.' If permission is granted at a lower level of the hierarchy, you may still need clearance from top management or senior executives. People who must grant their permission for you to gain access are sometimes called '**gatekeepers**.'

- Offer something in return: for example, a *final* report (if you provide a working draft, people may ask you to make changes that you would not consider acceptable). However, this strategy carries a risk of making the researcher a cheap consultant. Some writers on research methodology do not recommend offering something in return, although it is commonplace among researchers on formal organizations.

- Provide a clear explanation of your aims and methods. Suggest a meeting to deal with the participants' concerns and explain what will happen in terms that people who are not familiar with social research can understand.

- Be prepared to negotiate; almost no one gets complete access.

- Be frank about the amount of people's time you are likely to need. Time is an important issue for commercial organizations, and for many non-profit groups too.

ACCESS TO OPEN SETTINGS

Gaining access to people in open settings is similar in many ways. For instance, sometimes ethnographers have their paths smoothed by 'sponsors' and 'gatekeepers.' In seeking access to a group of soccer hooligans, Giulianotti (1995; see Box 9.3) sought out someone who could play both roles for him.

BOX 9.2 | The covert role in ethnography

Advantages

- *Easier access.* Adopting a covert role can help with access problems; no special permission to gain entry to a social setting or organization may be needed.

- *Less **reactivity**.* Because participants do not know they are being observed by a researcher, they will speak and act more naturally than they would otherwise.

Disadvantages

- *The problem of taking notes.* It is difficult and sometimes impossible to take notes without revealing that you are conducting research. However, notes are very important to an ethnographer, and it's too risky to rely on memory alone.

- *The problem of not being able to use other methods.* If the researcher is in a covert role, steering conversations in a certain direction can increase the risk of detection, and it is essentially impossible to conduct interviews.

- *Anxiety.* Ethnography is frequently a stressful research method, and worries about detection only add to the anxiety. Moreover, if the ethnographer is found out, the whole research project may be jeopardized. In extreme cases, such as covert research on gangs, being found out could even put the researcher's life at risk.

- *Ethical problems.* Covert observation transgresses two important ethical tenets: deception of participants and failure to obtain informed consent (see Chapter 11). It can also involve a violation of privacy. Indeed, many writers think covert investigations can harm the practice of research in general, since innocent researchers may be tarred with the same brush as outed covert observers, who are considered snoops or voyeurs (or worse). On the other hand, covert participant observation may be justified in some situations, as Lauder (2003) concluded regarding his investigation of the neo-Nazi Heritage Front.

Later, he was able to call on existing acquaintances to ease his entrée into a second group. In seeking access to female intravenous drug users, Taylor (1993) contacted a drug counsellor who introduced her to some local users and accompanied her on her first few research visits. A 'research bargain' (Becker 1970) was struck in which Taylor agreed in return to see any of the counsellor's clients who preferred to discuss issues with a woman.

'Hanging around' is another common access strategy. An example of the difficulties that await the researcher using this approach can be found in one of Whyte's (1955) early field encounters in Boston's North End in his classic case study *Street Corner Society*. The following incident occurred in a hotel bar:

> I looked around me again and now noticed a threesome: one man and two women. It occurred to me that here was a maldistribution of females that I might be able to rectify. I approached the group and opened with something like this: 'Pardon me. Would you mind if I join you?' There was a moment of silence while the man stared at me. He then offered to throw me

downstairs. I assured him that this would not be necessary and demonstrated as much by walking right out of there without any assistance (1955: 289).

Wolf (1991) used a hanging-around strategy to gain access to Canadian outlaw bikers. On one occasion he met a group of them at a motorcycle shop and expressed an interest in hanging out with them. But he tried to move too quickly in seeking information about them and was forced to abandon his plans. Eventually, Wolf's hanging-around strategy led to his being approached by the leader of a biker group (Rebels MC), who acted as his sponsor. To bring this off, Wolf ensured that he was properly attired in biker garb. Attention to dress and demeanour can be a very important consideration when seeking access to either public or closed settings.

As these anecdotes suggest, gaining access to social settings is a crucial first step in ethnographic research. But it is also difficult and in some cases dangerous—for example, when the group in question is engaged in violent or criminal activities. Caution is essential when choosing an access strategy.

BOX 9.3   Access to soccer hooligans

Giulianotti (1995) sought access to two groups of soccer hooligans. Access to one was reasonably smooth in that he was a close friend of 3 of the 47 men caught by the police engaging in unruly behaviour at a soccer game. In addition he had known and socialized with many others at school, and in terms of 'age, attire, and argot' he was similar to the people he was studying. Gradually his contacts multiplied and eventually he 'began socializing freely with the gang at [soccer] matches, travelling to and from matches within the main grouping' (1995: 4).

Access to the other group of supporters was much more difficult for three reasons: absence of prior acquaintanceships; his background and accent; and a high level of negative newspaper publicity about them at the time he was seeking access, which made the hooligans wary of people writing about them. Giulianotti

sought out a sponsor who could ease his entry into the group. After some abortive attempts, he was finally introduced to someone at a game and this contact gave him access to more supporters. Eventually, he was able to negotiate access to the group as a whole by striking a 'research bargain': he would provide details of what rival fans thought of them. Giulianotti described his overall research strategy as:

regularly introducing myself to new research acquaintances; renegotiating association with familiar casuals; talking with them, drinking with them, and going to matches with them; generally participating with them in a variety of social situations; but disengaging myself from . . . participating in violence, within and outside of [soccer] match contexts (1995: 3).

ONGOING ACCESS

Access problems do not end after initial contact and entrée to the group. Maintaining access is an ongoing activity and is likely to prove a persistent problem in closed contexts such as organizations.

- People will be suspicious, perhaps seeing the researcher as an instrument of top management (it's very common for members of organizations to believe that researchers have been put in place to check up on them). When Sharpe (2000: 366) began research on prostitution in a red light area, she was thought to be 'anything from a social worker to a newspaper reporter with hidden cameras and microphones.' When conducting her research on the British on the Costa del Sol, O'Reilly (2000) was suspected of being a tax inspector.

- Group members will worry that what they say or do may get back to bosses or colleagues. Van Maanen (1991a) noted that when conducting ethnographic research among police officers, it's not unusual to observe activities that reflect badly on the police and may even be illegal. In such situations the researcher can establish credibility by using discretion.

- If the people being studied have concerns or suspicions about the researcher, they may appear to go along with the research but in fact sabotage it, engage in deception, provide

misinformation, or not allow access to 'back regions' (Goffman 1956).

There are three ways to smooth the path for ongoing access to closed settings:

- Play up your credentials: talk about your past work, your experience, your knowledge of the group, and your understanding of its problems.

- Don't give people a reason to dislike you: be non-judgmental when hearing about informal activities or about the organization; make sure that information given to you doesn't get back to others, whether bosses or peers.

- Play a role: this may involve constructing a 'front' using demeanour and dress, offering plausible explanations of why you are there, helping out occasionally with work, or offering advice. Be consistent: the various aspects of your role should complement one another.

Similar considerations apply to research in public settings:

- Make sure you have a plan for allaying people's suspicions. Giulianotti (see Box 9.3) simply said that he was doing research on soccer fans for a book.

- Be prepared for tests of either competence or credibility. Taylor (1993) reported that at a meeting at a drop-in centre, 'proper cups' for tea were put out. Afterwards, Taylor was told that, if she had crooked her 'wee finger' as the leader of the centre had done, her informant 'would have put [Taylor] down in such a way that you'd never want to speak to us again' (1993: 15). When doing research on gang members in a poor community, Horowitz wrote that she was frequently told 'confidential' stories (which turned out to be fictional) to see if she could keep a secret (Gerson and Horowitz 2002; see Box 9.6).

- Be prepared for changes in circumstances. Both Giulianotti (Box 9.3) and Armstrong (1993) found that newspaper exposés of the kinds of activities they were studying led to worries that they were not what they said they were.

KEY INFORMANTS

Ethnographers rely heavily on informants, especially those who develop an understanding of the research and are able to identify situations, events, or people likely to be helpful to the investigation. Whyte (1955) again provides an extreme example, quoting a key informant named Doc:

> You tell me what you want to see, and we'll arrange it. When you want some information, I'll ask for it, and you listen. When you want to find out their philosophy of life, I'll start an argument and get it for you. If there's something else you want to get, I'll stage an act for you (1955: 292).

Doc was also helpful in warning Whyte that he was asking too many questions, telling him to 'go easy on that "who," "what," "why," "when," "where" stuff' (1955: 303). Taylor (1993) said that in her participant observation of 50 female drug users, she carried out intensive interviews with 26 women, 8 of whom were key informants.

Key informants can also provide support that helps with the stress of fieldwork. However, undue reliance on them can lead researchers to see social reality through their eyes only rather than viewing things from the perspectives of several group members or the group as a whole.

In addition, ethnographers encounter many other people who will act as informants whose accounts may or may not have been solicited. Some researchers prefer unsolicited information because of its spontaneity and naturalism. Very often, research participants develop a sense of the events or encounters that the ethnographer will want to see. Armstrong (1993), in the course of his research on soccer hooligans, would sometimes get tips from a group of Sheffield United fans who called themselves 'Blades':

> I often travelled on the same coach as Ray [an informant]; he would then sit with me at matches and in pubs . . . giving me background information. Sometimes he would start conversations with Blades about incidents which he knew I wanted to know about and afterwards would ask 'Did you get all that down then?' . . . There was never one particular informant; rather, there were many Blades . . . who were part of the core and would always welcome a beer and a chat about 'It,' or tell me who I 'ought to 'ave a word wi' ' (Armstrong 1993: 24–5).

Unsolicited offers of information are highly attractive to ethnographers because of their apparent spontaneity. However, as Hammersley and Atkinson (1995: 130–1) observed, it's important to recognize that such offers may on occasion be staged for the ethnographer's benefit.

Solicited accounts can be obtained in two ways: by interviewing (see Chapter 10) or by casual questioning during conversations (though in ethnographic research the boundary between an interview and a conversation is by no means clear). When the ethnographer needs specific information on an issue that does not lend itself to direct observation or that is not cropping up during 'natural' conversations, solicited accounts are likely to be the only way forward.

Roles for ethnographers

Related to the issue of ongoing access is the question of the role an ethnographer adopts in relation to the social setting and its members. Often the various roles in fieldwork are arrayed along a continuum from complete involvement to complete detachment (see Figure 9.2). It should also be noted that the full gamut of roles may be employed at different times in the course of a single ethnographic project, and for different purposes.

For example, the participant observer can be a:

- *Complete participant*: a fully functioning member of a social setting but one whose true identity is unknown to members: in other words, a covert observer. In such cases the ethnographer is engaged in regular interaction with people and participates in their daily lives but assumes the researcher's role in private to write down notes once the situation has unfolded. This is what Humphreys (1970) did when he studied male homosexual encounters in public washrooms.

- *Participant-as-observer*: As above, except that members of the social setting are aware that the ethnographer is studying them. All four of the 'overt' studies listed in Figure 9.1—whether in open or closed settings—were of this kind, as was Giulianotti's research (see Box 9.3).

- *Observer-as-participant*: The researcher is mainly an interviewer and observer, and participates only marginally in the group's activities. This was Bell's (2007) role in his study of western Canadian separatists. Ethnographic research on the police is often similar, since the opportunities for genuine participation are limited by legal and safety restrictions. Norris (1993) described how as an observer-as-participant, he concentrated on gathering two types of data: 'naturally occurring inter-officer talk' and 'detailed descriptions of how officers handled "live" incidents' (1993: 126).

Involvement ⟵⟶ Detachment

| Complete participant | Participant-as-observer | Observer-as-participant | Complete observer |

FIGURE 9.2 Classification of participant observer roles (Gold 1958)

For another example of a situation in which minimal participation may be appropriate, see Box 9.5. Some critics question whether this kind of research is genuine ethnography, but in cases like these there may be no alternative.

- *Complete observer*: The final possibility is no interaction with the people observed. Most writers do not include this as a form of ethnography, since by definition there is little or no involvement or participation. There may be less risk of *reactivity* (subjects behaving unnaturally because they know they are being observed) because the researcher is at a distance; but there is also greatly reduced potential for *understanding* because the researcher does not ask questions or try in any way to get into the heads of the people under study.

BOX 9.4 | What is 'going native'?

Despite its vaguely racist overtones, the phrase 'going native' is commonly used in ethnography in a non-pejorative way. It refers to situations in which, as a result of prolonged immersion in the lives of the people under study, coupled with a commitment to seeing through their eyes, ethnographers become so wrapped up in the world of their subjects that they forget their role as researchers. Under such circumstances the ethnographer may find it difficult to maintain a social scientific perspective on the collection and analysis of data. As Hobbs (1988: 6) wrote of his own fieldwork, he 'often had to remind himself that [he] was not in a pub to enjoy [himself] but to conduct an academic inquiry, and repeatedly woke up the following morning with an incredible hangover, facing the dilemma of whether to bring it up or write it up.' He may have been on the brink of going native.

A related issue for Hobbs was involvement in illegal activity:

A refusal, or worse still an inquiry concerning the legal status of the 'parcel,' would provoke an abrupt conclusion to the relationship. Consequently, I was willing to skirt the boundaries of criminality on several occasions, and I considered it crucial to be willingly involved in 'normal' business transactions, legal or otherwise. I was pursuing an interactive, inductive study of an entrepreneurial culture, and in order to do so I had to display entrepreneurial skills myself. . . . [My] status as an insider meant that I was afforded a great deal of trust by my informants, and I was allowed access to settings, detailed conversations, and information that might not otherwise have been available (1988: 7, 15).

BOX 9.5 | Not going native

It should not be assumed that 'going native' is inevitable in ethnography. Nor is it the only risk that participant observers face in relation to the social situations they study. Lee-Treweek (2000) carried out research on auxiliary caregivers in two homes for the elderly. In one of them she reacted in a way that was the opposite of going native. She disliked the home and found the staff unappealing because of their uncaring approach and lack of sympathy for the elderly residents. Nonetheless, she felt she 'was gathering good data, despite [her] feelings of being an outsider' (2000: 120). Similarly, although Bell (2007) spent more than a year observing western Canadian separatists, at no point was he ever tempted to join the group. The lesson here is that going native is not inevitable, and that researchers must be careful not to let either positive or negative feelings for the people they study distort their findings.

BOX 9.6 | Narrowing the focus of an ethnographic study

Gerson and Horowitz (2002) started their work on young people in a very poor community in Chicago by asking some general research questions. What is really going on in such groups and communities? How do people make sense of their social worlds? In the early stages of her research, Horowitz used these general questions to guide her data collection, and it was 'only after some time in the field' that she 'began to focus on specifying the sociological issues' (2002: 202).

She found a great deal of variety in the behaviour, ambitions, orientations, patterns of interaction, and attitudes towards street life among the young people she observed. Horowitz began to ask questions about how well the world of these young people fit with two prominent models used to explain the worlds of the poor. She concluded that neither model 'account[ed] for young people's creativity or for the struggles they mounted and the choices that they made in the face of great obstacles' (2002: 202).

Each approach has advantages and disadvantages. In the case of covert ethnography, some of these are discussed in Box 9.2. The participant-as-observer role carries the risk of over-identification and hence of 'going native' (see Boxes 9.4 and 9.5), but at the same time it offers an opportunity to get close to people. The observer-as-participant role carries the risk of not understanding the social setting and its people sufficiently and therefore making incorrect inferences. In an interesting variant of this problem, Hessler *et al.* (2003) cautioned observers (in a study of adolescent risk behaviour) against the temptation to act as counsellors to respondents. See also Boxes 9.6 and 9.7.

Gans (1968) would add that even if it were possible, it is probably undesirable to adhere to a single role over the entire course of a project, since this would limit the ethnographer's flexibility in handling situations and people. In addition, the risks of either excessive involvement (going native) or excessive detachment would loom large.

ACTIVE OR PASSIVE?

How active or passive should the ethnographer be? In most studies—even when the researcher is mainly an observer rather than a participant—involvement in the group's activities will be unavoidable from time to time. For example, Fine's (1996) research on the work of chefs in restaurants was carried out largely through semi-structured interviews. In spite of this limited participation, he sometimes found himself in the kitchen washing dishes to help out during busy periods. Similarly, in a study of bouncers, the participant observer will not have the luxury of deciding whether to become involved in fights, since involvement comes with the territory (Winlow *et al.* 2001).

Sometimes ethnographers feel they have no choice about getting involved because a failure to participate might suggest a lack of commitment to the group. In such situations, standing back could lead to a loss of credibility in the eyes of the people studied. This situation can arise especially when the activities are illegal or dangerous. On the other hand, many writers counsel against active participation in criminal or dangerous activities. Both Armstrong (1993) and Giulianotti (1995; see Box 9.3) refused to fight while doing their research into soccer hooliganism. The latter wrote: 'My own rules are that I will not get involved in fighting or become a go-between for the two gangs in organizing fights' (1995: 10). That is an illustration of why it is not a good idea to

BOX 9.7 | Virtual participant observation

Kanayama (2003) was interested in the nature of an Internet community formed by a group of Japanese senior citizens that counted 120 members by 1991. Kanayama described her 10-month study as follows:

> I had participated in this group as a technical volunteer supporter for two years to help senior members use PCs and the Internet and . . . took a position as a non-active participant. . . . Many members, including representatives of the group, knew of [my] personal background. I also conducted in-depth interviews with six female and seven male members . . . by telephone (2003: 274).

She found that members of this virtual community operated well with the medium: they succeeded in constructing real social relationships in cyberspace and thus were able to provide a supportive environment for each other.

do covert research on criminals or those involved in dangerous actions: it is much more difficult for someone in such a role to decline to participate in group activities (see Box 9.4).

Field notes

Because of the frailties of human memory, ethnographers must jot down their observations. These should be fairly detailed summaries of events and behaviour, and the researcher's initial reflections on them. The notes need to specify the key dimensions of whatever is observed or heard. Here are some general principles:

- Write down notes, however brief, as soon as possible after seeing or hearing something interesting.
- Write up full field notes at the end of the day at the very latest, including details such as location, the people involved, what prompted the exchange or event, and date and time of day.
- You may also use a tape recorder for notes, but you will have to allow plenty of time for transcription.
- Notes must be vivid, clear, and complete. If in doubt, write it down.

It's obviously best to take notes as soon as something significant happens. However, wandering around with a notebook and continually scribbling in it can make the people you are observing feel self-conscious. Thus it may be necessary to take small amounts of time away from the group to write down your observations. In that case you must take care not to make the participants anxious or suspicious (see Box 9.1).

To some extent, strategies for taking field notes depend on how clearly delineated the research questions are. As we noted in Chapter 8, most qualitative research begins with general research questions, but there is considerable variation in their specificity. Obviously, when there is a clearly focused research question, the ethnographer's observations should be oriented to it. At the same time, it's important to maintain a fairly open mind, so that the study's flexibility with respect to the themes it explores—a strength of qualitative research—is not impaired.

In the context of her research on female drug users, Taylor (1993: 15) explained that in her early days in the field she tended to listen rather than talk because she 'did not know what questions [she] wanted to ask.' Armstrong (1993: 12) wrote in connection with his research on soccer hooliganism that his research 'began without a focus' and that as a result 'he decided to record everything.' Therefore a typical Saturday would mean 30 pages of handwritten notes. Such openendedness usually cannot last long, because trying to record the details of absolutely everything is so tiring. Eventually the ethnographer begins to narrow down the focus of the research, sometimes by relating the emerging findings to the socialscientific literature on the topic. This approach is implied by the sequence suggested in Figure 8.1.

For most ethnographers, the equipment needed for observation consists mainly of a notepad and pen (for example, Armstrong 1993: 28). A tape recorder may be useful but, as we have noted, transcribing what you record will take time. In addition, recording may be more obtrusive than writing notes. Although participants usually grow accustomed to the presence of the researcher over time, speaking into a tape recorder can rekindle fears about participating; and in some gatherings it may be difficult to use a tape recorder because of extraneous noise. Photography can be an additional source of data, and pictures do help to stir the ethnographer's memory, but in some kinds of research (especially involving crime and deviance) photography may not be feasible.

TYPES OF FIELD NOTES

Some writers have found it useful to classify the types of field notes generated in the process of conducting ethnography. The following classification is based on categories suggested by Lofland and Lofland (1995) and Sanjek (1990):

- *Mental notes*: particularly useful when it is inappropriate to be seen taking written notes; however, they should be put into writing at the earliest opportunity.

- *Jotted notes (also called scratch or rough notes)*: very brief notes to jog the memory about events that should be written up more fully later. Lofland and Lofland (1995: 90) described jotted notes as 'little phrases, quotes, key words, and the like.' Such notes need to be written inconspicuously, preferably out of sight, since writing in front of research participants may be off-putting for them.

- *Full field notes*: the main data source in ethnographic research. Full notes should be written as soon as possible, usually at the end of the day. Provide as much detail as possible about events, people, conversations, etc. A particular comment from a subject or an account of an event that you witnessed may not seem very important at the time, but its significance may become apparent later on, once you have developed an interpretive structure. Without good notes, valuable data may be lost. Write down, in brackets, initial ideas about your interpretations, impressions, and feelings.

It's worth adding that in field notes the ethnographer's presence is frequently evident. This can be seen in Whyte's account (above) of almost being thrown down the stairs. However, in the finished work the ethnographer is sometimes written out of the picture. Field notes, except for brief passages, are primarily for the researcher's own use (Coffey 1999), whereas the written report is for public consumption and has to be presented as a credible account of the social setting and culture in question. References to the ethnographer should be limited; otherwise the report will look more like an account of his or her activities than those of the group purportedly under study. This issue will be addressed in further detail in Chapter 17.

Methods in Motion

Applications to Canadian Society

Browne (2007) used ethnographic methods and participant observation to examine how the historic political, social, and economic inequalities experienced by Canadian Aboriginal women affected their present-day interactions with nurses in a hospital in western Canada. She explored how socially constructed notions of culture, 'race,' and ethnicity can influence the quality of the health care that First Nations women receive. Browne, who is both a nurse and a researcher, spent nine months conducting the study, which involved doing in-depth interviews with 14 registered nurses (four of whom were Aboriginal) and 14 First Nations female patients. She also shadowed the nurses as they worked with the Aboriginal patients.

One thing Browne noted was that the nurses tended to ignore or downplay historically based power inequalities when they tried to make sense of their patients' demeanour, which was often passive, quiet, and introverted. A common interpretation was that the patients' behaviour stemmed from cultural factors. As one nurse put it, '[This patient] wouldn't look at me. She wouldn't answer anything. She would nod occasionally. . . . I mean, it's a cultural thing' (2169). One of the patients explained things differently: '. . . a lot of native women, especially, don't want to say anything, don't talk. . . . I know my mom, for example, had a lot of fear in her from residential school' (2170). Browne points out that these misunderstandings can have serious health consequences, as in the case of an Aboriginal woman who did not mention that her intravenous needle had not been removed before she left the hospital. Her study shows how routine micro-level interactions, such as those between patients and nurses, may be influenced by larger, historically based relationships such as those between First Nations people and the dominant Euro-Canadian society and state.

Analytic memos   Most of the previous discussion focused on the mechanics of note-taking. But content is even more important. Notes can be taken on the setting, the people, the methodological problems encountered, and so on. In addition it's possible to create *analytic memos* recording some initial thoughts on what all those observations might mean. Analytic notes help to bridge the gap between the data and the concepts, interpretations, and theories that researchers develop to make sense of what they are observing. Such memos should be dated and reviewed regularly. They should also be kept separate from notes on actual observations because they are comments on data, not data themselves.

The rise of visual ethnography

The use of visual materials in social research is by no means new. For many years cultural anthropologists have used photographs in their portrayals of traditional societies. However, books such as Pink's (2001) *Visual Ethnography* suggest that the use of photos in social research has entered a new phase.

The discussion of visual materials (primarily photographs) in Chapter 7 focused on the use of images produced some time before the research began. Other visual materials are produced more or less exclusively for research purposes. This chapter emphasizes the latter: research-driven images, mainly photographs but also video recordings and other visual media. It's worth noting that although the term 'visual ethnography' is increasingly popular, it does not always refer to the kind of sustained immersion in a social setting that is the subject of this chapter.

Qualitative researchers have used visual materials in at least three ways:

1. as memory aids in the course of fieldwork, where they essentially become components of the ethnographer's field notes;
2. as sources of data in their own right; and
3. as prompts for discussion by research participants.

Pink (2001) drew an important distinction between two positions on visual materials. The traditional framework is a **realist** one in which the material simply captures an event or setting that then becomes a 'fact' for the ethnographer to interpret along with other data. The image and what it represents are presented as unproblematic, as a window on reality. This has been the dominant framework within which visual resources have been produced and analyzed. By contrast, Pink also drew attention to a position that she described as '**reflexive**.' This entails an awareness of and sensitivity to the ways in which researchers themselves determine what the visuals reveal. This sensitivity requires a grasp of the ways in which researchers' personal characteristics—age, gender, social background, academic proclivities, and so on—may influence what images they choose to record, and how those images are presented.

This approach to the visual is frequently collaborative in the sense that research participants may be involved in decisions about what visuals should be recorded and how they should be interpreted. Further, it acknowledges that different people may interpret the images in different ways. In Pink's research on Spanish bullfighters, enthusiasts interpreted the images she took of bullfights in terms of bullfighter performance. Other viewers might see the same images in a different interpretive framework—for example, one centred on animal rights and cruelty.

Plate 9.1 presents an image called *The Bullfighter's Braid*, from Pink's research. Showing a female bullfighter, it appealed to many connoisseurs of the sport who saw in it various artistic and other meanings. For Pink, it held additional significance in terms of her interests in gender and the broader discipline of social anthropology (for more information on this photograph see Pink 2001: 101, http://sunsite.ualberta.ca/reflexive-frames/1_rprf/_E/gal_pink_1.html [accessed July 16, 2011]). Further examples of the use of visual resources in ethnographic contexts are described in Boxes 9.8 and 9.9.

Visual materials have great potential for ethnographers and qualitative researchers in general. In her research on Niketown in Chicago, for instance, Peñaloza (1999) was interested in what she called 'spectacular consumption': turning what would otherwise be a mundane consumption event (purchasing sportswear) into a spectacle through the use of sporting images, sounds, and atmosphere. Including photographs in a study of the role the environment plays in creating a sense of spectacular consumption was very appropriate because spectacle is largely a visual phenomenon.

BOX 9.8 Photographs in a study of hospital wards

Radley and Taylor (2003a, 2003b) were interested in the role that the physical setting of a hospital ward plays in patient recovery. Nine patients in a ward were asked to take photographs on the ward a few days after their surgery. Each patient was supplied with a camera and asked to take up to 12 photographs of things in the hospital that they found personally significant. The only constraint was not to include people in their photographs (because of hospital restrictions). The researchers stayed with the patients while they took their photographs. Patients were interviewed a day after the photos were developed, and again a month or so later at home. On each occasion, patients were asked about all the photographs and which ones best reflected their experience in the hospital. This approach to interviewing—asking people to discuss photographs and their meaning and significance—is often referred to as *photo-elicitation* or *photo-voice*.

Most of the images taken appear to be very mundane, neither striking nor interesting. However, the photos took on considerable significance in the interviewees' narratives on the positive and negative aspects of their time in hospital. As the authors expressed it: 'The camera engaged the patients with the hospital setting in a critical way. This meant that the photographic prints also became part of the passage . . . from hospital to home, something we have found to be important in how patients manage their recovery.'

Source: www.lboro.ac.uk/departments/ss/visualising_ethnography/hospital.html, accessed 6 June 2008.

Visual research methods require researchers to 'read' images while being sensitive to the context in which they were generated, the potential for multiple meanings among researchers, study participants and others, and the potential for the researcher to influence the image and its presentation. In addition, researchers usually include non-visual research methods, such as interviews, in their investigations. This raises the question of the relative significance of words versus images in the analysis of data and the presentation of findings. Since words are the traditional medium, it's easy to slip into seeing the visual as less important, but this is not always justified. Finally, visual research methods raise certain ethical issues, such as invasion of privacy and anonymity.

The end

Knowing when to stop is not an easy or straight-forward matter in ethnography. Because of its unstructured nature and the absence of specific hypotheses for testing (other than those that may emerge during data collection and analysis), there is a tendency for ethnographic research to lack an obvious end point. Only occasionally will there be a natural end to the research; this was the case with Hier (2002) and Wilson (2002), in that the rave scene was waning when they studied it. Sometimes the rhythms of the ethnographer's occupational career or personal and family life—the end of a sabbatical leave, the need to submit a doctoral thesis by a certain date, exhaustion of funding—necessitate withdrawal from the field: Taylor (1993) wrote that one factor contributing to her departure from the field was the lengthy illness of her youngest son.

PLATE 9.1   The Bullfighter's Braid

BOX 9.9 | Visual ethnography?

Clancey (2001) described a study that used the extreme environment of the Canadian High Arctic to see how scientists might someday live and work on Mars. The research used a variety of methods and techniques, including ethnography (to understand how scientists like to work and live), photography, and time-lapse videos. He found this combination applicable to other multi-disciplinary field expeditions that are spread over a large terrain.

Also relevant is the fact that ethnographic research can be highly stressful for many reasons: the nature of the topic, which may place the fieldworker in tense situations (as in research on crime); the marginal position of the researcher in the social setting; the constant need to maintain a front; the often prolonged absence from one's normal life. Ethnographers may simply feel that they have had enough.

An important reason for bringing fieldwork to a close is that reasonable answers to the research questions have been formulated. The ethnographer may even feel a strong sense of *déjà vu* towards the end of data collection if new data simply reiterate what has already been discovered. In the language of grounded theory, all the researcher's categories may become thoroughly *saturated*, although Glaser and Strauss's (1967) approach suggests that one should be certain that there are no new questions to be asked and no new comparisons to be made.

In sum, the reasons for bringing ethnographic research to a close can range from personal factors to matters of research design. Whatever the reason, disengagement has to be *managed*. For one thing, this means that promises must be kept (was a report promised as a condition of entry?). It also means that ethnographers must provide good explanations for their departure. Subjects may know that the researcher is not a permanent presence in their social setting, but over a long period of time they can forget, especially if there has been genuine participation in activities within that setting; therefore farewells may have to be arranged. It's also essential to remember the ethnographer's *ethical* commitments, such as the need to ensure that persons and settings are kept anonymous—unless, of course, there has

been an agreement that the social setting can be disclosed (as often occurs in studies of religious sects and cults).

Can there be a feminist ethnography?

This heading is in fact the title of a widely cited article in which Stacey (1988) rebuts the view that there can be a distinctively feminist ethnography. Reinharz (1992) considered feminist ethnography important to feminism because:

- it documents women's lives and activities, which were previously regarded as marginal and subsidiary to men's;
- it understands women from their perspective, so that research that 'trivializes females' activities and thoughts, or interprets them from the standpoint of men in the society or of the male researcher' (1992: 52) is rejected; and
- it understands women in context.

Similarly, Skeggs (2001: 430) observed that many feminist researchers have considered ethnography 'with its emphasis on experiences and the words, voice and lives of the participants' well suited to the goals of feminism.

Such commitments and practices go only part of the way. Of great significance to feminist researchers is whether the ethnography allows for a non-exploitative relationship between the researcher and the researched. One of the main elements of such a strategy is for the ethnographer not to treat the relationship as a one-way process of extracting information from others, but as one in which the researcher can provide something in return. Skeggs's (1994, 1997) ethnographic research on young women represents one such attempt to create a non-exploitative relationship with the people being studied (see Box 9.10).

Stacey (1988), however, argued on the basis of her fieldwork experience that the various situations she encountered as a feminist ethnographer placed her

in situations of inauthenticity, dissimilitude, and potential, perhaps inevitable betrayal, situations that I now believe are inherent in fieldwork method. For no matter how welcome, even enjoyable the fieldworker's presence may appear to 'natives,' fieldwork represents an intrusion and intervention into a system of

BOX 9.10   A feminist ethnography

Skeggs's (1997) longitudinal ethnographic study of 83 working-class white women was 'based on research conducted over a total period of 12 years including 3 years' full-time, in-the-field participant observation. It began when the women enrolled in a "caring" course at a local college and it followed their trajectories through the labour market, education, and the family' (1997: 1).

The elements of a distinctively feminist ethnography can be seen in the following comments by the author:

- 'This ethnography was politically motivated to provide space for the articulations and experiences of the marginalized' (1997: 23).

- The 'study was concerned to show how young women's experience of structure (their class and gender positioning) and institutions (education

and the media) frame and inform their responses and how this process informs constructions of their own subjectivity' (1994: 74). This comment, like the previous one, reflects a commitment to documenting women's lives and allowing their experiences to come through, while also pointing to the significance of context.

Skeggs felt that her relationship with the women was not exploitative. For example, she wrote that the research enhanced the women's 'sense of self-worth' giving them 'the opportunity to be valued, knowledgeable, and interesting.' She claimed she was able to 'provide a mouthpiece against injustices' and listen 'to disclosures of violence, child abuse, and sexual harassment' (1994: 81)

---

relationships, a system of relationships that the researcher is far freer to leave (1988: 23).

Stacey also argued that when the research is written up, it is the feminist ethnographer's interpretations and judgments that come through and have authority, not those of the women who were studied. Skeggs responded by acknowledging that her academic career was undoubtedly enhanced by the study, but added that Stacey's views present women research participants as victims. Skeggs maintained that:

> The young women were not prepared to be exploited; just as they were able to resist most things which did not promise economic or cultural reward, they were able to resist me. . . . They enjoyed the research. It provided resources for developing a sense of their self-worth. More importantly, the feminism of the research provided a framework [for them

to see] . . . that their individual problems are part of a wider structure and not their personal fault (1994: 88).

Similarly, Reinharz (1992: 74–5) argued that, although ethnographic fieldwork relationships may sometimes seem manipulative, they often involve a clear undercurrent of reciprocity. The researcher may offer help or advice to her research participants, or she may give a public airing to normally marginalized voices (although the ethnographer is always the mouthpiece for such voices and as such may impose a particular 'spin' on them).

The question of whether there is or can be a feminist ethnography is clearly a subject of ongoing debate. The fact that female researchers are in careers that place them in a fairly desirable socioeconomic position while their subjects are often situated in less advantaged sectors of society is an issue that is not easily resolved. Of course, male researchers who study the socially marginalized face the same problem.

Key Points

- The ethnographer is typically a participant observer who also uses interviews and documents.
- The ethnographer may adopt an overt or covert role, but the latter comes with serious ethical difficulties.
- The method of access to a social setting depends in part on whether it is open (public) or closed (private or restricted).
- Key informants frequently play an important role in ethnography, but care is needed to ensure that their impact on the research is not excessive.

- Field notes are important memory aids for the ethnographer.
- Visual materials such as photographs and videos have attracted considerable interest among ethnographers in recent years, not just as adjuncts to data collection but as objects of interest in their own right.
- Ethnography conducted from a feminist standpoint has become increasingly popular, although the possibility of a feminist ethnography as such is open to debate.

Relevant Websites

For examples of ethnographic studies, take a look at the journal *Ethnography* and the *Journal of Contemporary Ethnography* (you may have to log on to your institution's library server to access them):

http://eth.sagepub.com/
http://www.sagepub.com/journals/Journal200975

Digital ethnography, in particular the use of videos in ethnographic projects, is explored at:

http://mediatedcultures.net/ksudigg/

[Websites accessed 20 July 2011]

Questions for Review

- To what extent can ethnography rely solely on observation? Can it be done successfully without additional data from interviews, documents and so on? Explain.

ACCESS

- 'Covert ethnography can make it easier to gain access to certain settings and therefore has much to recommend it.' Discuss.
- Does the problem of access end once the researcher has gained entry to a particular setting? Explain.
- What is the role of key informants in ethnographic research? Is there anything to be concerned about when using them?

ROLES FOR ETHNOGRAPHERS

- What does it mean to 'go native'?
- Should ethnographers be active or passive in their research settings? Explain.

FIELD NOTES

- Why are field notes important for ethnographers?
- Why is it useful to distinguish between different types of field notes?

THE RISE OF VISUAL ETHNOGRAPHY

- How can visual materials be used in ethnography?
- Do photographs provide unproblematic images of reality? Discuss.

THE END

- How do ethnographers decide when to bring their studies to a close?

CAN THERE BE A FEMINIST ETHNOGRAPHY?

- What are the main features of feminist ethnography?

- Assess Stacey's argument regarding the possibility of feminist ethnography, taking Skeggs's research (or that of any other feminist ethnographer) into consideration.

CHAPTER 10

Interviewing in Qualitative Research

CHAPTER OVERVIEW

This chapter is concerned with interviews in **qualitative research**. Two types are discussed: **unstructured** and **semi-structured interviews**. This chapter is concerned mainly with interviews with individuals, but the **focus group** method is also examined. The highlights of this chapter include:

- the differences between **structured** and qualitative interviewing;
- the main characteristics of and differences between unstructured and semi-structured interviewing;
- how to devise and use an **interview guide** for semi-structured interviewing;
- the kinds of questions that can be placed in an interview guide;
- the importance of recording and transcribing qualitative interviews;
- the potential uses and pitfalls of online interviewing;
- how focus groups should be conducted, including matters such as the number of participants, how to select them, and how direct the questioning should be;
- issues concerning the interactions between participants in focus group discussions;

- some practical difficulties with focus group sessions, such as loss of control over the proceedings and the potential for unwanted group effects;
- the significance of qualitative interviewing and focus groups in feminist research; and
- the advantages and disadvantages of qualitative interviewing relative to **ethnography**.

Practice makes perfect, so why not hone your qualitative interviewing skills in casual, everyday conversations? It's often said that the art of conversation is dying in modern times, but if you approach every discussion you have as a qualitative interview in the making, that may change. Everyday conversation rarely has a narrowly restricted, specific purpose, and neither does qualitative research. A good way to start a discussion is to ask other people where they grew up, or what their most memorable experiences were; then get them to expand on their answers, taking care to draw out how they felt about the experiences, what the experiences meant to them, how they affected their lives, and so on. If you're with a group of people at a party or on a long trip, you can even hold an impromptu focus group session, secretly appointing yourself the moderator. Besides being good practice, chance conversations and seemingly inconsequential interactions can spark some very good research ideas.

Introduction

The interview is probably the most widely used method in qualitative research. Ethnography usually involves a substantial amount of qualitative interviewing, and this undoubtedly contributes to its wide use. But it is possible to conduct qualitative interviews without doing a full-blown ethnographic study. In fact, the flexibility of the qualitative interview and its relatively low cost compared to ethnography make it an attractive option for many researchers. Although interviewing, transcribing interviews, and analyzing transcripts are all very time-consuming, they don't intrude on researchers' personal lives to the degree that spending extended periods of time with research subjects does.

There are two main types of qualitative interview: unstructured and semi-structured. A variety of specialized interview forms fall under those two headings and will be explored below, including focus groups, **oral history interviews**, and **life history interviews**.

Differences between structured and qualitative research interviews

Qualitative interviewing is quite different from interviewing in **quantitative research**:

- In quantitative research, the approach is highly structured to maximize **reliability** and **validity** in measuring key **concepts**. The researcher usually has a clearly specified set of research questions that the interview is designed to answer. Qualitative interviewing, on the other hand, is much less structured and tends to be more open-ended. It also allows greater freedom to modify and add research ideas once the investigation has begun.

- There is greater interest in the interviewee's perspectives and concerns in qualitative interviewing; in quantitative research, the interview is driven mainly by the research agenda of the person conducting the study.

- In qualitative interviewing, going off on a tangent is often encouraged. The interviewer may vary both the order and the wording of questions, and may even ask unplanned questions to follow up on interviewees' replies; the additional replies may provide new insight into what the interviewee sees as relevant and important. In quantitative research, departing from the **interview schedule** is usually discouraged because it diverges from the specific research plan and may affect reliability and validity.

- Qualitative interviewing tends to be flexible, responding to the direction in which interviewees take the interview and perhaps adjusting the emphases in the research as a result of the issues that emerge during the interview. By contrast, **structured interviews** are typically inflexible, because of the need to standardize the interactions with all interviewees.

- In qualitative interviewing, the researcher wants rich, detailed answers; in structured interviewing the interview is normally designed to generate specific answers that can be coded and processed quickly.

- In qualitative interviewing, it is not uncommon for the interviewee to be interviewed more than once (see Box 10.1 for an example). In structured interviewing, unless the research is longitudinal in character, the person is usually interviewed only once.

BOX 10.1 | Unstructured interviewing

Malbon (1999: 33) described his strategy for interviewing 'clubbers' (people who frequent nightclubs) as follows:

> interviews were very much 'conversational' in style, although all interviews were taped. The first interview was designed . . . to put the clubber at ease while also explaining fully and clearly in what ways I was hoping for help; to begin to sketch in details of the clubbers clubbing preferences, motivations and histories; and to decide how to approach the night(s) out that I would be spending with the clubber. . . . The main content of the second [more relaxed] interview consisted of comments, discussion, and questions about the club visits . . . and the nature of the night out as an experience. . . . [D]iscussion occasionally diversified . . . to cover wider aspects of the clubbers' lives.

Unstructured and semi-structured interviewing

As we have noted, there are two main types of qualitative interview:

- In an *unstructured interview* the researcher uses at most a memory aid: a small set of self-prompts to investigate certain topics. The interviewer may ask just a single question; then the interviewee is allowed to respond freely, with the interviewer pursuing points that seem worthy of follow-up. Unstructured interviewing tends to be similar in character to a conversation.

- In a *semi-structured interview* the researcher has a list of questions or fairly specific topics to be covered (an *interview guide*), but the interviewee still has a great deal of leeway in deciding how to reply (see Box 10.2 for an illustration). Questions may not follow the exact order in the guide and some questions not included on the list may be asked in response to what the interviewee says. Nonetheless, all of the questions are usually asked and similar wording is used from interviewee to interviewee. Box 10.3 illustrates these features, while Box 10.4 gives an example of the qualitative interviewing typical of life history research.

BOX 10.2 | Semi-structured interviewing

Lupton investigated Australian food preferences using 33 semi-structured interviews conducted by four female interviewers (including herself):

> Interviewees were asked to talk about their favourite and most detested foods; whether they thought there was such a thing as 'masculine' or 'feminine' foods or dishes; which types of foods they considered 'healthy' or 'good for you' and which not; . . . whether they liked to try new foods; which foods they had tasted first as an adult; whether there had been any changes in the types of food they had eaten over their lifetime; whether they associated different types of food with particular times, places or people; . . . whether they ate certain foods when in certain moods and whether they had any rituals around food (1996: 156, 158).

BOX 10.3 | Flexibility in semi-structured interviewing

Like Lupton (see Box 10.2), Beardsworth and Keil (1992) were interested in food-related issues, particularly in vegetarianism. They carried out 73 'relatively unstructured interviews' guided by an inventory of issues to be covered in each session. As the interview program progressed, interviewees themselves raised additional or complementary issues, and these formed an integral part of the study's findings. In other words, the interview program was not based on a set of relatively rigid pre-determined questions and prompts. Rather, the open-ended, discursive nature of the interviews permitted an iterative refinement, whereby lines of thought identified by earlier interviewees could be taken up and presented to later ones (Beardsworth and Keil 1992: 261–2).

In semi- and unstructured interviews, the process is designed to bring out how the *interviewees themselves* interpret and make sense of issues and events. Bell (2007), for example, wanted to understand what western Canadian separatists thought of Canadian federalism and the federal party system. Tastsoglou and Miedema (2003) sought to understand the meaning of community from the perspective of immigrant women, and Smith (2008) examined the meanings of pain for professional wrestlers. Projects like these, unlike quantitative studies, are usually not designed to test hypotheses or theories. In short, qualitative research is not just quantitative research without the numbers.

There is a growing tendency to refer to semi-structured and unstructured interviews collectively as *in-depth interviews* or *qualitative interviews*, although the semi- and unstructured types can produce very different results. The choice of one type rather than the other is affected by a variety of factors.

- Researchers who feel that using even the most rudimentary interview guide hinders genuine access to the worldviews of members of a social setting are likely to favour an unstructured approach. But even here the interview is rarely completely unstructured: the researcher usually has at least a general topic that is to be discussed.

BOX 10.4 | Life history interviews

One special form of interview associated with qualitative research is the life history interview. It is often combined with personal documents such as diaries, photographs, and letters. Subjects are invited to look back in detail across their entire life course, and to report their experiences and how they understood their world. Valuable insights may be gained from a life history regardless of whether other people have had the same experiences as the person described in the work. It also has the advantage of illustrating *process*: how events unfold and interrelate in people's lives over long periods of time.

An example of the life history interview approach is provided by Lewis (1961) in his research on the Sánchez family and their experiences in a Mexican slum:

> I asked hundreds of questions of [the five members of the Sánchez family]. . . . While I used a directive approach to the interviews, I encouraged free association, and I was a good listener. I attempted to cover systematically a wide range of subjects: their earliest memories, their dreams, their hopes, fears, joys, and sufferings; their jobs; their relationship with friends, relatives, employers; their sex life; their concepts of justice, religion, and politics; their knowledge of geography and history; in short, their total view of the world. Many of my questions stimulated them to express themselves on subjects that they might otherwise never have thought about (1961: xxi).

Miller (2000) points out that a recent resurgence of interest in the life history method reflects the growing popularity of 'narrative interviews' in which the person studied, instead of responding to an interviewer's questions, 'tells a story.' In the past this approach was associated with the study of a single life, or perhaps two, but today it is increasingly applied to several lives in a single project. M. Atkinson (2002, 2004), for example, conducted narrative interviews with women tattoo enthusiasts.

P. Atkinson (2004) observed that the duration of life story interviews varies considerably from study to study, but that it usually takes two or three sessions lasting 60 to 90 minutes each. He provided a catalogue of questions that can be asked, and divided them into the following groups (1990: 43–53):

- Birth and family of origin (e.g., 'How would you describe your parents?')
- Cultural traditions (e.g., 'Was your family different from others in town?')
- Social factors ('e.g., What were some of your struggles as a child?')
- Education (e.g., 'What are your best memories of school?')
- Love and work (e.g., 'How did you end up in the work you do or did?')
- Inner and spiritual life (e.g., 'What are the stresses of being an adult?')
- Major life themes (e.g., 'What were the crucial decisions in your life?')
- Vision of the future (e.g., 'Is your life fulfilled yet?')
- Closure questions (e.g., 'Have you given a fair picture of yourself?')

A variant of the life history interview is the *oral history* interview, a technique often used by historians. It is usually somewhat more specific in tone than the interviews described above in that the subjects may be asked to reflect on certain historical events or eras they have lived through. The emphasis is often on how the individual's life was affected by those things. The information gathered is sometimes combined with other sources of data, such as documents.

The chief problem with the oral history interview (a problem it shares with the life history interview) is the possibility of bias caused by memory lapses and distortions. Sugiman (2004) pointed out in her work on Japanese-Canadian women interned during the Second World War that remembering is a social and even political act, involving recall, forgetting, transforming, and shaping of recollections. On the other hand, oral history testimonies can give a voice to groups that are typically marginalized in historical research (this is true of life history interviews in general), either because of their lack of power or because they are regarded as unimportant.

- If the researcher is beginning the investigation with a fairly clear rather than a general focus, it is likely that the interviews will be semi-structured, so that they can address more specific issues.

- If more than one person is to carry out the fieldwork, semi-structured interviewing may be preferred, to ensure that interviewing styles are comparable.

- Multiple-case study research generally needs some structure to ensure cross-case comparability.

PREPARING AN INTERVIEW GUIDE

An interview guide is much shorter and less detailed than a structured interview schedule. In fact, it is often simply a brief list of memory prompts for areas to be covered in unstructured interviewing and a somewhat more elaborate list of issues to be addressed or questions to be asked in semi-structured interviewing. What is crucial is that the actual questioning is flexible, allowing interviewers to pursue leads offered by research participants as they begin to open up and reveal their view of the social world.

In preparing for qualitative interviews, Lofland and Lofland (1995: 78) suggested that researchers ask themselves 'Just what about this thing is puzzling me?' This question can be applied to each of the research questions generated; it can also serve as a mechanism for generating research questions. Lofland and Lofland suggested that puzzlement may be stimulated in various ways: by recording random thoughts in different contexts (writing them down as quickly as possible); through discussions with colleagues, friends, and relatives; and, of course, by reading the existing literature on the topic. The formulation of the research question(s) should not be so specific as to close off the alternative avenues of inquiry that may arise during fieldwork. Premature closure of the research focus would be inconsistent with qualitative research's prime purpose: to explore the worldview of the people being studied, rather than to test the researcher's own ideas about that world.

The interview guide should:

- establish a certain amount of order, so that questions flow reasonably well, but still allow for changes in the order of the questions and the impromptu asking of different questions;
- include questions or topics that address the research questions (without being too specific);
- use language that is comprehensible and familiar to those being studied;
- not ask leading questions—that is, questions that imply a 'correct' or socially acceptable answer (for example, 'Have you ever done something really stupid, like taking crack?'); and

- include prompts to remind the researcher to record basic information about the participant (name, age, gender, etc.) as well as more specific information that is relevant to the research questions (position in company, number of years employed, number of years involved in a group, etc.); such information is useful for putting people's comments into context.

There are also some practical details to attend to before the interview begins:

- Become familiar with the research setting, which in many cases will be the everyday surroundings of the interviewees. This will help to put their comments in context.
- Get a reliable tape recorder. Qualitative researchers (with the possible exception of ethnographers and people doing participant observation research) nearly always record and then transcribe their interviews. This is important for the detailed analysis required in qualitative research, and to ensure that the interviewees' answers are captured in their own terms. Simply taking notes makes it too easy to lose specific words and phrases.
- Make sure as far as possible that the interview takes place in a setting that is quiet (so that the quality of the recording will be as good as possible) and private (so that the interviewee won't worry about being overheard).
- Prepare for the interview by cultivating the traits of a quality interviewer suggested by Kvale (1996) (see Box 10.5).

After the interview, make notes about:

- how the interview went (was interviewee talkative, cooperative, nervous, etc.?);
- where the interview took place;
- any other feelings about the interview (did it open up new avenues of interest?); and
- the setting (noisy/quiet, many/few other people in the vicinity).

The steps required to formulate questions for an interview guide in qualitative research are presented in Figure 10.1.

KINDS OF QUESTIONS

The kinds of questions asked in qualitative interviews are highly variable; Kvale (1996) suggested

BOX 10.5 : Kvale's ten traits of an effective interviewer (plus three others)

Kvale (1996) proposed that a successful interviewer has ten characteristics:

- *Knowledgeable:* is thoroughly familiar with the topic of the interview.
- *Structuring:* tells the interviewee the purpose of the interview; asks if the interviewee has questions.
- *Clear:* asks simple, easy, and short questions; no jargon.
- *Gentle:* lets people finish; gives them time to think; tolerates pauses.
- *Sensitive:* listens attentively both to what is said and to how it is said; is empathetic.
- *Open:* responds to what the interviewee considers important; is flexible.
- *Steering:* knows what needs to be found out.
- *Critical:* is prepared to challenge what is said when, for example, there is an inconsistency in the interviewee's replies.

- *Remembering:* relates what is said to what has previously been said.
- *Interpreting:* clarifies and extends the meaning of interviewees' statements but without imposing meaning on them.

To Kvale's list of traits, please add the following three:

- *Balanced:* does not talk too much, which can make interviewees passive, but does not talk too little, which can cause interviewees to feel that their responses are not satisfactory.
- *Ethically sensitive:* for example, assures the interviewee that all answers will be treated confidentially.
- *Non-judgmental:* does not communicate (even subtly) a moral judgment about what an interviewee has said or done; negative judgments may cause people to withhold information that could be useful to the study, while positive judgments may encourage them to focus on pleasing the interviewer rather than providing authentic commentary.

General research area → Specific research questions → Interview topics → Formulate interview questions → Review/revise interview questions → Pilot guide → Identify novel issues → Revise interview questions → Finalize guide

FIGURE 10.1 Formulating questions for an interview guide for social research

nine. Most interviews contain virtually all of them, although those that rely on lists of topics are likely to follow a somewhat looser format. Kvale's nine types are as follows:

- *Introducing questions*: 'Please tell me about when your interest in X first began'; 'Have you ever . . . ?'; 'Why did you go to . . . ?'

- *Follow-up questions*: These get the interviewee to elaborate on an answer; for example: 'What do you mean by that?'; even, 'Yeesss?' Kvale suggested repeating significant words in an answer to stimulate further explanation. See Box 10.6 for an example.

- *Probing questions*: These follow up what has been said through direct questioning; for example: 'Can you say some more about that?'; 'You said earlier that you prefer not to do X. Can you say what kinds of things have put you off it?'; 'In what ways do you find X disturbing?'

- *Specifying questions*: 'What did you do then?'; 'How did (name) react to what you said?'; 'What effect did (event) have on you?' See Box 10.6 for an example.

- *Direct questions*: 'Do you find it easy to keep smiling when serving customers?'; 'Are you

BOX 10.6 Using a semi-structured interview: research on female offenders

Two factors seem to have been instrumental in Davies' (2000) decision to use semi-structured interviewing with female offenders. First, she felt that her research questions—'exploring the types of crimes individuals engaged in and details of the ways in which they conducted them' (2000: 85)—were an important factor in her decision. A second factor was the consistency of semi-structured interviewing with the principles of feminist research 'because such interviews seek not to be exploitative but to be appreciative of the position of women' (2000: 86). Davies interviewed female offenders both in prison, which necessitated a lengthy series of negotiations about access, and in the community. Access to women in the community setting was provided by women already willing to be interviewed, who put Davies in touch with others. She described her interview strategy as follows: 'Most important is to listen, then prompt and encourage when appropriate without leading, and to steer the discussion back on track if it appears to be heading down a less promising avenue' (2000: 91). At one point, as a follow-up question, she repeated the interviewee's words—a tactic mentioned by Kvale (1996)—and then followed up the reply with what Kvale called a probing question (Davies is 'PD'):

> *PD*: You mentioned security tags and foil?
>
> *F*: It depended on the shops—some shops we would just. . . when we just started out we didn't know about the foil so we used ter take in a pair of wire clippers, take them off, and dump them in the changing room but they made one hell of a crack—have you heard wire being cut? It made a hell of a bang so we just used ter take them off and shove them anywhere—yer know what I meant—somewhere they wouldn't be found like in a pocket of someone else's coat and . . . then we found out about the foil an we started doing that.
>
> *PD*: How did you find out about that? (2000: 91).

Interviews were transcribed and written up within a day or two of their completion so that any particular nuances or impressions would not be forgotten.

---

happy with the way you and your husband decide how money should be spent?' Such questions are perhaps best left until later in the interview, in order not to influence the direction of the interview too much.

- *Indirect questions*: Before asking an indirect question—for example, 'What do most people around here think of the ways that management treats its staff?'—be sure to ask the interviewee for his or own view ('How do you feel about . . . ?').

- *Structuring questions*: 'Now I would like to move on to a different topic.'

- *Silence*: A pause will give the interviewee an opportunity to reflect and amplify an answer; just don't pause for so long that the interviewee feels embarrassed.

- *Interpreting questions*: 'Do you mean that your leadership role had to change from one of encouraging others to a more directive one?'; 'Is it fair to say that you don't mind being friendly towards customers most of the time, but you find it more difficult when they are unpleasant or demanding?'

As this list suggests, one of the main jobs of the interviewer is listening: being attentive to what the interviewee is saying or not saying. The interviewer must be active without being intrusive—a difficult balance. This means that the interviewer can't just sit back and relax, even if the interview is being recorded. In fact, the interviewer must be attuned and responsive not just to what is said and not said, but also to what the interviewee is doing. This is important because body language can indicate that the interviewee is becoming uneasy with a line of questioning. An ethically sensitive interviewer does not place undue pressure on an interviewee and is prepared to cut short any line of questioning that is clearly a source of anxiety.

It's likely that the kinds of questions asked will vary in the different stages of a qualitative interview. Charmaz (2002) distinguished three types of question in this connection. Note that questions about the past and factual matters come first, then questions about feelings, and finally questions of process and summing up.

- *Initial open-ended questions*: 'What events led to . . . ?'; 'What was your life like prior to . . . ?';

'Is this organization typical of others you have worked in?'

- *Intermediate questions*: 'How did you feel about . . . when you first learned about it?'; 'What immediate impact did . . . have on your life'; 'What do you like most/least about working here?'

- *Ending questions*: 'How have your views about . . . changed?'; 'What advice would you give to someone who is undergoing a similar experience . . . ?'; 'If you had to do it over, would you choose to work for this organization?'

Most questions are likely to be of the intermediate kind, and some categories are likely to overlap. Nonetheless, these are useful distinctions to bear in mind.

Remember as well that interviews include different kinds of topics, such as:

- values: of the interviewee, of the group, of the organization;

- beliefs: of the interviewee, of individual others, of the group;

- behaviour: of the interviewee, of others;

- formal and informal roles: of the interviewee, of others;

- relationships: of the interviewee, of others;

- places and locales;

- emotions: particularly of the interviewee, but also of others;

- encounters; and

- stories.

Try to vary the types of questions you ask (see Kvale's nine types) and, where appropriate, the topic areas (see the list above). Vague or overly general questions are usually best avoided; as Mason (2002*b*) pointed out, they only force interviewees to puzzle over them or to ask for clarification.

Vignette questions can be used to ground interviewees' ideas and accounts of behaviour in particular situations (Barter and Renold 1999). By presenting interviewees with concrete and realistic scenarios, the researcher can elicit a sense of how certain contexts mould behaviour. Hughes (1998) employed the technique in a study of perceptions of HIV risk among intravenous drug users. Context is important for this topic because drug users' willingness to engage in risky behaviour is influenced by situational factors. Scenarios depicting risk behaviour were presented and respondents were asked about the kinds of behaviour they felt that drug users *should* engage in (such as using prophylactics when having sex) and then about how they felt the hypothetical users *would* behave (when, for example, there was an opportunity for unprotected sex). Hughes argued that a scenario approach is particularly valuable with sensitive topics and for eliciting a range of responses to different contexts.

Using an interview guide: an example   Box 10.7 is taken from a study of visitors to Disney theme parks (Bryman 1999). The interviewees were a man in his sixties and his wife who was two years younger. They had visited Walt Disney World, and were very enthusiastic about the visit.

The sequence begins with the interviewer asking what is considered a 'direct question,' in terms of the nine question types suggested by Kvale (1996). The replies are very bland and do little more than reflect the interviewees' positive feelings about their visit to Disney World. The wife acknowledges this when she says, '. . . but I need to say more than that, don't I?' Interviewees frequently know that they are expected to be expansive in their answers. This sequence occurred about halfway through the interview, so by then the interviewees were primed to recognize that more details were expected. There is a tinge of embarrassment that the answer is so brief and not illuminating. The husband's answer is more expansive but not particularly enlightening.

Then the first of two important prompts by the interviewer follows. The husband's response after the initial prompt is more interesting in that he begins to wonder whether black people are underrepresented at attractions like the American Adventure, which tells the story of America via a debate between Mark Twain and Benjamin Franklin. The second prompt yields further useful reflection, this time that Third World countries are underrepresented in World Showcase in the Epcot Centre. The couple are clearly aware that it was the prompting that led them to these reflections: 'I hadn't really given this any consideration before you started asking about it.' This is the whole point of prompting: to get the interviewee to think more about the topic and to provide an opportunity for a more detailed response. It isn't

BOX 10.7 Part of the transcript of a semi-structured interview

Interviewer: OK. What were your views or feelings about the presentation of different cultures, as shown in, for example, Jungle Cruise or It's a Small World at the Magic Kingdom or in World Showcase at Epcot?

Wife: Well, I thought the different countries at Epcot were wonderful, but I need to say more than that, don't I?

Husband: They were very good and some were better than others, but that was down to the host countries themselves really, as I suppose each of the countries represented would have been responsible for their own part, so that's nothing to do with Disney, I wouldn't have thought. I mean some of the landmarks were hard to recognize for what they were supposed to be, but some were very well done. Britain was OK, but there was only a pub and a Welsh shop there really, whereas some of the other pavilions, as I think they were called, were good ambassadors for the countries they represented. China, for example, had an excellent 360-degree film showing parts of China and I found that very interesting.

Interviewer: Did you think there was anything lacking about the content?

Husband: Well I did notice that there weren't many black people at World Showcase, particularly the American

Adventure. Now whether we were there on an unusual day in that respect I don't know, but we saw plenty of black Americans in the Magic Kingdom and other places, but very few if any in that World Showcase. And there was certainly little mention of black history in the American Adventure presentation, so maybe they felt alienated by that, I don't know, but they were noticeable by their absence.

Interviewer: So did you think there were any special emphases?

Husband: Well, thinking about it now, because I hadn't really given this any consideration before you started asking about it, but thinking about it now, it was only really representative of the developed world, you know, Britain, America, Japan, world leaders many of them in technology, and there was nothing of the Third World there. Maybe that's their own fault, maybe they were asked to participate and didn't, but now that I think about it, that does come to me. What do you think, love?

Wife: Well, like you, I hadn't thought of it like that before, but I agree with you.

---

a leading question, since the interviewees were *not* asked whether they thought the Disney company failed to recognize the significance of black history or ignored the Third World. There is no doubt that the prompts elicited the more informative replies, which is precisely their role.

RECORDING AND TRANSCRIPTION

The point has been made several times that in qualitative research the interview is usually audio-recorded and then transcribed (not just listened to) whenever possible. Qualitative researchers are frequently interested not only in what people say but also in the way they say it. If this aspect is to be fully woven into an analysis, the complete series of exchanges in an interview must be available. Also, because interviewers are supposed to be highly alert to what is being said—following up on interesting points, prompting and probing where necessary, drawing attention to any inconsistencies in the interviewee's answers—it's best if they don't have to concentrate on writing down what is said as well. In addition, recording interviews

allows scrutiny by other researchers, who can evaluate the original analysis or even conduct a secondary analysis, which can help to counter accusations that the findings were influenced by the researcher's values or biases. Recording also makes it possible for the data to be reused

Practical Tip ▶ ▶ ▶ ▶

Transcribing interviews

A student doing research for a thesis may not have the resources to pay for professional transcription, and unless he or she is an accurate touch typist, transcription can take a lot of time. The usual estimate is five to six hours per hour of speech, although using a transcription device with a foot-operated stop-start mechanism makes the task much easier. The important thing is to allow sufficient time for transcription and to be realistic about how many interviews can be transcribed in the time available.

in ways other than those intended by the original researcher; for example, to be analyzed using new theoretical ideas or analytic strategies.

As with just about everything in social research, there is a cost (apart from the financial cost of buying recording equipment and tapes or disks) in that the use of a recorder can upset respondents, who may become self-conscious or alarmed at the prospect that their words will be preserved in that way. Most people will allow their interviews to be recorded, though it's not uncommon for a small number to refuse. When that happens (or when the tape recorder malfunctions), the interview can still proceed with the interviewer taking notes. Among those who do agree to be recorded, some will still be fearful and as a result their interviews may not be as informative as they otherwise would be.

Another consideration, as we have seen, is the time required to transcribe a recorded interview. There is some debate over who should do the transcribing: the interviewer (more familiar with what was actually said) or someone else (less time-consuming) (Rafaeli *et al.* 1997: 14). Furthermore, the vast amounts of text produced must then be read. Beardsworth and Keil (1992: 262) reported that their 73 interviews on vegetarianism (see Box 10.3) generated 'several hundred thousand words of transcript material.' Clearly, even though transcription has the advantage of keeping the interviewee's (and interviewer's) words intact, it does so by piling up the text to be analyzed. It's no wonder that writers like Lofland and Lofland (1995) advise researchers not to leave the analysis of qualitative data until all the interviews have been completed and transcribed. Insights may be gained by examining the content of early interviews, and it may be useful to pursue those points in greater detail in later interviews. Thus there are good grounds for making analysis an ongoing activity (see Box 10.3 for an example). Also, to wait until all interviews have been completed may make the task of transcription seem overwhelming.

Transcription may seem a relatively unproblematic matter of converting the spoken word into written form. However, given the importance of transcripts in qualitative research, the process should not be taken lightly. Transcribers need to be trained in much the same way that interviewers are. Moreover, even experienced transcribers can make mistakes. Poland (1995) provided some

Practical Tip ▶▶▶▶

Transcribing sections of an interview

It's not always to necessary to transcribe every word of an interview. Quite often you will find that large portions of a particular interview (even all of it) won't be useful, perhaps because the interviewee was reticent or because the comments made were not as relevant to the research topic as you had expected. For example, Gerson and Horowitz (2002: 211) found some of their qualitative interviews 'uninspiring and uninteresting.' There seems to be little point in transcribing such material. Before you begin transcribing, therefore, listen to the interviews closely once or twice, and then transcribe only the portions that seem useful or relevant. The same applies to focus group research, which is often more difficult and time-consuming to transcribe because of the number of speakers involved. The downside is that you may miss things, or certain comments may emerge as significant only later on. If that happens, you will have to go back to the tapes to get the needed material.

fascinating examples of the errors that can result from factors such as mishearing, fatigue, or carelessness. For example, one transcript contained the following passage:

> I think unless we want to become like other countries, where people have, you know, democratic freedoms . . .

But the actual words on the audiotape were:

> I think unless we want to become like other countries, where people have no democratic freedoms . . . (1995: 294)

Clearly, steps need to be taken to check on the quality of transcription.

In qualitative research there is often wide variation in the time that different interviews take. For example, in Wilson's rave study (2002), the interviews lasted between 45 minutes and 4 hours. Shorter interviews are not necessarily inferior, with the exception of those in which the interviewee was non-cooperative or anxious about being recorded. Indeed, when a long interview contains very little of significance, it may not be worth the time and cost of transcription. Thankfully, such occasions are relatively rare. People who have agreed to be interviewed are usually cooperative, and most loosen up once they get over their initial anxiety about the microphone. As a result, even short interviews are often quite revealing.

Flexibility in the interview Flexibility in interviewing means more than being responsive to what interviewees say and following up on the interesting points they make. A flexible interviewer is able to vary the order of questions and clear up inconsistencies in answers. Flexibility is also important when audio recording equipment breaks down, or when an interviewee refuses permission for recording to take place.

Another common problem for interviewers is knowing when to switch off their recording equipment. Often an interviewee will resume talking about the topic of interest as soon as the machine is turned off. It's usually not feasible to switch the machine back on again, so try to keep it going as long as possible. If that fails, take some notes either while the person is talking or as soon as possible after the interview. Such 'unsolicited accounts' can often be the source of revealing information. This is certainly what Parker found in his study of organizations: many interviewees offered 'unrecorded comments prefixed with a silent or explicit "well, if you want to know what I really think." . . . Needless to say, a visit to the toilet to write up as much as I could remember followed almost immediately' (2000: 236).

Focus groups: an introduction

Most people think of an interview as an exchange between one interviewer and one interviewee. The focus group technique, however, involves speaking with more than one (usually at least four) interviewees at the same time. Essentially it is a group interview in which the interviewees can speak to and interact with one another.

- Most focus group researchers work within a qualitative research tradition. They try to provide a fairly unstructured setting in which the person who runs the focus group, usually called the **moderator** or *facilitator*, guides the session but does not intrude. A focus group offers several advantages. One of the most important is that it allows the researcher to develop an understanding of *why* people feel the way they do. In individual interviews, subjects are often asked about their reasons for holding a particular view, but a focus group allows participants to probe one another's reasons. This can be more informative and revealing than the question-followed-by-answer method of ordinary interviews. For example, an individual who has already answered a certain question may decide, after hearing others' answers, to qualify or modify that response in some way. Some people may want to voice agreement with a view they might not otherwise have thought of. These possibilities permit focus groups to elicit a wide variety of perspectives on an issue.

- In conventional one-to-one interviewing, interviewees are rarely challenged; they may say things that are inconsistent with earlier replies or that patently cannot be true, but interviewers are often reluctant to point out such deficiencies. In a focus group, participants may argue and challenge one another's views. Arguing often produces more realistic accounts of what people think, because it forces them to defend and possibly revise their views.

- A focus group offers an opportunity to study how individuals collectively make sense of a phenomenon and construct meanings of it. It is a central tenet of theoretical positions such as **symbolic interactionism** that meanings and understandings are not derived by individuals in isolation: rather, they develop out of interactions and discussions with others. In this sense, focus groups reflect the processes through which meaning is constructed in everyday life, which allows them to be more **naturalistic** than individual interviews (Wilkinson 1998). On the other hand, it is not clear whether these new meanings persist beyond the focus group session.

Conducting focus groups

A number of practical aspects of conducting a focus group are considered below.

HOW MANY GROUPS?

How many focus groups are needed? Table 10.1 provides some data on this question, and on some other aspects of focus groups (cf. Deacon *et al.* 1999). As it suggests, there is a good deal of variation in the number of groups required for a particular study, but it generally ranges from 10 to 15.

A single group is unlikely to be sufficient, since the responses may not be typical of other groups. Nonetheless, there are good reasons for limiting the number of groups (besides saving time and resources). Once the moderator is able to anticipate fairly accurately what the next group is going to say, enough groups have participated. This notion is similar to **theoretical saturation** in grounded theory, discussed in Chapter 9.

One factor that can affect the number of groups required is whether the researcher thinks that the range of views is likely to be affected by socio-demographic factors such as age, gender, or social class. Many focus group researchers like to ensure that different demographic groups are included, which usually requires a large number of groups.

In connection with the research described in Box 10.8, Kitzinger (1994) wrote that a large number of groups is preferred in order to capture as many different perspectives as possible. On the other hand, conducting more groups increases the complexity of the analysis. For example, Schlesinger *et al.* (1992: 29; see Table 10.1 and Box 10.9) reported that their 14 tape-recorded hour-long sessions produced more than 1400 pages of transcription for analysis.

Size of groups and selecting participants

How large should a single focus group be? Morgan (1998*a*) suggested 6 to 10 members. To control for the problem of 'no-shows,' researchers often

---

BOX 10.8 | Focus group in action: AIDS in the Media Research Project

Focus groups were part of Kitzinger's research on the representation of AIDS in the mass media. The focus groups were concerned with how 'media messages are explored by audiences and how understandings of AIDS are constructed. We were interested not solely in what people thought but in how they thought and why they thought as they did' (Kitzinger 1994: 104).

Details of the groups are given in Table 10.1. Since one goal of the research was to emphasize the role of interaction in the construction of meaning, it was important to provide a platform for doing that. Accordingly, 'instead of working with isolated individuals,

or collections of individuals drawn together simply for the purposes of the research, we elected to work with pre-existing groups—people who already lived, worked or socialized together' (Kitzinger 1993: 272). As a result, the people in each group were known to each other: a team of civil engineers working on the same site, six members of a retirement club, five intravenous drug users, and so on. The sessions themselves were 'conducted in a relaxed fashion with minimal intervention from the facilitator—at least at first' (Kitzinger 1994: 106). Each session lasted approximately two hours and was tape-recorded.

BOX 10.9 | Asking about violence

Researchers usually want to inject some structure into their focus group sessions. An example can be seen in the research conducted by Schlesinger *et al.* (1992; see Table 10.1) on women viewing a film that featured varying levels of violence. For a rape scene, reactions were gleaned through 'guiding questions' under five main headings, the first three of which had several more specific elements:

- Initially, participants were given the opportunity to discuss the film in terms of things such as its purpose, its realism, and its storyline.

- The questioning then moved on to reactions to the characters: the woman who was raped, the three rapists, the female lawyer, the male lawyers.

- Participants were then asked about their reactions to particular scenes, including the rape; the

female lawyer's decision to support the case after initially not supporting it; and the victory in court.

- Participants were asked for their reactions to the inclusion of the rape scene.

- Finally, they were asked to give an assessment of the film's value, in particular whether the fact that it was American made a difference to their reactions.

While the research by Schlesinger and colleagues examined a lot of specific topics, initial questions were designed to generate relatively open-ended reactions. Such a general approach to questioning is fairly common in focus group research. It allows the investigator to address the research questions, ensures that there is some comparability between sessions, and permits participants to raise issues that *they* see as significant.

find themselves over-recruiting (for example, Wilkinson 1999a: 188). Morgan recommended small groups when the participants are likely to have a lot to say, as often occurs when they are emotionally involved with the topic, when the topic is controversial or complex, or when exploring personal interpretations. A larger group is appropriate when the researcher wants 'to hear numerous brief suggestions' (1998a: 75).

For most topics there is no need to select a particular kind of participant; however, the topic should be relevant to those taking part. A wide range of people is often required, but participants may be put into separate groups on the basis of age, gender, education, whether they have (or have not) had a certain experience, and so on. The aim is to look for any variation in how the different groups discuss the matter at hand. For example, to examine women's responses to scenes of violence, Schlesinger *et al.* (1992) showed 14 groups (see Table 10.1) four levels of mass-media violence:

incidental violence, moderate violence, marital violence, and an extremely vivid sexual assault scene. The authors concluded:

> Having a particular experience or a particular background does significantly affect the interpretation of a given text. The four programs screened are obviously open to various readings. However, on the evidence, *how* they are read is fundamentally affected by various socio-cultural factors and by lived experience (1992: 168; emphases in original).

A slight variation on this approach is Kitzinger's (1994) study of reactions to media representations of AIDS (see Box 10.8 and Table 10.1). Her groups were made up of people in a variety of situations. Some were what she called 'general population groups' (for example, a team of civil engineers working on the same site) but others were made up of people likely to have a special

TABLE 10.1 Composition of groups in focus groups research

AUTHORS	FROHLICH ET AL. (2002)	KITZINGER (1993, 1994)	LUPTON (1996)	MACNAGHTEN AND JACOBS (1997)	MIRAFTAB (2000)	SCHLESINGER ET AL. (1992)
Area of research	A contextual understanding of pre-adolescent smoking behaviour	Audience responses to media messages about aids	Responses to diet and health controversies	Understanding and identification with sustainable development	Housing experiences of Kurdish and Somali refugees in Vancouver	Responses of women to watching violence
Number of groups	Not specified	52	12	8 (each group had 2 sessions)	Not specified	14
Size range of groups	Probably 12	Not specified but appears to be 3, 9, or 10	3–5	6–10	10–15	5–9
Average (mean) size of groups	na	6.75	4.1	approximately 8	na	6.6
Criteria (if any) for inclusion	4 groups out of 32 Quebec communities	No, but groups made up of specific groups (e.g., retirement club members, male prostitutes)	Gender	Age, ethnicity, gender, occupation/ retired, rural/ urban location	None, except being recent immigrant	Experience of violence, Scottish/ English, ethnicity, class
Natural groups	No	Yes	Yes	No	No	Some

interest in AIDS, such as male prostitutes and intravenous drug users. Increasingly, focus group practitioners try to discern patterns of variation by putting together groups with particular attributes.

A further issue in designing a focus group is whether to select people who are unknown to each other, or to use natural groups (for example, friends, co-workers, or students in the same class). Some researchers prefer to exclude people who know each other, fearing that known status differences or pre-existing patterns of interaction would contaminate the session. Others prefer to select natural groups whenever possible. Holbrook and Jackson (1996) reported that, for their research on shopping centres, they initially tried to secure participants who were unknown to each other, but this strategy attracted no takers. They then sought out participants in various social clubs. They defended this new approach on the grounds that, because their research questions concerned shopping in relation to the construction of identity and how it relates to people's sense of place, recruiting people who knew each other would be highly appropriate. Recruiting people from natural groups is not always feasible, however, because of the difficulty of getting everyone in the group to participate. Morgan (1998*a*) revealed another downside: because people in natural groups know one another, they may share certain assumptions that they feel no need to explain or justify. He suggested that in cases where it is important that such assumptions are made explicit, a group of strangers is a better choice.

ASKING QUESTIONS AND LEVEL OF MODERATOR INVOLVEMENT

There are different questioning strategies and approaches to moderating focus group sessions. Most lie somewhere between a rather open-ended style and a more structured one. Macnaghten and Jacobs' (1997) middle-of-the-road approach to question structuring can be seen in the following passage in which a group of working women express cynicism about government and experts regarding the reality of environmental problems (in this passage 'F' is 'female' and 'Mod' is moderator):

> *F*: They only tell us what they want us to know. And that's just the end of that, so we are left with a fog in your brain, so you just think—what have I to worry about? I don't know what they're on about.

> *Mod*: So why do Government only tell us what they want us to hear?
>
> *F*: To keep your confidence going. (All together)
>
> *Mod*: So if someone provides an indicator which says the economy is improving you won't believe it?
>
> *F*: They've been saying it for about 10 years, but where? I can't see anything!
>
> *F*: Every time there's an election they say the economy is improving (1997: 18).

In this exchange, the moderator focuses on the topic to be addressed but is also able to pick up on what the group says.

How involved should the moderator or facilitator be? As with question structuring, above, the most common approach is middle-of-the-road. There is a tendency to use a fairly small number of very general questions to guide a focus group session. Obviously, if the discussion goes completely off topic it may be necessary to refocus the participants' attention, but even then the moderator must be careful, because apparent digressions can often reveal something of significance. More direction is probably needed if the participants are not addressing the research questions, or if a particularly meaningful point made by one participant is not followed up by the others.

Both intervention and non-intervention carry risks. The style of questioning and moderating depends on the nature of the research topic; if it is embarrassing for some participants, for example, additional direction may be required from the moderator. Levels of interest and knowledge among the participants can make a difference as well. Limited interest or knowledge on the part of participants may require a somewhat more structured approach. If in doubt, the best advice is to err on the side of minimal intervention.

RECORDING AND TRANSCRIPTION

Recording is even more important with focus groups than it is in other forms of qualitative research. Writing down not only exactly what is said but who says it is too difficult. In an individual interview you may be able to ask a respondent to 'hold on' while you write down a response, but this is not feasible in an interview where several people are speaking rapidly, and would almost certainly break the flow of the discussion.

Transcribing focus group sessions is also more complicated and hence more time-consuming than it is with other interview forms. Sometimes voices are hard to distinguish, making it difficult to determine who is speaking. Also, people sometimes talk over each other, which can make transcription even more problematic. Therefore a very high-quality recording device, capable of picking up even faint voices from many directions, is a necessity. Focus group transcripts always seem to have more missing bits than transcripts from other sorts of interview, mainly because of audibility problems.

Group interaction in focus group sessions

Kitzinger (1994) observed that reports of focus group research frequently fail to take group interaction into account. This is surprising, given that such interaction is a distinguishing feature of focus groups. Wilkinson reviewed more than 200 focus group studies, published between 1946 and 1996, and concluded: 'Focus group data is most commonly presented as if it were one-to-one interview data, with interactions between group participants rarely reported, let alone analyzed' (1998: 112).

In the context of her research on the coverage of AIDS in the mass media, Kitzinger (1994) drew attention to two types of interaction in focus groups: complementary and argumentative. Complementary interaction allows collective interpretations and understandings to develop, with each participant building on the preceding remark, as in the following passage taken from Morgan and Spanish's (1985: 414) research on heart-attack victims:

No. 1: But I think maybe what we're saying here is that there's no one cause of heart attacks, there's no one type of person, there's probably umpteen different types of heart attacks and causes coming from maybe smoking, maybe obesity, maybe stress, maybe design fault, hereditary, overwork, change in life style. Any of these things in themselves could be . . .

No. 2: And when you start putting them in combination [unclear].

No. 3: Yeah, you may be really magnifying each one of these particular things.

No. 2: Yeah, and depending on how, and in each person that magnification is different. Some people can take a little stress without doing any damage, some people can take a little smoking, a little drinking, a little obesity, without doing any damage. But you take a little of each of these and put them together and you're starting to increase the chances of damage. And any one of these that takes a magnitude leap increases the chances.

This sequence brings out the emerging consensus around the question of who has heart attacks and why. No. 1 summarizes several factors that have been discussed; No. 2 then suggests the possible significance of some factors existing in combination; No. 3 agrees about the importance of combinations of factors; and No. 2 summarizes the group's position on the salience of combinations of factors, at the same time raising the possibility that for each person there may be unique combinations of factors that are responsible for heart attacks.

However, as Kitzinger (1994) suggested, argumentative interaction in focus groups can be equally revealing. In such cases moderators can play an important role in identifying differences of opinion and exploring with participants the factors that lie behind them. Disagreement can give participants a chance to revise their opinions or to think about why they hold them. A passage from Schlesinger *et al.* (1992; see Table 10.1) illustrates. The group is made up of women with no experience of violence, and the debate concerns a rape scene in a film:

Speaker 1: I think . . . that they could've explained it. They could easily leave [out] that rape scene.

Speaker 2: But it's like that other film we watched. You don't realize the full impact, like, the one we were watching, the first one, until you've got the reconstruction.

Speaker 3: Yeah, but I think with that sort of film, it would cause more damage than it would good, I mean, if someone had been raped, would you like to have [to] sit through that again?

The debate then moved on to consider the significance of the scene for men:

Speaker 1: Men would sit down and think, 'Well, she asked for it. She was enjoying it and look, the men around enjoyed it' (1992: 51–2).

It seems, then, that behind the unease some of the women expressed about the rape scene was the idea that some men might enjoy it and identify with the onlookers depicted in the film. This interpretation came out because of an earlier disagreement within the group, which allowed the women to give a fuller account of their reactions to the scene.

In sum, as Kitzinger (1994) argued, drawing attention to patterns of interaction in focus groups allows a researcher to determine how group participants view the issues at hand. The posing of questions by focus group members as well as the agreement and disagreement among them help to bring out this knowledge. The resolution of disagreements also forces participants to explain why they hold the views they do.

Limitations of focus groups

Focus groups are particularly useful in illustrating how meaning is jointly constructed. What, then, are their chief limitations?

- The researcher probably has less control over the proceedings than in individual interviews. As we have seen, not all writers on focus groups perceive this as a problem; indeed, feminist researchers often see it as an advantage. However, the question of control raises questions about the extent to which a researcher should allow the participants to 'take over' the discussion. There is clearly a delicate balance to be struck in deciding how involved moderators should be and how much a set of prompts or questions should be allowed to influence the conversation. What is not clear is the degree to which it is appropriate to surrender control,

Methods in Motion

Applications to Canadian Society

Social researchers are often not satisfied with their conventional activities as scholars and scientists, and instead seek a broader role by engaging in public debates and working with various stakeholder groups to take political action to improve social conditions or prevent undesirable social change. Lett *et al.* (2010) tried their hand at this kind of social activism, which they and others describe as 'public sociology' (Burawoy 2005). The authors examined the use of video surveillance (CCTV) as a crime prevention mechanism, focusing on its use on the downtown streets of Kelowna, British Columbia. They were concerned that there had not been sufficient public consultation prior to the introduction of the surveillance, particularly with seniors and 'street' populations. Another issue was the scarcity of empirical evidence to back up the claims of CCTV supporters that video surveillance actually reduces the incidence of violent crime.

The researchers conducted focus group interviews with four sets of people: ten residents of a homeless shelter; five individuals recruited at a drop-in centre for the homeless and impoverished; and two groups of seniors who lived in downtown seniors' homes. They found that all four groups had limited knowledge of the surveillance system, in particular the location of the cameras and the fact that they were separate from the monitoring systems used in banks and stores. The researchers concluded from this that the much-heralded public consultation process was rather ineffective.

The focus group participants generally supported the installation of the cameras, especially the seniors, even though they were skeptical about the idea that the surveillance enhanced their safety. Yet when the researchers pointed out the absence of social scientific evidence that CCTV reduces the level of violent crime, the participants were not won over: they continued to support installation of the cameras. With some resignation, Lett *et al.* concluded that 'In the field, . . . public sociology is easier said than done' (458).

especially when there is a set of research questions to be answered.

- An unwieldy amount of data is sometimes produced. For example, Bloor *et al.* (2001) suggested that one focus group session can take up to eight hours to transcribe—somewhat longer than an equivalent personal interview, because of variations in voice pitch and the need to identify who says what. Also, group recordings often include inaudible comments from participants sitting too far from the microphone, and these also affect transcription.

- The data may be difficult to analyze. Developing an analysis strategy that incorporates both the themes of the discussion and the patterns of interaction is not easy.

- Focus groups are difficult to arrange. It may be hard to get people to agree to participate, and harder still to get them to show up. Very small payments, such as book tokens, are sometimes offered to induce participation, but it is still common to find that some people will not turn up.

- Group effects may be a problem. This category includes the obvious challenge of dealing with participants who are either too reticent to speak up or who hog the stage. Krueger (1998) suggested that the people running the focus group should make it clear to participants that other people's views are definitely required; for example, he suggested saying something like 'That's one point of view. Does anyone have another point of view?' (1998: 59). As for those who are reluctant to speak, Krueger recommended that they be actively encouraged to say something.

It would be interesting to know whether agreement among focus group participants is more common than disagreement; if that is the case, one reason might be group pressure to conform. It's also possible that participants are more likely to express socially acceptable views in a group setting than in individual interviews. Morgan (2002) cited a study in which group interviews with boys on the topic of relationships with girls were compared with individual interviews with boys on the same subject. Alone, the boys expressed a degree of sensitivity that was not evident in the group context, where they tended to express more macho views. This suggests that in the group setting the boys were trying to impress each other or avoid embarrassment, and were influenced by peer pressure. But this does not mean that such data are tainted: in fact, it may be the gulf between privately and publicly held views that is of interest.

- Madriz (2000) proposed that there are circumstances when individual interviews are more appropriate. One is when participants are likely to disagree profoundly with each other; another is when participants are not comfortable in one another's presence (for example, people in hierarchical relationships). Finally, because of the potential for focus groups to cause discomfort among participants (for example, when intimate details of private lives need to be revealed), an individual interview or even a questionnaire may be better.

Online interviews and focus groups

Conducting qualitative interviews and focus groups online has become increasingly common as more and more members of the general public become familiar with the Internet. At the time of writing, online focus groups appear to be attracting greater attention than online personal interviews, perhaps because of the time and administrative effort that can be saved by conducting focus groups online. There is less to be gained in that regard with online personal interviews, unless face-to-face interviews would require a great deal of travel.

Doing this sort of research online has its pros and cons. Selecting participants may be difficult, since everyone taking part must have access to the necessary hardware and software. Carefully selected websites, online bulletin boards, and chat rooms are potential sources of recruitment.

ONLINE QUALITATIVE INTERVIEWS

Markham (1998) conducted Internet interviews with people she recruited after 'lurking' (reading but not participating) for some time in computer-mediated communication forums such as chat rooms. Questions were asked and answered in real time rather than via email, which could have meant delays of hours or days. Markham used an interview guide, and the interviews lasted between one and four hours. Such interviews are a challenge for both interviewer and interviewee because neither party can pick up on visual cues (puzzlement, anxiety) or auditory cues (sighs, groans).

One of Markham's research interests was the reality of online experiences. This can be seen in the following brief sequence (Markham is Annette):

Annette: How real are your experiences in the Internet?

Sherie: How real are experiences off the Internet? (1998: 115)

Markham noted that her notion of 'real' was different from that of her interviewees. For her, 'real' carried connotations of genuineness and authenticity, but for her interviewees it had more to do with distinguishing experiences that occur offline (real) from those online (not real). These distinctions between life online and life offline are likely to become less significant as everyday life is increasingly lived on the Internet.

Kendall (1999: 62) came up with similar findings. She spent three years as an online participant observer, in addition to conducting face-to-face interviews and attending gatherings in person. Interested in issues to do with identity and the online presentation of self, she found that participants gave higher status to actual experiences (real) than to virtual ones (online and not real).

ONLINE FOCUS GROUPS

Mann and Stewart (2000) suggested that an online focus group should have between six and eight people. Larger groups make it difficult for some people to participate, especially those with limited keyboard skills. Also, moderating the session can be more difficult with larger numbers, and as Adriaenssens and Cadman (1999) suggested, large groups can present administrative problems.

Before starting an online focus group session, moderators are advised to send out a welcome message introducing the research and laying out some of the ground rules for the discussion. There is evidence that participants respond more positively if the researchers reveal something about themselves (Curasi 2001). This can be done in the opening message or by creating links to a personal website.

In online focus groups, participants respond more or less immediately to whatever has just been 'said,' whether by the moderator or by other participants. As all are simultaneously online, contributions can be responded to as soon as they appear on the screen (and with some forms of software, the contributions can be seen as they are being typed). As Mann and Stewart (2000) observed, because several participants can type in a response to something at the same time, the convention of taking turns in regular conversation is largely sidelined.

Online focus groups are unlikely to replace their face-to-face counterparts, but they are likely to be used for certain kinds of research topics and/or samples. As regards the latter, people who are dispersed or inaccessible are especially suitable for online focus group research; slow typists are not. As Sweet (2001) pointed out, the most appropriate topics for online research are likely to be those involving sensitive issues or Internet use itself (as in Box 10.10).

Much research on the Internet treats the technology as a given, but recent studies examine how it is *interpreted* by users. Hine (2000: 9), for instance, presented the Internet 'as a product of culture . . . shaped by the ways in which it is marketed, taught, and used.' Box 10.11 summarizes the main advantages and disadvantages of conducting focus groups and personal interviews online compared to administering them in person. The two methods are combined because the tally of advantages and disadvantages applies more or less equally well to both of them.

Feminism and interviewing in qualitative research

Unstructured and semi-structured interviewing are prominent in feminist research. The popularity of qualitative research is attributable in part to the idea that it allows researchers to realize many feminist goals. One writer has observed: 'Whilst several brave women in the 1980s defended quantitative methods, it is nonetheless still the case that not just qualitative methods, but the in-depth face-to-face interview has become the paradigmatic "feminist method"' (Kelly *et al.* 1994: 34). Feminist researchers advocate a framework for conducting interviews that establishes:

- a high level of rapport between interviewer and interviewee;
- a high degree of reciprocity on the part of the interviewer;
- the perspective of the woman being interviewed; and
- a non-hierarchical relationship.

Feminist researchers continue to uphold these principles. However, more and more feminist

BOX 10.10 | An online focus group study

O'Connor and Madge (2001, 2003; see also Madge and O'Connor 2002) employed conferencing software in a virtual focus group study that examined the use of an online information website for parents. Initially, the researchers set up a web survey on the use of the site. When respondents sent in their questionnaires, they were thanked for their participation and asked via email whether they were willing to take part in an in-depth interview. Of the 155 respondents who returned the questionnaires, 16 agreed to be interviewed and were sent the software to install on their computers. The researchers tried to ensure that each group was asked more or less the same questions. For each session, the researchers introduced themselves and asked participants to do likewise. In addition, they placed descriptions and photographs of themselves on a website to which participants were directed. An important part of the process of building rapport was the fact that both of the researchers were mothers. They found that the relative anonymity afforded by the Internet gave participants greater confidence in asking embarrassing questions, a finding that has implications for online focus groups in general. This can be seen in the following excerpt:

> *Amy*: I feel better asking BW [Babyworld] than my health visitor as they're not going to see how bad I am at housekeeping!!!
>
> *Kerry*: I feel the same. Like the HV [health visitor] is judging even though she says she isn't

> *Kerry*: Although my HV has been a lifeline as I suffer from PND [post-natal depression]
>
> *Amy*: Also, there are some things that are so little that you don't want to feel like you're wasting anyone's time. Asking the HV or GP might get in the way of something mroe important, whereas sending an e-mail, the person can answer it when convenient.
>
> *Amy*: My HV is very good, but her voice does sound patronising. I'msure she doesn't mean it, but it does get to me . . .
>
> *Kerry*: Being anon means that you don't get embarrassed asking about a little point or something personal (O'Connor and Madge 2001: 10.4).

This extract reveals a good flow without intervention by the researchers. It contains several mistakes ('mroe,' 'I'msure'), but they are retained to preserve the authenticity of the interaction. Another plus is that there is no need to transcribe the material because it is already in textual form. Also, the fact that participants appear to relish the anonymity of the Internet has implications for online focus groups, since participants may find it easier to ask naïve questions or make potentially embarrassing comments online than in face-to-face focus groups.

researchers are now recognizing the potential of quantitative research (and the structured interview) to achieve feminist goals.

A dilemma arises when feminist researchers have to decide what to do if their own 'understandings and interpretations of women's accounts would either not be shared by some of the research participants, and/or represent a challenge or threat to their perceptions, choices, and coping strategies' (Kelly *et al.* 1994: 37). We will examine the first of these situations, in part because its implications go beyond feminism to the tricky question of how far the commitment to seeing through the eyes of those being studied can or should be stretched. Two examples are relevant. Reinharz (1992: 28–9) cited a study by Andersen in which 20 'corporate wives' came across in their interviews as happy with their lot and supportive of feminism only in relation to employment

discrimination. Andersen interpreted their responses as indicating a 'false consciousness'; in other words, she concluded that they did not really understand how gender relations work. When Andersen wrote an article based on her findings, the women wrote a letter rejecting her account, affirming that women can be fulfilled as wives and mothers. A similar situation confronted Millen (1997) when she interviewed 32 female scientists using semi-structured, in-depth individual interviewing. As Millen (1997: 5.6, 5.9) put it:

> From my external, academically privileged vantage point, it is clear that sexism pervades these professions, and that men are assumed from the start by other scientists, to be competent scientists of status whilst women have to prove themselves, overcome the barrier of their difference

BOX 10.11 Advantages and disadvantages of conducting focus groups and individual interviews online rather than face-to-face

Advantages

- Online interviews and focus groups are much less expensive to conduct than their face-to-face equivalents.

- People who would otherwise be inaccessible (for example, in another country) or reluctant to participate (for example, busy senior executives) are more easily brought into the study.

- Interviewees and focus group participants are able to read and reread their statements (and in focus groups, those of the other participants as well).

- Audio recording is not required; this eliminates both interviewee apprehension and the need for time-consuming and expensive transcription.

- Records of online interviews are more accurate because nothing has to be transcribed and problems of mishearing don't arise. This is a particular advantage with focus group discussions.

- Participants can use pseudonyms to conceal their identity, making it easier for them to discuss embarrassing issues or to divulge potentially unpopular views.

- In focus groups, shy or quiet people may find it easier to participate and overbearing participants are less likely to predominate, though variations in keyboard skills may still prevent equal participation.

- Focus group participants are less likely to be influenced by factors such as the age, ethnicity, appearance, and (if pseudonyms are used) possibly even the gender of the other participants.

- Similarly, interviewees and focus group participants are less likely to be affected by the characteristics of interviewers or moderators, and the latter are less likely to be affected by the participants' characteristics; in this way, reactivity is reduced.

- Online focus groups and interviews allow people to participate in an environment that is 'anonymous, safe and non-threatening' (O'Connor and Madge 2001: 11.2); this may be especially helpful for vulnerable groups.

- Similarly, researchers do not need to enter potentially unsafe environments to reach the people they are studying.

Disadvantages

- Online focus groups and interviews take longer than their face-to-face counterparts.

- Only people with access to online facilities and who are comfortable using them are likely to participate.

- It is more difficult for the interviewer to establish rapport with interviewees, though this is less of a problem when the topic is of particular interest to the participants.

- Probing is more difficult, though not impossible. Curasi (2001) reported some success in eliciting further information from respondents, but working online makes it is easier for them to ignore or forget about such requests.

- There is less spontaneity in responding since interviewees are able to reflect on their answers more carefully than is possible in a face-to-face situation. However, this can be construed as an advantage in some respects since interviewees are likely to give more considered replies.

- There is a tendency for non-response rates to be higher in online personal interviews.

- The researcher cannot be certain that the participants are who they say they are (though this may sometimes be the case in face-to-face interviews as well).

- Online interviews and focus groups require considerable commitment from interviewees and participants if they have to install software and remain online for extended periods of time. This is especially problematic if they have to pay for the software (though reimbursement may be possible), or if participation blocks their telephone lines.

- The interviewer/moderator may not be aware that the interviewee/participant is distracted by something and in such circumstances will continue to ask questions as if they have the person's full attention.

- Online connections may be lost and long breakdowns may ensue, interrupting the flow of the discussion.

- Interviewers cannot rely on body language to tell them when someone is puzzled or (in the case of focus groups) losing interest in the discussion.

Source: Adapted from Adriaenssens and Cadman (1999); Bampton and Cowton (2002); Clapper and Massey (1996); Curasi (2001); Mann and Stewart (2000); O'Connor and Madge (2001); Sweet (2001); Tse (1999).

before they are accepted. These women, on the other hand, do not generally view their interactions in terms of gendered social systems. There is therefore a tension between their characterization of their experience and my interpretation of it. . . .

Two important issues arise from these two accounts. First, how can such a situation come about? If the researchers were genuinely committed to seeing through the eyes of others, the 'tension' to which Millen referred should not have developed. Yet it did, and this suggests that qualitative researchers are more affected by their own perspectives and research questions than textbook accounts of the qualitative research process would suggest. Second, given that feminist research is often concerned with the wider political goal of emancipation, a tension between participants' world views and the researcher's position raises moral questions about the appropriateness of imposing an interpretation not shared by the research participants themselves. For researchers to place their own interpretations above those of the participants can hardly be regarded as consistent with the principle of non-hierarchical interview relationships.

These issues have a significance that extends beyond feminism. Any qualitative researcher—feminist or not—may have to decide what to do when she or he strongly disagrees with the views of the people under study.

THE FOCUS GROUP AS A FEMINIST METHOD

The use of focus groups by feminist researchers has grown considerably in recent years and Wilkinson (1998, 1999b) has argued for its great potential in this regard. Three aspects of the method are particularly compatible with the ethics and politics of feminism:

- Focus group research is less artificial than many other methods because it features group interaction, which is a normal part of social life. The tendency to recruit participants from naturally occurring groups reinforces the realistic quality of such research, since people are able to discuss matters in situations that are normal for them. As a result, there is greater likelihood that the researcher's findings will resonate with the 'lived experience' of women. However, not all writers accept the argument that focus groups are more natural than individual interviews. Even when pre-existing groups are used, gathering people to discuss a certain topic (such as a television program) is not inherently naturalistic, the critics claim,

---

BOX 10.12 | Focus group: a model of women-centred research

A recent qualitative study (Graham et al., 2004) used focus groups to investigate factors that promote or inhibit women's sexual arousal. The purpose of the study was to develop a questionnaire on the topic for women. One already existed for men and it could have been adapted for women with minor changes, but the researchers 'wanted to hear from women themselves' (2004: 528). The study focused on several themes, including 'feelings about one's body; concern about reputation; unwanted pregnancy/contraception; [and] feeling desired versus feeling used by a partner' (2004: 527). Data were gathered from nine groups of women who varied on a number of characteristics such as age, race, education, and sexual orientation.

In Canada, feminist research using focus groups includes Ristock (2001), Little (2001), and Wachholz and Miedema (2000). When Ristock examined how 70 feminist counsellors responded to clients reporting

abuse in a lesbian relationship, she found that even feminist models and therapies for heterosexual violence may need revision in such instances. Little looked at Ontario single mothers on welfare after their support services were reduced and enhanced measures were put in place to force them to look for work. Specifically, she conducted a secondary analysis of 200 focus group interviews done by Ontario Workfare Watch. As a result, she was able to dispel some of the myths about these women and draw attention to some of the ways they were forced to cope, from going hungry some days to moving in with abusive ex-partners. Finally, Wachholz and Miedema examined how immigrant women felt about the police intervention that followed official reports of spousal abuse. The 'solution' often brought with it the harm of extra economic hardships for immigrant women who were already socio-economically vulnerable.

because the interaction is so unusual and contrived. In real life, people are rarely asked to discuss, in a group, issues not of their choosing.

- Feminist researchers have expressed a preference for methods that study the individual within a social context. The tendency for most methods to treat the individual as an isolated entity devoid of a social context is disliked by many feminist researchers, who prefer to analyze 'the self as relational or as socially constructed' (Wilkinson 1999*b*: 229–30).

- As we noted earlier, feminist researchers are suspicious of methods that exploit participants and put the researchers in a position of power over the respondent. Wilkinson observed that the risk of exploitation is greatly reduced in focus groups because the participants are able to take control of the discussion and even subvert the goals the researcher had for the session. As a result, participants' points of view are much more likely to be revealed in a focus group than in a traditional interview.

Wilkinson did not argue that the focus group, or indeed any method, is inherently feminist: only that focus groups have considerable potential for feminist research. A key point is that they allow the voices of highly marginalized women to be heard. According to Madriz (2000: 843), for example, focus groups constitute a relatively rare opportunity for lower-socioeconomic-class women of colour to 'empower themselves by making sense of their experience of vulnerability and subjugation.'

Qualitative interviewing (without immersion in a social setting) versus ethnography

The aim of this section is to compare the merits and limitations of interviewing in qualitative research (without immersion in a social setting) with those of ethnography. They are probably the two most prominent methods of data collection in qualitative research, so there is some value in assessing their relative strengths.

ADVANTAGES OF ETHNOGRAPHY COMPARED TO QUALITATIVE INTERVIEWING

Seeing through others' eyes   As we noted in Chapters 1 and 8, seeing through others' eyes is one of the main purposes of qualitative research. On the face of it, ethnographers would seem to be especially well placed to gain insight into social reality in this way, because of their prolonged immersion in particular social settings. Ethnographers are not only in much closer contact with people for a longer period of time than interviewers are: they also participate in many of the same kinds of activity as the people they are studying. Research that relies on interviewing alone is likely to entail more fleeting contacts, although qualitative research interviews can last many hours and re-interviewing is not unusual.

Learning the local language   Becker and Geer (1957) argued that ethnographers are like social anthropologists visiting a distant land: to understand its culture, they must have a good grasp of its language. To penetrate the culture of particular group, it's particularly important to be familiar with its 'argot': its informal slang and special uses of words. Learning that informal language takes prolonged observation. See Chapter 16 for more on language analysis.

Things taken for granted   Because interviews rely primarily on the interviewees' accounts of their world, elements of that world that the interviewees take for granted may not be mentioned. For example, a street prostitute may never mention her relationship with the police, and an interviewer may never think to ask about it. By contrast, an ethnographer immersed in the street scene may learn that prostitutes have to deal with police surveillance on a regular basis, and that it is an important part of their daily lives.

Deviant and hidden activities   There are certain activities that most people are reluctant to talk about in one-on-one interviews: drug-taking, violence, shoplifting, illegal commerce, hooliganism, and so on. For that reason, much of what is known about criminal and deviant subcultures has been gleaned from ethnography. Ethnographers have also uncovered information about workplace resistance practices (such as working-to-rule and industrial sabotage) and groups that support deviant ideologies, such as white supremacists. Ethnographers are better positioned than interviewers to infiltrate the social worlds of people who are wary of talking to outsiders.

Sensitivity to context and flexibility   Extensive contact with a social setting allows the ethnographer to map the context of people's behaviour.

Interacting with people in a variety of different situations makes it possible to connect behaviour and context.

Naturalistic emphasis   Ethnography can be more naturalistic because the researcher confronts members of a social setting in their natural environments. Interviewing, which tends to interrupt the normal flow of events even when it is informal, is often less naturalistic. It's no surprise that when discussing naturalism as a tradition in qualitative research, Gubrium and Holstein (1997) referred mostly to ethnography.

ADVANTAGES OF QUALITATIVE INTERVIEWING IN COMPARISON TO ETHNOGRAPHY

Issues resistant to observation   Many issues are simply not open to observation, so asking people about them may be the only way to get information about them. For example, consider domestic violence. Would it be feasible for a researcher to hang around in other people's homes, waiting for the violence to unfold? Reactivity would impinge in a big way, since perpetrators would do their best to hide their violence.

Reconstruction of events and future plans   In-depth reconstruction of past events and plans for future behaviour is not possible through observation alone. Qualitative research entails reconstruction of events when interviewees are asked to think about how a series of previous activities might have created a current situation. Beardsworth and Keil (see Box 10.3) used the symbolic interactionist notion of *career* to understand how people become vegetarians. In fact, most qualitative studies ask about events that occurred before the study began; for example, questions may be asked about the early family experiences of gang members, recent immigrants, or prostitutes. Some call this 'retrospective interviewing.' See Box 10.13 for a further example.

Reactive effects   Reactive effects are by no means straightforward. As with structured observation (see Chapter 6), it can be anticipated that the presence of an ethnographer will lead people to behave unnaturally (although ethnographers, like researchers using structured observation, typically find that their subjects become accustomed to their presence and over time begin to behave more

naturally). Ethnography also suffers from the related problem that an observer disturbs the very situation under study, sparking conversations and interactions, both with and about the observer, that otherwise would not occur.

Less intrusive in people's lives   Ethnography can be costly in that the researcher is likely to take up more of the participants' time than would be the case with interviews alone. Interviews in qualitative research can sometimes be very long, and as we have noted, re-interviewing is not uncommon. Nevertheless, the impact of undergoing an interview is probably still less than the impact of having to deal with an ethnographer on a regular basis. Ethnography can be especially intrusive in terms of time when it is conducted in organizational settings, because it disrupts the rhythm of the work day.

Longitudinal research easier   Interviewing can be carried out within a longitudinal research design somewhat more easily than ethnography because repeat interviews may be easier to organize than repeat visits to the ethnographer's research settings.

Ethnography can be used for longitudinal studies, but the time that ethnographers can spend away from their normal lives is usually not more than two or three years, and this limits the extent to which an ethnographic study can be longitudinal. When research is conducted on an episodic basis, however, a longer time period may be feasible. Armstrong's (1993) research on soccer hooligans, mentioned several times in Chapters 8 and 9, entailed six years of participant observation, but since hooliganism was not a full-time occupation for his subjects, the research did not require any sustained absence from work and other personal commitments.

Greater breadth of coverage   Interviewing may allow access to a wider variety of people and situations. In ethnographic work, the researcher is invariably limited to a fairly restricted range of people, places, and incidents. An ethnographer observing a large organization, for example, is unlikely to have extensive knowledge of operations outside the area under study.

Specific focus   As we noted in Chapter 8, qualitative research sometimes begins with a specific focus; Silverman (1993) was even critical

---

BOX 10.13 | Information through interviews: research on prostitution

McKeganey and Barnard (1996) discussed their strategies for conducting research into prostitutes and their clients. Their approach was largely that of the observer-as-participant (see Figure 9.2), in that their research was based primarily on interviews with prostitutes and their clients, supplemented by (frequently accidental) observation of interactions and overheard conversations. The interviews they conducted were especially important in gaining information on matters such as how the prostitutes had moved into that line of work; permitted and prohibited sex acts; links with drug use; experience of violence; and management of identity. In the following passage, a prostitute reconstructs her movement into prostitution:

> I was 14 and I'd run away from home. I ended up down in London where I met a pimp. . . . He'd got me a place to stay, buying me things and everything and I ended up sleeping with him as well. . . . One night we got really drunk and stoned and he brought someone in. . . . [Then]

after it happened I thought it was bad, I didn't like it but at least I was getting paid for it. I'd been abused by my granddad when I was 11 and it didn't seem a million miles from that anyway (1996: 25).

One area of particular concern to McKeganey and Barnard was the spread of HIV/AIDS infection and its implications for prostitutes and their work. This topic was specifically addressed in the interviews. For example:

> I've got a couple of punters who'll say 'I'll give you so and so if you'll do it without [a condom].' But never, I always use a condom for anal sex, oral sex and even for hand jobs; there's no way I'll let them come anywhere near me (1996: 66).

> You still get the bam-pots [idiots] asking for sex without. I had one the other night—I said, 'where have you been living—on a desert island?' (1996: 66).

---

of the notion that it should be regarded as an open-ended form of research. Qualitative interviewing seems to be better suited for dealing with a specific issue, since an interview can address a particular matter in detail. Research by Bryman *et al.* (1996) had a very specific focus: namely, conceptions of leadership among police officers. Because of its clear focus, it was more appropriate to conduct the research using semi-structured interviewing than ethnography, since issues involving leadership are unlikely to emerge naturally on a regular basis.

OVERVIEW

When Becker and Geer (1957: 28) proclaimed half a century ago that the 'most complete form

of the sociological datum . . . is the form in which the participant observer gathers it,' Trow (1957: 33) reprimanded them for making such a universal claim. He argued that 'the problem under investigation properly dictates the methods of investigation.' The latter view is very much the one taken in this book. Specific research methods are appropriate for some issues but not for others. Our discussion of the merits and limitations of ethnography versus qualitative interviews is meant to draw attention to some of the factors that researchers should take into account if given the opportunity to choose one method or the other. The points raised can also be used to evaluate existing research.

☑ Checklist *of issues to consider in qualitative interviewing*

✔ Have you thought about how you will present yourself in the interview, such as how you will dress?

✔ Is there a clear and comprehensive way of introducing the research to interviewees?

✔ Does the interview guide clearly relate to the research questions?

✔ Has a pilot test been done with some appropriate respondents ?

✔ Have the interviewers been fully trained?

✔ Does the interview guide contain a good mixture of question types (e.g., probing, specifying, and direct questions)?

✔ Do the interviews allow novel or unexpected themes and issues to arise?

✔ Is the language in the questions free of jargon?

✔ Are the questions relevant to the people being interviewed?

✔ Have the questions been designed to elicit indepth responses so that interviewees are not tempted to answer simply 'yes' or 'no'?

✔ Do the questions offer a real prospect of seeing the world from the interviewees' point of view rather than imposing a frame of reference on them?

✔ Has the setting in which the interviews will take place been checked out? Has the recording equipment been put through a dry run? Have all aids to be used (e.g., visual aids, film clips, case studies) been pre-tested?

✔ Is there a plan in place if the interviewee does not turn up for the interview?

For a focus group:

✔ Have you planned what you will do if not all participants turn up for the session?

✔ Have the questions been designed to encourage group interaction and discussion?

✔ Is there a strategy for dealing with silences and for particular participants who are reluctant to speak?

✔ Is there a strategy for dealing with participants who speak too much and 'hog' the discussion?

✔ Is there a strategy to follow if the discussion goes off on a tangent?

Key Points

- Interviewing in qualitative research is typically unstructured or semi-structured.

- Qualitative interviewing is meant to be flexible in order to explore the world views of research participants.

- If an interview guide is used, it should allow some flexibility in the way questions are asked.

- Qualitative interviews should be recorded and then transcribed.

- Qualitative interviews can be conducted online.

- The focus group allows the researcher to explore the joint production of meaning.

- The selection of focus group participants requires several decisions—in particular, whether to use natural groups.

- The focus group moderator generally tries to give free rein to the discussion. However, there may be contexts in which it is necessary to ask specific questions.

- Group interaction is an important aspect of focus groups.

- The Internet offers significant opportunities for gaining access to potential focus group participants.

- Qualitative interviewing is a popular method of data collection in feminist studies; some writers also consider focus groups well suited to feminist research.

- Whether to use ethnography or qualitative interviews alone depends mainly on the research questions to be addressed. Still, ethnographers usually conduct some interviews in the course of their investigations.

Relevant Websites

For a qualitative interview that uses the life history approach to examine the experiences of a Holocaust survivor, go to:

> http://www.youtube.com/watch?v=-jJ6s7ob_Dg&feature=channel

For a clip of a focus group discussing the issue of race and politics in the United States, in particular Barack Obama's political appeal, see:

> http://www.youtube.com/watch?v=jGnePpo8JrM

For a focus group discussing Sarah Palin's political appeal, see:

> http://www.youtube.com/watch?v=cnV1pS7qVD8&feature=related

[Websites accessed 20 July 2011]

Questions for Review

DIFFERENCES BETWEEN STRUCTURED INTERVIEWS AND QUALITATIVE INTERVIEWS

- How does qualitative interviewing differ from structured interviewing?

UNSTRUCTURED AND SEMI-STRUCTURED INTERVIEWING

- What are the differences between unstructured and semi-structured interviewing?
- Can semi-structured interviewing compromise the flexibility of qualitative research? Explain.
- What are the differences between life history and oral history interviews?
- What considerations need to be borne in mind when preparing an interview guide?
- What kinds of question can be included in an interview guide?
- What skills does the interviewer need to develop for qualitative interviewing?
- Why is it important to record and transcribe qualitative interviews?
- What role can vignette questions play in qualitative interviewing?

INTRODUCTION TO FOCUS GROUPS

- What advantages can a focus group offer compared to an individual qualitative interview?

CONDUCTING FOCUS GROUPS

- Are there any circumstances in which it is an advantage to select participants who know each other?

GROUP INTERACTION IN FOCUS GROUP SESSIONS

- Why is it important to examine group interaction when analyzing focus group data?

LIMITATIONS OF FOCUS GROUPS

- How can group effects and the loss of control over the discussion damage a focus group study?

QUALITATIVE RESEARCH USING ONLINE PERSONAL INTERVIEWS

- Can online personal interviews really be personal interviews? Explain. To what extent does the absence of direct contact mean that the online interview cannot be a true interview?

QUALITATIVE RESEARCH USING ONLINE FOCUS GROUPS

- Is the role of the moderator in online focus groups different from that in the face-to-face variety? Explain.

FEMINIST RESEARCH AND INTERVIEWING IN QUALITATIVE RESEARCH

- Why are qualitative interviews so prominent in feminist research?
- What dilemmas does qualitative interviewing pose for feminist researchers?
- What dilemmas do focus groups pose for feminist researchers?

QUALITATIVE INTERVIEWING ALONE VERSUS ETHNOGRAPHY

- Outline the advantages and disadvantages of qualitative interviewing (without immersion in a social setting) compared to ethnography.

- Is one method more in tune with the research needs of qualitative researchers than the other? Explain.

PART IV

This part of the book examines research ethics. Although our discussion takes up only one chapter, we have placed it in its own section to emphasize that ethics are relevant for *all* research methods and come into play at *every stage* of research.

Research Ethics

CHAPTER OVERVIEW

Ethics are a primary concern in social research. They permeate every aspect of the research process, from the recruitment of subjects to the publishing of the results. This chapter discusses some general ethical principles and their applications to real research situations. The backdrop for the discussion is the *Tri-Council Policy Statement: Ethical Conduct for Research Involving Humans (TCPS2)* (2010), which governs most research practices in Canada. The *TCPS2* was prepared by the Canadian Institutes of Health Research (CIHR), the Natural Sciences and Engineering Council of Canada (NSERC), and the Social Sciences and Humanities Research Council of Canada (SSHRCC). It identifies three core principles, which are complementary and mutually reinforcing:

- *Respect for persons* stipulates that people's autonomy and their freedom to choose what will happen to them must be ensured. Research participants must therefore be made aware of everything the study will entail, so that their consent is not only freely given but fully informed. Consent must also be ongoing; thus participants should be allowed to withdraw from the study at any time.

- *Concern for welfare* covers all aspects of a person's life as well as the welfare of groups and communities. To protect the welfare of individuals and groups, a favourable balance between the risks and benefits of research must be sought.

- *Justice* requires that people be treated fairly and equitably, so that no segment of the population bears an undue burden of the risk associated with research, and no part of society is excluded from the benefits that research may bestow.

Each of these principles provides valuable guidance and can be used to identify research activities and practices that should be avoided for moral reasons.

You may be surprised to learn that there are stringent formal policies in place to ensure that research in Canada is conducted in an ethical manner. Why, you ask? Surely researchers are decent people, not mad scientists who take pleasure in abusing the people who participate in their studies. Of course. Still, every research situation has an ethical dimension to it, and the history of the social sciences is riddled with studies in which well-meaning researchers harmed their subjects in some way. In many cases the studies seemed quite acceptable when they were done, and it was only with the passage of time that the consequences for participants were recognized. How could things possibly have gone so wrong? And why are ethical dilemmas still endemic to social research?

Introduction

Ethical issues arise in every phase of a research project. How they are handled affects the integrity of specific research initiatives as well as the reputation of the social sciences as a whole, so understanding research ethics is crucial. If you have read the first ten chapters of this book you will already have a basic understanding of how research is conducted and will be in a good position to grapple with the ethical dilemmas that researchers typically face.

The first priority of a social researcher should be to ensure that the people being studied are not harmed by their participation. This idea is similar to a fundamental precept among physicians and surgeons: 'First do no harm.' Notice the word 'First': it means that the prevention of harm should override any other goal. The same principle lies at the heart of research ethics in the social sciences. What it means is that the welfare of research subjects should take priority over everything else, *including the acquisition of knowledge*, even if that knowledge would expand our understanding of humanity or lead to improvements in the human condition. To some degree this principle conflicts with the concept of academic freedom. But minimizing the risks of participation and striking a proper balance between the risks and benefits of research is compatible with social scientists' freedom to choose the topics of their research and, within reasonable bounds, the methods to be used.

It may seem obvious that research participants should not be harmed by taking part in research activities, whether they be **experiments**, field research studies, or any other kind of social scientific investigation. As with many moral rules, however, knowing how to put this principle into practice is anything but simple. For example, defining 'harm' and outlining its limits is more complicated than you might think. We all know that research participants should not be killed in the process of being studied, but is any and all harm unjustifiable? What about milder forms of harm, such as short-term anxiety or embarrassment? Is it morally acceptable to subject people to temporary discomfort if the research has the potential to improve our understanding of society or human behaviour in general? Similarly, most people would say that telling lies is generally not a good thing, in part because it may cause harm

to the person who is lied to. But what about situations in which some temporary deception is necessary in order to create a research environment in which people feel free to behave in a natural or unguarded way? Typically, it is these sorts of 'grey areas' that are debated in the discussion of research ethics, although egregious ethical violations have been known to occur.

Each method of social research comes with its own set of ethical issues. However, it's worth considering some general principles that pertain to all social scientific research. In Canada, most research must comply with the *TCPS2* (CIHR, NSERC and SSHRCC 2010). Different academic organizations may also have their own ethical policies and procedures. For example, sociologists in Canada are encouraged to follow the *Code of Ethics* of the Canadian Sociological Association (http://www.csa-scs.ca/code-of-ethics, accessed 4 Oct. 2010). Research in Canada is also subject to Canadian law, in particular the *Charter of Rights and Freedoms* (http://laws.justice.gc.ca/en/charter/1.html, accessed 4 Oct. 2010).

Before a research project involving human subjects begins—even before potential subjects are asked if they would like to participate in the study—a Research Ethics Board (REB) must review and approve the project. REBs are normally made up of researchers from a variety of disciplines and usually include a community member from outside the institution under whose auspices the research will take place (which in the case of social research is usually a university). If the institution with which the researchers are affiliated administers research funds issued by any of the three agencies that created the *TCPS2* (CIHR, NSERC, and SSHRCC), then its REB must abide by the *TCPS2* in making its judgments. What this means in practice is that REBs at virtually every university in Canada use the *TCPS2* in making their decisions and recommendations.

REBs may approve a research project, request modifications, or reject it outright. If the research is to be conducted over an extended period of time, the REB may also hold periodic reviews, or at least require that the researchers file an annual report. In addition, REB members themselves are required to follow procedures outlined in the *TCPS2*. For example, they must avoid any conflict of interest, such as having a financial stake in a project that is up for approval.

Van den Hoonaard (2001) has suggested that it may be more difficult to get ethics approval for **qualitative research** than for **quantitative** studies. Qualitative research is sometimes considered less scientific than the quantitative kind, and ethics committees may prefer the epistemology of the latter, with its derived hypotheses and specific plans. This can be a fatal problem, because if the REB rejects the research proposal, the work can neither receive funding nor be carried out. Also, whereas in quantitative research data are usually collected one-on-one, in qualitative research a whole group may be under observation, including some people who might not want the attention. One REB allowed a researcher to go ahead with her **ethnographic** work but required that she turn her head when someone who had not explicitly agreed to be part of the study entered her field of vision. This directive is an example of what some researchers would consider an overzealous attempt to prevent harm. The fact that *TCPS2* acknowledges the right of researchers to appeal REB decisions is a tacit admission that at times the latter can be overly restrictive. In any case, there is little doubt that REBs perform a valuable function in protecting the rights of research participants, as the discussion to follow will show.

General ethical principles

The first thing to note regarding general principles is that researchers themselves disagree on the ethical acceptability of certain research practices. There are disputes from the 1960s that are still being rehashed today. Also, although the *TCPS2*'s codes and guidelines provide some direction, they often allow for a degree of flexibility. Nonetheless, there is little disagreement that recognizing the ethical implications of doing social research is crucial if informed decisions are to be made.

The *TCPS2* outlines three core principles for the conduct of research involving human subjects: respect for persons, concern for welfare, and justice. Although they are listed separately, there is considerable overlap between them.

RESPECT FOR PERSONS

The principle of respect for persons maintains that humans should not be treated as mere 'objects' or means to an end. Even if the end is a worthy one, it cannot justify the use of unethical means. As we noted above, even if the knowledge a researcher is seeking will be of benefit to all humankind, the welfare of the individuals and groups under study is of paramount importance. Researchers must recognize that people have rights, including the right to be treated with dignity by social researchers. Respect for persons is arguably the most fundamental of all the principles considered here.

The starting point of respect for persons in research is the stipulation that subjects must give free, informed and ongoing consent to participate in the study. Most researchers now adhere to the principle that potential research subjects should not only be asked for their permission before they are placed in a study, but should also be informed of all the risks and benefits to which they would be exposed. To assess those risks and benefits, prospective participants need a basic idea of what the study will entail.

In most quantitative studies and in some forms of qualitative research, potential participants are given an *information sheet* outlining what the research is about, how it will be conducted, and what the risks and benefits of participation are. The information sheet normally includes the names of the people in charge of the research, their institutional affiliation, and contact information. Assurances of confidentiality are commonly found on the information sheet, along with a description of how the data will be stored and the form in which the results are to be published.

Prospective subjects should be encouraged to think about the project; they should also be given a chance to ask questions and seek clarification if necessary. If they have all the information required and are willing to participate, a *consent form* is provided for them to sign. The consent form usually includes a brief synopsis of the study and states explicitly that research subjects are free to leave the study at any time without penalty. Consent must be freely given and cannot be coerced.

In some forms of qualitative research, such as ethnography and participant observation, providing information sheets and consent forms may be impractical; in some cases it might even defeat the purposes of the study. In cases where a formal agreement between the researchers and the informants might signal a lack of trust, less formal approaches such as verbal assurances and ad hoc explanations may be employed. Whichever method they choose, researchers must provide REBs with documentation outlining how informed consent will be obtained.

The principle of free and informed consent seems straightforward, but putting it into practice can be difficult and usually involves some ethical trade-offs. Homan (1991: 73) observed that abiding by this principle 'is easier said than done.' At least two major points stand out here:

- It's extremely difficult to give prospective participants absolutely all the information required to make an informed decision about their involvement. Relatively minor transgressions of the principle of informed consent are pervasive in social research: for example, not giving all the details about the study for fear of contaminating people's answers to questions. On the other hand, Hessler *et al.*'s qualitative study of adolescent risk behaviour (2003) included a consent form that was quite elaborate.

- In ethnographic research, the researcher is likely to come into contact with a wide spectrum of people, and ensuring that absolutely everyone has the opportunity to give informed consent is not practicable. Even when all participants in a certain setting are aware that they are being observed, it's unlikely that all of them will have been similarly (let alone identically) informed about the nature of the research.

Experiments are particularly problematic when it comes to informed consent because researchers want the participants to behave naturally and authentically. If participants were to be fully informed regarding the purpose of the experiment, it would be difficult to avoid the **reactive effects** that occur when people know they are being observed. For this reason, experiments usually involve some deception.

For example, Milgram (1963) designed a series of studies in an effort to understand the brutality that occurred in Nazi concentration camps during the Second World War. In particular, he wanted to know how a person could be led to cause extreme harm to an innocent human being, and whether being ordered to do so by an authority figure had anything to do with it. Milgram devised a laboratory experiment in which a supposedly reputable researcher (the authority figure) asked participants to act as 'teachers' who would punish 'learners' by giving them increasingly severe electric shocks whenever they gave incorrect answers to questions. Neither the shocks nor the howls of pain coming from the

'learners' were real, but the 'teachers'/subjects did not know this. Some of them were further disadvantaged in that they could not see the 'learners': they could only hear the shrieks of pain supposedly coming from them.

In all instances, the 'teachers' were told that the shocks were part of the study and would not cause any permanent harm, despite the increasingly shrill cries of pain. The experiment continued until the 'teacher'/subject refused to administer more shocks. In the version of the study in which the 'teachers' could not see the 'learners,' a substantial majority (62%) of the former administered the strongest shocks possible. Further, in one variant of the experiment, the subjects were given the option of ordering another person (actually an accomplice of Milgram's) to administer the shocks; in this situation, more than 90% of them ordered the greatest shocks possible. Many of the participants were visibly upset as they carried out the experimenter's orders, but they still did what the authority figure told them to do.

Milgram saw these results as shedding light on the circumstances that led to the horrors of the Nazi concentration camps. It appeared that ordinary, everyday people were willing to inflict serious harm on innocent others if ordered to do so by an authority figure—a finding that may have important implications for the understanding of human atrocities and ultimately their prevention. Nonetheless, the study involved a number of ethically questionable elements. For one thing, the 'teacher'/subjects themselves suffered at least short-term harm; most felt very uncomfortable administering what they believed to be powerful shocks, and while the experiment was in progress many participants came to doubt the experimenter's claim that the 'learners' were not suffering any serious harm.

Another issue was the deception that the subjects experienced: they were told that the experiment was investigating how people learn, not how people come to commit cruel acts, and they were led to believe that the shocks were real. Thus to the extent that the participants were not fully informed about the purpose of the experiment, they were lied to, although once it was over they were *debriefed* (informed of the deception and the reason for it). Most people would agree that in everyday life, lying and deception should be avoided. On the other hand, the experiment would not have worked had the subjects known the truth from the outset. Imagine the outcome if subjects had been told, 'We're going to see whether you are willing to inflict severe pain on an innocent person.' But does that justify the deception? Was the knowledge gained worth the psychological discomfort the subjects experienced when they believed they were causing innocent persons to suffer? This is the sort of question that researchers and REB members must ponder.

It must be emphasized that Milgram is not alone in his use of deception: in fact, most social research experiments involve some kind of pretence. However, it is unlikely that an REB in North America would allow a similar study to proceed today. For that reason Milgram's experiment has rarely been replicated, except in other parts of the world where research ethics codes are less stringent.

As you think about the ethics of Milgram's study, keep in mind that REBs are not infallible and that REB members sometimes disagree among themselves about the ethics of a particular study. As a student, you need to make up your own mind about ethical issues. Don't feel obliged to accept the ethical claims of more experienced social researchers; history has shown that empirical, theoretical, or technological expertise is no guarantee of moral wisdom. But do listen carefully to the arguments of experienced researchers. It is incumbent on you to consider what is at stake in any research situation, especially the probable harms and benefits to the research subjects, and to think about the effects—both good and ill—that the knowledge produced by the study would generate for the world at large.

Deception can be a controversial issue in qualitative research as well. Punch (1994: 91), for example, observed that 'some dissimulation is intrinsic to social life and, therefore, to fieldwork.' He quoted Gans (1962: 44) in support: 'If the researcher is completely honest with people about his activities, they will try to hide actions and attitudes they consider undesirable, and so will be dishonest. Consequently, the researcher must be dishonest to get honest data.'

Goode (1996) argued that judgments about deception should be considered on a case-by-case basis. Some writers argue that if all ruses were disallowed, a great deal of useful information—about terrorists, cults, drug gangs, white-collar criminals, etc.—would be inaccessible, because finding out about their activities often requires some kind of disguised observation. Some social reformers might add that exposing the sins of the powerful would be another acceptable use of deception, but that argument opens the door to its use in other situations. Would it be acceptable to use deception to expose the transgressions of the underclass and the less powerful? Is lying to a priest to uncover pedophilia more acceptable than lying to an animal rights activist to reveal a plan to destroy a mink coat factory?

Sometimes it may be beyond the power of a qualitative researcher to obtain informed consent. For example, Van Maanen (1991*b*) used his experience as a ride operator in Disneyland as the basis for a study he produced many years after he had been employed there during school vacations. He never went back and asked permission from the people he described in his work; to do so would have been close to impossible. Is a lack of subject consent acceptable in such a situation? Is it a form of deception?

Although the use of deception can be controversial in both quantitative and qualitative research, there is consensus on a number of criteria regarding its use. First, deception should be used only as a last resort. Second, if deception is used, that use should be as sparing as possible. Finally, where feasible, anyone deceived should be debriefed as quickly as possible; specifically, the researcher must reveal the deception and explain why it was used. What might have happened had Milgram's subjects not been debriefed?

Another issue regarding informed consent is whether the researcher is obliged to reveal the names of all those who have sponsored the project, whether individuals or organizations. At one Ontario university, ethical rules prohibit any reference to the names of research sponsors on the information sheet. This rule reflects the possibility that some people might feel pressured or coerced if they knew that the research was sponsored by (for example) the Canadian Cancer Society. But another university considers it unethical *not* to supply that information, on the grounds that it is necessary to enable the participant to give informed consent. For instance, some people might not want the government to know anything about them, so if a department such as Fisheries and Oceans Canada were funding the study, they would want to be informed so they could decide not to participate. Yet even if the sponsor's name is revealed, participants' ability to give informed consent may not be guaranteed, since the name may be virtually unknown to the general public. Ethical issues are never simple.

Only people competent to make a decision about participating in a research study should be asked to give their consent. That category normally includes most adults, although for reasons of illness, other incapacitation, or language difficulties some adults may not be capable of making an informed decision and must have a competent person make the decision on their behalf. Similarly, children are not ordinarily considered capable of giving informed consent. Parents or legal guardians are usually given the information sheet as well as an opportunity to ask questions and seek clarifications about the research before signing the consent form for their child. Quite often a parent or guardian is required to be present when the child interacts with the researcher, especially if the study involves children who are very young. Exceptions include situations in which older children fill out questionnaires that the parents or guardians have seen and approved.

CONCERN FOR WELFARE

'Welfare' in this context covers all aspects of the well-being of the person, group, or community affected by the research, including physical, mental, emotional, spiritual, social, and economic well-being. A very basic 'welfare' concern in social research involves respect for privacy and confidentiality. REBs normally require that the identities and records of subjects remain confidential to prevent any embarrassment or harm, especially harm to their reputations or personal relationships. This injunction means that the research subjects should not be identifiable when the findings are published, although exceptions may occasionally be made in the case of historical work or of studies dealing with public figures. In quantitative research, subjects are usually identified by code numbers rather than names when the data are processed; their actual identities are stored in a secure location. In such studies research participants are normally told on the information sheet that the data they provide will form part of a statistical aggregate (as in '50% of respondents expressed some dissatisfaction with their romantic partner's listening skills') and therefore they will not be personally identifiable.

BOX 11.1   What About Research Using the Internet?

A great deal of research is now done online (see Chapters 4, 7, 10, and 12). All the ethics guidelines discussed in this chapter apply to online research, with a handful of exceptions. One exception involves material that is publicly available and protected by law, such as Statistics Canada public use files or data in public archives. In such cases the researcher is not required to obtain informed consent, although he or she must obey the relevant laws and regulations. Another exception applies to online information that is publicly accessible and does not involve any expectation of privacy. Such material would include films, newspaper materials, official publications, third-party interviews and any other online research that does not entail direct interaction with research subjects.

Any situation that does involve direct contact with research participants, including online surveys and interviews, is subject to the same ethics protocols as in-person research. The same goes for gaining access to online materials in situations where there is a reasonable expectation of privacy, as in the case of

Internet chat room discussions, email, and the postings of organizations having restricted memberships, such as self-help groups. In these sorts of situations, both researchers and research participants have to be especially vigilant, since it is relatively easy to conduct **covert research** online. It would be quite easy, for example, for a researcher to pose as a regular participant in a self-help chat room for sex addicts, and use the material as data for a qualitative study. But doing so would be equivalent to joining an in-person discussion group and not revealing one's identity as a researcher. (The ethical implications of covert research will be discussed later in this chapter.)

Sending research data over the Internet is another concern. If data containing identifiable information are to be transferred via the Internet, the data should be encrypted to ensure the security of the information. Even when sensitive data are merely stored on a computer that is connected to the Internet, encryption should be considered.

Researchers have to be especially resourceful in situations where participants prefer to remain anonymous. One method that is sometimes employed is the *random response technique*, which was originally designed for interview situations in which the respondent is asked about controversial or illegal activities. One reason for developing this technique was to protect researchers as well as respondents from the risk that police would examine the data and then bring the researchers into court as witnesses. (Can some harm be anticipated here, as when the still-free criminals repeat their crimes?)

The random response process begins with respondents flipping a coin but not revealing the results. About half of them should get heads, half tails. All respondents are then instructed: 'For the following question, if you have a head you must say yes, regardless of whether it is true or not. With tails you should answer the question truthfully.' Then comes the question: 'Have you ever used cocaine?' Even if no one had in fact used it, roughly 50% should say yes because they got heads.

Assume that 60% of respondents say yes. The excess over the 50% (heads who had to say yes) can be used to calculate how many people used cocaine. Here the excess is 10%, presumably representing people who got tails and have used the drug. Then, since one would expect roughly the same number of cocaine users in the heads group, that figure must be doubled to get the percentage of the total sample who had used cocaine.

One of the authors of this book did this as a class exercise and had students raise their hands to say yes or no. When the behaviour in question was shoplifting after the age of 16, 80% answered 'yes,' meaning a 60% (30% plus another 30%) shoplifting rate. When the topic was post-puberty homosexual behaviour, however, 'yes' responses came out at only 50%. Here there are several possibilities: no one had engaged in the activity; a few had, but because heads and tails rarely come out exactly 50–50, they were concealed in the difference; some 'heads' students were afraid their classmates would think a raised hand was an admission; or perhaps some 'tails' students who had engaged in the activity did not want to give any indication that they had, fearing that a 'yes' response would be interpreted as an admission.

In qualitative research, dealing with privacy and confidentiality issues is quite different, especially if the study involves in-depth analysis of a small number of people. Pseudonyms are typically used to protect people's identities, but quite often the detailed description of the physical and social setting, which qualitative researchers usually include to provide the needed context for the study, can offer enough clues to identify some of the participants. The study of an American town that Vidich and Bensman (1968) called 'Springdale' (not its real name) is instructive in this regard. Their book was uncomplimentary about the town and many of its leaders, and many people felt that its tone was patronizing. To make matters worse, it was possible to identify individuals in the published account. The town's inhabitants responded with a Fourth of July parade in which many of them wore badges citing their book pseudonyms, and an effigy of Vidich was set up so that it was peering into manure. The townspeople also announced their refusal to cooperate in any more social research; they were clearly upset by the publication, and to that extent were harmed by it.

Another area of controversy surrounding privacy and confidentiality in qualitative studies pertains to covert research: investigations in which the people being observed are not informed that they are part of a study. In spite of the widespread insistence on informed consent and privacy rights, and the recognition that covert observation is especially prone to violations of those principles, covert studies still appear from time to time. The defence is usually that the benefits of the research outweigh any harm that may come to the subjects. Virtually all codes of ethics allow covert research as a last resort, but most state that it should be avoided 'as far as possible.' Those who use this method argue that it is necessary to prevent research participants from changing their behaviour because they know they are being studied. Still, where informed consent has not been obtained prior to the commencement of the research, permission to use the data gathered should be obtained post hoc whenever possible. That is a general rule, but it is often broken in dealing with dangerous subjects such as pimps and other criminals. Where such permission has not been obtained, it is absolutely crucial to maintain the anonymity of the people observed.

One difficulty with the arguments justifying the use of covert methods is the assumption that it is impossible to obtain the data using other means.

Covert observers sometimes base their judgments on the *anticipated* difficulty of gaining access to a setting rather than the actual experience of being denied entry. For example, Homan justified his use of covert participant observation of a religious sect on the grounds that sociologists are viewed very negatively by group members; hence 'It seemed probable that the prevalence of such a perception would prejudice the effectiveness of a fieldworker declaring an identity as sociologist' (Homan and Bulmer 1982: 107).

One of the most famous and controversial cases of covert research can be found in Humphreys' *Tearoom Trade* (1970), a study that Desroches (1990) partially replicated in Canada using less contentious methods. The researchers (Humphreys himself and police acting for Desroches) observed homosexual encounters in public toilets ('tearooms'), taking the roles of 'watch queens'—people who watch out for possible intruders while other men meet and engage in sexual activity. Such 'voyeurism' was offensive to some critics.

As part of his research, Humphreys recorded some of the participants' car licence numbers. He was then able to track down their names and addresses, thus further compromising their privacy, and ended up with a sample of 100 active tearoom-trade participants. To reduce the risk of being recognized, Humphreys waited a year before contacting the respondents whose licence numbers he had written down, and also changed his hairstyle. After this deception, he then conducted an interview (Desroches did not do this) with a sample of the men about their health issues (a ruse), including some questions about marital sex. He did not tell them he knew about their activity, nor did he debrief them when the study was finished. Humphreys learned that many of the men he observed were actually married, respected members of the community—a finding that allowed him to challenge a popular stereotype of the day.

Was his research ethical? Those who say 'yes' argue that he had no choice but to do covert research because very few people engaging in gay sex in those days were willing to talk about it; in fact, sexual acts between men were against the law and the people committing them were subject to prison sentences. Humphreys' supporters also maintain that the knowledge his studies produced led to a better understanding of human sexuality and the treatment to which stigmatized

individuals are subjected. His detractors argue that the knowledge gained did not justify the deception and invasion of privacy that his subjects experienced. The debate continues to this day.

Regardless of one's position on the ethics of Humphreys' work, the public reaction when it was first published illustrates what can happen to the reputation of social researchers as a whole if there is a perception that one of their kind has committed serious ethical violations. The following is an excerpt from an article written in the *Washington Post* in 1970, shortly after the controversy erupted:

> We're so preoccupied with defending our privacy against insurance investigators, dope sleuths, counterespionage men, divorce detectives and credit checkers, that we overlook the social scientists behind the hunting blinds who're also peeping into what we thought were our most private and secret lives. But they are there, studying us, taking notes, getting to know us, as indifferent as everybody else to the feeling that to be a complete human involves having an aspect of ourselves that's unknown (Von Hoffman 1970).

The ethical quandaries surrounding privacy and confidentiality inherent in qualitative research are also illustrated in the work of O'Connell Davidson and Layder (1994). These researchers conducted a small-scale ethnographic project on a prostitute, whom they called Desiree, and her clients and assistants. While Desiree and the women who served as her receptionists were fully aware of O'Connell Davidson's status, the clients were not. Both researchers admitted their invasion of client privacy and failure to obtain consent from them, but were 'untroubled' by the intrusion because the clients were anonymous to O'Connell Davidson and she was not 'in a position to secure, store or disclose information that could harm them' (1994: 214). The fact that there was no harm to participants was regarded as the litmus test of the ethical status of the research. They offered a further defence by saying that ethical transgression is pervasive: 'Virtually all social research is intrusive and exploitative to some degree' (1994: 215). There was an acknowledged commitment to attend to the concerns of Desiree and her receptionists, as well as considerable sympathy for them, but these sentiments did not extend to her clients:

I have . . . no personal liking and no real sympathy for them. I have a professional obligation to preserve their anonymity and to ensure that they are not harmed by my research, but I feel no qualms about being less than frank with them, and no obligation to allow them to choose whether or not their actions are recorded (1994: 215).

Although an effort was made to follow ethics protocols, it appears that not all the participants received the same level of ethical protection, and that the researchers believed that not all research subjects *deserved* the complete range of ethics coverage. This sort of arrangement is more common than one might think and has far-reaching implications. It also illustrates how difficult it can be to resolve ethical dilemmas in social research. Do the clients of prostitutes have a right to choose to be excluded from research studies? What if they are abusing the prostitutes? What if they are not? Does it matter whether such studies contribute to a better understanding of the sex industry—for instance, by revealing the physical risks that prostitutes take? Such questions must be weighed carefully and are not easily answered.

Sometimes a researcher may feel obliged to disregard concerns about privacy and confidentiality if the research uncovers evidence of serious harm or criminal activity. In his ethnographic research, Totten (2001) wanted to know how youth gang members interpreted the violence they perpetrated against their girlfriends, and how they accounted for their racist and homophobic activities. One underlying factor he observed was their mental construction of masculinity, which was rather limited. Most had lived on the street, were themselves victims of severe child abuse and neglect, and had witnessed their mothers being beaten. They saw their own violence as affirming their masculinity.

That was the sociology, but what about the welfare of the people concerned? Here the researcher was in some instances compelled to act. By law, he had to report any abuse suffered by children under the age of 16, regardless of whether they were gang members or their victims. Second, those deemed at risk of suicide had to be referred to mental health providers. Finally, some of the gang members were on probation or living in treatment facilities, so the authorities there also had to be informed. Totten handled the confidentiality issue by studying only the boys who agreed to those limitations on confidentiality.

Another aspect of the 'concern for welfare' criterion, one that can affect the larger community or even the society as a whole, involves sponsored research. Most social research in Canada is funded either by SSHRCC or by the university with which the researcher is affiliated, but other government agencies, private individuals, corporations, unions, and non-profit organizations can also sponsor research. Ethical issues arise if the sponsor places conditions on the methodology to be used or the publication of the results, or has certain expectations regarding the findings. In the United States, a social researcher was asked by the owner of an apartment building to do a study of the behaviour of tenants in 'singles' apartments after neighbours complained about bad behaviour (Bailey 1994). The sponsor in this case made it clear that the research was expected to show that the tenants were in fact good people and desirable neighbours. Perhaps the most famous Canadian case of a sponsor trying to influence the research process involved Dr Nancy Olivieri, who took part in research on a drug designed to treat thalassaemia, a blood disease. She claimed that the drug was not effective and had harmful effects, and wanted to inform the research participants. A controversy arose when the pharmaceutical company that sponsored the research denied her claims and cited a confidentiality agreement that she had signed that would be violated if she were to contact the participants. Another famous case involved three Canadian scientists who claimed that their supervisors at Health Canada had tried to coerce them into approving certain drugs for use on cows and pigs even though the scientists objected that the drugs could have harmful effects on humans; the scientists were subsequently fired, although one was later reinstated. In 2010, the head of Statistics Canada resigned over the federal government's decision to discontinue the mandatory long-form census and replace it with a voluntary version, which in his view would not be adequate to fulfill Statistics Canada's mandate.

People conducting social research should be mindful of the perils of sponsored research. The *TCPS2* states that financial considerations do not reduce the need to abide by the principles that

Methods in Motion

Applications to Canadian Society

Did the implementation of formal ethics reviews stifle social research in Canada? Van den Hoonaard and Connolly (2006) examined this issue by gathering information on Canadian Master's theses completed in anthropology in the ten years from 1995 to 2004. The mid-point in that time span—2001—marked the year that the first edition of the *Tri-Council Policy Statement on Ethics in Human Research* (*TCPS*) (CIHR, NSERC and SSHRCC 1998) was implemented on a national basis. The authors chose anthropology theses in part because a large portion of the research done in that discipline is qualitative, and qualitative researchers have been the most vocal about the negative consequences that stringent ethics policies may have on social research.

One of the major complaints of qualitative researchers is that ethics policies in Canada and elsewhere have been designed according to a bio-medical model that calls for standard research protocols, signed consent forms, and other elements that are not compatible with qualitative and especially ethnographic studies. In qualitative research, topics and even methodologies may emerge out of the research process itself, so information sheets on the goals of the research, consent forms outlining the risks and benefits of participation, and other features of the bio-medical model can in many cases seriously interfere with the research: imagine how members of an outlaw motorcycle gang would respond to a researcher who handed them information sheets and consent forms

to sign. Such difficulties are often not addressed in national ethics regulations. Indeed, the authors point out that the original *TCPS* (1998) contained 476 paragraphs, of which only four pertained to 'natural observation research.'

Van den Hoonaard and Connolly (2006) found, contrary to expectation, that the number of anthropology Master's theses actually increased in the ten-year period under investigation, and that the number of research projects involving research participants (as opposed to archival documents, secondary data sources, and so on) also increased. This suggested that ethics reviews did not put a brake on anthropological research, although the authors noted that the data did not include cases in which research was abandoned because ethics rules were too strict. More ominously, however, they noted that the proportion of theses involving only qualitative interviewing rather than full-blown ethnography had increased since 2001. They suggested that this trend might be a consequence of overly stringent ethics regulations on ethnographic research.

The most recent *Tri-Council Policy Statement* (*TCPS2*), which came into effect in December 2010, was created with substantial input from qualitative researchers. There is now an entire chapter on qualitative research, and the new guidelines recognize that requiring formal consent documents and other elements of the bio-medical model may not be appropriate in all research situations.

underlie its policies, and that the scientific integrity of the research process must be upheld. Any conflict of interest, including a financial conflict of interest involving a relationship with a sponsor, must be reported to the appropriate REB. Most fundamentally, the public good, in particular the welfare of the research participants, 'takes precedence over the interests of researchers and sponsors' (CIHR, NSERC, and SSHRCC 2010: 147).

JUSTICE

Justice in the context of research ethics includes the idea that the burdens and benefits of research should be spread evenly across society. No person or group should be exploited in the research process or systematically excluded from its benefits. This is a major concern in health research, in

which care has to be taken that poor or vulnerable people are not treated as guinea pigs for the benefit of others, whether some interest group or the larger society. Similarly, medical researchers should not arbitrarily exclude from their studies certain categories of people (such as members of specific ethnic, gender, or age groups), especially if such people stand to benefit from experimental drugs or other treatments.

With regard to social research, inclusiveness is usually not a pressing issue, partly because social scientific studies lack the immediate life-and-death consequences that are common in medical research, and also because vulnerable and exploited groups are often sought out for study, particularly by sociologists and anthropologists. However, there is always a risk that members of disadvantaged groups will be abused, mistreated, or disrespected by the researchers who study them. For example, some street people might resent an ethnographer's implication, however subtle, that they need 'help' of some kind, or the assumption that the researcher has a superior sort of wisdom or political insight. Some Western anthropologists have been barred from re-entering the countries where they did their fieldwork because the locals found them to be intrusive and disrespectful.

Justice in a research context also includes the principle of minimizing harm to participants. As we suggested above, it is a rule of thumb when harm is expected that it must not outweigh the potential benefits of the research. But as the examples discussed earlier have shown, harms and benefits can be difficult to judge correctly, and assessments of them ultimately involve value judgments as well as scientific decisions. Most social scientists are not curing cancer or ending racism. How much suffering or harm, if any, can be justified in social scientific research? That is a key ethical question facing both researchers and the REBs that oversee their work.

Research likely to harm participants is regarded by almost everyone as unacceptable. But what is 'harm'? Harm can mean a number of things, including physical harm, loss of self-esteem, stress, or even a mild sense of shame. And what does 'likely' mean: a 1% chance? 10%? 50%?

Researchers should do their best to anticipate and guard against consequences for research participants that are expected to be harmful or disturbing. But it's not always easy to know where to draw the line. For example, in the Rosenthal and Jacobson (1968) study of teacher expectations discussed in Chapter 2, it is at least possible that the pupils not identified as 'spurters' (students expected to excel quickly) were adversely affected in their intellectual development by the increased attention given to the 'spurters.' After all, teachers have limited time and energy, and time spent with the 'spurters' meant time away from everyone else. Was that a violation of research ethics? Was the harm suffered by the 'non-spurters' outweighed by the knowledge gained by the researchers? Similarly, in the Festinger *et al.* (1956) study of a doomsday/UFO cult, the researchers joined the group at a crucial time (close to the projected end of the world), thereby deluding group members into thinking that they had succeeded

in recruiting new converts. Was that ethical? Was the harm to the cult members less important than the understanding of cults gained through this research project?

One of the problems with trying to balance harms and benefits is that it is not possible to identify all the circumstances in which harm is likely—although that fact should not be taken to mean that there's no point in seeking to protect research subjects. Kimmel (1988) noted this in connection with the 1939 Cambridge–Summerville Youth Study: an experiment conducted on 506 boys aged 5 to 13 who were identified either as likely to become delinquent or as having an average likelihood in that regard. The boys were randomly assigned either to an experimental group in which they would receive preventive counselling, or to a no-treatment control group. In the mid-1970s the boys (by then men) were examined and results were quite shocking:

> Treated subjects were more likely than controls to evidence signs of alcoholism and serious mental illness, died at a younger age, suffered from more stress-related diseases, tended to be employed in lower-prestige occupations, and were more likely to commit second crimes (1988: 19).

In other words, the treatment itself may have had unintended negative consequences, although given the complex and long-term nature of the forces that cause delinquency it seems likely that non-experimental factors contributed to the results. Nonetheless, the findings do illustrate the difficulty of anticipating harm to participants. Might a questionnaire on marital happiness lead a respondent to question and eventually leave a marriage? Could asking a grade eight boy in gym class about steroid use encourage him to experiment with a drug that until then was unknown to him? Some interviewees may be uncomfortable answering any question; some may find the cut and thrust of a focus group discussion stressful, especially if they inadvertently reveal more than they had intended. Does it follow that such studies should not be conducted? Is the risk of harm, even mild harm, worth the potential increase in knowledge that this kind of research may make possible? That is the crux of the issue when a researcher seeks a proper balance between harms and benefits. Most ethical codes maintain that if there is any prospect of harm to participants, and if the risks of the research are greater than the risks of everyday life, informed consent is a minimum requirement.

Clearly, the principle of justice in social research is closely tied in with the precepts discussed earlier, in particular the notions of informed consent, privacy, and confidentiality. People are certainly less likely to be harmed if they know what to expect in a research situation, and if they know that their participation is voluntary. Thus it is particularly important to inform subjects of their *right to withdraw from the study at any time*—and to honour that right.

A good illustration of what can go wrong when subjects are pressured into remaining in a study can be found in the Stanford mock prison study (Zimbardo 1971). In this experiment, psychologically healthy male university students were randomly selected to be either 'guards' or 'prisoners' in a simulated prison set up in the basement of a university building. 'Guards' were given uniforms, wooden batons, and reflective sunglasses (to avoid eye contact with the 'prisoners' and thus to de-humanize them), and were told to instil fear in the 'prisoners.' The 'prisoners' were given humiliating smocks and headgear to wear, and had to address the 'guards' in a respectful manner regardless of how they were being treated. The aim of the study was to see whether taking on the role of 'guard' would create feelings of omnipotence and lead to belligerent behaviour, and whether being treated like a prisoner would produce feelings of subservience, self-alienation, resentment, and hostility. In short, the aim of the study was to see whether placing ordinary people in these roles would lead to stereotypical prison behaviour.

The study was designed to last two weeks. Zimbardo describes what happened:

At the end of only six days we had to close down our mock prison because what we saw was frightening. It was no longer apparent to us or most of the subjects where they ended and their roles began. The majority had indeed become 'prisoners' or 'guards' no longer able to clearly differentiate between role-playing and self. There were dramatic changes in virtually every aspect of their behavior, thinking and feeling; human values were suspended, self-concepts were challenged, and the ugliest, most base, pathological side of human nature surfaced. We were horrified because we saw some boys ('guards') treat other boys as if they were despicable animals, taking pleasure in cruelty, while other boys ('prisoners') became servile, dehumanized robots *who thought only of escape*, of their own individual survival, and their mounting hatred of the guards (Zimbardo 1971; quoted in Aronson 1992: 10–11; emphasis added).

A whole host of ethical issues come into play in this experiment, but let's focus on the right to leave a study at any time. Many of the prisoners wanted to leave long before the study was terminated. Yet they were given every indication that they had no choice but to stay in the study, and were convinced that for all practical purposes they were in a prison. A few were allowed to leave early, but only after showing signs of extreme stress and even hysteria. It's hard to see how this was not a violation of research ethics. Looking back on what he had created, Zimbardo himself was appalled.

Another point this experiment illustrates is the need for REBs. Like the Milgram (1963) study, Zimbardo's research was conducted before the era of compulsory ethics reviews. REBs are absolutely necessary because even well-meaning researchers like Zimbardo and Milgram may be completely unaware that their work raises ethical problems—even if those problems seem quite obvious to others. For example, it simply did not occur to Zimbardo that his experiment was causing his research participants harm. It was not until a student research assistant told him she thought the treatment of the prisoners was awful that he relented and brought the study to an end. Presumably, an REB review would have spared the prisoners considerable agony.

Another issue related to harm to participants concerns payment for participation. In general, it is considered unethical to offer payment if that would lead subjects to take risks they would not otherwise accept. Similarly, payment should not put undue pressure on people to take part or remain in a study, and for that reason should not exceed the sorts of benefits to which subjects are accustomed.

The participants in the Dinovitzer *et al.* (2003) study of educational attainment among immigrants (discussed in Chapters 1 and 2) were offered five dollars to participate. It seems unlikely that anyone answered the questionnaire simply for the small amount of money involved. Still, some REBs do not allow subjects to be paid for their participation, except to cover the costs of taking part (parking, etc.). The purpose of this rule is to prevent poor people from 'selling themselves' to researchers. Few would be critical of Beagan's (2001) offer to medical students for a chance at a $200 draw (which technically got around the payment rule) for taking part in her study of discrimination. But would offering $10,000 for testing a promising drug with potentially dangerous side effects be acceptable? What about selling a kidney for research purposes? Fortunately, the risk of harm to participants in social scientific research is usually not as severe as the risks associated with medical research, so those sorts of questions rarely have to be considered.

Benefit in the social sciences is typically indirect; in most cases it follows from an increase in knowledge. However, direct benefits can accrue, for instance in cases where research findings inspire positive social reform or contribute to beneficial societal conservation. One way to maximize the benefit derived from social research is to conduct it in a methodologically sound manner. It is considered unethical to put research subjects through the rigours of participation if the study is not designed or conducted properly and therefore is of little or no value. As you will know by now if you've read previous chapters of this book, researchers can disagree over what constitutes a sound methodology. Nonetheless, each methodological perspective assumes that there are optimal ways of doing the research, and if these are ignored it's doubtful that anyone, including the researcher, will get the maximal benefit from it. Maximizing benefit is also related to the inclusiveness principle discussed above: no group or individual should be arbitrarily excluded from research.

Finally, justice in the conduct of social research includes fairness in the adjudication of research proposals by REBs. The procedures and protocols that REBs use have to be reasonable and equitable, and their decisions unbiased. In order to achieve those ends, REBs must be independent of the institutions in which they function. This means, for example, that universities cannot overturn the decisions of their REBs.

As we noted above, sometimes REBs can go too far in trying to protect the interests of research subjects. This is often a concern in survey research, which normally involves minimal risk to participants. J. Paul Grayson, a sociologist at York University, conducted a study in which he found evidence that the excessively formal and legalistic letters of introduction that some universities require researchers to send to prospective participants lowers participation rates (Charbonneau 2005). Low response rates may result in sample sizes that are too small for analysis and can lead to additional expenses for follow-up.

Conclusions

These ethical principles, and the larger discussion of research ethics contained in the *TCPS2* (CIHR, NSERC and SSHRCC 2010), provide an invaluable guide for the conduct of social research. Their implementation can be challenging, however, especially when acquiring informed consent might lead participants to behave less naturally than they otherwise would. Balancing harms and benefits can also be problematic. But be that as it may, wherever the principles outlined above are not followed, the onus is on the researcher to convince the REB that it would be appropriate to go ahead with the study.

Another kind of challenge arises when professional researchers disagree on the ethical status of a particular practice, such as the covert methods used by Humphreys (1970) in his *Tearoom Trade* study. There is no simple answer to these ethical dilemmas, especially if there is no way to measure harms and benefits directly. However, it is incumbent on researchers to be vigilant in protecting the rights of research participants, and to maximize the benefits and minimize the harm that is created by their research.

Key Points

The *TCPS2* outlines three core principles for the ethical conduct of research:

- *respect for persons* demands that research participants be able to give free, informed and ongoing consent;
- *concern for welfare* includes all aspects of the well-being of individuals, groups, and communities affected by the research; and
- *justice* covers all dimensions of fairness in the treatment of research subjects and researchers themselves.

Most social research in Canada has to abide by those principles. In most cases, before social research can be conducted it has to be approved by a Research Ethics Board (REB) that uses the *TCPS2* to guide its decisions.

It may be difficult to measure harms and benefits in social research, so the implementation of these principles is rarely simple and straightforward.

Researchers may disagree on how the three core principles are to be implemented, but they still must do everything they can to comply with them.

Relevant Websites

The *TCPS2* (CIHR, NSERC and SSHRCC 2010) is available online. This site includes a *TCPS2* tutorial that provides an excellent introduction to the document and gives users the opportunity to apply ethical principles to case studies involving research with human subjects:

http://www.pre.ethics.gc.ca/eng/policy-politique/initiatives/tcps2-eptc2/Default/

[accessed 5 August 2011]

Thomas Blass's *Stanley Milgram* website provides information on the famous psychologist whose work on obedience is discussed in this chapter and in Chapter 1:

http://www.stanleymilgram.com/

[accessed 15 October 2010].

The film version of the Stanford mock prison study can be viewed at:

http://topdocumentaryfilms.com/quiet-rage-the-stanford-prison-experiment/

[accessed 26 October 2010]

Questions for Review

- How are ethical issues relevant to the conduct of social research?
- Explain what is meant by 'harm to participants.' Does it refer to physical harm alone?
- What are some of the difficulties involved in implementing the principle of informed consent when doing ethnographic research?
- Can deception in social research ever be justified? Explain.
- Why is the issue of privacy and confidentiality so hotly debated? What are the main difficulties with following that ethical principle in qualitative research?

- What is meant by 'balancing harms and benefits'?
- Why is there not 100% agreement among social researchers regarding research ethics?
- How can Milgram's (1963) 'electric-shock' experiments be used to illustrate issues of research ethics?
- How can Humphreys' (1970) *Tearoom Trade* study be used to illustrate issues of research ethics?

THE DIFFICULTIES OF ETHICAL DECISION-MAKING

- How easy is it to satisfy ethical criteria in social research? Explain.

DEBATING POINTS

- Defend one of the following positions:
  - Milgram's (1963) 'electric shock' experiments can be justified on ethical grounds.
  - Milgram's (1963) 'electric shock' experiments cannot be justified on ethical grounds.
- Defend one of the following positions:
  - A replication of Zimbardo's (1971) 'mock prison' study should not be allowed because it would not conform to the *TCPS2*'s ethical principles.
  - A replication of Zimbardo's (1971) 'mock prison' study should be allowed because it could provide invaluable knowledge on the effects of prison life for both guards and prisoners.
- Defend one of the following positions:
  - Humphreys' (1970) *Tearoom Trade* study was, on balance, ethical.
  - Humphreys' (1970) *Tearoom Trade* study was, on balance, unethical.

PART V

This part of the book is devoted to sampling and the basics of quantitative and qualitative data analysis. Sampling is an important part of quantitative research, but it is also relevant to qualitative studies. Chapter 12 presents some of the main issues involved in choosing a sample and includes a brief discussion of statistics—the topic of Chapter 13—to wet your feet. Chapter 13 walks you through some basic statistics that are commonly used in the social sciences so you will not be completely at sea when you encounter quantitative research. Different approaches to qualitative data analysis are discussed in Chapter 14.

CHAPTER 12

Sampling

CHAPTER OVERVIEW

Sampling principles are not exclusively the concern of **survey** and other **quantitative** researchers; they also apply to the **qualitative** work you read about in Chapters 8, 9 and 10. In fact, this chapter discusses sampling as it is done in both quantitative and qualitative studies. Putting these topics together here reflects our view that these two approaches, despite their differences, share certain goals and can complement one another—a point that will be addressed in greater depth in later chapters. This chapter explores:

- the role of sampling in relation to the overall process of doing research;
- why **generalizable** findings (that is, findings that can be applied to some larger **population**) require a **representative sample**;
- the idea of a **probability sample**: one using a random selection process;
- the main types of probability sample: **simple random**; **systematic**; **stratified random**; and the multi-stage **cluster sample**;
- the main issues involved in deciding **sample** size;
- different types of **non-probability sampling**, including **quota sampling**, which is widely used in market research;
- potential sources of **sampling error** in survey research;

- sampling in **structured observation** research, where times and contexts are sampled;
- sampling strategies in **ethnography**, in particular **theoretical sampling**, which is associated with the **grounded theory** approach to qualitative data analysis;
- sampling in **content analysis**; and
- raising response rates.

Do you like to spend more time and money than is actually necessary to accomplish something? Most people would say no, and that includes social researchers, who inevitably face the prospect of doing their work with limited time and physical resources. Ideally, researchers would study huge populations, such as all women in Canada or all adults living in the Atlantic provinces, but the costs involved make that impossible. In other areas of life, reducing the time and money you devote to a project normally means a reduction in the quality of the final product—think of building a house on a limited budget. Fortunately, this is not necessarily the case with social research. With proper sampling techniques you can vastly reduce the time and resources needed to complete the research without seriously compromising the findings. You might think of sampling as 'how to do a lot with very little.' Under the right conditions, you can even calculate the probability that sample-based statistical findings are in error. This chapter introduces you to the techniques that make this possible.

Introduction

The term 'sampling' refers to the selection of individuals and other units of analysis for research. The key terms used in sampling are explained in Box 12.1. We'll begin with a discussion of sampling in studies involving **structured interviews** or **questionnaires**. The techniques used for other methods of quantitative research are then discussed, followed by sampling in qualitative research. Finally, ways to increase response rates are considered.

Suppose you are wondering about your fellow students' attitudes on certain matters, or perhaps about their behaviours or backgrounds. To examine any of these areas, either structured interviews or mailed questionnaires would be appropriate. However, let's say that there are around 30 000 students at your university. It would cost a great deal of money to send out 30 000 questionnaires, and the time and energy required to interview 30 000 people would be prohibitive. It's almost certain that a *sample* of students would have to suffice. In fact, the need to sample is almost universal in quantitative research.

But would any sample do? What if you gave questionnaires to everyone in your classes? Or if you stood in a busy location on campus and then interviewed anyone who agreed to speak with you?

If your goal is simply to get some experience in data gathering and analysis, or to conduct a pilot study, these samples woud be fine. However, if the object is to get a *representative sample*, one that can be used to make inferences about all 30 000 students, these samples would not do. Why? There are various reasons, but the following stand out:

- If you distribute questionnaires in your classes, anyone not taking a course with you will be

---

BOX 12.1   Basic terms and concepts in sampling

- *Element* or *unit*: a single case in the population. In the social sciences that element or unit is usually a person, but many other things can be sampled as well: nations, cities, regions, schools, firms, etc. Finch and Hayes (1994), for example, based part of their research on a random sample of wills of deceased people.

- *Population*: all the cases about which you are seeking knowledge, or all the cases to which your conclusions are meant to apply. For example, if you are studying voting behaviour, the population might be all the people in a particular jurisdiction who are eligible to vote. If the topic is hyperactivity among young children, the population might be all children aged 2 to 11. (Note that 'population' in this context means something different from 'population' in the everyday sense.)

- *Sampling frame*: the list of elements from which the sample will be selected.

- *Sample*: the elements selected for investigation, a subset of the population. The method of selection may involve probability or non-probability sampling (see below).

- *Representative sample*: a sample that is a microcosm of the population, one that 'represents' its essential characteristics. A sample like this is most likely to be selected when a probability sampling process is used (see next).

- *Probability sample*: a sample selected using a random process such that each unit in the population has a known chance of being selected. The aim of probability sampling is to keep sampling error (see below) to a minimum.

- *Non-probability sample*: a sample selected using a non-random method. Essentially, this implies that some units in the population are more likely to be selected than others.

- *Sampling error*: an error of estimation that occurs if there is a difference between the characteristics of a sample and those of the population from which it was selected. Sampling error can occur even when a random method is used. For example, if valid measures indicate that 45 per cent of a national probability sample is in favour of more public funding for the arts, but the actual figure in the population is 49 per cent, the difference is caused by sampling error.

- *Non-response*: occurs whenever some unit selected for the sample refuses to participate in the study, cannot be contacted, or for some other reason does not supply the required data.

- *Census*: if an attempt is made to collect data from all elements in the population rather than from a sample, the data are a census. The phrase 'the census' typically refers to the enumeration of all (or nearly all) members of the population of a nation state—that is, a national census.

excluded. How many music or engineering majors take sociology?

- If you go out looking for people to interview, your sample will exclude anyone who happens to be somewhere else at that particular time. Some students will be at work, others will have skipped classes that day, and many will have a timetable different from yours. Some students may never need to go where you are.

- Your decisions about which people to approach may be influenced by your judgments about how friendly or cooperative they appear to be. Gender, race, and age are only a few of the factors that could have an impact on your selection of prospective respondents.

The problem with these sampling methods is that they make the choice of possible participants dependent on non-universal criteria: availability in one case and personal judgment in the other. In the language of sampling, this means that the sample would be *biased*: it would not represent the population from which it was selected. It is extremely difficult to remove bias altogether and get a truly representative sample, but steps should be taken to keep it to a minimum.

Three sources of bias can be identified:

- *Not using a random method to pick the sample.* Essentially, a random method is one in which each element has the same chance of being selected, like numbers from a lottery cage (although in some circumstances that principle may be violated for technical reasons; for example, in order to get a sufficiently large number of people from a small subgroup into the sample). As we saw above, if a random method is not used, there is a risk that the selection process will be affected by human judgment, so that some members of the population are more likely to be selected than others. This source of bias is eliminated through the use of probability sampling, described later in this chapter.

- *The sampling frame or list of potential subjects is inadequate.* If the sampling frame excludes some cases or is otherwise inaccurate, the sample derived from it may not represent the population, even if a random sampling method is employed.

- *Some people in the sample refuse to participate or cannot be contacted—in other words,*

there is non-response. The problem with non-response is that those who agree to participate may differ from those who refuse or cannot be reached in ways relevant to the subject matter being investigated. If that is the case, the sample may not be representative. For example, if you are studying rates of criminal victimization and people who have been victims of violent crime decline to participate, that would skew the results.

If the data are available, a researcher can check to see how non-respondents differ from the population. It is often possible to do this in terms of characteristics such as gender or age, but these are not the only potentially relevant factors; in the case of a sample of university students, for example, you might want to find out whether non-respondents reflect the entire student body in terms of faculty of registration. However, it is usually impossible to check characteristics that go beyond basic demographic categories, such as attitudes towards separatism or patterns of smoking behaviour, because population data are generally not available on these topics.

Sampling error

To appreciate the significance of sampling error for achieving a representative sample, consider Figures 12.1 through 12.4. Imagine a population of 200 people and a sample of 50. Imagine as well that the topic is whether people watch soap operas, and that the population is divided equally between those who do (100) and those who do not (100). If the sample is representative, the sample of 50 should also be equally split in terms of this variable (see Figure 12.1). If there is a small amount of sampling error, so that the sample contains one person too many who does not watch soap operas and one too few who does, it would look like Figure 12.2. Figure 12.3 shows a more serious over-representation in the sample of people who do not watch soaps. This time there are three too many who do not watch them and three too few who do. Finally, Figure 12.4 shows a very serious over-representation of people who do not watch soaps: 35, as opposed to the 25 that would be there if the sample were perfectly representative.

It's important to appreciate that the possibility of sampling error can never be completely eliminated. Even with a well-crafted probability sample,

Watch soaps   Do not watch soaps

FIGURE 12.1 A sample with no sampling error

Watch soaps   Do not watch soaps

FIGURE 12.2 A sample with very little sampling error

Watch soaps   Do not watch soaps

FIGURE 12.3 A sample with some sampling error

Watch soaps   Do not watch soaps

FIGURE 12.4 A sample with a lot of sampling error

a degree of sampling error is likely to creep in, just as flipping a coin 100 times is likely to yield more 49Heads/51Tails and 51Heads/49Tails results *combined* than 50Heads/50Tails outcomes, even though the latter is the most probable single result. Ask your instructor to take a minute for an in-class experiment in which a coin is flipped 20 times and you'll see the surprisingly large number of outcomes that are not 10Heads/10Tails. However, probability sampling stands a better chance than non-probability sampling of minimizing sampling error, so it's very unlikely that the sample will end up looking like Figure 12.4 when it is used. Moreover, probability sampling allows you to employ tests of statistical significance that will permit you to make inferences about the population from which the sample was selected, with a known probability of error. This topic will be addressed in Chapter 13.

Types of probability sample

Imagine a study on the social variables related to alcohol consumption, to be done at a university that has 9000 full-time students. This hypothetical example will be used in the illustrations that follow.

SIMPLE RANDOM SAMPLE

The simple random sample is the most basic form of probability sample. With it, each unit of the population has an equal probability of inclusion in the sample. Suppose there is enough money to interview 450 students at the university. This means that the probability of inclusion in the sample is

$$\frac{450}{9000}, \text{ that is, 1 in 20}$$

This is known as the *sampling ratio* and is expressed as

$$n/N$$

where n is the sample size and N is the population size.

The key steps in devising a simple random sample are as follows:

1. Define the population. Here N is all full-time students at the university: 9000.
2. Select or devise a comprehensive **sampling frame**. In this case, let's assume that (a) the office that keeps student records has a list of all full-time students and (b) you have access

to it (you can consider the ethics of your having access to such a list some other time).

3. Decide on the sample size (n) you will use; here n is 450.
4. List all the students in the population and assign them consecutive numbers from 1 to N, here 1 to 9000.
5. Using a table of random numbers, or a computer program that can generate random numbers, select n (450) different random numbers from 1 to N (9000).
6. The students who match the n (450) random numbers constitute the sample. Two points are worth noting here. First, there is almost no opportunity for bias, since in this case the selection process is entirely random: students are not selected on the basis of subjective criteria such as whether or not they look friendly and approachable. Second, selection does not depend on availability: students do not have to walk by the interviewer in order to be included in the sample. The process of selection takes place without their knowledge, and they do not know they will be asked to be part of a social survey until they are contacted by someone associated with the study.

Step 5 mentions the possible use of a table of random numbers, found in the back of many statistics books or generated by computer software. Such tables are usually made up of columns of five-digit numbers; for example:

09188	08358
90045	28306
73189	53840
75768	91757
54016	87941

The first thing to notice is that, since these are five-digit numbers and the population size is just 9000 (a four-digit number), the only random numbers that might be appropriate are the two that begin with zeros, 09188 and 08358 (and the former is already larger than the largest possible case number for this study). To deal with this, drop one of the digits in each number—in this case the first digit. Using only the last four digits gives us the following:

9188	8358
0045	8306
3189	3840
5768	1757
4016	7941

Still, one of the resulting numbers—9188—exceeds 9000; no student has that case number. The solution is simple: ignore that number and go on to the next one. This means that the student assigned the number 45 will be the first to be included in the sample. Moving down the first column, the student assigned the number 3189 will be next; the student assigned 5768 next; and so on.

To avoid the risk of interviewing the same person twice, ignore any random number that appears more than once and continue down the list. This procedure produces what is called a simple random sample *without replacement*: no number is placed back in (replaced after having been selected) for a second chance at inclusion. Since virtually all simple random samples in social research are like this, the qualifier 'without replacement' is usually omitted. Strictly speaking, 'without replacement' means that the result is not a true simple random sample, as those chosen later have a greater chance of being selected than those selected earlier. (The first person chosen has one chance in 9000 of being selected; removing that person means person two has one chance in the remaining 8999. Thus the 450th person chosen will have one chance out of the 8551 people remaining; a chance of one in 8551 is greater than a chance of one in 9000.) Researchers generally overlook

this problem, since it is a small one compared with other sampling problems.

SYSTEMATIC SAMPLE

A systematic sample is selected directly from the sampling frame, without using random numbers.

In the present case, 1 student in 20 is to be selected (450/9000). That '1 in 20' figure is called the *sampling interval*. A *random start* begins the process, which in this case can be achieved by selecting at random a number from 1 to 20, possibly by using the last two digits in a table of random numbers. With the 10 random numbers above, the first relevant one is 54016, since it is the first one where the last two digits yield a number in the desired range (1–20), namely 16. This means that the 16th student in the sampling frame is the first one to be included in the sample. Thereafter, take every 20th student on the list; the sequence of case numbers would be: 16, 36, 56, 76, 96, 116, etc. Who is the last person in the sample? Case number 8996.

In systematic sampling, it is important to ensure that there is no inherent ordering or pattern in the sampling frame, a feature called *periodicity*. For example, imagine that the sampling frame was set up such that case 1 was male, case 2 female, case 3 male, case 4 female, and so on for all cases. In the example above, that would yield a sample of 450 females and 0 males, in all likelihood a very unrepresentative sample. If there is any pattern to the list, arrange the cases in random order or choose a different sampling method.

Note that with systematic sampling, not every possible combination of cases has an equal chance of being selected. Once that first case number (here 16) is chosen, every case number in the

TABLE 12.1	The advantages of stratified sampling		
FACULTY	POPULATION	STRATIFIED SAMPLE	HYPOTHETICAL SIMPLE RANDOM OR SYSTEMATIC SAMPLE
Humanities	1800	90	85
Social sciences	1200	60	70
Pure sciences	2000	100	120
Applied sciences	1800	90	84
Engineering	2200	110	91
TOTAL	9000	450	450

sample must end in six, and no even-numbered prefixes will qualify, such as 26, 86, or 166.

STRATIFIED RANDOM SAMPLING

In the imaginary study of university students discussed earlier, the student's discipline may be relevant to what you will be researching. Generating a simple random sample or a systematic sample *may* yield one in which, for example, the proportion of kinesiology students in the sample is the same as that in the student population, but usually it is not an exact match. Thus if there are 1800 students majoring in kinesiology, a sampling ratio of 1 in 20 should produce 90 students in the sample from this faculty. But because of sampling error there might be, say, 85 or 93.

So long as data are available on each student's faculty of registration, it's possible to ensure that students are exactly represented in terms of their faculty membership by using **stratified random sampling**. In the language of sampling, this means stratifying the population (dividing it into subgroups) by a criterion (in this case faculty) and selecting either a simple random sample or a systematic sample from each of the resulting strata. In the present example, five faculties mean five strata, with the sample in each stratum being one-twentieth of the total for each faculty, as in Table 12.1, which also shows a hypothetical outcome of a simple random or systematic sample, one that does not exactly mirror the population.

The advantage of stratified sampling is clear: it ensures that the sample is distributed in the same way as the population in terms of the stratifying criterion. Using a simple random or systematic sampling approach *may* result in a distribution like that of the stratified sample, but it is unlikely. On the other hand, this strategy requires that the relevant criteria for stratification be known in advance of the research, which is not always the case.

Two more points are relevant here. Stratified sampling is feasible only when it is relatively easy to identify and allocate units to strata. Five strata based on physical activity level, from 'competitive athletes' at one end to 'couch potatoes' at the other, would be very hard to set up, because it would require an initial study just to get the population data on activity level that you would need to create these strata. Second, more than one stratifying criterion can be used at the same time. In our example, we could stratify by faculty and gender, or faculty, gender, and whether students are undergraduates or postgraduates, etc., so long as the criteria are easy to use and relevant to the research question. But this approach is practicable only when data on the relevant stratifying criteria are available for the population. Does your school have an accessible list of female undergraduate engineering students?

MULTI-STAGE CLUSTER SAMPLING

In the previous example, the students to be interviewed all attend the same university, so no travel would be required. However, imagine a *national* sample of students. The travel involved would add a great deal to the time and cost of doing the research. This kind of problem can occur not only for national populations but even for a large city. Another problem with large populations is the general lack of an adequate sampling frame. Is there a list somewhere of all students registered at Canadian universities? No. Without a sampling frame, it's impossible to select a simple random or systematic sample.

One way to deal with these problems is to employ *cluster sampling*. With cluster sampling, the primary sampling unit (the first stage of the sampling procedure) is not the individuals or units of the population to be studied, but an aggregate of them, known as a *cluster*. Imagine a nationally representative sample of 5000 students. Using simple random or systematic sampling (if that were practicable) would yield a geographically dispersed sample and require a great deal of travel for interviewers. One solution is to sample universities and then students from each of the sampled universities, with a probability sample at each stage. For example, you could randomly sample 10 universities from the entire population of universities, yielding 10 clusters, and then interview 500 randomly selected students at each of the 10 universities selected.

Suppose the result of sampling 10 universities is the following:

- Alberta
- McGill
- Simon Fraser
- Winnipeg
- Dalhousie
- Guelph
- Brandon
- Western Ontario
- Nipissing
- Toronto

This list is fine, but a great deal of travel would still be required because the 10 universities are scattered across the country. And note the absence of universities in Saskatchewan, Newfoundland, and Prince Edward Island. An alternative solution would be to group all universities by region (assuming that the topic of interest does not vary significantly by region)—for example, Maritimes, Quebec, Ontario, Prairies, and BC—and then randomly sample two regions. Five universities can be sampled from each of the two lists of universities, and then 500 students from each of the 10 universities. These are the stages:

- group universities by region and sample two regions; then
- sample 5 universities from each of the two regions; then
- sample 500 students from each of the 10 universities.

Cluster sampling is a multi-stage approach involving first clusters and then subunits within clusters. If the clusters are not created judiciously the chances of having an unrepresentative sample may increase, but if done properly cluster sampling can be very effective. With large populations it is very economical compared to simple random or systematic sampling when doing in-person interviews (using this technique for research based on telephone interviews is less economical now than it once was because phone charges are so low).

In addition to reducing costs, cluster sampling solves the second problem: no adequate sampling frame. The student study described above does not require a list of all university students in Canada, something that would be hard to come by. With cluster sampling, no such list is ever required.

Quite often, cluster sampling also entails stratification. For example, you could stratify universities in terms of whether they are 'new' (having received their charters after the great university expansion of the 1960s) or 'old.' In each of the two selected regions, group universities along the old/new university criterion first and then select universities from each of the strata.

Box 12.3 presents an example of a multi-stage cluster sample. It entails four stages: the sampling of parliamentary constituencies, the sampling of polling districts, the sampling of addresses, and the sampling of individuals.

BOX 12.3 | An example of a multi-stage cluster sample

To study the influence of social class on voting in Canada, suppose the goal is to get 2000 interviews from a random selection of Canadian adults eligible to vote. This may involve:

- Sampling the 308 federal ridings
  - These are stratified by population size (not all ridings have the same number of people in them) into large, average, and small ridings; whether the riding is mostly rural or mostly urban; and dependence on federal transfer payments (high and low).
  - One hundred ridings are then randomly sampled.
- Sampling polling districts
  - Two polling districts are randomly chosen from each sampled riding.
- Sampling addresses
  - Ten addresses from each sampled polling district are systematically sampled.
- Sampling individuals
  - One person at each address is chosen according to some pre-defined random method.

The advantage of multi-stage cluster sampling should be clear by now: it allows interviews to be far more geographically concentrated than is the case for simple random or systematic sampling, and no population sampling frame is required. However, as we suggested above, even a very rigorous sampling strategy cannot eliminate all sampling error, as the example in Box 12.4 shows.

The qualities of a probability sample

Many researchers prefer probability samples because they allow one to make inferences from the sample to the population from which it was selected. In other words, with probability samples, the sample findings can be generalized to the population. This is not to say that the sample and population characteristics are exactly the same, but the first can be used to estimate the second with a known probability of error. In the example of alcohol consumption in the sample of 450 students, the mean number of units consumed by the sample $(\overline{X})$ was used to estimate the population

BOX 12.4   Generalizing from a random sample to the population

If an average of 9.7 units of alcohol is consumed in the previous seven days by respondents in a probability sample, would a similar figure be found in the population? The answer is complex but it is sketched out here and in Box 12.5. Assume for the sake of illustration that it would be possible to take an infinite number of random samples of the same size from a population. Not all the resulting sample means would be perfect estimates of the population mean. We can never know the population figure with 100 per cent certainty, but we can imagine another study with a sample mean of 9.6 units, another with 9.8, and so on. These outcomes, as long as there are enough of them and the sample size is sufficiently high, will take the form of a bell-shaped curve known as a normal distribution (see Figure 12.5) with the sample means clustering around the population mean. Of the sample means not exactly at the population mean, half will be below the population mean and half above it. Moving to the left or to the right (away from the population mean), the curve tails off, reflecting the smaller and smaller number of samples generating

FIGURE 12.5   A distribution of sample means

means that depart considerably from the population mean. The variation of sample means around the population mean is the *sampling error* and is measured using

a statistic known as the *standard error of the mean*. This is an estimate of the amount by which a sample mean is likely to differ from the population mean.

This consideration is important because sampling theory tells us that about 95 per cent of all sample means lie within (+ or −) 1.96 standard errors of the population mean (see Box 12.4). In other words, we can be 95 per cent confident that our sample mean lies within 1.96 standard errors of the population mean.

To illustrate further, if a sample has been selected according to probability sampling principles, we can be 95 per cent certain that the population mean lies between (a) [the sample mean] − [1.96 times the standard error of the mean]; and (b) [the sample mean] + [1.96 times the standard error of the mean]. This is known as the 95 per cent confidence interval. If the mean level of alcohol consumption in the previous seven days in our sample of 450 students is 9.7 units and the standard error of the mean is 1.3, we can be 95 per cent certain that the population mean lies between

$$9.7 - (1.96 \times 1.3)$$

and

$$9.7 + (1.96 \times 1.3)$$

that is, between 7.152 and 12.248 units of alcohol.

Under certain conditions, the standard error of the mean in a stratified sample is smaller than in other probability samples. In other words, stratification may inject an extra increment of precision into the probability sampling process (for example, stratifying by university when levels of alcohol consumption vary widely between universities), since it eliminates a possible source of sampling error.

By contrast, a sample without stratification may exhibit a larger standard error of the mean than a comparable sample with stratification. This occurs because a possible source of variability between students is disregarded.

mean (μ) with a known margin of error. Greek letters are used to denote population characteristics, the Latin alphabet (the one used to write in English) for sample characteristics.

To expand on this point it is necessary to use some basic statistical ideas. These are presented in Box 12.4 and can be skipped if all you need is a broad idea of sampling procedures.

Sample size

'How large should a sample be?' 'Is the sample big enough?' No issue in sampling raises more questions than sample size. Decisions about sample size are not straightforward, as we will see below. At the same time, the quest for the perfect sample is usually constrained by the practical considerations of cost and time.

BOX 12.5   Sampling distributions

Assume a population of five cases (scores = 6, 8, 10, 12, 14) from which a random sample of two cases is selected. The five scores sum to 50 and therefore the mean of the population is 50/5, or 10. Taking all possible random samples of two cases with replacement (meaning that after a case is chosen it goes back into the pool, so that two 6s or two 14s are possible), and calculating the means of each sample of size two, the following results:

		Value of First Observation in Sample				
		6	8	10	12	14
	6	6	7	8	9	10
Value of	8	7	8	9	10	11
Second Observation in	10	8	9	10	11	12
Sample	12	9	10	11	12	13
	14	10	11	12	13	14

Thus the 7, where 6 and 8 meet, is the mean of 6 + 8/2 = 7; the 13 is where 12 and 14 meet, 12 + 14/2 = 13. Now count the number of the sample means in the table; there are 25. There is only one mean of 14, in the bottom right corner, but five means of 10, on the diagonal. Thus five of the 25 sample means, or 20 per cent of them, have a value of 10, *the same as the population mean*. Sample means of 9 and 11 are the next most frequent at 32 per cent (a combined total of 8 of 25 means). With 8 and 12, another 24 per cent (6 of 25) are now counted. So sample means of 8, 9, 10, 11, and 12 represent 76 per cent of all possible sample means. The sample means furthest from the population mean, the 6 and 14 (in each corner), are the rarest, at 4 per cent (1 of 25) each.

Those percentages are really probabilities. The probability of getting a sample mean of 7 is 2 chances in 25 or, as it is usually expressed, 8 chances in 100 or 8 per cent.

The logic of a confidence interval should now be more apparent. A researcher normally takes only one sample, but most random sample results stay close to the population value. In our example, 76 per cent of the sample means are within (+/−) 2 units of the

population mean. When plotted, that is not exactly the bell curve shown in Box 12.3, but you can see the broad outline. Including more and more cases in the sample shapes the lines into a normal curve.

With a real sample, an extension can be created on each side of the sample mean to make it more likely to be correct than if the sample mean by itself were used. The extension for a 95 per cent confidence interval is equal to 1.96 times the standard error of the mean. (In Box 12.3 the sample mean was 9.7, and the extensions were +/− [1.96 × 1.3] or +/− 2.548). The extensions around the sample mean create what is called an interval. There is only a 5 per cent chance that the interval does not include the population mean for a 95 per cent confidence interval.

This is basically how athletes using banned substances are caught. They provide one bio-sample

	SAMPLE	
Mean	Frequency	%
14	1	4
13	2	8
12	3	12
11	4	16
10	5	20
9	4	16
8	3	12
7	2	8
6	1	4
	Σ 25	100

(actually two, but one is a backup), which the authorities then check against a more sophisticated version of the table above. For example, suppose that the population mean value for testosterone is 10 and athlete X comes in at 14. While that is a possible (non-drugged) outcome, it is rare. So if the doping committee is willing to be wrong 4 per cent of the time (the frequency with which an honest 14 occurs), the athlete can be accused. With a reputation at stake, however, a 4 per cent chance of error is too high. That is why the tests allow for only much less likely errors.

ABSOLUTE AND RELATIVE SAMPLE SIZE

People unfamiliar with the field may be surprised to learn that it is the *absolute* size of a sample that is important, not the proportion of the population that it comprises. This means that a national probability sample of 1000 Canadians has about as much validity as a national probability sample of 1000 Americans, even though the latter involves a much larger population.

Increasing the size of a sample increases the precision of the estimates derived from it; for instance, a larger sample size means that the 95 per cent confidence interval referred to in Box 12.4 is narrowed. However, a large sample cannot *guarantee* precision, so it might be better to say that increasing the size of a sample *probably* increases the precision of the estimates it can create. In other words, as sample size increases, sampling error tends to decrease. Common sample sizes are 100 (minimum) and then 400, 900, 1600, and 2500. These sample size increases cut the sampling error by half, then by one-third, then by one-fourth, and then by one-fifth respectively. (The reason has to do with the square roots involved in the denominator of the calculation; thus the original square root of 10 for a sample of 100 becomes 20, 30, 40, and 50 [the square root of 2500], yielding the one-half, one-third, one-quarter, and one-fifth.) Notice that the increases in precision become less pronounced (going from 100 to 400 reduces sampling error by half, but 400 to 900 reduces it by only one-third) and thus the rate of decline in the standard error of the mean declines. Sample size is likely to be profoundly affected by considerations of time and cost at such a juncture, since striving for smaller and smaller increments of precision becomes increasingly uneconomic as ever-larger samples become less and less cost-efficient.

Fowler (1993) warned against simple acceptance of this size criterion and argued that it is not normal for researchers to be able to specify in advance 'a desired level of precision' (1993: 34). Moreover, since sampling error is only one component of any error entailed in an estimate, the notion of a desired level of precision is not realistic. Instead, to the extent that this notion affects decisions about sample size, it usually does so in a general rather than a calculated way. It is usually cost that ultimately determines sample size.

NON-RESPONSE

Considerations about sampling error do not end with issues of sample size. It's also important to bear in mind the problem of non-response and its consequences for response rates.

The response rate is the percentage of the sample that actually participates in the study. It is often

a good deal less than 100 per cent, partly because there are usually some people in the sample who will either refuse or be unable to participate, who cannot be contacted, or who turn out to be unsuitable for the study; Beagan's (2001) response rate of only 59 per cent was not unusual. The above are not the only factors that may be taken into account, however. In addition, some researchers will exclude as 'unusable' the questionnaires of any respondents who left a large number of questions unanswered, or who clearly did not take the interview or questionnaire seriously. Thus the response rate could be calculated as follows:

$$\frac{\text{number of usable questionnaires}}{\text{total sample} - \text{unsuitable or uncontactable}} \times 100$$
$$\text{members of the sample}$$

Those who are chosen for the sample but do not participate must be examined, from whatever data exist on them, to see if they are different from those who do participate. Are the people who cannot be contacted richer and on vacation? Are they ill and in hospital? Such differences may be important (depending on the research topic) and may have to be taken into account in the analysis.

Given that 100 per cent response rates are rare, sample size normally has to be adjusted. For example, if the goal is a sample of 450 students and earlier surveys suggest that the response rate will be approximately 80 per cent, it may be advisable to sample 575 individuals, on the assumption that approximately 115 (20 per cent) will not participate, leaving 460 and still room for some additional refusals.

The issue of refusal to participate is of particular significance because many researchers are experiencing declining response rates to social surveys. In the US, estimates put the refusal rate at about 30 per cent. However, Smith (1995) showed that response rates are affected by things like the subject matter of the research, the type of respondent, and the effort expended on obtaining the cooperation of prospective respondents.

How far should researchers go to boost response rates? Later in the chapter, a number of steps that can improve response rates to mailed questionnaires (which are particularly prone to poor response rates) are discussed. However, boosting response rates can be expensive. Teitler *et al.* (2003) discussed the steps taken to increase the response rate of a US sample that was hard to reach, namely both unwed parents of newly born children. They found that although increasing the sample from an initial 68 per cent to 80 per cent of all couples meant that the final sample more closely resembled the population from which it had been taken, diminishing returns set in. This does not mean that steps should not be taken to improve response rates, however. For example, following up on people who do not respond to a mailed questionnaire usually results in an improved response rate, at little additional cost.

HETEROGENEITY OF THE POPULATION

Yet another consideration is the heterogeneity of the population from which the sample is to be taken. When a population is heterogeneous with regard to characteristics relevant to the topic under study, as a whole country or city normally is, the samples drawn are likely to be highly varied. When it is relatively homogeneous, such as a population of students or members of a particular occupation, the amount of variation is less. Generally, the greater the heterogeneity of a population, the larger a sample should be in order to maximize the chances that all groups will be adequately represented.

KIND OF ANALYSIS

Finally, researchers should bear in mind the *kind of analysis* intended. An example is a contingency table showing the relationship between two variables. In a 2×2 table there are four cells into which the cases can fall, let's say gender (M/F) × whether the person voted in the last election (Y/N). Suppose there were only 10 males and 10 females in the sample, and that 50 per cent of the men and 50 per cent of the women voted, showing no relationship between gender and voting. But suppose the sample by chance included one more woman who voted and one more man who did not. Now the figures show that 40 per cent of men voted versus 60 per cent of women—quite a difference. To prevent such a small change in the sample from having such a major impact on the estimate, a larger sample is required. You would probably want to have at least 50 males and 50 females. Because the population is approximately half male and half female, this is easy to achieve. But what if the variable is religion? Fifty Roman Catholics (or 50 Anglicans) are easy to find in any random sample of 1000, but what about 50

Jehovah's Witnesses or 50 Hindus? One strategy to achieve statistically meaningful results is to randomly over-sample some of these small groups, as Dinovitzer *et al.* (2003) did to guarantee sufficient social class variation. Similarly, the Canadian National Election Study usually over-samples the less populous provinces (such as Prince Edward Island) in order to make interprovincial comparisons. This illustrates how sample size depends in part on the analysis to be conducted.

Types of non-probability sampling

Non-probability sampling includes all forms of sampling that are not conducted according to the canons of probability sampling outlined earlier. It covers a wide range of different types of sampling strategy, at least one of which—the quota sample— is claimed by some practitioners to be almost as good as a probability sample. This section covers three common non-probability samples: the **convenience sample**; the **snowball sample**; and the quota sample.

CONVENIENCE SAMPLING

A convenience sample is one that is used simply because the elements are readily available to the researcher. Imagine a professor in a faculty of education who is interested in the qualities that teachers want in their principals, and who has several classes made up of teachers working part-time towards master's degrees. Now suppose that she decides to administer a questionnaire to those students—a sample of convenience. Chances are that she will receive all or almost all of the questionnaires back, thus achieving a high response rate. However, the use of the convenience sampling strategy makes it impossible to generalize the findings to teachers as a whole: the very fact that her students are taking this degree program marks them off as different from teachers in general. (In addition, of course, it's ethically questionable for a researcher to ask people who are dependent on her for a grade to take part in her research.)

This is not to suggest that convenience samples should always be avoided. In fact, they are used more often than you might think. Beagan's (2001) study of one class at a medical school was based on a convenience sample, as was MacKinnon and Luke's (2002) study of cultural change. Convenience samples are also good for pilot studies. Imagine that the education professor is developing a battery of questions to measure the leadership preferences of teachers. Since it is highly desirable to pre-test such a research instrument before actually using it, administering it to a group that is not part of the main study is a legitimate way of exploring issues such as whether respondents will reply honestly to questions on sensitive topics, and whether the questions are clear and comprehensible. A convenience sample may also be used to test newly created scales for reliability and to generate ideas for further research. Box 12.6 contains an example of a convenience sample.

SNOWBALL SAMPLING

Snowball sampling is a form of convenience sampling, but worth distinguishing because it has attracted quite a lot of attention over the years. With this approach, the researcher makes initial contact with a small group of people who are relevant to the research topic and then uses them to establish contact with others. Tastsoglou and Miedema (2003) used this approach to create a sample of immigrant women in the Maritimes. Box 12.7 describes the generation of a snowball sample of marijuana users for what is often regarded as a classic study of drug use.

Becker's comment on creating a snowball sample is interesting: 'The sample is, of course, in no sense "random"; [indeed] it would not be possible to draw a random sample, since no one knows the nature of the universe from which it would have to be drawn' (Becker 1963: 46). What Becker is saying here is that there is no accessible sampling frame for the population from which the sample is to be taken. The difficulty of creating such a sampling frame means that a non-probability approach is the only feasible one. Moreover, even if it were possible to create a sampling frame of marijuana users or British visitors to Disney theme parks, it would almost certainly become obsolete very soon, because those populations are constantly changing. People become and cease being marijuana users all the time, while new theme park visitors arrive every minute.

The problem with snowball sampling is that it is very unlikely to be representative of the population, although, as Becker's experience suggests, the very notion of a population is problematic in some circumstances. However, snowball sampling is generally used not within a quantitative research strategy, but within a qualitative one: both Becker's work on marijuana users and Bryman's studies on theme parks used a qualitative research framework, and concerns about the ability to generalize do not

---

BOX 12.6 | A convenience sample

Suppose you want to study university undergraduates to find out the extent of their part-time employment while at school. To save time and effort you decide to conduct the study at your own university. You could use probability sampling to get participants, but you think the research is not important enough to justify the cost. Instead you choose five faculties, and within each, one or two of the specific degree programs it offers: anthropology, visual arts, chemistry, electrical engineering, French, kinesiology, media studies, and psychology. This choice of subjects is designed to maximize variety in the types of degree programs represented while providing similar numbers of males and females (since in particular degree programs one gender frequently predominates). Questionnaires can then be given to students in first-, second-, third-, and fourth-year courses.

Together, these procedures represent a good attempt at generating a varied sample. It is a

convenience sample, because the choices of university, faculty, degree program, and course are made purposively rather than randomly. Because of the way the questionnaires are administered (in class), there is a very high response rate. On the other hand, students who are absent from class do not get a chance to fill out a questionnaire. An important question is whether absence from class is connected in some way to part-time work, the latter variable being the focus of your study. In other words, is absence higher among students who work part-time, perhaps because they are working at the time of the class? Are some students too tired to go to class because of their part-time work? If so, you will probably underestimate the proportion of students who work part-time. Also, because you have selected a convenience sample, you must say so in your research report, acknowledging that the results cannot be generalized to Canadian students as a whole or even to the student population at your university.

BOX 12.7 | A snowball sample of marijuana users

Becker (1963: 45–6) reported on how he generated a sample of marijuana users:

> I had been a professional dance musician . . . and my first interviews were with people I had met in the music business. I asked them to put me in contact with other [marijuana] users who would be willing to discuss their experiences with me . . . Although in the end half of the fifty interviews were conducted with musicians, the other half covered a wide range of people, including labourers, machinists, and people in the professions.

loom large in qualitative research. Indeed, Tastsoglou and Miedema (2003) warned their readers not to generalize from their 40 women to all immigrant women in the Maritimes, much less to those in the rest of Canada. This is not to suggest that

Practical TIP ▶ ▶ ▶ ▶

Sample size and probability sampling for students

For most quantitative researchers sample size does matter: the bigger the sample, the more representative it is likely to be (provided the sample is randomly selected), regardless of the size of the population from which it is drawn. However, students have to do their research with very limited resources and a truly random sample may not be feasible for them. The crucial point is to be clear about your sampling decisions and to justify what you have done. Explain the difficulties that you would have encountered in generating a random sample. Explain why you could not increase your sample size. Above all, though, don't make claims about your sample that are not warranted. Never claim that your sample is representative, or randomly selected, unless that is true. Also, even if your sample is small, it may have some good features: the range of people included, a good response rate, high levels of honesty. Make sure to play up these positive features while being honest about the sample's limitations. This is what professional researchers do.

snowball sampling is entirely irrelevant to quantitative research: when the researcher needs to focus on relationships between people, tracing connections through snowball sampling can be a better approach than conventional probability sampling. Statistically small groups—gay francophone lawyers in New Brunswick, for example—are researchable with a snowball approach. Taking a random sample from that population would not be feasible.

QUOTA SAMPLING

Quota sampling is not common in academic social research, but it is used intensively for commercial purposes such as market research and in political opinion polling in some countries. The aim of quota sampling is to produce a sample that reflects a population in terms of the relative proportions of people in different categories (gender, ethnicity, age, socioeconomic status, region of residence, etc.), or in combinations of these categories. Unlike a stratified sample, however, a quota sample is not random, since the final selection of people is left up to the interviewer. Information about the stratification of the Canadian population or about certain regions can be obtained from sources such as the census and from surveys based on probability samples such as the General Social Survey.

Once the categories and the numbers of people to be interviewed within each category (the *quotas*) have been decided, interviewers merely have to select people who fit those categories. The quotas are typically interrelated. As in stratified sampling, the population may be divided into strata covering several characteristics (for example, gender, employment, and age) all at once (see Table 12.2). Census data can identify the number of people who should be in each subgroup; thus the numbers to be interviewed in each subgroup reflect the population. Interviewers can then seek out individuals who fit the subgroup quotas. Accordingly, an interviewer may be told to find and interview five 25- to 44-year-old unemployed females at an assigned location, such as a mall. Interviewers will then ask people at that location about the relevant characteristics (though gender will presumably be self-evident) in order to determine their suitability for a particular subgroup. Once a subgroup quota (or a combination of subgroup quotas) is achieved, the interviewer moves on to another subgroup.

Many Canadians have been approached in a mall by a person toting a clipboard and interview schedule and asked about their age, occupation, and so on, before being asked a series of questions about a product. That person is almost certainly an interviewer with a quota sample to fill. Sometimes she will decide not to interview you because the quota for your group is already filled or you are in a group with no quota; students, for example, are often declared ineligible for inclusion.

TABLE 12.2	Strata for gender, age, and employment
Older, female, unemployed (5%)	Younger, female, unemployed (4%)
Older, female, employed (17%)	Younger, female, employed (20%)
Older, female, other (7%)	Younger, female, other (1%)
Older, male, unemployed (3%)	Younger, male, unemployed (6%)
Older, male, employed (15%)	Younger, male, employed (15%)
Older, male, other (6%)	Younger, male, other (1%)

A number of criticisms are frequently levelled at quota samples:

- The proponents of probability sampling argue that because the choice of respondent is left to the interviewer, a quota sample is not likely to be representative. As noted earlier, in their choice of people to approach, interviewers may be unduly influenced by their perceptions of friendliness or willingness to make eye contact (many people will look at the ground and shuffle past as quickly as possible, not wanting to be bothered).

- People who are in an interviewer's vicinity at interview times, therefore available to be approached, may not be typical. There is a risk, for example, that people not in full-time paid work may be overrepresented, especially in malls, making the sample unrepresentative.

- Judgments about eligibility may sometimes be incorrect, for instance regarding the respondent's age, and even more so for social class. For example, someone who is actually young enough to be eligible but looks older may not be asked because the quota of the older group is filled. In such cases an element of bias is introduced.

- It is not appropriate to calculate a standard error term from a quota sample; in fact, most statistical estimates are meaningless unless random sampling has been used.

All this makes the quota sample a poor bet if the goal is to make accurate inferences with confidence about some larger population. That is why it is not favoured by academic social researchers. It does have some arguments in its favour, however:

- Quota sampling is undoubtedly less expensive than obtaining a comparable probability sample. There is generally no travelling involved and it's easier to manage. There is no requirement to keep track of people who may need to be re-contacted or to record refusals. Still, patterns of refusal should be reported. For example, if it becomes apparent that most men (but not women) don't want to take part, this can signal a gender bias in the results.

- Quota samples can be obtained very quickly. This makes them invaluable when news outlets need to know how people feel about a particular election issue, or when a sudden major news event calls for a more or less instant picture of the community's views or responses.

- Like convenience sampling, quota sampling is useful for conducting tests on new measures or research instruments, or in exploratory work from which new theoretical ideas may be generated.

Structured observation and sampling

Structured observation, like survey research, necessitates decisions about sampling. However, the issues that have to be considered are not limited to sampling *people*. Several other sampling issues may be involved:

- If the structured observation is to take place in public areas, there will be no sampling frames (lists of people who frequent those areas). It would be very difficult, for example, to get a complete list of people who walk along a particular street, or of men who frequent certain 'tearooms.' One can, however, choose the people by using a table of random numbers: for example, the 3rd, then 7th, then 18th person seen in the public area. The same table can be used to establish random samples of time, place, or activity.

• Time sampling involves an observer recording whatever is happening at a particular time, for example, in a pub every 15 minutes after a random start time. This can be done on one person or on several individuals at once and the 15-minute figure can be varied using a table of random numbers. It may be necessary that individuals watched on more than one day not be observed at the same time of the day; the observation periods may have to be randomly selected. For example, it would be an error to observe a certain pupil in a school classroom always at the end of the day, when most students are tired, since tiredness could give a false impression of that pupil's behaviour.

Time sampling should be combined with the next strategy:

• Random sampling of specific places: for example, in a pub near the phone, at the bar, by the pool table, outside where the smokers congregate, the washroom area, and the booths; and

• 'Behaviour sampling,' whereby an entire group is watched and the observer records a particular kind of behaviour. Thus in that same pub, the researcher can observe the nth pick-up (second, then fifth, etc.) after the previous one was observed, using a random number table to determine the n.

Considerations relating to probability sampling derive largely from concerns about **external validity**. For example, if a structured observation study is conducted over a relatively short span of time, questions are likely to arise concerning the stability or representativeness of the findings over longer periods. If the research is conducted in schools, for example, observations conducted towards the end of the school year, when examinations are likely to loom large for both teachers and students, may produce different results than observations made at a different point in the academic year. Consequently, consideration has to be given to the timing of the observations. Furthermore, how are the sites in which structured observation is to take place selected? Are they representative? Using a random sampling procedure to select the schools would assuage any worries in this connection. However, gaining access to settings such as

schools and business organizations is usually difficult; thus settings that are willing to grant access may not be representative.

Limits to generalization

An important point, often not fully appreciated, is that even when a sample is selected using probability sampling, any findings can be generalized *only* to the population from which the sample was taken. This is an obvious point, but it is easy to think that findings from any study have a broader applicability. If the study is based on a random sample of adult Calgarians, for example, its findings cannot be generalized to the whole province of Alberta, much less to other regions of Canada. The opinions of Calgarians may be very different from those of Edmontonians or people who live in Lethbridge, and even more different from the opinions of Montrealers or residents of St John's.

One issue rarely discussed in this context, and almost impossible to assess, is whether there is a time limit on the findings generated. Quite aside from the fact that findings cannot (or at least should not) be generalized beyond the population sampled, is there a point at which one should say, 'Well, those findings applied *then*, but do they apply *now*?' To take a simple example: no one should assume that the findings of a 1980 study of university students' budgeting and personal finance habits apply to today's students. Ever-increasing costs have changed the ways students finance their education, increasing their reliance on part-time work, parents, and loans. But even when there is no definable or recognizable source of relevant change, there is still the possibility (even the likelihood) that the findings are time-specific. Changes over time are a major reason why it is important to conduct replications.

SAMPLING PROBLEMS

There is some evidence that quota samples are often biased. They underrepresent people in lower social strata, people who work in the private sector and manufacturing, and people at the extremes of income; and they overrepresent women in households with children and people from larger households (Butcher 1994). On the other hand, probability samples may be biased as well: for example, they may underrepresent men and employed people (Marsh and Scarbrough 1990), perhaps because such people are often both more difficult to contact and busier, thus less willing to participate.

Other errors related to sampling (see Figure 12.6) include the following:

- *Sampling error*, discussed earlier in this chapter and defined in Box 12.1, arises because it is rare to end up with a perfectly representative sample, even when probability sampling is employed.
- *Sampling-related error* arises from activities or events related to the sampling process. Examples include an inaccurate sampling frame and non-response; each reduces the generalizability or the external validity of findings.

FIGURE 12.6 Four sources of error in research

Qualitative sampling

The sampling of informants in ethnographic research is often a combination of convenience and snowball sampling, and usually involves taking information from whatever sources are available. Ethnographers often face opposition, or at least indifference, to their research and for that reason are often willing to listen to anyone who is prepared to divulge information or views. Convenience and snowball sampling seem to have been the essence of Taylor's (1993) strategy. Her female drug users were

> eventually obtained by a mix of 'snowballing techniques' . . .and my almost continuous presence in the area. . .. Rather than ask to be introduced or given names of others I could contact, when I met a woman I would spend as much time with her as she would allow, participating in her daily round, and through this come to meet others in her social circle. My continued presence in the area also led other women drug users to approach me when I was alone. . .. In addition, the drug worker in the area would mention my presence and interest to women with whom he came in contact and facilitate introductions where possible (1993: 16).

Methods in Motion

Applications to Canadian Society

Over the past forty years, families in Canada and several other countries have made the transition from a 'male breadwinner' model to one in which women are full participants in the paid labour force. Gaudet *et al.* (2011) used the 2001 General Social Survey (Cycle 15 on Family History) to explore Canadian women's participation in paid work after childbirth, focusing on the years 1970–99. This General Social Survey used a stratified sampling technique in which the ten provinces were divided into 27 geographical areas or strata. Random digit dialling was used in each stratum to select the sample, which was considered to be representative of the target population of non-institutionalized people over the age of 15 in the ten provinces. The researchers noted that since the 1970s, it has become increasingly common for women to engage in paid work within two years of giving birth.

Gaudet *et al.* wanted to know what factors influenced women's proclivity to enter the labour force within that two-year period, and whether those factors have changed over time. They found that after controlling for a number of socio-economic influences, the greater a woman's level of education, the more likely she was to be in the paid labour force within two years. They also found that this relationship did not change significantly in the years under study. They noted that this pattern suggests that women at lower levels of education are more likely to suffer the effects of poverty and other negative life-course events associated with being out of the labour force. Another key finding was that for the 1995 to 1999 cohort, women whose spouses were in the highest and lowest income categories were more likely to return to work than those whose spouses had middling levels of income. This suggests that women's decisions to return to work were also affected by how much money their spouses earned.

Ethnographers who take on a role closer to that of observer-as-participant rely somewhat more on formal requests for the names of other people who may have relevant information and who can be contacted.

Whichever strategy is adopted, questions remain as to whether the resulting sample of informants is representative. Probability sampling is almost never used in ethnographic research and is rarely employed even in qualitative research based on interviews. In many cases, a probability sample is not feasible because it is difficult, if not impossible, to map 'the population' from which a random sample may be taken. Instead, ethnographers have to ensure that they gain access to as wide a range of individuals as possible, so that many different perspectives and ranges of activity can be analyzed.

THEORETICAL SAMPLING

An alternative strategy is *theoretical sampling*, advocated by Strauss and Corbin (1998). In their view, because of its reliance on statistical rather than theoretical criteria, probability sampling is not appropriate to qualitative research. Theoretical sampling is meant to be an alternative strategy, used 'in order to discover categories and their properties and to suggest the interrelationships into a theory. Statistical sampling is done to obtain accurate evidence on distributions of people among categories to be used in descriptions and verifications' (Glaser and Strauss 1967: 62).

In theoretical sampling, the researcher simultaneously collects and analyzes the data, decides what data to collect next and where to find them, and develops a theory in the process. Data collection is influenced by the emerging theory and—unlike quantitative data collection—is an ongoing process, subject to change as the study progresses. For Charmaz (2000: 519), theoretical sampling is a 'defining property of grounded theory' and is concerned with refining ideas rather than boosting sample size.

Moreover, theoretical sampling can involve not only people but also settings and events. This can be seen in Strauss and Corbin's (1998: 201) definition: 'Data gathering driven by concepts derived from the evolving theory and based on the concept of "making comparisons," whose purpose is to go to places, people, or events that will maximize opportunities to discover variations among

FIGURE 12.7 The process of theoretical sampling

concepts and to identify categories in terms of their properties and dimensions.'

Figure 12.7 outlines the main steps in theoretical sampling. Data collection (observing, interviewing, and collecting documents) continues until the point of **theoretical saturation** is reached: 'This means, until (a) no new or relevant data seem to be emerging regarding a category, (b) the category is well developed in terms of its properties and dimensions demonstrating variation, and (c) the relationships among categories are well established and validated' (Strauss and Corbin 1998: 212). In the language of grounded theory, a category operates at a somewhat higher level of abstraction than a **concept** in that it may group together several concepts that have common features denoted by the category.

Saturation means that previous interviews/observations have both formed the basis for the creation of a category and confirmed its importance. Thus there is no longer any need to collect data in relation to that category. Instead, the researcher should move on and generate hypotheses out of the categories that are forming, and then collect data related to those hypotheses.

NOT JUST PEOPLE

As we pointed out in the last section, ethnographic sampling is not just about people. Time and context may also be sampled. Attending to time means that the ethnographer must make sure that people or events are observed at different times of the day and different days of the week, to avoid drawing inferences valid only for particular times (mornings, for example, or weekdays rather than weekends).

Because behaviour is influenced by contextual factors, it is also important to observe in a variety of locations. For instance, soccer hooliganism is not a full-time occupation. To understand the hooligans' culture and world view, writers like Armstrong (1993) and Giulianotti (1995) had to ensure that they interacted with their subjects in a variety of contexts other than soccer stadiums, such as the pubs where they engaged in general socializing. Rosenhan had to do the same in his study of psychiatric hospitals (see Chapter 6).

Content analysis sampling

There are several phases in the selection of a sample for content analysis. Applying content analysis to the mass media is explored here but the basic principles have broader applications.

SAMPLING MEDIA

Many studies of the mass media specify a research problem in the form of 'examining the representation of X in the mass media.' The X might be trade unions, women, food scares, crime, or drunk driving. But which mass medium to choose—newspapers, television, radio, chat rooms? If newspapers, will the study focus on tabloids, broadsheets, or both? Will it include Sunday papers, or free newspapers? Will it examine feature articles and letters to the editor, or news stories only? Beharrell's (1993) study of the reporting and representation of AIDS/HIV concentrated on national newspapers over three years and ended up with over 4000 news items.

SAMPLING DATES

Sometimes the decision about dates depends on when the phenomenon of interest occurs. For example, the time for studying squeegee kids in Toronto was dictated by their initial proliferation and then their legislated disappearance (Parnaby 2003). It would be impossible to study squeegee kids before they appeared on the scene, or to continue after their removal. Similarly, the time to study western Canadian separatism (Bell 2007) was when the movement was active, not when it was in a dormant phase. The matter of dates is

more open with an ongoing general phenomenon such as crime. In such cases probability sampling can be used to sample dates: for example, a systematic sample can be generated by randomly selecting one day and then selecting every nth day thereafter.

The time span analyzed in content analysis depends on the research questions, and often the key decision is when to stop selecting cases. If Jagger (1998) had wanted to look for long-term changes in how men and women represent themselves in dating advertisements (see Box 16.1), she would have had to examine the columns of earlier years. She could have taken comparable samples from 10 and 20 years earlier or gone back even further. Warde (1997) was interested in changes in representations of food (what should be eaten and how it should be eaten) in food columns in five of the most widely read women's weekly magazines. He looked at two years, 20 years apart, and within each year at the February, May, August, and November issues to ensure that seasonal factors did not overly influence the findings. (If he had selected magazines from November only, there might have been a preoccupation with Christmas fare, while findings from a summer issue might have been affected by the greater availability of certain foods, such as particular types of fruit.) The choice of the years and months to analyze was somewhat arbitrary, however.

Reducing non-response

There is little consistent evidence on whether response rates are lower for interviews conducted over the telephone rather than face-to-face (see Table 12.3). However, there is a general *belief* that telephone interviews achieve slightly lower response rates than personal interviews (Shuy 2002; Frey 2004). Developments in telephone communications such as the growing use of call screening and cell phones have certainly had an adverse effect on telephone survey responses.

Interviewers in both types of study play an important role in maximizing the response rate for a survey study. The following points should be borne in mind:

- Interviewers should be prepared to keep calling back if interviewees are unavailable. This requires taking into account people's likely work and leisure habits: there is no point in

TABLE 12.3 Comparing the strengths of different ways of contacting members of the chosen sample

	MODE OF SURVEY ADMINISTRATION				
	Face-to-face interview	Telephone interview	Posted questionnaire	Email	Web
RESOURCE ISSUES					
Is the cost of the mode of administration relatively low?	✓	✓✓	✓✓✓	✓✓✓	✓ (unless access to low-cost software)
Is the speed of the mode of administration relatively fast?	✓	✓✓✓	✓✓✓	✓✓✓	✓✓✓
Is the cost of handling a dispersed sample relatively low?	✓ (✓✓ if clustered)	✓✓✓	✓✓✓	✓✓✓	✓✓✓
SAMPLING-RELATED ISSUES					
Does the mode of administration tend to produce a good response rate?	✓✓✓	✓✓	✓	✓	✓
Is the researcher able to control who responds (that is, the person targeted is the one who answers)?	✓✓✓	✓✓✓	✓✓	✓✓	✓✓
Is the mode of administration accessible to all sample members?	✓✓✓	✓✓	✓✓✓	✓ (because of need for respondents to be accessible online)	✓ (because of need for respondents to be accessible online)
Is the mode of administration less likely to result in non-response to some questions?	✓✓✓	✓✓✓	✓✓	✓✓	✓✓

Notes: Number of ticks indicates the strength of the mode of administration of a survey in relation to each issue. More ticks correspond to more advantages in relation to each issue. A single tick implies that the mode of administering a questionnaire does not fare well in this area. Two ticks imply that it is acceptable and three ticks that it does very well. This table was influenced by Czaja and Blair (1996).

daytime calling for people who work during the day. People living alone may be reluctant to answer the door, especially after dark.

- Be optimistic; you may get a better response rate if you assume that people will agree to be interviewed than if you assume that they will refuse.
- Reassure people that you are not a salesperson. Because of the unethical tactics of organizations whose representatives say they are doing market or social research, many people have become very suspicious of anyone who says she would 'just like to ask a few questions.'
- When conducting in-person interviews, dress in a way that is acceptable to a wide spectrum of people.

- Make it clear that you are happy to find an interview time to suit the respondent.

IMPROVING RESPONSE RATES TO MAILED QUESTIONNAIRES
Mangione (1995: 60–1) classified response rates to mailed questionnaires as follows:

Over 85%	excellent
70–85%	very good
60–69%	acceptable
50–59%	barely acceptable
Below 50%	not acceptable

Because of the tendency for mailed questionnaires to generate lower response rates than structured interviews (and the implications this has for the validity

Response rates

The lower the response rate, the more likely it is that questions will be raised about the representativeness of the sample. Mailed questionnaires in particular are often associated with low response rates, and as Mangione's classification (page 227) illustrates, some authorities consider a response rate below 50 per cent unacceptable. Then again, a great deal of published research achieves only a low response rate, so don't despair. The key point is to recognize and acknowledge the negative implications of a low rate. Many students find mailed and other forms of questionnaire attractive because of their low cost and ease of administration. Don't be put off using such techniques just because they are associated with low response rates. There are other considerations.

Also, response rates are usually an issue only with randomly selected samples. Samples not selected using probability methods are not expected to be representative of a population even if all the people selected do participate. But here again, it is necessary to acknowledge the limitations of the sample.

of findings), a great deal of thought and research has gone into improving response rates for the former. The following steps are frequently suggested:

- Write a good covering letter explaining the reasons for the research, why it is important, and why the recipient has been selected; provide guarantees of confidentiality.

- Make it personal by including the respondent's name and address in the covering letter, and by ensuring that each letter is individually signed. A cover letter addressed to 'Occupant' will put most people off. The downside of the personal approach is that it may raise concerns: How did they know about me? Will my responses really be confidential? The researcher should try to deal with any potential fears in the letter.

- The mailed questionnaires should always be accompanied by a stamped return envelope or (at the very least) return postage.

- Don't allow the questionnaire to appear unnecessarily bulky. Some researchers reduce the size of the questionnaire to fit a booklet format. As with structured interviewing, begin with questions most likely to be of interest to the respondent.

- Follow up individuals who do not reply at first, possibly with two or three further mailings. The importance of reminders cannot be overstated—they do work. One approach is to send out a reminder letter to non-respondents two weeks after the initial mailing, reasserting the nature and aims of the survey and suggesting that the person contact a member of the research team to obtain a replacement copy of the questionnaire should the original one have been lost. Then, two weeks after that, those who still have not responded should be sent another letter along with a second copy of the questionnaire. These reminders have a demonstrable effect on the response rate. Some writers argue for even more than two mailings of reminder letters. If a response rate is worryingly low, further mailings are certainly desirable.

- Monetary incentives increase the response rate but can be deemed unethical. They are most effective if they arrive with the questionnaire (as opposed to after its return). Apparently, most respondents will not take the money and discard the questionnaire. The evidence also suggests that quite small amounts of money have a positive impact on the response rate, but that larger amounts do not necessarily improve the rate any further.

VIRTUAL SAMPLING ISSUES

A major limitation of online surveys is that not everyone is online and has the technical ability to handle questionnaires in either email or web formats. Other factors that make such surveys problematic include the following:

- Many people have more than one email address;

- Many people use more than one Internet Service Provider (ISP);

- Many households have one computer but several users;

- Internet users are a biased sample of the population in that they tend to be better educated, wealthier, younger, and not representative in ethnic terms (Couper 2000); and

- Few sampling frames exist for the general online population, and most of these are likely to be either confidential or too expensive to acquire.

Such issues make surveys using probability samples difficult to do. This is not to say that online surveys should not be considered. For example, in many organizations, most if not all non-manual workers are likely to be online and familiar with using email and the Internet. The same is true of most university students (Couper 2000).

The chief problem with virtual sampling strategies is that the representativeness of the sample is almost always in question. On the other hand, given the paucity of knowledge and understanding of online behaviour, one could argue that having some information about these areas is a lot better than having none at all, provided that the limited generalizability of the findings is appreciated.

There is growing evidence that online surveys typically generate lower response rates than mailed questionnaires (Tse 1998; Sheehan 2001). In the early years, response rates for email surveys were quite encouraging (Sheehan and Hoy 1999), but they later declined to the point where they were often lower than the response rates for most mailed questionnaires, though there were exceptions (Sheehan 2001). Two factors may account for the decline: the novelty of email surveys had worn off and the proliferation of 'spam' had sparked a growing antipathy towards unsolicited emails.

Various researchers have used the following strategies in an effort to boost response rates:

1. Contact prospective respondents before sending them questionnaires. This is regarded as basic 'netiquette.'
2. As with mailed questionnaires, send non-respondents at least one follow-up message.

Overview

Online surveys are still fairly new and have potential if only for their low cost. There is evidence that offering a web survey or email option can boost response rates for mailed questionnaires (Yun and Trumbo 2000). Several problems have been identified with web and email surveys, but it's too early to dismiss this type of data gathering: methodologists are only beginning to come to grips with it and may gradually develop ways of overcoming its limitations. Moreover, as more and more people and organizations go online, some of the problems are bound to diminish.

One last point

Sampling decisions are the last step for most researchers before going into the field, so this is a good time to review the relevant ethical principles. For a checklist, see below.

☑ Checklist *of ethical issues to consider before going into the field to collect data*

✔ Have you submitted your project to your institution's research ethics board? If only certain types of research need to be submitted for formal approval, is your research exempt, or does it require clearance?

✔ Have you ensured that there is no prospect of serious harm to participants?

✔ Does your research conform to the principle of informed consent, so that research participants understand:
  – what the research is about?
  – the purposes of the research?
  – the nature of the participant's involvement in the research?
  – how long their participation is going to take?
  – that participation is voluntary?
  – that they can withdraw from the study at any time, even after the research starts?
  – what is going to happen to the data (for example, how it will be kept, when it will be destroyed)?

✔ Are you sure that the privacy of the people involved in your research will not be violated and that the confidentiality of the data will be maintained?

✔ If deception is involved, have you ensured that research participants will be debriefed in a timely matter—that is, that they will get an explanation of the true purposes of the study as soon as possible?

✔ After the data have been collected, have you ensured that the names of research participants and/or organizations involved will be made unidentifiable? Do you have a strategy for archiving data in electronic form that complies with data protection legislation?

Key Points

- Probability sampling is a mechanism for reducing bias in sample selection.
- Key technical terms in sampling include representative sample, random sample, non-response, population, and sampling error.
- Randomly selected samples are important because they permit generalizations to the population of interest.
- Sampling error generally decreases as sample size increases.
- Under certain circumstances, quota samples can be an alternative to random samples, but they have some deficiencies.

- Convenience samples can provide useful data, but have limited generalizability.
- Sampling and sampling-related error are just two sources of error in social survey research.
- Sampling considerations in qualitative research differ from those addressed in quantitative research, in that issues of representativeness are less important.
- Sampling in qualitative research may be done on people, places, times, and even behaviours.
- Response rates vary by the medium of communication and most can be improved by persistent follow-up procedures.

Relevant Websites

Statistics Canada provides a good general introduction to sampling at:

http://www.statcan.gc.ca/edu/power-pouvoir/ch13/5214895-eng.htm

To get some familiarity with a complex sampling design, scroll down to the 'Sampling' heading at this website, which describes the sample selection and random digit dialling procedures for the 2010 General Social Survey Time Use study:

http://www.statcan.gc.ca/cgi-bin/imdb/p2SV.pl?Function=getSurvey&SDDS=4503&lang=en&db=imdb&adm=8&dis=2

These YouTube videos illustrate how to select a simple random, stratified and cluster sample:

http://www.youtube.com/watch?v=yx5KZi5QArQ&NR=1

http://www.youtube.com/watch?NR=1&v=sYRUYJYOpGO

http://www.youtube.com/watch?v=QOxXy-l6ogs&feature=related

[Websites accessed 31 August 2011]

Questions for Review

- What do each of the following terms mean: population; non-probability sampling; sampling frame; and representative sample?
- What are the goals of sampling?
- What are the main areas of potential bias in sampling?

SAMPLING ERROR

- How does sampling error affect the representativeness of a sample?

PROBABILITY SAMPLING

- What is probability sampling and why is it important?
- What are the main types of probability sample?
- How does a stratified random sample offer greater precision than a simple random sample?
- To conduct an interview survey of 500 people in Winnipeg, what type of probability sample would be best? Why?

- A researcher positions herself on a street corner and asks every fifth person who walks by for an interview until she has a sample of 250. List some of the kinds of people to whom she should not generalize her results.

SAMPLE SIZE

- What factors should be taken into account in deciding the size needed for a probability sample?

- 'Non-response makes even most probability samples non-representative and thus not really worth the extra cost.' Discuss.

NON-PROBABILITY SAMPLES

- Which form of non-probability sample is likely to be least useful? Which is likely the most useful? Explain.

- What circumstances make snowball sampling appropriate?

- 'Both quota samples and true random samples generate representative samples, with little difference between them. This accounts for the widespread use of quota samples in market research.' Discuss.

LIMITS TO GENERALIZATION

- 'The problem of generalization to a population involves more than getting a representative sample.' Discuss.

QUALITATIVE SAMPLING

- What is theoretical sampling?

- What is theoretical saturation and how does it relate to theoretical sampling?

REDUCING NON-RESPONSE

- Realistically, what can you do to improve the response rate to a mailed questionnaire?

CHAPTER 13

Quantitative Data Analysis

CHAPTER OVERVIEW

This chapter presents some of the most basic and frequently used methods for analyzing quantitative data. To illustrate them, we'll use an imaginary data set on attendance at a gym—the kind of data set that could be generated from a small research project suitable for most undergraduates.

The chapter explores:

- the importance of anticipating questions of analysis early in the research process, before all the data have been collected;

- the different kinds of **variables** generated in quantitative research; knowing how to distinguish them is crucial in deciding which statistic to use;

- methods for analyzing a single variable (**univariate analysis**);

- methods for analyzing relationships between two variables (**bivariate analysis**); and

- analysis of relationships among three or more variables (**multivariate analysis**).

If you're like many students in the social sciences, the idea of learning about statistics doesn't fill you with joy. How about communing with nature? Yes, that would be much better—open fields, wild winds, the bright sky, a riot of colour provided by the plants and animals around you. On the other hand, it's often said that mathematics is the language that nature speaks, and statistics is a form of applied mathematics. Communing with nature via statistics can be just as invigorating as communing any other way, especially if you work at it for a while. Feel better now? If not, remember that the best way to learn a new language is to start with the basics. That's what we'll do in this chapter. In fact, we're not going to go beyond a basic level, and we won't even be using any formulas—we'll leave that for your statistics courses. What we will do is introduce the logic of statistics, which will give you the conceptual foundations you need to do quantitative data analysis. We'll also discuss some important ways of organizing quantitative data.

Introduction

This chapter will discuss some basic techniques for analyzing quantitative data. It will not consider the formulas that underpin those techniques, in order to keep the discussion focused on methodological issues. One chapter could not do justice to the topic of numerical data analysis in any case; readers are advised to consult books that provide more detailed and advanced treatments (for example, Healey and Prus 2010; Agresti and Finlay 2009).

Before we begin, a warning is in order. The biggest mistake in quantitative research is to think that data analysis decisions can wait until after the data have been collected. Data analysis *is* carried out after that stage, but it's essential to be fully aware of what techniques will be used before data collection begins. The **questionnaire**, **observation schedule**, and **coding frame** should be designed with the data analysis in mind, for two main reasons:

- The statistical techniques that can be used depend on how a variable is measured. Inappropriate measurement may make it impossible to conduct certain types of data analysis.

- The size and nature of the sample also imposes limitations on the kinds of techniques that are suitable for the data set.

A small research project

The discussion of quantitative data analysis provided here is based on an imaginary piece of research carried out by an undergraduate for her honours thesis on leisure in modern society. She chose that topic because of her enthusiasm for gyms and workout facilities, and her interest in how and why such venues are used. She had a hunch that they might be indicative of a 'civilizing process' and used this theory as a framework for her findings (Rojek 1995: 50–6). She was also interested in issues relating to gender and body image, and suspected that men and women differ in their reasons for going to a gym as well as in their activities there.

She secured the permission of a gym close to her home to contact a sample of its members by mail. The gym had 1200 members and she decided to take a **simple random** sample of 10 per cent

of them (that is, 120 members). She mailed questionnaires to members of the sample with a covering letter testifying to the gym's support for her research. One thing she wanted to know was how much time people spent on each of the three main types of activity in the gym: cardiovascular equipment, weights, and other activities (for example, stretching exercises). She defined each of these carefully in the covering letter and asked members of the sample to note down how long they spent on each of the three activities on their next visit. They were then requested to return the questionnaires to her in a prepaid reply envelope. She ended up with 90 questionnaires out of the 120—a response rate of 75 per cent.

The entire questionnaire ran to four pages; 12 of the questions along with the responses of a fictional respondent are provided in Box 13.1. Questions 1, 3, 4, 5, 6, 7, 8, and 9 were **pre-coded**; the respondent simply had to circle the appropriate code. With the others, specific figures were requested, which were later transferred to the code column.

MISSING DATA

The data for all 90 respondents are presented in Box 13.2. Each of the 12 questions is designated initially as a numbered variable (var00001, var00002, etc.); the number corresponds to the question number in Box 13.1 (var00001 is question 1, var00002 is question 2, etc.). An important issue in data analysis is how to handle the '**missing data**' generated when respondents do not reply to a question—whether because they accidentally skip it, because they do not want to answer it, or because it does not apply to them. For example, respondent 24 failed to answer question 2 on age. This was coded as 999, a number chosen because it cannot be mistaken for a person's age and is also easy to remember. Also, question 9 has a large number of 8s, because for this variable an 8 means 'not applicable'—many people did not answer this question, having been filtered out by the previous one (that is, they do not have other sources of regular exercise). Everyone answered questions 10, 11, and 12, so there are no missing data for those variables; if there were, it would be necessary to code the missing data with another number that could not be mistaken for an actual number of minutes. The various missing data codes are

BOX 13.1   Part of a completed questionnaire on use of a gym

Questionnaire   **Code**

1. Are you male or female? (please tick)

   Male _✓_   Female ____   ① 2

2. How old are you?

   _21_ Years

3. Which of the following best describes your main reason for going to the gym? (please circle one code only)

Relaxation	____	1
Maintain or improve fitness	____	②
Lose weight	✓	3
Meet others	____	4
Build strength	____	5
Other (please specify)	____	6

4. When you go to the gym, how often do you use the cardiovascular equipment (treadmill, step machine, bike, rower)? (please tick)

Always	✓	①
Usually	____	2
Rarely	____	3
Never	____	4

5. When you go to the gym, how often do you use the weights? (please tick)

Always	✓	①
Usually	____	2
Rarely	____	3
Never	____	4

6. Generally, how frequently do you go to the gym? (please tick)

Every day	____	1
4–6 days a week	____	2
2 or 3 days a week	✓	③
Once a week	____	4
2 or 3 times a month	____	5
Once a month	____	6
Less than once a month	____	7

7. Do you usually go with someone else to the gym or usually on your own? (please circle one code only)

On my own	✓	①
With a friend	____	2
With a partner/spouse	____	3

BOX 13.1 | . . . Continued

8. Do you have sources of regular exercise other than the gym?

    Yes ____ No ✓   1 ②

    If you have answered No to this question,
    please proceed to question 10.

9. If you have replied Yes to question 8, please indicate the main source of regular exercise in the last
    six months from this list (please circle one code only)

    Sport   ____   1
    Cycling on the road   ____   2
    Jogging   ____   3
    Long walks   ____   4
    Other (please specify)   ____   5

10. During your last visit to the gym, how many minutes did you spend on the cardiovascular
     equipment (treadmill, step machine, bike, rower)?

     _33_ minutes   33

11. During your last visit to the gym, how many minutes did you spend on weights?

     _17_ minutes   17

12. During your last visit to the gym, how many minutes did you spend on other activities
     (e.g., stretching exercises)?

     _5_ minutes   5

stored in the information for each variable so they cannot be read by the computer as anything other than missing data.

Types of variables

Look at the different questions and notice that some of them call for answers in real numbers: questions 2 (*age*), and 10, 11, and 12. Questions 1 (*gender*) and 8 yield either/or answers, which are called dichotomies (only two possible responses). The rest of the questions take the form of lists of categories, but there are also differences among them. Some of the answers can be rank ordered: see questions 4, 5, and 6. Thus for question 6 the category 'every day' implies greater frequency than '4–6 days a week,' which in turn is a greater frequency than '2 or 3 days a week,' and so on. Compare this to questions 3, 7, and 9 where the categories *can't* be rank ordered. In the case of

question 3, for instance, 'relaxation' is neither more nor less of something than 'maintain or improve fitness' is.

In short, different types of variables can be generated in the course of research. The three main types are distinguished by looking at the relationship between the categories of the variable *as manifested by any one individual*. The three are:

- **Nominal variables**. These variables, also known as *categorical variables*, are composed of categories that have no relationship to one another except that they are *different*. In the case of religion, for example, the categories might be Roman Catholic, Protestant, Jewish, Muslim, Hindu, Other, and No Religion. Any two research participants will be either in the same category or in different categories: no other kind of comparison is possible. This means that the

BOX 13.2   Gym survey data

Case	var00001	var00002	var00003	var00004	var00005	var00006	var00007	var00008	var00009	var00010	var00011	var00012
1	1	21	2	1	1	3	1	2	8	33	17	5
2	2	44	1	3	1	4	3	1	2	10	23	10
3	2	19	3	1	2	2	1	1	1	27	18	12
4	2	27	3	2	1	2	1	2	8	30	17	3
5	1	57	2	1	3	2	3	1	4	22	0	15
6	2	27	3	1	1	3	1	1	3	34	17	0
7	1	39	5	2	1	5	1	1	5	17	48	10
8	2	36	3	1	2	2	2	1	1	25	18	7
9	1	37	2	1	1	3	1	2	8	34	15	0
10	2	51	2	2	2	4	3	2	8	16	18	11
11	1	24	5	2	1	3	1	1	1	0	42	16
12	2	29	2	1	2	3	1	2	8	34	22	12
13	1	20	5	1	1	2	1	2	8	22	31	7
14	2	22	2	1	3	4	2	1	3	37	14	12
15	2	46	3	1	1	5	2	2	8	26	9	4
16	2	41	3	1	2	2	3	1	4	22	7	10
17	1	25	5	1	1	3	1	1	1	21	29	4
18	2	46	3	1	2	4	2	1	4	18	8	11
19	1	30	3	1	1	5	1	2	8	23	9	6
20	1	25	5	2	1	3	1	1	1	23	19	0
21	2	24	2	1	1	3	2	1	2	20	7	6
22	2	39	1	2	3	5	1	2	8	17	0	9
23	1	44	3	1	1	3	2	1	2	22	8	5
24	1	999	1	2	2	4	2	1	4	15	10	4
25	2	18	3	1	2	3	1	2	1	18	7	10
26	1	41	3	1	1	3	1	2	8	34	10	4
27	2	38	2	1	2	5	3	1	2	24	14	10
28	1	25	2	1	1	2	1	2	8	48	22	7
29	1	41	5	2	1	3	1	1	2	17	27	0
30	2	30	3	1	1	2	2	2	8	32	13	10
31	2	29	3	1	3	2	1	2	8	31	0	7
32	2	42	1	2	2	4	2	1	4	17	14	6
33	1	31	2	1	1	2	1	2	8	49	21	2
34	2	25	3	1	1	2	3	2	8	30	17	15
35	1	46	3	1	1	3	1	1	3	32	10	5
36	1	24	5	2	1	4	1	1	2	0	36	11
37	2	34	3	1	1	3	2	1	4	27	14	12
38	2	50	2	1	2	2	3	2	8	28	8	6
39	1	28	5	1	1	3	2	1	1	26	22	8
40	2	30	3	1	1	2	1	1	4	21	9	12
41	1	27	2	1	1	2	1	1	3	64	15	8
42	2	27	2	1	2	4	2	1	4	22	10	7
43	1	36	5	1	1	3	2	2	8	21	24	0
44	2	43	3	1	1	4	1	2	8	25	13	8
45	1	34	2	1	1	3	2	1	1	45	15	6
46	2	27	3	1	1	2	1	1	4	33	10	9
47	2	38	2	1	3	4	2	2	8	23	0	16

BOX 13.2   . . . Continued

Case	var00001	var00002	var00003	var00004	var00005	var00006	var00007	var00008	var00009	var00010	var00011	var00012
48	1	28	2	1	1	3	3	1	2	38	13	5
49	1	44	5	1	1	2	1	2	8	27	19	7
50	2	31	3	1	2	3	2	2	8	32	11	5
51	2	23	2	1	1	4	2	1	1	33	18	8
52	1	45	3	1	1	3	1	1	2	26	10	7
53	2	34	3	1	2	2	3	2	8	36	8	12
54	1	27	3	1	1	2	3	1	3	42	13	6
55	2	40	3	1	1	2	2	1	4	26	9	10
56	2	24	2	1	1	2	1	1	2	22	10	9
57	1	37	2	1	1	5	2	2	8	21	11	0
58	1	22	5	1	1	4	1	1	1	23	17	6
59	2	31	3	1	2	3	1	1	4	40	16	12
60	1	37	2	1	1	2	3	2	8	54	12	3
61	2	33	1	2	2	4	2	2	8	17	10	5
62	1	23	5	1	1	3	1	1	1	41	27	8
63	1	28	3	1	1	3	3	2	8	27	11	8
64	2	29	2	1	2	5	2	1	2	24	9	9
65	2	43	3	1	1	2	1	2	8	36	17	12
66	1	28	5	1	1	3	1	1	1	22	15	4
67	1	48	2	1	1	5	1	1	4	25	11	7
68	2	32	2	2	2	4	2	2	8	27	13	11
69	1	28	5	1	1	2	2	2	8	15	23	7
70	2	23	2	1	1	5	1	1	4	14	11	5
71	2	43	2	1	2	5	1	2	8	18	7	3
72	1	28	2	1	1	4	3	1	2	34	18	8
73	2	23	3	1	1	2	1	2	8	37	17	17
74	2	36	1	2	2	4	2	1	4	18	12	4
75	1	50	2	1	1	3	1	1	2	28	14	3
76	1	37	3	1	1	2	2	2	8	26	14	9
77	2	41	3	1	1	2	1	1	4	24	11	4
78	1	26	5	2	1	5	1	1	1	23	19	8
79	2	28	3	1	1	4	1	2	8	27	12	4
80	2	35	2	1	1	3	1	1	1	28	14	0
81	1	28	5	1	1	2	1	1	2	20	24	12
82	2	36	2	1	1	3	2	2	8	26	9	14
83	2	29	3	1	1	4	1	1	4	23	13	4
84	1	34	1	2	2	4	2	1	8	24	12	3
85	1	53	2	1	1	3	3	1	1	32	17	6
86	2	30	3	1	1	4	1	2	8	24	10	9
87	1	43	2	1	1	2	1	1	2	24	14	10
88	2	26	5	2	1	4	1	1	1	16	23	7
89	2	44	1	1	1	4	2	2	8	27	18	6
90	1	45	1	2	2	3	3	2	8	20	14	5

order of the categories is arbitrary: it could have begun with No Religion and ended with Roman Catholic. Switching the order has no implications for the way the data are interpreted.

- **Ordinal variables**. With these variables the different categories can be rank ordered. That means that 'greater than' (>) and 'less than' (<) statements can be made about the categories and the people in them. For example, in question 5 'always' indicates greater frequency than 'usually,' which indicates greater frequency than 'rarely,' etc. Note also that it would be illogical to re-order the categories as, say, 'always, never, sometimes, usually.'

- The distance or amount of difference between the categories, however, may not be equal across the range. Thus the difference between the categories 'always' and 'usually' is probably not the same as the difference between 'usually' and 'rarely,' and so on. This is because no unit of measurement is used for this question. Ordinal variables are similar to words that have either a comparative '-er' or a superlative '-est' attached to them, as in 'slimmer' and 'slimmest.'

- **Interval/ratio variables**. These are variables for which a unit of measurement exists and thus the distances or amount of difference between the categories can be made identical across the range of categories. The values take the form of actual numbers (such as 1, 2, 7.5, etc.). In the case of variables var00010 to var00012, the unit is the minute and the difference between the categories is a one-minute interval. Thus a person who spends 32 minutes on cardiovascular equipment is spending one minute more than someone who spends 31. That difference is the same as the difference between someone who spends 8 minutes and another who spends 9 minutes on the equipment. At the interval/ratio level of measurement, it is possible to say that two scores are equal or not equal (as at the nominal level), for example, $32 \neq 31$; that they have greater or lesser values (as at the ordinal level), for example, $32>31$, $8<9$; and that the distance or amount of difference between them can be specified, for example, $32-31 = 1$. This is the highest level of measurement, the one that allows the widest range of analysis techniques, including addition, subtraction, multiplication, and division.

- Sometimes a distinction is made between interval and **ratio variables**. Ratio variables are interval variables with a fixed and non-arbitrary zero point (as in a wind speed of 0 kilometres per hour). Many social science variables exhibit this quality, for example, income, age, and years of school completed. In the discussions that follow we will use the more inclusive term 'interval/ratio,' but to understand, take two incomes: $30K and $45K. They are nominally unequal and the first is less than the second, in fact $15K less. But with that real 0, one can also say that the first is 2/3 of the second (or the second is 1.5 times the first). The first income can also be said to stand in a 2:3 *ratio* to the second.

The three main types of variable and illustrations from the gym survey are provided in Table 13.1. Strictly speaking, items that have Likert-style response categories (see Box 3.3) produce ordinal variables. However, many writers argue that they can be treated as though they produce interval/ratio variables because of the relatively large number of categories they generate. For a brief discussion of this issue, see Bryman and Cramer (2001: 58–9). Figure 13.1 provides guidance about how to identify variables of each type.

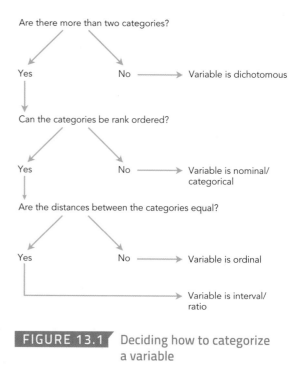

Are there more than two categories?

Yes　　　No ⟶ Variable is dichotomous

Can the categories be rank ordered?

Yes　　　No ⟶ Variable is nominal/categorical

Are the distances between the categories equal?

Yes　　　No ⟶ Variable is ordinal

⟶ Variable is interval/ratio

FIGURE 13.1　Deciding how to categorize a variable

TABLE 13.1 Types of variable

TYPE	DESCRIPTION	EXAMPLES IN GYM STUDY	VARIABLE NAME IN SPSS
Nominal	Variables whose categories cannot be rank ordered; also known as categorical	var00001 var00003 var00007 var00008 var00009	gender reasons accomp othsourc exercise
Ordinal	Variables whose categories can be rank ordered but the distances between the categories are not equal across the range	var00004 var00005 var00006	carduse weiuse frequent
Interval/ratio	Variables where the distances between the categories are identical across the range	var00002 var00010 var00011 var00012	age cardmins weimins othmins

Univariate analysis

Univariate analysis refers to the examination of one variable at a time. This section will outline several common approaches.

FREQUENCY TABLES

A frequency table provides the number and percentage of people (or whatever else constitutes a case in the study) belonging to each of the categories of the variable in question and can be created for all three variable types. An example of a frequency table for a nominal variable is provided for var00003 (**reasons**) in Table 13.2. The table shows, for example, that 33 members of the sample go the gym to lose weight and that they represent 36.7 per cent (percentages are often rounded in frequency tables) of the entire sample.

Frequency tables are typically created using software. A very commonly used software program for statistical analysis is SPSS (Statistical Package for the Social Sciences). In Appendix A of this book you will find instructions for using SPSS to perform the data analyses discussed in this chapter.

When an interval/ratio variable (such as age) is put in frequency table format, some of the categories may be combined in some way: 20–29, 30–39, and so on. Be sure that the categories you create don't overlap (as in 20–30, 30–40, etc.): if they do, you're likely to end up with some 30-year-olds in the first group and some in the second. This would violate the *mutually exclusive rule*, discussed in Chapter 5, that no one should be able to fall into more than one category (required for telling whether two cases are equal or not equal). Also recall from Chapter 5 the *exhaustive rule*: everyone must have a category, even if it is only 'missing data' or 'not applicable' (see Box 13.3).

Table 13.3 shows an example of a frequency table for an interval/ratio variable: var00002 (**age**). Not to group people in terms of age ranges would mean 40 different categories (one for each year from 18 to 57), which is too many to meaningfully describe. By creating 5 categories, you make the distribution of ages easier to comprehend. Notice that the sample totals 89 people, and that the 'Valid per cent' column is based on a total of 89 rather

TABLE 13.2 Frequency table showing reasons for visiting the gym

REASONS FOR VISITING

		Frequency	Per cent	Valid per cent	Cumulative per cent
Valid	Relaxation	9	10.0	10.0	10.0
	Fitness	31	34.4	34.4	44.4
	Lose weight	33	36.7	36.7	81.1
	Build strength	17	18.9	18.9	100.0
	Total	90	100.0	100.0	

than 90 because this variable contains one missing value (from respondent 24). Use the 'Valid per cent' column to cite percentages because the 'per cent' column includes missing values in the calculations.

DIAGRAMS

Diagrams are sometimes used to display quantitative data. With nominal or ordinal variables, the *bar chart* and the *pie chart* are two of the easiest to use. A bar chart of the data in Table 13.2 is presented in Figure 13.2. The height of each bar represents the number of people in each category. This figure and the next two were produced with SPSS.

Another way of displaying the same data is in a pie chart (Figure 13.3). This type of diagram

---

TABLE 13.3 | Frequency table showing ages of gym members

AGES OF GYM VISITORS

		Frequency	Per cent	Valid per cent	Cumulative per cent
Valid	20 and below	3	3.3	3.4	3.4
	21–30	39	43.3	43.8	47.2
	31–40	23	25.6	25.8	73.0
	41–50	21	23.3	23.6	96.6
	51 and over	3	3.3	3.4	100.0
	Total	89	98.9	100.0	
Missing	System	1	1.1		
TOTAL		90	100.0		

BOX 13.3 | Losing information

When an interval/ratio variable such as var00002 (**age**) is separated into categories (for example, 20 and under; 21–30; 31–40; 41–50; 51 and over), it is transformed into an ordinal variable. No longer can the data be added as is possible at the interval/ratio level. Where feasible, researchers avoid moving down to a lower level of measurement, because that involves losing information. Dinovitzer *et al.* (2003), however, did transform years of education, a ratio variable, into a four-level ordinal variable. In effect, they were saying that (for example) those with one to eight years of education were basically similar and that there was no need to differentiate a person with four years of education from one with five: both fall into the 'low' category. Ordinal variables can be dichotomous (for example, mild versus severe depression) but this is infrequent, since finer gradations are usually more meaningful.

Sometimes researchers, especially students, have no choice but to move to a lower level of measurement: that is, to give up some information. This problem may arise because they simply don't have enough cases for the detail they want. For example, examine the following data. Note that in some instances (for example, in the 'West secede' variable) where most people strongly disagree and only a few agree, feel neutral, or disagree, there could be too few people in the latter three categories to perform certain statistical analyses. In such cases one can collapse the data into a dichotomy (two parts); for example, any level of agreement versus any level of disagreement. Sometimes the data are combined into three, four, or more categories. When collapsing categories, be sure your decisions make conceptual and theoretical sense. For instance, for the NAFTA variable it would not be advisable to combine the people in the neutral category with those in either the agree or the disagree category.

	GUN-CONTROL (%)			PRO-CHOICE (%)			NAFTA (%)	WEST SECEDE (%)
Strongly agree	36	}	⎫	45	}	⎫	21	12
Agree	17	⎱	⎰	23	⎱	⎰	10	4
Neutral	2	}		1	⎰	⎱	40	2
Disagree	18	⎰		10	}	⎰	6	8
Strongly disagree	27	}		21	⎰	⎰	23	74

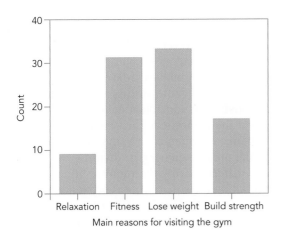

FIGURE 13.2 Bar chart showing main reasons for visiting the gym (SPSS output)

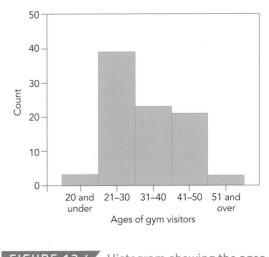

FIGURE 13.4 Histogram showing the ages of gym visitors (SPSS output)

FIGURE 13.3 Pie chart showing main reasons for visiting the gym (SPSS output)

also shows the size of the different categories but more clearly brings out the size of each relative to the total sample. The percentage of the whole sample that each slice represents is also given in this diagram.

To display an interval/ratio variable such as var00002 (**age**), a *histogram* is often employed. Figure 13.4 uses the same data and categories as Table 13.3. As in a bar chart, the bars represent the relative size of each of the age bands, but there is no space between the bars. This is to distinguish histograms, which show interval/ratio variables, from bar charts, which are used with nominal and ordinal variables.

More univariate analysis

MEASURES OF CENTRAL TENDENCY

Measures of central tendency provide, in one number, a typical or 'average' score for a distribution or group of scores. Three measures of central tendency are commonly used: the **mode**, the **median**, and the **mean**. Whether a particular one can be used depends on the level of measurement.

- *Mode*. This is the value that occurs most frequently in a distribution. The mode for var00002 (**age**) is 28, meaning that there are more 28s than any other score. The mode can be used with all types of variable but it is most applicable to nominal data.

- *Median*. This is the mid-point in a distribution of scores, derived by arraying all the scores in order (typically from the lowest to the highest) and then finding the middle one. If there is an even number of values, the median is calculated by taking the mean of the two middle numbers in the distribution. In the case of var00002, the median is 31. The median can be used with both interval/ratio and ordinal variables. It cannot be used with nominal data because those sorts of scores cannot be rank ordered.

- *Mean*. This is the average as it is understood in everyday use: that is, the sum of all numbers in a distribution, divided by the number of scores. The mean for var00002 is 33.6, meaning that the average age in our sample of gym visitors is about 34. This is slightly higher than the median because a few considerably older members (especially respondents 5 and 10) inflate it. The mean is vulnerable to such **outliers** (extreme values at either end of the distribution), which exert considerable upward or downward pressure on the mean. In such instances the median is recommended, as it is not affected in this way. (Some researchers exclude outliers and then calculate the mean, noting the removal in the text.)

MEASURES OF DISPERSION

The amount of variation in a sample—that is, its **dispersion**—can be just as important as its typical value. Two in-class tests can have the same mean of 60 per cent, but on one most people get between 50 and 70, while on the other the grades are evenly dispersed from the low 20s to 100 per cent. (In the language of testing, the first test would be described as one that does not discriminate: the brightest and least bright students get fairly close marks.) In the gym study, is there more or less variability in the amount of time spent on cardio-vascular equipment compared with weights?

The most obvious way of measuring dispersion is by calculating the **range**. This is simply the difference between the maximum and the minimum value in a distribution of interval/ratio scores. (Range can be applied to an ordinal variable too, but in that case it is more definitional than descriptive: for example, a range from working class to upper class.) The range is 64 minutes for the cardiovascular machines and 48 minutes for the weights. This suggests that there is more variability in the amount of time spent on the former, probably because some people spend almost no time on cardiovascular equipment. However, like the mean, the range is influenced by outliers, such as respondent 41, who spent 64 minutes on the cardio equipment.

Another measure of dispersion is the **standard deviation**, which is a measure of variation around the mean. It is calculated by taking the difference between each value in a distribution and the mean, squaring it, dividing the total of these differences by the number of values, and then taking the square root. The standard deviation for var00010 (**cardmins**) is 9.9 minutes and for var00011 (**weimins**) it is 8 minutes. This indicates that not only is the average amount of time spent on the cardiovascular equipment higher than for the weights, there is more deviation from the mean too. The standard deviation is also affected by outliers, which are sometimes excluded.

Bivariate analysis

Bivariate analysis examines whether there is a relationship between two variables. Several techniques are available for examining relationships, but their use depends on the level of measurement of the two variables being analyzed. Figure 13.5 details the main types of bivariate analysis according to the types of variable involved.

CONTINGENCY TABLES

Contingency tables are probably the most flexible of all methods of analyzing relationships in that they can be employed in relation to any pair of variables, from nominal to interval/ratio. They are not the most efficient method, however, especially

	Nominal	Ordinal	Interval/ratio
Nominal	Contingency table + chi-square (χ^2) + Cramér's V	Contingency table + chi-square (χ^2) + Cramér's V	Contingency table + chi-square (χ^2) + Cramér's V. If the interval/ratio variable can be identified as the dependent variable, compare means with eta.
Ordinal	Contingency table + chi-square (χ^2) + Cramér's V	Kendall's tau-b	Kendall's tau-b
Interval/ratio	Contingency table + chi-square (χ^2) + Cramér's V. If the interval/ratio variable can be identified as the dependent variable, compare means with eta.	Kendall's tau-b	Pearson's r

FIGURE 13.5 Methods of bivariate analysis, one variable on top, other variable on side

for interval/ratio data, which is the reason why the method is not recommended in all the cells in Figure 13.5. A contingency table is like a frequency table except that it allows two variables to be analyzed simultaneously, so that relationships between them can be examined. It is normal for contingency tables to include percentages, since they make the tables easier to interpret. Table 13.4 examines the relationship between gender and reasons for visiting the gym using our survey data. Gender is the presumed independent variable and for that reason becomes the column variable—a common preference among researchers. 'Reasons' is the presumed dependent or row variable (but see Box 13.4). In this case, gender is assumed to influence reasons for going to the gym; reasons for going to the gym cannot influence gender. The percentages are *column*

percentages, representing *the independent variable*. The number in each cell is calculated as a percentage of the total number in its column. Thus in the case of the top left-hand cell, the 3 men—of 42 in all—who go to the gym for relaxation represent 3/42 or 7 per cent of the men in the sample.

Contingency tables are generated to look for patterns of association. In this case, there are clear gender differences in reasons for visiting the gym. As our student anticipated, females are much more likely than males to go to the gym to lose weight. They are also somewhat more likely to go to the gym for relaxation. By contrast, men are much more likely to go to the gym to build strength. There is little gender difference in terms of fitness as a reason.

PEARSON'S *r*

Pearson's *r* is a statistic used to examine relationships between two interval/ratio variables. Its chief features are as follows:

- The coefficient has values from 0 (which indicates that there is no relationship whatever between the two variables) to +1 or −1 (the first indicating a perfect positive relationship, the second a perfect negative).
- The closer a positive coefficient is to 1, the stronger the relationship; the closer it is to zero, the weaker the relationship.
- Similarly, the closer a negative coefficient is to −1, the stronger the relationship is; the closer it is to zero, the weaker the relationship.

TABLE 13.4	Contingency table showing the relationship between gender and reasons for visiting the gym			
	GENDER			
	MALE		FEMALE	
Reasons	*No.*	*%*	*No.*	*%*
Relaxation	3	7	6	13
Fitness	15	36	16	33
Lose weight	8	19	25	52
Build strength	16	38	1	2
Total	42	100	48	100

BOX 13.4   Relationships not causality

Analyzing associations between variables reveals *relationships*, not *causes* (although finding associations helps in the search for causes). Similarly, the *direction* of causation cannot be determined by establishing that a relationship exists between two variables. Indeed, in some cases what appears to be a causal influence working in one direction may actually work the other way round. An example of the problem of causal direction was presented in Chapter 3, where Sutton and Rafaeli (1988) expected to find that a display of positive emotions (for example, smiling or friendliness) by retail checkout staff caused increased sales. In fact, the relationship appeared to flow in the opposite direction: levels of retail sales seemed to exert a causal

influence on the display of emotions. The more sales, the busier the staff, and the less time and inclination they had to smile!

There are times when one may feel confident in inferring a causal direction: the relationship between age and voting behaviour, for example. It is impossible for the way people vote to influence their age; so, if the two variables are related, age is the independent variable. It is not uncommon for researchers, when analyzing their data, to draw inferences about causal direction based on assumptions of this kind. However, some relationships may be **spurious** or non-causal: that is, caused by a third variable. That sort of relationship is discussed later in this chapter.

- The sign of the coefficient (positive or negative) indicates the *direction* of a relationship. Negative means that as one variable is going up, the other is going down; it doesn't matter which is which. Positive means that the two are going in the same direction, either both up or both down.

To be able to use Pearson's *r*, the relationship between the two variables must be broadly *linear*: when plotted on a scatter diagram, the values of the two variables will approximate a straight line (even though they may be scattered as in Figure 13.9), not a curve. A scatter diagram should be created to test for linearity before Pearson's *r* values are used in a study.

SCATTER DIAGRAMS

Scatter diagrams are shown in Figures 13.6 through 13.9. If one variable can be identified as likely to be the independent variable, it is by convention placed on the *X*-axis, the horizontal axis.

The scatter diagrams are based on the information in Box 13.5, which gives imaginary data for five interval/ratio variables. The scatter diagram for variables 1 and 2 is presented in Figure 13.6 and shows a perfect positive relationship, which yields a Pearson's *r* correlation of +1. This means that as one variable increases, the other variable increases as well, and the value of one variable perfectly predicts the value of the other. If the

FIGURE 13.6 Scatter diagram showing a perfect positive relationship

FIGURE 13.7 Scatter diagram showing a perfect negative relationship

FIGURE 13.8 Scatter diagram showing two variables that are not related

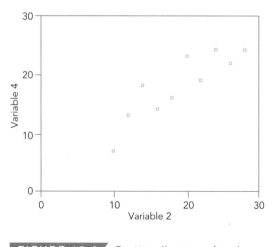

FIGURE 13.9 Scatter diagram showing a strong positive relationship

correlation is below 1, at least one other variable is affecting the relationship between them, possibly affecting variable 1 as well as variable 2.

The scatter diagram for variables 2 and 3 (Figure 13.7) shows a perfect negative relationship, which yields a Pearson's *r* correlation of –1. This means that as one variable increases, the other decreases, and that the values of one variable perfectly predict the values of the other. Here, as in the previous case, the line could be extended beyond the data to predict what would happen to either variable if the other moved beyond the range shown, although it is risky to go beyond what is known. Also, because social data usually include so many exceptions that few cases fall exactly on the line, predictions based on them tend to be general rather than specific.

If, as in Figure 13.8, there is no apparent pattern in the scatter diagram, there is no or virtually no correlation between the variables. In the case of variables 2 and 5, the correlation is close to zero, at –.041. This means that the variation in the dependent variable is probably associated with variables other than the one used in this analysis.

If a relationship is strong, a clear pattern will be evident in the variables. This is the case with variables 2 and 4, whose scatter diagram appears in Figure 13.9. There is clearly a positive

| BOX 13.5 | Imaginary data from five variables to show different types of relationship |

	Variables			
1	**2**	**3**	**4**	**5**
1	10	50	7	9
2	12	45	13	23
3	14	40	18	7
4	16	35	14	15
5	18	30	16	6
6	20	25	23	22
7	22	20	19	12
8	24	15	24	8
9	26	10	22	18
10	28	5	24	10

relationship; in fact, the Pearson's *r* is .88 (positive correlations are usually presented without the + sign). This means that the variation in the two variables is very closely connected, but that other variables also have some influence.

Going back to the gym survey, the correlation between **age** (var00002) and the time spent on

TABLE 13.5   Correlations output for age, weimins, and cardmins (SPSS output)

CORRELATIONS

Correlations of $p < 0.05$ are 'flagged' with asterisks

CORRELATIONS

		AGE	WEIMINS	CARDMINS
AGE	Pearson Correlation	1.000	–.273 **	–.109
	Sig. (2-tailed)	.	.010	.311
	N	89	89	89
WEIMINS	Pearson Correlation	–.273 **	1.000	–.161
	Sig. (2-tailed)	.010	.	.130
	N	89	90	90
CARDMINS	Pearson Correlation	–.109	–.161	1.000
	Sig. (2-tailed)	.311	.130	.
	N	89	90	90

** Correlation is significant at the 0.01 level (2-tailed).

Shows strength of relationship as indicated by Pearson's *r*

Shows number of cases, less any cases for which there are missing data for either or both variables

Shows level of statistical significance of computed value of Pearson's *r* weights, **weimins** (var00011), is –.27 (see Table 13.5): a weak negative relationship. This suggests that older people tend to spend less time on such equipment than younger ones, but that other variables also influence the time people spend there.

Kendall's tau-b

Kendall's tau-b is designed for pairs of ordinal variables, but is also used (as Figure 13.5 suggests) when one variable is ordinal and the other is interval/ratio. (Notice the general rule that data can be moved down a level, interval to ordinal, but not up.) It is exactly the same as Pearson's *r* in terms of possible outcomes in that the computed value of Kendall's tau-b can be positive or negative, and varies from 0 to ±1. In the gym study there are three ordinal variables: var00004 (**carduse**), var00005 (**weiuse**), and var00006 (**frequent**; see Table 13.1). Using Kendall's tau-b to calculate the correlation between the first two variables—frequency of use of the cardiovascular and weights equipment—it turns out to be very low. A slightly stronger relationship is found between var00006 (frequency of going to the gym) and var00010 (**cardmins**, the amount of time spent on the cardiovascular equipment): close to .4. Another option for relating two ordinal variables is to use **Spearman's rho** (though it can only accommodate a small number of ties: that is, cases with the same rank on a variable). It ranges from –1, a perfect negative relationship, to +1, a perfect positive relationship. For example, look at the participation rank (A) and popularity rank (B) of a group of seven people.

Person	Mary	John	Bill	Sally	Kim	Susan	Joe
A	1	2	3	4	5	6	7
B	1	2	3	4	5	6	7

Spearman's rho is 1.0; knowing a person's participation rank perfectly predicts the popularity rank.

It is called a rank correlation coefficient to remind you of its ordinal character and to distinguish it from Pearson's *r*.

CRAMÉR'S V

Cramér's *V* is suitable for examining the strength of a relationship between two nominal variables (see Figure 13.5). Its coefficient ranges from 0 to 1. It is always positive because nominal categories cannot be rank-ordered; its values cannot go up or down.

The value of Cramér's *V* for the relationship between **gender** and reasons for going to the gym (var00003, **reasons**) is .503, a moderate relationship. Cramér's *V* is usually reported with a contingency table and a **chi-square test** (see below). It is not normally presented on its own.

Comparing means and eta

There are many other bivariate statistics but we will present just one more. To examine the relationship between an interval/ratio variable and a nominal variable (if the latter can be construed as the independent variable), one can compare the means of the interval/ratio variable for each subgroup of the nominal variable. As an example, consider Table 13.6, which presents the mean number of minutes spent on cardiovascular equipment (var00010, **cardmins**) for each of the four categories of reasons for going to the gym (var00003, **reasons**). The four means shown suggest that people who go to the gym for fitness or to lose weight spend considerably more time on this equipment than those who go to the gym to relax or to build strength.

The statistic **eta** can be calculated with these variables; it expresses the level of association between them. Since one variable is nominal (meaning no rank ordering), its values are always positive. The eta for the data in Table 13.6 is .48, a moderate relationship between the two variables.

TABLE 13.6	Comparing subgroup means: time spent on cardiovascular equipment by reasons for going to the gym

	REASONS				
Time	Relaxation	Fitness	Lose weight	Build strength	Total
Mean number of minutes spent on cardiovascular equipment	18.33	30.55	28.36	19.65	26.47
n	9	31	33	17	90

Amount of explained variance

Squaring eta, Kendall's tau-b, Spearman's rho, and Pearson's *r* produces statistics that measure how much of the variation in one variable can be explained or predicted by the other variable. Thus if *r* is –.27 (the correlation between **weimins** and **age**), r^2 is .0729. This can be expressed as a percentage by multiplying r^2 by 100: thus 7.29 per cent of the variation in the time spent on weights can be predicted by age. This also shows that a strong correlation like .7 explains only 49 per cent of the variance. For nominal data, squaring Cramér's *V* (.503 for **gender** and **reasons**) provides an approximation of the explained variance, so about 25 per cent of the variation in reasons for visiting the gym is attributable to gender.

Statistical significance and inferential statistics

One difficulty with working on sample data is a lingering worry about whether the findings can be generalized to the **population** from which the sample was drawn. As we saw in Chapter 12, there is always the possibility of **sampling error**, even when **probability sampling** procedures are followed (as in the gym survey). If this happens, the sample is to some degree unrepresentative of the wider population. To make matters worse, there is no practical way of finding out for sure how extensive the sampling error is, as no one can afford the time or money to study every case in the population—that's why a sample is used in the first place. This is where various tests of **statistical significance** come in.

What is a test of statistical significance? It provides an indication of the risk we are taking when we use a particular sample statistic to estimate a population characteristic (see Box 13.6). For example, the mean age of the people in the gym sample is 33.6 years. Using the concept of the standard error of the mean, the 95 per cent confidence interval for the population mean extends from 31.72 to 35.47 years of age. The risk that this range does not contain the population mean is 5 per cent. Chapter 12 (see Box 12.3), in its discussion of the standard error of the mean, revealed some of the ideas behind statistical significance. The rest of this section looks at tests of significance for measures of bivariate association. All of the tests have a common structure, illustrated in the following steps.

- *Set up a* **null hypothesis**. A null hypothesis is a hypothesis that is to be disproved; for example, that there is no association between two variables, or that two populations do not differ on some characteristic. In the context of our gym survey, a null hypothesis might state that there is no relationship between gender and reasons for visiting the gym. If you can disprove that null hypothesis, you will have indirect support for the *research hypothesis* that there *is* a relationship in the population.

- *Establish an acceptable level of statistical significance.* This is essentially the level of risk

---

BOX 13.6 | What is the level of statistical significance?

There is always a chance that a rejected null hypothesis is actually true. The amount of risk associated with rejecting a true null hypothesis is called the level of statistical significance. The maximum acceptable risk in the social sciences is 5 chances in 100. This means that, in 100 samples, about 5 of them would exhibit a relationship when there is not one in the population. (We have to say 'about' 5 because this is based on probabilities, not certainties.) Any one sample of the 100 samples might be one of those five, but the risk is fairly small. This significance level is denoted by $p = .05$ (*p* means probability).

A significance level of $p = .1$ means that about 10 in 100 samples would show a relationship where none

exists in the population. Therefore, we would have less confidence in generalizing with that level of significance than with $p = .05$. If we want a more stringent test than the latter *p*-level provides (for instance, because of concern about the use that might be made of the results), we can choose the $p = .01$ level. This means that the risk is 1 in 100 that the results could have come about by chance alone (i.e., as result of sampling error). If $p = .01$ has been chosen, the null hypothesis should not be rejected if the results are statistically significant at the $p = .05$ level but not the $p = .01$ level. In what instances would it be appropriate to choose $p = .01$ rather than $p = .05$?

associated with rejecting the null hypothesis (implying that there *is* a relationship in the population) when in fact the null is correct (there is *no* relationship in the population). Levels of statistical significance are expressed as probability levels: that is, the probability of rejecting the null hypothesis when it is in fact true. The convention among most social researchers is that an acceptable level of statistical significance is $p \leq .05$, meaning that there are at most 5 chances in 100 that the sample shows a relationship not also found in the population. This risk level varies, depending on the circumstances. For example, 5 chances of error in 100 would be too many in the case of a drug being tested for its efficacy, especially a drug with side effects. Probably p would be set at .00001, accepting only one chance in 100 000 of an error.

- *Determine the statistical significance of the findings* (that is, use a statistical test such as chi-square, p. 249).

- *Decide whether to reject or not reject the null hypothesis.* Reject the null if the findings are statistically significant at the .05 level—that is, if the risk of error (i.e., getting a relationship as strong as the one that was found when in fact there is *no* relationship in the population) is no higher than 5 in 100. Such results are unlikely to have occurred by *chance* alone.

Two types of error are possible when inferring statistical significance (see Figure 13.10). A Type I error occurs when a null hypothesis that is actually true is rejected. This means that the results are the product of chance, and that the researcher was mistaken in concluding that there

was a relationship in the population. The level of significance is the probability of making a Type I error, so a $p = .05$ level of significance means a greater likelihood of making a Type I error than a $p = .01$ level of significance does.

The second type of error occurs when the null hypothesis should be rejected but is not. This is called a Type II error. These errors are more likely when the significance level is .01 than when it is .05, because using .01 makes it less likely that the null will be rejected. The two types of error cannot be minimized at the same time; if you decrease the chances of making a Type I error, you increase the chances of making a Type II error, and vice versa. Researchers usually make the conservative choice and seek to minimize Type I error; this makes it less likely that the null will be rejected in error, and hence less likely that the research hypothesis will be erroneously supported.

If an analysis reveals a statistically significant finding, this does not mean that the finding is important. It simply means that the results are probably not due to chance alone. For example, a study may find a correlation between time spent jogging per week and the amount of money spent on running shoes. Such a finding might be statistically significant, but is it important? Recall that statistical significance gets easier to achieve as sample size goes up. Also, it is important to appreciate that tests of statistical significance can be conducted only on probability samples.

CORRELATION AND STATISTICAL SIGNIFICANCE

Examining the statistical significance of a correlation from a randomly selected sample provides information about the likelihood that the correlation exists in the population. For instance, with a Pearson's r of $-.62$ in the sample, what is the likelihood that there is no relationship between the two variables in the population? How likely is a $-.62$ to occur by chance alone, that is, because of sampling error?

Whether a correlation coefficient is statistically significant or not is affected by two factors:

- the size of the computed coefficient; and
- the size of the sample.

This second factor may appear surprising, but it is true for all statistics. The larger a sample, the more likely it is that a computed correlation coefficient

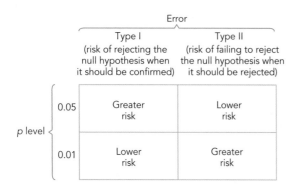

FIGURE 13.10 Type I and Type II errors

| **TABLE 13.7** | How chi-square is affected by increasing the size of *n* and not affected by changes to column headings | | | | | | | | |

	A			B			C		
Self-esteem	Contact sports	Non-contact sports	No sports	Contact sports	Non-contact sports	No sports	Contact sports	Non-contact sports	No sports
H	7	3	10	14	6	20	24	26	50
M	5	10	15	10	20	30	10	20	30
L	12	13	25	24	26	50	14	6	20
	$\chi^2 = 1.93$, not sig.			$\chi^2 = 5.08, p < .05$			$\chi^2 = 5.08, p < .05$		

is statistically significant. Thus, even though the correlation between age and the amount of time spent on weight machines in the gym survey is just −.27—a fairly weak relationship—it is statistically significant at the $p = .01$ level. This means that there is only one chance in 100 that there is no relationship between age and weights in the population. Because the statistical significance of a correlation coefficient depends so much on the sample size, it is important always to examine *both* the correlation coefficient *and* the significance level. This is true for any calculated statistic.

This treatment of correlation and statistical significance applies to both Pearson's *r* and Kendall's tau-b. A similar interpretation can also be applied to Cramér's *V* and the chi-square test.

THE CHI-SQUARE TEST

The chi-square (χ^2) test is applied to contingency tables like Table 13.4. It is a measure of the likelihood that a relationship between two variables in a sample would also be found in the population. The test works by calculating for each cell in the table an expected frequency—that is, one that would occur on the basis of chance alone. Think of the days of the week and crime: one might expect that 14.29 per cent (1/7) of all crimes would occur on each day of the week. That is what would be *expected* if there were no relationship between day of the week and crime. The data say otherwise; more crimes are committed on Friday and Saturday. The chi-square value, which for the data in Table 13.4 is 22.726, is calculated by taking the differences between the actual and expected values for each cell in the table and then summing those differences (the operation is slightly more complicated than this, but the details need

not concern us here). The chi-square value means nothing by itself and can be meaningfully interpreted only in relation to its associated level of statistical significance, which in this case is $p < .0001$. This means that there is less than one chance in 10 000 of rejecting a true null hypothesis (that is, inferring that there *is* a relationship in the population when none exists). We can be extremely confident that there is a relationship between gender and reasons for visiting the gym among all gym members, since the chance of obtaining a sample that shows this chi-square value when there is no relationship among all gym members is less than 1 in 10 000.

But a chi-square value is also affected by the number of cases. You want a large chi-square to reject a null hypothesis, and a larger *n* makes this easier to achieve. This is why it is necessary to look at the data and not just at the final statistic. Examine Table 13.7, which shows the level of self-esteem for three categories of people (those who engage in contact sports, those who engage in non-contact sports, and those who do not engage in any sports). Because the independent variable is nominal, chi-square is more appropriate than Kendall's tau-b. Note the information in the bottom row of the table.

The first two parts of Table 13.7, A and B, show that just by doubling the size of the sample, the results change from being very likely due to chance in A (thus the null hypothesis of no relationship cannot be rejected) to less than 5 chances in 100 that they occurred by chance in B, and thus a rejection of the null. This is problematic because it suggests that one could collect more and more data until the null can be rejected. Now look at the last part of the table, C. Why was it included?

When the data from B for high and low self-esteem are switched around in C, which in most instances should mean something, chi-square stays the same. This illustrates the point that statistical significance pertains only to whether the results may have resulted from chance alone, and says nothing about practical significance or importance. There is a big practical difference between a situation in which half the respondents at all levels of sports participation have low self-esteem and one in which half have high self-esteem, but that makes no difference to the level of statistical significance—it remains the same in each situation. The practical implications of a finding go beyond its level of statistical significance.

COMPARING MEANS AND STATISTICAL SIGNIFICANCE

A test of statistical significance called analysis of variance can be applied to the comparison of means in Table 13.6. This procedure entails treating the total amount of variation in the dependent variable—amount of time spent on cardiovascular equipment—as made up of two types: variation *within* each of the four subgroups that make up the independent variable, and variation *between* them. The latter is often called the *explained variance* (explained by the group one is in) and the former the *error variance*. A test of statistical significance for the comparison of means entails relating the two types of variance to form what is known as an *F* statistic, which expresses the amount of explained variance in relation to the amount of error variance. In the case of the data in Table 13.6, the resulting *F* statistic is statistically significant at the $p < .001$ level. This finding suggests that there is less than one chance in 1000 that there is no relationship between the two variables among all gym members.

Multivariate analysis

Multivariate analysis entails the simultaneous analysis of three or more variables, and can only be introduced here. It is sometimes called *elaboration* as it is more complicated and creates a more valuable picture than bivariate analysis: one rarely finds an adequate explanation of a particular phenomenon by looking at only one possible cause. (For more information on the techniques, consult a textbook on quantitative data analysis: for example, Healey and Prus 2010, Agresti and Finlay 2009.) There are three main contexts in which multivariate analysis is used. Each is explained below.

IS THE RELATIONSHIP SPURIOUS?

To establish a relationship between two variables, not only must there be logical and temporal evidence of a relationship but the relationship must be shown to be non-**spurious**. A spurious relationship exists when there appears to be a relationship between two variables, but the relationship is not real: it is being produced because each variable is itself related to a third variable. Think about the positive relationship between the number of fire engines at a fire and the fire damage: the more engines, the greater the devastation. Does this mean that the number of fire engines present *causes* the amount of fire damage? Of course not. The size of the fire accounts for both the number of engines responding and the damage. Variation in the two variables (number of fire engines and amount of damage) is caused by a third factor, the size of the fire.

Consider a social science example. Assume there is a positive relationship between income and voting behaviour such that the more income a person has, the more likely he or she is to vote for a conservative party. Does this mean that having more money *causes* people to move to the right? Or could this relationship be explained by age (see Figure 13.11)? The older one is, the more likely one is to have a higher salary; and the older one is, the more conservative one tends to be. If the apparent relationship between income and voting behaviour is in fact a function of age, that relationship is spurious.

IS THERE AN INTERVENING VARIABLE?

An **intervening variable** suggests that the relationship between the two original variables is not a direct one. Assume that there is a positive relationship between income and self-esteem—the higher one's income, the more positive one feels about oneself.

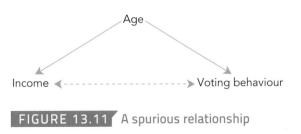

FIGURE 13.11 A spurious relationship

But maybe there is more to it than that. Maybe income affects overall levels of physical vibrancy (richer people tend to be more physically fit and to smoke less than poorer people), which in turn affects self-esteem: income → physical vibrancy → level of self-esteem. If this is true, what should happen to the relationship between income and self-esteem if physical vibrancy is controlled? (To control means to hold constant. Controlling in this instance might involve taking only people who had high levels of physical vibrancy, and seeing whether there is still a positive relationship between income and self-esteem among them.) If physical vibrancy were an intervening variable, that would weaken or eliminate the association between income and self-esteem. Also, notice the 'control' word? Yes, the purpose of controls is to make **cross-sectional** research more like an experiment in which random assignment makes all other things equal or controlled.

IS THERE AN INTERACTION?

If the relationship between two variables holds for some groups or situations but not for others, an interaction exists. The word 'interaction' is used in a statistical sense here, one that is different from its everyday meaning. In statistical terms, if the effect of one independent variable varies at different levels of a second independent variable, there is an interaction. In the gym study, for example, is the relationship between *age* and other sources of regular exercise (var00008, ***othsourc***) different for men and women? Table 13.8 shows the relationship between age and other sources of exercise and includes both men and women. (Age has been broken down into just three age bands to make the table easier to read.) The table suggests that the 31-to-40 age group is less likely to have other sources of regular exercise than

TABLE 13.8	Contingency table showing the relationship between age and whether gym visitors have other sources of regular exercise (percentages)

	AGE		
Other source of exercise	*30 and under*	*31–40*	*41 and over*
Other source	64	43	58
No other source	36	57	42
n	42	23	24

the 30-and-under and 41-and-over age groups. However, Table 13.9, which breaks the relationship down by gender, suggests that the patterns for males and females are somewhat different. Among males, the pattern shown in Table 13.8 is very pronounced (the 31-to-40 age group is less likely to have other sources of exercise than the other two age groups), but for females the likelihood of having other sources of exercise declines with age. We can say that the relationship between age and having other sources of exercise is moderated by gender. Another way to put this is that there is an interaction between age and gender.

OTHER USES FOR MULTIVARIATE ANALYSIS

Multivariate analysis can also be used to determine how much of the variation in the dependent variable is explained or predicted by the independent variables. In addition it provides a test to find out which, if any, of the independent variables are significant predictors after controlling for the others. These uses will be illustrated by examining *multiple linear regression*. Our brief discussion of this topic will also acquaint you with some key concepts in multivariate analysis.

TABLE 13.9	Contingency table showing the relationship between age and whether gym visitors have other sources of regular exercise for males and females (percentages)

	GENDER					
	Male			Female		
Other source of exercise	*30 and under*	*31–40*	*41 and over*	*30 and under*	*31–40*	*41 and over*
Other source	70	33	75	59	50	42
No other source	30	67	25	41	50	58
n	20	9	12	22	14	12

Consider the variable **weimins**, the number of minutes spent on weights. What might cause that to vary? One relevant factor might be **age**. Perhaps the older people get, the less likely they are to work out using weights. To test this idea, we could perform a bivariate regression with **weimins** as the dependent variable and **age** as the independent variable.

The first part of Table 13.10 shows an R Square value of .074, which indicates that **age** by itself explains 7.4 per cent of the variation in **weimins**—not very much. The value of R Square tends to be somewhat inflated, especially if the sample size is small (as in our example) or the number of independent variables is large (Agresti and Finlay 2009: 366). A more realistic estimate is the Adjusted R Square, which in our case has a value of .064 or 6.4 per cent.

The ANOVA section of the output indicates a significance or *p*-value of .010, which is the significance level of the model as a whole. Our model at this point consists of only one independent variable (**age**). The final section of the output, 'Coefficients,' has two subsections: 'Unstandardized coefficients' and 'Standardized coefficients.' The unstandardized coefficient for **age** is –.245, which represents the estimated change in the dependent variable for each unit change in the independent variable. In our example, the model predicts that for each one-year increase in age, the time spent on weights decreases by .245 minutes. The standardized coefficient of –.273 indicates that for every standard deviation increase in age, the time spent on weights decreases by .273 standard deviation units. Standardized coefficients (sometimes called *beta weights*) are useful in comparing the effect of independent variables that may be measured in different units: the higher the standardized coefficient, the more important the independent variable is considered to be. Finally, the significance level for **age** is shown to be .010, indicating that the probability that the association between **age** and **weimins** is due to chance alone is 1 in 100: this suggests it's a pretty safe bet that there is a relationship between those two variables in the population.

As we have noted, a single cause or independent variable is rarely if ever enough to provide a good explanation for anything. Let's see what happens if we put a second independent variable—**gender**—into the model. Normally, the variables used in linear regression have to be at the interval/

TABLE 13.10 | SPSS output showing results of bivariate regression

MODEL SUMMARY

Model	R	R Square	Adjusted R Square	Std. error of the estimate
1	.273[a]	.074	.064	7.72123

[a] Predictors: (Constant), age

ANOVA[b]

Model		Sum of squares	df	Mean square	F	Sig.
1	Regression	417.236	1	417.236	6.999	.010[a]
	Residual	5186.719	87	59.617		
	Total	5603.955	88			

[a] Predictors: (Constant), age
[b] Dependent variable: weimins

COEFFICIENTS[a]

Model		Unstandardized coefficients		Standardized coefficients		
		B	Std. error	Beta	t	Sig.
1	(Constant)	23.209	3.218		7.213	.000
	age	-.245	.093	-.273	-2.645	.010

[a] Dependent variable: weimins

ratio level of measurement, but a special procedure allows us to use nominal variables like **gender** as well. Such variables have to be converted to indicator or 'dummy' variables, a process that goes beyond the scope of our discussion here. Assume that the dummy variable we have created is called **gender2**, and that we have labelled it 'Gender dummy variable.'

Table 13.11 shows the output generated after **gender2** was added to the model. The 'Model Summary' shows that the R Square value has increased to .228 (or that 22.8 per cent of the variation in **weimins** can be explained or predicted by the new model), and that the more conservative Adjusted R Square has risen to .210 (or 21.0 per cent). This indicates that by adding **gender2** we have produced a much better model, although the majority of the variation in **weimins** is still unaccounted for. The ANOVA significance level is .000, which indicates that the findings for the new model as a whole (which includes both **age** and **gender2** as independent variables) have a probability of less than 1 in 1000 of being due to chance alone.

The 'Coefficients' sections show an unstandardized coefficient of −.260 for **age**, which means that, controlling for **gender2**, for each one-year increase in age, the model predicts a decline of .260 minutes spent on weights. The standardized coefficient for **age** is −.289, indicating a decrease of .289 standard deviation units in **weimins** for each standard deviation increase in **age** (controlling for **gender2**). The significance level for **age** is .003, which means that **age** remains significant even when **gender2** is held constant. Had the significance level exceeded .050, we would have had to consider dropping **age** from the model.

The 'Coefficients' section shows an unstandardized coefficient of 6.251 for **gender2**. Because of the way this dummy variable was coded, the coefficient means that, holding **age** constant, the model estimates that the average time men spend on weights is 6.251 minutes greater than that spent by women. The standardized coefficient of .393 tells us that according to the model, the average time men spend on weights is .393 standard

TABLE 13.11 Multiple Regression Output with *gender* (recoded) in the mode

MODEL SUMMARY

Model	R	R Square	Adjusted R Square	Std. error of the estimate
1	.478[a]	.228	.210	7.09088

a Predictors: (Constant), Gender dummy variable, age

ANOVA[b]

Model		Sum of squares	df	Mean square	F	Sig.
1	Regression	1279.830	2	639.915	12.727	.000[a]
	Residual	4324.125	86	50.281		
	Total	5603.955	88			

[a] Predictors: (Constant), Gender dummy variable, age
[b] Dependent variable: weimins

COEFFICIENTS[a]

Model		Unstandardized coefficients		Standardized coefficients		
		B	Std. error	Beta	t	Sig.
1	(Constant)	20.831	3.010		6.920	.000
	age	−.260	.085	−.289	−3.053	.003
	Gender dummy variable	6.251	1.509	.393	4.142	.000

[a] Dependent variable: weimins

deviation units higher than that of women (controlling for *age*). Also, *gender2* has a *p*-value of .000, indicating that the association observed between it and *weimins* (after controlling for *age*) has a probability of less than 1 in 1000 of being due to chance alone. Had the significance level been greater than .050, we would have had good reason to exclude *gender2* from the model. But with these results, it stays in.

Methods in Motion

Applications to Canadian Society

It would come as no surprise to working parents to learn that trying to balance family duties with employment responsibilities has been found to lead to stress and strain. But not all working parents experience the same levels of this sort of stress. What factors might add to the stress a person feels when trying to balance work and family activities?

Tézli and Gauthier (2009) examined this issue in Canadian families by using data on time use from the 2005 General Social Survey. Their sample was limited to employed people in two-parent households who had at least one dependent child less than 15 years of age. The authors devised a measure of time-related stress by combining six items that appeared on the survey, including 'How often do you feel rushed?' and 'How stressful are most of your days?' They then used multiple regression to determine what aspects of the parents' lives were associated with high levels of stress. After controlling for a number of variables, they found that gender was a factor, with women experiencing significantly higher levels of work–family stress than men. They also found that parents with long work hours had higher stress scores than those who worked less. Working parents who felt a strong sense of belonging to their local community showed lower levels of stress, presumably because they had greater access to social support networks.

One of the variables that did not have a significant association with time stress was government policy on family issues (such as affordable daycare and child tax credits) in the respondents' province or region. The expectation was that Quebec, which arguably has the most family-friendly policies in Canada (including $7 per day daycare), would have the lowest levels of work–family stress. But the results indicated that Quebec participants did not have significantly lower levels of stress than people in most other parts of the country (the exception was the Atlantic region). Tézli and Gauthier suggest that Quebec's relatively weak economy, including a high unemployment rate, may have increased the stress felt by Quebec families, neutralizing the effects of its family-friendly policies. They also point out that the demand for affordable childcare in the province is greater than the supply, and that many parents do not have access to quality childcare. As in other areas of social life, it seems that the ability of government to reduce levels of work–family stress is limited.

☑ Checklist *for performing and writing up quantitative data analysis*

✔ Have missing data codes been specified for all variables?

✔ Are the statistical techniques used appropriate for the level of measurement (that is, nominal, ordinal, or interval/ratio)?

✔ Are the most appropriate and powerful techniques for answering the research questions used?

✔ If the sample is not randomly selected, are inferences about a population avoided? If inferences are included, are their limitations outlined?

✔ If the data come from a cross-sectional design, have unsustainable inferences about causality been resisted?

✔ Does the analysis go beyond univariate to include bivariate and even multivariate analyses?

✔ Are the research questions answered, and only the analyses relevant to them presented?

Key Points

- Think about data analysis before designing research instruments.
- Know the difference between nominal, ordinal, and interval/ratio variables. Techniques of data analysis are applicable to some types of variable and not others.
- Become familiar with computer software such as SPSS, which is discussed in the Appendix A.
- Don't confuse statistical significance with importance or practical significance.

Relevant Websites

Statistics Canada offers a useful introduction to quantitative data analysis at:

http://www.statcan.gc.ca/edu/power-pouvoir/ch3/5214783-eng.htm

A YouTube video explaining levels of measurement:

http://www.youtube.com/watch?v=BOABvLa_u88

This YouTube video illustrates the notion of correlation:

http://www.youtube.com/watch?v=SaSpZdf1oHU

If you'd like to get a feel for SPSS software, their site offers some free trial downloads:

http://www-01.ibm.com/software/analytics/spss/products/

[Websites accessed August 31, 2011]

Questions for Review

- What are missing data and how do they arise?

TYPES OF VARIABLES

- Why is it important to be able to distinguish between the three types of variable outlined in this chapter: nominal, ordinal, and interval/ratio?
- Imagine answers to the following questions in an interview survey. Which of the three types of variable would each generate (nominal, ordinal, or interval/ratio)?

  1. Do you enjoy going shopping?
     Yes ___
     Unsure ___
     No ___

  2. How many times have you shopped in the last month? Please write the number here ___.

  3. For what items do you most enjoy shopping? Please tick one only.
     Clothes (including shoes) ___
     Food ___
     Things for the house/apartment ___
     Presents or gifts ___
     Entertainment (CDs, videos, etc.) ___

  4. How important is it to you to buy clothes with designer labels?
     Very important ___
     Fairly important ___
     Not very important ___
     Not at all important ___

UNIVARIATE ANALYSIS

- What is an outlier? How does the presence of an outlier affect the mean and the range?
- In conjunction with which measure of central tendency is the standard deviation usually reported: the mean, the median, or the mode?

BIVARIATE ANALYSIS

- Can one infer causality from bivariate analysis?
- Why are percentages crucial when presenting contingency tables?
- In what circumstances is each of the following used: Pearson's *r*, Kendall's tau-b, Cramér's *V*, Spearman's rho, eta?

STATISTICAL SIGNIFICANCE

- What does 'statistical significance' mean and how does it differ from 'importance' or 'practical significance'?
- What is a significance level?

- What does the chi-square test achieve?
- What does it mean to say that an eta of .42 is statistically significant at $p < .05$?

MULTIVARIATE ANALYSIS

- What are the uses of multivariate analyses?
- What is a spurious relationship?
- What is an intervening variable?
- What is a statistical interaction?
- How do multivariate analyses improve on bivariate (two-variable) analyses?

CHAPTER 14

Qualitative Data Analysis

CHAPTER OVERVIEW

Analyzing **qualitative** data from interviews or **participant observation** is never straight-forward. For one thing, such data typically take the form of a large body of unstructured textual material. Moreover, whereas **quantitative research** has clear-cut rules for data analysis, this is not the case in qualitative research. This chapter will examine some general approaches to qualitative data management. The most significant recent development in this area is the use of computer software for **coding**: the main feature of qualitative data analysis. This software, often referred to as computer-assisted qualitative data analysis software (**CAQDAS**), eliminates many if not most of the clerical tasks associated with the manual coding and retrieving of data. Although there is no industry leader among the different programs available for qualitative data analysis, this chapter introduces a relatively new entrant that is having a big impact: QSR NVivo (discussed in detail in Appendix A).

This chapter will explore:

- **grounded theory** as a general strategy of qualitative data analysis; its main features, processes, and outcomes are presented along with some criticisms;
- **coding** as a key process in grounded theory and in qualitative data analysis more generally; there is an extended

discussion of what it entails and some of its limitations;

- some of the debates about the desirability of using **CAQDAS**;
- the criticism that coding tends to fragment data; and
- the idea of **narrative analysis**, an approach that is gaining a following because it reduces that fragmentation.

Einstein once famously said that the most incomprehensible thing about the universe is that it is comprehensible. What is it that allows us to understand how the universe works? The simple fact that it shows certain regularities or patterns. Science, including social science, is all about finding those patterns, and then explaining them.

Qualitative social research may seem a long way away from Einsteinian physics, but in essence the 'concepts' and 'categories' that qualitative researchers look for as they navigate through vast seas of data are simply patterns. This suggests that the social world of meanings, perceptions and feelings is not chaotic, but has a coherence to it that we can know and describe if we use the right methodology. This chapter explores how qualitative researchers make sense of the data they gather, including how some of them use it to generate theory.

Introduction

Because of its reliance on words in the form of **field notes**, interview transcripts, or other documents, qualitative research rapidly generates a large, cumbersome database. Miles (1979) described qualitative data as an 'attractive nuisance'—attractive because of their richness and the apparent ease with which insight may be gained from them, but also a nuisance because that very richness can create analytical difficulties that are not always acknowledged.

Finding a path through the thicket of prose is not easy, especially for researchers confronting such data for the first time. 'What do I do with it now?' is a common refrain. In large part this is because there are few well-established and widely accepted rules for the analysis of qualitative data. Learning the techniques of quantitative data analysis can be challenging too, but at least there are unambiguous rules for handling such data. Analytic procedures for qualitative data analysis have not reached the same degree of codification, and many feel that would be undesirable anyway (cf. Bryman and Burgess 1994*b*). Nevertheless, there are some broad guidelines (Okely 1994) which we will explore. This chapter has two main sections:

- *General strategies of qualitative data analysis*: **analytic induction** and grounded theory.

- *Basic operations in qualitative data analysis*: coding and narrative analysis, the latter differing in style from both grounded theory and the secondary analysis of qualitative data.

General strategies of qualitative data analysis

ANALYTIC INDUCTION

One difference between qualitative and quantitative data analysis is that, with the latter, analysis occurs after all the data have been collected. Qualitative analysis, on the other hand, is often *iterative* (as noted in Chapter 8), meaning that analysis takes place after some of the data have been collected and then the implications of that analysis shape further data collection.

Analytic induction is an example of a type of qualitative research that uses an iterative process. It begins with a rough definition of a research question, proceeds to a hypothetical answer, and then moves to data collection. What makes it unique is that analytic induction seeks universal explanations of phenomena that permit no exception. If a case inconsistent with the hypothesis is encountered, the analyst either redefines the hypothesis to exclude the deviant or negative case or reformulates the hypothesis and proceeds with further data collection. With each new deviant case they find, analysts must choose again between reformulation and redefinition. Data collection continues until no new inconsistent piece of evidence is found. It is, in effect, a special case of grounded theory, one that holds 100 per cent of the time. But it is also rare, as the requirement to be able to explain all cases means that the explanation may become too broad to be useful. While analytic induction is an extremely rigorous method of analysis, it is not favoured by current qualitative researchers; in fact, most of the examples used in textbooks to illustrate analytic induction are not recent. A Canadian exception is research by Whitehead and Carpenter (1999) on unsafe sexual behaviour in the military. They found that the greater the social and cultural distance between sex partners, the greater the likelihood of condom use.

One further problem with analytic induction is that (unlike grounded theory) it does not provide useful guidelines on the number of cases required before the absence of negative cases can be assumed and the validity of the hypothetical explanation (whether reformulated or not) can be confirmed.

GROUNDED THEORY

In its most recent incarnation, grounded theory is defined as 'theory that was derived from data, systematically gathered and analyzed through the research process' (Strauss and Corbin 1998: 12). Its two central features are its development of theory out of data, and an iterative or recursive approach in which data collection and analysis proceed in tandem, repeatedly referring back to each other.

Grounded theory is by far the most widely used framework for analyzing qualitative data. Yet there is considerable controversy about what it entails (Charmaz 2000). For example, it is vague on the difference between **concepts** and categories. As we will see later in this chapter, it seems that the former term is increasingly being replaced by the latter, and this inconsistent use of key terms is not helpful either to practitioners of the craft or to people trying to understand the overall process.

Against such a background, defining grounded theory is not easy. As well, grounded theory cannot be described here in all its facets; we will simply outline its main features.

The basic features of grounded theory   Some of the basic features of grounded theory have been introduced in earlier chapters:

- *Coding*: the key process in grounded theory, whereby data are broken down into component parts and given names. It begins soon after the initial collection of data. According to Charmaz: 'Unlike quantitative research that requires data to fit into *preconceived* standardized codes, the researcher's interpretations of data shape his or her emergent codes in grounded theory' (emphasis in original) (2000: 515).

- *Constant comparison*: continuous comparison of new and existing data within a particular concept or category. Glaser and Strauss (1967) advised writing a *memo* (see p. 263) on each concept/category after a few phenomena have been coded. Comparison also entails sensitivity to differences between emerging concepts/categories.

- **Theoretical saturation**: the point at which there is nothing to be gained by further reviewing of old data or collection of new information to see how it fits with emerging concepts or categories; new data are no longer illuminating.

Coding in grounded theory   Coding in grounded theory entails reviewing transcripts and/or field notes and giving labels (names) to items that seem to share a similar theme, to be of potential theoretical significance, and/or to be particularly salient within the social worlds under investigation. As Charmaz (1983: 186) put it, 'Codes . . . serve as shorthand devices to *label*, *separate*, *compile*, and *organize* data' (emphases in original). This coding process differs from the coding used in the analysis of quantitative data (e.g., social **survey** data) in two ways. First, whereas quantitative analysis often involves testing a *pre-existing* theory, grounded theory uses coding as an important first step in the generation of theory. Second,

whereas in quantitative analysis coding is more or less a way of managing data that have already been at least broadly categorized, in grounded theory (and other approaches to qualitative data analysis), coding is more tentative and fluid. The data are treated as potential indicators of concepts/categories, and the indicators are repeatedly compared to see which concepts/categories they fit with best. Ad hoc compromises may have to be made when more than one researcher is doing the coding (Tastsoglou and Miedema 2003).

Strauss and Corbin distinguished three types of coding:

- *Open coding*: 'the process of breaking down, examining, comparing, conceptualizing, and categorizing data' (1990: 61); this process stays very close to the data and yields the concepts that are later grouped together to form categories. Thus concepts such as anger, jealousy, or affection could form the category 'emotion.'

- *Axial coding*: 'a set of procedures whereby data are put back together in new ways after open coding, by making connections between categories' (1990: 96). This is done by linking codes to contexts, consequences, patterns of interaction, and apparent causes. Thus the category of emotion, above, could be linked to the contexts in which it is expressed: for example, contexts of hardship or loss.

- *Selective coding*: 'the procedure of selecting the core category, systematically relating it to other categories, validating those relationships, and filling in categories that need further refinement and development' (1990: 116). A core category is the focus around which other categories are integrated—what Strauss and Corbin called the story-line that frames the account. In the case of hardship and loss, the core category might be 'adaptation.'

The three types of coding are really different levels of the same process, each relating to a different point in the process of elaborating concepts and categories. Not all grounded theory practitioners operate with this threefold distinction; the notion of axial coding has been especially controversial because it is sometimes perceived as closing off the coding process too quickly. Charmaz (2004) preferred to distinguish between open or initial coding and selective or focused coding. The former tends to be very detailed and may produce as much as one code per line of text. It is crucial at this stage of the research to be open-minded and to generate as many new ideas, and hence codes, as necessary to organize the data. Selective or focused coding emphasizes the codes that (a) appear most frequently and (b) seem most revealing. Combining the initial codes generates new codes. The data are then re-explored and re-evaluated in terms of the selected codes. Pidgeon and Henwood (2004: 638) provided a useful example in their study of 60 mother–daughter relationships:

> The initial coding led to the development of a long and varied, but highly unwieldy, list of instances under the label 'Relational Closeness.' . . . [A] closer reading and comparison of the individual instances indicated a much more mixed view of the emotional intensity of the relationships, ranging from a welcome but painful sense of gratitude and debt to a stance of hypersensitivity and a desire to flee from a relationship which involved 'confinement' or 'smothering.' . . . [T]his subdivision was retained and coded through their respective labels 'Closeness' and 'Overcloseness.'

Overall, then, the process of coding begins with the data themselves and then gradually moves to more selective and abstract ways of conceptualizing the phenomenon of interest.

Outcomes of grounded theory The following are the products of different phases of grounded theory.

- *Concepts*: the 'building blocks of theory' (Strauss and Corbin 1998: 101), concepts are the discrete phenomena produced through *open coding*.
- *Categories*: at a higher level of abstraction, a category subsumes two or more concepts. An especially crucial category may become a *core category* (see Box 14.1).
- *Properties*: attributes or aspects of a category.
- *Hypotheses*: initial hunches about relationships between concepts.
- *Theory*: 'a set of well-developed categories . . . that are systematically interrelated through statements of relationship to form a theoretical framework that explains some

relevant social . . . or other phenomenon' (Strauss and Corbin 1998: 22). In grounded theory there are two levels of theory: *substantive* and *formal*. A substantive theory pertains to a certain *empirical* instance of a phenomenon such as racial prejudice in a hospital setting (see Box 15.1). A formal theory is at a higher level of abstraction and has applicability to several substantive areas, such as prejudice generally or in a variety of spheres. The generation of formal theory requires data collection in different settings.

The various elements are portrayed in Figure 14.1. Any diagram is only an approximation, but this is particularly true in this instance, partly because there are different approaches to grounded theory and partly because it is difficult to convey diagrammatically the iterative nature of grounded theory—in particular, the recursive relationship between data collection and analysis (indicated by arrows pointing in both directions). The figure implies the following:

- The researcher begins with a general research question (step 1).
- Relevant people and/or incidents are **theoretically sampled** (step 2).
- Relevant data are collected (step 3).
- Data are coded (step 4), which may, at the level of open coding, generate concepts (step 4*a*).
- There is a constant movement backwards and forwards among the first four steps, so that early coding suggests a need for new data, which leads to **theoretical sampling**, and so on.
- Through constant comparison of indicators and concepts (step 5) categories are generated (step 5*a*). It's crucial to ensure a fit between indicators and concepts.
- Categories become saturated in the course of the coding process (step 6).
- Relationships between categories are explored (step 7) in such a way that hypotheses about connections between categories emerge (step 7*a*).
- Further data are collected via theoretical sampling (steps 8 and 9).
- The collection of data is likely to be governed by the theoretical saturation principle (step 10) and the testing of the emerging hypotheses (step 11), which leads to specification of

BOX 14.1 | Categories in grounded theory

Orona's (1997) study of sufferers of Alzheimer's disease and their relatives exemplifies many features of grounded theory. She began with an interest in the decision-making process that leads relatives to place Alzheimer's sufferers in institutions. She gradually realized from coding her interview transcripts that this process is not as crucial for relatives as she had anticipated, mainly because many of them simply feel they have no other choice. Instead, she was slowly taken by the significance for relatives of the 'identity loss' that they deemed sufferers to experience. This gradually became her core category. She conducted further interviews to flesh this notion out and reread existing transcripts in light of it. The link between indicators and category can be seen in relatives' references to the sufferer as 'gone,' 'different,'

'not the same person,' a 'stranger.' Orona was able to unearth four major themes surrounding the process of identity loss. A particularly significant theme was the one Orona called 'temporality,' revealed in relatives' comments such as the following:

> At the beginning . . .
> It got much worse later on.
> More and more, he was leaning on me.
> Before she would never have been like that.
> She used to love coffee (Orona 1997: 179–80).

Comments such as these became the building blocks of the category 'temporality,' which Orona eventually related to the 'core category' of identity loss. Relatives try to help sufferers maintain their identities, but in time the losses become undeniable.

---

substantive theory (step 11*a*). See Box 14.2 for an illustration.

- The substantive theory may eventually be explored using grounded theory processes in a different setting from the one in which it was generated (step 12). In this way a formal theory (step 12*a*)—relating to more abstract categories not specifically examined in the research— can be generated.

Note that Step 12 is relatively uncommon, because researchers using the grounded theory approach typically concentrate on one particular setting.

Sometimes researchers will claim to have used the 'grounded theory' approach when in fact they have not used it at all (Charmaz 2000) or have used just one or two features of it (Locke 1996). Concepts and categories are at the heart of the grounded theory approach, but coding, theoretical

---

BOX 14.2 | Grounded theory in action

Charmaz (1997) used grounded theory to examine the identity dilemmas of men with chronic but not terminal illnesses. She outlined clearly the chief steps in her analysis:

- Interviews with men and a small number of women.
- Exploring the interview transcripts for gender differences.
- Searching for themes in the men's interviews and published personal accounts such as autobiographies. An example was the theme of 'accommodation to uncertainty,' as the men found ways of dealing with the unpredictable paths of their illnesses.
- Building 'analytic categories from men's definitions of and taken-for-granted assumptions about their

situations' (1997: 39). Of particular significance in her work is the idea of 'identity dilemmas': the ways in which men approach and possibly resolve the assault on their traditionally masculine self-images. She showed that men often use strategies to re-establish earlier selves in order to preserve their identities, at least in their own eyes.

- Further interviews designed to refine the categories.
- Rereading personal accounts of chronic illness with a particular focus on gender.
- Reading a new group of personal accounts.
- Making 'comparisons with women on selected key points' (1997: 39).

Charmaz proposed a substantive theory that helped to explain the importance of notions of masculinity in maintaining an identity for chronically ill men.

Processes   **Outcomes**

1 Research question

2 Theoretical sampling

3 Collect data

4 Coding ————————————————→ 4a Concepts

5 Constant comparison ————————————→ 5a Categories

6 Saturate categories

7 Explore relationships ————————————→ 7a Hypotheses
   between categories

8 Theoretical sampling

9 Collect data

10 Saturate categories

11 Test hypotheses ————————————————→ 11a Substantive theory

12 Collection and analysis of ——————————→ 12a Formal theory
    data in other settings

FIGURE 14.1   Processes and outcomes in
grounded theory

sampling, and theoretical saturation are also key features. Again, Box 14.2 provides an illustration.

Memos   An important aid to grounded theory research is the *memo*: a note that researchers write for themselves or colleagues as a reminder of what a particular concept or category refers to. Memos can be very useful in helping researchers to crystallize their ideas and keep track of their thoughts on various topics; they also help to shape the researchers' reflections on broader issues. For an illustration, see Box 14.3.

Criticisms of grounded theory   Grounded theory has limitations:

- Some question whether researchers can fully suspend their awareness of existing theories or concepts until the late stages of analysis when their theories are supposed to emerge. Most social researchers are sensitive to the conceptual armoury of their disciplines and it seems unlikely that this awareness can be put aside. In fact, few people today believe that theory-neutral observation is possible. It is generally agreed that what is 'seen,' even in research, is conditioned by what is already known about the social world under study (in terms of both social scientific concepts and general, everyday ones). Many writers consider it an advantage to build on the work of others.

- In practical terms, the time required to transcribe recordings of interviews, for example, can make it difficult for a researcher with a tight deadline to carry out a genuine grounded theory analysis, given the constant interplay of data collection and conceptualization that it requires.

- It isn't clear that the grounded theory method necessarily results in *theory*. It offers a rigorous approach to the generation of concepts and categories, but it is often difficult to see what theory, in the sense of an *explanation* of something, is put forward. Moreover, although lip-service is frequently paid to the idea of generating formal theory, most grounded theories pertain only to the specific social phenomenon under investigation—not to a broader range of phenomena.

- Grounded theory tends to invite researchers to code their data into discrete chunks. However, some commentators believe that this kind of fragmentation results in a loss of context and narrative flow (Coffey and Atkinson 1996); we will return to this point later in this chapter.

That said, and even though many studies do not use it consistently, grounded theory is probably the most influential overall strategy in use today for qualitative data analysis. Many of its core elements, from coding and memos to the very idea of allowing theory to emerge from data, have also been very influential. It is striking that one of the main developments in qualitative data analysis

BOX 14.3 | A memo

In their research into the bus industry, Bryman *et al.* (1996) noticed that managers frequently mentioned that their companies still followed officially discontinued rules and practices. Managers often suggested that 'inherited' characteristics were holding them back in their efforts to adapt to a new competitive environment. 'Inheritance' is what Strauss (1987) called an *in vivo code*: one derived from the language of people in the social context under study, as opposed to a *sociologically constructed code*, which is a label created by the researcher. The following memo outlines the concept of inheritance, provides some illustrative quotations, and suggests some properties of the concept.

Memo for inheritance

Inheritance: Many of our interviewees suggest that they have inherited certain company traits and traditions that they themselves would not have chosen. The key point about this inheritance is that our interviewees see it as hindering their ability to respond to a changing environment.

Inherited features might include:

- expensive and often inappropriate fleets of vehicles and depots;

- the survival of attitudes and behaviour patterns, particularly among bus drivers, that are seen as inappropriate to the new environment (for example, lack of concern for customer service) and that hinder service innovation; and

- high wages from the earlier era, which make it possible for competitors who pay their drivers lower wages to enter the market and charge less for their services.

Sample comments:

'I suppose another major weakness is that we are very tied by conditions and practices we've inherited' (Commercial Director, Company G).

'We have what we've inherited and we now have a massive surplus of double decks [i.e., too many buses of the wrong size]. . . . We have to go on operating those' (Managing Director, Company B).

Managing Director of Company E said the company had inherited staff steeped in old attitudes: 'We don't have a staff where the message is "the customer is number one."'

---

in recent years—the use of computer software—has implicitly promoted grounded theory, because the software programs have in many cases been written with its processes in mind (Lonkila 1995).

Basic operations in qualitative data analysis

Coding (or *indexing*) is the starting point for most forms of qualitative data analysis. The principles involved have been well developed by writers concerned with grounded theory and other perspectives. Among the issues they consider in developing codes (cf. Lofland and Lofland 1995) are the following:

- Of what general category is this datum an instance?

- What does this datum represent?

- What is this datum about?

- What question does this datum suggest?

- What sort of answer to that question does this datum imply?

- What is happening here?

- What are people doing?

- What do people say they are doing?

- What kind of event is going on?

STEPS AND CONSIDERATIONS IN CODING

Following are some guidelines for coding:

- *Code as soon as possible (that is, as data are being collected), as grounded theory suggests.* This may sharpen an understanding of the data and help with theoretical sampling. It can also help to alleviate the feeling of being swamped by the data. At the very least, begin transcribing recorded interviews at a relatively early stage.

- *Read through the initial set of transcripts, field notes, documents, etc., without taking any notes or considering any interpretations.* Only when you have finished should you consider jotting down a few general notes about what seems especially interesting, important, or significant.

- *Do it again.* Read through the data again, but this time make marginal notes about significant remarks or observations—as many as possible. Initially, they will be very basic: perhaps keywords used by respondents or themes in the data. Now you are *coding*: generating terms that will help in interpreting the data.

- *Don't worry about generating too many codes—at least in the early stages of analysis.* Some will be fruitful, others not. The important thing is to be as inventive and imaginative as possible; tidying up can be done later. Remember that any one datum can, and often should, be coded in more than one way. An outburst of anger, for example, can be seen as an emotion, a cause of stress, or the beginning of a new level of integration. As a first stage, Charmaz (2004) recommended 'line by line coding,' in which virtually every line in the transcript (or other data source) has a code attached to it: this way, the qualitative researcher does not lose contact with the data and the perspectives and interpretations of those being studied. Although the line-by-line approach almost always results

in a proliferation of codes, this should not be alarming. What qualitative researchers need to do is ask what these codes have in common so that they can be combined into higher-order and more abstract codes.

- *Review the codes, possibly in relation to the transcripts.* Are two or more words or phrases being used to describe the same phenomenon? If so, remove one of them. Do some of the codes relate to concepts and categories in the existing literature? If so, would it make sense to use the existing terms? Are there connections between the codes? Is there evidence that respondents believe one thing tends to be associated with or caused by something else?

- *Consider more general theoretical ideas in relation to codes and data.* Now you can start generating some general theoretical ideas about the data. Try to outline connections between concepts and any developing categories. Consider in more detail how they relate

Methods in Motion
Applications to Canadian Society

One of the key insights of qualitative research is that people often interpret their situations in ways that an outsider might not expect. Take the example of women with eating disorders. You might think that they would definitely want to change their eating habits, but Whitehead (2010) found that that is not always the case. Instead, she found that some women suffering from anorexia nervosa and bulimia do not want to change that aspect of their lives, and in fact may seek to develop a collective identity with women in similar situations by interacting with them on pro-eating disorder (Pro-ED) websites. These sites are controversial in that they do not discourage eating disorders or recommend that sufferers seek treatment, but instead seek to foster a sense of solidarity and companionship for people who already have the condition and who do not want to change. Some openly revel in their situation, such as one woman who wrote that 'Ana [anorexia] loves me, She may use me, But she won't forget me. I am not her victim, I am one of her lovers. Every day I pray to be loved above the rest' (Whitehead 2010: 617).

The research involved 'virtual ethnography' in which the author regularly visited Pro-ED websites and closely monitored the postings made there. Since

the research was not conducted in person, Whitehead was not able to get information on the demographic characteristics of the participants and she makes no mention of their nationality. Like many other virtual interactions, the ones she observed were probably not limited to people from a single country, although much of what she describes is applicable to Canadian society.

Taking a grounded theory approach to the issue, Whitehead identified five practices that contributed to the development of a collective identity: encouraging surreptitious eating behaviours by sharing stories about how they had hidden their bulimia from their partners or family members; focusing on domestic tasks such as cooking (for example, sharing recipes for dishes that are delicious but not calorific and are easily purged); encouraging the idea that beauty, in particular thinness, is essential to self-worth; promoting friendships among people with eating disorders and even casting the disorder as a friend; and drawing inspiration from celebrity women who have battled eating disorders or who are simply thin and beautiful. One of the author's main conclusions is that these practices are 'gendered' in the sense that they reinforce and reproduce dominant norms and stereotypes about what it means to be a woman.

to the existing literature. Develop hypotheses about the linkages you perceive and go back to the data to see if they can be confirmed.

- *Finally, keep coding in perspective.* It's only one part (albeit an important part) of the analysis: a mechanism for thinking about the meaning of the data *and* for reducing the data to a manageable size. The larger task of interpretation awaits, including forging interconnections between codes, reflecting on the overall importance of the findings for the research literature, and pondering the significance of the coded material for the lives of the people who are the subjects of the research.

TURNING DATA INTO FRAGMENTS

The coding of materials such as interview transcripts typically entails writing marginal notes on them and gradually refining those notes into codes and then cutting and pasting (sometimes in the literal sense, with scissors and glue). It entails cutting transcripts into chunks of data (and of course carefully identifying the origins of each chunk with, for example, name, position in organization, date) for later data retrieval. Although word-processing programs can be used for this task, CAQDAS is becoming increasingly popular.

CAQDAS has been a growth area in terms of both the proliferation of programs and the numbers of people using them. Most of the best-known programs allow analysts to code text and later retrieve it, tasks that were once done manually. For example, the software can search for all chunks of text relating to a code, and then cut and paste them together. Human input is still crucial, however. CAQDAS cannot help with decisions about the codes, or the coding of textual materials, or the interpretation of findings. As with quantitative data analysis software such as SPSS, someone must still choose the variables to be analyzed and the analytic techniques to be used, and then make sense of the results. Each form of software requires creativity. CAQDAS differs from SPSS largely in terms of the type of data that can be used with it.

There is no CAQDAS industry leader, but NUD*IST (Non-numerical Unstructured Data Indexing Searching and Theorizing) is a package that most researchers would at least know by name, and was the software used by Tastsoglou and Miedema (2003). It became very popular

in the 1990s and has been improved with the development of QSR NUD*IST Vivo, known as NVivo. Appendix A outlines how to use NVivo for qualitative data analysis.

To use or not to use CAQDAS? With a very small data set, it is probably not worth the time and trouble required to become familiar with new software. Catterall and Maclaran (1997) have argued that CAQDAS is not very suitable for focus group data because the code and retrieve function tends to hide the communication process typical of focus groups. On the other hand, learning new software will give you skills that you may need in the future. CAQDAS is likely to be too expensive for personal purchase, though there are student and educational discounts. Demonstration copies of some of the main packages can be downloaded from the distributors' Internet sites.

There is no one correct approach to coding data. As we suggested earlier, grounded theory conceives of different types of code. Coffey and Atkinson (1996) pointed to three different levels of coding, applied below to a passage from an interview that first appeared in Box 10.7 (p. 172).

- First there is a very basic coding, which, in the case of the Box 10.7 material could be liking or disliking the visit to a Disney theme park. However, such a coding scheme is unlikely to provide anything more than a superficial analysis.

- A second level involves a deeper awareness of the content of what is said and is organized around the focus of the research. An example might be countries 'well-represented' and 'missing' at Disney World.

- A third level moves slightly away from what the respondent says to explore broader analytic themes. The responses in the Box 10.7 transcript were coded in terms of characteristics such as enthusiasm ('uncritical enthusiasm'), attitudes towards the Disney Corporation ('not critical of Disney'); comments made about typical visitors ('visitors' ethnicity'); and the nature of critical comments ('aesthetic critique,' 'ethnicity critique,' 'nationality critique'). Interestingly, the passage also reveals the potential for a code employed by Coffey and Atkinson (1996: 43–5): the use of a 'contrastive rhetoric' (making a point about one thing by comparing it to something else). This feature occurred when the husband made a point about the representation of British culture, which he regarded as poor compared to that of China.

As Coffey and Atkinson (1996) observed, following Strauss and Corbin's account (1990) of grounded theory, codes should not be thought of purely as mechanisms for the fragmentation and retrieval of text. They can do more than simply manage the data gathered. For example, examination of the interconnections between codes may reveal that some are dimensions of a broader phenomenon. For example, 'ethnicity critique' came to be seen as a dimension of 'ideology critique,' along with 'class critique' and 'gender critique.' In this way, a map of the more general or formal properties of the concepts under development can be started.

PROBLEMS WITH CODING

One of the most common criticisms of coding qualitative data is the risk of losing the context of what is said. (For a general critique of qualitative data analysis packages see Box 14.4.) By plucking chunks of text out of the context in which they appear, such as a particular interview transcript, the social setting can be lost. A second criticism of coding is that it results in fragmentation of the data, causing the narrative flow to be lost (Coffey and Atkinson 1996). Sensitivity to this issue has been heightened since the late 1980s by a growing interest in narrative analysis (see later in this chapter). Riessman (1993: vi) became concerned about fragmentation when coding themes in her structured interview study on divorce and gender:

> Some [interviewees] developed long accounts of what had happened in their marriages to justify their divorces. I did not realize these were narratives until I struggled to code them. Applying traditional qualitative methods, I searched the texts for common thematic elements. But some individuals knotted together

---

BOX 14.4 | Lack of agreement about the utility of CAQDAS

Whereas the use of computer software is almost universal in quantitative data analysis, among qualitative data analysts it is often avoided, for several reasons.

- Some writers worry that because qualitative data analysis packages make it so easy to quantify coded text, qualitative research will become subject to the reliability and validity criteria of quantitative research (Hesse-Biber 1995).

- Others feel that CAQDAS reinforces and even exaggerates the tendency towards a fragmentation of the textual materials (Weaver and Atkinson 1995), destroying the natural flow of interview transcripts and field notes. Awareness of context is crucial to many qualitative researchers, and they are concerned by the prospect that this awareness may be pushed to the sidelines. Stanley and Temple (1995) suggested that most of the coding and retrieval features needed for qualitative data analysis, such as search, cut, and paste, already exist in word-processing software. Using Microsoft Word, for example, would save not only money but also the time required to learn new software.

- Coffey et al. (1996) argued that the style of qualitative data analysis in most CAQDAS presumes a methodology—based on coding and retrieving text—that owes a great deal to grounded theory.

In their view, the emergence of grounded theory as a new standard is inconsistent with a key strength of qualitative research: its flexibility.

- On the other hand, several writers have extolled the virtues of such packages:

- CAQDAS, like NVivo, invites thought about 'trees' of interrelated ideas—a useful feature in that it encourages the analyst to consider possible connections between variables.

- Quantitative researchers often criticize the tendency towards 'anecdotalism' found in much qualitative research—that is, the tendency to use quotations from interview transcripts or field notes with little sense of how representative they might be. CAQDAS makes it possible to count the frequency with which a particular form of behaviour occurs or a particular viewpoint is expressed in interviews.

- CAQDAS enhances the transparency of qualitative data analysis. How qualitative data were analyzed is often unclear in published reports (Bryman and Burgess 1994b). CAQDAS may force researchers to be more explicit and reflective about the process of analysis, and may indirectly encourage replication, a feature often lacking in qualitative analysis.

several themes into long accounts that had coherence and sequence, defying easy categorization. I found myself not wanting to fragment the long accounts into distinct thematic categories.

Riessman's account is interesting because it suggests several possibilities: that the coding method can fragment the data; that some forms of data may be unsuitable for coding; and that researchers can produce narrative analysis, since what she provided in this passage is precisely a narrative. Interest in narrative analysis certainly shows signs of growing and in large part this trend parallels the rebirth of interest in the **life history** approach (see Box 10.4). Nonetheless, coding is unlikely to become less prominent, for several reasons: it is widely accepted in the research community; not all analysts are interested in research questions that lend themselves to narratives; grounded theory and the techniques associated with it are very influential; and the growing use of computer software for qualitative data analysis frequently invites a coding approach.

Regardless of analytical strategy, it is unacceptable to simply say: 'This is what my subjects said and did; isn't that incredibly interesting?' Interpretation and theorizing are necessary. Many researchers worry that focusing on those tasks may prevent them from doing justice to what they have seen and heard, or lead them to contaminate their subjects' words and behaviour. Those are real risks, but they must be balanced against the fact that findings acquire significance in an intellectual community only when they have been subject to reflection. The researcher has to do more than simply take notes or record answers.

NARRATIVE ANALYSIS

The term 'narrative analysis' covers a wide variety of approaches based on the search for and analysis of stories that people tell to understand their lives and the world around them. It has become particularly prominent in connection with the life history or biographical approach. However, as Box 14.5 shows, narrative analysis is not exclusively concerned with telling life histories. As Roberts (2002) observed, the term is often used to refer both to the research approach itself and to the accounts that it examines—the stories that people tell about their lives and other events. In general,

narrative analysis entails sensitivity to the connections between people's accounts of past, present, and future events and states of affairs; to people's sense of their place in those events and situations; to the stories they generate about them; and to the significance of context for the unfolding of events and people's sense of their roles in them. The way people forge connections between events and the sense they make of those connections are the raw material of narrative analysis. Riessman (2004b) helpfully distinguished four models of narrative analysis:

- *Thematic analysis* examines what is said rather than how it is said.

- *Structural analysis* emphasizes the way a story is told. Issues of content do not disappear, but attention is focused on the use of narrative mechanisms to increase the persuasiveness of a story.

- *Interactional analysis* looks at the dialogue between the teller of a story and the listener. The co-construction of meaning by the two parties is especially prominent, though content and form are also taken into account.

- *Performative analysis* analyzes narrative as a performance and explores the use of words and gestures to get a story across. This model of narrative analysis also examines audience responses to the narrative.

With narrative analysis, attention shifts from 'What happened?' to 'How do people make sense of what happened?' Proponents of narrative analysis argue that most approaches to the collection and analysis of data ignore the fact that people perceive their lives in terms of continuity and process, and that efforts to understand social life that do not take that fact into account may misunderstand the perspective of those being studied. Narrative analysis is obviously suitable for life history research, but its applications can be much broader. For example, it can also be applied to accounts of shorter episodes and their interconnections.

Some researchers apply narrative analysis to interviews. In her account of her 'click moment' as a narrative researcher, Riessman (1993) described how she applied narrative analysis to conventional interview transcript material, and then began to uncover the stories her interviewees were telling her. In this case, Riessman

BOX 14.5   Tattoo narratives

How can narratives be used to analyze a social trend such as the increasing popularity of tattoos for women?

As part of a three-year participant observation study of tattooing, Atkinson (2002, 2004) elicited tattoo narratives from the women he interviewed. The great increase in the numbers of women getting tattoos has clearly challenged the standard 'masculinity' explanations of male tattooing. Drawing on feminist theories about bodies, he found that these women are not misfits, and that they use tattoos to signify their 'established' or 'outsider' constructions of femininity. Ideas about femininity, including conformity to and resistance against cultural norms, are crucial in explaining women's tattooing.

was applying a narrative approach to materials gathered in a conventional way for conventional purposes. Other researchers start out with the intention of conducting a narrative analysis and deliberately ask people to recount stories (for example, Miller 2000). While stories can emerge in response to questions not designed to elicit a narrative, certain kinds of question are especially likely to produce them. Riessman (2004*a*) suggested that prompts such as 'Tell me what happened' followed by 'And then what happened?' are much more likely to elicit a narrative account than 'When did X happen?' While some narrative researchers prefer to start people off by asking them to tell their story of an event, Riessman argued that it is usually necessary to keep asking follow-up questions to stimulate the flow of details and impressions. For example, in her study of divorce, she often asked: 'Can you remember a time when . . . ?' and then followed it up with

'What happened that makes you remember that particular moment in your marriage?'

Coffey and Atkinson (1996) argued that a narrative should be examined in terms of the functions that it serves for the teller. The aim of narrative interviews is to elicit interviewees' reconstructed accounts of connections between events and links between events and contexts (see Box 14.6 for an example). Miller (2000) proposed that narrative interviews in life story or biographical research are far less concerned with eliciting facts than with drawing out interviewees' reflections and interpretations, as revealed in their accounts of their lives or families. Box 14.6 presents an example of narrative analysis beyond the life story approach. In this case, the author explored competing narratives explaining the failed implementation of an information technology system in a hospital.

Narrative analysis, then, is an approach to the analysis of qualitative data that examines the stories that people use to explain events. It can be applied to data that have been acquired through a variety of research methods (notably semi-structured and unstructured interviewing and participant observation), but it has also become an interviewing approach in its own right. Also, as we will see in connection with the writing of ethnographic research (see the section on 'Writing up ethnography' in Chapter 17), there is growing recognition of ethnography as a narrative designed to tell a story about a way of life.

Narrative analysis has been criticized. Bury (2001), while noting the increased interest in *illness narratives* (accounts of illnesses people have experienced), argued that there has been a tendency for narrative researchers to treat such stories uncritically. For example, he suggested that the frequent references in illness narratives to coping with and 'normalizing' illness may often represent attempts to convince the audience (whether the interviewer or the reader of the narrative) of the subject's competence; in other words, such accounts may be motivated more by the desire to be seen as a fully functioning member of society than by the desire to give a realistic account of coming to terms with a medical condition. However, as Bury recognized, the social conditions that prompt such narratives and the forms the narratives take are themselves revealing. In drawing attention to the motives behind illness narratives, he was not seeking to undermine narrative analysis but to show how the range of issues addressed in this form of research can be expanded.

BOX 14.6 | An example of organizational narratives in a hospital

Brown (1998) examined the competing narratives offered in the aftermath of the introduction of new information technology (IT) in a hospital, a project that was largely seen as unsuccessful because of cost over-runs and the absence of clear clinical benefits. Drawing on his unstructured and semi-structured interviews with key actors, Brown identified three contrasting narratives: those of the ward staff, the laboratory team, and the implementation team.

Together, the three narratives provide a very clear sense of the organization as a political arena in which groups and individuals contested the legitimacy of each other's interpretations of events. While the three groups claimed similar (though not identical) motivations for participating in the IT initiative, expressed mainly in terms of an ethic of patient care, they had different latent motivations and different interpretations of what went wrong (Brown 1998: 49).

With respect to latent motivations, the ward staff emphasized the desire to save doctors' and nurses' time; the laboratory team emphasized the importance of retaining the existing IT systems; and the implementation team emphasized the career advantages that might come with increasing dependence on their IT skills. With respect to what went wrong, the ward narrative suggested that the implementation team had failed to coordinate the initiative and meet deadlines; the laboratory team emphasized the implementation team's tendency not to listen or communicate; and the implementation team pointed to the ward staff's failure to communicate their needs and lack of cooperation from the laboratory staff, as well as poorly written software.

Key Points

- The collection of qualitative data frequently results in the accumulation of a large volume of information.

- Qualitative data analysis is not governed by codified rules to the same extent as quantitative data analysis is.

- There are different approaches to qualitative data analysis; grounded theory is probably the most prominent.

- Coding is a key process in most qualitative data analysis strategies, but it may have the effect of fragmenting and decontextualizing information.

- Narrative analysis emphasizes the stories that people tell in the course of interactions with a qualitative researcher; it has become a strategy for producing and analyzing qualitative data in its own right.

Relevant Websites

Website of the Grounded Theory Institute:

http://www.groundedtheory.com/

These YouTube videos discuss grounded theory, including coding and constant comparison:

http://www.youtube.com/ watch?v=4SZDTp3_New

http://www.youtube.com/ watch?NR=1&v=gn7Pr8M_Gu8

http://www.youtube.com/ watch?v=vi5B7Zo0_OE&NR=1

If you'd like to experiment with NVivo software, you can get trial downloads at:

http://www.qsrinternational.com/products_ free-trial-software.aspx

[Websites accessed 31 August 2011]

Questions for Review

- What did Miles (1979) mean when he described qualitative data as an 'attractive nuisance'?

GENERAL STRATEGIES OF QUALITATIVE DATA ANALYSIS

- What are the main components of analytic induction?

- What are the main features of grounded theory?

- What is the role of coding in grounded theory? What are the different types of coding?

- What is the role of memos in grounded theory?

- Charmaz wrote that theoretical sampling 'represents a defining property of grounded theory' (2000: 519). Why do you think she feels this way?

- What are some of the main criticisms of grounded theory?

BASIC OPERATIONS IN QUALITATIVE DATA ANALYSIS

- Is coding associated solely with grounded theory?

- What are the main steps in coding?

- To what extent does coding result in the fragmentation of data?

NARRATIVE ANALYSIS

- To what extent does narrative analysis provide a solution to data fragmentation?

- How does the emphasis on stories in narrative analysis represent a distinctive approach to the production and analysis of qualitative data?

- Can narrative analysis be applied to all kinds of qualitative interviews?

- Come up with a research question that can be answered using narrative analysis.

PART VI

This section explores areas of research that transcend the quantitative/qualitative divide. Chapter 15 invites readers to reconsider the distinction between those two approaches to social research. This may seem an odd thing to do, since this book has been organized around the differences between them. However, the aim is to show that the distinction is not hard-and-fast. Chapter 15 also considers the various ways in which quantitative and qualitative approaches can be combined; studies that do this are described as *multi-strategy research*. Chapter 16 examines content analysis, the study of media and other text, and applies qualitative strategies to it, including conversation analysis and discourse analysis; it also explores some quantitative aspects of such research. Chapter 17 looks at issues relating to the writing-up of social research, and discusses some features of good writing in both quantitative and qualitative research. Finally, Chapter 18 offers advice on conducting a small-scale research project.

These chapters return to issues raised in earlier sections, probing them in greater depth and making connections between them.

CHAPTER 15

Breaking Down the Quantitative/Qualitative Divide

CHAPTER OVERVIEW

This chapter is concerned with how far the **quantitative/qualitative** distinction should be taken. Although there are many differences between the two research strategies, there is also much that unites them, as we will see when we discuss how they can be combined. This chapter explores:

- aspects of qualitative research that can contain elements of the natural science model;

- aspects of quantitative research that can contain elements of **interpretivism**;

- the idea that research methods are more independent of **epistemological** and **ontological** assumptions than is sometimes supposed;

- ways in which the quantitative/ qualitative contrast may break down;

- studies in which qualitative research is used to analyze quantitative research and vice versa;

- the use of quantification in qualitative research;

- arguments against the combination of quantitative and qualitative research;

- two versions of the debate on combining quantitative and qualitative research, one concentrating on methods of research and the other on epistemological issues;

- different ways in which **multi-strategy research** has been carried out; and

- the claim that multi-strategy research is not inherently superior to research employing just one research strategy.

Philosophers of science sometimes use the term 'consilience' to refer to the notion that there is a unity or compatibility between all branches of knowledge. The word came into wide usage after the biologist E. O. Wilson published *Consilience: The Unity of Knowledge* (1998), in which he argued that the natural sciences, the social sciences, and even the humanities may one day have a unity of form and purpose that will allow for a more thorough and profound understanding of natural and social phenomena. This chapter is written in a similar spirit, seeking to show that quantitative and qualitative research strategies have a great deal in common and can complement each other. It makes the case that both are required to gain knowledge of the social world.

As you progress through your academic career, you may be tempted to take a dismissive attitude towards approaches and methodologies that are different from your own. Try to resist that temptation: giving in to it can lead to needless tensions and rivalries between researchers and can ultimately be quite destructive. Drawing on the insights of multiple perspectives is much more conducive to good research and produces a deeper level of understanding.

Introduction

Given the emphasis we have placed on the distinction between quantitative and qualitative research, it might appear perverse at this stage to suggest that the differences between them may be exaggerated. The dichotomy has been maintained to this point for two simple reasons:

- There *are* differences between quantitative and qualitative research strategies.
- Contrasting the two *is* a useful way of organizing research methods and approaches to data analysis.

As we have seen in earlier chapters, certain epistemological and ontological positions may be associated with particular research methods: for example, a natural science epistemology is often paired with social survey research, and an interpretivist epistemology with qualitative interviewing. However, the connections posited in Chapter 1 between epistemology and ontology, on the one hand, and research method, on the other, are best thought of as tendencies rather than definitive connections. The use of a **structured interview** or self-completion questionnaire does not *necessarily* imply a commitment to a natural science model; nor does ethnographic research *necessarily* mean an interpretivist epistemology.

Research methods are much more free-floating than is sometimes supposed. A method of data collection like **participant observation** can be employed in such a way that it is in tune with **constructionism**, but it can also be used in a way that reveals an **objectivist** orientation. Also, it's easy to underestimate the importance of practical considerations in determining how social research is carried out. It's not impossible to conduct a study of drug dealers by mailed questionnaire, but for practical reasons such a strategy is unlikely to succeed. The rest of this chapter will demonstrate why the distinction between quantitative and qualitative research should not be overstated.

It is of course possible to combine the two approaches so that their various strengths can be capitalized on and their weaknesses compensated for. Indeed, the number of studies that combine different strategies has been increasing since the early 1980s. However, not all research methodologists would agree that such integration is either feasible or desirable. In discussing the combination of quantitative and qualitative strategies, this chapter looks at three main issues:

- the arguments against integrating quantitative and qualitative methods;
- the different ways in which quantitative and qualitative strategies have been combined; and
- whether a combined research strategy is necessarily superior to one relying on a single approach.

This chapter uses the term *multi-strategy research* for work that integrates quantitative and qualitative approaches (sometimes referred to as mixed methods research). This term does not refer to the use of several quantitative methods in a single study, or the integration of two or more qualitative methods—for example, combining structured interviewing with **structured observation**, or ethnography with **semi-structured interviewing**. In the current discussion, 'multi-strategy research' refers only to studies that combine qualitative and quantitative methods in the same project.

The natural science model and qualitative research

One of the chief difficulties in linking issues of epistemology with research methods is the frequent characterization of the natural sciences as inherently **positivist** in orientation. But the term 'positivism' is often used in a polemical way, usually as an unhelpful criticism of another's work. Moreover, qualitative research frequently exhibits features associated with a natural science model. This tendency is revealed in several ways:

- *Empiricist overtones*. Although empiricism (see Chapter 1) is typically associated with quantitative research, many qualitative researchers place a similar emphasis on the importance of direct contact with social reality. They frequently stress the importance of direct experience with social settings, and advocate understanding social reality via that contact. The very idea that theory should be grounded in data (recall Chapter 8) is central to empiricism. It's not surprising, therefore, that some writers claim to detect 'covert positivism' in qualitative research.

  Another example of empiricist overtones can be seen in the idea that social reality must be studied from the vantage point of the research participants. The fact that ethnographers rely on extended contact to gain access to their subjects' perspectives implies acceptance of the empirical notion that meaning is accessible to the senses. The empiricism of qualitative research is perhaps most notable in **conversation analysis** (examined in Chapter 16), an approach that starts with precise transcriptions of speech and applies rules of analysis to them. The analyst is actively discouraged from speculating about intention or context; in other words, the empiricist notion that one should not stray too far from the data is strictly upheld.

- *A specific problem focus.* Qualitative research *can* investigate quite specific, tightly defined research questions of the kind normally associated with the natural science model.

- *Hypothesis-* and *theory-testing.* Following from the last point, qualitative researchers typically test hypotheses or theories generated in the course of conducting their research, as in **analytic induction** or **grounded theory**. This is well within the bounds of a natural science model, even if the natural sciences tend to be **deductive**. Also, there is no reason why hypothesis- or theory-testing in qualitive social research cannot be done with previously specified hypotheses or theories. In fact, this has been done on many occasions. For example, Wilson's qualitative study of raves (2002) used theory as a departure point. The research by Festinger *et al.* (1956) on a doomsday cult used the qualitative technique of participant observation to test a theory about how people respond when a belief they zealously endorse—in this case, the imminent end of the world—is disconfirmed. The authors argued that it is possible to imagine a number of conditions that, if met, would lead group members to embrace their belief even *more* fervently after its disconfirmation. They thought that the cult would provide an ideal opportunity for testing their theory. The researchers (and hired observers) pretended to be converts and gained entry to the group in order to make first-hand observations. The theory was substantiated when cult members decided that their faith had saved the world

and began proselytizing—an activity they had not engaged in before.

- *Realism.* Porter's (1993) critical realist ethnography (see Box 15.1) demonstrates how an ethnographic study can be based on an epistemological position derived from the natural sciences. It also relates to the previous point in providing a further illustration of hypothesis-testing in qualitative research.

BOX 15.1 | Critical realist ethnography

Porter (1993, 2002) took a critical realist stance in his ethnographic study of racism in a large Irish hospital where he spent three months as a staff nurse. He found that racism was expressed in the form of remarks made behind the backs of members of racial minorities. However, it did not intrude into work relationships, because more weight was given to achievements and performance (such as qualifications and medical skills) than to 'race' when judging members of professions. In part, this reflected the tendency of black and Asian doctors to emphasize their knowledge and qualifications during their interactions with whites, affirming their professional credentials. In terms of critical realism, one possible structural mechanism (racism) was countered by the operation of another structural mechanism (professional ideology). Only on rare occasions did tension surface, as when a minority doctor conducted a religious observance on his knees in the middle of a hospital unit (Porter 2002).

In addition, some qualitative researchers include explicitly quantitative elements in their research. Miller (2000), for example, engaging in what he called *neo-positivism*, made theoretically based predictions about people's lives using the **life history** method. Another illustration is Charmaz's (2000) suggestion that in spite of the differences that developed between Glaser (1992) and Strauss (for example, Strauss and Corbin 1998)—who were major proponents of grounded theory—both maintained that an objective, external reality exists (the position taken in the natural sciences). Each posited a social world beyond the researcher and maintained that it was the job of the social investigator to reveal its nature and functioning.

Quantitative research and interpretivism

Qualitative research would seem to have a near-monopoly on the ability to study meaning. Its proponents imply that only qualitative research makes it possible to see the social world through the eyes of the people studied. But this contention seems at odds with the widespread study of *attitudes* in social surveys based on interviews and questionnaires. For example, there is a huge literature on political attitudes, and many indexes and scales have been designed to measure them (see Robinson *et al.* 1999). The widespread inclusion of questions about attitudes in social surveys suggests that quantitative researchers are interested in matters of meaning too.

It may be objected that survey questions do not really tap issues of meaning because they are based on categories devised by the designers of the interview schedule or questionnaire and not by the subjects themselves. Two points are relevant here. First, the notion that qualitative research is better at gaining access to the point of view of those being studied is generally *assumed rather than demonstrated*. Qualitative researchers frequently claim to have tapped into participants' world views because of their extensive participation in the daily life of their subjects, the length of time they spend in the setting under investigation, or the lengthy and intensive interviews they conduct. However, the explicit demonstration that interpretative understanding has been accomplished—for example, through respondent validation (see Chapter 8)—is rarely undertaken. Second, if the design of attitude questions is based on prior questioning that seeks to bring out the range of possible attitudinal positions on an issue, attitudinal questions can certainly provide access to meaning.

Also, the practice in much survey research of asking respondents the reasons for their actions implies that quantitative researchers are frequently concerned with uncovering meaning. For example, in the research on delinquency in Box 1.2, the boys were asked to give the reasons for their actions in their own words and then to choose the sociological theories that came closest to explaining them. Examples such as these point to the possibility that the gulf between quantitative and qualitative research is not as wide as is sometimes supposed.

Quantitative research and constructionism

We noted in Chapter 1 that a keynote in qualitative analysis is constructionism: how people build up images or representations of the social world. Qualitative **content analysis** plays an important role in developing an understanding of how people construct their visions of reality, in the same way that **discourse analysis** (Chapter 16) does using materials such as newspaper reports and television programs.

Lantz and Booth's (1998) research on the social construction of breast cancer provides an example. As Box 1.7 makes clear, much of their understanding of the representation of breast cancer came from a qualitative content analysis, but they conducted a quantitative content analysis as well. The latter showed that 80 per cent of the women in the photographs attached to breast cancer articles were under age 50, and that 85 per cent of the anecdotes and case stories related to women in this age group. This emphasis on younger women helped to create the impression that they were the most at risk. But in reality, fewer than 20 per cent of new cases of breast cancer were in women under 50, and the mean age at diagnosis was 65. This inconsistency allowed Lantz and Booth to uncover how the media draw a connection between youthful lifestyles (working outside the home, postponing parenthood, greater sexuality) and breast cancer—a connection consistent with the articles' 'blame the victim' theme. The quantitative content analysis of articles on breast cancer played an important part in revealing the social construction of beliefs about the disease. More generally, this example shows how quantitative research can contribute to constructionist research.

Research methods and epistemological and ontological considerations

To review the argument so far:

- there may be differences between quantitative and qualitative researchers in their epistemological and ontological positions; *but*
- research strategies and epistemological and ontological assumptions do not necessarily go hand in hand. There is a *tendency* for quantitative and qualitative research to be associated with the epistemological and ontological positions outlined in Table 1.1, but the relationship is not perfect.

Nonetheless, some writers mistakenly suggest that each research method carries with it a full cluster of epistemological and ontological commitments. For example, it is sometimes assumed that researchers who use questionnaires necessarily embrace a natural science model and an objectivist world view. Similarly, the use of participant observation is often assumed to imply a commitment to interpretivism and constructionism. In fact, as we have seen, there is no perfect correspondence between research strategies and matters of epistemology and ontology. Any notion that a given method necessarily reflects certain underlying assumptions about knowledge and the nature of social reality is bound to break down.

Research methods are much more 'free-floating' in terms of epistemology and ontology than is often supposed. This can be seen in studies on social research itself. For example, Platt's (1986) historical research on American sociology suggested that the alleged connection between conservative functionalist theory (which is often associated with positivism) and survey research is greatly exaggerated. Her research indicated that 'the two originated independently, and that leading functionalists had no special propensity to use surveys and leading surveyors no special propensity for functionalism' (1986: 527). Moreover, Platt's general conclusion on the use of research methods in American sociology between 1920 and 1960 is very revealing:

> Research methods may on the level of theory, when theory is consciously involved at all, reflect intellectual . . . *post hoc* justifications rather than . . . carefully chosen fundamental assumptions. Frequently methodological choices are steered by considerations of a practical nature . . . and are just slogans and aspirations . . . (1996: 275).

Again, even when there are discernible links between research methods and assumptions about knowledge, the connections are not absolute.

Further evidence of the autonomy of research methods is the fact that both quantitative and qualitative approaches may be employed in a single piece of research, a point that will be illustrated later in this chapter.

Problems with the quantitative/ qualitative contrast

The contrasts between quantitative and qualitative research drawn in Chapter 8 suggest a sharp distinction between the two (see, in particular, Table 8.1). Here is a more nuanced view.

BEHAVIOUR VERSUS MEANING

A distinction is sometimes drawn between a quantitative focus on behaviour and a qualitative focus on meaning. Yet, as noted, quantitative research frequently seeks to study meanings in the form of attitudes. In recent decades the social sciences in general have increasingly recognized the importance of examining not only what people do, but also how they think and make sense of the world. The 'cognitive revolution' in psychology has made people's thoughts and feelings the topic of extensive research. The use of rational choice theory and game theory in economics, political science, and sociology reflects a similar emphasis on examining how people think and make choices. Many different perspectives in the social sciences now acknowledge the importance of meanings and interpretations in understanding social phenomena.

Looking at the other side of the divide, qualitative researchers frequently, if not invariably, examine *behaviour*, although they also pay close attention to the context in which it occurs. Qualitative researchers often seek to interpret people's behaviour in terms of the norms, values, and culture of the group or community in question. In other words, quantitative and qualitative researchers alike are typically interested both in what people do and in what they think, even if they go about their investigations in different ways. The degree to which quantitative and qualitative research reflect the 'behaviour versus meaning' distinction should not be overstated.

THEORIES AND CONCEPTS TESTED IN RESEARCH VERSUS THOSE EMERGING FROM THE DATA

A related point concerns the characterization of quantitative research as driven by theory testing. **Experimental** investigations probably fit this model well, but survey-based studies are often more exploratory in nature. Although **concepts** have to be measured, specific hypotheses are frequently not identified in advance. Surveys ask so many questions, and there are so many possible correlations and ways of organizing the findings, that hypotheses are often not formulated until *after* the data collection has taken place. The analysis of quantitative survey data is often more exploratory than is generally appreciated and consequently offers many opportunities for generating theories.

The common depiction of quantitative research as an exercise in theory testing also fails to take into account how often its findings can result in new theoretical departures and contributions. Reflecting on his career in survey research, Glock (1988: 45–6) provided the following example from his study of American church involvement. Having found that women, older persons, the poor, and those without families were more religiously active than people not in those categories, he suggested that such people might have more time than others to become involved. Alternatively (or in addition), these religiously active people might be compensating for some kind of deprivation relative to their counterparts—a conflict view that Marx would have appreciated. Since the existing data did not allow him to rule out either explanation, he collected *new* data to test them: in this way his original quantitative data led to new research ideas. Quantitative research commonly follows this path.

NUMBERS VERSUS WORDS

Even the most basic distinction between quantitative and qualitative research—numbers versus words—is problematic. Qualitative researchers will sometimes undertake to quantify a limited amount of their data in an effort to determine the generality of the phenomena they are describing. After observing doctor–patient interactions in public and private oncology clinics, for example, Silverman (1985) quantified some of his data to show that patients in private clinics have more influence over what goes on in the consultations. Still, Silverman warned that such quantification should reflect the research participants' own ways of understanding their social world.

It has often been noted that qualitative researchers engage in 'quasi-quantification' when they use terms such as 'many,' 'often,' and 'some' (see p. 279 below). The only difference in studies like Silverman's is that the researcher makes such estimates of frequency more precise.

ARTIFICIAL VERSUS NATURAL

The distinction between artificial and natural is similarly open to criticism. It is often assumed that because much quantitative research employs research instruments (such as questionnaires) that offer only limited and indirect indicators of people's lives, its account of the social world is artificial. Qualitative research tends to be considered more **naturalistic** in that it focuses on observing people in their natural settings, behaving as they normally do. This would seem to be particularly true of ethnographic research, since the participant observer studies people in their normal social worlds and contexts, as they go about their everyday activities. However, when qualitative research is based on interviews, the 'natural' label is less applicable. Interviews still have to be arranged and interviewees have to be taken away from activities they would otherwise be engaged in, even when the interviewing style is of the more conversational kind. Furthermore, little is known about interviewees' reactions to and feelings about being interviewed.

Phoenix (1994) reported on the responses of interviewees to in-depth interviews in connection with two studies: one focusing on mothers under the age of 20 and the other on the social identities of young people. Although many of her subjects seemed to enjoy being interviewed, they were clearly conscious of the fact that they had been engaged in interviews rather than conversations. This was revealed in some of their replies. For example, Phoenix reported one young black woman as saying that she had liked the interview, adding: 'I had the chance to explain how I feel about certain things and I don't really get the opportunity to do that much.' Another interviewee said it was a 'good interview' and added: 'I have never talked so much about myself for a long time, too busy talking about kids and their problems' (1994: 61). While such qualitative interviews are clearly valuable in allowing the perspectives of people whose voices are normally silent to surface, they don't fit the definition of 'naturalistic' used by critics of quantitative social science. Thus it would be incorrect to assume that artificiality is a problem only in quantitative research.

As we noted in Chapter 10, focus group research is often described as more natural than qualitative interviewing because it resembles the way people discuss issues in real life. Natural groups (people already known to each other) are often used to emphasize this element. Whether focus group participants see their interaction as 'natural' is unclear, however. In particular, since the participants are often paid strangers who have travelled some distance to discuss topics they rarely if ever talk about, it's clear that this sort of research may not be as natural as some have assumed.

In participant observation, the researcher can be a source of interference, making the research situation less natural than it might appear. It's difficult to estimate how much impact **reactivity** has on the research findings in such cases, but once again the naturalism of such studies is questionable. When the ethnographer also engages in interviewing (as opposed to casual conversation), the naturalistic quality is definitely compromised, although the research will probably be somewhat less artificial than it would be if quantitative methods were used.

These observations cast doubt on the rigidity of the quantitative/qualitative distinction. Once again, this is not to suggest that the usual contrasts are unhelpful: only that they should not be exaggerated. Quantitative and qualitative research strategies are not absolutely divergent.

Mutual analysis

The divisions between quantitative and qualitative research are also undermined when one approach is used to analyze research conducted using the other.

A QUALITATIVE APPROACH TO QUANTITATIVE RESEARCH

There has been growing interest in using some of the methods associated with qualitative research to examine quantitative research. In part, this trend reflects qualitative researchers' growing interest in ethnography. The qualitative study of quantitative research is part of this trend because it reveals that the written account of research constitutes not only the formal presentation of findings but an attempt to persuade readers of the credibility of those findings. This is true of the natural sciences as well; research by Gilbert and Mulkay (1984) showed that scientists, when writing up their findings, took pains to demonstrate that proper procedures were followed. They also learned from interviewing scientists that the research process was influenced by the scientists' personal biographies.

One way in which a qualitative approach has been applied to quantitative studies is through what Gephart (1988: 9) called *ethnostatistics*:

'the study of the construction, interpretation, and display of statistics in quantitative social research.' For example, Gephart showed that the use of statistics in itself can be regarded as a rhetorical device, because quantification makes social research look more like natural science—an association that tends to give it greater legitimacy and credibility. This is just one example of the way qualitative research can shed light on the nature of quantitative research.

A QUANTITATIVE APPROACH TO QUALITATIVE RESEARCH

When Hodson (1996) conducted a content analysis of workplace ethnographies (discussed in the next chapter; see Box 16.7), he essentially applied a quantitative content analysis to qualitative research. This type of research, sometimes called *meta-ethnography*, may have potential in other areas of social research where ethnography has been a popular method, such as the study of social movements, religious sects, and cults. Hodson's approach was one solution to the problem of comparing ethnographic studies in a given area. However, he largely ignored contextual factors in order to explore relationships between variables abstracted from the studies.

Among the key issues in a study of this kind is the selection of works suitable for analysis. Hodson chose to analyze just books, excluding articles because they usually contain only a limited amount of information. To qualify for selection, a book had to meet three criteria: '(a) the book had to be based on ethnographic methods of observation over a period of at least 6 months, (b) the observations had to be in a single organization, and (c) the book had to focus on at least one clearly identified group of workers. . . .' (Hodson 1999: 22). The application of these criteria resulted in the exclusion of 279 out of the 365 books he had considered. A second crucial issue was the coding of the studies (for an example, see Box 16.7, p. 307). Hodson stressed the importance of knowing the subject area, adopting clear coding rules, and pilot testing the coding schedule. In addition, he recommended checking the **reliability** of coding by having 10 per cent of the documents coded by two people. The process was time-consuming; each book took at least 40 hours to code.

Among the many attractions of this approach is the fact that it allowed a single researcher to investigate a varied set of organizations and provided more in-depth data than is typically gathered by quantitative researchers. It also allowed for the testing of hypotheses derived from established theories: for example, the 'technological implications' approach, which sees technology as having an impact on the experience of work (Hodson 1996). However, the loss of social context is likely to make Hodson's approach unattractive to many qualitative researchers.

Of particular significance is Hodson's remark that 'the fundamental contribution of the systematic analysis of documentary accounts is that it creates an analytic link between the in-depth accounts of professional observers and the statistical methods of quantitative researchers' (Hodson 1999: 68). In other words, the application of quantitative methods to qualitative research may provide a meeting ground for the two research strategies.

Quantification in qualitative research

As we noted in Chapter 8, perhaps the most basic difference between quantitative and qualitative research is the 'numbers versus words' distinction. Yet most qualitative research does contain some quantification. Three observations are worth making about quantification in the analysis and writing-up of qualitative data.

THEMATIC ANALYSIS

Chapter 8 noted that qualitative data analysis often takes the form of a search for themes in transcripts or field notes. The choice of themes to look for is often determined by how frequently certain incidents, words, phrases, and so on recur. This process may also account for the prominence given to some themes over others. In other words, a kind of implicit quantification probably influences both the identification of themes and the elevation of some themes over others.

QUASI-QUANTIFICATION IN QUALITATIVE RESEARCH

As we have noted, qualitative researchers engage in 'quasi-quantification' when they use terms such as 'many,' 'frequently,' 'rarely,' and 'some,' which by definition are based on the relative frequency of the phenomenon of interest. As expressions of quantity, however, these terms are imprecise, and it's often difficult to tell why they are being used

at all. When quantification is needed to support a point, it may be better to use actual numbers.

COMBATTING ANECDOTALISM THROUGH LIMITED QUANTIFICATION

Qualitative research is often criticized for the anecdotal nature of its data, which leaves the reader with no way of assessing their generalizability. Brief sequences of conversation, snippets from interview transcripts, and accounts of encounters between people say little or nothing about the prevalence of the phenomena that such evidence is supposed to indicate. There is also the related risk that the researcher may attribute undue significance to a particularly striking statement or unexpected activity.

At least partly in response to these problems, qualitative researchers sometimes undertake a limited quantification of their data. Gabriel (1998) collected 377 stories about organizational culture in the course of 126 interviews in five organizations. He identified different types of stories and noted the frequency of each type. For instance, there were 108 comic stories (usually a mechanism for the disparagement of others); 82 epic stories (survival against the odds); 53 tragic stories (undeserved misfortune); and 40 gripes (personal injustices). The stories could have been presented as anecdotes, but simple counting conveyed a clear sense of their relative prevalence.

Using actual numbers can counter the criticism that qualitative data are too anecdotal and do nothing to indicate the *extent* to which certain beliefs or behaviours occur. The precision of numbers also makes them superior to the estimates of frequency that must be inferred from quasi-quantification terms such as 'some' or 'many.'

We may see greater use of quantification in qualitative research in the future as a result of the growing use of software programs for qualitative data analysis. Most of the major software programs make it possible to produce simple counts for the use of a particular word or the incidence of a coded theme. In many cases, they can also produce simple cross-tabulations—for example, showing which sex uses the passive voice more often.

Multi-strategy research

The ways in which quantitative and qualitative research can complement each other can be seen most clearly in multi-strategy research, which by definition involves combining the two modes of investigation. However, there are two basic arguments against this sort of research.

ARGUMENTS AGAINST MULTI-STRATEGY RESEARCH

Arguments against multi-strategy research tend to be based on the following assumptions:

- that particular research methods are associated with particular epistemological and ontological positions; and
- that quantitative and qualitative research strategies are inherently incompatible on epistemological and ontological grounds.

These two positions are briefly reviewed below.

The embedded methods argument   Advocates of the first position, outlined earlier in this chapter, argue that every research method is permanently rooted in a particular set of epistemological and ontological commitments. For example:

> every research tool or procedure is inextricably embedded in commitments to particular versions of . . . knowing th[e] world. To use a questionnaire . . . to take the role of participant observer, to select a random sample . . . and so on, is to be involved in conceptions of the world which allow [the use] of these instruments (Hughes 1990: 11).

According to this view, a decision to employ (for example) participant observation is not simply a choice about data collection but a commitment to an epistemological position that is consistent with interpretivism and incompatible with positivism or a natural science model in general.

This view has led some writers to argue that multi-strategy research is not feasible. An ethnographer may collect questionnaire data about a slice of social life not amenable to participant observation, but this does not represent an integration of quantitative and qualitative research because the epistemological positions of the two methods are irreconcilable. The chief difficulty with this kind of argument is that the idea of research methods carrying fixed epistemological and ontological implications is very difficult to sustain.

The paradigm argument   The paradigm argument is closely related to the previous one. It conceives of quantitative and qualitative research as **paradigms**. A paradigm is a set of beliefs and assumptions about how the world works and how knowledge of it is to be gained. Kuhn (1970) popularized the term in his portrayal of natural science as going through periods of revolution, whereby 'normal' science (science carried out in terms of the prevailing paradigm) is increasingly challenged by new findings inconsistent with the assumptions and established findings of the discipline. The increasing frequency of such anomalies eventually sparks a crisis, which in turn sparks a revolution. The period of revolution comes to an end when a new paradigm gains acceptance and a period of the new 'normal' science sets in. An important feature of paradigms is that they are incommensurable: inconsistent with each other because of their divergent assumptions and methods. Disciplines in which no paradigm has emerged as pre-eminent, such as sociology and other social sciences, are deemed 'pre-paradigmatic.'

The paradigm argument maintains that quantitative and qualitative research approaches are based on incompatible paradigms in which epistemological assumptions, values, and methods are inextricably intertwined (Morgan 1998*b*). Therefore, when researchers combine participant observation with a questionnaire, they are not really combining quantitative and qualitative research, since the paradigms are incompatible: the integration is only superficial and within a single paradigm.

The problem with the paradigm argument, as with the embedded methods claim, is that it rests on a connection between method and epistemology that has not been demonstrated. Moreover, although Kuhn (1970) argued that paradigms are incommensurable, it is by no means clear that quantitative research and qualitative research are in fact separate paradigms. As we have suggested throughout this chapter, there are areas of overlap and commonality between them.

Two positions in the debate over quantitative and qualitative research

There are two opposing arguments regarding the question of whether quantitative and qualitative research can be combined.

- An *epistemological argument*, as in the embedded methods and paradigm positions discussed above, which sees quantitative and qualitative research as grounded in incompatible epistemological principles (and ontological ones too, though these tend to be given less attention). According to this version, multi-strategy research is not possible in principle.

- A *technical argument*, in which research methods are perceived to be independent of any specific epistemological position. According to this view, a research method from one research strategy can be pressed into the service of another: quantitative and qualitative methods can be fused. This is the position taken by most researchers whose work is mentioned in the next section.

The technical argument views the two research strategies as compatible, and multi-strategy research as both feasible and desirable. It is in that spirit that we will now consider the ways in which quantitative and qualitative research can be combined.

Approaches to multi-strategy research

Hammersley (1996) proposed three approaches to multi-strategy research:

- **Triangulation**: the use of quantitative research to corroborate qualitative research findings or vice versa.
- *Facilitation*: the use of one research strategy to aid research using another.
- *Complementarity*: the use of two different research strategies so that diverse aspects of an investigation can be combined.

THE LOGIC OF TRIANGULATION

Triangulation entails using more than one method in the study of social phenomena. The term has been used somewhat more broadly by Denzin (1970: 310) to refer to an approach that uses 'multiple observers, theoretical perspectives, sources of data, and methodologies,' but the emphasis has tended to be on methods of investigation and sources of data. One of the reasons Webb *et al.* (1966) called for greater use of **unobtrusive methods** is their potential for triangulation (see Box 6.5). Triangulation can operate within and across research strategies. It was originally conceptualized by Webb *et al.* (1966) as a way of developing additional measures, resulting in greater confidence in findings, and was strongly

associated with a quantitative research strategy. However, triangulation can also take place within qualitative research. In fact, ethnographers often check their observations with interview questions to look for possible misunderstandings. Bloor (1997) reported that he tackled the process of death certification in two ways: interviewing clinicians responsible for certifying causes of deaths, and asking the same people to complete dummy death certificates based on case summaries he had prepared. Increasingly, triangulation refers to the cross-checking of findings from both quantitative and qualitative research (Deacon *et al.* 1998).

An illustration of a triangulation approach is Hughes *et al.*'s (1997) study of the consumption of 'designer drinks' (fortified wines and strong white ciders) by young people. The authors used two main research methods:

- a qualitative method: 8 focus groups with 56 children and young adults, each discussion lasting around two hours; and
- a quantitative method: a survey administered in two parts to a multi-stage cluster sample of 824 12- to 17-year-olds. The first part was an interview and the second was a questionnaire designed to elicit more sensitive information.

The results achieved with the two research strategies were mutually reinforcing. The qualitative findings showed age differences in attitudes towards designer drinks and other types of alcohol: the youngest people (12- and 13-year-olds) tended to adopt a generally experimental approach; the 14- and 15-year-olds thought of drinking as a way of having fun and losing inhibitions, and felt that designer drinks met their needs well; the oldest group (16- and 17-year-olds) were mainly concerned with appearing mature and establishing relationships with the other sex, and tended to think of designer drinks as targeted at immature younger drinkers. These connections with age were confirmed by the quantitative evidence, which also corroborated the suggestion from the qualitative evidence that the consumption of designer drinks was largely associated with a desire to get drunk.

In this study the use of triangulation appears to have been planned, but this need not always be the case. Researchers may start out using different research strategies for different purposes but in the process discover that they have generated quantitative and qualitative findings on related issues, and that they can treat their overlapping results as a triangulation exercise.

Whether triangulation is planned or unplanned, there is always the possibility that the two sets of findings will not corroborate one another. In the event that the results are inconsistent, the solution is *not* to arbitrarily decide which set of findings is correct. Usually, further research is required to resolve the matter.

Deacon and colleagues (1998) used several quantitative and qualitative research methods to gather information, without intending to conduct a triangulation exercise. But analysis of their data revealed an inconsistency: the quantitative data suggested a broad consensus between journalists and social scientists on the reporting of social scientific research in the media, but the qualitative findings suggested some conflict of approaches and values between the two groups. Instead of favouring one set of findings over the other, the researchers re-examined the data and found that social scientists tended to answer questions about media coverage of their work differently, depending on the research instrument. In response to survey questions they typically expressed relief that the coverage was not as bad as they had expected, whereas in interviews they tended to emphasize 'war stories' of wounding encounters with the media. In general, then, the questionnaires showed social scientists to be relatively pleased with the reporting of their research, but their replies were more negative when they were encouraged to reflect on specific problems in the past.

Another example of triangulation can be found in Fenton *et al.*'s (1998) study of the same topic. It employed both quantitative and qualitative methods:

1. content analysis of news and current affairs coverage (local and national newspapers, TV, and radio);

2. mailed questionnaires soliciting social scientists' views about media coverage and their own practices (674 replies);

3. mailed questionnaires soliciting the views of social scientists identified in the content analysis as having received media coverage (123 replies);

4. semi-structured interviews with 20 of the latter;

5. semi-structured interviews with 34 journalists identified in the content analysis;

6. semi-structured interviews with 27 representatives of funding bodies and government;

7. observing journalists' movements and activities at three conferences; and

8. focus group analysis of audience reception of media coverage (13 focus groups).

QUALITATIVE RESEARCH FACILITATES QUANTITATIVE RESEARCH

Here are two ways in which qualitative research can serve as a guide for quantitative research:

- *By suggesting hypotheses.* Because of its tendency toward unstructured, open-ended methods of data collection, qualitative research is often a source of hypotheses that can be tested using a quantitative strategy. An example is Phelan's (1987) research in which she conducted qualitative interviews and conversations with people attending a treatment program for families dealing with incest. After a considerable amount of qualitative data had been collected, Phelan became aware of differences between biological fathers and stepfathers in how they interpreted their incestuous acts, and in the frequency with which certain behaviours occurred. Quantifiable data were collected through interviews with family counsellors that supported her hypothesis that 'the process of incest in structurally different families may vary' (Phelan 1987: 39). Similarly, Bell's (2007) study of western Canadian separatism started out as a qualitative investigation involving attendance at separatist events and hanging out with separatists. Analysis of these data led to the hypothesis that support for separatism was associated with a neo-liberal ideology and a partisan dislike for the ruling federal Liberal Party, a view that was later substantiated in a multiple regression analysis using survey data.

- *By aiding measurement.* The in-depth knowledge of social contexts acquired through qualitative research can be used to inform the design of survey questions for structured interviewing and self-completion questionnaires. Johnson and colleagues (2003) used data from unstructured interviews to develop highly structured questions for later interviews with adolescent smokers. Walklate (2000) explained that for her research on fear of crime and safety issues in high-crime areas, a survey using traditional questions about victimization was used. However, the questions were amended to reflect the local context following six months of interviews, ethnography, and examination of local newspapers. Similarly, the survey questions that Bell (2007) used in his study of western Canadian separatism were prompted in part by his experiences in gathering qualitative data.

QUANTITATIVE RESEARCH FACILITATES QUALITATIVE RESEARCH

One way in which quantitative research can prepare the ground for qualitative work is through the selection of people to be interviewed. This can occur in several ways. In the case of Fenton *et al.*'s (1998) research on the reporting of social science research in the mass media, discussed above, a media content analysis (method 1) was used as a source of data. However, it also served as a means of identifying journalists who had reported relevant research (method 5). In addition, replies to questions in the general survey of social scientists (method 2) were used to help identify two groups of social scientists, those with high and those with low levels of media coverage of their research, who were then interviewed with a semi-structured approach (method 4). Similarly, Jamieson (2000) administered a questionnaire to a sample of young men on their criminal activity. On the basis of their replies, qualitative interviews were conducted with equal numbers of young men in each of three categories: those who had never committed a criminal offence; those who had offended but not recently; and persistent offenders.

FILLING IN THE GAPS

When the researcher cannot rely on either a quantitative or a qualitative method alone, a multi-strategy approach can be used to fill in the gaps. For example, ethnographers may employ structured interviewing or self-completion questionnaires if not everything they need to know is accessible through direct observation, or if they have difficulty gaining access to certain groups of people.

Morgan (1998*b*) suggested a two-step approach to planning multi-strategy research:

- The priority decision: Will the principal data-gathering tool be qualitative or quantitative?
- The sequence decision: Should the 'complementary' method be used first, as a preliminary to the principal method, or second, as a follow-up?

These decisions yield four possible types of research design (see Figure 15.1).

FIGURE 15.1 Morgan's classification of approaches to multi-strategy research

One difficulty with using Morgan's typology is that it may be difficult to know whether quantitative or qualitative research had priority, and which one came first in the sequence. Sometimes research uses both strategies and several methods, but no single one is dominant.

STATIC AND PROCESS FEATURES

Together, the characteristics listed in Table 8.1 suggest that quantitative research presents a static picture of social life, while qualitative research presents a more dynamic picture, emphasizing process. In some contexts 'static' may be considered a negative term, but in this case it's positive. In fact, it is the regularities revealed by quantitative research that allow the analysis of process. A multi-strategy research approach makes it possible to combine the two. An illustration is provided by MacKinnon and Luke's (2002) study of cultural change from 1981 to 1995. Their main method of data collection was survey research, but to complete the picture they also examined census and public opinion data, as well as newspaper articles on historical events. They found that levels of homophobia and anti-Semitism decreased over that period, but that sympathy for First Nations also declined. They cautioned that their small sample (70) and what were essentially 'good guesses' meant that their conclusions, 'like the interpretations of an ethnographer [were] subject to alternative interpretations by others' (2002: 332).

RESEARCHER AND PARTICIPANT PERSPECTIVES

Sometimes researchers want to gather two kinds of data: qualitative data that show the general perspectives of their subjects, and quantitative data on specific issues. For example, Milkman (1997) was interested in the meaning of industrial work: in particular, whether factory conditions had changed since the 1950s, when they were portrayed very negatively. To find out, she employed semi-structured interviews and focus groups with GM car-production workers. She was also interested in a 'buyout' plan that the company's management introduced in the mid-1980s after it had initiated a variety of changes to work practices. The plan offered workers the opportunity to give up their jobs for a substantial cash payment. In 1988 and again in 1991, Milkman carried out a questionnaire survey of workers who had accepted the company's buyout offer. The surveys inquired about the reasons for taking the buyout, how those taking it had fared since leaving General Motors, how they felt about their current employment, and differences among social groups (in particular ethnic groups) in current earnings relative to those at General Motors.

THE PROBLEM OF GENERALITY

As we noted above, there is a tendency in qualitative research to present findings in an anecdotal fashion without sufficient evidence to show how typical the findings are, or how the group under study compares with some larger population. Partly to counter this problem, Tastsoglou and Miedema (2003) used quantitative national data on women's volunteer work to compare their admittedly non-random sample of immigrant women with the Canadian population; they found that the immigrant women actually volunteered more than the national average.

QUALITATIVE RESEARCH MAY HELP TO INTERPRET THE RELATIONSHIP BETWEEN VARIABLES

A frequent problem for quantitative researchers is how to explain relationships between variables.

One strategy is to look for an intervening variable: one that is influenced by the independent variable but in turn has an effect on the dependent variable. For example, in a relationship between ethnicity and occupation, education may be an intervening variable:

$$ethnicity \longrightarrow education \longrightarrow occupation$$

This sequence implies that the variable ethnicity has an impact on education (for example, ethnic groups differ in their levels of education), which in turn has implications for the jobs that people in different ethnic groups attain. Qualitative work could examine how different ethnic groups perceive education, which could lead to a fuller understanding of education as an intervening variable. It could also provide leads to a different theoretical perspective on the general topic of ethnicity, education, and occupation.

Another illustration is provided by Barnard and Frischer's (1995) research on HIV-related risk behaviour among drug injectors. Structured interviews with 503 injectors revealed that 'females report[ed] significantly higher levels of needle sharing, sexual activity, and AIDS awareness than their male counterparts,' and that 'women . . . co-habiting with sexual partners who [were] themselves injectors, [were] particularly likely to report high levels of risk behaviour and also AIDS awareness' (Barnard and Frischer 1995: 357). What produced this relationship between gender, risk behaviour, and cohabitation? Semi-structured interviews with 73 injectors suggested that the relationship between these variables could be explained 'by the tendency for women to be in sexual relationships with men who themselves inject and with whom they are unlikely to use condoms' (1995: 360). Here qualitative data were used to shed light on relationships among variables derived from quantitative research.

STUDYING DIFFERENT ASPECTS OF A PHENOMENON

There is a tendency to think of quantitative research as best suited to the investigation of 'macro' phenomena (such as social mobility and social stratification) and qualitative research as more appropriate for 'micro' issues (such as interactions between wait staff and their customers). The macro/micro distinction can also be discerned in Table 8.1. In the example outlined in Box 15.2, Wajcman and Martin (2002) used a quantitative method in the form of a questionnaire survey to explore the career patterns of male and female managers. However, they also carried out qualitative, semi-structured interviews to explore how managers *made sense* of their career patterns in terms of their identity. Thus the choice of methods was determined by the research question.

The use of multi-strategy research to study different aspects of a phenomenon can also be seen in the family-obligations studies conducted by Finch (1985) and Mason (1994). Focusing on the distribution within families of the obligation to care for relatives, this research had two main data collection elements: a survey of a sample of nearly 1000 people by structured interview, and semi-structured interviewing with 88 people. A major component of the survey interviewing was the use of the vignette technique described in Box 5.8. Mason described the purpose of integrating quantitative and qualitative research as follows:

> From the beginning . . . we were using the two parts of our study to ask different sets of questions about family obligations. Not only were we employing different methods to generate different types of data, but we also anticipated that these would tell us about different aspects of family obligations. . . . [O]ur view was that an understanding of kin obligations *in practice* would require an analysis of the relationship between the two data sets and the social processes they expressed (Mason 1994: 90–1).

What were the two sets of research questions to which Mason referred? The survey was designed to elicit information about '"the proper thing to do" for relatives in a variety of circumstances' (Mason 1994: 90). Through the semi-structured interviews, Finch and Mason tried 'to discover what people actually did in practice for their own relatives, and also the processes by which they came to do it and make sense of it: did a sense of obligation or responsibility have a role in the process? How did people in practice work out what to do for their kin, or ask of their kin?' (Mason 1994: 90).

BOX 15.2   Combining survey research and qualitative interviewing in a study of managers

Why do the findings from structured interviews often differ from those derived from semi-structured or unstructured interviews?

Wajcman and Martin (2002) used a questionnaire to survey male and female managers (470 in total) in six Australian companies and conducted semi-structured interviews with 136 managers in each company. The survey evidence showed that male and female managers were generally more similar than different in terms of career orientations and attitudes: contrary to what many had anticipated, women's career experiences and orientations were *not* found to be distinctive. They then examined the qualitative interviews for narratives of identity and found that both male and female managers depicted their careers in 'market' terms (they responded to the requirements of the managerial labour market by developing their skills and experience). But whereas for men narratives of career meshed seamlessly with narratives of domestic life, for women there was a disjuncture. Female managers found it harder to reconcile managerial identities with domestic ones and more often had to opt for one or the other. In this way, choices about career and family were still gendered. This example illustrates how a multi-strategy approach can work to reveal much more than could have been gleaned through the use of one method alone.

In multi-strategy research, then, the different methods may be geared to addressing different kinds of research questions. The research on the reporting of social science research in the British mass media by Fenton *et al.* (1998), discussed earlier, is a further example of a project that used quantitative and qualitative research to answer different types of questions:

- Questions about coverage; for example: How much coverage is there of social science research? What gets covered? Where? (method 1).

- Questions about the production of media coverage; for example: What kinds of attributes do journalists look for when deciding whether to write an item on social science research? (methods 5 and 7).

- Questions about social scientists' attitudes to media reports of research in general (method 2) and to the reporting of their own research (methods 3 and 4). Method 4 was designed to allow the findings reached through method 3 to be elaborated and more fully understood.

- Questions about reception; for example: How do readers/viewers interpret media reporting of social science research? (method 8).

- Questions about the communication environment; for example: What are the policies of universities, government departments, and funding bodies concerning the media reporting of research? (method 6).

This form of multi-strategy research entails making decisions about which kinds of research question are best answered using a quantitative method and which by a qualitative method. (Box 15.3 provides another example.) It also requires that researchers think about how best to interweave the different elements, especially since, as was suggested in the context of the discussion about triangulation, the outcomes of mixed-method research are not always predictable.

SOLVING A PUZZLE

The outcomes of research are not easy to anticipate. Although cynics sometimes claim that social scientists find what they want to find, or that what they 'uncover' is already obvious, the capacity of research to produce surprises should never be underestimated. When unexpected results occur, it can be helpful to revisit the question using a different research strategy. For example, if a quantitative investigation fails to produce the anticipated results, it may be possible to salvage the study using a qualitative approach (Weinholtz *et al.* 1995).

Like unplanned triangulation, this category of multi-strategy research is more or less impossible to plan in advance. Essentially, it offers quantitative researchers an alternative to either revising their hypotheses (see Box 15.4) or filing the inconsistent results away (and probably never looking at them again).

BOX 15.3   Research methods used in a study of gender and organization

Halford *et al.* (1997) conducted research on the role and significance of gender in organizational contexts in two very different British labour markets: an economically buoyant new town experiencing recruitment problems, and a larger metropolitan area suffering from manufacturing decline and high unemployment. They examined local government organizations, a bank, and a hospital in each place. In other words, their design was comparative in terms of both location (two areas experiencing different economic conditions) and organizational type (three distinct kinds of organization).

Three sources of data were employed. First, key informants supplied overall views on gender and career-related issues in all of the organizations and provided documentary materials. Second, a mailed questionnaire was sent to nearly 1000 employees, with a response rate of around 50 per cent. The questionnaire 'was designed to provide broad descriptive information about employees, careers, and [employees'] attitudes to their organization and to opportunities for women in particular' (Halford *et al.* 1997: 56). This material was used 'to describe broad patterns of response across a range of areas, such as occupational mobility, for different subgroups of the sample . . . or attitudes to the organization.' Third, semi-structured interviews with between 25 and 35 employees in each of the three sectors were used as 'filter[s] for choosing people to interview in-depth' (1997: 56). The researchers said that they 'frequently found the information provided by in-depth interviews more revealing' than the questionnaire data (1997: 59).

Revising the hypothesis to fit the data in positivist research

Imagine that your reading of the literature has led you to hypothesize that boys who are victims of sexual assault are less likely to report it than are victimized girls. Now suppose that analysis of your data, either quantitative or qualitative or both, reveals the counterintuitive opposite. What do you do? One unethical path would be to pretend that you always expected the boys to report assaults more often than girls, perhaps because of recent publicity regarding sexual abuse in churches and private schools. The review of the literature can then be rewritten to reflect this expectation. Another unethical option would be to pretend the study was an inductive one in which the hypothesis was developed after the data were gathered.

An ethical solution would be to leave the hypothesis and literature review intact, and then in the discussion explain why you think the hypothesis was not supported. The hypothesis could then be revised—for example, to maintain that in 'normal' times of little publicity on child sexual assault, the usual pattern of girls reporting more than boys should reappear. You would then outline how the new hypothesis could be tested with further research.

Reflections on multi-strategy research

There can be little doubt that multi-strategy research is becoming more common. Two particularly significant factors in this development are:

- a growing willingness to see research methods simply as techniques of data collection, unencumbered by epistemological and ontological baggage; and
- a softening in the attitude towards quantitative research among feminist researchers who in the past had resisted its use (see Chapter 8 for a discussion of this point).

Other factors are relevant, but these two are especially important. An example of their operation can be found in research on audience reception of media and cultural texts. In the past, researchers in the area relied mainly on qualitative methods (in particular, focus groups), but lingering unease regarding the reliability and generalizability of their findings has led some to recommend using quantitative research methods in tandem with qualitative methods (for example, Schrøder 1999).

However, multi-strategy research is not necessarily superior to one-method or one-strategy research. Four points must be borne in mind:

- Multi-strategy research must be competently designed and conducted: otherwise its findings will be suspect, no matter how many methods are employed.
- Multi-strategy research must be appropriate for the research questions asked. There is no point in collecting additional kinds of data on the assumption that 'more is better.'
- Multiple methods are likely to take considerably more time and financial resources than research using just one approach, and spreading resources too thinly can dilute the effectiveness of the research.
- Not all researchers have the skills and training required to carry out both quantitative and qualitative research, and their 'trained incapacities' may prevent them from integrating the different forms of research.

Multi-strategy research is not a panacea. It may provide a better understanding of a phenomenon than if just one method is used. It may enhance confidence in the findings, and it may even improve the chances of access to research settings. Milkman (1997: 192), for example, suggested in her research on a General Motors factory that her promise of 'hard,' quantitative data facilitated her entry to the plant even though she had no experience with this method. But the general point remains: multi-strategy research, while offering great potential in many instances, is subject to constraints similar to those in research relying on a single strategy.

Methods in Motion

Applications to Canadian Society

O'Shaughnessy and Kennedy (2010) used qualitative methods to address a paradox revealed by quantitative research: although women tend to show higher levels of concern for environmental issues than men, men are more likely to be environmental activists. To make sense of these apparently contradictory findings, the researchers conducted ethnographic interviews with 13 Alberta families who made a conscious effort to act in an environmentally responsible way. The researchers found that the paradox could be explained in part by the fact that environmental activism is typically defined in terms of public-sphere activities such as joining environmental political parties, participating in demonstrations, fundraising, and signing petitions.

Although women were less likely than men to engage in these forms of 'conventional activism,' they were prominent participants in 'relational activism,' which the authors describe as 'the acts behind activism' (555). Relational activism is less visible than the public kind, since it involves everyday activities conducted in networks of friends, family members, and local community residents. The authors note that although these sorts of behaviours tend to go unnoticed by social movement scholars, they are often necessary for more public behaviours to develop and be effective. One woman who was interviewed explained that simply promoting the use of bicycles in her neighbourhood had important implications for environmental sustainability:

> It turns out that our family can give a lot here and we get a lot back, just by doing what brings us joy. My husband loves bicycles and he can be . . . on the front porch and the neighbors come by and say, 'Oh can you help me with this?' And we also do free bike repairs once a year. In this way we . . . get more people to ride. If we help them fix their bicycles they'll ride more (562).

O'Shaughnessy and Kennedy conclude that women are not less inclined to be environmentally active than men: they simply tend to engage in a different *form* of environmental activism, one that emphasizes everyday relationships and activities.

Key Points

- It's important not to exaggerate the differences between quantitative and qualitative research.
- Connections between epistemology and ontology on the one hand, and research methods on the other, are not fixed or absolute.
- Qualitative research can exhibit features normally associated with a natural science model.
- Quantitative research can incorporate an interpretivist stance.
- The artificial/natural contrast used to distinguish quantitative and qualitative research is often exaggerated.
- A quantitative research approach can be used to analyze qualitative data, and qualitative research methods can be used to analyze the rhetoric of quantitative researchers.
- Some qualitative researchers employ quantification in their work.
- Although the practice of multi-strategy research has increased, not all writers support it.
- The view that there are epistemological and ontological impediments to the combination of quantitative and qualitative research is a barrier to multi-strategy research.
- There are several different ways of combining quantitative and qualitative research; some can be planned in advance, others cannot.

Relevant Websites

In this YouTube video, one of this book's authors (Professor Alan Bryman) discusses multi-strategy research in the social sciences:

> **http://www.youtube.com/ watch?v=OlZ3w8pKyJI**

If you find the video helpful, Part 2 can be found at:

> **http://www.youtube.com/ watch?v=ruEkdqM_KRw**

Professor Ashutosh Varshney discusses the use of quantitative and qualitative methods in the study of conflict in this YouTube video:

> **http://www.youtube.com/ watch?v=65ZlCgGYwXc**

For examples of multi-strategy research, there is the *Journal of Mixed Methods Research* at this address, although to access the journal you may have to go through your institution's library server:

> **http://mmr.sagepub.com/**

[Websites accessed on 5 September 2011]

Questions for Review

THE NATURAL SCIENCE MODEL AND QUALITATIVE RESEARCH

- Under what circumstances can some qualitative research use a natural science model?

QUANTITATIVE RESEARCH AND INTERPRETIVISM

- Under what circumstances can some quantitative research exhibit characteristics of interpretivism?

QUANTITATIVE RESEARCH AND CONSTRUCTIONISM

- Under what circumstances can some quantitative research be constructivist?

RESEARCH METHODS AND EPISTEMOLOGICAL AND ONTOLOGICAL CONSIDERATIONS

- How closely tied are research methods with epistemological and ontological positions? Explain.

- What is multi-strategy research?

PROBLEMS WITH THE QUANTITATIVE/ QUALITATIVE CONTRAST

- Outline some of the ways in which the quantitative/qualitative contrast is not as hard-and-fast as is often supposed.

THE MUTUAL ANALYSIS OF QUANTITATIVE AND QUALITATIVE RESEARCH

- What are some implications of Gilbert and Mulkay's (1984) research (on how scientists write up their findings) for the qualitative analysis of quantitative research?

- Assess the significance of ethnostatistics. What does it tell us about quantitative research?

- Assess the significance of Hodson's (1996, 1999) research on workplace ethnographies. What does it tell us about ethnography?

QUANTIFICATION IN QUALITATIVE RESEARCH

- To what extent is quantification a feature of qualitative research? Should there be more quantification in qualitative studies? Explain.

THE ARGUMENT AGAINST MULTI-STRATEGY RESEARCH

- What are the strengths and weaknesses of the embedded methods and paradigm arguments against multi-strategy research?

OPPOSING ARGUMENTS ABOUT COMBINING QUANTITATIVE AND QUALITATIVE RESEARCH

- What are the epistemological and technical arguments regarding the prospect of combining quantitative and qualitative research? What are their implications for multi-strategy research?

APPROACHES TO MULTI-STRATEGY RESEARCH

- What are the chief ways in which quantitative and qualitative research have been combined?
- What is the logic of triangulation?

- Traditionally, qualitative research is depicted as having a preparatory role in relation to quantitative research. To what extent do the different forms of multi-strategy research reflect this view?

REFLECTIONS ON MULTI-STRATEGY RESEARCH

- Why has multi-strategy research become more prominent?
- Is multi-strategy research necessarily superior to single-strategy research?

CHAPTER 16

Content Analysis

CHAPTER OVERVIEW

Content analysis involves the examination of various documents and **texts**, which may be printed, visual, aural, or virtual. It can be **quantitative**, focused on **coding** data into predetermined categories in a systematic and easily **replicable** manner, or **qualitative**, seeking to uncover deeper meanings in the materials. This chapter considers:

- the kinds of research question that content analysis can answer;
- the features of documents or texts that are commonly analyzed;
- how to code (a key part of content analysis);
- **semiotics** and **hermeneutics**;
- active and passive audiences;
- **conversation analysis** and its roots in **ethnomethodology**;
- the assumptions and analytic strategies of **discourse analysis**; and
- the advantages and disadvantages of content analysis.

Rebecca and her boyfriend Daniel were sitting at home watching TV on a Saturday night. Neither was in a particularly good mood; both thought there must be a more exciting way to spend the weekend. 'Have you ever noticed that there are way more food commercials—burgers, pizza, chicken—at night than in the daytime?' Rebecca asked. 'Are there?' Daniel replied. 'I know hockey games always seem to come with a lot of beer ads.'

'You ever notice how the women look in those ads?' Rebecca fumed. 'They're always in bathing suits or shorts, even if they're standing on a ski hill in winter. And by some miracle they all have perfect bodies.' 'Yeah,' said Daniel. 'It's a little different with the guys. A lot of them look like dorks, doing stupid things. But some guys look cool, and they're the ones who get the girls. They're better-looking and taller than the dorks.' 'We could probably do a study comparing men and women in beer commercials,' Rebecca said, her mood beginning to lighten. 'We could even throw in a comparison with detergent ads. Ever see a man selling detergent?' 'You could do that,' Daniel said. 'You'd just have to find a way to categorize the portrayals—flattering or unflattering, active or passive, the age of the people, how attractive they are, overtly sexual or non-sexual behaviour—that kind of thing.' 'That wouldn't be too hard to do,' Rebecca answered. 'Sounds like a lot more fun than watching this stupid stuff.'

Introduction

Suppose you are interested in how newspapers cover crime. You come up with the following questions:

- Do certain newspapers report more crimes than others?
- How much crime is reported? Where in the paper do crime stories appear—on the front page, or inside?
- Do columnists as well as reporters write about crime?
- Are some crimes given more attention than others?
- Do more crime stories appear during the week or on weekends?
- What sorts of crime predominate in newspaper articles (crimes against the person, property crime, crimes in which society is the victim)?

Most content analysis of the media is likely to entail several research questions, generally revolving around the same five W's that are the basis of any news report: *who* (does the reporting); *what* (gets reported); *where* (does the issue get reported); *why* (does the issue get reported); and *when* (does it get reported). But researchers are also interested in what media coverage omits. For example, interviews with the family of the accused are rare; such inattention is itself notable, revealing what is and is not important to writers and publishers.

Another common theme in content analysis is change in the coverage of an issue over time. For example, when Miller and Reilly (1995) studied newspaper coverage of a 'food scare' about salmonella in eggs, they found a massive amount of newspaper coverage for about 20 days following government statements about a particularly controversial incident. Over the subsequent 12 months, however, the coverage declined significantly, and it petered out further over the next 4 years, despite public health evidence that the incidence of salmonella poisoning was increasing. Apparently what was lacking was another 'headline' incident.

Content analyses of this kind yield a quantitative description of the characteristics of a communication. Those who perform content analysis claim to be objective and systematic, clearly specifying the rules for the categorization of the material in advance. Researchers try to create transparency in the coding procedures so that personal biases intrude as little as possible. The coding rules in question may, of course, reflect the researcher's interests and concerns and therefore be a product of subjective bias to some degree, but once the rules have been formulated, it should be possible to apply them without bias.

Content analysis can be performed on unstructured information, such as transcripts of semi- and unstructured interviews, and even qualitative case studies of organizations (for example, Hodson 1996). Until recently it was used mainly to examine printed texts and documents, but other sorts of materials may also be analyzed. If you were interested in gender roles or representations, for example, you might look at

- visual images in women's and men's magazines (to see how messages about bodily appearance are gendered) (Malkin *et al.* 1999);
- websites showing pictures of men and women, such as dating sites;
- animated cartoons (Thompson and Zerbinos 1995); and
- lyrics of popular songs (e.g., to look for changes in the representation of women) (Marcic 2002).

What things need to be counted?

Obviously, what is to be counted depends on the specific research questions. In quantitative studies, these elements are usually specified in advance in order to guide both the selection of the media to be analyzed and the construction of the coding schedule. They usually include the following:

WORDS

Determining the frequency with which certain words are used is often the first step in content analysis. Jagger (1998), for example, searched dating advertisements and counted words such as 'slim' and 'non-smoker' to compare women and men with respect to what each deemed desirable in a date (see Box 16.1). Simple counting of particular words can reveal emphasis, style of writing or presentation, and even the overplaying of certain events. For example, Dunning *et al.* (1988) noted a tendency for the British press to sensationalize disturbances at soccer matches by using emotive words such as 'hooligans' and 'louts' to refer to audience members, and terms such as 'battle' to refer to a game; less dramatic terms such as 'fans' or 'contest' would have encouraged more neutral responses among readers.

A variation on the search for individual keywords is the search for pairings of keywords. The growing availability of the written news media in electronic form, online, or on CD-ROM, greatly facilitates this kind of search. Hier (2002) found 'rave' and 'drug use' to be frequently linked, which may have encouraged readers to believe that raves must be controlled. Parnaby (2003), on the other hand, noted that 'squeegee kids' and 'homelessness' were not paired, even though many of the 'kids' were in fact homeless; as a result of this omission, he argued, the 'kids' were constructed 'as a social problem requiring a law and order resolution' (2003: 281). The search for pairings of keywords can be a starting point for a more in-depth analysis.

SUBJECTS AND THEMES

A more interpretative approach is required to code text in terms of subjects and themes. At this point, the analyst is searching not just for the obvious or *manifest* content, but also for some of the underlying or *latent* content as well. This occurs if the researcher wants to probe beneath the surface to ask deeper questions about what is happening. In reports on crime, for example, is the victim blamed along with the accused? Is the occupation of the accused or the victim stated? If not, is it implied in an address or a picture? Why is it that news stories about men who have been mugged sometimes mention their marital status? In seeking to answer these sorts of questions, what began as a quantitative content analysis may develop into a qualitative study.

VALUE POSITIONS

A further level of interpretation is likely when the researcher is seeking to demonstrate that the

---

BOX 16.1 | Finding love: Then and now

Jagger (1998) reported a content analysis of 1094 dating advertisements in four newspapers with a general readership. The sample was chosen over two four-week periods in 1996. Three research questions drove the study:

- What is 'the relative significance of monetary resources and lifestyle choices as identity markers and desirable attributes for men and women'?
- How do men and women vary in the ways they choose to market themselves and describe their preferred (or ideal) partners in terms of the body?
- To what extent are 'traditional stereotypes of masculinity and femininity . . . still in operation' (1998: 799)?

Jagger noted the tendency for considerable percentages of both men and women to market themselves in terms of their lifestyle choices (film preferences, clubs frequented, sports activities, etc.). She also found that women were far more likely than men to stress the importance of economic and other resources in a preferred partner. There was also a somewhat greater propensity for women to market themselves in terms of physical appearance. As an aside, men were just as likely to market themselves as 'slim,' suggesting that certain preferences in body shape were not exclusive to one gender. More generally, her results pointed to

the significance of the body in identity construction for both men and women. In a later publication, Jagger (2001) reported the findings from a qualitative content analysis of a sub-sample of the 1094 advertisements.

Much has changed in the years since Jagger did her research. The Internet dating site has eclipsed the classified newspaper advertisement as the medium of choice for people whose in-person activities do not provide adequate opportunities to meet a romantic partner. Since space is not at a premium, such sites allow participants to give far more information than was the case with newspaper ads, and of course the provision of photographs means that verbal descriptions of physical appearance have become far less important than they once were. However, many sites still feature 'dating profiles' in which people have a few paragraphs to describe themselves and to outline what they would like to find in a partner, and the content of these profiles is somewhat similar to the older-style ad descriptions. There are even sites that provide tips on writing a good dating profile. As with other social changes, the proliferation of online dating sites provides opportunities for social research. For example, a researcher could make a systematic comparison of the content found at online sites with what was contained in the older newspaper ads. How might that be done? What themes could be examined? What ethical issues would be relevant for a study like that?

writer of a particular text has taken a certain value position. For example, is a journalist who writes about crime sympathetic or hostile to the accused? Is all the blame put on the accused, with the implication that punishment is appropriate? Or is the focus on social conditions, with the assumption that less blame should be placed on the criminal? If there is no manifest indication of the writer's value positions, can inferences be made from the latent content?

Another way in which content analysis can reveal value positions is through the coding of ideologies, beliefs, and principles. Jagger (1998) coded dating advertisements in terms of whether stereotypical categories of masculinity and femininity were employed when advertisers described themselves (see Box 16.1). She found that women were more likely than men to advertise themselves in terms of their physical appearance, whereas men were more likely to advertise themselves in terms of their employment. It seemed that each group knew its audience.

Coding

As the foregoing has implied, coding is a crucial part of content analysis. There are two main elements to a content analysis coding scheme: designing a coding schedule and creating a **coding manual**. To illustrate, imagine that you are interested in crime reports in a local newspaper. To simplify, assume that your study is limited to crimes where the victim is a person rather than an organization, and that it considers these variables:

1. nature of the offence(s);
2. gender of perpetrator;
3. occupation of perpetrator;
4. age of perpetrator;
5. gender of victim;
6. occupation of victim;
7. age of victim;
8. depiction of victim; and
9. position of news item in the paper.

Content analysts are normally interested in a much larger number of variables, but this simple illustration can help to get across how a coding schedule and coding manual operate.

CODING SCHEDULE

The coding schedule is a form onto which the data are entered (see Figure 16.1). Each of the columns in Figure 16.1 is a dimension (indicated by the column heading) to be coded. The blank cells on the coding form are the places in which codes are to be written. One row is used for each media item coded. The codes can then be transferred to a computer data file for analysis with a software package such as SPSS.

CODING MANUAL

On the face of it, the coding schedule in Figure 16.1 seems bare, providing little information about what is to be done or where. This is where the coding manual comes in. It is a set of instructions to coders that includes all possible categories for each dimension to be coded. It provides a list of all the dimensions; the different categories subsumed under each dimension; the numbers (that is, *codes*) that correspond to each category; and guidance to coders on what should be taken into account in coding a particular dimension. Figure 16.2 shows a coding manual that corresponds to the coding schedule in Figure 16.1.

Our coding manual includes the occupation of both the perpetrator and the victim of the crime, using a simple social-class scheme. The offences are classified according to the categories used by the police in recording crimes. (Since police statistics have been criticized for weak **reliability** and **validity**—recall Chapter 7—a comparison between police data and crime reports in local newspapers

Case number	Day	Month	Nature of offence I	Gender of perpetrator	Occupation of perpetrator	Age of perpetrator	Gender of victim	Occupation of victim	Age of victim	Depiction of victim	Nature of offence II	Position of news item

FIGURE 16.1 Coding schedule

Nature of offence I
01. Violence against the person
02. Sexual offences
03. Robbery
04. Burglary in a dwelling
05. Burglary other than in a dwelling
06. Theft from a person
07. Theft of bicycle
08. Theft from shops
09. Theft from vehicle
10. Theft of motor vehicle
11. Other theft and handling stolen goods
12. Fraud and forgery
13. Drug offences
14. Other offences

Gender of perpetrator
1. Male
2. Female
3. Unknown

Occupation of perpetrator
01. Professionals, administrators, officials and managers in large establishments; large proprietors
02. Lower-grade professionals, administrators, and officials; higher-grade technicians; managers in small business and industrial establishments; supervisors of non-manual employees
03. Routine non-manual employees in administration and commerce
04. Personal service workers
05. Small proprietors, artisans, etc., with employees
06. Small proprietors, artisans, etc., without employees
07. Farmers and smallholders; self-employed fishermen
08. Lower-grade technicians, supervisors of manual workers
09. Skilled manual workers

10. Semi-skilled and unskilled manual workers (not in agriculture)
11. Agricultural workers
12. Other
13. Unemployed
14. Homemaker
15. Student
16. Retired
17. Unknown

Age of perpetrator
Record age (–1 if unknown)

Gender of victim
1. Male
2. Female
3. Unknown

Occupation of victim
Same as for occupation of perpetrator
If not applicable, code as 99

Age of victim
Record age (–1 if unknown)

Depiction of victim
1. Victim responsible for crime
2. Victim partly responsible for crime
3. Victim not at all responsible for crime
4. Not applicable

Nature of offence II (code if second offence mentioned in relation to the same incident; code 0 if no second offence)
Same as for Nature of offence I

Position of news item
1. Front page
2. Inside
3. Back page

FIGURE 16.2 Coding manual

is a possible research topic.) Finer distinctions can be used, but unless you are planning to examine a large sample of news items, broader categories are preferable. Note also that the coding schedule and manual permit the recording of two offences for any incident. If there are more than two, you will have to make a judgment concerning the two most significant offences.

The coding manual is crucial because it provides a complete listing of all categories for each dimension to be coded, as well as guidance on how to interpret the dimensions. It is on the basis of these lists that a coding schedule of the kind presented in Figure 16.1 is created. Detailed rules about how to code should be formulated, because reliability, both inter-coder and intra-coder, is always a concern (see below).

Here is a news report of a fictional road-rage

Case number	Day	Month	Nature of offence I	Gender of perpetrator	Occupation of perpetrator	Age of perpetrator	Gender of victim	Occupation of victim	Age of victim	Depiction of victim	Nature of offence II	Position of news item
001	24	11	01	1	10	26	1	16	68	2	00	2

FIGURE 16.3 Completed coding schedule

Case number	Day	Month	Nature of offence I	Gender of perpetrator	Occupation of perpetrator	Age of perpetrator	Gender of victim	Occupation of victim	Age of victim	Depiction of victim	Nature of offence II	Position of news item
002	25	12	06	1	13	32	2	16	86	3	01	2

FIGURE 16.4 Completed coding schedule with errors

incident. Two male motorists, one a retired schoolteacher aged 68, the other a 26-year-old assembly-line worker, got into an argument and the worker punched the retired man, causing him to fall, hit his head, and suffer a concussion. There was no second offence. The coding of the incident would then appear as in Figure 16.3 and the data would be entered into a computer program such as SPSS.

Suppose a second article, appearing the next day, described how an unemployed 34-year-old female took an 86-year-old woman's purse and then knocked her down. The code is provided in Figure 16.4 but with a few errors. Can you spot them? Forms like these would be completed for each news item within the chosen period(s) of study.

POTENTIAL PITFALLS IN DEVISING CODING SCHEMES

The potential dangers in devising a content analysis coding scheme are similar to those involved in designing **structured interview** and **observation schedules**. Points to recall include:

- *Mutually exclusive categories.* There should be no overlap in the categories supplied for each dimension. If the categories are not mutually exclusive, coders will not know how to code an item that fits into more than one category.

- *Exhaustive.* Every possible dimension should have a category.

- *Clear instructions.* Coders should be clear about what factors to take into account when assigning codes. Sometimes these have to be very elaborate. In quantitative content analysis, coders generally have little or no discretion in deciding how to code the units of analysis.

- *A clear unit of analysis.* For example, in the imaginary study of the reporting of crime in the local press, there is both a media item (for example, one newspaper article) and a topic to be coded (one of two offences). In practice, a researcher is interested in both but needs to keep the distinction in mind.

To enhance the quality of a coding scheme, it is advisable to conduct a pilot study to identify difficulties, such as finding there is no code to cover a particular case (not exhaustive). A pilot test will also help to reveal if one category of a dimension includes an extremely large percentage of items. When this occurs, it may be necessary to break that category down to allow for greater specificity.

As we have mentioned, the reliability of coding is a further concern. An important part of pre-testing the coding scheme is examining consistency between coders (inter-coder reliability) and, if time permits, **intra-coder reliability**. The process of gauging reliability is more or less the same as in **structured observation**, discussed in Chapter 6.

Qualitative content analysis

Qualitative content analysis involves a search for underlying themes and was used in several of the studies referred to earlier, such as Beharrell's study of the reporting of AIDS in the press (1993), and the Giulianotti (1997) study of Aberdeen soccer magazines. Kennedy (2006), in his study of the Canadian fathers' rights movement called 'Fathers For Justice,' used content analysis in conjunction with participant observation and semi-structured interviews to examine how the movement developed a collective identity. The content analysis was conducted on documents such as position papers submitted to government agencies, newsletters, pamphlets, and minutes from meetings, and was used mainly to make sense of the data gathered through participant observation and interviews. Similarly, Bell (2007) used pamphlets, speeches, newsletters, and other texts to arrive at an overall assessment of western Canadian separatism as a neo-liberal movement. The processes by which the themes are extracted in a qualitative content analysis are often left implicit, although they are usually illustrated with quotations from the text in question.

Lynch and Bogen (1997) examined core sociological textbooks and found that they contained recurring themes that presented an upbeat and scientific view of the discipline—one that, in the researchers' view, was biased and value-laden. Seale (2002: 109) examined newspaper reports about people with cancer. One of the phases of his analysis entailed an 'NVivo coding exercise, in which sections of text concerning themes of interest were identified and retrieved.' He was especially interested in gender differences in the representation of sufferers, and demonstrated that stories about men were much more likely than stories about women to discuss the role that the individual's character played in dealing with the disease.

Altheide (1996) outlined an approach he called *ethnographic content analysis* (ECA), which is typical of qualitative content analysis. He described his approach as differing from quantitative content analysis in that the researcher is constantly revising the themes or categories distilled from the examination of documents. As he put it:

> ECA follows a recursive and reflexive movement between concept development-sampling-data, collection-data, coding-data, and analysis-interpretation. The aim is to be systematic and analytic but not rigid. Categories and variables initially guide the study, but others are allowed and expected to emerge during the study, including an orientation to **constant discovery** and **constant comparison** of relevant situations, settings, styles, images, meanings, and nuances (1996: 16; emphases in original).

While quantitative analysis typically entails applying predefined categories to the sources, ECA allows for greater refinement of those categories as well as generation of new ones. For example, Parnaby's (2003) study of squeegee kids included a reflexive examination of the documents used (newspapers, magazines, government documents, official reports), which was done while the process of forming and confirming theoretical concepts was still under way; it was a process of continuing discovery and comparison. In addition, ECA emphasizes the context within which documents are generated. For instance, a study of newspaper reports of crime would require some understanding of news organizations and the work that journalists do (Altheide 2004).

SEMIOTICS

Another form of qualitative content analysis is semiotics, the *science of **signs***. In social research, semiotics involves analysis of the signs and symbols encountered in everyday life. It can be applied to documentary sources as well as many other kinds of data. The main terms employed in semiotics are as follows:

- the *sign* is something that stands for something else, such as a yellow traffic light; it has two components, a *signifier* and a *signified*;
- the *signifier* is the thing (here the yellow light) that points to an underlying meaning;
- the *signified* is the meaning to which the signifier points ('caution: stop if possible');
- the **denotative meaning** is the manifest or obvious meaning of a signifier and as such indicates its function (here to regulate traffic);
- a **connotative meaning** is one that can arise in conjunction with the denotative meaning (for example, 'speed up to beat the coming red light'); and
- *polysemy* refers to the notion that signs can be interpreted in many different ways.

Methods in Motion

Applications to Canadian Society

Puddephatt and Nelson (2010) did a qualitative content analysis of the promotional materials posted online by English-language sociology departments in Canada. The materials were designed to attract students and generally create a positive public profile for the departments' programs. The authors were concerned about the trend in Canada away from traditional approaches to higher education, which value intellectual development and critical thinking, towards what they perceived to be a more market-oriented, job-training perspective on the part of both students and university administrators.

As is typical in qualitative analyses, the researchers 'undertook a textual analysis of the program descriptions, coding the text as [they] went along, until a number of categories emerged' (411). Puddephatt and Nelson found some important differences in the promotional themes presented by large, comprehensive universities that offer doctoral degrees, compared to institutions that offer mainly undergraduate programs. For example, the latter were more likely to mention the benefits of a well-rounded liberal arts education (such as developing a passion for ideas that offer insight into life and the world at large), although those goals were often linked to their practical utility in the job market in an increasingly information–based society. In fact, both types of institution frequently listed specific career paths that could be taken with a sociology degree.

Another finding was that the promotional materials for the undergraduate institutions tended to emphasize acquisition of the knowledge needed to create social change, while the larger institutions more often referred to specific marketable skills. The authors lamented the fact that neither type of university appeared to place much importance on rigorous and challenging academic programs.

Semiotics seeks to uncover the hidden meanings that reside in texts, broadly defined. Consider, by way of illustration, the curriculum vitae (CV) in academic life. The typical academic CV contains information on matters such as degrees earned; previous and current posts; administrative responsibilities and experience; teaching experience; research experience; research grants acquired; and publications. It can be seen as a system of interlocking signifiers denotatively providing a summary of the individual's experience (its sign function). At the connotative level, it as an indication of an individual's value, particularly in connection with employability. Every CV is capable of being interpreted in different ways and is therefore polysemic, but there is a shared code among academics whereby certain attributes of CVs (such as lists of publications) are seen as especially desirable and are therefore less contentious in terms of their meaning. Applicants for posts know this and design their CVs to highlight the desired qualities and downplay others, so that the CV becomes a presentation of self, as Miller and Morgan (1993) suggested.

Box 16.2 outlines a semiotic study (Gottdiener 1997) in which the 'text' was Disneyland. The chief strength of semiotics lies in its invitation to see beyond and beneath the apparent ordinariness of everyday life and its manifestations. The main difficulty with semiotic analysis is that, although it may offer a compelling exposition of some aspect of everyday life, the interpretation may be somewhat arbitrary. For example, Gottdiener's association of 'Adventureland' with colonialism/imperialism might not be shared by other analysts. However, the results of a semiotic analysis may be no more arbitrary than those of any other interpretive approach. Indeed, it would be surprising not to be struck by a sense of arbitrariness in semiotics, given its emphasis on the principle of polysemy.

HERMENEUTICS

The hermeneutic approach has been used in understanding and interpreting the Bible, but it has also been employed in the analysis of other texts. It was influential in the formation of interpretivism as an **epistemology** (see Chapter 1) and has much in common with Weber's notion of *Verstehen*. The central idea behind hermeneutics is that the analyst of a text must seek its meanings from the perspective of its author, considering the social and historical context within which the text was produced. Qualitative content analysis and semiotics are hermeneutic when they are sensitive to context.

BOX 16.2 | A semiotic Disneyland

Gottdiener (1997: 108–15) proposed that Disneyland can be fruitfully explored through semiotic analysis. He concluded that its meaning is based on the contrast between the alienated daily lives of nearby Los Angeles residents and the life they experience at the theme park. He identified, through this principle, several sign systems contrasting the park with the surrounding environment: transportation, food, clothing, shelter, entertainment, social control, economics, politics, and family. The first of these sign systems—transportation—revealed a difference between the Disneyland visitor as pedestrian (walking with others in a group) and the Los Angeles resident as passenger (a car is necessary; danger on the congested freeways). A further component of his research entailed analysis of the connotations of the different 'lands' that make up the park. He suggested that each land was associated with one or more signifiers of capitalism. For example:

- Frontierland—predatory capital, conquering;
- Adventureland—colonialism/imperialism; and
- Tomorrowland—state capital for space exploration.

Phillips and Brown's (1993) hermeneutic study of the corporate image advertisements of a Canadian synthetic crude oil company was a 'formal analysis of the structural and conventional aspects of the text' (1993: 1563). For them this meant examining the texts of the advertisements in terms of their constituent parts and the writing conventions they reflected. They also relied on a large database of magazine and newspaper articles relating to the company for additional documentary materials. They showed how corporate image advertisements were used to mobilize support for company activities from government and the public, and to ward off the environmental legislation that threatened them.

Readers and audiences – active or passive?

Audience reception is a prominent area of inquiry in media and cultural studies. The key question is whether audiences/readers are active interpreters of what they see or hear. Do they passively accept the meanings that authors or designers infuse into their texts, as in the oil company advertisements just described, or do they resist those meanings and strive for independent readings?

Do they arrive at a middle point that incorporates both passive and active elements? Much of the research on this issue suggests that audiences frequently come up with readings different from those intended by authors (see Fenton *et al.* 1998 for a summary of some of this research).

Although the idea of the 'active audience' has not gone unchallenged (see, for example, McGuigan 1992), it is so well supported that many of the interpretations of texts offered by social scientists have been questioned. This suggests caution in reading Giulianotti's (1997) study of 'fanzines' or Hier's (2002) examination of city council minutes to understand the rave issue. Would other social scientists arrive at the same interpretations? Do their interpretations match those of the original readers or audiences? The social researcher is always putting a personal 'spin' on the texts analyzed. The same is true of all social science data: the conclusions derived from questionnaire or ethnographic data reflect the author's interpretations, not the complete set of possible interpretations. The point is that close scrutiny and critical thinking are always required.

Two approaches to the study of language

In this section two approaches to the study of language are examined: conversation analysis (CA) and discourse analysis (DA). While CA and DA do not exhaust the range of possibilities for studying language, they do represent two of the most prominent approaches, and each includes both quantitative and qualitative aspects. Both have developed a technical vocabulary and a set of techniques. This section outlines some of their basic elements and draws attention to their contrasting features.

Conversation analysis

The roots of CA lie in ethnomethodology, a sociological approach to communication focusing on the 'practical, common-sense reasoning' that people use in their everyday lives. It includes notions of cause and effect ('if I do this, then that will happen') and the generalizations that allow people to perform everyday tasks. This process of reasoning and communication is presented as a way in which social order is created. Social order is not seen as a pre-existing force constraining individual action, but as something that is worked at and achieved by people through interaction. Garfinkel, one of the pioneers of conversation analysis, claimed that the role of sociology is not to uncover 'objective' social facts as Durkheim suggested, but to see them as an accomplishment, as the eventually taken-for-granted patterns established through the activities of ordinary people going about their daily lives (Garfinkel 1967: vii).

Two ideas are particularly central to ethno-methodology and find clear expression in CA: *indexicality* and **reflexivity**. The former suggests that the meanings of words or utterances, includ-ing pauses and sounds, depend on the context in which they are used. Reflexivity means that talk is not a 'mere' representation of the social world, standing for something else, but is itself a real-ity. In these ways, ethnomethodology fits squarely with two aspects of qualitative research: a prefer-ence for a contextual understanding of action (see Chapter 8) and an **ontological** position associated with **constructionism** (see Chapter 1).

In the years following its introduction, ethno-methodological research sought to conduct fine-grained analyses of the sequences of interaction revealed in conversations recorded in naturally occurring contexts. As such, CA is a multifaceted approach, part theory, part method of data acqui-sition, part method of analysis. The predilection for the analysis of talk gleaned from naturally occurring situations suggests that CA fits well with another preoccupation among qualitative researchers: a commitment to **naturalism** (see Chapters 2 and 8).

Conversation analysts have developed a variety of ways to study talk. Psathas (1995: 1) described them as 'rigorous, systematic procedures' that can 'provide reproducible results.' Such a framework brings to mind the procedures used to generate valid, reliable, and replicable findings in quantita-tive research. It is not surprising, therefore, that CA is sometimes described as having a **positivist** orientation. Thus some features that are broadly in tune with qualitative research (contextual and naturalistic analysis without prior theoretical commitments) are married to traits associated with quantitative research.

However, the emphasis on context in CA is somewhat at variance with contextual under-standing as it is normally thought of in quali-tative research. For CA practitioners, context refers to the specific here-and-now context of immediately preceding talk, whereas for most qualitative researchers it has a much wider focus, encompassing phenomena such as the broader culture of the group within which the social action occurs, including their values, beliefs, and typical modes of behaviour. This is precisely the kind of attribution that CA practitioners seek to avoid. To import elements that are not specifically grounded in the here and now of what has just been said during a conversation is to risk impos-ing an understanding that is not grounded in the participants' immediate concerns. It is no wonder, therefore, that writers like Gubrium and Holstein (1997) treated CA as a separate tradition within qualitative research, whereas Silverman (1993) found it difficult to fit CA into broad descriptions of qualitative research.

ASSUMPTIONS OF CONVERSATION ANALYSIS

Analysts often begin practising conversational analysis when they notice something significant about the way a speaker says something and this recognition generates interest in the function that the turn of phrase serves. To illustrate, Clayman and Gill (2004) referred to the way a child will often begin a conversation with an adult by say-ing 'You know what, Daddy [or whoever]?' The question generally produces a 'What?' reply that allows the child to find a slot in a sequence of com-munications, or to inaugurate such a sequence. The use of a question, rather than a declarative statement, may reflect the child's lesser power.

Once such a focus has been identified, conversa-tion analysts typically follow certain basic assump-tions. Heritage (1984, 1987) proposed three:

- *Talk is structured.* Talk comprises patterns, and participants are implicitly aware of the rules that underpin these patterns. As a result, conversation analysts do not attempt to infer the motivations of speakers from what they say, or to ascribe their talk to purely personal characteristics. Such information is unneces-sary, since the conversation analyst is oriented to the underlying structures that are revealed in pauses, emphases, questions followed by answers, etc.

- *Talk is forged contextually.* Talk must be ana-lyzed in terms of its context and understood in terms of the talk that has preceded it.

- *Analysis is grounded in data.* Conversation analysts shun prior theoretical schemes and argue that the characteristics of talk and social order must be derived from the data.

In doing a project based on CA, it is important not to collect too much data. The real work of CA is the painstaking analysis that its underlying theoretical stance requires. It may be that just one or two portions of transcribed text will be sufficient to answer the research questions.

TRANSCRIPTION AND ATTENTION TO DETAIL

The transcript in Box 16.3 includes some basic symbols used by conversation analysts

> We:ll A colon indicates that the sound that occurs directly before the colon is prolonged. More than one colon means further prolongation (e.g., Ye: : : :s).
>
> .hh A row of h's preceded by a dot indicate an intake of breath. If no dot is present, it means breathing out. The more h's, the longer the breath.
>
> (0.8) A figure in parentheses indicates a period of silence, usually measured in tenths of a second. Thus (0.8) indicates eight-tenths of a second of silence.
>
> you and knowing An underline indicates an emphasis in the speaker's talk.
>
> you- you A hyphen means the speaker was interrupted or stopped speaking.
>
> (.) Indicates a very slight pause.

The attention to detail in the sequence of talk in Box 16.3 is striking, but what is significant in it? Silverman (1994) drew two main inferences. First, *P* initially tries to deflect any suggestion that there may be a special reason why she needs an HIV test. As a result, the disclosure that she has been engaging in potentially risky behaviour is delayed. Second, *P*'s use of 'you' depersonalizes her behaviour. Silverman argued that sequences like these show how 'people receiving HIV counselling skilfully manage their talk about delicate topics' (1994: 75). The hesitations are designed by patients to establish that issues like these are not the subject of normal conversation. The rather general replies to questions indicate that the speaker is not the kind of person who immediately launches into a discussion about difficult sexual

---

BOX 16.3 | Conversation analysis showing a question and answer adjacency pair

Silverman (1994: 72) provided the following extract from a conversation between an HIV counsellor (*C*) and a patient (*P*):

1. *C*: Can I just briefly ask why: you thought about having
2. an HIV test done:
3. *P*: .hh We:ll I mean it's something that you have these
4. I mean that you have to think about these da: ys, and
5. I just uh: m felt (0.8) you- you have had sex with
6. several people and you just don't want to go on (.)
7. not knowing.

---

matters with a stranger. As an aside, Silverman suggested that *P*'s hesitancy and depersonalization are minimal. Others stall more, lie, or totally refuse to answer (1994: 76).

SOME BASIC CHARACTERISTICS OF CONVERSATIONS

There are recurring features in the way talk is organized that can be discerned in sequences of conversation. Among them are the following.

Turn-taking One of the most basic features of everyday conversation is the fact that the participants take turns speaking. Only one speaker tends to talk at a time, the other listening, and turns are taken with minimal gaps between them (Hutchby and Wooffitt 1998: 47). Turn-taking is particularly important to conversation analysts because it points to the existence of shared codes indicating the ends of utterances. Without such codes, conversation could not proceed in an organized manner, with smooth transitions between speakers.

Of course, things sometimes go wrong, as when people speak at the same time. Silverman (1993: 132) described some repair mechanisms for instances in which turn-taking conventions are not followed:

- when one participant starts to speak before the other has finished, the interrupted speaker stops talking before completing his or her turn;

- when a turn transfer does not occur at an appropriate point (for example, when someone does not respond to a question), the first speaker may speak again, perhaps reinforcing the need for the other person to speak (for example, by re-phrasing the question).

The crucial point to note about such repair mechanisms is that they allow the rules of turn-taking to be maintained even after the rules have been breached.

Adjacency pairs   One feature of turn-taking is the tendency for an exchange to have two linked phases known as an **adjacency pair**; for instance, a question followed by an answer, as in Box 16.3; an invitation followed by a response (accept/decline); or a greeting followed by a returned greeting. The first phase assumes that the other part of the adjacency pair will be forthcoming, for example, that an invitation will get a response. The second phase is of interest to the conversation analyst not just because it invites a response in its own right but because compliance with the model indicates recognition of the way one is supposed to respond to the initial phase. In this way 'intersubjective understandings' are continuously reinforced. This does not mean that the second phase *always* follows the first. Failure to respond appropriately—for example, when one answers a question with another question—has itself been the focus of attention for conversation analysts.

Preference organization   Some responses are clearly preferred to others. An example is when an invitation or a request is proffered: acceptance is the *preferred response* and refusal the *non-preferred response*. To illustrate, Potter (1996: 59) contrasted a sequence in which an offer is met with a straightforward acceptance—'thank you'—with a sequence (reproduced in Box 16.4) in which an invitation is declined.

According to Potter, A's response is fairly typical of rejections, which have their own standard features. For example, A delays the start of his or her response and fills it with 'hehh.' In addition, the rejection is 'softened' by A's saying 'I don't think I can make it' (which suggests that acceptance is still possible) and then offering an explanation for his or her failure to provide the preferred response. The key point is that the participants recognize the preference structure of this kind

> **BOX 16.4** Conversation analysis in action: a non-preferred response
>
> 1. *B*: Uh if you'd care to come over and visit a little while
> 2. this morning I'll give you a cup of <u>coffee</u>.
> 3. *A*: hehh
> 4. Well
> 5. that's awfully sweet of you,
> 6. I don't think I can make it this morning. hh uhm
> 7. I'm running an ad in the paper and-and uh I have to
> 8. stay near the phone (Atkinson and Drew 1979: 58; quoted in Potter 1996: 59).

of adjacency pairing and that this recognition affects the response (hesitancy, acknowledgment of the invitation, explanation of failure). Acceptance of an invitation does not have to be justified, whereas refusal generally does, in order to protect the relationship between the two parties from the harm that the non-preferred response might otherwise do.

Conversational patterns can be a good subject for student research to see if different groups, such as men and women, or students and professors, exhibit varying patterns. (Keep in mind that status hierarchies can sometimes determine who the interrupters are, who defers to the interrupters, etc.) Your class could go to an eating area on campus to collect data, each student listening to different conversations. To catch body movements, video recordings can be used (Heath 1997), so long as ethical protocols have been followed.

A FINAL NOTE ON CONVERSATION ANALYSIS

CA considers it illegitimate to invoke cultural factors when analyzing conversations. However, some researchers see that principle as unnecessarily restrictive. In many exchanges, much of the talk is informed by the participants' shared knowledge of contexts, including cultural contexts, yet the prohibition against cultural arguments limits CA to research questions that pertain to talk itself. On the other hand, CA reduces the risk of making unwarranted speculations about what is happening in social interaction, and has contributed to our understanding of how social order is created—one of the classic concerns of social theory.

Discourse analysis

Discourse analysis incorporates aspects of CA, but is more flexible and can be applied to forms of communication other than talk. It puts less emphasis on naturally occurring talk, so the language used in research interviews can also be a legitimate subject of analysis. According to Potter, DA 'emphasizes the way versions of the world, of society, events and inner psychological worlds are produced in discourse' (1997: 146). For continental philosophers such as Foucault (1926–84), 'discourse' refers to the way a particular set of linguistic categories relating to an object frames people's understanding of that object.

For example, a certain discourse concerning mental illness can produce particular conceptions of what mentally ill persons are like, the nature of their illness, how they should be treated, and who is legitimately entitled to treat them. In this way discourse serves to justify the power of those who provide such treatment as well as the treatment regimens they prescribe. This discourse is much more than language: it is part of the social world of mental illness.

Several different approaches fall under the DA heading (Potter 1997). The version discussed here is one associated with writers such as Potter (1997), Potter and Wetherell (1994), and Billig (1991). This version of DA exhibits two distinctive features at the level of epistemology and ontology (Potter 1997).

- It is generally anti-realist in that it denies the existence of an external reality awaiting a definitive portrayal by the researcher. It therefore disavows the notion that researchers can arrive at accurate and objective accounts of the social world.

- It is *constructionist* in that it gives priority to the versions of reality propounded by members of the social setting being investigated. More specifically, it recognizes that discourse analysis entails a selection from many possible interpretations of a given situation. For example, is a person who speaks to herself dangerous or harmless? Is she more in need of treatment or social support? In the process of answering such questions, a particular reality is constructed.

Discourse is not simply a neutral device for imparting meaning. After all, there are many things that people seek to accomplish when they talk or write. DA is concerned with the strategies they employ in order to create different kinds of effect. This is illustrated in three basic questions that DA asks:

- What is this discourse doing?
- How is it constructed to make this happen?
- What resources are available to perform this activity? (Potter 2004: 609).

This action orientation is revealed in a study of the first few moments of telephone calls to the helpline of the UK's National Society for the Prevention of Cruelty to Children. Through analysis of these call openings, Potter and Hepburn (2004) showed that a variety of actions are performed during the first few moments:

- The callers spell out the details of their concerns.

- The callers seek to establish, in collaboration with the 'experts' on the line (the child protection officers) that the incidents they are reporting do in fact require some kind of intervention.

- The callers convey the idea that the activity they are describing is serious and that they are concerned about it, but not so concerned that the police should be contacted immediately.

- The child protection officers show a willingness to treat the reports as serious, without making judgments as to their actual truth or seriousness.

Analysis of these brief moments of conversation shows that the flow of discourse achieves a number of objectives for both parties and in that sense constitutes action. On the other hand, as Gill (1996) suggested, what is said is always a way of *not* saying something else. Either way, discourse can be seen as providing a solution to a problem (Widdicombe 1993).

DA shares with CA a preference for locating contextual understanding in terms of the situational specifics of talk. As Potter (1997: 158) put it, discourse analysts prefer 'to see things as things that are worked up, attended to, and made relevant in interaction rather than being external determinants.' However, DA practitioners are less wedded to this principle than are conversation analysts.

Discourse analysts resist the idea of codifying their procedures and argue that such codification is probably impossible. Potter (1997: 147–8) described his work as 'a craft skill, more like bike riding or chicken sexing than following [a] recipe.' Gill (2000) suggested adopting a posture of 'skeptical reading.' This means searching for a purpose lurking behind the way things are said or presented. Gill proposed that DA can be usefully thought of in terms of four main themes, outlined in Box 16.5.

The bulk of the exposition of DA that follows is based on a study of a television program about success in the treatment of cancer (see Box 16.6).

PRODUCING FACTS

In this section, the emphasis is on the strategies employed to convey allegedly factual knowledge. Among them is *quantification rhetoric*: the various ways in which statements involving numbers or quantities can be made to either support or refute arguments. The interest in this issue lies partly in the importance of quantification in everyday life, but also in the tendency of many social scientists to use this strategy themselves (John 1992). In their analysis of data such as the portions of transcript cited in Box 16.6, Potter *et al.* (1991) and Potter and Wetherell (1994) show how these sorts of devices are used.

Using variation as a lever   The authors drew attention to the phrase '1 per cent of a quarter of a million' because it incorporates two different types of quantitative expression: a relative expression (a percentage) and an absolute frequency (quarter of a million). The difference is important, because it allowed the program-makers to emphasize the very low cure rate (just 1 per cent) compared with the very large number of cases diagnosed each year. Instead, they could have pointed to the absolute number of people who are cured (2500), but the impact would have been less dramatic. It's also worth noting that the phrase 'a quarter of a million' not only exaggerates the number of new cases (adding 7000 to the actual 243 000) but also sounds significantly larger.

Reading the detail   Discourse analysts, like conversation analysts, attend to the details of discourse. For example, Potter and Wetherell suggested that the description of the three 'curable cancers' as 'amongst the rarest cancers' was deployed to make the point that these are atypical cancers, and that it would be unwise to generalize from them to all cancers.

BOX 16.5 | Four themes in discourse analysis

Gill (2000) drew attention to four prominent themes in DA:

1. *Discourse is a topic.* In other words, discourse is a focus of inquiry itself and not just a means of gaining access to the aspects of social reality that lie behind it. This idea contrasts with the view traditionally taken by research interviewers, in which language simply reveals what people think, or serves as a mechanism for learning about their behaviour and the reasons for it.

2. *Language is constructive.* Discourse is a way of constituting a particular view of social reality. Moreover, in order to create that view, choices have to be made regarding the most appropriate way of presenting it, and these choices reflect the disposition of the person concerned.

3. *Discourse is a form of action.* As Gill put it, language is considered 'a practice in its own right' (2000: 175). Language is a way of accomplishing acts, such as attributing blame, presenting oneself in a particular way, or getting an argument across. Moreover, a person's discourse is affected by the situation he or she is in. For instance, the reasons given for wanting a job may vary depending on whether the job seeker is talking to a prospective employer, a family member, or a friend.

4. *Discourse is rhetorically organized.* DA practitioners recognize that discourse is concerned with 'establishing one version of the world in the face of competing versions' (Gill 2000: 176). In other words, the version of events that a person presents is intended to persuade others.

BOX 16.6 | Discourse analysis in action: producing facts through quantification rhetoric

The study of the television program *Cancer: Your Money or Your Life* (Potter *et al.* 1991; Potter and Wetherell 1994) used a variety of sources, including

- a video recording of the program;
- the observations of one of the people making the program (who acted as a participant observer while it was being made);
- drafts of the script;
- recordings of editing sessions;
- entire interviews (of people such as cancer research specialists and heads of charities) conducted for the program; and
- research interviews with some of the latter people as well as some of the people involved in making the program.

With regard to the coding process, the authors reported that they

> made a list of about a dozen keywords and phrases that related to the sequence—percentage, cure rates, death rates, 1 per cent, etc.—and then ran through each of the interview and interaction files, looking for them with a standard word-processor. . . . Whenever we got a 'hit' we would read the surrounding text to see if it had relevance to our target sequence. When it did we would copy it across to an already opened coding file . . . noting the transcript page numbers at the same time. If we were not sure if the sequence was relevant we copied it anyway, for, unlike the sorts of coding that take place in traditional content analysis, the coding is not the analysis itself but a preliminary to make the task of analysis manageable (Potter and Wetherell 1994: 52).

Below is a sequence used in the research. It occurred roughly halfway through the program, following interviews with cancer scientists who had cast doubt on whether their research, much of it funded by charities, resulted in successful treatment:

Commentary: The message from these scientists is clear—exactly like the public—they hope their basic research will lead to cures in the future—although at the moment they can't say how this will happen. In the meantime, their aim is to increase scientific knowledge on a broad front and they're certainly achieving this. But do their results justify them getting so much of the money that has been given to help fight cancer? When faced with this challenge the first thing the charities point to is the small number of cancers which are now effectively curable.

[on screen: *Dr. Nigel Kemp Cancer Research Campaign*]

Kemp: The outlook for individuals suffering from a number of types of cancer has been totally revolutionized. I mean for example—children suffering from acute leukemia—in the old days if they lived six months they were lucky—now more than half the children with it are cured. And the same applies to a number of other cancers—Hodgkin's Disease in young people and testicular tumours in young men (Potter and Wetherell 1994: 52-3).

At this point a table showing the annual incidence of 34 types of cancer begins to scroll on the screen. The total incidence is 243 000 and the individual incidences range from placenta (20) to lung (41 400). The three forms of cancer mentioned by Kemp and their levels of incidence are highlighted in yellow: childhood leukemia (350), testis (1000), and Hodgkin's Disease (1400). The program continues while the table is scrolling.

Commentary: But those three curable types are amongst the rarest cancers—they represent around 1 per cent of a quarter of a million cases of cancers diagnosed each year. Most deaths are caused by a small number of very common cancers.

Kemp: We are well aware of the fact that [pause] once people develop lung cancer or stomach cancer or cancer of the bowel sometimes—the outlook is very bad and obviously one is frustrated by the s[low], relatively slow rate of progress on the one hand but equally I think there are a lot of real opportunities and positive signs that advances can be made—even in the more intractable cancers (Potter and Wetherell 1994: 53).

Looking for rhetorical detail   Attention to rhetorical detail entails sensitivity to the way arguments are constructed. During the editing of the film, the program-makers' discourse suggested they were looking for ways to present a convincing argument to show that cancer remains largely incurable in spite of the money spent on it. The program-makers very consciously devised the strategy outlined in the discussion of 'using variation as a lever' of playing down the numerical significance of the cancers that are amenable to treatment. Another element of their strategy was to employ a tactic that Potter *et al.* (1991) called a 'preformulation,' the discounting of a possible counterargument, as when the commentary says: 'When faced with this challenge the first thing the charities point to is the small number of cancers which are now effectively curable.'

OVERVIEW

DA draws on insights from CA, particularly when analyzing strings of talk. The CA injunction to focus on the talk itself and the ways in which intersubjective meaning is arrived at in sequences of talk is also incorporated into DA. However, DA practitioners break with their CA counterparts when they speculate on motives. It is precisely this practice of speculating on things that are not directly discernible in the sequences of talk that conversation analysts reject, as when Schegloff (1997: 183) wrote of DA: 'Discourse is too often made subservient to contexts not of its participants' making, but of its analysts' insistence.' For their part, discourse analysts object to the restrictions that CA imposes, because those restrictions cause conversation analysts to 'rarely raise their eyes from the next turn in the conversation, [which] is not an entire conversation or sizeable slice of social life but usually a tiny fragment' (Wetherell 1998: 402).

Both CA and DA practitioners dismiss the notion of a pre-existing material reality that can constrain individual behaviour. This anti-realist inclination has been a source of controversy, as the resulting lack of attention to material reality has proved to be too much for some social researchers and theorists. Writing from a **critical realist** position, Reed (2000) argued that discourses should be examined in relation to social structures, such as the power relationships that create

the discourses. Similarly, Hier (2002) described his analysis of raves as critical discourse analysis. These studies showed how discourses work through existing structures, transforming discourse from a self-referential concept in which nothing of significance exists outside itself, into a 'generative mechanism.' Thus while many DA practitioners are anti-realist, a realist position in relation to discourse is feasible. That position is perhaps closer to the classic concerns of the social sciences than an anti-realist stance.

Advantages of content analysis

Content analysis has several advantages:

- In its most quantitative form, it is a very transparent research method, making replication relatively easy. It is because of this transparency that content analysis is often said to be an 'objective' method of analysis.

- It allows for longitudinal analysis. For example, a crime study can be expanded to examine changes in newspaper crime reporting over two different time periods.

- Content analysis is an unobtrusive, non-reactive method (see Box 6.5). Newspaper articles and television scripts are generally not written with the expectation that a content analysis might one day be carried out on them. On the other hand, if the object of analysis is an interview transcript or ethnography (for example, Box 16.7), its content may have been at least partly influenced by anticipation of such scrutiny and thus may contain some reactive error.

- Content analysis is a highly flexible method, applicable to several different kinds of unstructured information. Although it is primarily applied to mass media outputs, it has a much broader applicability. Box 16.8 illustrates an unusual but still interesting application.

- Content analysis can permit the study of social groups that are difficult to access. For example, much of what social scientists know about the social backgrounds of elite groups, such as company directors and top military personnel, comes from content analyses of publications such as *Who's Who* and the business pages of newspapers.

BOX 16.7 A content analysis of qualitative research on the workplace

As we noted in Chapter 15, Hodson reported the results of a content analysis of 'book-length ethnographic studies using sustained periods of direct observation' (1996: 724). (The idea of ethnography was explored in detail in Chapter 9.) As a method, ethnography relies on long periods of participant observation to understand the culture of a social group. Hodson (1996) performed a content analysis on ethnographic studies of workplaces published in book form (articles were excluded because they rarely included sufficient detail). Thousands of case studies from around the world were assessed for possible inclusion in the sample, but in the end 86 ethnographies were selected and 106 cases analyzed (several published ethnographies studied more than one case). Each case was coded into one of five types of workplace organization: craft, direct supervision, assembly line, bureaucratic, and worker participation. That was the independent variable. Various dependent variables were also coded. Here is one of the variables and its codes:

Autonomy

1 = none (workers' tasks are completely determined by others, by machinery, or by organizational rules); 2 = little (workers occasionally have a chance to select among procedures or priorities); 3 = average (regular opportunities to select procedures or to set priorities within definite limits); 4 = high (significant latitude in determining procedures and setting priorities); 5 = very high (significant personal interpretation is needed in order for the worker to reach broadly specified goals) (Hodson 1996: 728).

Hodson's findings suggested that some negative accounts of worker participation schemes (for example, accounts claiming such schemes did not genuinely permit participation, and did not necessarily have a beneficial impact on workers) were not thorough enough in their assessment of the programs. A more detailed treatment of this research can be found in Hodson (1999).

Disadvantages of content analysis

Like all research techniques, content analysis suffers from certain limitations:

- A content analysis can only be as good as the documents it explores. Recall that Scott (1990) recommended assessing documents in terms of criteria such as authenticity (the document is what it purports to be); credibility (there are no grounds for thinking that its contents have been distorted in any way); and representativeness (the specific documents examined are representative of all possible relevant documents). These issues were explored in Chapter 7.

- Even in quantitative content analysis, it's almost impossible to devise coding manuals that do not require some interpretation by the coder. It seems unlikely that there is ever a perfect correspondence of interpretation between different coders.

- Problems of interpretation are especially likely to arise when the aim is to identify *latent* meanings (as opposed to the more readily apparent *manifest* meanings). For example, in searching for traditional markers of masculinity and femininity (see Box 16.1), the potential for conflicting interpretations is magnified. A related distinction is sometimes made between

BOX 16.8 Just burp the cover and you get a perfect seal

Vincent (2003) combined qualitative and quantitative strategies in a study of Tupperware in relation to the changing roles of women. She began with a qualitative content analysis of the available literature, including literature produced by the company itself. What image of women did the company show? A housewife who did not work outside the home and would sell Tupperware in order to earn a small amount of money? A woman so busy juggling career and family that she needed time-saving, economical Tupperware? Vincent then turned to census data to acquire macro-sociological information on women's economic roles over the previous fifty years. She concluded that Tupperware 'continues to solve the problems of preserving freshness and maintaining order in the kitchen, at the same time as it helps women mediate tensions between their domestic and income-earning roles,' adding that '[a]s long as women must contend with responsibilities in both spheres, Tupperware's success seems secure.'

mechanical analysis (in particular, counting certain words) and analysis that emphasizes themes in the text, which entails a higher level of abstraction and a correspondingly greater risk of measurement invalidity.

- Content analysis is generally not helpful in answering 'why?' questions. For example, Jagger's analysis of dating advertisements clearly showed that both men and women put less emphasis on the 'attractiveness, shape and size' they desired in a partner than they did on their own appearance (1998: 807; see Box 16.1). But further research would be needed to determine *why* this was the case. Similarly, Fenton *et al.* (1998) found that sociology was only the fourth most common discipline explicitly referred to (after psychology, economics, and social policy) when social science research was reported in the mass media, but it was by far the most frequently *inferred*

discipline (not directly mentioned, but apparently the discipline under discussion). Again, however, the reasons behind this phenomenon could only be a matter for speculation (Fenton *et al.* 1998).

- Some content analysis studies are accused of being atheoretical, and it's easy to see why. The emphasis on measurement in content analysis can easily lead researchers to focus on what is measurable rather than what is theoretically significant or important. However, content analysis is not necessarily atheoretical. Jagger (1998), for instance, placed her findings on dating advertisements in the context of current ideas about consumerism and the body. And Hodson's (1996) content analysis of workplace ethnographies (Box 16.7) was underpinned by theoretical ideas derived from research on developments in workplace organization and their impact on workers.

Key Points

- Content analysis is most often associated with the quantitative research tradition, but it can be qualitative as well.

- Although it has traditionally been applied to mass media content, it is a flexible method applicable to a wide range of phenomena.

- It's important to have clear research questions and to be explicit about what is to be analyzed.

- The design of a coding schedule and preparation of a coding manual are crucial steps in content analysis.

- Content analysis can be particularly controversial when it is used to search for latent meanings and themes.

- Semiotics and hermeneutics are qualitative approaches to content analysis.

- There is disagreement over whether readers of documents are active or passive consumers of the messages they receive.

- Both CA and DA approaches make language itself a focus of research.

- Conversation analysis is a systematic approach based on the principle that talk is structured by certain rules.

- Practitioners of CA avoid making inferences about talk that are not grounded in its immediate context.

- Discourse analysis shares many features with CA but comes in several different versions and can be applied to a wider variety of phenomena.

- DA sees discourse as a means of conveying meaning and generally relates meaning in talk to contextual factors.

- As with all research methods, there are advantages and disadvantages to content analysis.

Relevant Websites

Information on ethnomethodology and conversation analysis can be found at

http://www.paultenhave.nl/EMCA.htm

The journal *Discourse & Society*, which is an international journal that features articles on discourse analysis, can be found at this address (although you may have to go through your institution's library sever to access the material):

http://das.sagepub.com/

A YouTube video describing how to do qualitative content analysis can be found at

http://www.youtube.com/watch?v=BhQX-zKultw

An overview of the software available to do content analysis can be found at

http://www.audiencedialogue.net/soft-cont.html

A tutorial on conversation analysis is available at

http://www-staff.lboro.ac.uk/ssca1/intro1.htm

[Websites accessed on 9 September 2011]

Questions for Review

- To what kinds of documents and media can content analysis be applied?
- What is the difference between manifest and latent content? What are the implications of that distinction for content analysis?

RESEARCH QUESTIONS

- Why are precise research questions crucial in content analysis?
- What kinds of things can be counted in a content analysis?

CODING

- What is the difference between a coding schedule and a coding manual?
- What potential pitfalls need to be guarded against when devising coding schedules and manuals?

QUALITATIVE CONTENT ANALYSIS

- What is a sign? How central is it to semiotics?
- What is the difference between denotative and connotative meaning?
- What lessons can be learned from the hermeneutic approach used by Phillips and Brown (1993)?

CONVERSATION ANALYSIS

- Explain what each of the following means: turn-taking, adjacency pairs, preference organization, repair mechanism. How do they relate to the production of social order?
- Evaluate the argument that CA should examine a participant's motives.

DISCOURSE ANALYSIS

- What is the significance of saying that DA is anti-realist and constructionist?
- What are the chief differences between CA and DA?

ADVANTAGES OF CONTENT ANALYSIS

- 'One of the most significant virtues of content analysis is its flexibility, that is, that it can be applied to a wide variety of documents.' Discuss.

DISADVANTAGES OF CONTENT ANALYSIS

- To what extent does the need for coders to interpret meaning undermine latent content analysis?
- Must content analysis be atheoretical?

CHAPTER 17

Writing Up Social Research

CHAPTER OVERVIEW

One of the main tasks of any researcher, regardless of the project's size, is to report the findings. Report writing is crucial, because an audience must be persuaded that the research is credible and important. This chapter explores:

- why writing, and especially good writing, is important to social research;
- how **quantitative** and **qualitative** research are typically written up;
- the influence of **postmodernism** and its implications for writing; and
- key issues in the writing of **ethnography**, an area in which discussions about writing have been especially prominent.

As with other skills, the best way to become proficient at writing up social research is to do it as often as you can. And be patient with yourself—even the best writers edit and revise their work many times over before they consider it finished. It's also helpful to get a knowledgeable person to read your work and offer advice.

There are structural and technical requirements that vary depending on the type of work you've done, but it's equally important to pay attention to the quality of your writing as *writing*. Writing up a report shouldn't be drudgery: think of it as an art to be cultivated.

One of the best ways to become a good writer is to become a great reader. The more you read, the better you will understand the subject matter and the more familiar you will become with the structure of social science writing. In the process, you will come to recognize that some texts are better written than others and begin to absorb the techniques of good writing as if by osmosis. Becoming a collector of words also helps. Keep a good dictionary on hand (or online) while you read, and be sure to look up any word that you aren't sure you understand, even if it isn't a technical term. Finally, and perhaps most important, try to bring your enthusiasm for your work to the page. If you find it hard to get excited about a particular project, think about how it relates to some larger societal or theoretical issue, and keep that in mind as you write.

Introduction

The main purpose of this chapter is to discuss some principles of good writing that are relevant and useful to students. This is an important issue for two reasons:

- no matter how well research is conducted, readers have to be convinced that its findings are credible; good writing is *persuasive* and *convincing*, whereas flat, lifeless writing does not have the necessary power to persuade; and
- many researchers find it more difficult to write up their work than to do the research itself.

We will begin by considering whether quantitative and qualitative research studies call for different approaches to writing. Two published articles are examined to uncover some helpful features, one based on quantitative research and the other on a qualitative study. When Bryman (1998) compared qualitative and quantitative research articles, he found the differences between them to be less pronounced than the methodological literature had led him to expect. One difference he did notice, however, was that quantitative researchers often gave more detailed accounts of their research design and methods than qualitative researchers. This was surprising, because in *books*, qualitative researchers usually provide detailed accounts of these areas. Wolcott (1990) also noticed this tendency:

> Our [qualitative researchers'] failure to render full and complete disclosure about our data-gathering procedures gives our methodologically-oriented colleagues fits. And rightly so, especially for those among them willing to accept our contributions if we would only provide more careful data about our data (1990: 27).

Simply to inform readers that a study is based on a year of **participant observation** or a particular number of **semi-structured interviews** is not enough to establish credibility. On the other hand, the differences between quantitative and qualitative articles may not be as great as one might anticipate.

Writing up quantitative research: an example

To illustrate some of the characteristics of writing up quantitative research for academic journals, we will use the article by Kelley and De Graaf (1997) that was referred to in several chapters (see especially Boxes 1.3 and 3.3). 'National Context, Parental Socialization, and Religious Belief' is based on a **secondary analysis** of **survey** data on religion in 15 nations and was accepted for publication in one of the most prestigious journals in sociology—the *American Sociological Review*. The vast majority of articles published in academic journals have undergone a blind review process in which two or three peers read the draft article and then comment anonymously on it; their assessments then help the editors decide whether it is worthy of publication.

Many articles are rejected. With highly prestigious journals, that is the fate of more than 90 per cent of them. Moreover, it is unusual for an article to be accepted on its first submission. Usually, the referees will suggest areas that need revising and the author must then respond to that feedback. A revised version may then be sent back to the referees for further comment. At that point, the author will often have to revise the draft yet again. Thus an article like Kelley and De Graaf's is not just the culmination of a research process: it is also the product of a reviewer feedback process. The fact that it was accepted for publication when so many others are rejected shows that it met the standards of the journal. This does not mean that the article is perfect, but passing the refereeing process is an indication that it does possess certain crucial qualities.

The article has the following components, aside from the abstract and bibliography:

1. introduction;
2. theory;
3. data;
4. measurement;
5. methods and models;
6. results; and
7. conclusion.

INTRODUCTION

The opening four sentences of the Introduction attempt to grab the reader's attention, give a clear indication of the article's focus, and provide an indication of the likely significance of the findings. This is what the authors wrote (Kelley and De Graaf 1997: 639):

> Religion remains a central element of modern life, shaping people's world-views, moral

standards, family lives, and in many nations, their politics. But in many Western nations, modernization and secularization may be eroding Christian beliefs, with profound consequences that have intrigued sociologists since Durkheim. Yet this much touted secularization may be overstated—certainly it varies widely among nations and is absent in the United States (Benson, Donahue, and Erickson 1989: 154–7; Felling, Peters, and Schreuder 1991; Firebaugh and Harley 1991; Stark and Iannaccone 1994). We explore the degree to which religious beliefs are passed on from generation to generation in different nations.

This is an impressive start: in just over a hundred words, the authors set out both what the article is about and what its significance is. Look at what each sentence achieves:

- The first sentence presents the research as addressing an aspect of modern society that touches many people's lives.

- The second sentence notes that in many Western nations Christian belief may be eroding in response to secularization and modernization, and that this could have 'profound consequences.' At the same time, it makes the point that this topic has long been of interest to sociologists and, by mentioning Durkheim, one of sociology's most venerated figures, implicitly underlines the importance of the authors' research.

- The third sentence introduces the idea that the extent of secularization may have been exaggerated and cites several fairly recent articles in support of this proposition. In this sentence, the authors move away from the idea of social change that was the focus of the two opening sentences and indicate that the rationale for their research is primarily sociological.

- In the fourth sentence the authors establish their specific contribution to this area of study: they will explore the passing on of religious beliefs between generations in different countries.

So, in just four sentences the authors outline the contribution they propose to make and situate it within the established literature on the topic. This is quite a powerful start.

THEORY

In this section, existing ideas and research on the topic of religious socialization are presented. The authors point to the impact of parents and other people on children's religious beliefs, but then assert that 'a person's religious environment is also shaped by factors other than their own and their parents' religious beliefs, and hence is a potential cause of those beliefs . . .' (Kelley and De Graaf 1997: 641). The authors go on to argue that 'prominent among these "unchosen" aspects of one's religious environment is birthplace' (1997: 641). Their ruminations on this issue lead them to propose the **hypothesis** that contextual factors have an impact on religious beliefs. They suggest that family background has a greater impact on a person's religious beliefs in predominantly secular societies than in devout societies. In the former, they suggest, parents and other family members are more likely to isolate children from secularizing influences. In devout societies, by contrast, such insulation is less necessary and the influence of national factors greater. These hypotheses are derived directly from the research questions, which are stated in the article's Abstract: 'How much does a nation's religious environment affect the religious beliefs of its citizens? Do religious nations differ from secular nations in how beliefs are passed on from generation to generation?' (1997: 639).

DATA

In this section the authors outline the data sets they used. The sampling procedures are outlined along with **sample** sizes and response rates.

MEASUREMENT

Here Kelley and De Graaf explain how their main **concepts** are measured. The concepts are *religious belief* (for the questionnaire items see Box 3.3, p. 52); *parents' church attendance*; *secular and religious nations* (that is, the scoring procedure for indicating the degree to which a nation is religious or secular on a five-point scale); *other contextual characteristics of nations* (for example, whether or not it is a former Communist nation); and *individual characteristics* (for example, age and gender).

METHODS AND MODELS

This is a very technical section, which outlines both the different ways in which the relationships between the **variables** can be conceptualized and the implications of using different **multivariate data analysis** methods.

RESULTS

Here the authors provide a general description of their findings and then consider whether their hypotheses are supported; it turns out they are. The significance of other contextual characteristics of nations and individual differences are discussed separately.

CONCLUSIONS

In this final section, Kelley and De Graaf return to the issues that have been driving their investigation, namely those presented in the Introduction and Theory sections. They begin with a strong statement of their findings: 'The religious environment of a nation has a major impact on the beliefs of its citizens: people living in religious nations acquire, in proportion to the orthodoxy of their fellow citizens, more orthodox beliefs than those living in secular nations' (Kelley and De Graaf 1997: 654). They then reflect on the implications of the confirmation of their hypotheses for understanding the process of religious socialization and religious beliefs. They also address the ramifications of their findings for the theories about religious beliefs in modern society outlined in the Theory section:

> Our results also speak to the long-running debate about US exceptionalism (Warner 1993): They support the view that the United States is unusually religious. . . . Our results do not support Stark and Iannaccone's (1994) 'supply-side' analysis of differences between nations which argues that nations with religious monopolies have substantial unmet religious needs, while churches in religiously competitive nations like the US do a better job of meeting diverse religious needs (Kelley and De Graaf 1997: 655).

The final paragraph spells out inferences about the impact of social change on a nation's level of religious belief. The authors suggest that factors such as modernization and the growth of education depress levels of religious belief, resulting in a precipitous rather than gradual fall in levels of religiosity. In their final three sentences, they discuss societies undergoing such change:

> The offspring of devout families mostly remain devout, but the offspring of more secular families now strongly tend to be secular. A self-reinforcing spiral of secularization then sets in, shifting the nation's average religiosity ever further away from orthodoxy. So after generations of stability, religious belief declines abruptly in the course of a few generations to the modest levels seen in many Western nations (Kelley and De Graaf 1997: 656).

It may be argued that these reflections are somewhat risky, because the data from which the authors derived their findings are cross-sectional rather than longitudinal. They were clearly extrapolating from their scoring of the 15 nations in terms of levels of modernization to the impact of social change on national levels of religiosity. However, these final sentences make for a strong conclusion, which may inspire further research.

LESSONS

What lessons can be learned from Kelley and De Graaf's article?

- A strong opening statement can both grab the reader's attention and act as a signpost indicating what the article is about.

- It's important to spell out the rationale for the research (in this case, the authors point to the continued significance of religion in many societies and refer explicitly to the literature on religious beliefs and secularization).

- The research questions and any hypotheses derived from them should be clearly formulated. (As we noted in Chapter 3, not all quantitative research is driven by hypotheses.)

- The nature of the data, the measurement of concepts, the sampling, the research methods employed, and the approaches to the analysis of the data should be clearly and explicitly summarized.

- The presentation of the findings should be oriented very specifically to the research questions and their related hypotheses.

- The conclusion should return to the research hypotheses and spell out the implications of the findings both for them and for the theories cited. This is an important point: linking the findings of the study to the hypotheses and theories introduced earlier allows the authors to discuss whether the hypotheses or theories are supported, and what the implications are for further research.

There is also a clear sequential process connecting the formulation of the research hypotheses, the description of the data, the presentation of the findings, and the presentation of the conclusions. Each stage follows from its predecessor. The structure used by Kelley and De Graaf is a common one in quantitative research reported in social science journals, although sometimes a separate Discussion section is included between the Results and the Conclusion.

Writing up qualitative research: an example

Now consider an example of a journal article based on qualitative research. The article is one that has been referred to in several previous chapters (see Chapter 2 and Box 10.3): a study of vegetarianism by Beardsworth and Keil (1992). 'The Vegetarian Option: Varieties, Conversions, Motives and Careers' was based on semi-structured interviews and published in the *Sociological Review*, a leading British journal.

The structure runs as follows:

1. introduction;
2. analysis of the social dimensions of food and eating;
3. studies of vegetarianism;
4. the design of the study;
5. the findings of the study;
6. explaining contemporary vegetarianism; and
7. conclusions.

What is immediately striking about the structure is that it is fairly similar to that of Kelley and De Graaf's (1997) article. Nor should this be surprising. After all, a structure that runs

Introduction $\rightarrow$ Literature review $\rightarrow$ Research design/methods $\rightarrow$ Results $\rightarrow$ Discussion $\rightarrow$ Conclusions

is not associated with any particular research strategy. As we will see, however, the presentation and discussion of the results tend to be more interwoven in articles based on qualitative research.

INTRODUCTION

The first four sentences give an immediate sense of what the article is about:

> The purpose of this paper is to offer a contribution to the analysis of the cultural and sociological factors that influence patterns of food selection and food avoidance. The specific focus is contemporary vegetarianism, a complex of inter-related beliefs, attitudes and nutritional practices which has to date received comparatively little attention from social scientists. Vegetarians in Western cultures, in most instances, are not life-long practitioners but converts. They are individuals who have subjected more traditional foodways to critical scrutiny, and subsequently made a deliberate decision to change their eating habits, sometimes in a radical fashion (Beardsworth and Keil 1992: 253).

Like Kelley and De Graaf's, this is a strong introduction. Look at what each sentence achieves:

- The first sentence makes it clear that the research is concerned with the study of food.
- The second sentence describes the specific research focus, the study of vegetarianism, and makes a claim for attention by suggesting that this topic has been under-researched by sociologists. Interestingly, this is almost the opposite of the claim made by Kelley and De Graaf in their second sentence, in that the latter point to a line of sociological interest in religion going back to Durkheim. Both are legitimate strategies for gaining the attention of readers.
- Interest is further piqued by the idea of vegetarians as converts.
- The fourth sentence elaborates on the idea that for most people vegetarianism is a choice rather than a tradition into which they were born.

Again, just a hundred words are enough to give readers a clear idea of the focus of the research and alert them to the fact that the authors' work is a significant contribution to the literature on a subject that has not been widely studied by sociologists.

ANALYSIS OF THE SOCIAL DIMENSIONS OF FOOD AND EATING

This section's review of existing theory in the area of food serves as a backdrop to the issue of vegetarianism. Beardsworth and Keil propose that 'there exists a range of theoretical and empirical resources which can be brought to bear upon the issue of contemporary vegetarianism' (1992: 255).

STUDIES OF VEGETARIANISM

This section examines the social scientific literature on vegetarianism. The review includes opinion poll and survey data pointing to the likely proportion of vegetarians in the British population at the time of writing; debates about animal rights; a sociological analysis of vegetarian ideas; and a reference to a dated survey research study of vegetarians in the US (Dwyer *et al.* 1974).

THE DESIGN OF THE STUDY

The first sentence of this section forges a link with the preceding one: 'The themes outlined above appear to warrant further investigation, preferably in a manner which allows for a much more richly detailed examination of motivations and experiences than is apparent in the study by Dwyer *et al.*' (Beardsworth and Keil 1992: 260). This opening gambit allows the authors to suggest that the literature in this area is scant and that there are many unanswered questions. In this way they distance themselves from the one existing sociological study of vegetarians and justify their preference for qualitative research. The authors then explain

- who was studied and why;
- how respondents were recruited and the difficulties encountered with recruitment;
- the semi-structured interviewing approach and its rationale;
- the number of people interviewed and the interview context; and
- the approach to analyzing the interview transcripts, largely through identifying themes.

THE FINDINGS OF THE STUDY

The chief findings are outlined under separate headings: respondents' characteristics, types of vegetarianism, the process of conversion, motivations, nutritional beliefs, social relations, and dilemmas. For example, in the final sentence reporting findings relating to nutritional beliefs, the authors write (Beardsworth and Keil 1992: 276):

> Just as meat tended to imply strongly negative connotations for respondents, concepts like 'fruit' and 'vegetable' tended to elicit positive reactions, although less frequently and in a more muted form than might have been anticipated on the basis of the analysis of the ideological underpinnings of 'wholefoods' consumption put forward by Atkinson (1980, 1983), or on the basis of the analysis of vegetarian food symbolism advanced by Twigg (1983: 28).

EXPLAINING CONTEMPORARY VEGETARIANISM

In this section, the meaning and significance of the findings are discussed in light of the study's research questions on food selection and avoidance. The results are also related to many of the ideas encountered in the two literature sections. The authors develop an idea emerging from their research which they call 'food ambivalence.' This concept encapsulates the anxieties and paradoxes concerning food that can be discerned in the interview transcripts (for example, the idea that food can be construed simultaneously as a source of strength and energy and as a source of illness). Vegetarianism is in many respects a response to the dilemmas associated with food ambivalence.

CONCLUSIONS

In this section the authors return to many of the ideas and themes that drove their research. They spell out the significance of the idea of food ambivalence, which is probably the article's main contribution to research in this area. The final paragraph outlines the importance of food ambivalence for vegetarians, but the authors are careful not to imply that it is the sole reason for the adoption of vegetarianism. In the final sentence they write that 'for a significant segment of the population [vegetarianism] appears to represent a viable device for re-establishing some degree of peace of mind when contemplating some of the darker implications of the carefully arranged message on the dinner plate' (Beardsworth and Keil 1992: 290). The sentence neatly encapsulates one of the article's main themes—vegetarianism as a response to food ambivalence—and through the reference to 'the carefully arranged message' alludes to semiotic analyses of meat and food.

LESSONS

- What lessons can be learned from Beardsworth and Keil's article? As in Kelley and De Graaf's article, strong opening sentences attract attention and give a good indication of the nature and content of the article.

- The rationale for the research is clearly identified, a key point being the paucity of sociological investigations of vegetarianism.

- Research questions are specified but—in keeping with the general orientation of qualitative research—they are somewhat more open-ended than in Kelley and De Graaf's article. The research questions revolve around the issue of vegetarianism as a dietary choice and the motivations for that choice.

- The research design and methods are outlined. In fact they are spelled out in greater detail than is usually the case with qualitative research articles.

- The presentation and discussion of the findings are geared to the broad research questions that sparked the researchers' interest in vegetarianism. The 'explaining contemporary vegetarianism' section provides an opportunity to explore the idea of food ambivalence and its dimensions. The **inductive** nature of qualitative research means that the concepts and theories generated by an investigation must be clearly identified and discussed, as in this case.

- The conclusion elucidates in a more specific way the significance of the results for the research questions. It also explores the implications of food ambivalence for vegetarians, emphasizing one of the article's major theoretical contributions.

Postmodernism and its implications for writing

Postmodernism is an extremely difficult idea to pin down. It questions the very notion of a pre-existing external reality that can be revealed by dispassionate social scientists, and does not consider any single account of social reality to be authoritative. 'Knowledge' of the social world is relative; thus, as Rosenau (1992: 8) put it, postmodernists 'offer "readings" not "observations," "interpretations" not "findings". . . .'

For postmodernists, a report of findings in a journal article represents merely one perspective on the topics investigated, so they are interested in investigating the bases and forms of those sorts of knowledge claims. While all types of social science writing are potentially in the postmodernist's firing line, texts produced by ethnographers have been particularly frequent targets. The ethnographic text 'presumes a world out there (the real) that can be captured by a "knowing" author through the careful transcription and analysis of field materials (interviews, notes, etc.).' Postmodernists claim that such accounts are problematic because there 'can never be a final, accurate representation of what was meant or said, only different textual representations of different experiences' (Denzin 1994: 296).

However, it would be wrong to depict the growing attention given to ethnographic writing as exclusively a product of postmodernism. Atkinson and Coffey (1995) argued that other intellectual trends in the social sciences also stimulated this interest. One such trend was concerned with distinctions between rhetoric and logic and between the observer and the observed; another, with doubts about the possibility of a neutral language through which the natural and social worlds can be revealed. Atkinson and Coffey also pointed to the antipathy within feminism towards the image of the neutral 'observer-author' who assumes a privileged stance in relation to members of the social setting under investigation. This stance is regarded as one of domination by the observer-author over the observed that is inconsistent with the goals of feminism (revisit Chapter 8 for an elaboration of this general point). This concern has led to an interest in the way 'privilege' is conveyed in ethnographic texts and how voices, particularly of marginal groups, are suppressed.

The concerns in these and other traditions have led to innovations in writing ethnography (Richardson 1994). An example is the use of a 'dialogic' form of writing that seeks to raise the profile of the multiplicity of voices that can be heard in the course of fieldwork. As Lincoln and Denzin put it:

Slowly it dawns on us that there may . . . be . . . not one 'voice,' but polyvocality; not one story, but many tales, dramas, pieces of fiction, fables, memories, histories, autobiographies, poems, and other texts to inform our sense of lifeways, to extend our understandings of the Other . . . (1994: 584).

As an example of the postmodern preference for allowing a variety of voices to come through within an ethnographic text, Manning (1995) cited Stoller's (1989) research in Africa. Manning (1995: 260) described the text as a dialogue, not a monologue by the ethnographer, one 'shaped by interactions between informants or "the other" and the observer.' This postmodern preference for seeking out multiple voices and turning the ethnographer into a 'bit player' reflects postmodernists' mistrust of 'meta-narratives,' that is, positions or grand accounts that implicitly question the possibility of alternative versions of reality. By contrast, 'mini-narratives, micro-narratives, local narratives are just stories that make no truth claims and are therefore more acceptable to postmodernists' (Rosenau 1992: xiii).

Postmodernism has also encouraged a growing **reflexivity** about the conduct of social research, and the growing interest in the writing of

ethnography is very much a manifestation of this trend (see Box 17.1). Reflexivity can be discerned in the way ethnographers turn inwards to examine the truth claims inscribed in their own classic texts (the focus of our next section).

In the end, postmodernism produces an acute sense of uncertainty. In questioning how one can ever know or capture a social reality that belongs to another, it points to an unresolvable tension that affects ethnographic work in particular. To quote Lincoln and Denzin (1994: 582) again: 'On the one hand there is the concern for validity, or certainty in the text as a form of . . . authenticity. On the other hand there is the sure and certain knowledge that all texts are socially, historically, politically, and culturally located. Researchers, like the texts they write, can never be transcendent.'

Writing up ethnography

The term 'ethnography,' as we noted in Chapter 9, refers to both a method of social research and the finished product of that research. In recent years, the production of ethnographic texts has become a focus of interest in its own right, particularly the rhetorical conventions employed in their production.

Ethnographic texts are designed to convince readers of the *reality* of the events and situations described, and the plausibility of the analyst's

---

BOX 17.1	What is reflexivity?

Reflexivity has a number of meanings in social science. To ethnomethodologists it refers to the fact that speech and action do more than merely act as indicators of deeper phenomena (see Chapter 16). Another meaning of the term carries the connotation that social researchers should reflect on the implications that their methods, values, biases, and decisions have for the knowledge of the social world that they generate. Reflexivity entails sensitivity to the researcher's cultural, political, and social context. Thus 'knowledge' generated from a reflexive position is always a reflection of a researcher's location in time and social space. This notion is the basis of Pink's (2001) formulation of a reflexive approach to the use of visual images (see Chapter 9).

There has been a growing trend towards reflexivity in social research, documented in books that collect

details on the inner workings of the actual research process as distinct from the often sanitized versions presented in research articles (for example, Bryman 1988). The confessional tales referred to in Box 17.2 are manifestations of this development. However, the rise of reflexivity largely predates the growth of postmodern thinking. What distinguishes the reflexivity that has followed in the wake of postmodernism is a greater acknowledgment of the role that the researcher plays in the construction of knowledge. A researcher is not just someone who extracts knowledge from observations and conversations with others and then transmits that knowledge to an audience. Rather, the researcher is seen as implicated in the construction of knowledge both through the observer stance assumed in relation to the observed, and through the ways in which an account is transmitted in the form of a written text.

explanations. The ethnographic text does not simply present a set of findings: it endeavours to provide an 'authoritative' account, with strong claims to truth, of the group or culture in question. Stylistic and rhetorical devices are used to persuade the reader to enter into a shared framework of facts, interpretations, observations, and reflections. Ethnographic writing, like the writing found in reports of quantitative social research, is typically **realist** in orientation: the researcher tries to present an authoritative, dispassionate account of an external, objective reality. In this respect, there is very little difference between the writing styles of quantitative and qualitative researchers. Van Maanen (1988) described ethnography texts that conform to this model (one of three he identified; see Box 17.2) as *realist tales*. This is the most common form of ethnographic writing, though its realism can take different forms. Van Maanen distinguished four characteristics of realist tales: experiential authority, typical forms, the subject's point of view, and interpretive omnipotence.

EXPERIENTIAL AUTHORITY

In ethnography, as in much quantitative research writing, the author disappears from view. Readers are told what the members of a group—the only people directly visible in the text—say and do. An invisible author provides the narrative, giving the impression that the findings presented are what any reasonable, similarly placed researcher would have found. Readers have to accept that this is what the ethnographer experienced. This strategy essentially plays down the risk that the findings will be suspected of bias arising from the personal subjectivity of the author/ethnographer (for example, suspicion that, as a fieldworker, he or she might have become too involved with the people under study). To this end, when writing up their ethnographic work, authors play up their academic credentials and qualifications, their previous experience, and so on. All this enhances the impression that they are reliable witnesses.

Another way in which authors often seek to underline their experiential authority is by emphasizing the intensity of their research work: they spent so many months in the field, interviewed countless individuals, worked hard to establish rapport, and so on. Drawing the reader's attention to the hardships of the fieldwork—the dangerous setting, the poor food, the disruptive effect on normal life, the feelings of isolation and loneliness, and so on—creates sympathy for the author or (less charitably) deflects potential criticism of the findings.

Also worth mentioning are the extensive quotations from conversations and interviews that invariably form part of the ethnographic report. These quotations serve not only as evidence in support of the author's findings, but also to establish the credibility of the report in that they

---

BOX 17.2   Three forms of ethnographic writing

Van Maanen (1988) distinguished three major types of ethnographic writing:

- *Realist tales*: apparently definitive, confident, and dispassionate third-person accounts of a culture and the behaviour of its members. This is the most prevalent form of ethnographic writing.

- *Confessional tales*: personalized accounts in which the ethnographer is fully implicated in the data-gathering and writing-up processes. These are warts-and-all accounts of the trials and tribulations of doing ethnography. They have become more prominent since the 1970s and reflect a growing emphasis on reflexivity in qualitative research. Several of the sources referred to in Chapter 10 are confessional tales (for example, Armstrong 1993; Giulianotti 1995). However,

confessional tales are less concerned with presenting findings than with detailing how research is carried out. Very often the confessional tale is published separately from the project's findings: for example, it may appear as a chapter in a book of similar tales, while the main findings are written up in realist tale form.

- *Impressionist tales*: accounts that feature 'words, metaphors, phrasings, and . . . the expansive recall of fieldwork experience' (1988: 102). There is an emphasis on stories of dramatic events that provide 'a representational means of cracking open the culture and the fieldworker's way of knowing it' (1988: 102). However, as Van Maanen noted, impressionist tales 'are typically enclosed within realist, or perhaps more frequently, confessional tales' (1988: 106).

demonstrate the author's ability to engage people in talk. Copious descriptive details—of places, patterns of behaviour, contexts, and so on—suggest that the author was ideally placed to bear witness to the people and activities described in the study.

TYPICAL FORMS

Authors will often generalize about recurring features of the group under study in order to illustrate a typical behaviour or thought pattern. Examples based on particular incidents or people may be used, but basically the emphasis is on recurrent forms of behaviour. For example, in her conclusion to her ethnographic research on female drug users, cited several times in Chapter 9, Taylor wrote:

> Yet the control exercised over women through the threat to remove their children highlights a major factor differentiating female and male drug users. Unlike male drug users, female drug users, like many other women, have two careers: one in the public sphere and one in the private, domestic sphere' (1993: 154).

This statement portrays a pattern among women drug users, making any individual woman important only insofar as she can be seen as illustrating the general tendency.

THE SUBJECTS' POINTS OF VIEW

A commitment to seeing through the eyes of their subjects is important for qualitative researchers because it is part of their strategy for getting at the meaning of those people's social reality. However, it is also helps to establish the authority of the ethnographer. Claiming to have taken the subjects' points of view implies that the author can speak authoritatively about the group in question. Ethnographies frequently include numerous references to the steps taken by the ethnographer to get close to the people under investigation, and their success in that regard. In her research on female drug users, Taylor (1993: 16) wrote:

> Events I witnessed or took part in ranged from the very routine (sitting around drinking coffee and eating junk food) to accompanying various women on visits to . . . the HIV clinic; I accompanied

them when they were in court, and even went flat-hunting with one woman. I went shopping with some, helping them choose clothes for their children and presents for their friends. I visited them in their homes, rehabilitation centres, and maternity wards, sat with them through withdrawals, watched them using drugs, and accompanied them when they went 'scoring' (buying drugs).

INTERPRETATIVE OMNIPOTENCE

When writing ethnography, authors rarely suggest alternative interpretations of an event or pattern of behaviour. Instead, they tend to portray the phenomenon in question as having a single meaning or significance, which only they have been able to identify. The evidence is carefully marshalled to support the singular interpretation placed on the event or pattern of behaviour. It seems obvious or inevitable that anyone would draw the same inferences the author drew when faced with such evidence.

The above characteristics imply that the research process is only the first stage in the creation of a convincing realist tale. Persuading readers that one has in fact figured out the nature of a different culture also requires that the written ethnography *represent* the fieldwork in an effective way. Recall that for postmodernists, any realist tale is merely one 'spin'—one interpretation that has been formulated in relation to the culture in question.

Bibliography

No one likes to write bibliographic entries. That is why most bibliographies contain an error or two. The problem with errors is that they indicate a lack of attention on the author's part. Here is a bibliography taken from an earlier version of this text with errors deliberately added. Look over all the entries to familiarize yourself with the form they take, and then see how many errors you can find. Errors in bibliographic entries will not stop true scholars from finding your source, but they will slow them down. The answers are at the end of the next chapter (p. 334).

Abraham, J. (1994), 'Bias in Science and Medical Knowledge: The Opren controversy,' *Sociology*, 28: 717–36.

Armstrong, D, Gosling, A., Weinman, J., and Marteau, T. (1997), 'The Place of Inter-Rater

Reliability in Qualitative Research: an Empirical Study,' *Sociology*, 31: 597-606

Atkinson, R. (1998), *The Life Story Interview* (Thousand Oaks, CA: Sage).

Barnard, M., and Frischer, M. (1995), 'Combining Quantitative and Qualitative Approaches: Researching HIV-Related Risk Behaviours among Drug Injectors', *Addiction Research*, 351–62.

Barter, C., and E. Renold (1999) 'The Use of Vignettes in Qualitative Research,' *Social Research Update*, 25.

Blaikie, A. (2001), 'Photographs in the Cultural Account: Contested Narratives and Collective Memory in the Scottish Islands,' *Sociological Review*, 49- 345–67.

Buchanan, D. R. (1992), 'An Uneasy Alliance: Combining Qualitative And Quantitative Research Methods,' *Health Education Quarterly*, *19*: 117–35.

Charmaz, K., (2000), 'Grounded Theory: Objectivist and Constructivist Methods,' in Denzin, N.K. and Lincoln, Y.S. (eds.), *Handbook of Qualitative Research*, 2nd ed. (Thousand Oaks, CA: Sage).

B. Czarniawska. (1998), *A Narrative Approach to Organization Studies* (Thousand Oaks, XA: Sage).

Giulianotti, R. (1995), 'Participant Observation and Research into Football Hooliganism: Reflections on the Problems of Entrée and Everyday Risks,' *Sociology of Sport Journal*, 12: 1–20.

Reinharz, S, 1992, *Feminist Methods in Social Research* (New York).

Okely, J. (1994), 'Thinking through Fieldwork, in A. Bryman and R G. Burgess (eds.), *Analyzing Qualitative Data* (London: Routledge).

Sheehan, K. (2001), 'E-Mail survey response rates: A review,' *Journal of Computer-Mediated Communication*, 6. www.ascusc.org/jcmc/vol6/issue2/sheehan.html.

DO NOT ALPHABETIZE the authors' names in items with multiple authors. The existing order reflects their choice, or at least the choice of the most powerful one in the group. (The first author listed is generally considered to be the lead author; the remaining ones are presented in descending order of importance.) What ethical issues arise in determining authorship order? Some online bibliographies include only the first author, as does part of the *Social Science Citation Index*.

Practical TIP ▶▶▶▶

Referring to websites

It is a common practice in academic work when referring to a website to include the date when it was last consulted. This convention has arisen because a subsequent researcher, perhaps wanting to follow up some findings, may find that the website is no longer there or that it has changed.

Key Points

- Good writing is probably just as important as good research practice. Indeed, it should probably be considered part of good research practice.

- In writing up research, a clear statement of the research questions and an effective structure for the report are essential.

- The writings of social scientists are designed to do more than simply report findings; they must also convince and persuade.

- Our emphasis on the importance of writing to convince and persuade is not meant to imply that there is no external social reality. It is intended merely to point out that readers' understanding of that reality is profoundly influenced by the way the writer represents it.

- While postmodernism in particular has promoted recognition of this last point, writers working within other traditions have also drawn attention to it.

- Quantitative and qualitative research articles are broadly similar in structure, as are the rhetorical devices used to produce them.

Relevant Websites

This website provides commentary and tips on writing up a research project in sociology, political science and economics:

http://www.ssric.org/node/144

Advice on writing up a qualitative study can be found at:

http://www.psy.dmu.ac.uk/michael/qual_writing.htm

General tips on writing papers for university courses is found at:

http://www.youtube.com/watch?v=jtP5Or78 g9k&feature=related

This video outlines how to organize your activities when starting the research for a paper for a university course, and how to write things up as you go along:

http://www.youtube.com/ watch?v=BuJLRjd9vAc&NR=1

If you found the above video helpful, you may want to look at the next one in the series as well: it outlines how to read articles and books when preparing a paper for a university course:

http://www.youtube.com/watch?v=HgwAmr SQZLo&feature=relmfu

[Websites accessed on 11 September 2011]

Questions for Review

- Why is it important to think about the ways in which social research is written up?

WRITING UP QUANTITATIVE RESEARCH: AN EXAMPLE

- Read an article based on quantitative research in a Canadian sociology journal (such as the *Canadian Journal of Sociology* or the *Canadian Review of Sociology*). To what extent does it exhibit the characteristics identified in Kelley and De Graaf's (1997) article?

- Why are strategies to convince and persuade important in writing up quantitative social research?

WRITING UP QUALITATIVE RESEARCH: AN EXAMPLE

- Read an article based on qualitative research in a Canadian sociology journal. To what extent does it exhibit the characteristics identified in Beardsworth and Keil's (1992) article?

- How does the structure of Beardsworth and Keil's article differ from that of Kelley and De Graaf's piece?

POSTMODERNISM AND ITS IMPLICATIONS FOR WRITING

- Why has postmodernism stimulated interest in the writing-up of social research?
- What is reflexivity?

WRITING UP ETHNOGRAPHY

- Is it true that ethnographic writing is typically oriented towards realism? Explain.
- The realist tale is one form of ethnographic writing. What other forms can such writing take?
- What are the main characteristics of the realist tale?

CHAPTER 18

Conducting a Research Project

CHAPTER OVERVIEW

The goal of this chapter is to guide you through a small-scale research project from beginning to end. The guidance offered goes beyond the discussions presented in previous chapters. A wide variety of issues is explored, including:

- time management when doing research;
- generating research questions;
- dealing with existing literature on your subject; and
- writing a compelling account of your findings.

When one of the authors of this book was a graduate student and had his first meeting with his dissertation advisor, the advisor listened to his research proposal, offered a few suggestions, and then said, somewhat acerbically, 'Just *do* it!' (This was years before that phrase became a marketing slogan.)

Those three words contain a lot of wisdom. It's easy to overthink things and waste time worrying that your plans aren't worthwhile or that you're not up to the task. You should always plan your research carefully, whether it be for a small class project, a term paper, or a graduate thesis or dissertation. But don't wait for the perfect time to start. Imagine you're at work and your boss has given you an unbreakable deadline. You'll find that once you get absorbed in the task, your inspiration and motivation will pick up even if they were minimal when you began. It also helps if you think of the project as a series of small jobs rather than one monumental undertaking.

The same goes for the writing. Try to write something related to the project—*anything*—every day. And for your first draft, allow yourself to be sloppy. Don't worry about finding the perfect word or crafting the perfect sentence or ensuring that the logic flows perfectly. Those issues can be dealt with later, at the editing stage. When Michael Jackson was asked about how he wrote his songs, he replied, 'Don't get in the way of the music.' That advice applies to writing too: don't get in the way of the words. Just let them flow. Write first and evaluate later. Just do it.

Introduction

This chapter provides some advice for those readers carrying out their own small-scale research projects. The previous 17 chapters have provided helpful information about the choices available and how to implement them. Here we will examine how you can use that knowledge to conduct a small project of your own, such as an honour's thesis or a course assignment. Students in graduate programs will also find some of the observations helpful. Finally, the advice is tailored for students engaged in empirical research, that is, studies in which they either collect new data or conduct analyses of existing data.

Know what is expected by your institution

Quite often a course instructor will have specific guidelines and requirements for class projects. Look them over carefully and follow them. People doing undergraduate theses or those in graduate programs should be aware that their institution or department may have specific requirements concerning everything from binding and page margins to the format for referencing, the inclusion of an abstract, the structure of the presentation, plagiarism, and deadlines.

IDENTIFYING RESEARCH QUESTIONS

Most students want to conduct research in areas of personal interest. This is not a bad thing; as we noted in Chapter 1, many professional social researchers want to do the same thing (see also Lofland and Lofland 1995: 11–14). However, even open-ended qualitative research must begin with the formulation of research questions. Although Chapter 9 referred to some studies that were not driven by specific research questions, open-ended research is risky. It can lead to the collection of data that will never be used, and to serious problems in data organization and analysis. The lack of focus can also cause the project to take too long or even to be abandoned. So, unless your supervisor or instructor advises you to the contrary, you need to formulate some research questions that are not completely open-ended. What is it about your area of interest that you want to know?

Research questions are important because they provide a focus that will:

- guide the literature search;
- limit the scope of the project (see Figure 18.1);
- guide decisions about what data to collect;
- guide the analysis of data;
- guide the writing-up of the findings; and
- reduce the risk of going off on unnecessary tangents.

Research questions should exhibit the following characteristics:

- They should be clear.
- They should be researchable. This means that they cannot be formulated in terms so abstract that they cannot be investigated. Nor should they be so grand in scope that it would be impossible to answer them in the time available.
- They should have some connection with established theory and research. Linking your questions to an existing literature will help illuminate how they should be approached and how they relate to the larger discipline. Even if your topic has not been directly addressed by social scientists, there will be relevant material available on related or parallel topics.
- If you have more than one research question (which is very common), they should be linked to each other so an argument can be developed in the paper. To construct a coherent argument from unrelated research questions is almost impossible, even for experienced researchers.
- They should hold out the prospect of making an original contribution—however small—to the knowledge on the topic.

If you're unsure of how to formulate research questions (or any other phase of the research process), look at journal articles or research monographs to see what others have done. Look at past student papers for ideas as well. Talk things over with your advisor or course instructor. Gary Marx (1997) suggested a wide range of sources for research questions (see Box 18.1).

Using a supervisor

Most institutions will assign a student writing a thesis or dissertation to a supervisor or advisor. However, the kind and amount of assistance you can expect varies greatly. Of course, students also

Research area

(Example: Concerns about risks to personal safety)

⇓

Select aspect of research area

(Causes of the variations in concerns about risks to personal safety)

⇓

Possible research questions

(What personal safety risks are of greatest concern to people? Do age, gender, social class, or education affect the perception of risk? Do parents worry more than non-parents about risks to personal safety? What is the main source of people's knowledge about issues relating to such risk—newspapers, television, family? Do concerns about these risks have an impact on how people conduct their daily lives, and if so in what ways? Do worries about personal safety result in fatalism?)

⇓

Select research questions

(What personal safety risks are of greatest concern to people? Do age, gender, social class, or education affect the perception of risk? Do parents worry more than non-parents about risks to personal safety? Why?)

FIGURE 18.1 Steps in selecting research questions

vary in what they ask of their advisors. Our advice here is simple: use supervisors or advisors to the fullest extent allowable and give due consideration to their suggestions. Such people are usually well versed in the research process and can provide help and feedback at all stages of the project, subject to your institution's strictures in this regard. If they criticize your research questions, interview schedule, early drafts, or whatever, try to respond positively. Criticism isn't a personal attack. Such comments are usually accompanied by the reasons for them and some suggestions for revision. Be thankful for the opportunity to address problems *before* your work is formally examined. Supervisors have to go through the same process themselves whenever they apply for a research grant or submit an article to a peer-refereed journal.

Students who get stuck or fall behind in their work will sometimes avoid their supervisors. But the longer they wait, the harder it is to ask for help. Then, because the work has been put off, it has to be rushed at the end, and in some cases is never completed. Try to avoid this situation by confronting any difficulties head-on and getting advice on how to deal with them as soon as possible.

Undergraduate students doing course projects should follow the same basic advice. Consult your course instructor if you run into difficulties, and the sooner the better. Even if there are no apparent problems, it's always worthwhile to discuss your research with your instructor, who may pick up on issues that you have missed.

Managing time and resources: start thinking early about the research area

Students are usually asked to start thinking about a potential research topic well before they are expected to start work on the project. That thinking is worth doing, because all research is constrained by time. Two pieces of advice are relevant here:

- Work out a timetable, preferably with your supervisor or instructor, detailing the different stages of the research (including the literature review and the writing up). The timetable should specify the different stages and the specific dates for starting and finishing them (see Figure 18.2 for an example of a quantitative research outline). Some stages are likely to be ongoing—for example, searching the literature

BOX 18.1 | Marx's (not Karl) sources of research questions

What types of research question could emerge from a close investigation of new media technologies and social networking websites?

Marx (1997) suggested the following possible sources of research questions:

- Intellectual puzzles and contradictions;
- The existing literature;
- Replication;
- A feeling that a certain theoretical perspective or notable piece of work is misguided (in this case you would explore the reasons for the shortcomings).

- A social problem in need of a social scientific (for example, sociological) explanation.
- 'Gaps between official versions of reality and the facts on the ground' (1997: 113). Examine the standard explanations offered by governments, the media, or social researchers for social phenomena such as poverty, substance abuse, international conflict, or anything else of interest. Are those explanations consistent with what you know or have experienced? If not, develop some research questions pertaining to the phenomenon in question, including questions about the validity of the conventional wisdom on the topic.
- The counterintuitive; for example, cases in which social scientific truths seem to fly in the face of common sense, as they did when a doomsday cult began to proselytize rather than slink away in embarrassment when 'doomsday' passed and life carried on as usual (Festinger et al., 1956)
- '[E]mpirical examples that trigger amazement' (1997: 114); for example, atypical events, cases that contradict widely accepted theories, etc.
- New methods and theories. How can they be applied in new settings?
- 'New social and technical developments and social trends' (1997: 114).

for references (see below)—but that should not delay the development of a timetable.

- Find out what resources, if any, are available for carrying out your research. For example, can your institution help with the cost of photocopying, postage, stationery, and so on? Can it lend you hardware to record and transcribe interviews? Does it have the necessary software, such as SPSS or NVivo? This kind of information will help you decide whether your research design and methods are financially feasible and practical. The fictional 'gym study' in Chapter 12 is an example of a project feasible within the kind of time frame usually allocated to undergraduate projects. However, it would require resources for photocopying covering letters and questionnaires; postage both for sending the questionnaires out and for follow-up letters; and return postage for the questionnaires.

In addition, quantitative data analysis would require software such as SPSS.

Searching the existing literature

Online bibliographical databases (accessible at most university libraries) are an invaluable source of references. The best one for students is probably *Sociological Abstracts*. It allows searches by keyword (topic), author, title, journal, and other descriptors. The focus is easily narrowed by specifying language, year, and type of presentation. For example, 'English, post-2005, journal articles only' can be searched and listed from latest to earliest. The 'journal articles only' restriction removes papers presented at meetings and dissertations, which are too hard for most students to access in any event. Searches can be conducted using keywords in different combinations with the Boolean operators 'and,' 'or,' and 'not.' Thus a search for material on 'sexism and universities' will produce

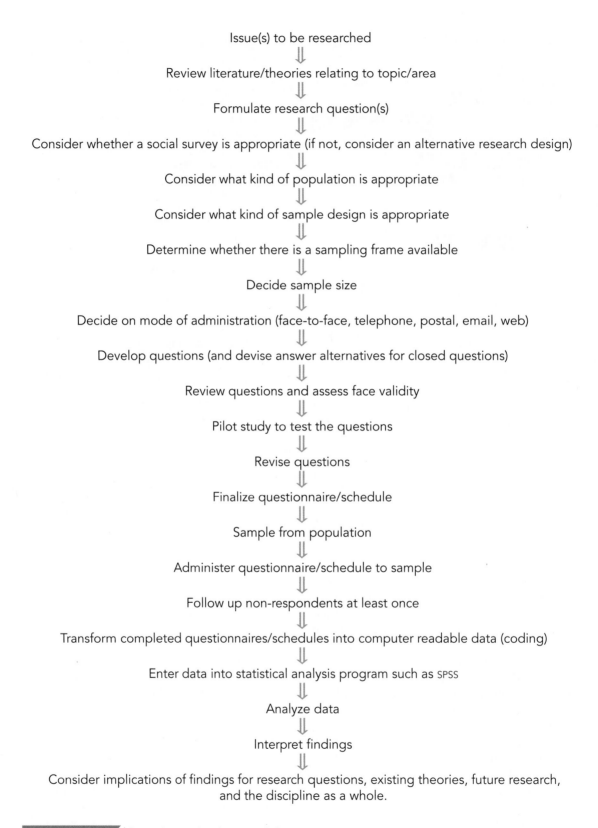

Issue(s) to be researched
⇓
Review literature/theories relating to topic/area
⇓
Formulate research question(s)
⇓
Consider whether a social survey is appropriate (if not, consider an alternative research design)
⇓
Consider what kind of population is appropriate
⇓
Consider what kind of sample design is appropriate
⇓
Determine whether there is a sampling frame available
⇓
Decide sample size
⇓
Decide on mode of administration (face-to-face, telephone, postal, email, web)
⇓
Develop questions (and devise answer alternatives for closed questions)
⇓
Review questions and assess face validity
⇓
Pilot study to test the questions
⇓
Revise questions
⇓
Finalize questionnaire/schedule
⇓
Sample from population
⇓
Administer questionnaire/schedule to sample
⇓
Follow up non-respondents at least once
⇓
Transform completed questionnaires/schedules into computer readable data (coding)
⇓
Enter data into statistical analysis program such as SPSS
⇓
Analyze data
⇓
Interpret findings
⇓
Consider implications of findings for research questions, existing theories, future research, and the discipline as a whole.

FIGURE 18.2 Steps in conducting a social survey

articles that deal with both topics in the same piece. Choosing 'sexism or universities' will produce those articles plus articles on each one alone. That is probably not a good choice—it's too broad. 'Universities and sexism or prejudice' is better because it expands the first option above to cover university prejudice in addition to university sexism. Finally, 'not' restricts the search. 'Sexism not universities' will find articles about sexism in places other than universities. You can experiment with the use of keywords and Boolean options; if you don't find what you need, ask a librarian for help.

Following these procedures will produce a list of journal articles in which the keyword(s) appears, with full citation details and an abstract. Other indices are more specialized: examples include the *Canadian Periodicals Index Quarterly* (formerly the *Canadian Periodical Index*) and the *Population Index*, as well as collections of abstracts, such as *Sage Race Relations Abstracts* and *Women Studies Abstracts*. (The *Readers' Guide to Periodical Literature* covers more popular pieces of the kind that appear in magazines, so it is generally not useful for finding academic research.) Mark the records you want and email them to yourself for a permanent record. The bibliographies in the articles you find can provide additional sources to examine.

A particularly interesting tool is the *Social Sciences Citation Index*, which looks forward from the original article to later ones that cite it, revealing what others have thought of it. Perhaps some who cited the article were critical; perhaps others accepted or expanded on it. In this way a history of the research in the area of interest can be built up. To some professors, this index provides a measure of how often they have been cited. To those granting tenure and raises, it can be a crude indicator of merit, following the logic of 'more citations, better researcher.'

The library catalogue is an obvious tool for finding books, even those held at other universities. Again, ask a librarian if you run into difficulty. However, since books are often dated, checked out, or too specialized for student papers, the above sources may be preferable. The rule of thumb is similar to the idea of theoretical saturation in qualitative research: stop searching when the same items keep appearing.

Why review the existing literature? The most obvious reason is to find out what is already known about your area of interest, in order to avoid 'reinventing the wheel.' In addition, the process of reviewing the literature will help you revise and refine your research questions. Beyond this, the existing literature on your topic will help you develop an argument regarding the significance of your research and where it will lead. The metaphor of a *story* is sometimes used in this context (see below). A competent review of the literature will help to establish your credibility as someone knowledgeable in your chosen area.

As you explore the existing literature, look for answers to the following questions:

- What is already known about this area?
- What concepts and theories are relevant?
- What research methods and strategies have been employed in studying this area?
- Are there any significant controversies?
- Are there any inconsistencies in the findings relating to this area?
- Are there any unanswered research questions?

While reading, take good notes, and be sure to record full citations for all the materials you consult. It's infuriating to find that you've forgotten some detail, such as the volume number of an article, when you come to assemble your bibliography. Also keep in mind that your written review of the literature should be critical as well as descriptive. How does a particular article relate to others you have read? Does it contradict them? Are there any apparent strengths or deficiencies—for example, in the methods used or the conclusions drawn? What theoretical ideas influenced the author(s)?

In some areas of research you will find huge numbers of references. Try to identify the major ones and work outwards from there. Move on to the next stage of the research at the point you identified in your timetable (see above) so that you can dig yourself out of the library. This is not to say that your literature search will cease: only that you need to force yourself to move on. Ask your supervisor or instructor for advice on whether you need to extend your search of the literature.

Preparing for research

In choosing a methodology you need to consider its ethical implications and what you will do to prevent any potential ethical violations. Keep in mind the various ethical issues discussed in

Chapter 11 and flagged throughout this book (see also Box 18.2).

Don't begin collecting data until you have clearly identified your research questions, and design your data collection instruments with those questions in mind. If at all possible, conduct a small pilot study to see how well your research instruments work. You will also need to think about access to research sites. If the research requires entry to a closed setting such as an organization, you need to get permission at the earliest opportunity. This usually takes so long that many advisors do not recommend using closed settings for student research. You also need to consider how you will go about gaining access to people. This issue leads you into sampling considerations, such as the following:

- Whom do you need to study in order to answer the research questions?

- Is an adequate sampling frame available?

- What kind of sampling strategy is feasible—probability, quota, theoretical, convenience?

Doing research and analyzing results

This is what the bulk of this book has been about. Here are some practical reminders:

Practical Tip ▶ ▶ ▶ ▶

Reasons for writing a literature review

The following are reasons for writing a literature review:

1. To find out what is already known in a research area, and what remains to be researched.

2. To learn from other researchers' mistakes.

3. To learn about different theoretical and methodological approaches to the research area.

4. To get help in developing an analytic framework.

5. To find additional variables to include in the research.

6. To search for further research questions.

7. To view examples of how findings can be interpreted.

8. To compare and contrast your findings with those of other researchers.

9. It's expected.

BOX 18.2 : Ethical approval for student work

By this point you will be aware of many of the ethical issues involved in doing social research. Schools usually hold supervisors or instructors responsible for preventing unethical practices on the part of students. Still, teachers have limited time to oversee students' work, and situations may arise in the field that require quick decisions. In the end the project is yours, and so is the ethical responsibility.

The following are examples of tricky ethical issues taken from actual research. To refresh your memory, see if you can identify the ethical dilemma in each case and explain how it can be avoided or resolved.

- You are supposed to interview Ms Jones. Her mother answers the door and asks to be interviewed. She is lonely, so you interview her and then throw the data away; later you interview Ms Jones.

- Introductory psychology students are invited to participate in two experiments during the year. They are told that participation is optional, but that those not taking part have to write a five-page paper.

- To reduce lying, the question 'Have you ever masturbated?' is rephrased as 'At what age did you begin masturbating?'

- To determine whether the answers given in an interview are truthful, some questions may be repeated with slightly different wording. In one variation, respondents are asked about reading books or seeing movies that do not exist.

- Respondents are told that the questionnaires they are answering are anonymous, but in fact each questionnaire has been marked with a unique series of pinholes in the last page, in order to keep track of non-respondents needing a reminder. This will save a lot of time and money.

- After a three-hour interview, the respondent asks that her case not be used and that all the information she has provided be destroyed.

- Keep good records. A research diary can be helpful, but there are several other points to bear in mind. For example, in a mailed questionnaire survey, you need to keep track of who has replied so you know who needs a reminder. If participant observation is a component of the research, it's imperative to keep good field notes: to rely on memory is a serious mistake.

- Practise operating any hardware that you will be using (such as tape recorders for interviewing) and make sure it is in good working order, with fresh batteries and extras on hand, just in case.

- Don't wait until all your data have been collected to begin **coding**. This recommendation applies to both quantitative and qualitative research. If you're using a questionnaire, begin coding data and entering them into a software package such as SPSS as soon as you have a reasonable number of completed questionnaires. In the case of qualitative data, such as interview transcripts, the same advice applies; according to the grounded theory approach, data collection and data analysis should be intertwined.

- Remember that it takes a long time to transcribe even one recorded interview. Allow at least six hours of transcription for every one hour of recorded talk, at least in the early stages of the research.

- Become familiar with any software packages you will need as early as possible.

- Never put your personal safety at risk when doing research (see Box 18.3).

Writing up research

Once the data gathering and analysis have been completed, the findings must be conveyed to an audience. The first bit of advice is to . . .

START EARLY

There are good reasons for beginning the writing process early on. It forces you to think about issues such as how best to present and justify the research questions, and how to structure the discussion of the literature cited. A second reason is entirely practical: many people find it difficult to get started and tend (often unwittingly) to use

---

BOX 18.3   Safety in research

In 2002, a 19-year-old British female sociology student was supposed to interview a homeless person in Manchester. Because of safety concerns, her advisor recommended that she take a friend with her and conduct the interview in a public place. When she did not return, she was reported missing (Barkham and Jenkins 2002). Four days later she showed up in Dublin, where she claimed to have fled after the man robbed her; however, it was later suggested that her disappearance might in fact have been sparked by a family argument.

Whether or not her story was true, there is an important lesson in it: social research can place you in potentially dangerous situations. Avoid situations where personal harm is a real possibility. Just as you should ensure that no harm comes to research participants (as prescribed in the discussion of ethical principles in Chapter 11), individuals conducting research should not place themselves in unsafe situations. The advice given by the student's advisor—to take someone with you and conduct the interview in a public place—is sensible. If you have a cell phone, keep it nearby and switched on. Establish a routine whereby you keep in regular contact

with friends or family members. Even in seemingly safe situations, a researcher can be faced with a sudden outburst of abuse or threatening behaviour; you can't always predict how people will react to a particular trigger, such as an interview question. If there are signs that trouble is imminent (for example, through body language), withdraw from the situation. Further guidelines on these issues can be found in Craig (2004).

Lee (2004) drew an important distinction between two kinds of danger in fieldwork: ambient and situational. 'Ambient danger' refers to situations in which danger is endemic to the context. Fieldwork in conflict situations of the kind encountered by the researcher who took on the role of a bouncer (Winlow *et al.* 2001) is an example. 'Situational danger' occurs when a researcher attracts aggression, hostility, or violence from particular participants in an otherwise safe setting (Lee 2004). It is more difficult to foresee than ambient danger.

Other possible hazards can be even less obvious. For instance, it was only after she began her research in a hospital laboratory that Lankshear (2000) realized that the project could expose her to dangerous pathogens.

procrastination strategies. But putting off the inevitable almost always results in rushed, last-minute writing. Writing under that kind of pressure is not ideal, to say the least. How you present your findings and conclusions is a crucial aspect of the research process, and if you fail to produce a convincing account of your findings because of time pressures, you will not do your work justice.

BE PERSUASIVE

This point is crucial. Writing up research does not mean mechanically reporting findings and drawing conclusions. Above all, the writing must be *persuasive* in order to convince readers that your conclusions are credible. To comment that a particular finding is 'interesting' is not enough. Readers must be convinced that your findings and conclusions are both plausible and significant.

GET FEEDBACK

Try to get as much feedback on your writing as possible, and respond positively to whatever comments you receive. Your supervisor or instructor is likely to be the main source of feedback; show as many drafts of your work as regulations allow, leaving plenty of time for a response. You will not be the only student seeking advice, and if comments are rushed, they may not be particularly helpful. You can also ask others in your program or class to read your drafts and comment on them, and they may ask you to do the same. Their comments may be very useful, but those from your supervisor or instructor are likely to be the most valuable.

AVOID SEXIST, RACIST, AND OTHER PREJUDICIAL LANGUAGE

Remember that writing should be free of sexist, racist, and other prejudicial language. The Social Sciences and Humanities Research Council of Canada publication *On the Treatment of the Sexes in Research* (1985) by M. Eichler and J. Lapointe is helpful.

STRUCTURE YOUR WRITING

A 10 000- to 15 000-word research project entailing data collection is typically structured as follows.

Title page   Your institution or class may have specific requirements. Typically a title page should include your name, your instructor's name, the course, and the date, as well as the title of the paper.

> ## *Practical* TIP ▶ ▶ ▶ ▶
>
> ### Non-sexist writing
>
> One of the biggest challenges (though by no means the only one) when trying to write in an inclusive way is how to avoid those awkward 'she/he' and 'his/her' formulations. The easiest solution is to write in the plural where possible. For example:
>
> > 'I wanted to give each respondent the opportunity to complete the questionnaire at a time and location that was convenient for him or her.'
>
> This sentence, although grammatically correct, can be rephrased as:
>
> > 'I wanted to give all respondents the opportunity to complete their question-naires at times and locations that were convenient for them.'

Acknowledgments   You may want to acknowledge the help of people such as gatekeepers who gave you access to an organization and those who read your drafts and provided you with feedback or advice.

Table of contents (if applicable)   Your institution or class may have recommendations or prescriptions about the form this should take.

An abstract   An abstract is a brief (less than one page) summary of your work. Not all institutions or instructors ask for this component, so find out if it is required. Most journal articles include abstracts; draw on them for ideas and models.

Introduction   The purpose of the Introduction is to explain what you are writing about and why it is important. It should also

- describe in general terms the theoretical perspective you have chosen to take;
- explain your choice; and
- outline your research questions (remember that in qualitative studies, research questions are often more open-ended than is the case with quantitative work).

The opening is often the most difficult of all. Becker (1986) strongly advised against 'vacuous' opening sentences on the model of 'This study deals with the problem of careers.' This kind of sentence 'is evasive, pointing to something without saying anything, or anything much, about it. *What* about careers?' (Becker 1986: 51). To those concerned that too much detail might give away the plot, he countered that it is much better to give readers a quick and clear indication of what is going to be presented. Kelley and De Graaf's (1997) and Beardsworth and Keil's (1992) opening sentences do rather well in this regard (see Chapter 17).

Literature review   As we have seen, the literature review provides an overview of the main ideas and research done in the area of interest. However, your review should do more than simply summarize the relevant literature.

- Remember that, whenever appropriate, your approach should be critical.

- You should use your review of the literature to show why your research questions are important. For example, suppose that the basis for your research questions is the idea that although a lot of research has been done on *X* (a general topic or area, such as food consumption), little research has been done on *Y* (an aspect of *X*, like vegetarianism). In that case the literature review is where you should justify this assertion. Alternatively, it may be that there are two competing positions with regard to *Y* and you are going to investigate to see which one provides a better understanding. In the literature review, you should outline the differences between the competing positions. The literature review, then, locates your own research within a tradition of related research.

- Bear in mind that you will return to points made in the review when you present your findings and write up the conclusions.

- Don't try to get everything you've read into the literature review. Forcing it all in (because of the effort you've put into finding and reading the material) will not help. The literature review is there to assist you in developing an argument, and if you stuff it with material of passing relevance you will undermine your ability to get your argument across.

- Recall that reading the relevant literature should continue more or less throughout the research process. This means that a literature review written before the data collection begins is provisional. If you find that you want to revise your initial review, go ahead. *Just be sure that you don't attempt to make the new review conform to unexpected findings you have uncovered.* Leave that to another study.

- Additional reflections on producing a literature review are presented in Box 18.4. They were derived from a review of qualitative studies of organizations, but they also apply to quantitative research.

Research methods   The term 'research methods' is a kind of catch-all for several things that need to be outlined: research design; sampling approach; how access was achieved (if relevant); specific procedures used (for example, in the case of a mailed questionnaire, whether and how non-respondents were contacted for follow-up); and, where relevant, the nature of the questionnaire, interview schedule, participant observation, observation schedule, or coding frame. Although copies of these usually appear in an appendix, you should comment on matters such as your style of questioning or observation and why you asked the questions you did. Other issues to be discussed in this section include procedures for note-taking and data analysis. When discussing each of these matters, you should describe and defend the choices you made: for example, why you decided to use a mailed questionnaire rather than a structured interview, or why you chose a particular population for sampling.

Results   In this section you present the gist of your findings. If you will be including a separate Discussion section, the results should generally be presented with little or no commentary on how they relate to the claims made in the literature. If there is no Discussion to follow, you need to include some reflections on the significance of your findings for your research questions and for the literature. Bear the following points in mind:

- If you are presenting tables, graphs, and so on, you need to comment on each one; otherwise readers will be left wondering why they were included. Don't just summarize what a table shows: direct the reader to the parts of it that are especially striking from the point of view

BOX 18.4   Presenting qualitative research literature

In their examination of journal articles reporting qualitative research on organizations, Golden-Biddle and Locke (1993, 1997) argued that good articles in this area develop a story; that is, a clear and compelling framework around which the writing is structured. This idea is very much in tune with Wolcott's (1990: 18) advice on writing up qualitative research: 'determine the basic story you are going to tell.' Golden-Biddle and Locke suggest that establishing how your research relates to the existing literature on the topic is an important component of storytelling. They identified two things that are done to effectively review the literature and convey the relevance and significance of your research.

- **Constructing inter-textual coherence:** the author shows how existing contributions to the literature relate both to each other and to the research that will be reported. Golden-Biddle and Locke distinguished three approaches to the coherence question:
  - *synthesized coherence*—the author pieces together theory and research previously regarded as unconnected;
  - *progressive coherence*—the author traces the building of consensus in a particular area of knowledge;
  - *non-coherence*—the author emphasizes disagreements in the contributions to a certain research program.

Each of these strategies is designed to leave room for the writer to make his or her own contribution to the field.

- **Problematizing the situation:** The literature is then criticized by identifying a problem; for example:
  - *incomplete*—there is a gap in the existing literature;
  - *inadequate*—the existing literature has overlooked useful ways of looking at the phenomenon; alternative perspectives or frameworks are then introduced.

According to Golden-Biddle and Locke, the authors they studied used their accounts of the literature in various ways:

- They demonstrated their knowledge and competence by referring to prominent writings in the field.
- They developed their review of the literature in such a way as to highlight the contribution they would make in the article.
- They explained how the gaps or problems they identified in the literature corresponded to their research questions.

The idea of writing up research as storytelling serves as a useful reminder that reviewing the literature, which is part of the story, should link seamlessly with the rest of the article.

of your research questions. Ask yourself what story you want the table to convey; then relay that story to your readers.

- Whichever approach you choose, remember not to include *all* your results. You should present and discuss only those findings that relate directly to your research questions. Omitting some of your findings can be painful but it's necessary to ensure that the thread of your argument is not lost. This is especially true in the case of qualitative research. As one experienced qualitative researcher put it: 'The major problem we face in qualitative inquiry is not to get data, but to get rid of it!' (Wolcott 1990: 18). If you don't leave out some of your results, you will not only obscure your argument but run the risk that your account of your findings will appear too descriptive and lack an analytical edge. This is why it's essential to use the research questions as a focus and to orient your presentation of the findings to them.

Discussion   If you are including a Discussion, it should address the implications of the findings for your research questions. If you have specified hypotheses, as Kelley and De Graaf (1997) did, the discussion should revolve around whether or not they were confirmed. If they were not, you might speculate about the reasons. Was the sample too small? Did you forget a key variable? In this section you can also bring out the main theoretical contributions of your research and explore their implications.

Conclusion   The main guidelines are as follows:
- A conclusion is not the same as a summary. However, it is frequently useful to briefly recapitulate your main arguments at the beginning of the Conclusion section. Once that is done, hammer home to readers the significance of your research.
- This is the place to draw attention to any limitations of your work that cannot be rectified without unduly expanding the scope of the research.

☑ Checklist *of issues to consider for writing up research*

✔ Is there a good correspondence between the title of the project and its contents?

✔ Have you clearly specified your research questions?

✔ Have you clearly linked the literature cited to your research questions?

✔ Is your discussion of the literature critical and not just a summary of what you have read?

✔ Have you clearly outlined your research design and research methods? Make sure you have explained

– why you chose a particular research design or method;

– why you implemented your research design in the way you did (for example, how the interview questions relate to the research questions, or why you observed people in particular situations);

– how you selected your research participants;

– whether you experienced any problems with cooperation (for example, response rates);

– if your research required access to an organization, how and on what basis the agreement was achieved;

– any difficulties encountered in implementing your research;

– the steps taken to ensure that the research was ethical;

– how the data were analyzed.

✔ Have you presented your data in such a way that they clearly relate to your research questions?

✔ Are your interpretations of the data fully supported with tables, figures, or segments from transcripts?

✔ Is every table and/or figure properly labelled with a title and number?

✔ Is every table and/or figure commented on in the text?

✔ Does the discussion of the findings relate to the research questions?

✔ Does that discussion show how the findings shed light on the literature presented?

✔ Do the conclusions clearly establish what your research contributes to the literature?

✔ Have you explained the limitations of your study?

✔ Do your conclusions consist solely of a summary of findings? If so, rewrite them, explaining their significance.

✔ Do the conclusions provide clear answers to your research questions?

✔ Have you broken up the text in each chapter or section with appropriate subheadings?

✔ Have you provided signposts so that readers know what to expect next, and why it is there?

✔ Does the writing avoid sexist, racist, and other prejudicial language?

✔ Have you checked to ensure that the text does not make excessive use of jargon?

✔ Have you included all the necessary appendices (for example, interview schedule, letters requesting access, communications with research participants)?

✔ Does the list of references include all the items referred to in your text?

✔ Does the format of the references follow precisely the style required by your institution or instructor?

✔ Have you met all requirements regarding matters such as word count (so that the paper is neither too long nor too short) and inclusion of an abstract and table of contents?

✔ Have you ensured that you do not quote excessively when presenting the literature?

✔ Have you fully acknowledged the work of others, so that you cannot be accused of plagiarism?

✔ Have you acknowledged, preferably in an 'acknowledgments' section, the help of others where appropriate (for example, your supervisor, people who helped with interviews, people who read drafts)?

✔ Finally, have you checked to make sure that your tenses, margins, pagination, and capitalization are consistent? Many forms may be acceptable, but all must be used consistently.

• You may also suggest avenues for further research.

Two things to avoid are (a) engaging in speculations that either take you too far from your data or cannot be substantiated by the data, and (b) discussing issues or ideas that have not already been introduced.

Appendices Researchers often have some material that would help readers assess their work, but is too detailed or technical to include in the main text. Such material—questionnaires, coding frames, observation schedules, letters sent to those sampled, letters to and from gatekeepers, and so on—can be included in appendices.

References Be sure to include all the sources cited in the text. Follow the format suggested by your department or instructor. The format is usually a variation of the one used in this book.

FINALLY

Remember to fulfill any obligations you have incurred, such as supplying a copy of your report to those who have been promised one. Maintain the confidentiality of the information given and the anonymity of informants and other research participants by securing and later destroying all the primary data.

ANSWERS Bibliography errors in Chapter 17 are found at *X*

Abraham, J. (1994), 'Bias in Science and Medical Knowledge: The Opren X controversy,' *Sociology*, 28: 717-36.

Armstrong, D, Gosling, A., Weinman, J., and Marteau, T. (1997), 'The Place of Inter-Rater Reliability in Qualitative Research: X an Empirical Study,' *Sociology*, 31: 597-606 *X*

Atkinson, R. (1998), *The Life Story Interview* (Thousand Oaks, CA: Sage).

Barnard, M., and Frischer, M. (1995), 'Combining Quantitative and Qualitative Approaches: Researching HIV-Related Risk Behaviours among Drug Injectors', *X Addiction Research*, *X*351-62.

Barter, C., and *X*E. Renold (1999)*X* 'The Use of Vignettes in Qualitative Research,' *Social Research Update*, 25*X*.

Blaikie, A. (2001), 'Photographs in the Cultural Account: Contested *X* Narratives and Collective Memory in the Scottish Islands,' *Sociological Review*, 49*X*- 345-67.

Buchanan, D. R. (1992), 'An Uneasy Alliance: Combining Qualitative *X*And Quantitative Research Methods,' *Health Education Quarterly*, *X(font)* 19: 117   35.

Charmaz, K., (2000), 'Grounded Theory: Objectivist and Constructivist Methods,' in Denzin, *X*N.K. and Lincoln, *X*Y.S. (eds.), *Handbook of Qualitative Research*, 2nd ed. (Thousand Oaks, CA: Sage).

*X*B. Czarniawska. (1998), *A Narrative Approach to Organization Studies* (Thousand Oaks, *XX*A: Sage). SPACING*X*

Giulianotti, R. (1995), 'Participant Observation and Research into Football Hooliganism: Reflections on the Problems of Entrée and Everyday Risks,' *Sociology of Sport Journal*, 12: 1-20.

Reinharz, S. *X*1992, *Feminist Methods in Social Research* (New York*X*).

*X*ALPHABETIZATION

Okely, J. (1994), 'Thinking through Fieldwork*X*, in A. Bryman and R*X* G. Burgess (eds.), *Analyzing Qualitative Data* (London: Routledge).

Sheehan, K. (2001), 'E-Mail *X*survey *X*response *X*rates: A *X*review,' *Journal of Computer-Mediated Communication*, 6*X*. www.ascusc.org/jcmc/vol6/issue2/sheehan.html

---

Relevant Websites

Sociological Abstracts, *PsycINFO*, *Worldwide Political Science Abstracts*, the *Social Work Abstracts*, the *Canadian Periodicals Index Quarterly*, the *Population Index*, *Sage Race Relations Abstracts*, *Women Studies Abstracts* and the *Social Sciences Citation Index* (through the *Web of Knowledge*) are all accessible online. To use them, log on to your institution's library server and call them up from there.

This video discusses the fundamentals of doing a literature review:

http://www.youtube.com/watch?v=2IUZWZX 4OGI&feature=related

This website walks you through a hypothetical social science project in a step-by-step manner:

http://www.trinity.edu/mkearl/research. html

This video discusses how to choose and narrow down a research topic:

http://www.youtube.com/ watch?v=jSHXb83Xtsk

[Websites accessed 16 September 2011]

Chapters 13 and 14 described a number of methods for analyzing quantitative and qualitative data. This appendix illustrates how to perform those analyses using SPSS and NVivo software.

Quantitative data analysis using SPSS

The gym survey described in Chapter 13 will be used to illustrate how SPSS software is used. Learning new software requires some perseverance, but is well worth the effort. It would take far longer to perform the calculations by hand (even on the small gym survey sample of 90) than to learn the software. With more advanced techniques and larger samples, the time saved is even more substantial. Imagine calculating the mean age of 2500 people by hand!

Getting started in SPSS

INTRODUCTION

SPSS (short for *Statistical Package for the Social Sciences*) is the software most widely used for this kind of analysis, probably because it is relatively straightforward. It has been in existence since the mid-1960s and over the years has undergone many revisions, particularly since the arrival of personal computers. The version used in preparing this section is IBM SPSS Statistics 19.

SPSS operations are presented in **bold** (e.g., **Analyze**). The names given to variables are in ***bold italics*** (e.g., ***gender*** or ***reasons***). Labels (longer versions of names; see p. 336) given to values or to variables are also in bold but are not italicized (e.g., **reasons for visiting** or **male**). A right-pointing arrow ($\rightarrow$) means 'left click once with the mouse' to make selections. Box A.1 presents a list of basic operations in SPSS.

If you have SPSS software loaded onto the hard disk of the computer you are using, you can start by double clicking on the SPSS icon on the computer screen. If there is no icon, click the **Start** button in the bottom left-hand corner of the screen and select SPSS from the menu of programs. A series of follow-on menus will appear: select IBM SPSS Statistics $\rightarrow$ IBM SPSS Statistics 19. If you don't have SPSS software on your computer, it may be available from a special server provided by your university.

After SPSS loads, an opening dialogue box with the title 'What would you like to do?' and a list of options may appear. If so, disable it: $\rightarrow$**Cancel**. This will give you the SPSS **Data Editor**, made up of two components: **Data View** and **Variable View**. Move between these two by selecting the appropriate button at the bottom left of the screen. The **Data View** provides a spreadsheet grid into which data are entered (see Plate A.1). The columns represent *variables*—in our example, information about the characteristics of each person in the gym study sample, such as ***gender*** and ***age***. Until data are entered, each column simply has **var** as its heading. The rows represent *cases*, which can be people (as in this example) or other units of analysis. Each block in the grid is referred to as a 'cell.' Note that when the data are entered in the SPSS spreadsheet, they will look different: for example, 1 becomes 1.00 (this can be adjusted if necessary).

ENTERING DATA IN THE DATA VIEW

To input the data into the **Data View**, make sure that the top left-hand cell in the grid is highlighted (Plate A.1). If it is not, simply click once in that cell. Then type the appropriate number in that cell—that is, 1. This number goes directly into that cell and into the box beneath the toolbar. Although you can use the mouse, many people find it easier to use the arrow keys on their keyboard to move from cell to cell. If you make a mistake, simply click once in the cell in question, type in the correct value, and click once more in that cell. The last piece of data goes into the bottom right-hand cell of what will be a perfect rectangle of data. Plate A.2 shows the **Data View** with the data from the gym survey entered (though only part of the data set is visible: the first 23 of the 90 respondents and 11 of the 12 variables). The first row of data contains the coded answers (provided by the first respondent) from the completed questionnaire in Box 13.1.

BOX A.1   Basic operations in SPSS

- The IBM SPSS Statistics **Data Editor**. This is the mode in which data may be entered and subsequently edited and defined. It is made up of two screens: **Data View** and **Variable View**. Move between these two views by selecting the appropriate button at the bottom left of the screen.

- **Data View**. This is the spreadsheet into which the data are entered. It appears when SPSS is started.

- **Variable View**. Another spreadsheet, this one displays information about each of the variables (such as the variable name, the variable labels, and value labels) and allows that information to be changed (see below).

- IBM SPSS Statistics **Viewer**. After a statistical analysis or the production of a graph (sometimes called a 'chart' in SPSS), the output is deposited here. The output window superimposes itself over the Data Editor after an analysis has been performed or a graph has been generated.

- **Variable Name**. This is the name given to a variable (for example, *gender*). Until it is given a name, the variable is referred to as var00001, var00002, etc. Once it is given a name, the name appears in the column for that variable in the Data View window. It is generated from the Variable View.

- **Variable Label**. This is a label attached to a particular variable, and is optional. It is usually longer than the variable name and therefore more explanatory. Spaces can be used: for example, **reasons for visiting**. The label appears in any output generated and comes from the Variable View.

- **Value Label**. This is a label attached to the code used when entering the data. Thus for var00001, the label **male** can be attached to 1 and the label **female** to 2. In output, such as a frequency table or chart, the labels for each value appear, making the interpretation of output easier than if the code were used. It is generated from the Variable View.

- **Missing Values**. If data for a particular variable are missing, you must specify how missing values are coded so that the computer can omit them from the calculations. Missing values are generated from the Variable View.

- **Analyze**. This is the button on the menu bar along the top of the Data Editor from which (via a drop-down menu) the method of analysis is selected. Note that whenever a menu item appears with a right-pointing arrowhead after it, a further sub-menu is available.

- **Graphs**. This is the button (at the top of the Data Editor) used to get access to the **Chart Builder** (via a drop-down menu), which can be used to create various graphs and charts.

- **Chart Builder**. This feature is used to make charts and graphs. A very useful tutorial is available from the **Data Editor** by clicking **Help** →**Tutorial** → **Creating and editing charts**.

- **Chart Editor**. This is used to make various changes to graphs. To activate it, double-click anywhere in the graph. A small Chart Editor window appears along with a version of the main graph and stays until the Chart Editor is exited.

To proceed further, SPSS works in the following typical sequence for selecting variables and analyzing data.

1. Make a selection from the menu bar at the top of the screen, for example, →**Analyze**.

2. From the menu that will appear, make a selection, for example, → **Descriptive Statistics**.

3. This will bring up another menu where you will specify which statistics you want—for example, **Frequencies**.

4. This will bring up a *dialogue box* in which you provide further information, such as the variables to be analyzed.

5. Very often, further information is needed; → a button that brings up a *sub-dialogue box*.

6. Provide the information in the sub-dialogue box and then go back to the dialogue box. Sometimes, a further sub-dialogue box is required before you can return to the dialogue box.

When you have finished going through the entire procedure, → OK. The toolbar beneath the menu bar allows shortcut access to certain SPSS operations.

DEFINING VARIABLES: VARIABLE NAMES, MISSING VALUES, VARIABLE LABELS, AND VALUE LABELS

Once you have finished entering the data, prepare the variables. The following steps explain how this is done:

Each row represents a case.

Each column represents a variable.

For the Variable View to examine each variable in detail, click on this tab.

PLATE A.1 The SPSS Data Editor **Data View**

This row shows the data for the first person who answered the questionnaire in Box 13.1.

PLATE A.2 The **Data View** with the 'gym study' data entered

1. → the **Variable View** tab at the bottom left of the **Data Editor** (opens the window shown in Plate A.3).

2. To name a variable, click on the current variable name (for example, **var00003**) and type a name for it (for example, *reasons*). This name, which cannot include spaces, is the identification needed for instructing the computer to perform an analysis with this variable. It can be anything you like, but you should choose a name that indicates what the variable is measuring.

3. To give the variable a more detailed designation, known in SPSS as a **variable label**, → the cell in the **Label** column for this variable. Then type in the label (for example, **reasons for visiting**). This label will appear on your output, just as a designer label appears on a piece of clothing. If no variable label is specified, the variable name will be used for the output.

4. Provide 'value labels' for the values of the variables, where appropriate. The procedure generally applies to variables that are not interval/ratio. The latter do not need value labels (unless you are grouping them in some way). To assign value labels, → in the cell in the **Values** column for the variable in question. A small button with three dots on it appears. → the button. The **Value Labels** dialogue box appears (Plate A.4). → the box to the right of **Value**: and begin to define the value labels. To do this, enter the value (for example, 1) in the area to the right of **Value**: and then type in the value label (for example, **relaxation**) in the area to the right of **Label**:. Then → **Add**. Do this for each value. When finished → OK. A variable name for question one on the questionnaire could be *gender*, the variable label 'gender of respondent,' and the value labels, 1 'male' and 2 'female.' The computer reads only numbers (male is 1, female 2) so the value labels are optional, but if you omit them the output will tell you about 1s and 2s instead of males and females.

To insert Value Labels for var00003, click here.

	Name	Type	Width	Decimals	Label	Values	Missing	Columns	Align	Measure	Role
1	var00001	Numeric	8	2		None	None	8	Right	Scale	Input
2	var00002	Numeric	8	2		None	None	8	Right	Scale	Input
3	var00003	Numeric	8	2		None	None	8	Right	Scale	Input
4	var00004	Numeric	8	2		None	None	8	Right	Scale	Input
5	var00005	Numeric	8	2		None	None	8	Right	Scale	Input
6	var00006	Numeric	8	2		None	None	8	Right	Scale	Input
7	var00007	Numeric	8	2		None	None	8	Right	Scale	Input
8	var00008	Numeric	8	2		None	None	8	Right	Scale	Input
9	var00009	Numeric	8	2		None	None	8	Right	Scale	Input
10	var00010	Numeric	8	2		None	None	8	Right	Scale	Input
11	var00011	Numeric	8	2		None	None	8	Right	Scale	Input
12	var00012	Numeric	8	2		None	None	8	Right	Scale	Input

gym data ORIGINAL.sav [DataSet1] - IBM SPSS Statistics Data Editor

File   Edit   View   Data   Transform   Analyze   Graphs   Utilities   Add-ons   Window   Help

Data View   **Variable View**

IBM SPSS Statistics Processor is ready

start   *Output1 [Document...   gym data ORIGINAL....   Untitled2 [DataSet2] ...   A.2 old 12.2 - Paint   3:41 PM

PLATE A.3   The Data Editor **Variable View**

Remember to click here after entering each Value and Value Label.

PLATE A.4 The **Value Labels** dialogue box

5. Designate missing values. In the case of *reasons*, missing data are given a value of 0. To assign the missing value, → the cell for this variable in the **Missing** column. Again, → the button that has three dots on it. This will generate the **Missing Values** dialogue box (Plate A.5). In the **Missing Values** dialogue box, enter the missing value (0) below **Discrete missing values** and then → OK.

To simplify the following presentation, *reasons* is the only variable for which a variable label and missing values are defined.

PLATE A.5 The **Missing Values** dialogue box

SAVING THE DATA

To save the data for future use, make sure that the **Data Editor** is the active window. Then,

→ **File** → **Save As...**

The **Save Data As** dialogue box will appear. It needs a name for the data, which is placed after **File name**: and a place to save the data—for example, onto a portable disk or the hard drive of your computer. To select the destination drive, → the downward pointing arrow to the right of the box by **Look in**:. Then choose the drive on which to save the data and → **Save**.

This procedure saves the data *and* any work done on it—for example, value labels and missing values specifications. If you do more work on the data, such as creating a new variable, the data must be saved again or the new work will be lost. SPSS gives you a choice of renaming the data—in which case there will be two data files (one with the original data and one with the revised data)—or keeping the same name. In the latter case the original file is lost but its name is retained and applied to the modified file.

RETRIEVING DATA

To retrieve a data file, → **File** → **Open** → **Data**... The **Open Data** dialogue box will appear. Go to the location in which the data are deposited to retrieve the file containing the data and then → **Open**.

COMPUTING A NEW VARIABLE

The total amount of time a respondent spent in the gym is made up of three variables: *cardmins*, *weimins*, and *othmins* (questions 10, 11, and 12 respectively in Box 13.1, referring to cardiovascular equipment, weights, and other activities). Adding them up gives the total number of minutes spent on various activities in the gym, and a new variable, *totalmin*, can be created for that purpose. To do this, take the following steps:

1. →**Transform** → **Compute Variable**... [opens the Compute Variable dialogue box shown in Plate A.6]

2. under Target Variable: type **totalmin**

3. under **Function group**:, select **Statistical**; under Functions and Special Variables, select **Sum**; then click on the button with an upward-pointing arrowhead to send it into the box under **Numeric Expression**:

PLATE A.6   The **Compute Variable** dialogue box

4. from the list of variables at the left, →
   cardmins → adjacent button [puts ***cardmins***
   in box after **SUM**]; → ***weimins*** → button [puts
   weimins in box after ***cardmins***]; → ***othmins*** →
   button [puts ***othmins*** in box after ***weimins***]; be
   sure to put commas (but not spaces) between
   the variable names, and to delete any '?' that
   remain in the Numeric Expression box.

5. → **OK**.

The new variable ***totalmin*** is created and appears
in the **Data Editor**.

RECODING VARIABLES
Sometimes you will need to recode variables—for
example, to group scores together, as was done

to produce Table 13.3 for an interval/ratio variable (var00002, now given the variable name ***age***).
SPSS offers two choices: change ***age***, or keep ***age*** as
it is and create a new variable. The latter option is
appropriate here, because you may need the data
for ***age*** in its original form for some other analysis.
We will preserve the original variable and create
a new one, ***agegp***, for age groups, with five age
categories, as in Table 13.3.

1. → **Transform** → **Recode into Different
   Variables** [opens Recode into Different
   Variables dialogue box shown in Plate A.7]

2. → ***age*** → adjacent button [puts ***age*** in Numeric
   Variable → Output Variable: box] → box
   beneath Output Variable Name: and type

Original name
of variable.

Recoded name
of variable.

PLATE A.7   The **Recode into Different Variables** dialogue box

agegp → **Change** [puts *agegp* in the Numeric Variable → Output Variable: box] → **Old and New Values** ... [opens Recode into Different Variables: Old and New Values sub-dialogue box shown in Plate A.8]

3. If there are missing values for a variable (as in this case), in the **Old Value** box, → the circle by **System- or user-missing**, and in the **New Value** box, → **System-missing**, then → **Add**.

4. In the **Old Value** box, → circle by **Range: LOWEST through value** and type 20 in the box. In the **New Value** box, → circle by **Value:** and type 1 → **Add** [the new value appears in the Old → New: box]

5. In the **Old Value** box, → first circle by **Range:** and type 21, and in box after 'through' type 30. In the **New Value** box, → circle by **Value:** and type 2 → **Add**

6. In the **Old Value** box, → first circle by **Range:** and type 31 and in box after 'through' type 40. In the **New Value** box, →circle by **Value:** and type 3 → **Add**

7. In the **Old Value** box, → first circle by **Range:** and type 41, and in box after 'through' type 50. In the **New Value** box, → circle by **Value:** and type 4 → **Add**

8. In the **Old Value** box, → circle by **Range: value through HIGHEST** and type 51 in the box. In the **New Value** box, →circle by **Value:** and type 5 → **Add** → **Continue** [closes the Recode into Different Variables: Old and New Values sub-dialogue box shown in Plate A.8 and returns to the Recode into Different Variables shown in Plate A.7]

9. → **OK**

PLATE A.8 The **Recode into Different Variables: Old and New Values** sub-dialogue box

The new variable *agegp* is created and appears in the **Data View**. To generate value labels for the five age bands and a variable label, repeat the approach described above for those procedures.

GENERATING A FREQUENCY TABLE
To produce a frequency table like the one in Table 13.2:

1. → **Analyze** → **Descriptive Statistics** → **Frequencies**... [opens the **Frequencies** dialogue box shown in Plate A.9].

2. → *reasons* → adjacent button [puts *reasons* into **Variable(s):** box]

3. → **OK**

4. The table then appears in the IBM SPSS Statistics **Viewer** (see Plate A.10)

Note that in the **Frequencies** dialogue box, the variable name appears. If you would prefer to work with variable labels (which provide more information on what the variable measures), go into the **Data Editor**, → **Edit** → **Options** →

General, and in the top left-hand corner you can select variable labels to be used. Similarly, if you

Click here to send selected variables into Variable(s) list.

Select variable(s) to be analyzed from here.

PLATE A.9 The **Frequencies** dialogue box

Number of cases in each category.

Percentage of cases in each category.

Percentage of cases in each category taking missing values into account.

PLATE A.10   The IBM SPSS Statistics **Viewer**

prefer that the variables be arranged in alphabetical order, you can specify that there.

GENERATING A BAR CHART

To produce a bar chart like the one in Figure 13.2:

1. → **Graphs** → **Chart Builder...** [opens **Chart Builder** dialogue box]

2. → **Gallery** → **Bar,** and drag the type of bar chart you want into the 'canvas,' the large area above the Gallery [see plate A.11]

3. drag *reasons* into the *X*-axis box at the bottom of the canvas

4. → **OK**

As mentioned earlier, for some useful details on this procedure, do the tutorial available in the **Data Editor** at **Help** → **Tutorial** → **Creating and editing charts**.

GENERATING A PIE CHART

To produce a pie chart like the one in Figure 13.3:

1. → **Graphs** → **Chart Builder...** [opens **Chart Builder** dialogue box]

2. → **Gallery** → **Pie/Polar**, and drag the pie chart into the 'canvas,' the large area above the Gallery.

3. right-click *reasons* in the **Variables: list** and choose nominal

PLATE A.11 The **Chart Builder** dialogue box

4. drag *reasons* into the 'Slice by?' drop zone at the bottom of the canvas

5. → **OK**

6. *double-click* anywhere in the chart to bring up the **Chart Editor** (Plate A.12). → **Elements** → **Show data labels**. This will place the percentage in each category in the appropriate slices of the pie [see Plate A.13].

This pie chart is in colour, but if you only have access to a monochrome printer, you can change the colours into patterns. Get into the **Chart Editor**, which enables editing of all figures: → **Edit** → **Properties** → **Variables**. By **reasons for visiting** (the variable label) select **Style: Colour**, and change that to **Style: Patterns** → **Apply**. Use the same procedure for all charts. Once again, for some useful details on this procedure, do the tutorial available in the **Data Editor** at **Help** → **Tutorial** → **Creating and Editing Charts**.

GENERATING A HISTOGRAM

Producing the histogram in Figure 13.4 is just as simple except that it requires you to define the ages to be grouped together. The general procedure for doing this is → **Chart Builder** → **Gallery** → **Histogram** → **Element Properties** → **Statistic** → **Histogram** → **Set Parameters**. However, since we have already recoded age into the categories we want, you can use the newly created *agegp* variable. Make sure that *agegp* is defined as a scale [interval/ratio] variable by right-clicking on it in the **Variables: list** while in the **Chart Builder**. Other ways of presenting interval/ratio data, such as measures of central tendency and dispersion, will be discussed below.

PRINTING OUTPUT

To print all the output in the IBM SPSS Statistics **Viewer**, make sure that the **Viewer** is the active window and then → **File** → **Print**... When the

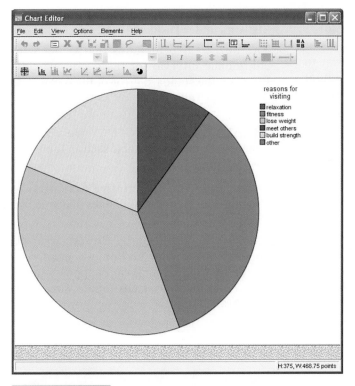

PLATE A.12   The **Chart Editor**

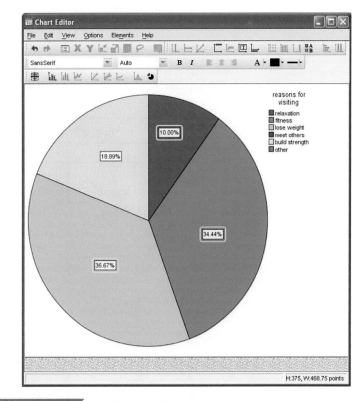

PLATE A.13   The **Chart Editor** showing pie chart percentages

Print dialogue box appears, → **OK**. To print just some of the output, hold down the Ctrl button on the keyboard and click once on the parts of the output you want to print. The easiest way to do this is to select the elements from the output summary in the left-hand segment of the **Viewer** shown in Plate A.10. Then bring up the **Print** dialogue box. When the **Print** dialogue box appears, make sure **Selected output** under **Print Range** is selected.

GENERATING THE ARITHMETIC MEAN, MEDIAN, STANDARD DEVIATION, AND RANGE

To produce the mean, median, standard deviation, and the range for an interval/ratio variable like *age*, follow these steps:

1. → **Analyze** → **Descriptive Statistics** → **Explore ...** [opens the **Explore** dialogue box]
2. → *age* → the button to the left of **Dependent List:** [puts *age* in the **Dependent List:** box] → **Statistics** under **Display** → **OK**

3. The output also includes the 95 per cent confidence interval for the mean, which is based on the standard error of the mean. The output is in Table A.1.

GENERATING A CONTINGENCY TABLE

To generate a contingency table such as Table 13.4 follow this procedure:

1. → **Analyze** → **Descriptive Statistics** → **Crosstabs...** [opens the **Crosstabs** dialogue box shown in Plate A.14]
2. → *reasons* → button by **Row(s):** [*reasons* appears in the **Row(s):** box] → *gender* → button by **Column(s):** [*gender* appears in the **Column(s):** box] → **Cells** [opens **Crosstabs: Cell Display** sub-dialogue box shown in Plate A.15]

TABLE A.1 Explore output for *age* [SPSS output]

EXPLORE

CASE PROCESSING SUMMARY

| | Cases | | | | | |
| | Valid | | Missing | | Total | |
	N	Per cent	N	Per cent	N	Per cent
AGE	89	98.9%	1	1.1%	90	100.0%

DESCRIPTIVES

			Statistic	Std. Error
AGE	**Mean**		33.5955	.9420
	95% Confidence	Lower bound	31.7235	
	Interval for mean	Upper bound	35.4675	
	5% Trimmed mean		33.3159	
	Median		31.0000	
	Variance		78.971	
	Std. deviation		8.8866	
	Minimum		18.00	
	Maximum		57.00	
	Range		39.00	
	Interquartile range		14.0000	
	Skewness		.446	.255
	Kurtosis		−.645	.506

3. Make sure **Observed** in the **Counts** box is selected. Make sure **Column** under **Percentages** is selected. If either of these was not selected, simply click at the relevant point. → **Continue** [closes **Crosstabs: Cell Display** sub-dialogue box and return to the **Crosstabs** dialogue box shown in Plate A.14]

4. → **Statistics...** [opens the **Crosstabs: Statistics** sub-dialogue box shown in Plate A.16]. For example, suppose Cramér's *V* is needed (because of having two nominal variables). → **Chi-square** → **Phi and Cramér's** *V* → **Continue** [closes **Crosstabs: Statistics** sub-dialogue box and returns to the **Crosstabs** dialogue box shown in Plate A.14]

5. → **OK**

The resulting output is in Table A.2. Cramér's *V* is just one of the available statistics.

GENERATING SCATTER DIAGRAMS

The production of scatter diagrams, known as *scatterplots* in SPSS, is illustrated in the relationship between *age* and *cardmins*. If one variable can be identified as likely to be the independent variable, it is by convention placed on the *X*-axis (the horizontal axis). Since *age* is bound to be the independent variable, follow these steps:

1. → **Graphs** → **Chart Builder** → **Gallery** → **Scatter/Dot**

2. drag the Simple Scatter diagram into the canvas

3. drag *age* into the **X-Axis?** box at the bottom of the canvas

4. drag *cardmins* into the **Y-Axis?** box at the left side of the canvas

5. → **OK**

PLATE A.14   The **Crosstabs** dialogue box

TABLE A.2   Contingency table for **reasons for visiting** by *gender* (SPSS output)

CROSSTABS

CASE PROCESSING SUMMARY

	Cases					
	Valid		Missing		Total	
	N	Per cent	N	Per cent	N	Per cent
reasons for visiting * GENDER	90	100.0%	0	.0%	90	100.0%

REASONS FOR VISITING * GENDER CROSSTABULATION

			GENDER		
			male	female	Total
reasons for visiting	relaxation	Count	3	6	9
		% within GENDER	7.1%	12.5%	10.0%
	fitness	Count	15	16	31
		% within GENDER	35.7%	33.3%	34.4%
	lose weight	Count	8	25	33
		% within GENDER	19.0%	52.1%	36.7%
	build strength	Count	16	1	17
		% within GENDER	38.1%	2.1%	18.9%
Total		Count	42	48	90
		% within GENDER	100.0%	100.0%	100.0%

CHI-SQUARE TESTS

This is the X^2 value referred to in the text →

	Value	df	Asymp. Sig. [(2-sided)]
Pearson Chi-Square	22.726[a]	3	.000
Likelihood Ratio	25.805	3	.000
Linear-by-Linear Association	9.716	1	.002
N of Valid Cases	90		

[a] 2 cells (25.0%) have expected count less than 5. The minimum expected count is 4.20.

Since this is not a 2 × 2 table, interpret Cramér's *V*

SYMMETRIC MEASURES

		Value	Approx. Sig.
Nominal by Nominal	Phi	.503	.000
	Cramer's *V*	.503	.000
N of Valid Cases		90	

[a] Not assuming the null hypothesis.
[b] Using the asymptotic standard error assuming the null hypothesis.

Shows level of statistical significance of computed value of Cramér's *V*

Shows strength of relationship

Must be selected for number of cases in each cell to be included in table.

Select to provide the X^2 statistics for the contingency table.

Select to give the percentage of cases of each category of the column variable.

Select to generate Phi/Cramér's V.

PLATE A.15   The **Crosstabs: Cell Display** sub-dialogue box

PLATE A.16   The **Crosstabs: Statistics** sub-dialogue box

GENERATING PEARSON'S r

To produce Pearson's r, in particular the correlation between *age*, *weimins*, and *cardmins* shown in Table 13.5, follow these steps:

1. → **Analyze** → **Correlate** → **Bivariate...** [opens **Bivariate Correlations** dialogue box shown in Plate A.17]

2. → *age* → button → *cardmins* → button → *weimins* → button [*age*, *cardmins*, and *weimins* should now be in the **Variables:** box] → **Pearson** [if not already selected] → **OK**

The resulting output is shown in Table A.3

To produce Kendall's tau-b, follow the same procedures but instead of selecting **Pearson**, → **Kendall's tau-b**. Somer's d and Kendall's tau-c are other options, but for clarity are not explained here.

COMPARING MEANS

To produce a table like Table 13.6, follow these steps:

1. → **Analyze** → **Compare Means** → **Means...** [opens the **Means** dialogue box shown in Plate A.18]

2. → *cardmins* → button to the left of **Dependent List:** → *reasons* → button to the left of **Independent List:** → **Options** [opens the **Means: Options** sub-dialogue box]

3. → **Anova table and eta** underneath **Statistics for First Layer** → **Continue** [closes the **Means: Options** sub-dialogue box and returns to the **Means** dialogue box shown in Plate A.18] → **OK**

GENERATING A CONTINGENCY TABLE WITH THREE VARIABLES

To create a table like Table 13.9, do as follows:

1. → **Analyze** → **Descriptive Statistics** → **Crosstabs...** [opens the **Crosstabs** dialogue box shown in Plate A.14]

2. → *othsourc* → button by **Row(s):** [*othsourc* appears in the **Row(s):** box]

3. → *age3* [this is the name given to a newly created variable with *age* recoded into three categories] → button by **Column(s):** [*age3* appears in the **Column(s):** box] → *gender* → button beneath **Previous** [*gender* appears in the box underneath **Layer 1 of 1**] → **Cells** [opens **Crosstabs: Cell Display** sub-dialogue box shown in Plate A.15]

All variable(s) to be correlated go here.

Select Pearson or Spearman depending on the kinds of variables being analyzed.

PLATE A.17 **Bivariate Correlations** dialogue box

TABLE A.3 Correlations output for age, weimins, and cardmins (SPSS output)

CORRELATIONS

Correlations of $p < 0.05$ are 'flagged' with asterisks

CORRELATIONS

		AGE	WEIMINS	CARDMINS
AGE	Pearson Correlation	1.000	−.273 **	−.109
	Sig. (2-tailed)	.	.010	.311
	N	89	89	89
WEIMINS	Pearson Correlation	−.273 **	1.000	−.161
	Sig. (2-tailed)	.010	.	.130
	N	89	90	90
CARDMINS	Pearson Correlation	−.109	−.161	1.000
	Sig. (2-tailed)	.311	.130	.
	N	89	90	90

** Correlation is significant at the 0.01 level (2-tailed).

Shows strength of relationship as indicated by Pearson's r

Shows number of cases, less any cases for which there are missing data for either or both variables

Shows level of statistical significance of computed value of Pearson's r

Dependent variable(s) go here.

Independent variable(s) go here.

PLATE A.18   The **Means** dialogue box

PLATE A.19   The **Linear Regression** dialogue box

4. Make sure **Observed** in the **Counts** box has been selected. Make sure **Column** under **Percentages** has been selected. If either has not, simply click at the relevant point. → **Continue** [closes **Crosstabs: Cell Display** sub-dialogue box and returns to the **Crosstabs** dialogue box shown in Plate A.14]

5. → **OK**

The resulting table looks somewhat different from Table 13.9 in that *gender* appears as a row rather than as a column variable.

REGRESSION

To perform a bivariate regression in SPSS:

1. → **Analyze** → **Regression** → **Linear**. This will produce the **Linear Regression** dialogue box shown in Plate A.19.

2. → *wiemins* → button to put it in the **Dependent:** box.

3. → *age* → button to put it in the **Independent(s):** box.

4. → **OK**. The output appears in Table 13.10.

To perform multiple regression, simply add additional independent variables to the model. Once you are in the **Linear Regression** dialogue box (described above and shown in Plate A.19), just click on whatever variable you would like to add, then click the arrow button to put the variable in the **Independent(s):** box along with *age*.

Questions for Review

GETTING STARTED IN SPSS

- Outline the differences between variable names, variable labels, and value labels.

- In what circumstances is it appropriate to recode a variable?

- In what circumstances is it appropriate to create a new variable?

EXERCISES: DATA ANALYSIS WITH SPSS (SEE TABLE 13.1 TO IDENTIFY THE VARIABLES)
Using the gym survey data, create:

- a frequency table for the variable *exercise*;

- a bar chart and pie chart for *exercise* and compare their usefulness;

- a histogram for *cardmins*;

- measures of central tendency and dispersion for *cardmins*;

- a contingency table and Cramér's *V* for *gender* and *exercise*;

- a scatter diagram for *age* and *cardmins*;

- Pearson's *r* for *age* and *cardmins*;

- Kendall's tau-b for *carduse* and *weiuse*; and

- a difference of means analysis for **reasons for visiting** and *totalmin*.

Qualitative data analysis using NVivo

Introduction

To illustrate how to use NVivo software, version 9, we will use the interview transcripts from a study of visitors to Disney theme parks, discussed in Chapter 14. This illustration of NVivo and its functions addresses just its most basic features. There is a very good help facility included with this program as well as tutorials that are recommended for more in-depth instruction. As in the discussion of SPSS, in the following account → signifies 'click once with the left-hand button of your mouse.'

Getting started with NVivo

On opening NVivo, you will be presented with a welcome screen (Plate A.20). This screen shows any existing NVivo projects and is the springboard for either opening one of the existing projects or starting a new one. If you are starting a new project, as in the example that follows, → **File** → **New Project**. The **New Project** dialog box appears and you are asked to provide a **Title** for your project. For this exercise, the title 'Disney Project1' was chosen. You are also asked to give a **Description** of the project, though this is an optional feature. When you have done this, → **OK**.

You then need to import the documents you want to code. In this case, they will be interview transcripts from the project on visitors to Disney theme parks, referred to in Box 10.7 and Chapter 14. Other kinds of documents can be imported such as fieldwork notes. NVivo 9 can accept documents in both rich text (.rtf) and Word (.doc, .docx) formats. To import the documents, → **Internals** (below **Sources** at the top of the **Navigation view**) → **External Data** on the **Ribbon** → **Document** button on the **Find bar** [opens the **Import Internals** dialog box] → **Browse** to locate the documents that are to be imported. → the documents to be imported (you can hold down the Ctrl key to select several documents; if you want to select all of them, hold down the Ctrl key and tap the A key) → **Open**

PLATE A.20   The opening screen

(see Plate A.21 for the series of steps). The documents will then be visible in the **Document Viewer** [this is the term used to describe the general screen shown in Plate A.22]. Once the documents have been imported, they can be read and edited. All you need to do is to double-click on the yellow icon to the left of each interview in the **List view**.

Coding

Coding your data is obviously one of the key phases in the whole process of qualitative data analysis. For NVivo, coding is accomplished through nodes. NVivo's help system in earlier releases defined coding as 'the process of marking passages of text in a project's documents with *nodes*' (emphasis added). Thus nodes are the route by which coding proceeds. In turn, the latest release defines a node as 'a collection of references about a specific theme, place, person or other area of interest.' When a document has been coded, the node will incorporate references to those portions of documents in which the code appears. Once established, nodes can be changed or deleted.

There are several ways of going about the coding process in NVivo. The approach taken in relation to the coding of the Disney Project was as follows:

- The interviews, both in printed form and in the **Document Viewer** (Plate A.22), were read through. The viewer is treated as having a number of different components or sections and these are highlighted in Plate A.22.
- Some codes that seemed relevant to the documents were created.
- The documents were then coded using NVivo.

An alternative strategy is to code while browsing the documents.

CREATING NODES

The nodes that were relevant to the passage in Box 10.7 are presented in Figure A.1. Prior to NVivo 9, when creating a node, the researcher had to choose either a free node or a tree node. The latter is a node that is organized in a hierarchy of connected nodes, whereas free nodes were not organized

1. Select **Internals**.

2. Select **External Data** and then **Documents**. This brings up the **Import Internals** dialogue box.

3. In the **Import Internals** dialogue box, click on **Browse...** to locate the documents to be imported.

4. Select the documents to be imported from the location identified in step 3.

5. Click on **Open**. The documents will then be imported into NVivo.

PLATE A.21   Stages in importing documents into NVivo

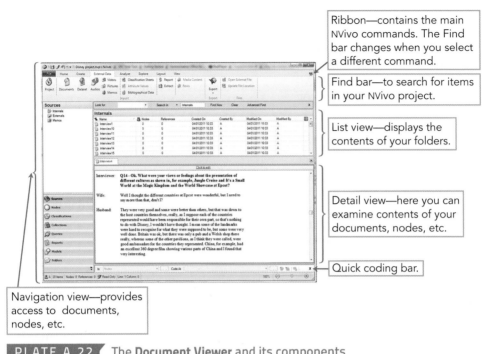

Ribbon—contains the main NVivo commands. The Find bar changes when you select a different command.

Find bar—to search for items in your NVivo project.

List view—displays the contents of your folders.

Detail view—here you can examine contents of your documents, nodes, etc.

Quick coding bar.

Navigation view—provides access to documents, nodes, etc.

PLATE A.22   The **Document Viewer** and its components

Hierarchical nodes   Critique

Aesthetic critique   Ideological critique   Content critique   Other critique

Class critique   Ethnicity critique   Gender critique   Nationality critique

Visitors

Visitors' age   Visitors' gender   Visitors' class   Visitors' ethnicity

Significance

Educational significance   Recreational significance   Ideological significance   Other significance

Non-hierarchical nodes

Uncritical enthusiasm
Not critical of Disney

FIGURE A.1   Nodes used in the Disney project

in this way. This distinction has been dropped in NVivo 9, and the software assumes that a tree node is being created. Two points are crucial to note here for users of earlier releases of the software. First, the tendency now is not to refer to 'tree nodes' but to treat them as hierarchically organized nodes. Second, free nodes (that is, nodes that are not hierarchically organized) can still be created; they are simply nodes without 'children' (to use the latest NVivo terminology).

Notice that there are three groups of *hierarchically organized nodes* and two *non-hierarchically organized nodes* in Figure A.1. The nodes can be created in the following way.

Creating non-hierarchically organized nodes   This sequence of steps demonstrates how to create the non-hierarchically organized node *not critical of Disney*.

1. While in the **Document Viewer** → **Create** in the Ribbon

2. → **Node** in the **Find bar** [opens the **New Node** dialog box—see Plate A.23]

3. Enter the node **Name** [*not critical of Disney*] and a **Description** (the latter is optional)

4. → **OK**

1. Select **Create**.

2. Select **Node**.

3. In the **New Node dialogue box**, enter the node **Name** and a **Description** (the latter is optional).

4. Click on **OK**.

PLATE A.23 Stages in creating a non-hierarchically organized node

Creating hierarchically organized nodes To create a hierarchically organized node, the initial process is exactly the same as with a non-hierarchically organized node. The following example will show how to create the hierarchically organized node *Class critique*, which is a child of the hierarchically organized node *Ideological critique*, which is itself a child of the hierarchically organized node *Critique* (see Figure A.1). The following steps will generate this node.

1. While in the **Document Viewer** → **Create** in the Ribbon

2. → **Node** in the **Find bar** [opens the **New Node** dialog box—see Plate A.24]

3. Enter the node **Name** [*Critique*] and a **Description** (the latter is optional)

4. → **OK**

5. → *Critique* in the list of nodes in the **List viewer**

6. → **Node** in the **Find bar** [opens the **New Node** dialog box—see Plate A.24]

7. Enter the node **Name** [*Ideological critique*] and a **Description** (the latter is optional). This node will form a child of the hierarchically organized node [make sure that in Hierarchical name it reads **Nodes\\Critique**, as this will mean it is a child of **Critique**]. See Plate A.24.

8. → *Ideological critique* in the list of nodes in the **List viewer**

9. → **Node** in the **Find bar** [opens the **New Node** dialog box—see Plate A.24]

10. Enter the node **Name** [*Class critique*] and a **Description** (the latter is optional). This node will form a child of the hierarchically organized node [make sure that in Hierarchical name it reads **Nodes\\Critique\Ideological critique**, as this will mean it is a child of **Ideological critique**, which is itself a child of **Critique**]. See Plate A.24.

11. → **OK**

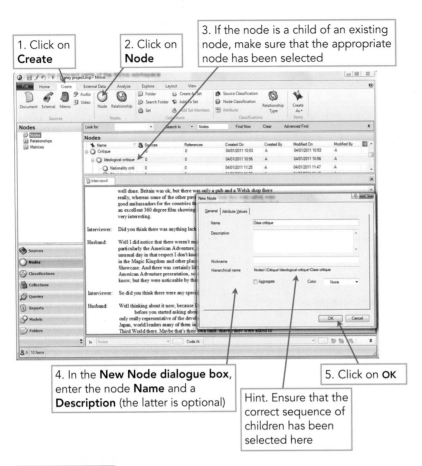

1. Click on **Create**

2. Click on **Node**

3. If the node is a child of an existing node, make sure that the appropriate node has been selected

4. In the **New Node dialogue box**, enter the node **Name** and a **Description** (the latter is optional)

Hint. Ensure that the correct sequence of children has been selected here

5. Click on **OK**

PLATE A.24   Stages in creating a hierarchically organized node

Applying nodes in the coding process   Coding is carried out by applying nodes to segments of text. Once you have set up some nodes (remember that you can add and alter them at any time), you can look at a document in the viewer and highlight the area of the document that you want to code; then right-click on the mouse while holding the cursor over the highlighted text. If the node that you want to use has not been created yet, highlight the text you want to code, right-click on the highlighted text, and then → **Code Selection** → **Code Selection at New Node...** This opens the **New Node** dialog box. You can then create a new node in the manner outlined in the previous sections. If the code you want to use has been created, NVivo 9 allows you to drag and drop text into it (see Plate A.25). To do this, highlight the text to be coded and then, holding down the left-hand button, drag the text over to the appropriate node in the **List view**.

Alternatively, you can highlight the text you want to code and right-click over it. Then → **Code Selection** → **Code Selection at Existing Nodes**, which opens the **Select Project Items** dialog box (see Plate A.26). Tick the node(s) you want to use. Thus, in the example in Plate A.26, the tick by *Uncritical enthusiasm* will code the highlighted text at that node. If you also wanted to use a hierarchically organized node, you would need to find the appropriate parent in the list of nodes within the **List view** and then click on the plus to the left of it. To *uncode* at any point, simply highlight the passage to be uncoded, and → the button with a red cross in it in the Quick coding bar (see Plate A.22). Alternatively, you can right-click on the highlighted text and → **Uncode**.

Coding stripes   It's very helpful to be able to see the areas of text that have been coded and

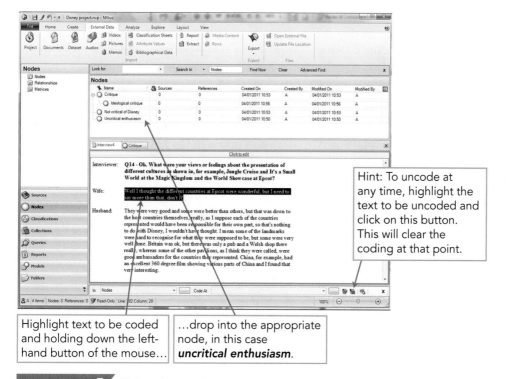

Hint: To uncode at any time, highlight the text to be uncoded and click on this button. This will clear the coding at that point.

Highlight text to be coded and holding down the left-hand button of the mouse...

...drop into the appropriate node, in this case *uncritical enthusiasm*.

PLATE A.25 Using drag and drop to code

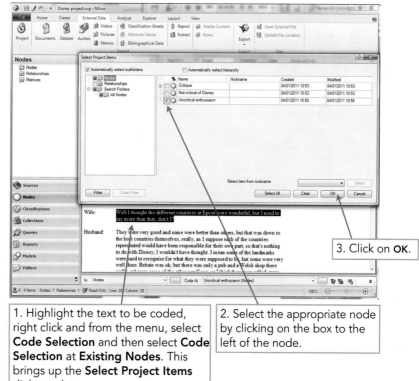

3. Click on **OK**.

1. Highlight the text to be coded, right click and from the menu, select **Code Selection** and then select **Code Selection** at **Existing Nodes**. This brings up the **Select Project Items** dialogue box.

2. Select the appropriate node by clicking on the box to the left of the node.

PLATE A.26 Coding in NVivo

the nodes applied to them. To this end NVivo has a useful aid called *coding stripes*. Selecting this feature allows you to see multi-coloured stripes that represent portions of coded text and the nodes that have been used. Overlapping codes do not represent any problem at all.

To activate this feature, → **View** in the **Ribbon** and then → **Coding Stripes** in the **Find** bar → **Show Nodes Recently Coding**. Plate A.27 shows these stripes. We can see that some segments have been coded at two or more nodes (for example, ***Visitors' ethnicity*** and ***Ethnicity critique***). All the nodes that have been used are clearly displayed.

SEARCHING TEXT

Once you have coded your data, however preliminary that coding may be, at some point you will want to conduct a search of your data. For instance, suppose that you want to retrieve all occurrences of a particular node. NVivo allows you to trawl rapidly through all your documents and find all the text that was coded at a particular node. This is very easy to do in NVivo 9.

To search for occurrences of a single node   These steps describe how to conduct a search for sequences of text that have been coded in terms of the node ***Ethnicity critique***. The stages are outlined in Plate A.28.

1. While in the **Document Viewer** → **Nodes** in the **Navigation view**. This will bring up your list of nodes in the **List view**.
2. If you cannot find the parents of ***Ethnicity critique***, → on the little box with a + sign to the left of ***Critique*** [this brings up a list of all branches of the node ***Critique***].
3. → on the + to the left of ***Ideological critique*** [this brings up a list of all branches of the node ***Ideological critique***].
4. Double-click on *Ethnicity critique*.
5. All instances of coded text at the node ***Ethnicity critique*** will appear at the bottom of the screen, as in Plate A.28.

To search for the intersection of two nodes   This section is concerned with searching for sequences

PLATE A.27   Coding stripes

1. Click on **Nodes**.

2. Locate the node to be analyzed and double click on it.

PLATE A.28   Stages in retrieving text from a node

of text that have been coded at two nodes: ***Aesthetic critique*** and ***Not critical of Disney***. This type of search is known as a 'Boolean search.' It will locate text coded in terms of the two nodes together (that is, where they intersect), *not* text coded in terms of each of the two nodes. The steps are as follows:

1. In the Document Viewer, → Queries in the Navigation view

2. → the **Explore** tab in the **Ribbon**

3. → **New Query** on the **Find** bar and select **Coding...** from the menu of options [opens the **Coding Query** dialogue box in Plate A.29]

4. → Coding Criteria tab

5. → Advanced tab

6. In the **Define more criteria**: panel, → **Coded at** from the drop-down menu

7. → **Select**. You then need to choose the two nodes to be analyzed

8. → Once the nodes have been selected, → **Add to List**

9. Make sure **AND** has been selected immediately below **Define more criteria**:

10. → Run

To search for specific text   NVivo can also perform searches for specific words or phrases, often referred to as 'strings' in computer jargon. For example, to search for **Magic Kingdom**, you would:

1. → Home on the Ribbon

2. → **Find...** [opens the **Find Content** dialog box in Plate A.30]

3. Insert **Magic Kingdom** to the right of **Text**

4. To the right of **Look in**, make sure **Text** has been selected

5. → Find Next

Text searching can be useful for the identification of possible *in vivo* codes (introduced in Chapter 14). You would then need to go back to the documents to create nodes to allow you to code in terms of any *in vivo* codes.

3. Select **New Query** and then **Coding...** from the menu of options. This brings up the **Coding Query** dialogue box.

2. Select **Explore**.

4. Select the **Coding Criteria** tab.

5. Select the **Advanced** tab.

9. Ensure **AND** has been selected.

10. Click on **Run**.

1. Click on **Queries**.

6. Select **Coded at**.

7. Click on **Select**.

8. Choose the nodes to be analyzed and click on **Add to List**. They will appear here.

PLATE A.29   The **Coding Query** dialogue box (searching for the intersection of two nodes)

PLATE A.30   The **Find Content** dialogue box

OUTPUT

To find the results of coding at a particular node, → the **Nodes** button in the bottom left. This will bring up your node structure. Find the node that you are interested in and simply double-click on it. This will bring up all text coded at that node along with information about which interview(s) the text comes from.

MEMOS

In Chapter 14 we noted that one feature of the grounded theory approach to qualitative data analysis is the use of memos in which ideas and illustrations might be stored. Memos can be easily created in NVivo. The steps, which are outlined in Plate A.31, are as follows:

1. In the Navigation View, → Sources
2. Under Sources → **Memos**
3. → **Create** tab on the **Find bar** and then
4. → **Memo** [opens the **New Memo** dialogue box shown in Plate A.31]
5. To the right of **Name**, type in a name for the memo (e.g. **Gender critique**). You can also provide a brief description of the document in the window to the right of Description, as in Plate A.31
6. → **OK**

SAVING AN NVivo PROJECT

When you have finished working on your data, you will need to save it for future use. To do this, on

2. Select **Memos**.

3. Select **Create**.

4. Select **Memo**. This brings up the **New Memo** dialogue box.

1. Select **Sources**.

5. Enter the memo **Name** and **Description** here.

6. Click on **OK**.

PLATE A.31 Stages in creating a memo

the menu bar at the top, →**File** → **Save**. This will save all the work you have done. You will then be given the opportunity to exit NVivo or to create or open a project without worrying about losing all your hard work. You might also consider backing up the project.

OPENING AN EXISTING NVivo PROJECT
To retrieve a project you have created, at the Welcome screen, → **File** → **Open**. This opens the **Open Project** dialogue box. Search for and then select the project you want to work on. Then → **Open**. Alternatively, simply click on the project you want to retrieve on the opening screen.

You can also open a NUD*IST project, or one designed using an earlier release of NVivo, by selecting the appropriate project type from the drop-down menu to the right of **File name:**.

FINAL THOUGHTS
As with SPSS, space limitations allow us to introduce only the most basic features of the NVivo software. In so doing, we hope to have given readers unfamiliar with CAQDAS a sample of how the system works. No doubt some will decide that they prefer the tried-and-tested scissors and paste approach. On the other hand, the software warrants serious consideration because of its power and flexibility.

For useful online help with NVivo, see the Online QDA website and the CAQDAS Networking Project website at:

http://onlineqda.hud.ac.uk/
http://caqdas.soc.surrey.ac.uk/

[Websites accessed 7 January 2011]

Questions for review

LEARNING NVIVO

- What is a node?
- What is the difference between a hierarchically organized node and a node that has not been hierarchically organized?
- What is *in vivo* coding?
- Do nodes have to be set up in advance?

- In NVivo, what is the difference between a document and a memo?
- How do you go about searching for a single node and the intersection of two nodes?
- Why might it be useful to display coding stripes?
- How do you search for specific text?

Appendix B: The Ideal Stages of Research

We describe what follows as 'ideal' not because it represents the best way to do things, but rather to indicate that it is an abstraction, a simplification of a more complex reality. There is no single best way to do research, any more than there is a single best way to build a house or paint a portrait. Sometimes the order of the tasks presented in Figure B.1 can be rearranged. Also, it's not uncommon to go from one step to the next and then backtrack to adjust something in a previous step. Nonetheless, some general points and observations can be made that outline how research may progress from its initial stages to its completion.

IN THE BEGINNING: MOTIVATION
Where does research begin?

Sometimes research begins with a sense of wonder, a feeling of amazement with the social world that is accompanied with a strong desire to understand it. Sometimes it begins with a sense of crisis, as when a society is strained to the breaking point and scholars are looking for solutions. This motivation has been around since the beginnings of social science in the eighteenth century. Since then, the challenges posed by urbanization, industrialization, ethnic conflict, and gender inequality (to name only a few) have provided the impetus for countless research projects. In other cases, the process of inquiry may begin with simple curiosity: as one wag put it, if you walk by a house with its curtains closed and wonder what goes on inside, you'd probably make a good social scientist.

Not all research begins with lofty motivations. In fact, the reasons for conducting a study are often quite mundane. For example, research may be done to enhance the career of the researcher, especially if it is supported by substantial funding. Sometimes researchers compete with one another to see who can produce the most publications. Similarly, graduate students (and some undergraduates) may do research simply in order to fulfill degree requirements. In most instances, the motivations for research are probably some combination of the exalted and the mundane.

THE RESEARCH QUESTION(S)
Once the decision has been made to do research in a particular area, the first task is to come up with a research question, or a set of research questions, that will give the study a specific focus or goal. A good research question should allow you to contribute to the existing knowledge of the topic, if only in a modest way. As we have mentioned at various points in this book, research questions in quantitative studies tend to be much more precise and explicit than those found in qualitative research. But even qualitative researchers must have at least a general idea of what they are trying to accomplish. With both types of inquiry, it's fairly common to revise research questions as the project proceeds, especially in the early stages.

LITERATURE REVIEW
Chances are that you won't be the first person to investigate your topic or to use the methodology you have in mind. Reading up on what others have done will help you understand your topic more fully and will prevent you from 'reinventing the wheel.' A good knowledge of the literature may also reveal contradictions or gaps in the existing understanding of your topic, which can form the basis of your project. Sometimes a review of the literature can lead to substantial revisions in research questions: for example, if you encounter a finding that lacks a compelling explanation and decide to make it the focus of your inquiry. Reviewing the literature may also spark ideas about how various methodologies could be applied to your topic.

CHOOSING A GENERAL RESEARCH ORIENTATION: QUANTITATIVE AND/OR QUALITATIVE
Once you've come up with your research question(s) and reviewed the existing literature in the area, you can decide on your general research orientation. However, it's not uncommon to decide on a particular orientation even before reviewing the literature or formulating any questions. For example, researchers specializing in qualitative studies are likely to start with the assumption

Motivation

↓

Research Question(s)

↓

Literature Review

↓

Choose general orientation

↕   ↕

Quantitative   **Qualititative**
(choose design)   (choose design)

↓   ↓

Experiments   Ethnography
Surveys   Participant Observation
– Structured interviews   Unstructured interviews
– Questionnaires   Semi-structured interviews
Structured observation   Life history
Case studies   Oral History
                                     Narrative analysis
↓   Focus groups
                                     Content analysis
Ethics review   – Ethnographic
                                     – Semiotics
↓   – Hermeneutics
                                     – Conversation analysis
Gather data   – Discourse analysis

↓   ↓

Analyze data   **Ethics review**

↓   ↓

Findings   **Gather data**

                                     ↕
Conclusions
– Do the findings support the hypotheses?   **Analyze data**
– Implications for existing theories?
– New hypotheses, concepts, or theories   ↓
  generated?
– Implications for further research?   **Findings**

                                     ↓

                                     Conclusions
                                     – Do the findings provide a new interpretation
                                       of a person, group, setting, event, or text?
                                     – Implications for existing theories?
                                     – New hypotheses, concepts, or theories
                                       generated?
                                     – Implications for further research?

FIGURE B.1   The Ideal Stages of Research

that their research will be qualitative rather than quantitative in nature. Likewise, a researcher who has done a number of survey projects may well design a study with surveys in mind, and may not even review the qualitative literature relevant to the topic of interest.

Of course it's also possible to combine quantitative and qualitative approaches in a single study, as the arrows below 'Choose general orientation' in Figure B.1 suggest. In practice, however, most studies are predominantly of one sort or the other.

PICKING A RESEARCH DESIGN FROM THE ONES AVAILABLE WITHIN A GENERAL RESEARCH ORIENTATION

Once your research orientation has been decided, a number of research designs are available for consideration. The choice of the research design depends on a number of things, but your first concern should be to find a design that's appropriate for your research questions. For example, if you've chosen to explore political attitudes using quantitative methods and want to be able to apply your findings to some larger population, a survey design would be appropriate. Similarly, if you want to do a qualitative study of how professional jazz dancers cope with the pressures of auditions, then unstructured or semi-structured interviews would be a reasonable choice of design. Another consideration is whether a cross-sectional or longitudinal design would be most appropriate to answer the research questions.

Other factors that affect the choice of design include things like the availability of resources such as funding and time. If you can't afford to select a large probability sample, a full-blown survey analysis will be out of reach. Similarly, ethnography might be your design of choice, but time and travel constraints could rule that out. In most cases, some sort of compromise has to be made between the best possible research design and what is feasible under the circumstances.

ETHICS REVIEW

As we have emphasized at various points in this text, ethics are an important consideration at every stage of a research project, including the writing-up of results. Once a research design has been picked, researchers in most cases have to present an ethics committee with a proposal that outlines how ethical considerations will be

handled in each phase of the project. Note that this step can usually be skipped if the research does not involve human or animal subjects; for instance, if the goal is to offer a new interpretation of a body of theoretical work without gathering empirical data.

GATHER DATA

Data gathering can begin as soon as the ethics committee grants its approval. Sometimes a pilot study is conducted to determine whether the chosen method of data collection needs any refinement. For example, a pilot study can be used to find out whether the questions prepared for use in a survey are clear enough for respondents to understand, or whether potential participants in a qualitative study react strongly to the presence of the observer.

ANALYZE DATA

In quantitative studies, data analysis usually begins after all the data have been gathered. In qualitative research, by contrast, the process is often iterative, with preliminary data analysis leading to a change in either the kind of information to be sought or the way it is to be gathered. That is why there is a two-headed arrow between 'Gather data' and 'Analyze data' in the qualitative section of Figure B.1. At this stage software may be used (for example, SPSS for quantitative analysis or NVivo for qualitative).

FINDINGS

The findings are the results of the data analysis. For instance, a quantitative researcher might find that support for a particular government policy is strongly associated with age and ethnicity. Or a qualitative study of heroin addicts in Vancouver's downtown east side might find that they resent the people from whom they purchase their drugs.

CONCLUSIONS

Finally, what does it all mean? At this point an effort is usually made to relate the findings of the study to existing theories or knowledge on the topic. This is where you enter the debate about the subject matter with other scholars.

Quantitative social scientists will discuss whether their findings support their hypotheses (if they had specific hypotheses to begin with—not all of them do). Support for a hypothesis could provide substantiation for a particular theory. For instance, findings indicating that economic development leads to greater similarity in gender roles would support a version of modernization theory. If the hypotheses are not supported or if the findings are not consistent with the theory, a case can be made that the theory has to be revised or abandoned. Sometimes the findings will generate new hypotheses, concepts, or theories. In virtually all cases, the researcher will be able to suggest ways in which further research could be beneficial—perhaps different variables should be examined, or maybe the key variables need to be measured differently.

Qualitative researchers will discuss whether their findings suggest a new interpretation of the subject matter. For example, findings derived from interviews with 15-year-old single mothers might reveal something new about how certain young people view sexuality and their relationships with their peers—something quite different from what is currently believed. Like quantitative work, qualitative analysis may produce new hypotheses, concepts, or theories. Similarly, qualitative researchers can usually outline the ways in which further research would be desirable—for instance, by expanding the study of 15-year-old single mothers to include 15-year-old boys.

Glossary

Terms in *italic* type are defined elsewhere in the Glossary.

action research An approach in which the researcher and client collaborate to diagnose a problem and develop a solution based on the diagnosis.

adjacency pair Two kinds of talk activity that are linked together, such as an invitation and a response.

analytic induction An approach to the analysis of qualitative data in which the collection of data continues and the hypothesis is modified until no cases inconsistent with it are found.

arithmetic mean What everyday language refers to as the 'average': the sum of all the scores divided by the number of scores. Also known simply as the **mean**.

biographical method See *life history method*.

bivariate analysis Examination of the relationship between two variables, as in *contingency tables*; *correlation*.

CAQDAS An abbreviation of **c**omputer-assisted (or -aided) **q**ualitative **d**ata **a**nalysis **s**oftware.

case study A *research design* that entails detailed and intensive analysis of either a single case or (for comparative purposes) a small number of cases.

causality A causal connection between variables, as opposed to a mere *correlation* between them.

cells The areas in a table where the rows and columns intersect and data are inserted.

census A count of an entire *population*; by contrast, a *sample* counts only some units of a population.

chi-square test Chi-square (χ^2) is a test of *statistical significance* used to establish confidence that a finding displayed in a *contingency table* can be generalized from a *probability sample* to the *population* from which it is drawn.

closed, closed-ended question A question in an *interview schedule* or *questionnaire* that presents the respondent with a fixed set of possible answers to choose from; also called a **fixed-choice question**.

cluster sampling A procedure in which the researcher first samples sets of cases ('clusters') and then samples units within them, usually using a *probability sampling* method.

code, coding In *quantitative research*, codes are the tags used to assign the data on each *variable* to a category of the variable in question. Numbers are usually assigned to each category to allow easier computer processing. In *qualitative research*, coding is the process in which data are broken down into component parts, which are then assigned names.

coding frame or **coding manual** A list of the codes to be used in the analysis of a particular set of data. For answers to a structured interview schedule or questionnaire, the coding frame delineates the categories used for each *open question*. With *closed questions*, the coding frame is essentially incorporated into the fixed answers from which respondents must choose; hence the term 'pre-coded question.'

concept A general or abstract idea; a category that serves to organize observations and ideas about some aspect of the social world.

concurrent validity A type of validity that is tested by relating a measure to an existing criterion or a different indicator of the concept to see if one predicts the other; one of the main forms of *measurement validity*.

connotation A term used in *semiotics* to refer to the meanings of a *sign* associated with the social context within which it operates: a sign's connotations are supplementary to its *denotation* and less immediately apparent.

constant An attribute on which cases do not differ; compare with *variable*.

constructionism, constructionist An *ontological* position (the antithesis of *objectivism*) according to which social phenomena and their meanings are continually being created by social actors; also known as **constructivism**.

construct validity 1) Same as *measurement validity*; 2) a type of measurement validity that is established by determining whether the concepts being measured relate empirically in a manner that would be predicted by relevant theories.

content analysis An approach to the analysis of documents and texts that seeks to quantify content in terms of predetermined categories in a systematic and replicable manner. The term is sometimes used in connection with qualitative research as well; see *qualitative content analysis*.

contingency table A table made up of rows and columns that shows the *relationship* between two *variables.* Usually, at least one of the variables is a *nominal variable* or *ordinal variable.* Each *cell* in the table shows the number or (more often) the percentage of cases for that specific combination of the two variables.

control group   See **experiment**.

convenience sample   A sample that is selected because of its availability to the researcher; a form of *non-probability sample.*

conversation analysis   The fine-grained analysis of talk (recorded in naturally occurring situations and then transcribed) to uncover the underlying structures in interaction that make social order possible. Conversation analysis is grounded in *ethnomethodology.*

correlation   An approach to the analysis of relationships between *interval/ratio variables* and/or *ordinal variables* that seeks to assess the strength and direction of the relationship between the variables concerned. *Pearson's r* and *Spearman's rho* are both correlational measures. The corresponding term **measure of association** is often used with *nominal variables.*

covert research   A term frequently used in connection with *ethnographic* research in which the researcher does not reveal his or her true identity and/or intentions. Such research may violate the ethical principle of *informed consent.*

Cramér's V   A statistical measure used to assess the strength of the relationship between two *nominal variables.*

critical realism   A *realist* epistemology according to which the study of the social world should be concerned with the identification of social structures in order to change them and thereby counteract inequalities and injustices. Unlike positivism, which is an *empiricist* epistemology, critical realism maintains that the structures may not be directly perceivable.

cross-sectional design   A *research design* in which data are collected at a single point in time.

deduction, deductive   An approach to inquiry that begins with the statement of a theory from which hypotheses may be derived and tested; compare with *inductive.*

denotation   A term used in *semiotics* to refer to the principal and most manifest meaning of a *sign*; compare with *connotation.*

dependent variable   A *variable* that is caused (or assumed to be caused) by an *independent variable.*

diary   A written memoir. Three types of diary are discussed in this book: personal diaries that are

spontaneously produced and can be analyzed as *personal documents*; diaries written at the behest of a researcher; and diaries written by researchers to log their activities and reflections.

dichotomous variable   A variable with just two categories.

dimension   An aspect of a *concept.*

discourse analysis   An approach to the analysis of talk and other forms of communication that emphasizes the way language can create versions of reality.

dispersion   The degree of variation in a set of scores. Commonly used measures of dispersion include the *range* and the *standard deviation.*

ecological fallacy   The error of assuming that inferences about individuals can be made from data on the characteristics of groups.

ecological validity   A type of validity that is achieved when social scientific findings are applicable to people's everyday, natural social settings.

empiricism   An approach to the study of reality according to which only knowledge gained by observation through the senses is acceptable.

epistemology, epistemological   A branch of philosophy concerned with what constitutes knowledge and how knowledge is to be acquired; see *positivism, realism,* and *interpretivism.*

eta   A test of the strength of the *relationship* between two *variables.* The *independent variable* is usually a *nominal variable* while the *dependent variable* must be an *interval variable* or *ratio variable.*

ethnography, ethnographer, ethnographic   Like *participant observation,* a research method in which the researcher is immersed in a social setting for an extended period of time, observing behaviour, asking questions, and analyzing what is said in conversations both between subjects and with the fieldworker. As a term, 'ethnography' is more inclusive than 'participant observation,' which emphasizes the observational component. Written accounts of ethnographic research are often referred to as **ethnographies**.

ethnomethodology   A sociological perspective concerned with the way social order is established and maintained through talk and interaction; the intellectual foundation of *conversation analysis.*

evaluation research   Research that concentrates on the evaluation of real-life interventions, such as policy changes.

experiment   A *research design* that rules out alternative explanations of findings deriving from it (in other words, that possesses *internal validity*) because it involves (a) both an experimental group, which is exposed to a treatment, and a control group, which is not, and (b) *random assignment* to the two groups.

experimental group See **experiment**.

external validity A type of validity that is achieved if the results of a study can be generalized beyond the specific research context in which they were generated.

face validity A type of validity that is achieved if, on inspection, an *indicator* appears to measure the *concept* in question.

facilitator See **moderator**.

factor analysis A statistical technique used for large numbers of *indicators* to establish whether there is a tendency for groups of them to be interrelated. It is often used with *multiple-indicator measures* to see if they cluster into one or more groups (factors).

field experiment A study in which the researcher directly intervenes in and/or manipulates a natural setting to observe what happens as a consequence.

field notes A detailed *ethnographic* account of events, conversations, and behaviour, and the researcher's initial reflections on them.

focus group A form of group interview in which there are several participants (in addition to the *moderator/facilitator*); there is an emphasis in the questioning on a particular topic or related topics; and interaction within the group and the joint construction of meaning is observed.

frequency table A table that displays the number and/or percentage of units (for example, people) in different categories of a variable.

gatekeeper A non-researcher who controls researchers' access to a research setting.

generalization, generalizability To **generalize** a research finding is to apply it to people or groups who were not in the study.

grounded theory An approach to the analysis of qualitative data in which the goal is to use the data to generate theory; the data collection and analysis proceed in an iterative (recursive) fashion.

hermeneutics An approach to the interpretation of texts that emphasizes the need to understand them from the perspective of their authors.

hypothesis An informed speculation, which is set up to be tested, about the possible relationship between two or more variables.

independent variable A *variable* that has (or is assumed to have) a causal impact on a *dependent variable*.

index See **scale**.

indicator Something employed to measure a *concept* when no direct measure is available.

induction, inductive, inductivist An approach to inquiry that begins with the collection of data, which are then used to develop theories, hypotheses, and concepts; compare with *deductive*.

informed consent The principle that prospective participants in social research should be given as much information as they need to make a sound decision about whether to participate in a study; a key principle in social research ethics.

inter-coder reliability The degree to which two or more individuals agree on the *coding* of an item; a frequent concern in the *coding* of answers to *open questions* in research based on *questionnaires* or *structured interviews*.

internal reliability or **internal consistency** The degree to which the items that make up a *scale* or *index* are consistent or correlated.

internal validity A type of validity that is achieved if there is sufficient evidence that a *causal* relationship exists between two or more variables.

interpretivism, interpretivist An *epistemological* position that requires the social scientist to grasp the subjective meanings that people attach to their actions and behaviours.

intersubjectivity A condition in which two or more observers of the same phenomenon are in agreement as to what they have observed. *Empiricists* assume that intersubjectivity is possible insofar as knowledge is based on data acquired through the senses.

interval variable A *variable* for which the intervals between the categories are identical and quantifiable.

intervening variable A *variable* that is affected by a another variable and in turn has a causal impact on a third. Taking an intervening variable into account often facilitates the understanding of the relationship between two variables. An intervening variable is the 'Y' in 'X $\longrightarrow$ Y $\longrightarrow$ Z.'

interview guide A brief list of memory prompts regarding areas to be covered in *unstructured* and *semi-structured interviewing*.

interview schedule A collection of questions designed to be asked by an interviewer; always used in a *structured interview*.

intra-coder reliability   The degree to which an individual coder is consistent over time in the *coding* of an item; likely to be an issue in the coding of answers to *open questions* in research based on *questionnaires* or *structured interviews*.

Kendall's tau-b   A test of the strength of the *relationship* between two *ordinal variables*.

key informant   Someone who offers the researcher, usually an *ethnographer*, particularly perceptive information about the social setting, important events, and individuals.

life history interview   An *unstructured interview* that is similar to an *oral history interview*, but designed to gather information on the entire biography of a respondent.

life history method   A method (often referred to as the *biographical method*) that emphasizes the inner experience of individuals and its connections with larger societal events throughout the life course. It usually entails *life history interviews* and the use of *personal documents* as data.

Likert item, Likert scale   A widely used format in which respondents are typically asked their degree of agreement with a series of attitude statements that together form a *multiple-indicator* measure. The scale is designed to measure the intensity of respondents' feelings about an issue.

longitudinal research   A *research design* in which data are collected on at least two separate occasions.

mail questionnaire   The traditional term for what is now more commonly known as a *postal questionnaire*.

mean   See **arithmetic mean**.

measure of central tendency   A measure that summarizes the magnitude of a set of scores; examples includes the *arithmetic mean*, *median*, and *mode*.

measure of dispersion   A measure (such as the *range* or *standard deviation*) that summarizes the amount of variation in a set of scores.

measurement validity   The degree to which a measure of a concept actually measures what it is supposed to measure; see also *face validity* and *concurrent validity*.

median   The mid-point in a set of scores that is arranged in order.

member validation   See **respondent validation**.

meta-analysis   A method for determining the relationship between variables by drawing together the findings from several research studies. It is typically achieved through quantitative measurement and the use of statistical procedures.

missing data   Data that are not available; for example, when a respondent in social survey research does not answer a question. These are referred to as 'missing values' in SPSS.

mode   The score that occurs most frequently in a set of scores.

moderated relationship   A *relationship* between two *variables* is said to be 'moderated' when the effect of the independent variable varies at different levels of a second independent variable (also known as a statistical interaction).

moderator   The person who guides the questioning of a *focus group*, also called a *facilitator*.

multiple-indicator measure   A measure that uses more than one *indicator*.

multi-strategy research   Research that combines *quantitative* and *qualitative* approaches.

multivariate analysis   The examination of relationships among three or more *variables*.

narrative analysis   An approach focused on the search for and analysis of stories that people use to understand their lives and the world around them.

naturalism, naturalistic   A style of research designed to minimize disturbance to the natural or everyday social world.

negative relationship   A *relationship* between two *variables* in which one decreases as the other increases.

nominal variable   A *variable* comprised of categories that cannot be ranked; also known as a categorical variable.

non-probability sample   A sample selected using a non-random sampling method. Essentially, this means that some units in the population are more likely than others to be selected.

non-response   Occurs if someone in a sample refuses to participate in the study, cannot be contacted, or for some other reason does not supply the required data.

null hypothesis   A *hypothesis* of no relationship between two variables; the hypothesis that the researcher hopes to disprove.

objectivism, objectivist   An *ontological* position according to which social phenomena have an existence independent of social actors or their perceptions; compare with *constructionism*.

observation schedule A device used in *structured observation* that specifies the categories of behaviour that are to be observed and gives instructions on how behaviour should be allocated to those categories.

official statistics Data compiled by (or on behalf of) state agencies in the course of conducting their business.

ontology, ontological A branch of philosophy concerned with the nature of reality: for example, whether social entities can and should be considered objective entities with a reality external to specific social actors, or as social constructions built up through the perceptions and actions of these actors. See *objectivism* and *constructionism*.

open, open-ended question In an *interview schedule* or *questionnaire,* a format that does not present the respondent with a set of possible answers to choose from; compare with *closed question*.

operational definition A definition that spells out the operations that are to be performed to measure a *concept*.

oral history interview A largely *unstructured interview* in which respondents are asked to recall and reflect on events they have experienced.

ordinal variable A variable whose categories can be rank-ordered, but the distances between the categories are not equal or known across the range.

outlier An extreme value (either very high or very low) in a distribution of scores. If a *variable* has an outlier, it will distort both the *arithmetic mean* and the *range*.

paradigm A cluster of beliefs and assumptions, often unstated, that influence views on what should be studied, how research should be done, and how results should be interpreted.

participant observation Research in which fieldworkers are immersed in a social setting for an extended period of time, observing behaviour, asking questions, and analyzing what is said in conversations both between the people under study and with the researcher. It usually includes interviewing *key informants* and studying documents. In this book, 'participant observation' refers to the observational aspect of *ethnography*.

Pearson's r A measure of the strength and direction of the *relationship* between two *interval/ratio variables*.

personal documents Documents not written for an official purpose that provide first-person accounts of the writer's life and events within it. Examples include *diaries*, letters, and autobiographies.

population All cases or people covered by a theory or explanation; the universe of units from which a *sample* is selected.

positive relationship A *relationship* between two *variables* whereby both move in the same direction, either increasing or decreasing simultaneously.

positivism, positivist An *epistemological* position that advocates using the methods of the natural sciences in the study of social reality.

postal questionnaire A *questionnaire* that is sent out and returned by regular (non-electronic) mail.

postmodernism A position that questions the notion of a pre-existing external reality that dispassionate social scientists can simply uncover, and argues that no single account of social reality can be authoritative. Postmodernists prefer qualitative methods.

pre-coded question Another name for a *closed question*; used because a numerical *code* has been pre-assigned to each of the predetermined answers (hence there is no need for a *coding frame*).

probability sample A sample, selected at random, in which each unit in the population has a known probability of being selected.

QSR NVivo A CAQDAS package that derives from but goes beyond NUD*IST (Non-numerical Unstructured Data Indexing Searching and Theorizing).

qualitative content analysis An approach to constructing the meaning of documents and text that allows categories to emerge out of data analysis and recognizes the significance of the context in which items appear.

qualitative research Inquiry that uses mainly words, images, and other non-numerical symbols as data and involves little or no quantification. As a research strategy it tends to be *inductivist, constructivist,* and *interpretivist*, but qualitative researchers do not always subscribe to all three features; compare with *quantitative research*.

quantitative research Inquiry using quantitative data-gathering techniques and statistical analysis. As a research strategy it tends to be *deductivist* and *objectivist* and to incorporate a natural science model of the research process (in particular, one influenced by *positivism*), but quantitative researchers do not always subscribe to all three features; compare with *qualitative research*.

quasi-experiment A *research design* that resembles an *experiment* but does not meet all the requirements and therefore does not exhibit complete *internal validity*.

questionnaire A collection of written questions or response items that the respondent completes without the aid of an interviewer.

quota sample A type of *non-probability sample* that matches the proportions of people in different categories in the *population*.

random assignment The random allocation of research participants to either the experimental or the control group(s) in an *experiment*.

random sampling The form of sampling in which all units of a *population* have the same chance of being selected.

range The difference between the maximum and the minimum score in a set of scores associated with an *interval* or *ratio variable*.

ratio variable An *interval variable* with a true zero point.

reactivity, reactive effect The effect on research participants of knowing that they are being studied, which may result in atypical or inauthentic behaviour.

realism, realist An epistemological position according to which reality is independent of the senses but is to some degree accessible to the researcher's tools and theoretical speculations. See also *critical realism*.

reflexive, reflexivity Terms used to refer to social researchers' awareness of the implications that their methods, values, biases, decisions, and mere presence in the situations they investigate have for the knowledge they generate.

relationship An association between two variables whereby the variation in one variable coincides with variation in another variable.

reliability The degree to which a measure of a concept is stable or consistent.

replication, replicability The degree to which a study can be repeated using the same methods.

representative sample A sample that is similar to the *population* in all important respects.

research design The term used in this book to refer to a framework for the collection and analysis of data. The choice of research design reflects the goals that the researcher hopes to achieve (for example, *generalization*, establishing *causality*, or producing empathetic understanding).

respondent validation A process whereby researchers provide the people on whom they conducted research with an account of their findings and request their feedback on it; sometimes called **member validation**.

response set A term for the tendency for some people, when responding to *multiple-indicator* measures, to respond to every item in the same way, suggesting that their answers are motivated by something other than their actual feelings. Three of the most common response-set effects are 'acquiescence,' 'social desirability,' and 'laziness or boredom.'

sample The segment or subset of the *population* selected for research. The selection may be based on either *probability* or *non-probability sampling*.

sampling error Differences between the characteristics of a *random sample* and the *population* from which it is selected.

sampling frame A listing of units in the *population* from which a *sample* is to be selected.

scale A term usually used interchangeably with **index** to refer to a *multiple-indicator measure* in which the scores an individual respondent gives for each component *indicator* are summed to produce a composite score for that person.

secondary analysis The analysis of data (quantitative or qualitative) by researchers other than those responsible for their collection, often for purposes that the latter may not have envisaged.

semiotics An approach to the analysis of documents and other materials that emphasizes the importance of *signs* and symbols, seeking out their deeper meaning and exploring their intended effects.

semi-structured interview A type of interview in which the interviewer has a series of questions in the general form of an *interview guide* and is able to vary the sequence of questions. The questions are typically more general than those specified by a *structured interview* schedule, and the interviewer usually has some latitude to ask further questions in response to replies that appear significant.

sensitizing concept A *concept* that is not fixed in advance (as with an *operational definition*) but rather is treated as a guide that suggests what may be relevant or important in an investigation.

sign A term used in *semiotics*. Each sign has two parts: the signifier (manifestation of a sign) and the signified (the deeper meaning to which the signifier refers).

simple random sample A *sample* in which each unit selected from the *population*, and each combination of units, has an equal probability of being included.

snowball sample A *non-probability sample* in which the researcher makes initial contact with a small group of people connected to the research topic and then uses them to establish contact with others.

social desirability bias Distortion of data caused by respondents' efforts to construct accounts that conform to a socially acceptable model of behaviour.

Spearman's rho [ρ] A measure of the strength and direction of the *relationship* between two *ordinal variables*.

SPSS Statistical Package for the Social Sciences: a computer program that facilitates the management and analysis of quantitative data.

spurious relationship A *relationship* in which two *variables* are *correlated* but not *causally* related. It is produced by the impact of a common third variable on each of the two variables. When the third variable is controlled, the relationship disappears.

standard deviation A measure of how widely the scores that make up a set are dispersed around the *mean*.

standard error of the mean An estimate of the degree to which a *sample mean* is likely to differ from the *population mean*.

statistical significance (test of) A test (such as the *chi-square* test) that allows analysts to estimate the probability that the results of a study of a randomly selected *sample* are generalizable to the *population* from which the sample was drawn. Note that statistical significance has nothing to do with substantive significance or importance. Using a test of statistical significance to generalize from a sample to a population is known as **statistical inference**.

stratified random sample A *sample* in which units are *randomly sampled* from a *population* that has been previously divided into sub-groups (strata).

structured interview One in which all respondents are asked exactly the same questions in the same order with the aid of a formal *interview schedule*.

structured observation Often called **systematic observation**, this is a research method in which the researchers follow explicitly formulated rules regarding not only what they should look for, but when and where, and how they should record what they have observed.

survey research A *research design* in which data are collected from respondents, mainly by *questionnaire* or *structured interview*; typically, the data are then examined to detect *relationships* among *variables*.

symbolic interactionism A theoretical perspective in which social interaction is understood to be based on the meanings that actors attach to their actions and the contexts in which they occur.

systematic sample A *probability sampling* method in which units are selected from a *sampling frame* at fixed intervals (for example, every fifth unit).

text A written document or, in more recent years, anything (from paintings to buildings to theme parks) that may be 'read' and analyzed for its symbolic value.

theoretical sampling A term used mainly in the context of *grounded theory* to refer to sampling carried out in such a way that emerging theoretical considerations guide the collection of data and/or the selection of cases (usually research participants). This process is supposed to continue until a point of *theoretical saturation* is reached.

theoretical saturation In *grounded theory*, the point where emerging *concepts* have been fully explored and no new insights are being generated. See also *theoretical sampling*.

thick description A term coined by Geertz (1973) to refer to detailed accounts of a social setting or people's experiences that can form the basis for general statements about a culture and its significance in peoples' lives.

transcription, transcript The verbatim written record of a taped *interview* or *focus group* session.

triangulation The use of more than one method or source of data so that findings may be cross-checked.

trustworthiness A general criterion (composed of four more specific criteria) used by some writers in assessing the quality of *qualitative research*.

turn-taking In *conversation analysis*, the idea that taking turns to speak is a rule that helps to maintain order in everyday conversation.

univariate analysis The analysis of one *variable* at a time.

unobtrusive measures, unobtrusive methods, unobtrusive observations Measures that do not cause *reactivity* because they do not make research participants aware that they are being studied.

unstructured interview An interview in which the interviewer is free to explore any topic, although an *interview guide* is often used. The questioning is usually informal and the content, phrasing and sequencing of questions may vary from one interview to the next.

validity A research criterion concerned with the integrity of the conclusions generated by a particular study. There are several types of validity: see, in particular, *measurement validity, internal validity, external validity,* and *ecological validity*. When used on its own, *validity* is usually taken to refer to *measurement validity*.

variable   An attribute or characteristic that may vary over time or from case to case. See also *dependent variable* and *independent variable*; compare with *constant*.

vignette technique   A method in which people are presented with 'vignettes' (hypothetical scenarios) and then asked how they would respond if they faced the circumstances depicted in the scenarios.

References

Abraham, J. (1994), 'Bias in Science and Medical Knowledge: The Opren Controversy,' *Sociology*, 28: 717–36.

Achille, M., and Ogloff, J. (1997), 'When Is a Request for Assisted Suicide Legitimate?' *Canadian Jour. of Behavioural Sci.*, 29: 19–27.

Adams, M. (2003), *Fire and Ice* (Toronto: Penguin).

Adriaenssens, C., and Cadman, L. (1999), 'An Adaptation of Moderated E-mail Focus Groups to Assess the Potential of a New Online (Internet) Financial Services Offer in the UK,' *Jour. of the Market Research Society*, 41: 417–24.

Agresti, A., and Finlay, B. (2009), *Statistical Methods for the Social Sciences* (Upper Saddle River, NJ: Prentice-Hall).

Alford, J.R., Funk, C.L., and Hibbing, J.R. (2005), 'Are Political Orientations Genetically Transmitted?' *American Political Science Review*, 99: 153–67.

Altheide, D.L. (1996), *Qualitative Media Analysis* (Thousand Oaks, CA: Sage).

——— (2004), 'Ethnographic Content Analysis,' in M. Lewis-Beck, A. Bryman, and T. Liao (eds.), *The Sage Encycl. of Soc. Sci. Research Methods* (Thousand Oaks, CA: Sage).

Anderson, K., Sebaldt, R., Lohfeld, L., Burgess, K., Donald, F., and Kaczorowski, J. (2006), 'Views of Family Physicians in Southwestern Ontario on Preventive Care Services and Performance Incentives,' *Family Practice*, 23: 469–71.

Andrews, K., Smith, L., Henzi, D., and Demps, E. (2007), 'Faculty and Student Perceptions of Academic Integrity at U.S. and Canadian Dental Schools,' *Jour. of Dental Education*, 71: 1027–39.

Armstrong, D., Gosling, A., Weinman, J., and Marteau, T. (1997), 'The Place of Inter-Rater Reliability in Qualitative Research: An Empirical Study,' *Sociology*, 31: 597–606.

Armstrong, G. (1993), 'Like that Desmond Morris?' in D. Hobbs and T. May (eds.), *Interpreting the Field: Accounts of Ethnography* (Oxford: Clarendon Press).

——— (1998), *Football Hooligans: Knowing the Score* (Oxford: Berg).

Aronson, E. (1992), *The Social Animal: Sixth Edition* (New York: W.H. Freeman and Company).

Atkinson, J.M., and Drew, P. (1979). *Order in Court: The Organization of Verbal Interaction in Judicial Settings* (London: Macmillan).

Atkinson, M. (2002), 'Pretty in Ink: Conformity, Resistance and Negotiation in Women's Tattooing,' *Sex Roles*, 47: 219–35.

——— (2004), 'Tattooing and Civilizing Processes,' *Canadian Rev. of Sociology and Anthropology*, 41: 125–46.

Atkinson, P. (1981), *The Clinical Experience* (Farnborough: Gower).

——— (1990), *The Ethnographic Imagination: Textual Constructions of Society* (London: Routledge).

——— (2004), 'Life Story Interview,' in M. Lewis-Beck, A. Bryman, and T. Liao (eds.), *The Sage Encycl. of Soc. Sci. Research Methods* (Thousand Oaks, CA: Sage).

——— and Coffey, A. (1995), 'Realism and Its Discontents: On the Crisis of Cultural Representation in Ethnographic Texts,' in B. Adam and S. Allan (eds.), *Theorizing Culture: An Interdisciplinary Critique after Postmodernism* (London: UCL Press).

Baer, D., Curtis, J., and Grabb, E. (2001), 'Has Voluntary Association Membership Declined? Cross-national Analyses for Fifteen Countries,' *Canadian Rev. of Sociology*, 38: 249–74.

Bahr, H., Caplow, T., and Chadwick, B. (1983), 'Middletown III: Problems of Replication, Longitudinal Measurement, and Triangulation,' *Annual Rev. of Sociology*, 9: 243–64.

Bailey, K. D. (1994), *Methods of Social Research: Fourth Edition* (Toronto: Maxwell Macmillan Canada).

Bales, Robert (1951), *Interaction Process Analysis* (Cambridge, MA: Addison-Wesley).

Bampton, R., and Cowton, C.J. (2002), 'The E-Interview,' *Forum Qual. Social Research*, 3 (2): www.Qual.-research.net/fqs/.

Barkham, P. and Jenkins, R. (2002), 'Fears for Fresher Who Vanished on Mission to Talk to the Homeless,' *The Times* [London], 13 December.

Barnard, M., and Frischer, M. (1995), 'Combining Quantitative and Qualitative Approaches: Researching HIV-Related Risk Behaviours among Drug Injectors,' *Addiction Research*, 2: 351–62.

Barter, C., and Renold, E. (1999), 'The Use of Vignettes in Qualitative Research,' *Social Research Update*, 25.

Beagan, B. (2001), 'Micro Inequities and Everyday Inequalities: "Race," Gender, Sexuality and Class in Medical School,' *Canadian Jour. of Sociology*, 26: 583–610.

Beardsworth, A., and Keil, T. (1992), 'The Vegetarian Option: Varieties, Conversions, Motives and Careers,' *Sociological Rev.*, 40: 253–93.

——— (1997), *Sociology on the Menu: An Invitation to the Study of Food and Society* (London: Routledge).

——— Bryman, A., Ford, J., and Keil, T. (n.d.), '"The Dark Figure" in Statistics of Unemployment and Vacancies,' discussion paper, Department of Social Sciences, Loughborough Univ.

——— Keil, T., Goode, J., Haslam, C., and Lancashire, E. (2002), 'Women, Men and Food: The Significance of Gender for Nutritional Attitudes and Choices,' *Brit. Food Jour.*, 104: 470–91.

Becker, H. (1958), 'Problems of Inference and Proof in Participant Observation,' *Amer. Sociological Rev.*, 23: 652–60.

——— (1963), *Outsiders: Studies in the Sociology of Deviance* (NY: Free Press).

——— (1967), 'Whose Side Are We On?' *Social Problems*, 14: 239–47.

——— (1970), 'Practitioners of Vice and Crime,' in R. Habenstein (ed.), *Pathways to Data* (Chicago: Aldine).

——— (1986), *Writing for Social Scientists: How to Start*

and Finish Your Thesis, Book, or Article (Chicago: Univ. of Chicago Press).

———— and Geer, B. (1957), 'Participant Observation and Interviewing: A Comparison,' *Human Organization*, 16: 28–32.

Beharrell, P. (1993), 'AIDS and the British Press,' in J. Eldridge (ed.), *Getting the Message: News, Truth and Power* (London: Routledge).

Belk, R., Sherry, J., and Wallendorf, M. (1988), 'A Naturalistic Inquiry into Buyer and Seller Behaviour at a Swap Meet,' *Jour. of Consumer Research*, 14: 449–70.

Bell, E. (2007), 'Separatism and Quasi-Separatism in Alberta,' *Prairie Forum*, 32: 335–55.

———— Aitken Schermer, J., and Vernon, P.A. (2009), 'The Origins of Political Attitudes and Behaviours: An Analysis Using Twins,' *Canadian Jour. of Political Science*, 42: 855–79.

———— Jansen, H., and Young, L. (2007), 'Sustaining a Dynasty in Alberta: The 2004 Provincial Election,' *Canadian Poli. Sci. Rev.*, 1: 27–49.

Beres, M.A., Crow, B., and Gotell, L. (2009), 'The Perils of Institutionalization in Neoliberal Times: Results of a National Survey of Canadian Sexual Assault and Rape Crisis Centres,' *Canadian Jour. of Sociology*, 34: 135–63.

Berthoud, R. (2000a), 'Introduction: The Dynamics of Social Change,' in R. Berthoud and J. Gershuny (eds.), *Seven Years in the Lives of British Families: Evidence on the Dynamics of Social Change from the British Household Panel Survey* (Bristol: Policy Press).

———— (2000b), 'A Measure of Changing Health,' in R. Berthoud and J. Gershuny (eds.), *Seven Years in the Lives of British Families: Evidence on the Dynamics of Social Change from the British Household Panel Survey* (Bristol: Policy Press).

Bhaskar, R. (1989), *Reclaiming Reality: A Critical Introduction to Contemporary Philosophy* (London: Verso).

Billig, M. (1991), *Ideology and Opinions: Studies in Rhetorical Psychology* (Cambridge: Cambridge Univ. Press).

Blaikie, A. (2001), 'Photographs in the Cultural Account: Contested Narratives and Collective Memory in the Scottish Islands,' *Sociological Rev.*, 49: 345–67.

Blauner, R. (1964), *Alienation and Freedom: The Factory Worker and His Industry* (Chicago: University of Chicago Press).

Blaxter, M. (1990), *Health and Lifestyles* (London: Routledge).

Bloor, M. (1997), 'Addressing Social Problems through Qualitative Research,' in D. Silverman (ed.), *Qualitative Research: Theory, Method and Practice* (London: Sage).

————, Frankland, S., Thomas, M., and Robson, K. (2001), *Focus Groups in Social Research* (London: Sage).

Blumer, H. (1954), 'What Is Wrong with Social Theory?' *Amer. Sociological Rev.*, 19: 3–10.

———— (1956), 'Sociological Analysis and the "Variable,"' *Amer. Sociological Rev.*, 21: 683–90.

———— (1962), 'Society as Symbolic Interaction,' in A. Rose (ed.), *Human Behavior and Social Processes* (London: Routledge & Kegan Paul).

Bottomore, T.B., and Rubel, M. (1963), *Karl Marx: Selected Writings in Sociology and Social Philosophy* (Harmondsworth, UK: Penguin).

Bourdieu, P. (1987), 'The Historical Genesis of a Pure Aesthetic,' *Jour. of Aesthetics and Art Criticism*, 46 (Analytic Aesthetics): 201–10.

Brannigan, A. (2004), *The Rise and Fall of Social Psychology: The Use and Misuse of the Experimental Method* (Hawthorne, NY: Aldine de Gruyter).

Brannigan, A., Gemmell, W., Pevalin, D., and Wade, T. (2002), 'Self-control and Social Control in Childhood Misconduct and Aggression: The Role of Family Structure and Hyperactivity,' *Canadian Jour. of Criminology*, 44: 119–42.

Braverman, H. (1974), *Labour and Monopoly Capital: The Degradation of Work in the Twentieth Century* (London: Monthly Rev. Press).

Brayfield, A., and Rothe, H. (1951), 'An Index of Job Satisfaction,' *Jour. of Applied Psych.*, 35: 307–11.

Bridgman, P. (1927), *The Logic of Modern Physics* (NY: Macmillan).

Brown, A. (1998), 'Narrative, Politics and Legitimacy in an IT Implementation,' *Jour. of Management Studies*, 35: 35–58.

Brown, S., and Lightfoot, G. (2002), 'Presence, Absence, and Accountability: E-mail and the Mediation of Organizational Memory,' in S. Woolgar (ed.), *Virtual Society? Technology, Cyberbole, Reality* (Oxford: Oxford Univ. Press).

Browne, A.J. (2007), 'Clinical Encounters between Nurses and First Nations Women in a Western Canadian Hospital,' *Social Science & Medicine*, 64: 2165–2176.

Bryman, A. (1988a), *Quantity and Quality in Social Research* (London: Routledge).

———— (1992), 'Quantitative and Qualitative Research: Further Reflections on Their Integration,' in J. Brannen (ed.), *Mixing Methods: Qualitative and Quantitative Research* (Aldershot: Avebury).

———— (1994), 'The Mead/Freeman Controversy: Some Implications for Qualitative Researchers,' in R. Burgess (ed.), *Studies in Qual. Methodology, Volume 4* (Greenwich, CT: JAI Press).

———— (1995), *Disney and His Worlds* (London: Routledge).

———— (1998), 'Quantitative and Qualitative Research Strategies in Knowing the Social World,' in T. May and M. Williams (eds.), *Knowing the Social World* (Buckingham: Open Univ. Press).

———— (1999), 'Global Disney,' in P. Taylor and D. Slater (eds.), *The American Century* (Oxford: Blackwell).

———— and Burgess, R. (1994a), 'Developments in Qualitative Data Analysis: An Introduction,' in A. Bryman and R. Burgess (eds.), *Analyzing Qualitative Data* (London: Routledge).

———— (1994b), 'Reflections on Qualitative Data Analysis,' in A. Bryman and R. Burgess (eds.), *Analyzing Qualitative Data* (London: Routledge).

———— (1999), 'Introduction: Qualitative Research Methodology: A Review,' in A. Bryman and R. Burgess (eds.), *Qualitative Research* (London: Sage).

———— and Cramer, D. (2001), *Quantitative Data Analysis with SPSS Release 10 for Windows: A Guide for Social Scientists* (London: Routledge).

————— (2004), 'Constructing Variables,' in M. Hardy and A. Bryman (eds.), *Handbook of Data Analysis* (London: Sage).

————— Haslam, C., and Webb, A. (1994), 'Performance Appraisal in UK Universities: A Case of Procedural Compliance?' *Assessment and Evaluation in Higher Educ.*, 19: 175–88.

————— Stephens, M., and Campo, C. (1996), 'The Importance of Context: Qualitative Research and the Study of Leadership,' *Leadership Quarterly*, 7: 353–70.

Buckle, A., and Farrington, D. (1994), 'Measuring Shoplifting by Systematic Observation: A Replication Study,' *Psych., Crime and Law*, 1: 133–41.

Bulmer, M. (1980), 'Why Don't Sociologists Make More Use of Official Statistics?' *Sociology*, 14: 505–23.

————— (1984), 'Facts, Concepts, Theories and Problems,' in M. Bulmer (ed.), *Social Research Methods* (London: Macmillan).

Burawoy, M. (2005), '2004 American Sociological Association Presidential Address: For Public Sociology,' *British Jour. of Sociology*, 56: 259–294.

Burman, M., Batchelor, S., and Brown, J. (2001), 'Researching Girls and Violence: Facing the Dilemmas of Fieldwork,' *Brit. Jour. of Criminology*, 41: 443–59.

Burrell, I., and Leppard, D. (1994), 'Fall in Crime a Myth as Police Chiefs Massage the Figures,' *Sunday Times*, 16 Oct.: 1, 5.

Bury, M. (2001), 'Illness Narratives: Fact or Fiction?' *Sociology of Health and Illness*, 23: 263–85.

Buston, K. (1997), 'NUD*IST in Action: Its Use and Its Usefulness in a Study of Chronic Illness in Young People,' *Sociological Research Online*, 2: www.socresonline.org.uk/socresonline/2/3/6.html.

Butcher, B. (1994), 'Sampling Methods: An Overview and Review,' *Survey Methods Centre Newsletter*, 15: 4–8.

Camerer, C. (1997), 'Taxi Drivers and Beauty Contests,' *Engineering and Sci.*, 60: 11–19.

Canadian Institutes of Health Research, Natural Sciences and Engineering Council of Canada, and Social Sciences and Humanities Research Council of Canada (1998, with 2000, 2002, 2005 amendments), *Tri-Council Policy Statement: Ethical Conduct for Research Involving Humans* (Public Works and Government Services Canada).

Canadian Institutes of Health Research, Natural Sciences and Engineering Council of Canada, and Social Sciences and Humanities Research Council of Canada (2010), *Tri-Council Policy Statement: Ethical Conduct for Research Involving Humans* (Her Majesty the Queen in Right of Canada).

Carroll, L. (2009 [1865]), *Alice's Adventures in Wonderland* (Toronto: Penguin Group).

Catterall, M., and Maclaran, P. (1997), 'Focus Group Data and Qualitative Analysis Programs: Coding the Moving Picture as well as Snapshots,' *Sociological Research Online*, 2: www.socresonline.org.uk/socresonline/2/1/6.html.

Charbonneau, L. (2005), 'Ethics Boards Harming Survey Research, Says York Professor,' *University Affairs*, June 6: http://www.universityaffairs.ca/ethics-boards-harming-survey-research-says-york-professor.aspx [accessed August 24, 2011]

Charles, N., and Kerr, N. (1988), *Women, Food and Families* (Manchester: Manchester Univ. Press).

Charlton, T., Gunter, B., and Coles, D. (1998), 'Broadcast Television as a Cause of Aggression? Recent Findings from a Naturalistic Study,' *Emotional and Behavioural Difficulties*, 3: 5–13.

————— Coles, D., Panting, C., and Hannan, A. (1999), 'Behaviour of Nursery Class Children before and after the Availability of Broadcast Television: A Naturalistic Study of Two Cohorts in a Remote Community,' *Jour. of Social Behaviour and Personality*, 14: 315–24.

Charmaz, K. (1983), 'The Grounded Theory Method: An Explication and Interpretation,' in R. Emerson (ed.), *Contemporary Field Research: A Collection of Readings* (Boston: Little, Brown).

————— (1997), 'Identity Dilemmas of Chronically Ill Men,' in A. Strauss and J. Corbin (eds.), *Grounded Theory in Practice* (Thousand Oaks, CA: Sage).

————— (2000), 'Grounded Theory: Objectivist and Constructivist Methods,' in N. Denzin and Y. Lincoln (eds.), *Handbook of Qualitative Research*, 2nd ed. (Thousand Oaks, CA: Sage).

————— (2002), 'Qualitative Interviewing and Grounded Theory Analysis,' in J. Gubrium and J. Holstein (eds.), *Handbook of Interview Research: Context and Method* (Thousand Oaks, CA: Sage).

————— (2004), 'Grounded Theory,' in M. Lewis-Beck, A. Bryman, and T. Liao (eds.), *The Sage Encycl. of Soc. Sci. Research Methods* (Thousand Oaks, CA: Sage).

Chin, M., Fisak, B., and Sims, V. (2002), 'Development of the Attitudes Toward Vegetarianism Scale,' *Anthrozoös*, 15: 333–42.

Christakis, T., Christakis, P., Chipman, M., and Christakis, J. (2008), 'Medical Students' Attitudes on Diversity When Applying to Toronto's Ophthalmology Residency Program,' *Canadian Jour. of Ophthalmology*, 43: 218–21.

Cicourel, A. (1964), *Method and Measurement in Sociology* (NY: Free Press).

————— (1982), 'Interviews, Surveys, and the Problem of Ecological Validity,' *Amer. Sociologist*, 17: 11–20.

Clairborn, W. (1969), 'Expectancy Effects in the Classroom: A Failure to Replicate,' *Jour. of Educational Psych.*, 60: 377–83.

Clancey, W. (2001), 'Field Science Ethnography: Methods for Systematic Observation of an Arctic Expedition,' *Field Methods*, 13: 223–43.

Clapper, D., and Massey, A. (1996), 'Electronic Focus Groups: A Framework for Exploration,' *Information and Management*, 30: 43–50.

Clayman, S., and Gill, V.T. (2004), 'Conversation Analysis,' in M. Hardy and A. Bryman (eds.), *Handbook of Data Analysis* (London: Sage).

Cobanoglu, C., Ward, B., and Moreo, P.J. (2001), 'A Comparison of Mail, Fax and Web-based Survey Methods,' *Intnatl. Jour. of Market Research*, 43: 441–52.

Coffey, A. (1999), *The Ethnographic Self: Fieldwork and the Representation of Reality* (London: Sage).

————— and Atkinson, P. (1996), *Making Sense of Qualitative Data: Complementary Research Strategies* (Thousand Oaks, CA: Sage).

————— Holbrook, B., and Atkinson, P. (1996), 'Qualitative Data Analysis: Technologies and Representations,'

Sociological Research Online, 2: www.socresonline.org. uk/socresonline/1/1/4.html.

Coleman, C., and Moynihan, J. (1996), *Understanding Crime Data: Haunted by the Dark Figure* (Buckingham: Open Univ. Press).

Coleman, H., Grant, C., and Collins, J. (2001), 'Inhalant Use by Canadian Aboriginal Youth,' *Jour. of Child and Adolescent Substance Abuse*, 10: 1–20.

Collins, M. (1997), 'Interviewer Variability: A Review of the Problem,' *Jour. of the Market Research Society*, 39: 67–84.

Collins, R. (1994), *Four Sociological Traditions*, rev. ed. (NY: Oxford Univ. Press).

Conger, J., and Kanungo, R. (1998), *Charismatic Leadership in Organizations* (Thousand Oaks, CA: Sage).

Cook, T., and Campbell, D. (1979), *Quasi-Experimentation: Design and Analysis for Field Settings* (Boston, MA: Houghton Mifflin).

Corti, L. (1993), 'Using Diaries in Social Research,' *Social Research Update*, 2.

Coté, J., and Allahar, A. (1994), *Generation on Hold: Coming of Age in the Late Twentieth Century* (Toronto: Stoddart).

Couper, M. (2000), 'Web Surveys: A Review of Issues and Approaches,' *Public Opinion Quarterly*, 64: 464–94.

———— and Hansen, S. (2002), 'Computer-assisted Interviewing,' in J. Gubrium and J. Holstein (eds.), *Handbook of Interview Research: Context and Method* (Thousand Oaks, CA: Sage).

Coxon, A. (1994), 'Diaries and Sexual Behaviour: The Use of Sexual Diaries as Method and Substance in Researching Gay Men's Response to HIV/AIDS,' in M. Boulton (ed.), *Challenge and Innovation: Methodological Advances in Social Research on* HIV/AIDS (London: Taylor & Francis).

Craig, G. (2004), 'Managing Safety in Policy Research,' in S. Becker and A. Bryman (eds.), *Understanding Research for Social Policy and Practice: Themes, Methods, and Approaches* (Bristol: Policy Press).

Cramer, D. (1998), *Fundamental Statistics for Social Research* (London: Routledge).

Crook, C., and Light, P. (2002), 'Virtual Society and the Cultural Practice of Study,' in S. Woolgar (ed.), *Virtual Society? Technology, Cyberbole, Reality* (Oxford: Oxford Univ. Press).

Curasi, C. (2001) 'A Critical Exploration of Face-to-face Interviewing vs. Computer-mediated Interviewing,' *Intnatl. Jour. of Market Research*, 43: 361–75.

Czaja, R., and Blair, J. (1996), *Designing Surveys: A Guide to Decisions and Procedures* (Thousand Oaks, CA: Sage).

Dale, A., Arber, S., and Proctor, M. (1988), *Doing Secondary Analysis* (London: Unwin Hyman).

Davies, P. (2000), 'Doing Interviews with Female Offenders,' in V. Jupp, P. Davies, and P. Francis (eds.), *Doing Criminological Research* (London: Sage).

Deacon, D., Bryman, A., and Fenton, N. (1998), 'Collision or Collusion? A Discussion of the Unplanned Triangulation of Quantitative and Qualitative Research Methods,' *Intnatl. Jour. of Social Research Methodology*, 1: 47–63.

————, Pickering, M., Golding, P., and Murdock, G. (1999), *Researching Communications: A Practical Guide to Methods in Media and Cultural Analysis* (London: Arnold).

Demaiter, E.I., and Adams, T.L. (2009), '"I Really Didn't Have Any Problems with the Male–Female Thing Until . . . ": Successful Women's Experiences in IT Organizations,' *Canadian Jour. of Sociology*, 43: 31–53.

Demers, A. (1996), 'Effect of Support Groups on Family Caregivers to the Frail Elderly,' *Canadian Jour. on Aging*, 15: 129–44.

Deng, J., Walker, G., and Swinnerton, G. (2006), 'A Comparison of Environmental Values and Attitudes Between Chinese in Canada and Anglo-Canadians,' *Environment and Behavior*, 38: 22–47.

Denzin, N. (1970), *The Research Act in Sociology* (Chicago: Aldine).

———— (1994), 'Evaluating Qualitative Research in the Poststructural Moment: The Lessons James Joyce Teaches Us,' *Intnatl. Jour. of Qual. Studies in Educ.*, 7: 295–308.

Desroches, F. (1990), 'Tearoom Trade: A Research Update,' *Qual. Sociology* 13: 39–61.

Dickinson, H. (1993), 'Accounting for Augustus Lamb: Theoretical and Methodological Issues in Biography and Historical Sociology,' *Sociology*, 27: 121–32.

Dinovitzer, R., Hagan, J., and Parker, P. (2003), 'Choice and Circumstance: Social Capital and Planful Competence in the Attainments of Immigrant Youth,' *Canadian Jour. of Sociology*, 28: 463–88.

Ditton, J. (1977), *Part-time Crime: An Ethnography of Fiddling and Pilferage* (London: Macmillan).

Dobash, R.E., and Dobash, R.P. (2000), 'Evaluating Criminal Justice Interventions for Domestic Violence,' *Crime & Delinquency*, 46: 252–70.

Dommeyer, C., and Moriarty, E. (2000), 'Comparison of Two Forms of an E-Mail Survey: Embedded vs. Attached,' *Intnatl. Jour. of Market Research*, 42: 39–50.

Duncan, L. (2010), 'Money and Membership: Effects of Neighbourhood Poverty, Income Inequality and Individual Income on Voluntary Association Membership in Canada,' *Canadian Jour. of Sociology*, 35: 573–93.

Dunning, E., Murphy, P., and Williams, J. (1988), *The Roots of Football Hooliganism: An Historical and Sociological Study* (London: Routledge).

Durkheim, E. (1938), *The Rules of Sociological Method*, trans. S. Solavay and J. Mueller (New York: Free Press).

———— (1952), *Suicide: A Study in Sociology*, trans. J. Spaulding and G. Simpson (London: Routledge & Kegan Paul).

Dwyer, J., Mayer, L., Dowd, K., Kandel, R., and Mayer, J. (1974), 'The New Vegetarians: The Natural High?' *Jour. of the Amer. Dietetic Assoc.*, 65: 529–36.

Dyer, W., and Wilkins, A. (1991), 'Better Stories, Not Better Constructs, to Generate Better Theory: A Rejoinder to Eisenhardt,' *Academy of Management Rev.*, 16: 613–19.

Edin, K. and Kefalas, M. (2005), *Promises I Can Keep: Why Poor Women Put Motherhood Before Marriage* (Berkeley: University of California Press).

Eichler, M., and Lapointe, J. (1985), *On the Treatment of the Sexes in Research* (Ottawa: Social Sciences and Humanities Research Council of Canada).

Elliott, H. (1997), 'The Use of Diaries in Sociological Research on Health Experience,' *Sociological Research Online*, 2: http://www.socresonline.org.uk/socresonline/2/2/7.html.

Fenton, N., Bryman, A., and Deacon, D. (1998), *Mediating Social Science* (London: Sage).

Festinger, L., Riecken, H., and Schachter, S. (1956), *When Prophecy Fails* (NY: Harper & Row).

Finch, J. (1985), '"It's Great to Have Someone to Talk to": The Ethics and Politics of Interviewing Women,' in C. Bell and H. Roberts (eds.), *Social Researching: Politics, Problems, Practice* (London: Routledge & Kegan Paul).

———— (1987), 'The Vignette Technique in Survey Research,' *Sociology*, 21: 105–14.

———— and Hayes, L. (1994), 'Inheritance, Death and the Concept of the Home,' *Sociology*, 28: 417–33.

———— and Mason, J. (1990), 'Decision Taking in the Fieldwork Process: Theoretical Sampling and Collaborative Working,' in R. Burgess (ed.), *Studies in Qual. Methodology*, 2: 25–50.

Fine, G. (1996), 'Justifying Work: Occupational Rhetorics as Resources in Kitchen Restaurants,' *Administrative Sci. Quarterly*, 41: 90–115.

Foddy, W. (1993), *Constructing Questions for Interviews and Questionnaires: Theory and Practice in Social Research* (Cambridge: Cambridge Univ. Press).

Foran, C. (2010), *Mordecai: The Life and Times* (Toronto: Knopf Canada).

Forster, N. (1994), 'The Analysis of Company Documentation,' in C. Cassell and G. Symon (eds.), *Qualitative Methods in Organizational Research* (London: Sage).

Foster, J. (1995), 'Informal Social Control and Community Crime Prevention,' *Brit. Jour. of Criminology*, 35: 563–83.

Fowler, F. (1993), *Survey Research Methods*, 2nd ed. (Newbury Park, CA: Sage).

———— and Mangione, T. (1990), *Standardized Survey Interviewing: Minimizing Interviewer-Related Error* (Beverly Hills, CA: Sage).

Frazer, R., and Wiersma, U. (2001), 'Prejudice vs. Discrimination in the Employment Interview: We May Hire Equally, but Our Memories Harbour Prejudice,' *Human Relations*, 54: 173–91.

Frean, A. (1998), 'Children Read More after Arrival of TV,' *The Times*, 29 April: 7.

Frey, J. (2004), 'Telephone Surveys,' in M. Lewis-Beck, A. Bryman, and T. Liao (eds.), *The Sage Encycl. of Soc. Sci. Research Methods* (Thousand Oaks, CA: Sage).

Frohlich, K., Potvin, L., Chabot, P., and Corin, E. (2002), 'A Theoretical and Empirical Analysis of Context: Neighbourhoods, Smoking, and Youth,' *Social Sci. and Medicine*, 54: 1401–17.

Gabor, T., Hung, K., Mihorean, S., and St-Onge, C. (2002), 'Canadian Homicide Rates: A Comparison of Two Data Sets,' *Canadian Jour. of Criminology*, 44: 351–63.

Gabriel, Y. (1998), 'The Use of Stories,' in G. Symon and C. Cassell (eds.), *Qualitative Methods and Analysis in Organizational Research* (London: Sage).

Gans, H. J. (1962), *The Urban Villagers* (NY: Free Press).

———— (1968), 'The Participant-Observer as Human Being: Observations on the Personal Aspects of Field Work,' in H. Becker (ed.), *Institutions and the Person: Papers Presented to Everett C. Hughes* (Chicago: Aldine).

Garfinkel, H. (1967), *Studies in Ethnomethodology* (Englewood Cliffs, NJ: Prentice-Hall).

Gaudet, S., Cooke, M. and Jacob, J. (2011), 'Working after Childbirth: A Lifecourse Transition Analysis of Canadian Women from the 1970s to the 2000s,' *Canadian Review of Sociology*, 48: 153–180.

Gazso-Windlej, A., and McMullin, J. (2003), 'Doing Domestic Labour: Strategising in a Gendered Domain,' *Canadian Jour. of Sociology*, 28: 341–66.

Geertz, C. (1973), 'Thick Description: Toward an Interpretive Theory of Culture,' in C. Geertz, *The Interpretation of Cultures* (NY: Basic Books).

Gephart, R. (1988), *Ethnostatistics: Qualitative Foundations for Quantitative Research* (Newbury Park, CA: Sage).

Gerson, K., and Horowitz, R. (2002), 'Observation and Interviewing: Options and Choices,' in T. May (ed.), *Qualitative Research in Action* (London: Sage).

Giddens, A. (1984), *The Constitution of Society* (Cambridge, UK: Polity).

Gidengil, E., Everitt, J., Blais, A., Fournier, P., and Nevitte, N. (2006), 'Gender and Vote Choice in the 2006 Canadian Election,' paper prepared for the Annual Meeting of the American Political Science Association, Philadelphia.

Gilbert, G., and Mulkay, M. (1984), *Opening Pandora's Box: A Sociological Analysis of Scientists' Discourse* (Cambridge: Cambridge Univ. Press).

Gill, R. (1996), 'Discourse Analysis: Practical Implementation,' in J. Richardson (ed.), *Handbook of Qualitative Research Methods for Psychology and the Social Sciences* (Leicester: BPS Books).

———— (2000), 'Discourse Analysis,' in M. Bauer and G. Gaskell (eds.), *Qualitative Researching with Text, Image and Sound* (London: Sage).

Ginn, J., and Arber, S. (1995), 'Exploring Mid-life Women's Employment,' *Sociology*, 29: 73–94.

Giulianotti, R. (1995), 'Participant Observation and Research into Football Hooliganism: Reflections on the Problems of Entrée and Everyday Risks,' *Sociology of Sport Jour.*, 12: 1–20.

———— (1997), 'Enlightening the North: Aberdeen Fanzines and Local Football Identity,' in G. Armstrong and R. Giulianotti (eds.), *Entering the Field: New Perspectives on World Football* (Oxford: Berg).

Gladney, A., Ayars, C., Taylor, W., Liehr, P., and Meininger, J. (2003), 'Consistency of Findings Produced by Two Multidisciplinary Research Teams,' *Sociology*, 37: 297–313.

Glaser, B. (1992), *Basics of Grounded Theory Analysis* (Mill Valley, CA: Sociology Press).

———— and Strauss, A. (1967), *The Discovery of Grounded Theory: Strategies for Qualitative Research* (Chicago: Aldine).

Glock, C. (1988), 'Reflections on Doing Survey Research,' in H. O'Gorman (ed.), *Surveying Social Life* (Middletown, CT: Wesleyan Univ. Press).

Glucksmann, M. (1994), 'The Work of Knowledge and the Knowledge of Women's Work,' in M. Maynard and J. Purvis (eds.), *Researching Women's Lives from a Feminist Perspective* (London: Taylor & Francis).

Goffman, E. (1956), *The Presentation of Self in Everyday Life* (NY: Doubleday).

———— (1963), *Stigma: Notes on the Management of Spoiled Identity* (Harmondsworth, UK: Penguin).

Gold, R. (1958), 'Roles in Sociological Fieldwork,' *Social Forces*, 36: 217–23.

Golden-Biddle, K., and Locke, K. (1993), 'Appealing Work: An Investigation of how Ethnographic Texts Convince,' *Organization Sci.*, 4: 595–616.

——— (1997), *Composing Qualitative Research* (Thousand Oaks, CA: Sage).

Goode, E. (1996), 'The Ethics of Deception in Social Research: A Case Study,' *Qual. Sociology*, 19: 11–33.

Gottdiener, M. (1997), *The Theming of America: Dreams, Visions and Commercial Spaces* (Boulder, CO: Westview Press).

Gouldner, A. (1968), 'The Sociologist as Partisan,' *Amer. Sociologist*, 3: 103–16.

Goyder, J., Guppy, N., and Thompson, M. (2003), 'The Allocation of Male and Female Occupational Prestige in an Ontario Urban Area: A Quarter-century Replication,' *Canadian Rev. of Sociology and Anthropology*, 40: 417–39.

Grabb, E., and Curtis, J. (2004), *Regions Apart: The Four Societies of Canada and the U.S.* (Don Mills, ON: Oxford University Press).

Graham, C.A., Sanders, S.A., Milhausen, R.R., and McBride, K.R. (2004), 'Turning On and Turning Off: A Focus Group Study of the Factors That Affect Women's Sexual Arousal,' *Archives of Sexual Behavior*, 33: 527–38.

Green, A.I. (2010), 'Queer Unions: Same-sex Spouses Marrying Tradition and Innovation,' *Canadian Jour. of Sociology*, 35: 399–436.

Greene, J. (1994), 'Qualitative Program Evaluation: Practice and Promise,' in N. Denzin and Y. Lincoln (eds.), *Handbook of Qual. Research* (Thousand Oaks, CA: Sage).

——— (2000), 'Understanding Social Programs through Evaluation,' in N. Denzin and Y. Lincoln (eds.), *Handbook of Qual. Research*, 2nd ed. (Thousand Oaks, CA: Sage).

Griffin, J. (1961), *Black Like Me* (Boston: Houghton Mifflin).

Guba, E., and Lincoln, Y. (1994), 'Competing Paradigms in Qualitative Research,' in N. Denzin and Y. Lincoln (eds.), *Handbook of Qual. Research* (Thousand Oaks, CA: Sage).

Gubrium, J., and Holstein, J. (1997), *The New Language of Qualitative Method* (NY: Oxford Univ. Press).

Guppy, L., and Siltanen, J. (1977), 'A Comparison of the Allocation of Male and Female Occupational Prestige,' *Canadian Rev. of Sociology and Anthropology*, 14: 320–30.

Halford, S., Savage, M., and Witz, A. (1997), *Gender, Careers and Organisations: Current Developments in Banking, Nursing and Local Government* (London: Sage).

Hallgrimsdottir, H., Phillips, R., and Benoit, C. (2006), 'Fallen Women and Rescued Girls: Social Stigma and Media Narratives of the Sex Industry in Victoria, B.C., from 1980 to 2005,' *Canadian Rev. of Sociology and Anthropology*, 43: 265–80.

Hammersley, M. (1992a), 'By What Criteria Should Ethnographic Research Be Judged?' in M. Hammersley, *What's Wrong with Ethnography* (London: Routledge).

——— (1992b), 'Deconstructing the Qualitative–Quantitative Divide,' in M. Hammersley, *What's Wrong with Ethnography* (London: Routledge).

——— (1996), 'The Relationship between Qualitative and Quantitative Research: Paradigm Loyalty versus Methodological Eclecticism,' in J. Richardson (ed.), *Handbook of Research Methods for Psychology and the Social Sciences* (Leicester: BPS Books).

——— (1997), 'Qualitative Data Archiving: Some Reflections on Its Prospects and Problems,' *Sociology*, 31: 131–42.

——— and Atkinson, P. (1995), *Ethnography: Principles in Practice*, 2nd ed. (London: Routledge).

——— Scarth, J., and Webb, S. (1985), 'Developing and Testing Theory: The Case of Research on Pupil Learning,' in R. Burgess (ed.), *Issues in Educational Research: Qualitative Methods* (London: Farwin).

Hamplová, D., and Le Bourdais, C. (2008), 'Educational Homogamy of Married and Unmarried Couples in English and French Canada,' *Canadian Jour. of Sociology*, 33: 845–872.

Hanson, R. K., Broom, I., and Stephenson, M. (2004), 'Evaluating Community Sex Offender Treatment Programs: A 12-Year Follow-Up of 724 Offenders,' *Canadian Jour. of Sociology*, 36: 87–96.

Healey, J. (2002), *Statistics: A Tool for Social Research*, 6th ed. (Belmont, CA: Wadsworth).

Healey, J., and Prus, S. G. (2010), *Statistics: A Tool for Social Research*, *First Canadian Edition* (Toronto: Nelson Education).

Heath, C. (1997), 'The Analysis of Activities in Face to Face Interaction Using Video,' in D. Silverman (ed.), *Qualitative Research: Theory, Method and Practice* (London: Sage).

Heritage, J. (1984), *Garfinkel and Ethnomethodology* (Cambridge, UK: Polity).

——— (1987), 'Ethnomethodology,' in A. Giddens and J. Turner (eds.), *Social Theory Today* (Cambridge, UK: Polity).

Hesse-Biber, S. (1995), 'Unleashing Frankenstein's Monster? The Use of Computers in Qualitative Research,' *Studies in Qual. Methodology*, 5: 25–41.

Hessler, R., Downing, J., Beltz, C., Pelliccio, A., Powell, M., and Vale, W. (2003), 'Qualitative Research on Adolescent Risk Using E-mail: A Methodological Assessment,' *Qual. Sociology*, 26: 111–24.

Hier, S. (2000), 'The Contemporary Structure of Canadian Racial Supremacism; Networks, Strategies, and New Technologies,' *Canadian Jour. of Sociology*, 25: 471–94.

——— (2002), 'Raves, Risks and the Ecstasy Panic: A Case Study in the Subversive Nature of Moral Regulation,' *Canadian Jour. of Sociology*, 27: 33–57.

Hiller, H., and DiLuzio, L. (2004), 'The Interviewee and the Research Interview: Analyzing a Neglected Dimension in Research,' *Canadian Rev. of Sociology and Anthropology*, 41: 1–26.

Hine, V. (2000), *Virtual Ethnography* (London: Sage).

Hirsch, J. (1981), *Family Photographs* (NY: Oxford Univ. Press).

Ho, K., Baber, Z., and Khondker, H. (2002) 'Sites of Resistance: Alternative Websites and State–Society Relations,' *Brit. Jour. of Sociology*, 53: 127–48.

Hobbs, D. (1988), *Doing the Business: Entrepreneurship, the Working Class and Detectives in the East End of London* (Oxford: Oxford Univ. Press).

——— (1993), 'Peers, Careers, and Academic Fears: Writing as Field-work,' in D. Hobbs and T. May (eds.), *Interpreting the Field: Accounts of Ethnography* (Oxford: Clarendon Press).

———, Hadfield, P., Lister, S., and Winlow, S. (2003), *Bouncers: Violence and Governance in the Night-time Economy* (Oxford: Oxford Univ. Press).

Hochschild, A. (1983), *The Managed Heart* (Berkeley and Los Angeles: Univ. of California Press).

Hodson, R. (1996), 'Dignity in the Workplace under Participative Management,' *Amer. Sociological Rev.*, 61: 719–38.

———— (1999), *Analyzing Documentary Accounts* (Thousand Oaks, CA: Sage).

Holbrook, A., Green, M., and Krosnick, J. (2003), 'Telephone Versus Face-to-face Interviewing of National Probability Samples with Long Questionnaires: Comparisons of Respondent Satisficing and Social Desirability Response Bias,' *Public Opinion Quarterly*, 67: 79–125.

Holbrook, B., and Jackson, B. (1996), 'Shopping Around: Focus Group Research in North London,' *Area*, 28: 136–42.

Homan, R. (1991), *The Ethics of Social Research* (London: Longman).

———— and Bulmer, M. (1982), 'On the Merits of Covert Methods: A Dialogue,' in M. Bulmer (ed.), *Social Research Ethics* (London: Macmillan).

Houghton, E. (1998), 'Sex Is Good for You,' *Guardian*, 92 (Jan.): 14–15.

Howell, J., and Frost, P. (1989), 'A Laboratory Study of Charismatic Leadership,' *Organizational Behavior and Human Decision Processes*, 43: 243–69.

Huey, L. (2003), 'Explaining Odlin Road: Insecurity and Exclusivity,' *Canadian Jour. of Sociology*, 28: 367–86.

Hughes, E. (1943), *French Canada in Transition* (Chicago: Univ. of Chicago Press).

Hughes, G. (2000), 'Understanding the Politics of Criminological Research,' in V. Jupp, P. Davies, and P. Francis (eds.), *Doing Criminological Research* (London: Sage).

Hughes, J. (1990), *The Philosophy of Social Research*, 2nd ed. (Harlow: Longman).

Hughes, K., MacKintosh, A. M., Hastings, G., Wheeler, C., Watson, J., and Inglis, J. (1997), 'Young People, Alcohol, and Designer Drinks: A Quantitative and Qualitative Study,' *Brit. Medical Jour.*, 314: 414–18.

Hughes, R. (1998), 'Considering the Vignette Technique and its Application to a Study of Drug Injecting and HIV Risk and Safer Behaviour,' *Sociology of Health and Illness*, 20: 381–400.

Humphreys, L. (1970), *Tearoom Trade: Impersonal Sex in Public Places* (Chicago: Aldine).

Hutchby, I., and Wooffitt, R. (1998), *Conversation Analysis* (Cambridge, UK: Polity).

Jagger, E. (1998), 'Marketing the Self, Buying an Other: Dating in a Post Modern, Consumer Society,' *Sociology*, 32: 795–814.

———— (2001), 'Marketing Molly and Melville: Dating in a Postmodern, Consumer Society,' *Sociology*, 35: 39–57.

Jamieson, J. (2000), 'Negotiating Danger in Fieldwork on Crime: A Researcher's Tale,' in G. Lee-Treweek and S. Linkogle (eds.), *Danger in the Field: Risk and Ethics in Social Research* (London: Routledge).

Jayaratne, T., and Stewart, A. (1991), 'Quantitative and Qualitative Methods in the Social Sciences: Current Feminist Issues and Practical Strategies,' in M. Fonow and J. Cook (eds.), *Beyond Methodology: Feminist Scholarship as Lived Research* (Bloomington, IN: Indiana Univ. Press).

John, I.D. (1992), 'Statistics as Rhetoric in Psychology,' *Australian Psychologist*, 27: 144–9.

Johnson, J., Bottorff, J., Moffat, B., Ratner, P., Shoveller, J., and Lovato, C. (2003), 'Tobacco Dependence: Adolescents' Perspectives on the Need to Smoke,' *Social Sci. and Medicine*, 56: 1481–92.

Jones, K. (2000), 'Constructing rBST in Canada: Biotechnology, Instability, and the Management of Nature,' *Canadian Jour. of Sociology*, 25: 311–41.

Kanayama, T. (2003), 'Ethnographic Research on the Experience of Japanese Elderly People Online,' *New Media and Society*, 5: 267–88.

Karabanow, J. (2002), 'Open for Business: Exploring the Life Stages of Two Canadian Street Youth Shelters,' *Jour. of Sociology and Social Welfare*, 29: 99–116.

Katz, J. (2002), 'From How to Why: On Luminous Description and Causal Inference in Ethnography (Part 2),' *Ethnography*, 3: 63–90.

Katz, J., Kuffel, S., and Coblentz, A. (2002), 'Are There Gender Differences in Sustaining Dating Violence?' *Jour. of Family Violence*, 17: 247–71.

Kelley, J., and De Graaf, N. (1997), 'National Context, Parental Socialization, and Religious Belief: Results from 15 Nations,' *Amer. Sociological Rev.*, 62: 639–59.

Kelly, L., Burton, S., and Regan, L. (1994), 'Researching Women's Lives or Studying Women's Oppression? Reflections on What Constitutes Feminist Research,' in M. Maynard and J. Purvis (eds.), *Researching Women's Lives from a Feminist Perspective* (London: Taylor & Francis).

Kendall, L. (1999), 'Recontextualizing "Cyberspace": Methodological Considerations for On-line Research,' in S. Jones (ed.), *Doing Internet Research: Critical Issues and Methods for Examining the Net* (Thousand Oaks, CA: Sage).

Kennedy, R. (2006), 'Researching the Intersection Between Collective Identity and Conceptions of Post-separation and Divorced Fatherhood: A Case Study; Fathers For Justice, Fathers For Just Us, or Fathers Are Us,' *Qualitative Sociology Rev.*, 2: 75–97.

Kent, R., and Lee, M. (1999), 'Using the Internet for Market Research: A Study of Private Trading on the Internet,' *Jour. of the Market Research Society*, 41: 377–85.

Kerr, D. (2004), 'Family Transformations and the Well-being of Children: Recent Evidence from Canadian Longitudinal Data,' *Jour. of Comparative Family Studies*, 35: 73–90.

Kerr, D., and Michalski, J. (2007), 'Family Structure and Children's Hyperactivity Problems: A Longitudinal Analysis,' *Canadian Jour. of Sociology*, 32: 85–112.

Kimmel, A. (1988), *Ethics and Values in Applied Social Research* (Newbury Park, CA: Sage).

Kitzinger, J. (1993), 'Understanding AIDS: Researching Audience Perceptions of Acquired Immune Deficiency Syndrome,' in J. Eldridge (ed.), *Getting the Message: News, Truth and Power* (London: Routledge).

———— (1994), 'The Methodology of Focus Groups: The Importance of Interaction between Research Participants,' *Sociology of Health and Illness*, 16, 1994: 103–21.

Krosnick, J., Holbrook, A. *et al.* (2002), 'The Impact of "No Opinion" Response Options on Data Quality: Non-Attitude Reduction or an Invitation to Satisfice?' *Public Opinion Quarterly*, 66: 371–403.

Krueger, R. (1998), *Moderating Focus Groups* (Thousand Oaks, CA: Sage).

Kuhn, T. (1970), *The Structure of Scientific Revolutions*, 2nd ed. (Chicago: Univ. of Chicago Press).

Kusow, A. (2003), 'Beyond Indigenous Authenticity: Reflections on the Insider/Outsider Debate in Immigration Research,' *Symbolic Interaction*, 26: 591–9.

Kvale, S. (1996), *InterViews: An Introduction to Qualitative Research Interviewing* (Thousand Oaks, CA: Sage).

Lankshear, G. (2000), 'Bacteria and Babies: A Personal Reflection on Researcher's Risk in a Hospital,' in G. Lee-Treweek and S. Linkogle (eds.), *Danger in the Field: Risk and Ethics in Social Research* (London: Routledge).

Lantz, P., and Booth, K. (1998), 'The Social Construction of the Breast Cancer Epidemic,' *Social Sci. and Medicine*, 46: 907–18.

LaPiere, R.T. (1934), 'Attitudes vs. Actions,' *Social Forces*, 13: 230–7.

Laplante, B. (2006), 'The Rise of Cohabitation in Quebec: Power of Religion and Power over Religion,' *Canadian Jour. of Sociology*, 31: 1–24.

Lauder, M. (2003), 'Covert Participant Observation of a Deviant Community: Justifying the Use of Deception,' *Jour. of Contemporary Religion* 18: 185–96.

Laurenceau, J.-P., and Bolger, N. (2005), 'Using Diary Methods to Study Marital and Family Processes,' *Jour. of Family Psychology*, 19: 86–97.

Layder, D. (1993), *New Strategies in Social Research* (Cambridge, UK: Polity).

————, Ashton, D., and Sung. J. (1991), 'The Empirical Correlates of Action and Structure: The Transition from School to Work,' *Sociology*, 25: 447–64.

Leake, J. (1998), 'Police Figures Hide Poor Clear-up Rate,' *The Times*, 21 June: 1.

LeCompte, M., and Goetz, J. (1982), 'Problems of Reliability and Validity in Ethnographic Research,' *Rev. of Educational Research*, 52: 31–60.

Lee, R.M. (2000), *Unobtrusive Methods in Social Research* (Buckingham: Open Univ. Press).

———— (2004), 'Danger in Research,' in M. Lewis-Beck, A. Bryman, and T. Liao (eds.), *The Sage Encycl. of Soc. Sci. Research Methods* (Thousand Oaks, CA: Sage).

Lee-Treweek, G. (2000), 'The Insight of Emotional Danger: Research Experiences in a Home for the Elderly,' in G. Lee-Treweek and S. Linkogle (eds.), *Danger in the Field: Risk and Ethics in Social Research* (London: Routledge).

Leidner, R. (1993), *Fast Food, Fast Talk: Service Work and the Routinization of Everyday Life* (Berkeley and Los Angeles: Univ. of California Press).

Lett, D., Hier, S.P., and Walby, K. (2010), 'CCTV Surveillance and the Civic Conversation: A Study in Public Sociology,' *Canadian Jour. of Sociology*, 35: 437–62.

Levitas, R., and Guy, W. (1996), in R. Levitas and W. Guy (eds.), *Interpreting Official Statistics* (London: Routledge).

Lewis, O. (1961), *The Children of Sánchez* (NY: Vintage).

Li, P. (2003), 'Initial Earnings and Catch-up Capacity of Immigrants,' *Can. Public Policy*, 29: 319–37.

Liebling, A. (2001), 'Whose Side Are We On? Theory, Practice and Allegiances in Prisons Research,' *Brit. Jour. of Criminology*, 41: 472–84.

Lincoln, Y., and Denzin, N. (1994), 'The Fifth Moment,' in N. Denzin and Y. Lincoln (eds.), *Handbook of Qual. Research* (Thousand Oaks, CA: Sage).

———— and Guba, E. (1985), *Naturalistic Inquiry* (Beverly Hills, CA: Sage).

Lipset, S. (1990), *Continental Divide: The Values and Institutions of the United States and Canada* (NY: Routledge).

Little, M. (2001), 'A Litmus Test for Democracy: The Impact of Ontario Welfare Changes for Single Mothers,' *Studies in Political Economy*, 66: 9–36.

Locke, K. (1996), 'Rewriting *The Discovery of Grounded Theory* after 25 Years?' *Jour. of Management Inquiry*, 5: 239–45.

Lofland, J., and Lofland, L. (1995), *Analyzing Social Settings: A Guide to Qualitative Observation and Analysis*, 3rd ed. (Belmont, CA: Wadsworth).

Lonkila, M. (1995), 'Grounded Theory as an Emergent Paradigm for Computer-assisted Qualitative Data Analysis,' in U. Kelle (ed.), *Computer-aided Qualitative Data Analysis* (London: Sage).

Lupton, D. (1996), *Food, the Body and the Self* (London: Sage).

Lynch, M., and Bogen, D. (1997), 'Sociology's Asociological "Core": An Examination of Textbook Sociology in the Light of The Sociology of Scientific Knowledge,' *Amer. Sociological Rev.*, 62: 481–93.

Lynd, R., and Lynd, H. (1929), *Middletown: A Study in Contemporary American Culture* (NY: Harcourt Brace).

———— (1937), *Middletown in Transition: A Study in Cultural Conflicts* (NY: Harcourt Brace).

McCall, M.J. (1984), 'Structured Field Observation,' *Annual Rev. of Sociology*, 10: 263–82.

McGuigan, J. (1992), *Cultural Populism* (London: Routledge).

McKee, L., and Bell, C. (1985), 'Marital and Family Relations in Times of Male Unemployment,' in B. Roberts, R. Finnegan, and D. Gallie (eds.), *New Approaches to Economic Life* (Manchester: Manchester Univ. Press).

McKeganey, N., and Barnard, M. (1996), *Sex Work on the Streets* (Buckingham: Open Univ. Press).

MacKinnon, N., and Luke, A. (2002), 'Changes in Identity Attitudes as Reflections of Social and Cultural Change,' *Canadian Jour. of Sociology*, 27: 299–338.

Macnaghten, P., and Jacobs, M. (1997), 'Public Identification with Sustainable Development: Investigating Cultural Barriers to Participation,' *Global Environmental Change*, 7: 5–24.

Madge, C., and O'Connor, H. (2002), 'On-line with E-Mums: Exploring the Internet as a Medium of Research,' *Area*, 34: 92–102.

Madriz, M. (2000), 'Focus Groups in Feminist Research,' in N. Denzin and Y. Lincoln (eds.), *Handbook of Qual. Research*, 2nd ed. (Thousand Oaks, CA: Sage).

Malbon, B. (1999), *Clubbing: Dancing, Ecstasy and Vitality* (London: Routledge).

Malinowski, B. (1967), *A Diary in the Strict Sense of the Term* (London: Routledge & Kegan Paul).

Malkin, A.R., Wornian, K., and Chrisler, J.C. (1999), 'Women and Weight: Gendered Messages on Magazine Covers,' *Sex Roles*, 40: 647–55.

Mangione, T.W. (1995), *Mail Surveys: Improving the Quality* (Thousand Oaks, CA: Sage).

Mann, C., and Stewart, F. (2000), *Internet Communication and Qualitative Research: A Handbook for Researching Online* (London: Sage).

Manning, P. (1995), 'The Challenge of Postmodernism,' in J. Van Maanen (ed.), *Representation in Ethnography* (Thousand Oaks, CA: Sage).

Marcic, D. (2002), *Respect: Women and Popular Music* (New York: Texere).

Markham, A. (1998), *Life Online: Researching the Real Experience in Virtual Space* (London and Walnut Creek, CA: AltaMira Press).

Marsh, C., and Scarbrough, E. (1990), 'Testing Nine Hypotheses about Quota Sampling,' *Jour. of the Market Research Society*, 32: 485–506.

Marshall, G., Newby, H., and Vogler, C. (1988), *Social Class in Modern Britain* (London: Unwin Hyman).

Marx, G.T. (1997), 'Of Methods and Manners for Aspiring Sociologists: 37 Moral Imperatives,' *Amer. Sociologist*, 28: 102–25.

Marx, K. (1998 [1845]), *The German Ideology including Theses on Feuerbach and Introduction to the Critique of Political Economy* (Amherst: Prometheus Books).

Mason, J. (1994), 'Linking Qualitative and Quantitative Data Analysis,' in A. Bryman and R. Burgess (eds.), *Analyzing Qualitative Data* (London: Routledge).

———— (2002a), *Qualitative Researching*, 2nd ed. (London: Sage).

———— (2002b), 'Qualitative Interviewing: Asking, Listening, Interpreting,' in T. May (ed.), *Qualitative Research in Action* (London: Sage).

Mauthner, N., Parry, O., and Backett-Milburn, K. (1998), 'The Data Are Out There, or Are They? Implications for Archiving and Revisiting Qualitative Data,' *Sociology*, 32: 733–45.

Mayhew, P. (2000), 'Researching the State of Crime' in R. King and E. Wincup (eds.), *Doing Research on Crime and Justice* (Oxford: Oxford Univ. Press).

Maynard, M. (1994), 'Methods, Practice and Epistemology: The Debate about Feminism and Research,' in M. Maynard and J. Purvis (eds.), *Researching Women's Lives from a Feminist Perspective* (London: Taylor & Francis).

———— (1998), 'Feminists' Knowledge and the Knowledge of Feminisms: Epistemology, Theory, Methodology and Method,' in T. May and M. Williams (eds.), *Knowing the Social World* (Buckingham: Open Univ. Press).

Mead, M. (1928), *Coming of Age in Samoa* (New York: Morrow).

Menard, S. (1991), *Longitudinal Research* (Newbury Park, CA: Sage).

Merton, R. (1938), 'Social Structure and Anomie,' *Amer. Sociological Rev.*, 3: 672–82.

———— (1967), *On Theoretical Sociology* (NY: Free Press).

Michaud, S. (2001), 'The National Longitudinal Study of Children and Youth—Overview and Changes after Three Cycles,' *Canadian Studies in Population*, 28: 391–405.

Midgley, C. (1998), 'TV Violence Has Little Impact on Children, Study Finds,' *The Times*, 12 Jan.: 5.

Mies, M. (1993), 'Towards a Methodology for Feminist Research,' in M. Hammersley (ed.), *Social Research: Philosophy, Politics and Practice* (London: Sage).

Miles, M.B. (1979), 'Qualitative Data as an Attractive Nuisance,' *Administrative Sci. Quarterly*, 24: 590–601.

Milgram, S. (1963), 'A Behavioural Study of Obedience,' *Jour. of Abnormal and Social Psych.*, 67: 371–8.

Milkman, R. (1997), *Farewell to the Factory: Auto Workers in the Late Twentieth Century* (Los Angeles: Univ. of California Press).

Millen, D. (1997), 'Some Methodological and Epistemological Issues Raised by Doing Feminist Research on Non-Feminist Women,' *Sociological Research Online*, 2: www.socresonline.org.uk/socresonline/2/3/3.html.

Miller, D., and Reilly, J. (1995), 'Making an Issue of Food Safety: The Media, Pressure Groups, and the Public Sphere,' in D. Maurer and J. Sobal (eds.), *Food and Nutrition as Social Problems* (NY: Aldine de Gruyter).

Miller, D. Disney (1956), *The Story of Walt Disney* (NY: Dell).

Miller, N., and Morgan, D. (1993), 'Called to Account: The CV as an Autobiographical Practice,' *Sociology*, 27: 133–43.

Miller, R.L. (2000), *Researching Life Stories and Family Histories* (London: Sage).

Miraftab, F. (2000), 'Sheltering Refugees: The Housing Experience of Refugees in Metropolitan Vancouver, Canada,' *Canadian Jour. of Urban Research*, 9: 42–63.

Morgan, D. (1998a), *Planning Focus Groups* (Thousand Oaks, CA: Sage).

———— (1998b), 'Practical Strategies for Combining Qualitative and Quantitative Methods: Applications for Health Research,' *Qual. Health Research*, 8: 362–76.

———— (2002), 'Focus Group Interviewing,' in J. Gubrium and J. Holstein (eds.), *Handbook of Interview Research: Context and Method* (Thousand Oaks, CA: Sage).

———— and Spanish, M. (1985), 'Social Interaction and the Cognitive Organization of Health-relevant Behaviour,' *Sociology of Health and Illness*, 7: 401–22.

Morgan, R. (2000), 'The Politics of Criminological Research,' in R. King and E. Wincup (eds.), *Doing Research on Crime and Justice* (Oxford: Oxford Univ. Press).

Myles, J., and Hou, F. (2004), 'Changing Colours: Spatial Assimilation and New Racial Minority Immigrants,' *Canadian Jour. of Sociology*, 29: 28–58.

Nemni, M., and Nemni, M. (2006), *Young Trudeau: Son of Quebec, Father of Canada, 1919–1944*, trans. W. Johnson (Toronto: Douglas Gibson Books).

Nettleton, S., Pleace, N., Burrows, R., Muncer, S., and Loader, B. (2002), 'The Reality of Virtual Social Support,' in S. Woolgar (ed.), *Virtual Society? Technology, Cyberbole, Reality* (Oxford: Oxford Univ. Press).

Neuman, W.L. (2003), *Social Research Methods* (Toronto: Pearson Canada).

Nippard, E., and Murphy, E. (2007), 'Social Presence in the Web-based Synchronous Secondary Classroom,' *Canadian Jour. of Learning and Technology*, 33.

Nixon, K., Tutty, L., Downe, P., Gorkoff, K., and Ursel, J. (2002), 'The Everyday Occurrence: Violence in the Lives of Girls Exploited through Prostitution?' *Violence against Women*, 8: 1016–43.

Norris, C. (1993), 'Some Ethical Considerations on Field-work with the Police,' in D. Hobbs and T. May (eds.), *Interpreting the Field: Accounts of Ethnography* (Oxford: Clarendon Press).

Oakley, A. (1981), 'Interviewing Women: A Contradiction in Terms,' in H. Roberts (ed.), *Doing Feminist Research* (London: Routledge & Kegan Paul).

———— (1998), 'Gender, Methodology and People's Ways

of Knowing: Some Problems with Feminism and the Paradigm Debate in Social Science,' *Sociology*, 32: 707–31.

O'Connell Davidson, J., and Layder, D. (1994), *Methods, Sex, and Madness* (London: Routledge).

O'Connor, H., and Madge, C. (2001), 'Cyber-Mothers: Online Synchronous Interviewing Using Conferencing Software,' *Sociological Research Online*, 5: www.socresonline.org. uk/5/4/o'connor.html.

——— (2003), '"Focus Groups in Cyberspace": Using the Internet for Qualitative Research,' *Qual. Market Research*, 6: 133–43.

Okely, J. (1994), 'Thinking through Fieldwork,' in A. Bryman and R. Burgess (eds.), *Analyzing Qualitative Data* (London: Routledge).

O'Reilly, K. (2000), *The British on the Costa del Sol: Transnational Identities and Local Communities* (London: Routledge).

Orona, C.J. (1997), 'Temporality and Identity Loss due to Alzheimer's Disease,' in A. Strauss and J. Corbin (eds.), *Grounded Theory in Practice* (Thousand Oaks, CA: Sage).

O'Shaughnessy, S., and Kennedy, E. H. (2010), 'Relational Activism: Reimagining Women's Environmental Work as Cultural Change,' *Canadian Jour. of Sociology*, 35: 551–572.

Pahl, J. (1990), 'Household Spending, Personal Spending and the Control of Money in Marriage,' *Sociology*, 24: 119–38.

Parker, M. (2000), *Organizational Culture and Identity* (London: Sage).

Parnaby, P. (2003), 'Disaster through Dirty Windshields: Law, Order and Toronto's Squeegee Kids,' *Canadian Jour. of Sociology*, 28: 281–307.

Pawson, R., and Tilley, N. (1997), *Realistic Evaluation* (London: Sage).

Peñaloza, L. (1999), 'Just Doing It: A Visual Ethnographic Study of Spectacular Consumption at Niketown,' *Consumption, Market, and Culture*, 2: 337–400.

Perrucci, R., Belshaw, R., DeMerritt, A., Frazier, B., Jones, J., Kimbrough, J., Loney, K., Pappas, J., Parker, J., Trottier, B., and Williams, B. (2000), 'The Two Faces of Racialized Space at a Predominantly White University,' *Intnatl. Jour. of Contemporary Sociology*, 37: 230–44.

Pettigrew, A. (1997), 'What Is a Processual Analysis?' *Scandinavian Jour. of Management*, 13: 337–48.

——— and Whipp, R. (1991), *Managing Change for Competitive Success* (Oxford: Blackwell).

Phelan, P. (1987), 'Comparability of Qualitative and Quantitative Methods: Studying Child Sexual Abuse in America,' *Educ. and Urban Society*, 20: 35–41.

Phillips, N., and Brown, J. (1993), 'Analyzing Communications in and around Organizations: A Critical Hermeneutic Approach,' *Academy of Management Jour.*, 36: 1547–76.

Phoenix, A. (1994), 'Practising Feminist Research: The Intersection of Gender and "Race" in the Research Process,' in M. Maynard and J. Purvis (eds.), *Researching Women's Lives from a Feminist Perspective* (London: Taylor & Francis).

Pidgeon, N., and Henwood, K. (2004), 'Grounded Theory,' in M. Hardy and A. Bryman (eds.), *Handbook of Data Analysis* (London: Sage).

Pink, S. (2001), *Visual Ethnography* (London: Sage).

Platt, J. (1986), 'Functionalism and the Survey: The Relation of Theory and Method,' *Sociological Rev.*, 34: 501–36.

——— (1996), *A History of Sociological Research Methods in America 1920–1960* (Cambridge: Cambridge Univ. Press).

Plomin, R., Defries, J.C., McClearn, G.E., and McGuffin, P. (2008), *Behavioural Genetics*, 5th ed. (New York: Worth).

Podsakoff, P., and Dalton, D. (1987), 'Research Methodology in Organizational Studies,' *Jour. of Management*, 13: 419–44.

Poland, B.D. (1995), 'Transcription Quality as an Aspect of Rigor in Qualitative Research,' *Qual. Inquiry*, 1: 290–310.

Porter, S. (1993), 'Critical Realist Ethnography: The Case of Racism and Professionalism in a Medical Setting,' *Sociology*, 27: 591–609.

——— (2002), 'Critical Realist Ethnography,' in T. May (ed.), *Qual. Research in Action* (London: Sage).

Potter, G. (2003), '*Sui generis* Micro Social Structures: The Heuristic Example of Poker,' *Canadian Jour. of Sociology*, 28: 171–202.

Potter, J. (1996), *Representing Reality: Discourse, Rhetoric and Social Construction* (London: Sage).

——— (1997), 'Discourse Analysis as a Way of Analysing Naturally Occurring Talk,' in D. Silverman (ed.), *Qual. Research: Theory, Method and Practice* (London: Sage).

——— (2004), 'Discourse Analysis,' in M. Hardy and A. Bryman (eds.), *Handbook of Data Analysis* (London: Sage).

——— and Hepburn, A. (2004), 'The Analysis of NSPCC Call Openings,' in S. Becker and A. Bryman (eds.), *Understanding Research for Social Policy and Practice: Themes, Methods, and Approaches* (Bristol: Policy Press).

——— and Wetherell, M. (1994), 'Analyzing Discourse,' in A. Bryman and R. Burgess (eds.), *Analyzing Qualitative Data* (London: Routledge).

——— and Chitty, A. (1991), 'Quantification Rhetoric— Cancer on Television,' *Discourse and Society*, 2: 333–65.

Pratt, A., and Valverde, M. (2002), 'From Deserving Victims to "Masters of Confusion": Redefining Refugees in the 1900s,' *Canadian Jour. of Sociology*, 27: 135–62.

Psathas, G. (1995), *Conversation Analysis: The Study of Talk-in-Interaction* (Thousand Oaks, CA: Sage).

Puddephatt, A., and Nelson, R.W. (2010), 'The Promise of a Sociology Degree in Canadian Higher Education,' *Canadian Review of Sociology*, 47: 405–30.

Punch, M. (1994), 'Politics and Ethics in Qualitative Research,' in N. Denzin and Y. Lincoln (eds.), *Handbook of Qual. Research* (Thousand Oaks, CA: Sage).

Radley, A., and Chamberlain, K. (2001), 'Health Psychology and the Study of the Case: From Method to Analytic Concern,' *Social Sci. and Medicine*, 53: 321–32.

——— and Taylor, D. (2003*a*), 'Images of Recovery: a Photo-Elicitation Study on the Hospital Ward,' *Qual. Health Research*, 13: 77–99.

——— (2003*b*), 'Remembering One's Stay in Hospital: A Study in Photography, Recovery and Forgetting,' *Health: An Interdisciplinary Jour. for the Social Study of Health, Illness and Medicine*, 7: 129–59.

Rafaeli, A., Dutton, J., Harquail, C.V., and Mackie-Lewis, S. (1997), 'Navigating by Attire: The Use of Dress by Female Administrative Employees,' *Academy of Management Jour.*, 40: 9–45.

Reed, M. (2000), 'The Limits of Discourse Analysis in Organizational Analysis,' *Organization*, 7: 524–30.

Reiner, R. (2000*a*), 'Crime and Control in Britain,' *Sociology*, 34: 71–94.

———— (2000*b*), 'Police Research,' in R. King and E. Wincup (eds.), *Doing Research on Crime and Justice* (Oxford: Oxford Univ. Press).

Reinharz, S. (1992), *Feminist Methods in Social Research* (NY: Oxford Univ. Press).

Ricciardelli, R. and Clow, K. (2009), 'Men, Appearance, and Cosmetic Surgery: The Role of Self-esteem and Comfort with the Body,' *Canadian Jour. of Sociology*, 34: 105–34.

Richardson, L. (1990), 'Narrative and Sociology,' *Jour. of Contemporary Ethnography*, 19: 116–35.

———— (1994), 'Writing: A Method of Inquiry,' in N. Denzin and Y. Lincoln (eds.), *Handbook of Qual. Research* (Thousand Oaks, CA: Sage).

Riches, G., and Dawson, P. (1998), 'Lost Children, Living Memories: The Role of Photographs in Processes of Grief and Adjustment Among Bereaved Parents,' *Death Studies*, 22: 121–40.

Riessman, C.K. (1993), *Narrative Analysis* (Newbury Park, CA: Sage).

———— (2004*a*), 'Narrative Interviewing,' in M. Lewis-Beck, A. Bryman, and T. Liao (eds.), *The Sage Encycl. of Soc. Sci. Research Methods* (Thousand Oaks, CA: Sage).

———— (2004*b*), 'Narrative Analysis,' in M. Lewis-Beck, A. Bryman, and T. Liao (eds.), *The Sage Encycl. of Soc. Sci. Research Methods* (Thousand Oaks, CA: Sage).

Rinehart, J. (1996), *The Tyranny of Work*, 3rd ed. (Toronto: Harcourt Brace).

————, Huxley, C., and Robertson, D. (1998), *Not Just Another Auto Plant* (Ithaca, NY: Cornell Univ. Press).

Ristock, J. (2001), 'Decentring Heterosexuality: Responses of Feminist Counsellors to Abuse in Lesbian Relationships,' *Women and Therapy*, 23: 59–72.

Roberts, B. (2002), *Biographical Research* (Buckingham: Open Univ. Press).

Robinson, J., Shaver, P., and Wrightsman, L. (1999), *Measures of Political Attitudes* (Toronto: Academic Press).

Roethlisberger, F., and Dickson, W. (1939), *Management and the Worker* (Cambridge, MA: Harvard University Press).

Rojek, C. (1995), *Decentring Leisure: Rethinking Leisure Theory* (London: Sage).

Rose, G. (2001), *Visual Methodologies* (London: Sage).

Rosenau, P.M. (1992), *Post-Modernism and the Social Sciences: Insights, Inroads, and Intrusions* (Princeton: Princeton Univ. Press).

Rosenhan, D.L. (1973), 'On Being Sane in Insane Places,' *Science*, 179: 350–8.

Rosenthal, R., and Jacobson, L. (1968), *Pygmalion in the Classroom: Teacher Expectation and Pupils' Intellectual Development* (NY: Holt, Rinehart & Winston).

Rosnow, R.L., and Rosenthal, R. (1997), *People Studying People: Artefacts and Ethics in Behavioral Research* (NY: W.H. Freeman).

Rubin, H.J., and Rubin, I.S. (1995), *Qualitative Interviewing: The Art of Hearing Data* (Thousand Oaks, CA: Sage).

Rushton, J. (2000), *Race, Evolution and Behaviour: A Life History Perspective* (Port Huron, MI: Charles Darwin Research Institute).

Russell, R., and Tyler, M. (2002), 'Thank Heaven for Little Girls: "Girl Heaven" and the Commercial Context of Feminine Childhood,' *Sociology*, 36: 619–37.

Sampson, H., and Thomas, M. (2003), 'Lone Researchers at Sea: Gender, Risk and Responsibility,' *Qual. Research*, 3: 165–89.

Sanderson, S.K. (2001), *The evolution of human sociality: a Darwinian conflict perspective* (Lanham, Md.: Rowman & Littlefield).

Sanjek, R. (1990), 'A Vocabulary for Fieldnotes,' in R. Sanjek (ed.), *Fieldnotes: The Making of Anthropology* (Ithaca, NY: Cornell Univ. Press).

Sarsby, J. (1984), 'The Fieldwork Experience,' in R. Ellen (ed.), *Ethnographic Research: A Guide to General Conduct* (London: Academic Press).

Schaeffer, D., and Dillman, D. (1998), 'Development of a Standard E-mail Methodology,' *Public Opinion Quarterly*, 62: 378–97.

Schegloff, E. (1997), 'Whose Text? Whose Context?' *Discourse and Society*, 8: 165–87.

Schlesinger, P., Dobash, R.E., Dobash, R.P., and Weaver, C. (1992), *Women Viewing Violence* (London: British Film Institute).

Schrøder, K.C. (1999), 'The Best of Both Worlds? Media Audience Research between Rival Paradigms,' in P. Alasuutari (ed.), *Rethinking the Media Audience* (London: Sage).

Schuman, H., and Presser, S. (1981), *Questions and Answers in Attitude Surveys: Experiments on Question Form, Wording, and Context* (San Diego, CA: Academic Press).

Schutz, A. (1962), *Collected Papers I: The Problem of Social Reality* (The Hague: Martinus Nijhof).

Scott, J. (1990), *A Matter of Record* (Cambridge, UK: Polity).

Seale, C. (1999), *The Quality of Qualitative Research* (London: Sage).

———— (2002), 'Cancer Heroics: A Study of News Reports with Particular Reference to Gender,' *Sociology*, 36: 107–26.

Shalla, V. (2002), 'Jettisoned by Design? The Truncated Employment Relationship of Customer Sales and Service Agents under Airline Restructuring,' *Canadian Jour. of Sociology*, 27: 1–32.

Sharf, B.F. (1999), 'Beyond Netiquette: The Ethics of Doing Naturalistic Discourse Research on the Internet,' in S. Jones (ed.), *Doing Internet Research: Critical Issues and Methods for Examining the Net* (Thousand Oaks, CA: Sage).

Sharpe, K. (2000), 'Sad, Bad, and (Sometimes) Dangerous to Know: Street Corner Research with Prostitutes, Punters, and the Police,' in R. King and E. Wincup (eds.), *Doing Research on Crime and Justice* (Oxford: Oxford Univ. Press).

Sheehan, K. (2001), 'E-mail Survey Response Rates: A Review,' *Jour. of Computer-Mediated Communication*, 6: www.ascusc. org/jcmc/vol6/issue2/sheehan.html.

———— and Hoy, M. (1999), 'Using E-mail to Survey Internet Users in the United States: Methodology and Assessment,' *Jour. of Computer-Mediated Communication*, 4: www.ascusc.org/jcmc/vol4/issue3/sheehan.html.

Shuy, R.W. (2002), 'In-person versus Telephone Interviewing,' in J.F. Gubrium and J.A. Holstein (eds.), *Handbook of*

Interview Research: Context and Method (Thousand Oaks, CA: Sage).

Silverman, D. (1984), 'Going Private: Ceremonial Forms in a Private Oncology Clinic,' *Sociology*, 18: 191–204.

——— (1985), *Qualitative Methodology and Sociology: Describing the Social World* (Aldershot: Gower).

——— (1993), *Interpreting Qualitative Data: Methods for Analysing Qualitative Data* (London: Sage).

——— (1994), 'Analysing Naturally Occurring Data on AIDS Counselling: Some Methodological and Practical Issues,' in M. Boulton (ed.), *Challenge and Innovation: Methodological Advances in Social Research on HIV/AIDS* (London: Taylor & Francis).

Silverman, R., Sacco, V., and Teevan, J. (2000), *Crime in Canadian Society* (Toronto: Harcourt Canada).

Skeggs, B. (1994), 'Situating the Production of Feminist Ethnography,' in M. Maynard and J. Purvis (eds.), *Researching Women's Lives from a Feminist Perspective* (London: Taylor & Francis).

——— (1997), *Formations of Class and Gender* (London: Sage).

——— (2001), 'Feminist Ethnography,' in P. Atkinson, A. Coffey, S. Delamont, J. Lofland, and L. Lofland (eds.), *Handbook of Ethnography* (London: Sage).

Smith, D. (2004), 'Women's Perspective as a Radical Critique of Sociology.' In S. Harding, ed., *The Feminist Standpoint Theory Reader: Intellectual and Political Controversies* (New York: Routledge).

——— (2005), *Institutional Ethnography: A Sociology for People* (Walnut Creek, CA: AltaMira Press).

Smith, D.J., and McVie, S. (2003), 'Theory and Method in the Edinburgh Study of Youth Transitions and Crime,' *Brit. Jour. of Criminology*, 43: 169–95.

Smith, N., Lister, R., and Middleton, S. (2004), 'Longitudinal Qualitative Research,' in S. Becker and A. Bryman (eds.), *Understanding Research for Social Policy and Practice: Themes, Methods, and Approaches* (Bristol: Policy Press).

Smith, R. (2008), 'Pain in the Act: The Meanings of Pain Among Professional Wrestlers,' *Qualitative Sociology*, 31: 129–48.

Smith, T.W. (1995), 'Trends in Non-response Rates,' *Intnatl. Jour. of Public Opinion Research*, 7: 157–71.

Stacey, J. (1988), 'Can There Be a Feminist Ethnography?' *Women's Studies Intnatl. Forum*, 1: 21–7.

Stake, R.E. (1995), *The Art of Case Study Research* (Thousand Oaks, CA: Sage).

Stanley, L., and Temple, B. (1995), 'Doing the Business? Evaluating Software Packages to Aid the Analysis of Qualitative Data Sets,' *Studies in Qual. Methodology*, 5: 169–97.

Stoller, P. (1989), *The Taste of Ethnographic Things* (Philadelphia: Univ. of Pennsylvania Press).

Strauss, A. (1987), *Qualitative Analysis for Social Scientists* (NY: Cambridge Univ. Press).

——— and Corbin, J. (1990), *Basics of Qualitative Research: Grounded Theory Procedures and Techniques* (Newbury Park, CA: Sage).

——— (1998), *Basics of Qualitative Research: Techniques and Procedures for Developing Grounded Theory* (Thousand Oaks, CA: Sage).

——— Schatzman, L., Ehrich, D., Bucher, R., and Sabshin, M. (1973), 'The Hospital and Its Negotiated Order,' in G. Salaman and K. Thompson (eds.), *People and Organizations* (London: Longman).

Sudman, S., and Bradburn, N. (1982), *Asking Questions: A Practical Guide to Questionnaire Design* (San Francisco: Jossey-Bass).

Sugiman, P. (2004), 'Memories of the Internment: Narrating Japanese-Canadian Women's Life Stories,' *Canadian Jour. of Sociology*, 29: 359–88.

Sullivan, O. (1996), 'Time Co-ordination, the Domestic Division of Labour and Affective Relations: Time Use and the Enjoyment of Activities within Couples,' *Sociology*, 30: 79–100.

Sutton, R.I. (1992), 'Feelings about a Disneyland Visit: Photography and the Reconstruction of Bygone Emotions,' *Jour. of Management Inquiry*, 1: 278–87.

——— and Rafaeli, A. (1988), 'Untangling the Relationship between Displayed Emotions and Organizational Sales: The Case of Convenience Stores,' *Academy of Management Jour.*, 31: 461–87.

——— (1992), 'How We Untangled the Relationship between Displayed Emotion and Organizational Sales: A Tale of Bickering and Optimism,' in P. Frost and R. Stablein (eds.), *Doing Exemplary Research* (Newbury Park, CA: Sage).

Sweet, C. (2001), 'Designing and Conducting Virtual Focus Groups,' *Qual. Market Research*, 4: 130–5.

Tastsoglou, E., and Miedema, B. (2003), 'Immigrant Women and Community Development in the Canadian Maritimes: Outsiders Within?' *Canadian Jour. of Sociology*, 28: 203–34.

Taylor, A. (1993), *Women Drug Users: An Ethnography of an Injecting Community* (Oxford: Clarendon Press).

Taylor, S. (1999), 'Covert Participant Observation: Unguarded Moments in Organizational Research,' *Notework: The Newsletter of the Standing Conference on Organizational Symbolism*, May: 8–18.

Teevan, J., and Dryburg, H. (2000), 'First Person Accounts and Sociological Explanations of Delinquency,' *Canadian Rev. of Sociology and Anthropology*, 37: 77–93.

Teitler, J., Reichman, N., and Sprachman, S. (2003), 'Costs and Benefits of Improving Response Rates for a Hard-to-reach Population,' *Public Opinion Quarterly*, 67: 126–38.

Tézli, A. and Gauthier, A. H. (2009), Balancing Work and Family in Canada: An Empirical Examination of Conceptualizations and Measurements,' *Canadian Jour. of Sociology,* 34: 433–61.

Thompson, T., and Zerbinos, E. (1995), 'Gender Roles in Animated Cartoons: Has the Picture Changed in 20 Years?' *Sex Roles*, 32: 651–73.

Tilley, N. (2000), 'Doing Realistic Evaluation of Criminal Justice,' in V. Jupp, P. Davies, and P. Francis (eds.), *Doing Criminological Research* (London: Sage).

Totten, M. (2001) 'Legal, Ethical, and Clinical Implications of Doing Fieldwork with Youth Gang Members Who Engage in Serious Violence,' *Jour. of Gang Research*, 8: 35–49.

Tourangeau, R., and Smith, T.W. (1996), 'Asking Sensitive Questions: The Impact of Data Collection Mode,

Question Format, and Question Context,' *Public Opinion Quarterly*, 60: 275–304.

Trow, M. (1957), 'Comment on "Participant Observation and Interviewing: A Comparison,"' *Human Organization*, 16: 33–5.

Tse, A. (1998), 'Comparing the Response Rate, Response Speed and Response Quality of Two Methods of Sending Questionnaires: E-mail vs. Mail,' *Jour. of the Market Research Society*, 40: 353–61.

———— (1999), 'Conducting Electronic Focus Group Discussions among Chinese Respondents,' *Jour. of the Market Research Society*, 41: 407–15.

Turnbull, P. (1973), *The Mountain People* (London: Cape).

Van Brunschot, E.G., Laurendeau, J., and Keown, L.A. (2009), 'The Global and the Local: Precautionary Behaviours in the Realms of Crime, Health, and Home Safety,' *Canadian Jour. of Sociology*, 34: 403–30.

van den Hoonaard, W.C. (2001), 'Is Research-ethics Review a Moral Panic?' *Canadian Rev. of Sociology and Anthropology,* 38: 19–36.

———— and Connolly, A. (2006), 'Anthropological Research in Light of Research-Ethics Review: Canadian Master's Theses, 1995–2004,' *Jour. of Empirical Research on Human Research Ethics*, 1: 59–69.

Van Maanen, J. (1988), *Tales of the Field: On Writing Ethnography* (Chicago: Univ. of Chicago Press).

———— (1991*a*), 'Playing Back the Tape: Early Days in the Field,' in W. Shaffir and R. Stebbins (eds.), *Experiencing Fieldwork: An Inside View of Qualitative Research* (Newbury Park, CA: Sage).

———— (1991*b*), 'The Smile Factory: Work at Disneyland,' in P. Frost, L. Moore *et al.* (eds.), *Reframing Organizational Culture* (Newbury Park, CA: Sage).

Vidich, A., and Bensman, J. (1968), *Small Town in Mass Society* (Princeton, NJ: Princeton Univ. Press).

Vincent, S. (2003), 'Preserving Domesticity,' *Canadian Rev. of Sociology and Anthropology,* 40: 171–96.

Von Hoffman, N. (1970), 'The Sociological Snoopers,' *Washington Post*, January 30.

Wachholz, S., and Miedema, B. (2000), 'Risk, Fear, Harm: Immigrant Women's Perceptions of the "Policing Solution" to Woman Abuse,' *Crime, Law, and Social Change,* 34: 301–17.

Wacjman, J., and Martin, B. (2002), 'Narratives of Identity in Modern Management,' *Sociology*, 36: 985–1002.

Walby, S., and Myhill, A. (2001), 'New Survey Methodologies in Researching Violence against Women,' *Brit. Jour. of Criminology*, 41: 502–22.

Walklate, S. (2000), 'Researching Victims,' in R. King and E. Wincup (eds.), *Doing Research on Crime and Justice* (Oxford: Oxford Univ. Press).

Walsh, M., Hickey, C., and Duffy, J. (1999), 'Influence of Item Content and Stereotype Situation on Gender Differences in Mathematical Problem,' *Sex Roles*, 41: 219–40.

Walters, D. (2004), 'A Comparison of the Labour Market Outcomes of Postsecondary Graduates of Various Levels and Fields over a Four-cohort Period,' *Canadian Jour. of Sociology*, 29: 1–27.

Warde, A. (1997), *Consumption, Food and Taste* (London: Sage).

Weaver, A., and Atkinson, P. (1995), *Microcomputing and Qualitative Data Analysis* (Aldershot: Avebury).

Webb, E.J., Campbell, D.T., Schwartz, R.D., and Sechrest, L. (1966), *Unobtrusive Measures: Non-reactive Measures in the Social Sciences* (Chicago: Rand McNally).

Weber, M. (1947), *The Theory of Social and Economic Organization*, trans. A.M. Henderson and T. Parsons (NY: Free Press).

Weick, K.E. (1990), 'The Vulnerable System: An Analysis of the Tenerife Air Disaster,' *Jour. of Management*, 16: 571–93.

Weinholtz, D., Kacer, B., and Rocklin, T. (1995), 'Salvaging Quantitative Research with Qualitative Data,' *Qual. Health Research*, 5: 388–97.

Westergaard, J., Noble, I., and Walker, A. (1989), *After Redundancy: The Experience of Economic Insecurity* (Cambridge, UK: Polity).

Wetherell, M. (1998), 'Positioning and Interpretative Repertoires: Conversation Analysis and Post-structuralism in Dialogue,' *Discourse and Society*, 9: 387–412.

White, J. (1990), *Hospital Strike* (Toronto: Thompson Educ. Publishing).

Whitehead, K. (2010), '"Hunger Hurts but Starving Works": A Case Study of Gendered Practices in the Online Pro-eating-disorder Community,' *Canadian Jour. of Sociology*, 35: 595–626.

Whitehead, P., and Carpenter, D. (1999), 'Explaining Unsafe Sexual Behaviour: Cultural Definitions and Health in the Military,' *Culture, Health, and Sexuality*, 1: 303–15.

Whyte, W.F. (1955), *Street Corner Society*, 2nd ed. (Chicago: Univ. of Chicago Press).

Widdicombe, S. (1993), 'Autobiography and Change: Rhetoric and Authenticity of "Gothic" Style,' in E. Burman and I. Parker (eds.), *Discourse Analytic Research: Readings and Repertoires of Text* (London: Routledge).

Wilkinson, P., and Whitworth, D. (1998), 'Fat Is Fanciable, Says the Body of Evidence,' *The Times*, 7 Jan.: 3.

Wilkinson, S. (1998), 'Focus Groups in Feminist Research: Power, Interaction, and the Co-production of Meaning,' *Women's Studies Intnatl. Forum*, 21: 111–25.

———— (1999*a*), 'Focus Group Methodology: A Review,' *Intnatl. Jour. of Social Research Methodology*, 1: 181–203.

———— (1999*b*), 'Focus Groups: A Feminist Method,' *Psych. of Women Quarterly*, 23: 221–44.

Williams, M. (2000), 'Interpretivism and Generalization,' *Sociology*, 34: 209–24.

Wilson, B. (2002), 'The Canadian Rave Scene and Five Theses on Youth Resistance,' *Canadian Jour. of Sociology,* 27: 373–412.

Wilson, E. O. (1998), *Consilience: The Unity of Knowledge* (New York: Knopf).

Winkler, C. (1995), 'The Ethnography of the Ethnographer,' in C. Nordstrom and A. Robben (eds.), *Fieldwork under Fire: Contemporary Studies of Violence and Survival* (Berkeley: Univ. of California Press).

Winlow, S., Hobbs, D., Lister, S., and Hadfield, P. (2001), 'Get Ready to Duck: Bouncers and the Realities of Ethnographic Research on Violent Groups,' *Brit. Jour. of Criminology*, 41: 536–48.

Wolcott, H. (1990), *Writing Up Qualitative Research* (Newbury Park, CA: Sage).

Wolf, D. (1991), 'High Risk Methodology: Reflections on Leaving an Outlaw Society,' in W. Shaffir and R. Stebbins (eds.), *Experiencing Fieldwork: An Inside View of Qualitative Research* (Newbury Park, CA: Sage).

Wright, K.B. (2005), 'Researching Internet-Based Populations: Advantages and Disadvantages of Online Survey Research, Online Questionnaire Authoring Software Packages, and Web Survey Services,' *Jour. of Computer-Mediated Communication* 10: article 11.

Yin, R. (1984), *Case Study Research: Design and Methods* (Beverly Hills, CA: Sage).

Yun, G.W., and Trumbo, C.W. (2000) 'Comparative Response to a Survey Executed by Post, E-mail, and Web Form,' *Jour. of Computer-Mediated Communication*, 6: www.ascusc.org/ jcmc/vol6/issue1/yun.html.

Zimbardo, P.G., (1971) 'The psychological power and pathology of imprisonment.' A statement prepared for the U.S. House of Representatives Committee on the Judiciary, Subcommittee No. 3, Hearings on Prison Reform, San Francisco, Calif., October 25, 1971.

Photo Credits

Index